Herbert Haines

A Manual of Monumental Brasses

Comprising an Introduction to the Study of these Memorials and... Part II

Herbert Haines

A Manual of Monumental Brasses
Comprising an Introduction to the Study of these Memorials and... Part II

ISBN/EAN: 9783744728508

Printed in Europe, USA, Canada, Australia, Japan

Cover: Foto ©ninafisch / pixelio.de

More available books at **www.hansebooks.com**

A MANUAL OF Monumental Brasses:

COMPRISING AN

INTRODUCTION TO THE STUDY OF THESE MEMORIALS

AND

A LIST OF THOSE REMAINING IN THE BRITISH ISLES.

With Two Hundred Illustrations.

BY THE

REV. HERBERT HAINES, M.A.,

OF EXETER COLLEGE, OXFORD; SECOND MASTER OF THE COLLEGE SCHOOL,
AND CHAPLAIN OF THE COUNTY ASYLUM, GLOUCESTER.

"....EXPRESSI VULTUS PER AHENEA SIGNA,
....MORES ANIMIQUE VIRORUM
CLARORUM APPARENT."—HORAT. EPIST. ii. I.

PART II.

Oxford and London:
J. H. AND JAS. PARKER.
1861.

(With the Sanction of the Oxford Architectural Society.)

PART II.

A LIST

OF THE

Monumental Brasses

IN THE

BRITISH ISLES.

ABBREVIATIONS, &c.

A., Aisle; N.A., North Aisle; S.A., South Aisle.
A.T., Altar Tomb.
acad., academical dress.
æt., ætatis.
arm., armour.
C., Choir, Chancel; N.C., North Chantry; S.C., South Chantry.
c., circa—about.
Ch., Church.
chil., children.
coh., coheir.
covd., covered.
dau., daus.—daughter, daughters.
dec., deceased.
det., dets.—detail, details.
eff., effs.—effigy, effigies.
eleg. (Latin) elegiac.
Eng., English.
engr., engraved.
Evang. symbs.—Evangelistic symbols.
fem., female.
Fr., French.
frag., fragments.
hf., half.
Hy. Trin., Holy Trinity.
inscr., inscrs.—inscription, inscriptions.
Introd., Introduction.
kng., kneeling.
Lat., Latin.
Lomb., Lombardic.
m., married.
marg., marginal.
mcht., merchant.
mcht's. mk., merchant's mark.
mur., mural—against the wall.
mutil., mutilated.
N., Nave.
pecul., peculiar,—generally used of a brass engraved by a provincial artist.
pos., posuit, posuerunt—placed.
qd. pl., quadrangular plate.
rel., relaid.
SS., Saints.
sh., shs.—shield, shields.
sm. small.
Tr., Transept; N.Tr., North Transept; S. Tr., South Transept.
vv., verses.
w., ws.—wife, wives.

Unless otherwise stated, the following particulars are to be taken for granted:—mural brasses have the figures kneeling and of small size; Ecclesiastics are in eucharistical vestments; Knights, Esquires, and Gentlemen before 1550 are represented in armour, after that date in civil costume; and canopies have as many pediments as there are principal figures beneath them.

Words or dates enclosed in rectangular brackets contain information which cannot be ascertained from the present state of the brass. When the inscription, &c., is described as *lost*, the brackets are omitted.

The dates in Clarendon type are those of the engraving of the brasses, usually the date of decease.

Figures less than eighteen inches in length are described as *small*, above three feet and a half as *large*.

The author has examined rubbings of those brasses which have not the marks * † attached to them. An asterisk prefixed to a notice of a brass, or to the name of a church containing one or more brasses, indicates that the description has been obtained from recent communications or publications, and is most probably correct. The mark †, placed before a few notices of brasses, implies that their present existence or the accuracy of their description is uncertain. Notices of Inscriptions of slight interest or unauthenticated are generally omitted.

The reference to pages of the Introduction is placed at the end of the description of the brasses. The titles of works in which engravings of brasses are to be found are printed in italics.

A LIST

OF THE

Monumental Brasses

IN THE

BRITISH ISLES.

Bedfordshire.

AMPTHILL. I. Wm. Hicchcok, wolman, mcht., and "locum tenens" of the Staple of Calais, mutil., **1450**, and widow, "domina" Agnes. II. John Lodyngton, junr., eff. lost, **1485**, and w. Margt., sm., worn. III. John Barnard, chapman, **1506**, and w. Ellen, sm.; inscr., 4 sons and 3 daus. lost. *Fisher's Lithograph*, No. 32. IV. Sir Nich. Harve, in arm., **1532**, with marg. inscr., once on A.T., now under moveable floor, N.A. *Fisher's Lith.*, No. 2. INSCR. V. Seven Eng. vv., Hy. Trin. seated on a rainbow lost, p. 223. *Fisher's Lith.*, No. 31. All these brasses, except No. IV., were loose in the parvise, April, 1857.

ASPLEY GUISE. I. *A Priest, in cassock, kng., and St. John Bapt. standing, a cross between them and marg. inscr. gone, c. **1410**, p. 77. *Fisher's Collections for Bedfordshire*, pl. 6. II. —— Guise, Esq., c. **1490**, inscr. lost, p. 116. *Fisher's Beds.*, pl. 5. Both brasses are under seats.

BARFORD, GREAT. A Man in arm., and w., c. **1525**, lately loose, now lost? pp. 232, 260.

BARFORD, LITTLE. Thos. Perys, **1535**, and w. Agnes, pecul., sm., N., p. 244. *Fisher's Lith.*, No. 3.

BARTON-IN-THE-CLAY. I. Rich. Brey, rector, hf. efl., c. **1370**. *Anonymous*. II. A civilian, c. **1490**, sm. INSCR. III. Philip de Lee, rector, c. **1360**.

*BEDFORD, ST. MARY'S. I. Robt. Hawse, Gent., thrice mayor, **1627**, æt. 52. *Fisher's Beds.*, pl. 12. II. Mary, dau. of Dr. Giles Thorne, **1663**, and three daus., mur.

BEDFORD, ST. PAUL'S. Sir Wm. Harper, lord mayor of London [1561], founder of Bedford Grammar-school [and Almshouses], **1573**, æt. 77, and w. Margt., rel., A.T., S.C., p. 91. *Fisher's Beds.*, pl. 11. Simon de Beauchamp, **1208**, lost, p. 43.

BIDDENHAM. I. Wm. Faldo and w. Agnes, below John Faldo, c. **1490**, sm., S.C. *Fisher's Beds.*, pl. 15.   II. Helen, dau. of Geo. Nodes, of Shephall, Esq., and w. of Wm. Boteler, Esq., **1639**, qd. pl., with bust, mur., N.C.   INSCRS. III. John Aylyff, rector, N.C.: 6 Lat. vv. to the same, mur.

BIGGLESWADE. I. Wm. Halsted, head lost, **1449**, and ws. Isabella (lost) and Alice, N., p. 33.   II. John Rudyng, prebendary [of Lincoln], archdeacon of Bedford, rector of St. Michael's, Gloucester, [dec. **1481**, rebuilder of C., c. 1467]; eff. and canopy with SS. John Bapt., Anna, Elizth., and Mary of Egypt, lost; figures of death, angels, &c., inscr. in 16 Lat. vv., and mutil. marg. inscr. in 10 Lat. vv. left, slab very large and powdered with crescents and escallops, all lost but 2, C., pp. 105, 112. *Gough*, vol. ii., pl. 102, p. 272.

BLUNHAM. Rich. Maulaye, mercer, **1506**, and w. Alice, C.

BROMHAM. [Sir John Dyve], **1535**, and mother Elizth., h. of Thos. Wilde, Esq. [1497], and w. Isabella, h. of Sir Ralph Hastings, with fine canopy, and mutil. marg. inscr. in Lat. vv., large. Palimpsest, originally commemorating Thos. Wideville, Esq., **1435**, and ws. Elizth. and Alice, C., pp. 50, 189, 252. *Lysons' Mag. Brit.*, vol. i. p. 163.

CADDINGTON. I. John Hawll (or Hawtt), alias Cryseyan, **1505**, and w. Elizth., with 4 sons and 4 daus., N.   II. Edw. Dormer, yeoman, **1518**, and ws. Joan (with 7 sons and 7 daus.) and Elizth., N.C.

CAMPTON. Rich. Carlyll, Esq., not in arm., and w. Joan, both dec. Feb. 14th, **1489**, N. *Fisher's Lith.*, No. 4.

CARDINGTON. I. [Sir Wm. Gascoigne, comptroller of the household to Cardinal Wolsey, and 2 ws., Jane, dau. of Wm. (?) Pickering, of Northumberland, and Elizth., dau. and h. of Rich. Mowbray (?) : see Harl. MS., 1,531, p. 135], in heraldic dresses, c. **1540**, inscr. lost, A.T., C., p. 113.   II. Sir Jarrate Harvye, second son of John Harvye, of Thurley, Esq., **1638**, æt. 69, in arm., and w. Dorothy, a coh. of John Gascoigne, of Cardington Manor, Esq., and 6 sons and 6 daus., A.T., C., p. 236.   Sir Gerard was knighted by the Earl of Essex for his bravery at the siege of Cadiz, being the first man who entered the town.

CLIFTON. I. John Fysher, Esq., son of Sir Mich. Fysher, **1528**, and w., a dau. lost, pp. 29, 235. *Fisher's Beds.*, pl. 23. INSCR. II. †Wm. Haryson, priest, **1516** eff. lost.

COPLE. I. Nichol Rolond and w. Pernel, with Fr. inscr., c. **1410**, C., p. 90. *Fisher's Beds.*, pl. 27.   II. Walter Rolond, in arm.,

c. **1415**, with Fr. inscr., head covd., C., p. 189. *Fisher's Beds.*, pl. 26.
III. John Launceleyn, Esq., **1435**, and w. Margt., C., p. 189.
Fisher's Beds., pl. 25.   IV. Thos. Gray, in arm., and w. Benet
[Launceleyn ?], c. **1520**, inscr. in 14 Eng. vv., pecul., A.T., S.C.
V. Sir Walter Luke, justice, **1544**, and w. Anne, "Norysthe" (nurse)
to King Hen. VIII., and a dau. and h. of John Launceleyn, Esq., in
heraldic mantle, 1538, Hy. Trin. and scrolls lost, mur., C., p. 91.
VI. Robt. Bulkeley, Esq., 1550, in arm., and w. Joan, dau. of Sir
Wm. Gascoyne, **1556**, with 6 sons and 4 daus., qd. pl., mur., S.C.
VII. Nich. Luke, Esq., a baron of the exchequer, **1563**, and w.
Cecyle, dau. and h. of Sir Thos. Wanton, mur., N.A., p. 91.
VIII. Thos. Spencer, Gent., **1547**, and w. Anne, dau. of Robt.
Bulkeley, Esq., and 2 sons and 2 daus., all lost except the daus.
and inscr., S.C., p. 57.   A Priest, c. **1430**, 2 ft. 2¾ in. long, once
in N., lost. A brass like No. VI. to Wm. Bulkeley, Esq., **1568**, and
w. Jane, dau. of baron Luke (No. VII.), and chil., Chas., Wm.
(dec.), John, Joyse, Judyth, Susan, Cisseley, lost since 1840.

DEAN. Thos. Parker, rector, prebendary of St. Mary's, Shrewsbury, in almuce, **1501**, Hy. Trin. lost, A.T., p. 79.

DUNSTABLE. I. Laurence Pygot, wolman, feet lost, **1450**, and
w. Alice (both effs. with mcht's. mks., fastened to a board), with 6
daus. and a son [? Laurence Cantelowe]; inscr. and 3 sons lost, N.,
p. 261.   II. A Civilian and w., c. **1460**, sm., partly covd., N.
III. John Pedder, **1463** (loose), and ws. Margt., Matilda, and Agnes,
sm., one w. lost, two ws. and inscr. fastened to a board, once in S.A.
IV. John Blunte, **1502**, (now with inscr. on a board,) and w. Elizth.,
with 7 daus.; 8 sons, and Hy. Trin. lost, N.   V. Rich. Pynfold,
1516, and w. Margt., with 4 sons; 7 daus. lost, N.   VI. Henry
Fayrey, **1516**, and w. Agnes, in shrouds, with 5 sons 4 daus. gone,
N., p. 171. *Fisher's Beds.*, pl. 32.   VII. Robt. Alee, **1518**, and
ws. Elizth. (with 1 son and 3 daus.) and Agnes (with 2 sons and
4 daus.), in shrouds; one w., inscr., and 2 sons now on a board;
male eff. loose, engr. in *Introd.*, p. 171, N.A.   VIII. A Civilian
and w., c. **1520**, partly covd., N.   IX. Nich. Purvey, **1521**, and
ws. Elizth. and Alys, eff. of 2nd w. on a board, 3 sons loose,
2 daus. lost, N.   X. Rich. Fynche, citizen and mcht.-tailor of
London, **1640**, æt. c. 81, and parents, Thos. Fynche, 1586, and
Elizth. Fynche, 1607, with marg. inscr., another inscr. now on a
board, N., pp. 119, 216. Ch. visited Jan. 1858.   The brass of
Wm. Mulso and wife, if it be not No. II., is lost, p. 173.

EATON-BRAY. I. Lady Jane Bray, w. of Sir Edm. Bray, and dau.
and h. of Rich. Halwell, Esq. (son of Sir John Halwell, of Devon),

and his w. Anne (dau. and h. of Sir John Norbery), **1558**, with 1 son and 10 daus., mur., C.   INSCR. II. †Jane, dau. of Edm. Lord Bray, **1539**, eff. lost. *Fisher's Lith.*, No. 33.

EATON-SOCON.   I. John Covesgrave and w., c. **1400**, marg. inscr. lost, N.A., p. 164. *Fisher's Lith.*, No. 9.   II. Fem. eff., worn, sm., c. **1450**, husband and inscr. lost, N. FRAGS., 2 sons and a sh., c. **1610**, A.T., C.

ELSTOW.   I. Margery, dau. of Ralph [Corbet?], of Richard's Castle [co. Hereford?], twice a widow, marg. inscr. in Lat. vv., mutil., S.C. She married first John Hervey? and secondly Sir John Argentine, and died **1427**. See The Topog. and Geneal., pt. i. p. 71. *Gough*, vol. ii. pl. cxxii. p. 346.   II. Dame Elizth. Herwy, abbess, **15—** [dec. 1524?], with marg. inscr., S.C., pp. 87, 88. *Gough*, vol. ii. pl. cxxii. p. 346; *Fisher's Beds.*, pl. 37; *Waller*, pt. xv.

*EYWORTH. Rich. Gadburye, Gent., **1624**, æt. c. 63, and second wife Margt., dau. of Thos. Anderson, late of Castlethorpe, Lincolnshire, Esq., with dau. Magdalenna: he left in trust 6 acres of arable land at Wrestlinworth and 8 acres at Dunton for the poor, C.

FELMERSHAM.   A Civilian and w., c. **1610**, worn, sm., C.

FLITTON.   I. Lady Eleanor, widow of Sir Hen. Conquest, **1434**, head lost, N.   II. Thos. Waren, Gent., in arm., **1544**, and w. Elizth., inscr. palimpsest, male eff. and chil. lost, sm., N.A., p. 48. III. Harry Gray, son and h. of Sir Harry Gray, **1545**, in arm., now in N.C., p. 230. *Fisher's Beds.*, pl. 43.   IV. Thos. Hill, Gent., receiver-general to Reginald, Hen., and Chas., earls of Kent, **1628**, æt. 101, inscr. in 4 Eng. vv., C.   INSCR. V. Alice, w. of Mr. Reginald Hill, **1594**, and son Wm.

GOLDINGTON.   I. Rich. Fyssher, **1507**. *Fisher's Beds.*, pl. 45. II. Robt. Hatley, Esq., **1585**, in arm., inscr. in 8 Lat. and 12 Eng. vv., mur., C.

*GRAVENHURST, LOWER.   I. Benj. Pigott, Esq., **1606**, æt. 55, and 3 ws.: 1st, Mary, dau. of Ralph Astrey, Esq., of Harlington, Beds. (with 1 son); 2nd, Anne, dau. and coh. of Thos. Wiseman (with 2 sons and 2 daus.); 3rd, Bridget, dau. of John Nedham, of Wymondly, Herts. (with 2 sons and 7 daus.): with genealogical inscr., mur., C.   INSCR. II. Sir Robt. de Bilhemore, [c. **1362**?] rebuilder of Ch., inscr. in Fr., at the Rectory in 1859. *Fisher's Beds.*, pl. 47.

HATLEY COCKAYNE.   I. A Man in arm., c. **1430**, p. 189.   II. A Lady, c. **1480**, now placed beside No. 1.   III. *Edmond Cockayn, Esq., **1515**, and w. Elizth., with 12 sons and 4 daus., p. 223. *Fisher's Lith.*, No. 8.   IV. *Wm. Cokyn, Esq., **1527**, and ws. Dorothy and Kath., with 4 sons and 6 daus., pp. 29, 234. *Fisher's Lith.*, No. 7. The brasses are rel. in N., and misplaced.

HAWNES. Anth. Newdegate, Esq., "curic generalium supervisorum terrarum quondam regis Henrici Octavi dum steterit auditorium unus," **1568**, not in arm., mur., C.

HOLWELL. A chalice and host, two woodmen, and inscr. to Robt. Wodehowse, rector, **1515**, benefactor to Ch., pecul., pp. 125, 132. *Fisher's Lith.*, No. 12; *The Topog. and Geneal.*, pt. i. p. 74.

HOUGHTON CONQUEST. I. Rich. Conquest, in arm., and w. Isabella, **1493**, with 9 sons and 5 daus., and John Conquest (father of Rich.), lord of Houghton, A.T., C., p. 198. II. Rich. Conquest, Esq., **1500**, and w. Elizth.; 6 sons and 2 daus. and Hy. Trin. lost, very sm., C., p. 199. *Fisher's Lith.*, No. 13. Male eff. and portions of brass No. I. loose at the Rectory 1847. The brass of Thos. Awdley, **1531**, and w., with 1 son and 2 daus., A.T., C., is now lost, p. 5. *Fisher's Beds.*, pl. 56, (tomb only engr.)

HOUGHTON REGIS. I. John Waleys, vicar, c. **1400**, hf. eff., and his kinsman Wm. Waleys (eff. lost), p. 63. II. Sir Wm. Walley, vicar, **1506**, C.

LANGFORD. Thos. Hundon, vicar, **1520**, worn, C.

LEIGHTON BUZZARD. I. Wm. Jackmain, of Billington, Gent., **1592**, and sons Wm. and Reginald, inscr. with 6 Lat. vv., qd. pl., mur., C. II. *Francis Welles, Gent., **1646**, and first w. Margt., dau. of Rich. Saunders, Gent., qd. pl., mur., C. III. *Cath. Whitlock, w. of Rich. Whitlock, Gent. and mcht. of London, **1649**, æt. 54, qd. pl., mur., C.

LIDLINGTON. Wm. Goldyngton, Gent., '149-, and w. Margt., with 2 sons and 4 daus., Hy. Trin. and mutil. marg. inscr., C. *Fisher's Lith.*, No. 14.

LUTON. I. Hugh atte Spotyll, w. Alice (eff. lost), and their son John, a priest (eff. loose and mutil.), c. **1425**, C., p. 63. *Fisher's Lith.*, No. 16. II. John Hay, steward of the Abp. of Canterbury for thirty years, repairer of the Ch. and roads, **1455**, and ws. Anne (with 3 chil.) and Isabella; the inscr. in 12 Lat. lines, and the eff. of 2nd. w. (with part of the shaft of a canopy on reverse), only now remain, and are loose, N.A., p. 47. III. A Widow Lady, c. **1490**, under triple canopy, marg. inscr. lost, A.T., N.C. IV. A Civilian, c. **1500**, loose, w. and inscr. lost. V. Edw. Sheffeld, LL.D., canon of Lichfield, vicar of Luton, rector of Camborne, Cornwall, and Yate, Glouc., c. **1510**, in cap and almuce, inscr. loose, C., p. 79. *Fisher's Lith.*, No. 35. VI. John Lamar and w. Elynor, **1512**, with 6 sons and 4 daus., w. lost, the daus. loose, N. VII. John

Sylam, **1513**, in arm., and ws. Elizth. and Joan; 1 son and 6 daus. lost? C. VIII. John Acworth, Esq., **1513**, and ws. Alys and Amy, with 8 sons and 9 daus., and mutil. marg. inscr., N.Tr., p. 224. *Fisher's Beds.*, pl. 64. IX. John Barbar, **1515** (lost), and w. Agnes; 2 chil. and a male eff. below lost, inscr. loose, N. X. Robt. Su......, and 2 ws., —— (with 2 sons and 4 daus. lost) and Annys, c. **1520**, loose and much mutil., N. XI. Robt. Colshill, mcht.-tailor of London, and w. Anne, dau. of Thos. Waren, Gent., **1524**, N.Tr., p. 119. *Fisher's Beds.*, pl. 15. XII. Geo. Rotherham, of Farley, Esq., **1593**, and 2 ws., Elizth. dau. of Edm. Bardolfe (with chil., Geo., Ralf, and Elizth.), and Anne, dau. of Wm. Gower, Esq. (with chil., Isaac, Thos., Edm., and Anna): only the 2nd w., a sm. part of the 1st w., and the chil. now remain, and are loose, except chil. of 1st w., N.T. INSCRS., &c. XIII. Scroll from brass of John Penthelyn, vicar, **1444**, loose. XIV. Mutil. marg. inscr. to Thos. [Rotherham, **1504**?] and w. [Kath.?], loose. XV. Roland Staper, clothworker of London, 1558, w. Dorothy, **1565**, and 6 chil., mur., N.C. XVI. Lady Penelope Napeir, **1658**, mur., S.C. Ch. visited Jan. 1858; the loose brasses were then in a chest.

MARSTON MORTEYNE. I. Walter Papley, rector, **1420**, hf. eff., C. *Fisher's Lith.*, No. 36. II. Thos. Reynes, Esq., lord of the manor, **1451**, and widow Alice, with 9 sons, several daus. lost, C., p. 193. *Fisher's Beds.*, pl. 66. III. Wm. Lentthorpe, **1506**, in shroud, upper part of eff. gone, C. INSCR. IV. Mary Lentton, w. of Thos. Reynes, Esq., **1506**, loose, with shs., S A.

MAULDEN. I. Rich. Faldo, Esq., **1576**, in arm., and w. Amphilicia Chamberlin, with 4 sons, a dau. lost, with mutil. marg. inscr., once on A.T.? now mur. N.A. II. Anne, dau. of Rich. Faldo, Esq., **1594**, æt. 18, mur. N.A. *Fisher's Beds.*, pl. 67.

*MEPSHALL. I. John Mepertyshale, Esq., **1440**, and w. Kath. lost. p. 192. *Fisher's Beds.*, pl. 68. II. John Boteler, Esq., and w. Elizth., a dau. and h. of Nich. Kymbell, Esq., **1441**, p. 192. *Fisher's Beds.*, pl. 69. These brasses are now nailed to pews in S.Tr.

PUDDINGTON. I. John Howard, **1518**, N. *Fisher's Lith.*, No. 20. II. Sir Clement Edmonds, **1622**, æt. 58, in arm., and w. Mary, 1622 æt. 53, sm.

RENHOLD. Edm. Wayte, Gent., **1518**, not in arm., and w. Agnes, a son and 2 daus. gone, sm., A.T., C., p. 215.

SALFORD. John Peddar, **1505**, and w. Alice, with 6 sons and 6 daus. (2 of the daus. lost). *Fisher's Lith.*, No. 37.

SHARNBROOK. I. Wm. Cobbe, smith, **1522**, w. Alice, 1522, and

Thos. their son, some chil. lost, p. 212. *Fisher's Lith.*, No. 21. II. *Sir Oliver Boteler, **1618**, and w., with genealogical inscr., mur. INSCR. III. Sibell, dau. of Thos. Cobbe, Gent., and w. of Wm. Payne, of Podington, Gent.; also Elizth., dau. of Thos. Cobbe (Sybell's brother), **1603**. This inscription and No. I. were loose at the vicarage, Jan. 1860.

SHILLINGTON. I. Matthew de Asscheton, rector of the churches [of Shitlington and ———, and canon of York] and Lincoln, **1400**, in cope, large, with marg. inscr., N.C. *Fisher's Beds.*, pl. 88. II. Thos. Portyngton, rector, and treasurer of York Cath., **1485**, in cope, sm., marg. inscr. lost, pecul., N.C., p. 76. *Fisher's Lith.*, No. 22.

STEVINGTON. Thos. Salle, Esq., **1422**, N., p. 189. *Gent. Mag.*, vol. lxxxii. 1812, pt. ii. p. 9.

SUTTON. A cross fleury and inscr. to Thos. Burgoyn, **1516**, and w. Elizth., N.A., p. 222. *Fisher's Beds.*, pl. 93.

THURLEIGH. A Man in arm., c. **1430**, marg. inscr. lost, p. 189. *Fisher's Lith.*, No. 24.

TILBROOK. I. A Civilian, with anelace, and w., c. **1400**, p. 202. *Fisher's Lith.*, No. 23; *Boutell's Series*. II. John Carter, **1600**, æt. 67, and w. Agnes, dau. of Thos. Taylor, of Lidlington, (with sons John, Thos., and daus. Dorothy, Mary, Lucy, Penelope.)

*TINGRITH. Robt. Hogeson, Esq., **1611**, mur., C.

TOTTERNHOE. I. John Warwckhyll, vicar, **1524**, with chalice and host. II. †Wm. Michell, child, **1621**.

TURVEY. I. *A Priest in almuce, c. **1500**, inscr. lost, S.A. II. A Civilian, c. **1480**, inscr. lost, sm., S.A. *Fisher's Lith.*, No. 26. III. Alice, w. of Rich. Bernard, Esq., and dau. of John Chubnoll, of Astwood, Esq., **1606**, æt. 64, S.A. *Fisher's Lith.*, No. 25.

WILSHAMPSTEAD. Wm. Carbrok, chaplain, c. **1450** or earlier, hf. eff., N.A. *Fisher's Beds.*, pl. 105.

WIMINGTON. I. John Curteys, lord of the manor, rebuilder of the Ch., mayor of wool staple of Calais, **1391**, with anelace, and widow Albreda, under good canopy, marg. inscr., A.T., C. *Lysons' Mag. Brit.*, vol. i. p. 151. II. Margt., dau. of Sir Edw. Seynt Jon, h. of Lord Vessy, and w. of Sir Thos. Brounflet, by whom she had 5 sons and 1 dau. [**1407**], in mantle, marg. inscr. in 12 Lat. vv., C. *Gough*, vol. ii. pl. xxxi. p. 96. III. Sir Thos. Brounflet, cup-bearer to Rich. II., treasurer of the household to Hen. IV., **1430**, inscr. in 14 Lat. vv., large, C., p. 62. *Gough, ibid.; Hartshorne's Sep. Mon.*, p. 39; *Boutell, Mon. Br.*, p. 65. IV. John Stokys, rector, c. **1510**, with chalice and wafer, N. *Fisher's Lith.*, No. 27.

YIELDEN. I. John Heyne, rector, **1433**, C. *Fisher's Lith.*, No. 29.
II. Thos. Barker, rector, M.A., fellow of New Coll., Oxford, born at
Soulgrave, Northants., dec. **1617**, æt. 54; inscr. in 9 Lat. vv., his
brothers pos., qd. pl., mur., C.   III. Christ. Stickland, Gent.,
1628, æt. 80, qd. pl. *Fisher's Beds.*, pl. 112.

INSCRIPTIONS, &c.

ARLSEY. *Rich. Edwards, **1638**, inscr. and sh.   COLMWORTH.
Alianora, w. of Sir Gerard Braybrook, and dau. and h. of Almaric
de St. Amand, 1389, engr. c. **1460**? sh. gone, now mur., C. *Fisher's
Lith.*, No. 6.   EVERSHOLT. 6 sons and 6 daus., c. **1450**, parents
gone.   MELCHBOURN. *Robt. Paveley, Esq., **1377**.   MILBROOK.
Robt. Were, priest, c. **1430**, with Eng. inscr., lost at the funeral of
Lady Holland, p. 260. *Fisher's Beds.*, pl. 70.   ROXTON. *Roger
Hunt, A.T.   WILLINGTON. *Robt. Gostwyk, Esq., 1315. *Joan
Gostwyk, 1326, both inscrs. in N. and engr. c. **1530**.

Berkshire.

ABINGDON, ST. HELEN'S. 1. Geoffrey Barbur, mcht. of Abingdon,
and once bailiff of Bristol, **1417**, hf. eff., S.A., p. 252.   II. Wm.
Heyward, S.T.D., vicar, **1501**, in acad., partly covd., worn, N., p. 84.

APPLETON.   John Goodryngton, gent., **1518**, emaciated eff. in
shroud; after his dec. his w. Dorothe "toke relygyon in ye monastary of Syon," C., p. 89.

ASHBURY. I. John de Walden, c. **1360**, hf. eff. in hood and cape,
mutil., sm., inscr. in 2 Lat. vv., C.   II. Thos. de Busshbury,
rector, canon of Hereford, **1409**, in cope, eff. headless, and loose in
Ch. chest in 1859, C.   III. Wm. Skelton, LL.B., 'prepositus' of
Wells Cath., rector of Ashbury, and St. Vedastus, London, **1448**,
in cope, C.

BINFIELD.   Water de Annesfordhe, priest, [**1361**,] hf. eff., with
Fr. inscr.

BISHAM. I. Thos. Crekett, fishmonger of London, **1517**, w.
Annes and a child gone, rel., N. p. 119.   II. John Brinckhurst,
citizen and mercer of London, and mcht. adventurer, and ws. Elizth.
Blundell, **1581**, and Jane Wodfoorde, C., p. 110.

BLEWBURY. I. John Balam, vicar, **1496**, C.   II. A Man in arm.
and 2 ws., each with 2 sons and 3 daus., of which 3 daus. only are left;
c. **1515**, effs. now separated and mur. in C. and S.Tr., inscr. lost; a
sh. with arms of Isbery left in S.A.   III. Sir John Daunce, counsellor and surveyor-general to Hen. VIII., and w. Alice, dau. of Thos.

Latton, Gent., **1523**, in heraldic dresses, with 5 sons and 2 daus., A.T., S.C.   IV. John Latton, Esq., of Chilton, **1548**, in tabard, and w. Ann, with 6 sons (mutil.) and 9 daus., Wm., Thos., Anth., John, Barth., John, Alice, Elizth., Mary, Margt., Dorothy, Fryswythe, Jane, Susan; eff. of another w. lost, C.   V. A figure of Faith and inscr. to Eliza, w. of Rev. J. Macdonald, vicar, 1849, æt. 53, and their son John, **1841**, æt. 13, C.   INSCR. VI. John Bouldre (?), **1499**, N.   VII. John Casberde, "one of the good benefactours to this Churche," c. **1500**, N.

BRAY.   I. Sir John de Foxle, **1378**, and ws., [Matilda, dau. of Sir John Brocas, of Beaurepaire, Hants., and Joan, dau. of —— Martin,] in heraldic dresses, on a bracket, canopy and marg. inscr. lost, S.A., pp. 31, 131, 160, 169. *Waller*, pt. xiv.   II. Sir Wm. Laken, justice of the King's Bench, and son of Sir Rich. Laken, **1475**, with rosary and anelace, and widow Sibilla, a dau. and h. of John Syferwast, lord of the manor of Clewer, w. and inscr. lost, S.A., p. 90. *Gough*, vol. ii. pl. lxxxvii. p. 230.   III. Wm. Smyth, and ws. Agnes and Matilda, with 7 sons and 5 daus., c. **1490**, S.A.   IV. [—— Smith?] M.A., Fellow of —— Coll., Oxford, and w., c. **1600**, m. 35 years, inscr. with 10 Eng. vv., qd. pl., mur., C.   V. Arthur Page, of Walter Okelye in Bray, Gent., **1610**, and w. Sessely, dau. of Wm. Brownesopp, Esq., 1598, with their infant son Edward, qd. pl., mur. *Fairholt's Costume*, p. 261 (fem. eff.)   INSCRS. VI. Thos. Attelude, chaplain, c. **1430**, eff. lost, sm., N.   VII. Wm. Dyer, vicar, **1440**, eff. lost, sm., N.   VIII. *Wm. Smyth, Esq., "ad arma et scutellas serviens" to Queens Mary and Elizth., **1594**, æt. 84, with shs.   Ursula Morris, **1560**, lost, p. 57.

BRIGHTWELL.   I. John Scolffyld, priest, **1507**, with chalice and host.   II. Robt. Court, auditor to Prince Arthur, **1509**, and w. Jane.   III. Rich. Hampden and w. Jane, **1512**, sm.

BUCKLAND.   *John Yate, Esq., **1578**, and w. Mary, dau. and h. of Wm. Justice, of Reading, with 5 sons and 7 daus., once on A.T., now mur., N.Tr.

BURGHFIELD.   †Nich. Williams, Esq., **1568**, in arm., and ws. Elizth. and Mabel, and daus. Rason and Sara.

CHILDREY.   I. Wm. Fynderne, Esq., **1444**, and w. Elizth. [Chelrey?], widow of Lord John Kyngeston, both in heraldic dresses, under a fine canopy, with marg. inscr. in 20 Lat. vv., large, C., p. 190. *Waller*, pt. xiii.; *Relton's Sketches of Churches*.   II. A Priest, c. **1480**, marg. inscr., mutil., C.   III. Wm. Walrond, Gent., not in arm., and w. Elizth., c. **1480**, inscr. mutil., C. *Relton*. IV. A Priest, c. **1490**, with chalice, head and inscr. lost, sm., nailed to window-sill in C.   V. Joan, dau. of Thos. Walrond, and w. of Robt. Strangbon, **1507**, in shroud, with Hy. Trin., inscr. in 7 Eng. vv., S.Tr., p. 102.   *Relton.   Gent. Mag.*, 1850, vol. xxxiii. N.S., p. 579 (Hy. Trin.)   VI. John Kyngeston, Esq., **1514**, and w. Susan, with Hy. Trin., C., p. 54.   *Relton.*   VII. A Man and his w., c. **1520**, in shrouds, rising from tombs, mur., S.Tr., p. 171.   VIII. Thos. Wolrond, Gent., **1480**, not in arm., and w. Alice, dau. of Nich. Englefield, **1477**, with Hy. Trin., mur., engr. c. **1520**, S.Tr. IX. Bryan Roos, LL.D., parson of Ch., **1529**, in acad., C., p. 82. Inscrs. X. Dame Agnes, w. of John Fynderne, **1441**, C.   XI. Wm. Feteplace, Esq., and w. Elizth., **1516**, founders of the chantry, S.Tr., probably belonging to No. VII.   A matrix of a Civilian and w., c. **1380**, N.Tr.

CHOLSEY.   I. John Mere, vicar, **1471**, with chalice, worn, sm., C. Inscrs. II. John Barfoot, **1361**, Fr. inscr., S.Tr.   III. John Bate, vicar, **1394**, C.

COMPTON.   *Rich. Pygott and w. Alice, c. **1520**, N.   *Hewett's Hundred of Compton*, p. 68.

COOKHAM.   I. John Babham, **1458**, and w. Muriel, hf. covd., sm., N.A.   II. Wm. Andrew, **1503**, John Monkeden, and their w. Margt., sm., N.A.   III. Robt. Pecke, Esq., "master clerke of the Spycery" with Hen. VI., **1510**, and w. Annes, with Hy. Trin., sm., A.T., C.   IV. Raffe More, Gent., **1577**, and w. [Mary, dau. of John Babham, Esq.], with marg. inscr. and 10 Eng. vv., much mutil., N.A.   Probably others remain under pews.

COXWELL, GREAT.   I. Wm. Morys, farmer, c. **1500**, with 2 sons and a dau., N., p. 62.   *Bib. Top. Brit.*, vol. iv. pl. vi.   II. Joan, w. of Wm. Morys, c. **1500**, N.   *Ibid.*

CUMNOR.   I. Anthony, fourth son of Rich. Forster, of Ightfield, Sa'op, in arm., and w. Ann, dau. of Rainold Williams, Esq., with 3 sons, John, Robt., Hen., c. **1570**, they had also two daus., Cynthia and Penelope, inscr. in 32 eleg. vv., mur., A.T., C.   II. Kath., w. of Hen. Staverton, Gent., and dau. of Raynold Wylliams, of Borgfield, Berks., Esq., **1577**, mutil., 3 chil. lost, C., p. 245.   *Oxford Manual for the Study of Mon. Brasses*, p. 107, and *Introd.*, p. 246 (part of eff.)   III. —— Stavertoon and w. Edith, dau. of Raygnald Wyllyams, of Borfeld, Berks., Esq., c. **1580**, sm., C.

DENCHEWORTH.   I. Oliver Hyde, Esq., **1516**, in arm., and w. Agnes, they had 4 sons and 4 daus., N.C.   II. *Wm. Hyde, Esq., **1557**, in arm., and w. Margery, **1562**, with 12 sons and 8 daus., and punning inscr., mur., S.C.   III. Wm. Hyde, Esq., **1567**, in arm., and w. Alice, they had 5 sons and 5 daus., N.C.   Several inscrs.

FARRINGDON. I. Petronilla, w. of John Parker, mcht. of the staple of Calais, **1471**. II. John Parker, **1485**, and w. Margt., with marg. inscr. nearly all lost, worn. III. John Sadler, vicar of Inglesham, **1505**, sm. IV. Sir Alex. Unton, **1547**, in tabard, with 7 sons, and 2 ws. in heraldic mantles, Mary, and Lady Cecyll [Bulstrode] with 3 daus., mur., N.C. INSCR. V. Rich. Lenton, vicar, **1410**, benefactor to Ch., C. In a MS. given by Geo. IV. to the Brit. Museum (case vii. 3), is a drawing of the brass of Thos. Faryndon, Esq., **1396**, and w. Margt., **1402**, and their dau. Kath. Pynchepole, **1443**, once in N.C.

FAWLEY. *Mary, dau. of Thos. Cresswell, Gent., and w. of Humfrey Gunter, Gent., **1621**, æt. 36, with 1 son, her husband pos., inscr. with 8 vv., qd. pl., mur., C.

FINCHAMPSTEAD. Elizth., dau. and h. of John Taylor, of Finchampstead, Gent., and w. of John Blighe, **1635**, and dau. Jane, then 5 years old, rel., p. 247.

HAGBOURN, EAST. I. *Hugh Keate, of Hodcott, Esq., 1614, buried at West Ilsley, and w. Christian, **1627**, and 8 chil., Hugh, John, Francis, Wm. (who pos.), Mary, Margt., Christian, Elenor, qd. pl., mur., S.C. INSCRS. II. Claricia Wyndesore "domina de Westhakborn," w. of John York, and founder of a chapel, **1403**. III. John York, founder of [S. ?] Aisle, 1413, engr. c. **1445**. IV. John Yorke, and w. Joane, both dec. Sept. 5th, **1445**.

HAMPSTEAD, EAST. Thos. Berwyk, "nuper in societate M. J. Fowler de Capella Regis Hen. VI^{ti}.," 1443, hf. eff., C.

HANNEY, WEST. I. [John] Seys, rector, c. **1370**, on a bracket now lost, marg. inscr. mutil., large, C. p. 137. *Introd.*, p. 142 (det.); *Gough*, vol. ii. pl. liii. p. 149. II. Humfrey, second son of John Cheynie, of Westwoodday, **1557**, in arm., dec. childless, with 12 Eng. vv., and text from Job xix. 25—27 on marg. inscr., C., p. 222. III. John Ayshcombe, of Lyfford, Gent., **1592**, and 2 ws.; by the second w. (Margery, a dau. of Oliver Welsborne, of West Hanney) he had 10 sons and 4 daus., marg. inscr., C. IV. Sir Christopher Lytcot, **1599**, in arm., twice high sheriff of Berks., m. Jane, widow of Thos. Essex, Esq., of Beckett House, Berks., and Cath., widow of Wm. Younge, of Bastledon, Esq., and was "knighted in the campe before Roane the xvjth of November · 1591 · by the hands of the french Kinge, Henry the fovrth of y^t name & king of Navarre. who after his travailes in Germany, Italy and Fravnce," died at Bastledon, C., p. 237. V. *Francis Wellesborne, Esq., **1602**, in arm., and ws. Alice and Eleanor, dau. of Thos. Stafford, of Broadfield, with 3 daus., Frances, Cath., and Anne, marg. inscr., A.T., S.Tr. VI. Oliver Ayshcombe,

Gent., **1611**, a benefactor to the poor, and w. Martha, a dau. of Thos. Yeate, of Lyfford, Esq., 1611, with 4 sons and 2 daus. C.

*HARWELL. John Jenneus, **1599**, and w. Margt., with 6 sons and 5 daus., N.

*HENDRED, EAST. I. Hen. Eldysley and his brother Roger Eldysley, **1439**, mchts., one eff. lost, C.   II. John Eyston, **1589**, in arm., æt. 58, and w. Jane (Burington [Burton]), with 4 sons and a dau., inscr. in 10 cleg. vv., S.C.   *Front.*, *Relton*.   INSCR. Wm. Whitwey, clothier and wolman, **1479**, S.C.

HURST. I. [Rich.?] Warde, "aulæ proquæstor" to Hen. VIII., Edw. VI., Mary, and Elizth., in arm., and w. Colubra, **1574**, with 8 sons and 9 daus., inscr. in 14 eleg. vv., mur., A.T., N.A.   II. Alice, eldest dau. of Rich. Ward, Esq., cooferer to Queen Elizth., and w. of Thos. Harison, Esq., dec. in childbed of her only son Rich., father of Sir Rich. Harison, c. **1600**, in a bed, qd. pl., inscr. cut in stone? p. 221.

KINTBURY. Mr. John Gunter, 1624, æt. 89, and w. Alice (buried at Cirencester), **1626**, æt. 86, Jos. Plat, Esq., their son-in-law and executor, pos., C., p. 54.

LAMBOURN. I. John de Estbury, and w. Agnes, c. **1400**, hf. effs.; Fr. inscr. and two Evang. symbs. lost, N., p. 164.   *Boutell's Christian Monuments*, p. 150.   II. John Estbury, Esq., founder of chantry, 1372, not in arm., and his son Thos., c. **1410**, hf. effs., E.A. of S.Tr., pp. 45, 52.   III. John Estbury, Esq., founder of chapel, chantry [and almshouse], c. **1485**, in tabard, with marg. inscr., A.T., S.C., p. 112.   IV. Thos. Garrard, Gent. (eldest son of Thos. Garrard by his second w. Alice), **1619**, and w. Anne, dau. of John Jutt, Esq., 1610; Thos. their son pos., C.   INSCR. V. Thos. Garord, **1530**, mur., C.

LANGFORD. Walter Prunes, Gent., 1594, and w. Mary, dau. of Thoby Playdell, of Great Farringdon, Berks., Esq., **1609**, with marg. inscr.

LOCKING, EAST. *Edw. Keate, Gent., third son of Sir Wm. Keate, of East Hagbourn, **1624**, æt. 83, and w. Joan, eldest dau. of John Doe, Gent., 1624, æt. 79, m. in 1565, and had 11 chil., Edw., Wm., Francis, John, Anne, Jane, Agnes, Christian, Elenor, Mary, and Dorothy, inscr. cut in the slab, S.A.

READING, ST. GILES. John Bowyer, tanner, **1521**, and w. Jone, worn, N.

READING, ST. LAURENCE. I. John Kent, burgess, and w. Joan, c. **1415**, hf. effs., C.   II. Walter Barton, Gent., **1538**, inscr. with 2 Lat. vv. *Views of Reading Abbey and Churches*, 1805, vol. i. p. 54.

III. Edw. Butler, Gent., 5 times mayor, **1584**, æt. 72, and w. Alce, 1583, æt. 72, with 3 daus., Alce, Mary, and Elizth. [Alce m. Wm. Buttell, Esq., and had 3 sons and 4 daus.; Mary m. Wm. Powell, D.D., and had 2 sons and 1 dau.; Elizth. m. Rich. Staverton, Esq., and had 2 daus.]; eff. of w., the second and third daus., the grandchil. and marg. inscr. lost, once on A.T., C., p. 225. INSCRS. IV. John Andrew, priest, **1428**, inscr. with 4 Lat. vv., C., eff. sm., now lost, but engr. in *Views of Reading Abbey, &c.*, vol. i. p. 54. V. Wm. Hunt, mayor, **1463**, and ws. Alice and Isabella, effs. lost, worn, once in N.A., now in N.

READING, ST. MARY. I. A cross fleury and several scrolls for Wm. Baron, **1416**, mutil., S.A., pp. 173, 179. INSCR. II. John Boome, dec. in his third mayoralty, **1558**, and w. Alice, 1558, m. 37 years, had 1 son and 5 daus., 8 Eng. vv., effs. lost. Eff. of w. and inscr. engr. in *Views of Reading Abbey, &c.*, vol. i. p. 46; inscr. now in wooden frame.

SANDHURST. Rich. Geale, **1608**, and w. Elizth., with 4 sons and 5 daus., sm.

SHEFFORD, LITTLE. John Fetyplace, Esq., **1524**, and w. Dorothy, with 4 daus., 3 sons and Hy. Trin. lost, mur., C.

SHOTTESBROOKE. I. A Priest and a Frankelein, c. **1370**, under fine canopy, inscr. lost, large, once in C., now in N.Tr., pp. 138, 163. *Waller*, pt. ii. *Bib. Top. Brit.*, vol. iv. p. 105 (effs.) II. [Margt., w. of Sir Fulk] Pennebrygg, mutil. marg. inscr. in Fr., N.Tr., p. 68. *Gough*, vol. ii. pl. v. p. 11. She was the dau. of Sir Wm. Trussel, founder of the Ch. in 1337, and dec. **1401**. III. Rich. Gyll, Esq., "sergeaūt of the Bakehous" with Kings Hen. VII. and VIII., and "bayly of the vij hundreds of Cokam and Bray," **1511**, N.Tr., p. 232. *Fairholt's Costume in England*, p. 282. IV. Thos. Noke, "comenly called Father Noke," created Esq. by Hen. VIII., "and for his Excellencie in artilarie made Yoman of the Crowne of Englond," **1567**, æt. 87, not in arm., and 3 ws., with 3 sons and 3 daus. of 2nd. w., 1 son and 3 daus. of 1st. w., and a dau. of 3rd. w. lost. Thos. Noke left surviving his w. Julian, 2 brothers, 1 sister, 1 son and 2 daus., inscr. and 6 eleg. vv., N.Tr., pp. 95, 239. *Oxford Man.*, p. 105, and *Introd.*, p. 240 (male eff.) INSCR. V. Wm. Throkmarton, priest, LL.D., "late garden of this church," **1535**, with 4 eleg. vv., placed over an alabaster eff., C.

SPARSHOLT. I. Wm. de Herleston, priest, c. **1360**, cross and marg. inscr. nearly all lost, eff. loose in Ch. chest, C., p. 136. Persons of this name were prebendaries of Lichfield in 1322, and Hereford in 1351. II. Thos. Bothe (?), c. **1495**, lower part lost, with 2 sons?

loose in Ch. chest, 2 daus. lost, slab partly covd. III. A Lady, c. **1510**, sm., loose in Ch. chest. IV. John Fettiplace, Gent., **1602**; he m. Margt. Androwes, widow, a dau. of Thos. Braybrooke, of Abington, Gent.; eff. loose in Ch. chest, inscr. with 4 eleg. vv. in C. Others under pews (?).

STANFORD-DINGLEY. Margt., w. of Wm. Dyneley, "Esquire to the King," **1444**, N.A.

STANFORD-IN-THE-VALE. Roger Campedene, rector, **1398**, hf. eff., with Evang. symbs., large, C.

STEVENTON. Rich. Do, **1476**, and ws. Agnes and Joan, 1 w. and inscr. lost, sm., C., p. 202.

STRATFIELD-MORTIMER. I. Rich. Trevet, alias Hasylwode, valectus, **1441**, in arm., N.A., p. 190. II. Johanna, w. of Rich. Trevet, **1441**, N.A.

STREATLEY. I. Griffin, the son of Thos. and Elizth. Clarke, **1583**, sm. II. Margt., w. of Wm. Buryngton, Gent., **1570**, eff. covd. by a pew, C. III. Thos. Clarke, Gent., **1600**, and w. Elizth., a dau. and coh. of Griffeth Barton, Esq., 1598, with 4 chil., Griffeth, Agnes, Elizth., and Margt., C. IV. Thos. Buriton, Esq. (son and h. of Wm., third son of Thos. Buriton, of Hereford, Esq.), **1603**, and w. Joan (Wier), by whom he had 6 sons (then dec.) and 11 daus., his w. pos., partly covd. by pew, N. Another under pews (?).

SUNNING. I. Laurence Fyton, Esq., bailiff of Sunning, **1434**, p. 189. II. Wm. Barker, steward and receiver of the lordship of Sunning, **1549**, and w. Anne, with 1 dau. [Anne]. III. Wm. Barker, Esq., [**1575**], eff. lost, and w. Anne (Stowghton), with 6 sons and 5 daus., 12 Eng. vv., C. IV. Anne, dau. and h. of Wm. Barker, Esq. [No. II.], and w. of Wm. Staverton, of Oakingham, Berks., Gent., **158[9]**, with 4 sons, Fraunces, Wm., Geo., and John. V. Elizth., dau. of Sir Geo. and Dame Anne Chute, **1627**, æt. three years and a half, inscr. with 6 Eng. vv., very sm., C.

SWALLOWFIELD. I. Margery, w. of Thos. Letterford, Esq., c. **1450**, sm., C. II. Christopher Lytkott, Esq., **1554**, and w. Kath., dau. of Robt. Cheyne, of Chesham Bois, Bucks., Esq., with 4 chil., John, Leonard, Christopher, and Dorothy, C., pp. 235, 236, 245. *Introd.*, pp. 235, 245.

TIDMARSH. I. Margt., w. of Thos. Wode, (a justice of the Court of Common Pleas,) and formerly w. of Robt. Leyneham, Esq., lord of the manor, **1499**, N. *Views of Reading Abbey, &c.*, vol. i. p. 26. II. Robt. (?) Leyneham, Esq., c. **1500**, in tabard, mutil., inscr. lost. N. *Ibid.*

TILEHURST. Gauwin More, Gent., a marshall of the king's

hall, **1469**, not in arm., and w. Isabella, 1469, with 3 sons and 2 daus., sm., S.A.

UFTON-NERVET. *Wm. Smith, Gent., **1627**, æt. 70, and w. Constance, dau. of Geo. Tettersale, Esq., 1610, sm., N.C.

WALTHAM, BRIGHT. John Newman, **1517**, and w. Ellen, with their son Thos., sm.

WALTHAM, WHITE. I. Margt., w. of John Hille, **1445**, under seats, C.   II. Joan, dau. and h. of Thos. Beauchamp, Esq., and w. of Rich. Decons, Esq., **1506**, sm., C.

WANTAGE. I. A Priest, c. **1320**? hf. eff., now mur., C., p. 143. *Boutell's Series.*   II. Sir Ivo Fitzwaryn, **1414**, large, now mur., N.C., p. 188. *Boutell's Series; Relton.*   III. A Civilian, c. **1460**, head and feet lost, loose.   IV. A Priest, c. **1510**, in acad., now mur., sm.   V. Walter Tawbott, **1522**, and ws. Agnes and Alice, with 5 sons, 4 daus. lost, loose.   VI. *Wm. Willmott, Gent., 1618, æt. 76, (eff. lost), and w. Cecilia, a dau. of Hugh Hyde, Esq., of Letcomb Regis, 1612, eff. loose, and engr. in *Relton;* they had 6 chil., Hugh, Geo., Cicilye, Martha, Fraunces, Bridget; their sons-in-law, Thos. Garrard and Thos. Tempest, pos., **1619**, C.   INSCRS. VII. Roger Merlawe, **1460**, and w. Kath., 1459, loose, belonging to No. III. (?), S.Tr.   VIII. Wm. Geddyng, vicar of Wantage, and of All Hallows' Barking, London, **1512**, marg., belonging to No. IV.(?)

WARFIELD. I. Houmfrey, third son of Rich. Staverton, Esq., **1592**, N.A. *Views of Reading Abbey, &c.,* vol. i. p. 35.   INSCRS. II. Elizth., dau. of Humfrey Staverton, and m. 5 years to John Reade, Gent., **1587**, æt. 25, loose.   III. Letice, dau. of Wm. Lovelace, Gent., and m. 30 years to Humfrey Staverton, **1587**, æt. 51, loose.

WELFORD. I. John Westlake, priest, c. **1490**, in acad., sm., C., p. 84.   II. John Young, c. **1530**, he had 4 chil., John, Thos., Ellen, and Susan, sm., C., p. 84. Both brasses now on one slab.

WINDSOR, OLD. *Humfrey Michell, Esq., surveyor of Windsor Castle, 1598, æt. 71, and 2nd. w. Frances, only dau. and h. of Francis Waller, Esq., **1621**, by whom he had Sam. (dec.), Dorcas, Elizth., Susanna (dec.), and Sara; by Kath. Hobbs, his 1st. w., he had Francis, mur., C.

WINDSOR, ST. GEORGE'S CHAPEL. I. Wm. Mugge, priest, first warden [**1380**], eff. in cope lost, super-canopy and mutil. marg. inscr. only left, p. 25.   II. Sir Thos. Sellynger [St. Leger], founder of chapel, and w. Anne, Duchess of Exeter, and sister to Edw. IV., **1475**, in heraldic dresses, with Hy. Trin., qd. pl., curious, mur., Rutland Chapel, pp. 21, 96. *Sandford's Geneal. Hist.,* 1707, p. 396;

Pote's Windsor Castle, p. 31. III. Robt. Honywode, LL.D., archdeacon of Taunton and canon of Windsor, **1522**, in almuce, with S. Cath. and B.V. M. and Child, under a canopy, with diapered background, curious, qd. pl., mur., Rutland Chapel, pp. 21, 34. IV. Dorothy, dau. of John King, D.D. and prebendary, and of his w. Mary, **1630**, æt. 8 months, in cradle, marg. inscr. and 8 Eng. vv., King's Chapel. V. Wm. King, second son of John and Mary King, **1633**, æt. 10 weeks, close by and similar to the last. INSCR. VI. John Robyns, learned in astronomy, physical science, divinity, &c., 16 eleg. vv., now mur., Rutland Chapel; eff. in canon of Windsor's habit, lost. He was S. T. B., and chaplain to Hen. VIII. and Queen Mary, and dec. **1558**. See also brasses in private possession—J. B. Nichols, Esq.

WINKFIELD. Thos. Mountague, yeoman of the guard, **1630**, æt. nearly 92, hf. eff., curious, qd. pl., mur., S.A., pp. 122, 127.

WITTENHAM, LITTLE. I. John Churmound, rector, **1433**, C. II. David Kidwelly, porter of the palace of Henry VI., **1454**, sm., partly covd., C. III. Cecilia, w. of Geoff. Kydwelly, **1472**, N. IV. Geoff. Kidwelly, Esq., **1483**, not in arm., A.T., C., p. 204. *Introd.*, p. 203. V. John Barnes, Esq., "gentleman porter of the Towne and Castle of Guysnes in ffraunce when it was Englishe," dec. at London, **1588**, in arm., his only sister, Mary, m. Wm. Dunche, Esq., and had 2 sons, Edm. and Walter, eff. mur., inscr. on floor, C. VI. Anne, dau. of Henry and Anne Dunch, **1683**, æt. 10 months, qd. pl., inscr. with 8 Eng. vv., sm., C. FRAG. VII. Lower part of fem. eff., c. **1570**?

WOKINGHAM. I. A Civilian and 2 ws., c. **1520**, inscr. and one w. with her chil. lost, N. II. Civilian and w., c. **1590**, inscr. in 8 Eng. vv., mur., S.A.

WYTHAM. A Man in arm. and w., c. **1455**, much mutil., inscr. lost., rel., C., p. 191. Male eff. engr. in *Oxford Man.*, p. 86, and *Introd.*, p. 191. Perhaps Rich. de Wygtham and w. Alice, a dau. of Walter Daundsey of Oxford, or else their dau. Agnes and her husband Wm. Browning.

INSCRIPTIONS, &c.

CLEWER. Martine Expence, who "shott with 100 men him selfe alone at ould fielde at Bray," 6 Eng. vv., mur., S.C. HATFORD. Three shs. and inscr. to Frauncis Pigott, son and h. of Robt. Pigott, of Colwicke, **1614**, by his w. Margt., dau. of Alban Butler, Esq., of Aston, Northants., he had 7 sons and 3 daus. HUNGERFORD. *A brass with Hy. Trin. HURLEY. A crest, 2 scrolls, and 6 eleg. vv.

to John Doyly, **1492**, date in Arabic numerals, C.   ILSLEY, EAST. *A sh. loose, and inscr. to ——, w. of Wm. Hildsley, she survived him 30 years, **1606**, 8 Lat. vv., her dau. Cath. pos., eff. now lost, but engr. in *Hewett's Hundred of Compton*, pl. 14, p. 50.   MORETON, NORTH. Thos. Mayne, yeoman, **1479**, S.A.   NEWBURY. I. John Smalwode, alias Wynchcom, **1519**, and w. Alice, effs. lost, N.A.   For an account of John Winchcombe, the celebrated 'Jack of Newbury,' see Burke's Fam. Romance, vol. i. p. 126.   II. Mr. Hugh Shepley, rector, born at Prescott, Lanc., dec. **1596**, 10 Eng. vv.; his son John, citizen and broderer of London, pos.   III. Francis Trenchard, Esq., of Normanton, Wilts., **1635**, left a dau. Elizth.   SULHAMSTEAD ABBOTS. Ralph Eyer, rector, **1521**, mur., C., p. 44.

The brasses are lost at BEENHAM, ENGLEFIELD, FIFIELD, MARCHAM (p. 259), SHELLINGFORD (p. 140). The brass of Wm. Carter, Gent., **1586**, formerly at Beenham, is engr. in *Views of Reading Abbey, &c.*, vol. i. p. 30. In a MS. given to the Brit. Mus. by Geo. IV. (case vii. 64 b), is a drawing of the eff. and inscr. of Sir Robt. Corbet de Haddley, **1403**, with w. Beatrix (eff. lost), lately at Marcham.

Buckinghamshire.

AMERSHAM. I. Hen. Brudenell, Esq., **1430**, with anelace, and w. Alianora, dau. of Hugh, the son of Sir Thos. Preston, S.Tr., p. 203.   II. Thomas Carbonell, Esq., **1439**, not in arm., and w. Elizth., 14-7 or 14-4, N.A.   III. A Civilian, c. **1450**, head lost, worn, N.A.   III. John de la Penne, 1537, and w. Elizth., dau. of Peter Hally, Esq., **1521**, S.Tr., p. 45.   V. John Drake (son of Francis Drake, of Esher, Surrey, Esq., by his w. Joan, dau. of Wm. Tothill, of Sharlons, and of his w. Kath.), **1623**, æt. 4 years, sm., kng., inscr. with 6 Eng. vv.

ASTWOOD.   *John Chibnale, **1534**, and ws. Emma and Alice, now mur., S.A.

BEACHAMPTON. I. Wm. Bawdyn, blacksmith, **1600**, inscr. with 4 Eng. vv., N. *Lipscomb's History and Antiquities of the County of Buckingham*, 1831-47, vol. ii. p. 533.   II. Alice, dau. of Wm. Mathew, of Calverton, Esq., and w. of Geo. Baldwyn, **1611**, æt. 30, died in childbed, and 4 chil., Wm., Geo., Jane, Isabell, sm., S.A. INSCRS. III. Address to his flock from Mathew Pigot, 20 years their pastor, he dec. **1598**, mur.   IV. Wm. Elmor, **1652**.

BEACONSFIELD. John Waren, **1609**, æt. 60, and w. Elizth., m. 23 years, with 6 chil., Rich., Hen., Wm., John, Fillis, Elizth., worn, N.   There is an incised slab to Thos. Waller, Esq., 1627, and w. Dorothy [Garrard], 1626, holding 2 flaming hearts conjoined, N.A.

BLEDLOW. Wm. Herū, B.A., vicar, 1525, now mural in aumbry, sm., C.

BLETCHLEY. Thos. Sparke, D.D., rector, 1616, æt. 68, a bust in an oval, with 3 sons and 2 daus., and figures of death, fame, &c.; Thos. his son and h. pos., qd. pl., mur., C., pp. 30, 217. There is an incised slab to Rev. Edw. Tayler, 1693, C., p. 230.

BURNHAM. I. Gyles Eyre and w. Elizth., c. 1500, several chil. lost, sm., N. II. [Edmund Eyre, Gent., 1563], and w., with 3 sons and 2 daus., N. III. Thos. Eyer, Gent., late owner of the manor of Allerds, 1581, and 3 ws., the second w. with 4 sons and 3 daus., inscr. with an acrostic in 10 Eng. vv. (see Appendix B.), on same slab as No. II., p. 225. INSCRS., &c. IV. Wm. Aldriche and w. Agnes, c. 1520 (effs. lost), with 9 sons and 15 daus., N. V. Jacomyne, dau. of Robt. Littell, m. for 20 years to Wm. Tyldsley, 1556, 8 Lat. vv., N. VI. Wm. Tyldsley, Esq., 1563, C. VII. Anna, dau. of —— Wentworth, and w. of —— Knatchbull; 4 Lat. vv.

CAVERSFIELD. I. —— Langston, 1435, head lost, loose, a figure of St. Laurence and inscrs. lost, pp. 140, 202. II. John Langston [1506], in arm., and w. Amice, with 11 (?) sons and 10 (?) daus.; w., inscr., and 3 shs. loose; male eff. (?) and chil. under a pew, C. III. Two hands holding a heart, with 3 scrolls, for [Thos?] Denton [1533?], inscr. lost, C. p. 108. INSCR. IV. Rauf, son of Wm. Heydon, Esq., 1592, loose. The loose brasses were in a chest, April, 1858.

CHALFONT ST. GILES. I. A Priest, c. 1470, inscr. lost, sm., N.A., p. 25. II. A Lady, c. 1510, inscr. lost, N. III. Wm. Gardyner, Esq., 1558, in arm., and w. Anne, with 5 sons and 4 daus. IV. Thos. Fletewoode, Esq., born at Heskyn, co. Lanc., 'lord of the vache, treasurer of mynte,' knight of the parliament for Bucks., and late sheriff of Bucks. and Beds., 1570, æt. 52, in arm., and 2 ws.; 1st, Barbara [Francis], with 2 sons and 2 daus.; 2nd, Bridgett, dau. of Sir John Springe, with 8 sons and 6 daus., mur., C. *Lipscomb*, vol. iii. p. 235.

CHALFONT, WEST, or ST. PETER. I. Wm. Whappelode, senior, 1398, in arm., and w. Elizth., the widow of Wm. Restwold, Esq., engr., c. 1446, pp. 45, 51, 193. II. Wm. Whappelode, son of No. I., and steward of Hen. [Beaufort], cardinal of England and bp. of Winchester, 1446, in arm., and w. Margery, on same slab as No. I., p. 193. III. †A Priest, c. 1520, p. 78. IV. Sir Robt.

Hanson, vicar of Chalfont St. Peter and of Little Missenden, **1545**, palimpsest, sm., p. 50.

CHEARSLEY. *John Frankeleyn and w. Margt., "which ordeyned leystowe to this Chirche, and divine service to be doone every holydaye, in the yere," **1462**, C. *Lipscomb*, vol. i. p. 125.

CHENIES, or ISENHAMPSTEAD. I. John Waliston, smith, **1469**, and ws. Isabella and Joan, worn, N.   II. Edmund Molyneux, Esq., **1484**, and w. Agnes, [dau. of Wm. Cogenhoe, of Northants., and] widow of Lord John Cheyne [dec. 1494?] with canopy, C., p. 197. *Lipscomb*, vol. iii. p. 255.   III. Lady Anne, widow of Sir David Phelip, lady of the manors of Thorno, Northants., and Isenhampstead, **1510**, holding a heart with 2 scrolls, under a canopy, C., p. 107. *Ibid.*, p. 254.   IV. Agnes Johnson, widow, mother of Robt. Leyff, rector, **1511**.   V. Elizth., dau. of John Broughton, Esq., **1524**, with marg. inscr., once on A.T. (?), p. 214.   INSCR. VI. Sir Nich. Smythe, 'late person of late mars' (Latimer), **1517**, C.

CHESHAM BOIS. I. Elizth., w. of Robt. Cheyne, Gent., **1516**, and Robert Cheyne, Esq., **1552**, in arm., C., pp. 54, 226, 236. *Lipscomb*, vol. iii. p. 272; *Introd.*, p. 241 (det.)   II. Benedict Lee, 'crysome,' son of Roger Lee, Gent., c. **1520**, sm., C., p. 220. *Introd.*, p. 220.

CHICHELEY. I. Anth. Cave, Esq., mcht. of the Staple of Calais, lord of the manor of Chicheley, **1558**, in arm., and w., N.A. *Lipscomb*, vol. iv. p. 97.   II. —— [Cave]. a skeleton, recumbent, in shroud, c. **1560** (?), inscr. in 4 Lat. and 5 Eng. vv., qd. pl., sm., N.A.

CLAYDON, MIDDLE. I. Isabella Gifford, **1523**, rel., N., p. 241. *Lipscomb*, vol. i. p. 194.   II. Alex. Anne, priest, **1526** (hf. eff.), with chalice and host, rel., N., p. 115. *Ibid.*, p. 192.   III. Roger Gyffard, Esq., **1542**, and w. Mary [Nansegles], with 13 sons and 7 daus., large, N., pp. 31, 235. *Ibid.*, p. 193. Lipscomb states that they built the C. in 1519.

CLIFTON REYNES. I. Sir John Reynes, **1428**, legs lost, p. 190. II. A Man and w., c. **1500**, in shrouds, inscr. lost, N.C. Perhaps John Reynes and second w. Agnes, dau. of John Tyringham, Esq.

CRAWLEY. *John Garbrand, D.D., parson, and benefactor to the poor of North Crawley, **1589**, æt. 47, qd. pl., mur., C., p. 222. *Lipscomb*, vol. iv. p. 132.

CRENDON, LONG. *John Canon, 1460, and w. Agnes, **1468**, with 3 sons and 8 daus., N.

DATCHET. I. Mr. Rich. Hanbery, citizen and goldsmith of London, and w. Alice, **1593**, æt. 56, with 2 daus.; one m. Mr. Wm. Combe, of the Middle Temple, Esq., the other, Mr. Edm. Wheler, goldsmith of London, qd., pl., mur., C., p. 119.   INSCR. II. Lady Kath., dau. of Rt. Hon. Wm. Blount, Lord Mountjoy, and w. of Sir Mores Barkeley, **1559**, with sh., mur., C.

DENHAM. I. Walter Duredent, Esq., **1494**, and 2 ws.; Agnes (with 9 sons and 10 daus.), and Margt. (with 3 sons and 4 daus.), N., p. 198. *Fisher.* II. Dame Agnes Jordan, abbess of Syon, c. **1540**, dec. 1544; shs. with the 5 wounds, and marg. inscr. lost, C., pp. 45, 87. *Aungier's Hist. of Syon and Isleworth,* p. 89; *Waller,* pt. xv.; *Introd.,* p. 88. III. Sir Leonard Hurst, parson, **1560**, partly covd., inscr. lost, C., p. 229. *Introd.,* p. 229. INSCUS., &c. IV. Margt. (?) Peckham, **1512** (?), with shs., nearly covd., C. V. Thos. Bedyll, **1528**, and ws. Margt. and Joan; all lost but 3 sons and a dau. of the first w., S.A. VI. Rich. Thornhill, of Tuxford, Notts., parson, **1612**, loose. A Priest, hf. eff., lost, C., p. 142. *Introd.,* p. 143. Amphillis, dau. of Sir Edm. Pekham, **1545**, lost, C., p. 214. An incised slab to Mr. Philip Edelen, preacher, 1656, æt. 58, mur., C., p. 230.

*DINTON. I. John Compton, **1424**, in arm., and w., sm., p. 190. II. Wm. Lee, of Morton, **1486**, and w. Alice (mutil.), N. III. Francis Lee, Gent., **1508**, and w. Elizth., with 7 sons and 8 daus., worn, sm. IV. Thos. Grenewey, Esq., 1538, and w. Elizth., **1539**, with 3 daus., mutil., inscr. loose (?), C. V. Rich. Grenewey, Esq., son and h. of Thos. Grenewey, Esq., **1551**, in arm., and w. Joan, dau. and h. of John Tylney, Esq., of Leckhampstead (eff. lost), on same slab as No. IV. VI. Simon Mayne, Esq., 1617, in arm., and w. Colubery [Lovelace], **1628**, with their chil. Simon and Colubery, N., p. 238. Simon the son was one of the regicides, and died in the Tower in 1660-1. INSCR. VII. John Lee, **1506**.

DRAYTON BEAUCHAMP. I. Thos. Cheyne, Esq., shield-bearer to Edw. III., **1368**, inscr. lost, large, once in S.A., now mur., C., pp. 158, 160. *Waller,* pt. i.; *Boutell's Series; Introd.,* p. 158 (det.) II. [Wm.] Cheyne, **1375**, in arm., with mutil. marg. inscr., large, now mur., C., pp. 150, 160, 173. *Lipscomb,* vol. iii. p. 335; *Waller,* pt. viii. III. Hen. Fazakyrley, priest, **1531**, with chalice and host, headless, sm., C.

DUNTON. I. John Sotton, **1518**, and w. Agnes, effs. c. **1420**, sm., N. II. —— Collys, w. of Rich. ——, c. **1510**, with 1 son standing behind, inscr. mutil., sm., N. Both brasses partially recut (?).

EDLESBOROUGH. I. John, son and h. of John Rufford, Esq., **1540**, in arm., and 3 ws. (all on one plate), Bryggett, Anne, and Elynore, N.C. II. *John Pigott and w., **1592**, mur., N. INSCR. III. Hen. Brugis, Gent., who m. Frances Pygott, **1647**, æt. 88, mur., N. See also p. 110, and brasses in private possession —Ashridge House.

ELLESBOROUGH. I. —— Hawtrey, Esq., c. **1535**, and w., with 10 sons and 7 daus., inscr. lost, sh., palimpsest (?), S.A.   INSCRS. II. Thos. Hawtrey, Esq., **1544**, and w. Sybell, S.A. (belonging to No. I.?) III. Mary, w. of Wm. Hawtrey, Esq., **1555**, dec. in childbirth, on same slab as No. II.

EMBERTON.   John Mordon, alias Andrew, rector, c. **1410**, C. *Lipscomb*, vol. iv. p. 141. See inscr. in Appendix B.

ETON COLLEGE CHAPEL. I. Dr. Thos. Barker, fellow, and for 18 years vice-provost of Eton College, rector of Petworth, **1489**, in cap and almuce, inscr. in 16 Lat. vv., sm., now mur., S.C.   II. Hen. Bost, provost, **1503** (?), in almuce, under triple canopy lately repaired, inscr. in 16 eleg. vv., worn, large, now mur. in S.C., p. 79. *Lipscomb*, vol. iv. p. 485.   III. Rich. Ardern, fellow, **1509**, with chalice and host, worn, sm.   IV. A Priest, M.A. (?), c. **1510**, inscr. lost, perhaps John Gregoray, 1512.   V. A Lady, c. **1520**, inscr. lost.   VI. Rich. Grey, 'Lord Grey, Cotenore, Wylton, and Ruthyn,' h. apparent to Rich. Earl of Kent, son of Edm. Lord Grey, brother and h. to Geo. Lord Grey and Thos. Lord Grey, and henchman to Hen. VIII., **1521**, pp. 50, 198.   VII. Wm. Boutrod, pety-canon of Windsor, **1522**, in cope.   VIII. [Wm.?] Horman, **1535**, with chalice and host, inscr. in 12 eleg. vv., sm., p. 179. IX. Roger Lupton, provost of Eton and canon of Windsor, c. **1536**, inscr. lost, mur., S.C., p. 81.   X. Thos. Edgcomb, fellow and vice-provost of Eton, **1545**, ¾ eff. in hood, on reverse portions of 10 Lat. vv., inscr. in 10 eleg. vv., sm., p. 86.   XI. Robt. Stokys and w. Elizth., both dec. **1560** (male eff. and chil. lost); on reverse of inscr. one to Walter Haugh, **1505**, and ws. Margt. and Isabella.   XII. Thos. Allen, fellow of Eton and other colleges, and a benefactor, **1636**, kng.   INSCRS. XIII. John Chelde and 3 ws., Margt., Isabel, and Alice, **15—**, effs. lost.   XIV. Thos. Smith, fellow, M.A. of King's Coll., Camb., **1572**, 4 Eng. vv., p. 226.   XV. Edw. Underhyll, citizen and haberdasher of London, **1606**.   XVI. Edm., son of Sir Hen. Hobart, 'alumnus,' **1607**.   XVII. *Philip Boteler, **1613**. XVIII. *Elizth. Francklin, **1641**.   XIX. Jane, dau. of Edm. Woodhall, Esq., and w. of G. Goad, **1657**, inscr. on a large heart. Most of these brasses have been lately removed from the floor to the walls of the ante-chapel. See also list of brasses in private possession, &c.—British Museum.

*HADDENHAM. I. A Priest, c. **1420**, inscr. lost.   II. Thos. Nassh, priest, **1428**, hf.-eff., C.   INSCR. III. Giles Wodbryge, **1539**, and w. Elizth., effs. lost, now placed under No. II.

HALTON.   Hen. Bradschawe, Esq., chief baron of the exchequer,

1553, and w. Joan [Hurst], with 4 sons and 4 daus., mur., C., p. 54. *Lipscomb*, vol. ii. p. 225.

HAMBLEDON. I. A Civilian, c. 1460, lower part of off. lost, loose, sm. *Lipscomb*, vol. iii. p. 575. II. John White, 1497, (upper part of cff. gone), and w. Alice, sm., S.Tr. III. A Man in arm. and widow with inlaid mantle [Robt. Scrope, 1500 ? and w. Cath. ?] kng., inscr. lost, sm., p. 9. *Lipscomb*, vol. iii. p. 575. IV. A Civilian, lower part of off. lost, c. 1500. V. A Civilian and w. (upper part of off. lost), c. 1600, with 2 sons, loose. VI. —— Sheepwash and 2 ws., c. 1620, inscr. lost, qd. pl., sm., nailed to a pew. INSCRS., &c. VII. John Shipwash, 1457, and w. Joan, with arms and initial on 4 shs., N.A. To this belong (?) No. I., and 4 sons now loose, 3 daus. gone. VIII. John Berde and w. (?), 1492. IX. Wm Shypwasshe and w. Margery, c. 1500 ?

*HAMPDEN, GREAT. I. John Hampden, Esq., 1496, and w. Elizth. [Sydney], engr. c. 1525, with 4 sons and 6 daus., C. *Lipscomb*, vol. ii. p. 289. II. Sir John Hampden, 1553, in arm., and 2 ws.; 1st., Elizth. Savage (with 3 daus.), 2nd., [Philippa, dau. of John Wilford, of London], C., p. 33. *Ibid.*, p. 290. INSCRS. III. Griffith Hampden, Esq., 1591, and second w., Anne, dau. and h. of Anthony Cave, of Chicheley, 1594, with sh., C. *Ibid.*, p. 291. Some shs. with arms of Hampden and Horsey, 5 sons and 3 daus., probably under flooring within communion rails.

*HANSLOPE. I. Mary, dau. of Thos. Birchemore, 1602, æt. 6, sm., N. INSCR. II. Eight Eng. vv., —— Troughton, and w. ——, dau. of —— Hampden, N.A.

HARDMEAD. Francis Catesby, Gent., youngest son of Anth. Catesbye, of Whyston, Esq., 1556, feet gone, C.

HAVERSHAM. I. Alice, w. of Thos. Payn, Esq., 1427, C. II. John Maunsell, Gent., 1605, æt. 66 years, 4 months, and 5 days, a skeleton, qd. pl., C.

HEDGERLEY. I. Robt. Fulmer, 1498, and w. Joan, with 2 sons and 2 daus., sm., N. II. Margt., w. of Edw. Bulstrode, Esq., 1540, with 10 sons and 3 daus., mostly palimpsest, C., pp. 45, 46, 103.

HITCHAM. I. Thos. Ramsey, 1510, in arm., and w. Margt., with 4 sons and 3 daus., N. II. Nich. Clarke, Esq., son and h. to "syr John Clarke of Weston Knt. that tooke the Duke of Longevyle prisoner," [see Thame, Oxon., 1539], 1551, in arm., with 4 chil., Jane, Wm., Dorothy, and John, the daus. lost; he m. Elizth., dau. and h. of Thos. Ramsey, Esq., A.T., C., p. 223. *Lipscomb*, vol. iii. p. 284. INSCRS. III. Jane Clarke, 1563, dec. young, with 6 Eng.

vv., below No. II.   IV. Sir Francis, youngest son of Sir Wm. Clarke, **1631**, and w. Grizzell, dau. of Sir David Woodroffe, of Poyle, Surrey, and 8 chil., John, Wm., Edm., Grizzell, Dorothy, Frances, Mary, and Elizth., C.

HITCHENDON.   *Robt. Thurloe, priest, **1493**.

HORWOOD, GREAT.   Hen. Virgine (?), rector, **1487**, in acad., sm., worn, C.

IVER.   I. Rich. Blount, Esq., **1508**, and w. Elizth., dau. and h. of Wm. Forde, Esq., with 3 sons and 3 daus., marg. inscr., once on A.T., C., p. 232.   INSCRS. II. Raufe Awbrey, Gent., "late cheyffe clerke of the kechyn with prince Arthur."   III. Joan, dau. of Wm. Hytchcocke, Gent., of Bread-street, London, and w. of Hen. Moncke, Gent., of Iver, **1601**, and 3 sons, Thos., Hen., and Hen., with 5 shs., C.

IVINGHOE.   I. Rich. Blackhed, **1517**, and w. Maude; 2 sons and 2 daus. lost (?), loose, sm., N.Tr.   II. Thos. Duncombe, **1531**, headless, and 4 daus., Margt., Margt., Elizth., Anne; w. Joan, sons, and inscr. lost; 6 sons, c. **1595**, placed on the slab, S.Tr.   III. Wm. Duncumbe, Gent., **1576** (loose), and 2 ws.; 1st, Mary, with 5 chil., Elizth., Mary, Roger, Thos., John; 2nd, Alice, with 6 sons and 5 daus., [Wm., Edw., Edith]; effs. of ws. and of chil. of 2ud w. lost, N.A. IV. John Douncombe, **1594**, æt. 80, and w. Alice (eff. lost), with 7 chil., Roger, Hen., Thos., Wm., Elizth., Alice, Agnes, now on same slab as No. II., S.Tr. *Lipscomb*, vol. iii. p. 395.   INSCR. V. Ralf Fallywolle, 1349, and w. Lucy, **1368**, Fr. inscr., hf. effs. lost, N.

LANGLEY MARSH.   I. John Bowser, Gent., son of Thos. Bowser, of Colebroke, dec. "in the 50 yeare of the peace of the Gospell in England," **1608**, æt. 64, leaving 1 son and 1 dau.; 2 shs. with knots and initials.   INSCRS. II. *Elizth., dau. of Roger Giffard, and w. of Nich. Clopton, **1434**, N.A.   III. John Boteler and w. Matilda, and dau. Alice, c. **1440**(?), N.   IV. Thos. Bowsare, **1572**, 2 Eng. vv. V. Julian, w. of Edw. Higgins, and dau. of Christ. and Elizth. Meale, **1603**, with 4 Eng. vv.

LILLINGSTONE DAYRELL.   I. Paul Dayrell, Esq., **1491**, and w. Margt., A.T., C., pp. 171, 198. *Lipscomb*, vol. iii. p. 36. *Introd.*, p. 194 (det.)   II. Rich. Blakysley, rector, **1493**, headless, sm., C., p. 227. See Addenda and Corrigenda.

LINFORD, GREAT.   I. Roger Hunt, **1473**, and w. Joan, marg. inscr., with 8 Eng. vv. stating he paved the Ch., chil. lost, N.   II. Thos. Malyn, Gent., **1536**, and w. Elizth., with 1 dau., N.   III. John Uvedall, Gent., and w. Anne, **1611**, æt. 62, sm., with 5 sons and 3 daus., C.

LINSLADE. *A Civilian, c. **1500**, and 3 ws., and 12 chil. by 1 w., and 3 or 4 (lost) by another, N.

LOUGHTON. Hugh Parke, M.A., B.D., rector [**1514**], hf. eff., C.

LUDGERSHALL. *Three fem. effs. and chil., with inscrs. to Anne, w. of Mihil Englishe, sheriff of London in 1523, she dec. **1565**; Anne Englishe, w. of John Gyfford, Esq., and her dau. Anne Neele, æt. 4 years, rel., A.T., C. *Lipscomb*, vol. i. p. 321.

MARLOW, LITTLE. *Nichol Ledewich, founder of Ch. or C. (eff. lost), and w. Alice, **1430**, inscr. in 6 Lat. vv., A.T., C.

MARSTON, NORTH. I. Rich. Sanders, Gent., **1602**, æt. 67, inscr. in 10 Eng. vv., qd. pl., mur., C. *Lipscomb*, vol. i. p. 347. INSCRS. II. John Yngrave (or Yngrame), bailiff, **1499**, N.A. III. Elizth. Saunders, **1613**. IV. Elizth. Cookson, **1656**, C.

*MARSWORTH. I. Nich. West, master in Chancery, **1586**, in arm. (eff. loose in 1859), and w. Joan, 1585 (eff. gone), with 4 sons (legs only left) and 2 daus., S.C. II. Mary (Clare), w. of Edm. West, Esq., **1606**, with shrouded child, S.C. III. Edmund West, serjeant-at-law, son of Edm. West, **1681**, æt. 51, in arm., and w. Sarah, dau. of Alex. Croke, of Studley, Oxon., with 3 sons and 3 daus., and figure of death, qd. pl., mur., S.C., pp. 215, 218. *Lipscomb*, vol. iii. p. 414. INSCR. IV. John Scelke and w. Cristina, S.C.

MILTON KEYNES. *Adam Babyngton, rector, **1427**, C.

*MISSENDEN, GREAT. I. A Lady, c. **1450** (?), husband and inscr. lost. II. A Civilian, sm., c. **1520**. These brasses are now mur. in S.A., and are engr. by *Lipscomb*, vol. ii. p. 381, who also engr. the brass of John Iwardby, Esq., and w. Kath., dau. and h. of Bernard de Missenden, **1436**, now lost (?), p. 208. INSCR. III. Zacheus Metcalfe, Gent., 1595, and mother, Margt. (w. of Christ. Metcalf), **1596**, mur., S.A.

MISSENDEN, LITTLE. †John Style, Gent., **1613**, N.

MOULSOE. *Rich. Ruthall (?), in arm., **1528** (?), and w. ——— (Lee?), inscr. lost, N.C., p. 232. *Lipscomb*, vol. iv. p. 255.

NETTLEDEN. Sir Geo. Cotton, vice-chamberlain to Prince Edward, dec. "post longam egritudinem," **1545**; Rich., his brother, who was comptroller [of the household?] of Prince Edward, pos., C., p. 230.

NEWPORT PAGNELL. A Civilian, c. **1440**, headless, inscr. lost, worn, large, N.

PENN. I. Elizth. Rok, **1540**, in shroud, pecul., S.A., p. 223. II. John Pen, Esq., **1597**, and w. Ursula (lower part of effs. lost), with 6 sons, inscr. in 4 Lat. vv. III. Wm. Pen, Esq., **1638**, in arm., and w. Martha, 1635, with 1 son and 2 daus., C. IV. Susan,

w. of Sir Hen. Drury, and mother of Mrs. Sarah Pen, **1640**, p. 25.
V. John Pen, Esq., **1641**, in arm., and w. Sarah, dau. of Sir Hen.
Drury, with 5 sons and 5 daus., C., pp. 25, 238. *Lipscomb*, vol. iii.
p. 291.

QUAINTON. I. Joan Plessi, c. **1360**, hf. eff., sm., with Fr. inscr.,
C., pp. 166, 213. *Lipscomb*, vol. i. p. 428.   II. *John Lewys,
rector, **1422**, in cassock, kng., sm., C. *Ibid.*, p. 432.   III. *John
Spence, rector, **1485**, in cope, C. *Ibid.*, p. 431.   IV. Margery,
dau. of Mr. John Iwardby, Esq., and w. of Sir Rauff Verney, **1509**,
with 1 son and 3 daus., C.   V. Rich., son of Nich. Iwardby, **1529**,
C. *Ibid.*, p. 429.   VI. †Elizth., w. for 26 years, 8 months, and
15 days to John Chester, Gent., **1593**, inscr. lost. *Ibid.*, p. 429.

RISBOROUGH, MONKS. I. Robt. Blundell, rector, **1431**, inscr.
lost, C. *Lipscomb*, vol. ii. p. 422.   II. A Civilian and w., c. **1460**,
hf. effs., inscr. lost, N.   III. Two sons and 5 daus., c. **1520**, parents
lost, S.A.

SAUNDERTON. Isabella, dau. of Wm., and sister of Bernard,
Saunterdon, c. **1430**, hf. eff., on a pew, sm., inscr. lost (?).

SHALSTON. Dame Susan Kyngeston, "vowes," eldest dau. of
Rich. Fetyplace, of East Shefford, Berks., and w. of John Kyngeston,
of Childrey, Berks., **1540**, once in C., now rel. and mur., N.A.,
pp. 54, 89.

SLAPTON. I. Reginald Manser, rector, **1462**, hf. eff., C.   II.
*Jas. Tornay, yeoman of the crown to Hen. VIII., **1519**, and ws.
Amy and Elizth., with 4 sons and 5 daus., pp. 127, 239.

*SOULBURY. I. John Turney, **1512**, and w. Agnes, worn, N.
II. John Mallet, **1516**, and w. Alice (?), one eff. and inscr. lost,
N.A.

STOKE POGES. I. Sir Wm. Molyns, **1425**, and widow, Lady
Margery, [dec. 1439?], C., p. 190. *Lipscomb*, vol. iv. p. 566.   II.
Edm. Hampdyn, Esq., c. **1560**, and w. ——, dau. of Rich. Curson, of
Waterpery, Oxon., Esq.; 2 daus., Mary and El[izth.], lost, mutil.
marg. inscr., C.   INSCR. III. Elenor Mullens, w. 1stly, of Lord
Robt. Hungurforde, and 2ndly, of Lord Oliver Manyngham, [**1476**?],
eff. in shroud, with chil. lost, 2 shs. left, C.

*STONE. I. Wm. Gurney, of Bisshopston, **1470**, and w. Agnes,
N.   II. Thos. Gorney, **1520**, and w. Agnes, with 5 sons and 3 daus.,
palimpsest, N.

STOW. I. Anna Saunders, **147[9?]**, inscr. mutil., sm.   II. John,
2nd son of Thos. Temple, Esq., and his w. Hester, **1592**, æt. 2
months, sm.   There is a sm. incised eff. in stone of Hester Pemston,
1612, æt. 3 months.

*SWANBOURN. I. Thos. Adams, yeoman, and freeman of London, who "in prime of youth by bloudy theves was slaine, In Liscombe ground his blood y⁰ grasse did staine," 1626, and w. Elizth., with 4 chil., Robt., Thos., Alice, and Joan, inscr. with 6 Eng. vv., once on A.T., now mur., C. INSCR. II. Robt. Addams, 1616, and w., N.

TAPLOW. I. Nichole de Aumberdene [Ambrosden, *Oxon.*], "iadis pessoner de Londres," c. 1350, eff. sm., in the head of a fine floriated cross with the stem resting on a dolphin, N., pp. 140, 162. *Gough,* vol. ii. pl. liii. p. 149; *Lipscomb,* vol. iii. p. 300; *Boutell,* p. 121. *Specimens of Ancient Ch. Plate, Sepulchral Crosses, &c.* (cross). *Oxford Man.,* p. 72, and *Introd.,* p. 162 (eff.) II. Rich., son and h. of Robt. Manfeld, 1455, æt. 19, with his maiden sister Isabel, and brother John in shroud, inscr. in 8 Eng. vv. (see Appendix B.), curious, C., pp. 116, 171, 213. *Gough,* vol. ii. pl. lx. p. 167; *Lipscomb,* vol. iii. p. 300. III. Thos. Manfeld, Esq., 1540, and 2 ws., Agnes, a dau. and h. of John Trewonwall, Gent., of Molasshe, Kent, and widow Kath., N. INSCRS. IV. Robt. Manfyld, in the service of Kings Hen. V. and VI., 1459 (?), mutil. marg. inscr., with shs., once on A.T., C. V. *Robt. Manfyld, Esq., 1512, and w. VI. *Hen. Manfeld, 1568. VII. Ursula, w. of Thos. Jonys, 12 Eng. vv. and shs., c. 1570. VIII. Thos. Jones, Esq., who served Kings Hen. VIII. and Ed. VI., and Queens Mary and Elizth., 1584, with shs. IX. Hester, w. of Hen. Manfeild, 1617, "who died in yᵉ catholique Romane faith," 4 Eng. vv., p. 225. These brasses are now incorrectly rel. in the new Ch.

THORNTON. I. Robt. Ingylton, lord of the manor of Thornton, lawyer [chancellor of the Exchequer], 1472, in arm., and 3 ws.; [Margaret], with 3 sons and 5 daus.; [Clemens], with 2 sons and 3 daus.; and [Isabella], with 1 son and 2 daus., under quadruple canopy, mutil. marg. inscr. and 6 Lat. vv., once on A.T., pp. 179, 197. *Lipscomb,* vol. iii. p. 122 (male eff.) II. Jane, dau. and h. of Robt. Yngleton, Esq., dec., and w., 1stly, of Humph. Tyrrill, Esq. (by whom she had a son, Geo., æt. 27 at her decease), 2ndly, of Alex. Seynct Johns, Esq., 1557, æt. 55, with marg. inscr., once on A.T.

TINGEWICK. Erasmus Williams, rector, 1608, hf. eff., curious, qd. pl., mur., pp. 30, 216. *Lipscomb,* vol. iii. p. 124.

TYRINGHAM. I. Rich. Node (?), rector, 1494 (?), worn, very sm. II. Mary, w. of Anthony Catesby, Esq., and dau. of John Tyryngham, Esq., 1508, C.

TURWESTON. I. A Priest, c. 1450, inscr. lost, C. II. Thos. Grene and ws. Joan and Agnes, very sm., c. 1490, N., p. 214.

*TWYFORD. I. John Everdon, rector, [and canon of Lincoln], **1413**, hf. eff. *Lipscomb*, vol. iii. p. 134.   II. Thos. Giffard, **1550**, in arm., he m. Mary, dau. of Wm. Staveley, Esq., of Bignell; once on A.T.

UPTON.   I. Agnes Bulstrode, **1472**, kng., in shroud, effs. of husband Wm. and of 9 sons and 2 daus., with inscr., lost, sm., rel. See Appendix B.   II. Edw. Bulstrode, Esquire for the body with Kings Hen. VII. and Hen. VIII., **1517**, and ws., Mary, Ellen, and Margt., with 4 sons and 6 sons and 2 daus., eff. of 1 w. and inscr. lost, rel.   III. Edw. Bulstrode, Esq., **1599**, in arm., and w. Cecill, a dau. of John Croke, Esq., with 4 sons, Hen., Thos., Edw., Wm., and 6 daus., Elizth., Margt., Anne, Cecill, Magdalen, and Dorothy, Hebrew inscr., now placed under No. I., C., p. 237.   INSCR. IV. Maria, dau. of Thos. Read, Esq., of Barton, near Abingdon, and w. of Hen. Bulstrod (son of No. III.), **1614**, and chil., Thos., Hen., Elizth., Mary, Edw., Cecily, and Dorothy, placed below No. III.

WADDESDON. *Hugh Brystowe, parson, **1548**, in shroud, inscr. in curious Eng. vv., C. *Lipscomb*, vol. i. p. 510.

WENDOVER. Wm. Bradschawe, Gent., **1537**, and w. Alice, and 9 chil., Hen., Joan, Agnes, Alice, Bridget (dec.), Elizth., Margery (dec.), Wm. (dec.), Sibil (unmarried), with the names of their several chil., sm., kng., mur., S.A., p. 3. *Lipscomb*, vol. ii. p. 491.

WESTON TURVILLE. *A Civilian, c. **1580**, inscr. lost, C. *Lipscomb*, vol. ii. p. 501.

WESTON UNDERWOOD. Elizth., dau. of Lord Hussey, and w., 1st, of Walter Hungerford, then of Sir Robt. Throkmarton, **1571**, headless, 5 daus. lost (?), S.A. *Lipscomb*, vol. iv. p. 405.

*WHADDON. I. Thos. Pygott, serjeant-at-law, **1519**, and ws., Agnes [Forster], with 2 sons and 3 daus., and Elizth., dau. and h. of John Iwardeby, Esq., with 3 sons and 2 daus., Hy. Trin. lost, A.T., N.C., p. 90.   II. Margt. Myssenden (?), **1612**, and son (a skeleton), mur., N.

†WINCHENDON, NETHER. I. A Man in arm. [John Hamperotis, or Hampekons?], c. **1420**, C., p. 189. *Lipscomb*, vol. i. p. 533. II. John Barton, alias Bayle, **1487**, and w. Margt. *Ibid.*

*WINCHENDON, OVER. I. Sir John Stodeley, vicar, **1515** [or 1502], in dress of an Austin canon (?), his mother, Emmot, buried under the same stone, inscr. in Eng. vv., C., p. 87. *Waller*, pt. xiii.; *Boutell's Series*.   INSCR. II. John Goodwyn, Esq., **1558**, and w. Kath., with 18 chil., 3 shs., 4 Eng. vv., C. *Lipscomb*, vol. i. p. 571.

WING. I. Harry Blaknall, 1460, and w. Agnes, **1489**, N.

II. A Civilian and w., c. **1490**, inscr. gone, sm.   III. Thos. Cotes, porter at Ascott Hall, **1648**, inscr. in 6 Eng. vv., see Appendix B., Geo. Houghton, pos., qd. pl., N., p. 129.

WINSLOW.   Thos. Fige, Gent., **1578**, and w. Jane, with 2 sons and 5 daus., sm.

WOOBURN.   I. John Godwyn, **1488**, and w. Pernell (eff. lost), "ffirst founders of the Stepull of Obourne Deyncourt," N.A.   *Gough*, vol. ii. pl. lxxv. p. 305; *Langley's Desborough*, p. 451.   II. Christopher Askowe, Gent., c. **1500** (not in arm.), and w. Margery, who had a son Wm.   III. Thos. Swayn, S.T.B., prebendary of Aylesbury, and chaplain to Wm. Atwater, Bp. of Lincoln, **1519**, in cope, C.   IV. A Mcht., in shroud, c. **1520**, w. gone, with Hy. Trin. and inscr. in 10 Eng. vv., C., pp. 118, 119, 224.   V. Arthur, only son of Philip Lord Wharton, and Dame Jane, dau. and h. of Arthur Goodwin, Esq., **1642**, æt. 9 months, recumbent on A.T., with inscr. in 6 Eng. vv., and a marg. inscr. cut in stone, sm., qd. pl.   An inscr., p. 97.

WORMINGHALL.   *Philip King, Gent. (educated by his uncle, Bp. King of Oxford), **1592**, and w. Elizth. [Conquest], with 5 sons and 6 daus., and infant dec., Elizth. pos., mur., C.   *Lipscomb*, vol. i. p. 581.

WOOTTON UNDERWOOD.   *Edw. Greneville, Esq., **1587**, and w. Alice, dau. of Wm. Haselwood, and infant son dec., marg. inscr. and 4 Eng. vv., p. 225.   *Lipscomb*, vol. i. p. 613.

WYRARDISBURY.   I. John, son of Walter Stonor, Esq., **1512**, sm., C., p. 86.   *Introd.*, p. 85.   INSCR. II. Dame Elizth. Hobby, dau. and h. of Sir Walter Stonor, of Stonor, Oxon., and w. to Walter Walsh, Esq., of Elmeley, Worc., servant of the privy chamber to Hen. VIII., 1560, and her son Walter, **1561**, with 3 shs.

INSCRIPTIONS, &c.

*BROUGHTON.   I. John, son of Robt. de Broughton, **1403**.   II. Agnes, w. of John Broughton, **1399**.   FARNHAM ROYAL.   Eustace [Mabeall?], clerk of the works to Cardinal Wolsey [at Ch. Ch., Oxford], and chief clerk of accompts for 17 years for the buildings of Hen. VIII. within 20 miles of London, dec. **1567**, being then ["pistile reader] in Windsor Castell," mutil.   LECKHAMPSTEAD. *Reginald Tylney, son of Ralf Tylney, Gent., citizen and alderman of London, **1506**, and 3 daus., Elizth., Joan, and Joan, effs. lost, C. MEDMENHAM.   Rich. Levyng, 1412, and w. Alice, **1419**.

The brasses are lost at PRESTON BISSET, SHERRINGTON, and GREAT MARLOW.   Impressions of 2 formerly at Great Marlow are preserved in the British Museum (see Introd., p. 257). I. Wm., John, Lodiwic, and John, sons of Lord John and Lady [Joan] Salesbury, **1383**, kng., with scrolls, and mutil. marg. inscr.   II. John Warner, rector, [**1421** ?], with mutil. marg. inscr., large.

Cambridgeshire.

ABINGTON-IN-THE-CLAY. A Civilian (of the Pigott family?), c. **1460**, with 8 sons and 8 daus., w. and marg. inscr. lost, C. FRAG. II. A Scroll, C.

BALSHAM. I. John Sleford, rector, master of the wardrobe to King Edw. III., canon of Ripon and Wells, rebuilder of the Ch. and erector of the stalls, **1401**, in cope, with SS. B. V. Mary and Child, John Evang., Kath., Paul, Mary Magd.—John Bapt., Etheldreda, Peter, Margt., Wilfrid (Bp.), under triple canopy, with seraphim, &c., marg. inscr. in 14 Lat. vv., very large, C., pp. 104, 106, 115. *Lysons' Mag. Brit.*, vol. ii. p. 66.   II. Dr. John Blodwell [Dean of St. Asaph's], "longo tempore cecus erat," **1462**, in cope, with SS. Mich., Jas., Kath., Gabriel, Margt., and others, under fine canopy, having at the sides these SS., John Bapt., Peter, Asaph (Bp.), Brigida—John Evang., Andrew, Nich. (Bp.), Wenefreda, 12 Lat. vv. and marg. inscr., very large, N., pp. 77, 92, 104, 112, 175. *Illustrations of Monumental Brasses*, published for the Cambridge Camden Society, No. iii. p. 73.   III. A Man in arm., c. **1475**, N.

BARTON. John Martin and w. Margt., both dec. c. 1593, engr. c. **1600**, sm., C.

BASSINGBOURN. Edw. Turpin, Gent., **1683**, and w. Elizth.; the inscr. mentions John Turpin, Gent., 1494, and w. Margt.; Wm. Turpin, Esq., principall of New Inn, 1573 (or 75), and Jane Turpin, widow, a benefactor to the Ch. and poor; Thos. Turpin, Gent., 1627, and w. Ann, the parents of Edw., p. 215.

BURWELL. John Lawrence, of Wardeboys, abbot of Ramsey, **1542**, original eff. c. 1510, altered from episcopal to canonical vestments (almuce, surplice, &c.), with triple canopy, its centre pediment with eff. of our Blessed Lord only left, on its reverse part of a foreign (?) brass of a deacon, c. 1320 (?), marg. inscr. lost, C., pp. 29, 47, 67, 68, 74, 104.   *Camb. Antiq. Soc. Publications.   Introd.*, p. 68 (part of eff.)

CAMBRIDGE, ST. BENET'S. Rich. Billingford, D.D., Master of Benet. Coll., **1442**, in acad., kng., inscr. lost, N.A., pp. 82, 256. *R. Masters' Hist. of C. C. Coll., Camb.*, 1753, pl. 2, p. 39; *Oxf. Man.*, p. 36; and *Introd.*, p. 82.

CAMBRIDGE, CAIUS COLL. A Man in arm., c. 1500, pecul.

CAMBRIDGE, CHRIST'S COLL. I. [Thos. Fowler, usher of the chamber to Edw. IV.,] and w. Edith, late gentlewoman to Margt. Countess of Richmond, c. 1520, with mutil. marg. inscr. partly covd. II. An Ecclesiastic, in acad., c. 1540, usually assigned to Edw. Hauford, D.D., master for 24 years, 1582-3, pecul., inscr. lost, p. 171. *C. C. Soc. Illustr.*, No. iv. p. 109.

CAMBRIDGE, ST. JOHN'S COLL. I. Eudo (?) de la Zouch, priest, master of the suppressed hospital, c. 1410, in acad., head gone, with triple canopy, worn, large, p. 84. II. A Priest, c. 1430, nearly effaced. INSCR. III. Nich. Metcalf, for 20 years master, 1537; he was also prebendary of Lincoln.

CAMBRIDGE, KING'S COLL. I. Wm Town, D.D., fellow, [provost, and prebendary of Lincoln], 1496, in acad., with scroll from hands, N.C., p. 82. II. John Argentein, [D.D. and M.D., provost, 1507], inscr. in 4 Lat. vv., marg. inscr. lost, eff. loose (?), pp. 29, 82. III. [Robt. Hacombleyn, provost, 1528], in almuce, with marg. inscr., another inscr. lost, S.C., pp. 29, 79, 102. IV. Robt. Brassie, S.T.P, provost, 1558, in almuce, S.C., p. 79. *INSCR. V. John Stokys, 1559, Math. Stokys, esquire bedel, and fellow, pos.

CAMBRIDGE, ST. MARY-THE-LESS. †John Holbrook, master of Peter House, 1418-1431, chancellor to the University, chaplain to Hen. VI., and a famous mathematician, inscr. in 6 cleg. vv., beginning "Quem tegit iste lapis *cavus* cognomine *torrens*" (Hollow-brook), much mutil., under floor (?). In Cole's MS. (Brit. Mus. Add.), 5,803, fol. 50. a, is a sketch of this brass, also of a hf. eff. of a Doctor, both like that at King's Coll., 1496.

CAMBRIDGE, QUEEN'S COLL. I. A Priest, in cope, c. 1480, head and inscr. gone. II. A Priest, c. 1535, in acad., inscr. lost, sm., pp. 29, 82. III. *Robt. Whalley, Gent., born at Nottingham, fellow, 1591, æt. 28, marg. inscr. and 10 eleg. vv., p. 240. INSCR. IV. *John Stokes, S.T.P., master, 1568; he left property at Ockley, of the value of £9 13s. 4d., to found 4 scholarships; eff. lost, (upper part sketched in Cole's MS., 5,803, fol. 14. b,) marg. inscr. and 8 cleg. vv.

CAMBRIDGE, TRINITY HALL. I. Walter Hewke, D. Can. L., 151- [dec. 1517], in cope, with the 12 Apostles on the orphrey, head gone, inscr. in 3 Lat. vv., large, pp. 92, 105. *C. C. Soc. Illustr.*, No. i. p. 7. II. A Priest, c. 1530, in acad., pp. 29, 82. III. *Thos. Prestone, a native of Lancashire, "scholarem quem dixit princeps Elizabetha suum," LL.D., master, 1598, æt. 60, his w. Alice pos., inscr. in 8 cleg. vv. and marg. inscr.

CAMBRIDGESHIRE. 33

DRY-DRAYTON. —— Hutton, Esq., and w., c. 1530, inscr. covd. by a pew, S.A., p. 235.

ELY CATHEDRAL. I. [Thomas] Goodryke, [c. 20 years Bp. of Ely,] often a foreign ambassador, a counsellor of Edw. VI., lord high chancellor [1554], canopy and 1 inscr. lost, marg. inscr. mutil., large, S.A. of C., pp. 70, 73, 78, 111, 123. *Bentham's Ely*, ed. 1812, pl. xxv. p. 191; *C. C. Soc. Illustr.*, No. I., p. 13; *Boutell's Series*. II. Umphry Tyndall, of a Norfolk family, D.D., 4th dean, master of Queen's Coll., Camb., 1614, with marg. inscr., very large, S.A. of C., p. 230. Dean Tyndall, in the reign of Queen Elizabeth, was offered the crown of Bohemia, which he refused. *Bentham's Ely*, pl. xxv. p. 191.

FORDHAM. Wm. Cheswryght, 1521, and Matilda, pecul., worn, pp. 239, 243.

FULBOURN. I. A Priest, c. 1390, with scroll from hand, mutil., inscr. lost, N., p. 141. II. Wm. de Fulburne, canon of St. Paul's, London, [baron of the exchequer, 1391,] in cope, with fine canopy, marg. inscr. mutil., very large, C., pp. 138, 141, 144. *Lysons' Mag. Brit.*, vol. ii. p. 64; *Rees' Cyclopædia*, plate of Early British Engravings, fig. 3. *Boutell's Series* (eff.) III. Geoff. Bysschop, vicar, 1477, nailed to a seat, inscr. lost, N., pp. 25, 61. IV. A Civilian (eff. lost) and w., c. 1480, with 2 sons (1 a priest in acad.), all kng., scrolls and inscr. lost, S.A., p. 84. FRAGS. V. Eight sons and a scroll, c. 1470, S.A. VI. A shield, civilian with badge or rebus (?) beneath lost, N.

GIRTON. I. Wm. Malster, "in decretis licenciatus," rector, canon of York, (prebend of Fenton,) 1492, in cope, C. II. Wm. Stevyn, in decr. licenc., rector, canon of Lincoln, 1497, in cope, C. In Cole's MS., 5,805, fol. 24. a, are sketches of small brasses of the Collyn family now lost.

HADDENHAM. I. Wm. Noion, last rector, canon of York, Lincoln, and Chichester, 1405, eff. in cope, lost, with double canopy, C., pp. 92, 176. II. John Godfrey, (who roofed chapel), 1454, and w. Margt. (head gone), N.A.

HATLEY, EAST. *A Lady, c. 1520, husband and inscr. lost.

HATLEY ST. GEORGE. Sir Baldwin Seyntgorge, 1425, p. 189.

HILDERSHAM. I. Robt. de Paris, of Caermarthen, 1379 (?), and widow Alienora (?), kng. beside a floriated cross with Hy. Trin. in the head, inscr. lost, C., pp. 102, 136, 163. *Waller*, pt. vi. *Introd.*, p. 163 (male eff.) II. Hen. Paris, Esq., 1427 (?), and w. Margt. (Poche), marg. inscr. lost, A.T., C., p. 188. *Oxf. Man.*, p. 84, and *Introd.*, p. 188 (male eff.) III. Hen. Paris, Esq., 1466 (?), with

F

mutil. canopy with Hy. Trin. at the finial, inscr. lost, C., p. 194. *Waller*, pt. ix.   IV. A Skeleton, c. **1530**.

HINXTON. Sir [Thos. de] Skelton, steward of John [Duke of Lancaster, and of the Duchy of Lancaster to Hen. IV., **1416**,] and 2 ws. [Margt. and] Kath., marg. inscr. mutil., S.C., p. 188.

HORSEHEATH.   I. Sir John de Argentine, **1382**, canopy and inscr. lost, large, C., p. 160. *Boutell's Series.*   II. *Robt., son of Sir Giles Allington, **1552**, he m. Margt., dau. of Wm. Coningsbie, head and inscr. gone, under seats, C.   INSCRS. III. Joan Alyngt[on, a sister and h.] of John Argentein, the son of John, [son of Wm. Argentein, **1429**,] mutil., C.   IV. Six Lat. vv. to Mary Cheyne, w. of John Alvington, c. **1470** (?), C.

IMPINGTON. John Burgoyn, Esq., **1505**, and w. Margt., in heraldic dresses, with 7 sons and 2 daus., marg. inscr., N.

ISELHAM.   I. Sir John Bernard, **1451**, and w., under mutil. canopy, inscr. lost, S.Tr., pp. 113, 176.   *Gough*, vol. ii. pl. lx. p. 167 (effs.)   II. Thos. Peyton, Esq., **1484**, and ws. Margt. [Bernard] and Margt. [Francis], under canopy, A.T., C., pp. 33, 104, 171, 197. *Lysons' Mag. Brit.*, vol. ii. p. 68.   III. *Sir Rich., 3rd son of Sir Robt. Payton, a student and reader at Gray's Inn, **1574**, and w. Mary [Hyde], m. 10 years, inscr. in 12 Eng. vv., S.Tr., p. 125.   INSCRS. IV. Sir John Bernard, 1451, and his ws., 1st, Lady Elena Swynerton, dau. and h. of Sir John Mallorre, of Northants., 1440, and 2nd, Elizth. Sakevyle, **1464**, now placed above the canopy of No. I.   V. Elizth. Peyton, a cross lost, **1516**, pp. 171, 222.   VI. Sir Robt., son of Sir Robt. Peyton, **1550** (?), he m. Frauncys, dau. and h. of Frauncys Hassylden, Esq.

KIRTLING.   *Edw. Myrfin, Gent., born at London, travelled through Europe, Greece, to Aleppo, Armenia, Syria, Jerusalem, Damascus, &c., **1553**, æt. 27, mur.

LINTON.   I. Nich. (?) Paris, Esq., **1425** (?), partly covd., pp. 188, 190.   FRAGS. II. Two shs. from the brass of Wm., son of Philip and Margt. Parys, **1538**, and w. Elizth., C.   III. Three shs., loose, from the brass of Ferdinand Parys and w. Frances, dau. of —— Moore, of Whaddon, c. **1590**, eff. of w. sketched in Cole's MS., 5,802, fol. 35. a.

MARCH.   I. Wm. ["Andrei Jordan" (Cole), Andrei yoman?], **1501**, and w. Joan, pecul., worn, N.   II. Anth. Hansart, in arm., and w. Kath., sister of Sir Robt. Southwell, chancellor to Hen. VII. and Hen. VIII., kng., in heraldic dresses, below 2 daus., and a sh. with crests as supporters, curious, sm., N.A., pp. 105, 223.   INSCR. III. Symond Payne, **1510**, N.A.

MILTON. I. Wm. Coke, justice of the common pleas, **1553**, and w. Alice (who pos.), with 2 sons and 3 daus., marg. inscr. and 8 eleg. vv., A.T., C., pp. 91, 97. *Boutell's Series; Gent. Mag.*, vol. xxx. New Ser., 1848, p. 606. II. *John Harris, **1664**, and fam., mur., S.A.

QUY. John Ansty, Esq., c. **1465**, and w. Joan (eff. lost), with 12 sons, in tabards, and 4 daus., kng., marg. inscr. mutil., N., pp. 112, 190, 193. *Oxf. Man.*, p. 88, and *Introd.*, p. 193.

SAWSTON. I. A Civilian, c. **1420**, feet gone, loose. II. A Man in arm., c. **1480**; head, w., and marg. inscr. gone, S.A., p. 115. III. A Man and w., c. **1500**, in shrouds, with 5 daus., inscr. and 4 (?) sons lost, N. Probably the brass of Robt. Lockton, Esq., and w. Joan, dau. of Robt. Allington, of Horseheath. See Cole's MSS., vol. xxxi. p. 155. *Gent. Mag.*, vol. lxxxv. 1815, pt. ii. p. 25. IV. Wm. Richardson, alias Byggyns, rector of Raynham-mare, dioc. Norw., **1527**, with chalice, pecul., sm., S.A., p. 78. INSCRS. V. *Sh. and marg. inscr. to Hera, dau. and h. of Thos. Lord Bradstone, and w. of Sir Walter Delapole, **1423**, A.T., C. VI. *Sir John Huddilston, privy counsellor to Queen Mary, **1557**, A.T., C. VII. *John Huntington, Esq., 1558, and w. Joyce, **1564**, benefactors, mur., N.

SHELFORD, GREAT. I. Thos. Pattesle, rector, rebuilder and benefactor of Ch., prebendary of Southwell, **1418**, in cope, with canopy, much mutil., inscr. lost (see Appendix B.), C., p. 132. *Gent. Mag.*, vol. lxix. 1799, pt. ii. p. 561. FRAG. II. A Sh. with curious arms; eff. of Edw. Risley, **1511**, in arm., and inscr. lost, A.T., C.

SHELFORD, LITTLE. I. Robt. de Frevile, brother and h. of John de Frevile, 1393, in arm., and w. Claricia, 1399, engr. c. **1405** (?), N. p. 61. II. Thos., son and h. of Robt. Frevile, **1405** (or 1400), in arm., and widow Margt., "postea sacre maiestatis amica professa" (Dodsworth's MS. in Bodl., No. 5,029, vol. lxxxviii. fol. 13. A.), 1410, N., p. 61. The male effs. are armed similar to Sir John Wylcotes, 1410, Great Tew, Oxon. (see Introd., p. 186), but have no plate gorgets. Both brasses are engr. in *Camb. Ant. Soc. publ.*, illustrating a geneal. hist. of the Freville Fam., by A. W. Franks, Esq. In the same work are three facsimiles of sketches in Cole's MSS., of brasses formerly at Shefford: to Sir Rich. Freville, 1375, eff. in arm., in a cross; Elena de Freville, 1380 (?), Flemish (?); and Wm. Freville, Esq., 1460, and ws. [Anna and] Margt. III. A Priest, c. **1480**, in acad., C., p. 84. INSCR. IV. An Inscr., **1632**, stating that a seat and side-chapel of the Frevilles belonged to Priscilla, widow of John Banckes, Esq.

STAPLEFORD. Wm. Lee, born at Batley, Yorks., vicar for 43 years, **1617**, pecul., qd. pl., sm., N., p. 230.

STRETHAM. Dame Joan, widow, 1st of Wm. Rypphingham, and then of John Swan, both mchts. of Kingston-upon-Hull, and of the staple of Calais, **1497**, her sons, John and Robt. Rypphingham, were rectors of Stretham, canopy and inscr. gone, C., p. 209. *Introd.*, p. 209 (det.) A matrix of the brass of Nich. de Kingeston, rector, hf. eff., with Lomb. inscr., temp. Edw. II.

SWAFFHAM PRIOR. I. John Tothyll, Gent., **1462**, and w., sm., S.C., p. 194. II. Rich. Water, **1515**, and w. Alice, 4 sons and about 5 daus. lost, N.A., p. 29. III. Wm. Water, **1521**, and w. Alice, with 6 sons, 2 (?) daus. gone, N.A., p. 29. IV. A Civilian and w., c. **1530**, pecul., N. V. *Robt. Chambers, Esq., **1638**, not in arm. All these brasses are under moveable seats in N.

TRUMPINGTON. Sir Roger de Trumpington, a crusader c. 1270, **1289**, large, marg. inscr. (of more recent date?) lost, A.T., N.C., pp. 43, 139, 146. *Ant. Repert.*, vol. iii. p. 322; *Lysons' Mag. Brit.*, vol. ii. p. 65; *C. C. Soc. Illustr.*, pt. ii. p. 65; *Waller*, pt. iv.; *Glossary of Architecture; Boutell's Mon. Br.*, p. 30; *Oxf. Man.*, p. 65, and *Introd.*, p. 146.

WESTLEY WATERLESS. Sir John de Creke, c. **1325**, and w. Alyne (Clopton, or Chamberleyn), canopy and marg. inscr. lost, large, S.A., pp. 25, 137, 150, 153, 165, 166. *Gough*, vol. i. pl. lvii. p. 142; *Lysons' Mag. Brit.*, vol. ii. p. 64; *Waller*, pt. viii.; *Boutell*, p. 39; *Bloxam's Mon. Arch.*, p. 150; *Introd.*, pp. 25 (det.), 151. *Gloss. of Arch.*, and *Oxf. Man.*, p. 68 (male eff.)

WESTON COLVILLE. *A Man in arm., inscr. lost, N.

WICKEN. I. Margt., [dau. of Sir John Gernon, and] w. of Sir John Peyton, **1414**, sm. II. John, son of Sir Robt. Peyton, c. **1520**, head lost, sm.

WILBRAHAM, LITTLE. Wm. Blakwey, M.A., rector, **1521**, in acad., kng., sm., A.T., C., pp. 29, 84, 203. *Introd.*, p. 84.

WILBURTON. I. Rich. Bole, archdeacon of Ely, **1477**, in cope, canopy mutil., marg. inscr. nearly all lost, large, C. II. John Hyll, **1506**, and w. Margt., with Evang. symbs., pecul. III. Wm. Byrd, **1516**, and w. Margt., with 3 sons and 5 daus., pecul., N. In Cole's MS., 5,805, fol. 58. a, is a sketch of the brass of Robt. Wetheringset, archdeacon of Ely and prebendary of Lincoln, **1444**, in cope, with SS. and triple canopy now lost. A skeleton brass is also sketched at fol. 60. b.

WIMPOLE. I. Thos. Worsley, LL.B., residentiary of Beverley, benefactor to St. Mary's Chantry, **1501**, in cope, above B. V. Mary,

inscr. in 6 Lat. vv., large, N.C. II. A Civilian, c. **1500**, inscr. lost.
III. A Lady, c. **1535**, with 6 daus., pecul., inscr. lost, p. 244. INSCR.
IV. Edw. Marshall, parson, **1625**, æt. 63, 8 Eng. vv. This inscr.,
a sh., and Nos. II. and III. are now placed on one slab in N.C.

WISBEACH. [Thos. de Braunstone,] "conestable du Chastel de
Wisebeche, **1401**, in arm., canopy lost, Fr. inscr. marg. and mutil.,
very large, much worn, S.A., p. 186. *Gough*, vol. ii. pl. iii. p. 8;
Lysons' Mag. Brit., vol. ii. p. 67; *Boutell's Series.*

WOOD DITTON. Hen. Englissh, **1393**, in arm., and w. Margt., her
head and the canopy lost, large, S.A., p. 160. *Boutell's Series.*

INSCRIPTIONS, &c.

BRINKLEY. A son and dau., c. **1520**, parents and inscr. lost,
2 shs. left, one with arms of White (?).   CHEVELEY. *An Evang.
symb., part of a brass of the Cotton family (?).   DUXFORD, ST.
JOHN'S. Thos. Wyntworth, vicar, B. of Can. Law, official of the
archdeacon of Colchester, **1489**. A Priest, hf. eff., xv. cent., now
lost, is sketched in Cole's MS., 5,802, fol. 19. a.   LANDBEACH.
Hen. Clifford, parson for 47 years, **1616**, æt. 77, mur., C.   LAND-
WADE. *Some scrolls, now mur., from the brass of Wm. Cotton,
Esq. (?), **1453**, sketched in Cole's MS., 5,802, fol. 42. b.   OVER.
Seven daus., c. **1530**.

Good matrices of crosses remain at CHERRY-HINTON, SAWSTON,
GREAT and LITTLE SHEFFORD, and RAMPTON. At BOTTISHAM is
the indent of a large eff. of a priest in chasuble, under canopy, with
Lomb. marg. inscr. to Elyas de Bekingham, the celebrated upright
judge, **1298**. *Anastatic drawing* by C. R. M. In Cole's MS., 5,803,
fol. 40. b, is a sketch of the brass of a civilian formerly at St. Peter's-
on-the-Hill, Cambridge; in MS. 5,802, fol. 17. b, a chalice at
Pampisford; and in MS. 5,804 (fol. 169), some civilians and ws.
at Swaffham Bulbec.

Cheshire.

CHESTER CATHEDRAL. *Thos. Madock, 1761, and w., **1792**, a long
inscr. with angels and a skeleton, sm., S.Tr.

MACCLESFIELD. Roger Legh, **1506**, and w. Elizth. [Sutton],
1489, kng., with 6 sons and 6 daus., w. and daus. now lost, curious,
mur., in wooden frame, River's Chapel, pp. 101, 104. *J. Burroughs's
View of Popery*, 1735, pp. 152, 154, and *Gent. Mag.*, vol. lxiv. 1794,
pt. ii. p. 980 (inscrs.); *Anastatic Camb.*, 1848 (det.)

MIDDLEWICH. Elizth., eldest dau. of Sir Wm. Brereton, and w.

of Thos. Venables, Esq., baron of Kynderton, **1591**, and son Thos. dec., æt. 11, and daus. Elizth. and Mary, qd. pl., sm., N.C.

OVER. Hugh Starky, Esq., of Olton, gentilman usher to Hen. VIII., son of Hugh Starky, Esq., of Olton, and rebuilder of Ch., c. **1510**, A.T., C.

TARVIN. †Four Eng. vv. to Hen. Hardware, alderman and twice mayor of Chester, **1584**, C.

WILMSLOW. Sir Robt. del Bothe, lord of the manors of Bolyn, Thorneton, and Dunham, [slain at the battle of Blore Heath,] **1460**, and w. Douce [Venables], 1453, canopy lost, marg. inscr. much mutil., C., pp. 62, 194, 214. *Boutell's Series.*

WYBUNBURY. Ralf Dellvys, **1513**, in arm., and w. Kath., 3 daus. lost, now mur., N.

The brasses of Randall Dod, 1634, and w. Elizth., in shrouds, once at LITTLE BUDWORTH, are lost, p. 5.

Cornwall.

ANTHONY, EAST. Margt. Arundell, dau. of Sir Warin Erchedeken, **1420**, under canopy, C. *Gilbert's Historical Survey and Heraldry of Cornwall*, 1817-1820, vol. ii. p. 388.

BLISLAND. John Balsam, rector, **1410**, C., p. 78.

ST. BREOCK. *A Civilian and 2 ws. (1 w. lost), of the Tredinnick family (?), c. **1510**, with 5 sons and 7 daus., and 1 son and 3 daus., S.C.

ST. BUDOCK. John Killigrew, Esq., of Arwenach, lord of the manor of Killigrew, made the first captain of Pendennis Castle by Hen. VIII., and succeeded by his son Sir John at his dec., **1567**; in arm., and w. Elizth. Trewinnard, C.

CALLINGTON. Nich. Assheton, justice, rebuilder of Chapel [**1465**], and w. Margt., about 5 sons and 6 daus. lost, 12 cleg. vv. and mutil. marg. inscr., C., p. 90.

CARDYNHAM. Thos. Awmarle, rector, c. **1400**, sm., now mur., C., pp. 90, 96.

*COLAN. I. Francis Bluet, Esq., **1572**, and w. Elizth. (Colan), with 13 sons and 9 daus., mur. II. —— Coswarth, Esq., and w., **1573**.

ST. COLUMB. I. John Arundell, knt. of the Bath and knt. banneret, receiver of the duchy of Cornwall, **1545**, and 2 ws., 1st, Elizth. (Grey), dau. of the Marq. of Dorset, and 2nd, Kath., dau. of Sir Thos. [Greenvill]; several chil. lost, 5 left, Thos., Jane, Elenor, (Mary). II. Sir John Arundel, 1590, æt. 60, in arm., and w. Anna (Stanley), dau. of the Earl of Derby, 1602, æt. 71, with chil., John, Geo., Dorothy, Elizth., Cicily, Margt., Gertrude, engr. c. **1630**, p. 52. III. John Arundel, son of No. II., [**1633**?], æt. 70, in arm., and w. Anne (Jarnegan), and chil. John, Mich., Thos., Geo., Mary, Magd., Mary, Anne, Cath., Dorothy, Winefreda, on same stone as No. II., pp. 52, 238. *Introd.*, p. 238 (male eff.)

CONSTANTINE. I. Rich. Geyrveys, Esq., **1574**, and w. Jane, dau. of Thos. Trefusis, Esq., hands clasped, with 8 sons and 6 daus. (others gone), qd. pl., with canopy, detached marg. inscr., pecul. II. John Pendarves, Gent., **1616**, and w. Melior, dau. of Rich. Gearveis, Esq., 1607, and chil. Sam. and Mary, qd. pl., sm.

CROWAN. I. Geoff. St. Aubyn, 1400, and w. Elizth., dau. and h. of Piers Kymyel, of Clowance, engr. c. **1420**, w. and inscr. lost. II. Geoffrey [St. Aubyn], c. **1490**, and w. Alice, dau. and h. of John Tremure, of Launevet, Esq., with 4 sons, 4 daus. gone, inscr. mutil., p. 198. III. [Thos. Seintabbyn], c. **1550** (?), and w. Matilda (dau. and h. of John Trenowyth), 1512, upper parts of effs. lost. These brasses, and probably three others of the same family (1599-1626), were removed to Clowance in 1859, during the restoration of the Ch. They were all in the C., with marg. inscrs., and are engr. in *Polwhele's Cornwall*, vol. iv. p. 119.

FOWEY. I. †Two Civilians (one headless), and a lady (of the Treffry family?), c. **1450**, inscr. lost. *II. John (?) Rashleigh, **1582** (?). III. Alice, dau. of Wm. Lanyon, Esq., and w. of John Rashleigh, Esq., 1591, they had 1 son (who pos.) and 6 daus., **1602**.

ST. GLUVIAS. Thos. Kyllygrewe, Gent. [**1484**], not in arm., and ws. Joan [and Elizth.], partly covd.

GRADE. *Jas. Eryssy, **1522**, in arm., and w. Margt., with 5 sons and 5 daus., S.Tr.

HELSTON. Thos. Buggins, mcht., **1602**, w., and 3 chil., fastened to door (?), chil. and inscr. lost (?).

ILLOGAN. Jas. Bassett, Esq., **1603**, æt. 43, in arm., and w. Jane, dau. of Sir Francis Godolphin, they had 5 sons and 5 daus., now mur.

ST. IVES. Oto Trevnwyth, Gent., **1462** (eff. lost), and w. Agnes, kng., with St. Michael and a scroll, sm., loose in 1859.

ST. JUST. A Priest, c. **1520**, in plain cope, pecul., inscr. lost, pp. 30, 76.

LANDRAKE. Edw. Cowrtney, Esq., 2nd son of Sir Wm. Cowrtney, of Powderham, sm., **1509**.

LANTEGLOS-JUXTA-FOWEY. I. Thos. de Mohun, c. **1440**, in arm., he was son of John, the son and h. of Sir Reg. de Mohun and his w.

Elizth., dau. and h. of Sir John Fitzwilliam, also 2nd brother of John, last lord of Mohun, with marg. inscr., p. 192. II. John Mohun, Esq. (son and h. of Wm. Mohun, Esq., and his w. Florence, a sister of Edw. Courtney, Earl of Devon,) and w. Anne, dau. of Rich. Code, Esq., both dec. 1508, with 5 sons and 4 daus., engr. c. **1525**, pp. 223, 232.

LAUNCESTON. A Lady, æt. 65, married 41 years, and had 15 chil., lived 3 years at Launceston, c. **1620**, mur., N., pp. 30, 215.

LOSTWITHIEL. Tristram Curteys, Esq., **1423**, worn, p. 190.

MADRON. John Clies, mcht., twice mayor of Penzance, **1623**, æt. 55, and w. Blanche, only dau. of Hugh Trevanion, Esq., with 1 son and 5 daus., 12 Eng. vv. and marg. inscr.

MAWGAN-IN-PYDER. 1. A Priest, c. **1420**, in cope, sm. II. Cecily, dau. of Sir John Arundell and his w. Elizth., **1578**, æt. 52, 12 Eng. vv. and mutil. marg. inscr., 5 pieces loose, 1 palimpsest. III. A Civilian, c. **1580**, ". . . de Tregonon generosus," marg. inscr. mutil. IV. Jane, unmarried dau. of Sir John Arundell and his w. Kath., she served 5 queens, c. **1580**, æt. 72, eff. loose, on reverse of it portions of 2 Flemish brasses, c. 1375, inscr. an acrostic in 12 Eng. vv., on reverse pieces of 2 Flemish brasses; 6 pieces are loose of mutil. marg. inscr., pp. 46, 225. *Transactions of the Exeter Dioc. Arch. Soc.*, vol. iii. p. 16, and *Introd.*, pp. 16, 17 (palimpsests). INSCRS. V. Mary, dau. of Sir John Arundell and w. Elizth., **1578**, æt. 49, marg. in 6 loose pieces. VI. Edw. Arundell, dec. at Fleet-street, London, **1586**, with 8 eleg. and 18 Eng. vv., marg. inscr. loose in 3 pieces. Ten or 12 fragments of marg. inscrs. of Geo. Arundell, Esq., **1573**, and w.; Cath. (?), dau. of Sir Pierse Edgcomb, with 14 Lat. vv.; and Elizth., dau. of Gerard Danet, Esq., and 2nd w. of Sir John Arundell, **1564**. The loose inscrs. are at Lanherne nunnery.

ST. MELLIONS. Peter Coryton, Esq., **1551**, in arm., and w. Jane, dau. and h. of John Tregasoo, with 24 chil. (?), marg. inscr., now mur., and partly covd., N.A., p. 222.

MENHENIOT. †Ralph Carmynolls.

MEGAVISSEY. †Otwell Hill, Esq., of Penwarne, son of Alan Hill, **1614**, and w. Mary (who pos.), with 8 Eng. vv.

MINSTER. Four very sm. qd. pls., worn, each with kng. effs. of a man and his w., 2 in arm., of the Hender family (?).

ST. MINVER. Roger, son of Nich. Opy and his w. Elizth., dau. of John Carmynow, Esq., **1517**, with marg. inscr.

MYLOR. †Thos. Kyllygrave, Gent., and w., c. **1500**.

PENKEVIL, ST. MICHAEL. I. John Trenowyth, Esq., **1497**, S.A.,

p. 199. II. John Trembras, M.A., parson, **1515**, in acad., C., p. 84. III. Edw. Boscawen and Nancarrow, Gent., 7th son of Hugh Boscawen, Esq., **1619**, æt. 63, and w. Jane, dau. of Wm. White, Gent., of St. Agnes. IV. John Boscawen, Esq., son and h. of Hugh Boscawen, of Tregothnan, Esq., 1564, in arm., with trophy and 8 Eng. vv., Nich. his brother and h. pos., qd. pl., mur., engr. c. **1640**. V. Mary, 4th dau. of Hugh Boscawen, Esq., and widow of Peter Coffin, Gent., **1622**, æt. 71.

PROBUS. John Wulvedon, **1514**, and w. Cecilia, 1512, 1 son and 2 (?) daus. lost, S.A.

QUETHIOCK. I. Roger Kyngdon, **1471**, and w. Joan, with 11 sons and 5 daus., S.Tr., pp. 79, 127, 172. *Proceedings of Soc. of Ant.*, vol. iv. p. 72 (3 sons). II. Rich. Chiverton, Esq., 1617, and w. Isabell [May?], **1631**, with 5 sons and 6 daus., 24 Eng. vv., mur., pp. 30, 215.

STRATTON. Sir John Arundell, of Trerise, **1561**, in arm. and helmet, and 2 ws., with 10 chil., Rich., John, Roger, Margt., Mary, Jane, Phelipe, Grace, Margery, Annes, p. 235.

TINTAGEL. Joan Bon, mother of John Kelly, dean of St. Crantoch's Coll., c. **1430**, hf. eff.

TRURO. I. A Civilian, c. **1580**, with 2 sons and 4 daus., and arms of Williams (?) and Truro, w. and inscr. gone, under reading-desk, C. II. Cuthbert Sydnam, woollen-draper, mayor in 1627, dec. **1630**, æt. 54; he had 8 chil., Humph., Cuthbert, Anne, Margt., Blanch (all dec.), Wm., Cuthbert, Jane; his w. Jane pos. INSCR. Eight Eng. vv. to Thos. Haselle, **1567**.

WENDRON. I. Warin Penhallinyk, "in decretis baccallareus," prebendary of Glaseney Coll., rector of St. Just, vicar of Wendron and Stithians, **1535**, in cope, head gone, marg. inscr. II. A Civilian and w., c. **1580**, lower part of effs. and inscr. lost, with 7 sons and 8 daus.

INSCRIPTIONS, &c.

LANDULPH. I. Theodore Paleologus, descended from the Imperial lyne of the last Christian Emperors of Greece, **1636**, see Appendix B., mur. II. Dame Elizth., w. of Sir Nich. Lower, of Clifton, **1638**. III. Sir Nich. Lower, **1635**, and w. Elizth., dau. of Sir Hen. Killegrve, of London. ST. STEPHENS-BY-SALTASH. I. An Evang. symb. and mcht's. mk., c. **1480**, man and w. lost. II. Mary (Stradlinge), w. of Sam. Rolle, **1613**.

At CAMBORNE is a cast-iron plate to Alex. Pendarves, **1655**, æt. 24, with eff., kng., and 12 Eng. and 6 Lat. vv., mur., p. 1.

Cumberland.

CARLISLE CATHEDRAL. I. Rich. Bell, bp., before prior of Durham [**1496**], with triple canopy, marg. inscr. and 4 Lat. vv., large, C., pp. 73, 125. *Gough*, vol. ii. pl. cxvi. p. 329. II. Hen. Robinson, bp., **1616**, curious, qd. pl., mur., C., pp. 30, 54, 72. See Queen's Coll., Oxford.

CROSTHWAITE. Sir John Ratclif, **1527**, and w. Alice; knt.'s head and shs. badly restored, A.T., pp. 53, 97, 232.

EDENHALL. Wm. Stapilton, Esq., lord of Edenhall, **1458**, in tabard, and w. Margt., dau. and h. of Nich. de Vipont and Lady of "Aldeston Mor.," pp. 62, 196. *Lysons' Mag. Brit.*, vol. iv. p. 197.

*GREYSTOKE. I. Rich. Newport, **1451**, S.A. INSCRS. II. William le Bone, Baron de Graystok, **1359**, Fr. inscr., shs. gone, C. III. Jas. Moresby and w. IV. Thos. Eglisfelde and Walter Readman, provosts of Greystoke, **1509**. V. John Whelpdale, master of the Coll., **1526**. VI. Wm. Bewley, **1543**, and dau. VII. Wenefrid Newport, **1547**.

Derbyshire.

ASHBOURN. I. Francis, son of Sir Thos. Cockayne, **1538**, in tabard, and w. Dorothy, dau. and h. of Thos. Marow, serjeant-at-law, 1505, under low triple canopy, about 4 sons and 3 daus., also nearly all the marg. inscr., lost, A.T., N.Tr., p. 29. INSCR. II. Dedication of Ch., **1241**, p. 43. *Anonymous.*

ASHOVER. I. James Rolleston "de le ley" (Lea), in arm., and w. Anna, dau. of John Babyngton "de dedyk" (Dethick), Esq., **1507**, with 4 sons and 9 daus., marg. inscr., p. 234. *Glover's Derbyshire*, vol. ii. p. 62. II. A Priest, c. **1510**, above head a matrix of a chalice (?), C. *Ibid.* INSCR. III. †Thos. Babington, son and h. of Thos. Babington and his w. Isabel, dau. and h. of Robt. Dethick, Esq., **1518**, mur., N.A.

CHESTERFIELD. I. Sir Godfrey Foljambe, one of the King's council, 1541 (?), and w. Kath., dau. of John Leake, Esq., of Sutton, **1529**, in heraldic dresses, inscr., 1 son, and 7 daus. lost, once on A.T., C. *Gent. Mag.*, vol. lxvii., 1797, pt. i. p. 280. INSCRS. II. John Verdon, rector of Lyndeby, Notts., chaplain of St. Michael's Chantry, Chesterfield, **1500**, mur., S.Tr., p. 96. III. John Potts, **1676**. The brass of Hen. Foljambe, Esq. (father of No. I., 1519), and w. Bennett, c. **1510**, on A.T., is lost, pp. 59, 60.

*CRICH. I. Ephraim, [son of Rev. Thos.] Shelmerdine, child,

1637, in swaddling clothes, qd. pl., with roses, &c., mur., C. INSCRS. II. Robt. Marshall and w. Margt., m. above 50 years, and had 7 sons and 3 daus., N.   III. John Kirkeland, yeoman, **1652**, on pew-door.

DRONFIELD. I. Thos. Gomfrey, of Wormehul, rector, **1399**, and his brother Rich., rector of Tatenhull, and prebendary of Somerschell, in the King's chapel of Penkeriche; inscr. states that Roger Braylisforde, rector of Dronfield, is buried under the stone; worn, C., pp. 63, 78, 130.   II. †John Fanshawe, 1578, and w. Margt. (Eyer), 1573, both æt. c. 74, and 6 chil., Thos., Hen. (dec. 1545), Robt., Godfrey, Elizth. (dec. 1537), Margt., engr. **1580**, worn.

EDENSOR. †John Beton, Esq., an attendant on Mary Queen of Scots, an aider of her escape from Lochleven Castle, and her ambassador to Chas. IX. of France and Queen Elizth., dec. at Chatsworth, **1570**, æt. 32, in arm., sm., his brothers, Jas., Abp. of Glasgow, and Andrew, pos.

ETWALL. I. Hen. Porte, **1512** (eff. lost), and widow Elizth., with 9 sons and 8 daus., effs. of our Blessed Lord and B. V. Mary and Child, N., p. 102. *Fairholt's Costume*, p. 245 (fem. eff.)   II. Sir John Porte (son and h. of Sir John Porte, a justice of the king's bench), **1557**, in tabard, and 2 ws. in heraldic mantles, Elizth. [dau. of Sir Thos. Giffard, of Chillington, Stafford, dec. 35 Hen. VIII.], with 2 sons and 3 daus., and Dorothy [dau. of Sir Anth. Fitzherbert, of Norbury], mur., A.T., C.   Sir John founded the hospital at Etwall and Grammar-school at Repton.

HATHERSAGE. I. Robt. Eyr, Esq., 1459, and w. Joan [Padley], **1463**, with 14 chil., Robt., Nich., Roger, Rich., Rauff, Hugh, Philip, Hen., Edm., Stephen, Joan, Elizth., Joan, Margt., A.T., C., p. 194. *Introd.*, p. 194 (det.)   II. —— Eyre and w., c. **1500**, in heraldic dresses, with 4 sons, Thos., John, Christ., John (2 others lost?), and 2 daus. [Elizth. and ——], gilt, mur., in wooden frame, perhaps the brass of Ralph Eyre, of Offerton, 1493, and w. Elizth.   III. Sir Arthur Eyre (son of Robt., son of Robt., son of Robt., or Robenet, [No. I.]), c. **1560**, in tabard, and 1st w. Margt., dau. of Sir Robt. Plompton, of Yorks., in heraldic mantle, kng., C.   By Margt., Sir Arthur had Robt., Harry, Edm., and Kath., Margt., Anne (m. to Sir Thos. Fitzherbert, justice of the chief bench), Joan; by his 2nd w. Alice, dau. of Thos. Coffyn, Esq., of Devon, he had Geo.; all his chil. but Anne dec. young; his 3rd w. was Dorothy, dau. of Humph. Okever, Esq., of Stafford.   INSCR. IV. Robt., eldest son of Robt. Eyre, Esq., dec. at Trin. Coll., Camb., **1615**, æt. 20.

KEDLESTON. Rich. Curzon, **1496**, in arm., and w. Alice (Willoughby, of Wollaton), with 8 daus., 4 sons and inscr. lost, C.

MORLEY. I. John Stathum, Esq., Nov. 6th, **1454**, and w. Cecily, 1444, "which yaf to yis Churche iij belles & ordeyned iijs. iiijd. yerely for brede to be done in almes among pou'e folk of y^{is} pish ī ye day of ye obit of dame Godith̄ sometyme lady of y^s towne;" kng., with St. Christopher, C., pp. 193, 105.   II. Sir Thos. Stathum, **1470**, and 2 ws., Elizth., dau. of Robt. Langley, Esq., and Thomasine, dau. of John Curson, Esq., with SS. Anne, B. V. Mary, Christopher, A.T., C., p. 105.   III. Hen. Stathum, **1481**, in arm., and 3 ws., Anne, dau. of Thos. Bothe, of Barton; Elizth., dau. of Giles Seyn'clow; and widow Margt., dau. of John Stanhop, with 1 son and 4 daus., A.T., C., p. 197.   IV. John Sacheverell, Esq., son and h. of Ralph Sacheverell, Esq., lord of the manors of Snetterton and Hopwell, slain at Bosworth Field 1485, and w. Joan, dau. and h. of Hen. Stathum, Esq., engr. c. **1525**, p. 232.   V. Sir Hen. Sacheverell, **1558**, in arm., and w. Isabella.   INSCRS. VI. Godithe de Stathum and son Rich., who built the Ch. and tower, **1403**, C.   VII. Ralph de Stathum, builder of chapel, dec. 1380, and w. Godythe, **1418**, N.A.   VIII. John Stathum, Esq., benefactor to the Ch., dec. Nov. 7th, **1453**, and w. Cecilia, 1444, C.   IX. A list of prayers ordained by John Stathum to be said for the souls of his family (see Appendix B), mur., C.

MUGGINTON. Nich. [Kniveton, lord of the manors of Mercaston and Underwood, in arm., and w. Joan], c. **1475**, with 4 sons, detached, in arm., a 5th gone, and 1 dau., marg. inscr. mutil., A.T., pp. 116, 214.

NORBURY. Sir Anth. Fitzherbert, justice of the common pleas, "Lorde and patrone" of Norbury, **1538** (head lost), and 2nd w. (in heraldic mantle) Mawde, a dau. of Rich. Coton, of Hampstall Rydware, by whom he had 5 sons and 5 daus.; his 1st w. was Dorothy, dau. of Sir Hen. Willoughby; marg. inscr. nearly all lost, C., pp. 91, 125.   Sir Anth. was the author of " De Natura Brevium," and other works.

SAWLEY. I. Roger Bothe [brother of Laurence?], bp. of Durham, **1467**, in arm., and w. Kath. [Hatton], 1466, parents of [John Bot]he, treasurer of Lichfield, with 7 sons and 11 daus., marg. inscr., C., pp. 113, 192.   II. [Robert, son of] Roger Bothe, and brother of John Bothe, archdeacon of Durham, and of Ralph Bothe, archdeacon of [York?], **1478**, and widow Margt., with 6 daus., Kath., Isabell, Dowce, Jane, Aunes, Eme, 2 sons (1 in almuce) lost, marg. inscr., pp. 113, 116, 197.

STAVELEY. I. Peter F[rechwell, Esq.], pos. c. **1480**, in tabard, head lost, with Hy. Trin. and marg. inscr., A.T., C., p. 56. II. Peyrs Freychwell, "Squier" to Hen. VI., patron of Ch. and benefactor to it, **1503**, in arm., and w. Mawde [dau. of Sir Nich. Wortley], with 8 sons and 7 daus., B. V. Mary and Child, mur., A.T., C., p. 56.

TADDINGTON. †Rich. Blackwall, **1500**, w. and chil.

*TIDESWELL. I. Hy. Trin., scrolls, and long inscr., with account of life, to Sir Sampson Meverell, **1462**, who m. Isabel, dau. of Sir John Leche, and served in France under the Earl of Salisbury and Duke of Bedford, who knighted him, A.T., C. Beneath is a stone emaciated eff. of the deceased, p. 1. *C. C. Soc. Illustr.*, No. I., p. 27. (Hy. Trin.) II. Robt. Lytton, **1483**, and w. Isabella, 1458, with marg. inscr. III. Robt. Pursglove, born at Tideswell, educated by his uncle Wm. Bradshaw, prior of Gisburn, Yorks., suffragan bp. of Hull, archdeacon of Nottingham, provost of Rotherham Coll., endower of 2 grammar-schools and a hospital, **1579**, in episcopal vestments, inscr. with 20 Eng. and 2 Lat. vv., marg. inscr. with 4 Eng. vv., C., pp. 73, 78, 222, 224. *Gent. Mag.*, vol. lxiv. 1794, pt. ii. p. 1101; *C. C. Soc. Illustr.*, No. I., p. 19.

WALTON-ON-TRENT. A Priest, c. **1490**, with chalice and host, probably engr. by same artist as the brasses at Charwelton, Northants., marg. inscr. and scrolls lost, pp. 30, 78, 123.

WILNE. Hugh Wylloughby, Esq., of Rysley, **1513**, and son and h. Thos., both in tabards, and w. Anne, dau. of Rich. Wentworth, Esq., with 4 daus., Hy. Trin., mur., A.T.. C.

WIRKSWORTH. I. Thos. Blakewall, **1525**, and w., with 6 sons and 1 dau., N.C. II. A Civilian and w., c. **1510**, with 8 sons and 10 daus. Probably the brass of John Blackwall, 1520, or of Elizth., dau. of Rich. Blackwall, and w. of —— Wigley, 1500.

YOULGRAVE. *A Lady, c. **1600**.

INSCRIPTIONS, &c.

ALFRETON. *Genealogical inscr. to John Ormond, Esq., 1503, and w. Joan, dau. and h. of Sir Wm. Chaworth, **1507**, effs. lost, mur., A.T., C. †DARLEY. I. Anth. Senior, Gent. **1654**. II. Rich., son of No. I., æt. 4, **1656**, p. 30. HUCKNALL. Rich. Pawson, vicar, **1537**. NORTON. —— Spencer, lost, p. 220.

Devonshire.

ALLINGTON, EAST. I. John Fortescue, Esq., **1595**, æt. 70, and w. Owner, or Olivier. INSCR. II. John Fortesty and w. Margt., 17th cent.

ATHERINGTON. Sir Arthur Basset and 2 ws., Honora, dau. of Sir Thos. Grenville, with 1 son and 4 daus., and Ann, dau. of John Dennis, Esq., with 3 sons and 4 daus., c. **1540**, rel. and misplaced (?), marg. inscr. lost, A.T., N.C. *Mon. Brasses of Devon, by W. R. Crabbe, Esq., in Transactions of the Exeter Diocesan Architectural Society,* vol. vi. pt. i. pl. 2.

BIGBURY. I. *A Lady, c. **1440**, inscr. lost, below arms of Burton imp. Bigbury; perhaps the same person as No. II. *Trans. of Exeter Soc.,* vol. vi. pt. ii. pl. 2. II. Robt. Burton (?), (eff. lost), and w. Lady Elizabeth, [formerly ?] w. of Thos. Arundell, c. **1460**, in mantle, marg. inscr. mutil., p. 125. *Trans. of Exeter Soc.,* vol. v. pt. ii. pl. 11. According to Lysons (Mag. Brit., vol. vi. p. cccxxxvii.), the lost eff. was that of Wm. Bigbury, Elizth.'s first husband.

BLACKHAUTON. *Nich. Forde, **1582**, and w. Margt. [Fountain ?].

BRAUNTON. *Lady Elizth. Bowcer [Bourchier], dau. of John Erle, of Bath, and w. of Edw. Chechester, Esq., **1548**, kng., on reverse of eff. the head of a knt. in bascinet and camail, inlaid in slab with incised cross, pp. 47, 57. *Trans. of Exeter Soc.,* vol. vi. pt. i. pl. 7.

CHITTLEHAMPTON. I. John Coblegh and 2 ws., Isabella, late w. of Robt. Cornew, Esq., 1466, and Joan, **1480**, with 1 dau., N.Tr. *Trans. of Exeter Soc.,* vol. v. pt. iii. pl. 20. INSCR. II. Hen. Coblegh, **1470**, and w. Alice, parents of John Coblegh (No. I.), N.Tr. *Ibid.*

CLOVELLY. I. Robt. Cary, Esq., son and h. to Sir Wm. Cary, **1540**, rel. (?) in incised slab, p. 57. *Trans. of Exeter Soc.,* vol. v. pt. ii. pl. 14. II. —— Cary (?), c. **1540**, in arm., inscr. lost. INSCR. III. Geo. Cary, Esq., **1601**.

CLYST, ST. GEORGE. Julian, dau. of —— Bonifant, and m. 30 years to —— Osborne, survived him 40 years, **1614**, æt. nearly 100, Eng. vv., qd. pl., mur. *Trans. of Exeter Soc.,* vol. vi. pt. i.

DARTMOUTH, ST. PETROCK'S. I. ——, son of John Roope, mcht., **1609**, dec. young, large, mutil. marg. inscr., S.A. II. †Barbara Plumleigh, **1610**. III. †Dorothy Roup, **1614**. Nos. II. and III. are under seats.

DARTMOUTH, ST. SAVIOUR'S. I. John Hauley, founder of C. [**1408**], in arm., and 2 ws., Joan (whose hand he holds), 1394, and

Alice, 1403, under mutil. canopy, large, C., pp. 61, 92, 149, 187, 205. *Boutell's Series. Trans. of Exeter Soc.*, vol. iii. pl. 12 (effs.) John Hauley was probably the merchant of Dartmouth, "who in 1390, waged the navie of shippes of the ports of his owne charges, and tooke foure-and-thirty ships laden with wine to the summe of fifteene hundred tunns." Stowe's "Annals," quoted by Lysons, (Mag. Brit., vol. vi. p. 154). II. A Lady, c. **1470**, sm., inscr. lost, N.A. III. Gilbart Staplehill, once mayor, c. **1600**, 6 Eng. vv. and mutil. marg. inscr., C. *Trans. of Exeter Soc.*, vol. vi. pt. i. pl. 3.

ERMINGTON. Wm. Strachleigh, Esq., **1583**, and w. Anne, dau. and h. of John Gould, Esq., of Dore, with their only child Christian, who m. Christopher, son and h. of Sir Rich. Chudleigh, and had John, Strachleigh, John, Robt., Elizth., Elizth., Mary, and Anne, kng., mur. *Trans. of Exeter Soc.*, vol. vi. pt. ii. pl. 12.

EXETER CATHEDRAL. I. Sir Peter Courtenay, son of the Earl of Devon, "Regis cognatus, Camerarius intitulatus, Calesie gratus Capitanius, ense probatus," [knight of the garter,] **1409**, very large, with canopy, marg. inscr. mutil., and with badges at the corners, two lost, very much worn, N., pp. 114, 117. *Hewett's Exeter Cath.; Trans. of Exeter Soc.*, vol. iii. pls. 14, 15. II. Wm. Langeton, canon of Exeter, and kinsman of Edw. Stafford, bp. of Exeter, **1413**, in cope, kng., Lady-chapel, p. 114. *Gough*, vol. ii. pl. cxxiii. p. 353; *Trans. of Exeter Soc.*, vol. iii. pl. 15.

*FILLEIGH. I. Rich. Fortescue, **1570**, in arm., 6 Eng. vv., his brother Drake pos., qd. pl., mur., now in a wooden frame, p. 55. *Trans. of Exeter Soc.*, vol. vi. pt. i. pl. 8. II. A similar brass to the same person.

*ST. GILES-IN-THE-WOOD. I. Alyanora, dau. of John Copleston, and w. of John Pollard, **1430**. *Trans. of Exeter Soc.*, vol. v. pt. iii. pl. 23. II. Margt., dau. of John Forde, and w. of John Rolle, of Stevenston, **1592**, and chil., Hen., Rich., Valentyne, Alex., Geo., Joachyme, Robt., John, Honor, and Margerye, 8 Eng. vv., marg. inscr. mutil., but recently restored. *Ibid.* III. Joan, dau. of Geo. Pollard, Esq., of Langley, and w. of Wm. Risdon, Gent., of Winscott, **1610**, æt. 63, she had 2 sons and 1 dau., mur. INSCR. IV. John Rolle, Esq., **1570** [husband of No. II.?]

HACCOMBE. I. Nich. Carew, Esq., **1469**, 8 Lat. vv., C., p. 196. *Trans. of Exeter Soc.*, vol. v. pt. iii. II. Thos. Carewe, Esq., **1586**, æt. 68, in arm., C., p. 236. *Ibid.* III. Maria, dau. of Wm. Huddye, Esq., of Dorset, and w. of Thos. Carewe, Esq., **1589**, C. IV. Elizth., dau. of Robt. Hill, Esq., of Shilston, and w. of John Carewe, Esq., **1611**, C. *Ibid.*, vol. vi. pt. i. V. Thos. Carew,

Esq., and w. Anne, they dec. Sept. 6th, 8th, **1656**, qd. pl., mur. *Ibid.*

HARFORD. I, Thos. Williams, Esq., twice appointed reader in Court, speaker in Parliament, **1566**, æt. 52, in arm., 8 Eng. vv., p. 93. *Trans. of Exeter Soc.*, vol. v. pt. iii. pl. 19. II. John Prideaux, of Stoford, and w. Agnes, with 7 sons (the 4th in doctor's gown) and 3 daus.; John Prideaux, the 4th son, D.D. and Regius Prof. of Div. at Oxford, rector of Exeter Coll., and Chaplain to Prince Hen., Jas. I., and Chas. I., pos., **1639**, qd. pl., mur., S.A.

KENTISBEARE. I. John Whiting, Esq., **1529**, and w. Anne, A.T., S.A., pp. 232, 260. *Trans. of Exeter Soc.*, vol. v. pt. ii. Stolen in Feb. 1858. INSCR. II. *Lady Mary, dau. of Sir Robt. Wotton, of Kent, w. to Sir Hen. Guildeford, (knight of the garter, comptroller of the household and one of the privy counsel to Hen. VIII.,) and then to Sir Gawyn Carew, knt., **1558**.

*MONKLEIGH. I. A Man in arm., kng., c. **1580**, mur., C. II. Two Angels holding a scroll with inscr. to Jas. Seyntleger, Esq., **1509**. *Trans. of Exeter Soc.*, vol. vi. pt. i. pl. 6.

OKEHAMPTON. †Thomasin, w. of Thos. Peter, Gent., **1608**, 8 Eng. vv., and 2 daus., qd. pl., mur. *Trans. of Exeter Soc.*, vol. vi. pt. i. pl. 5. Destroyed (?) at the burning of the Ch., 1842.

†OTTERTON. I. Rich. Duke, Esq., **1641**, with 5 sons and 2 daus. II. Sarah, dau. and coh. of Rich. Reynell, Esq., of Creedy, and w. of Robt. Duke, Esq., **1641**, with 3 sons and 5 daus.

*OTTERY ST. MARY. I. John Sherman, Gent., 1542, Wm. his son, 1583, and Rich. his grandson, c. **1620** (?), 10 eleg. vv., N.C. FRAG. II. Part of the inscr. of a fine brass to John de Northwode, D.D., chancellor of Oxford, and archdeacon of Totness, **1348**.

PETROCKSTOW. Hen. Rolle, Esq., 4th son of Geo. Rolle, of Stevenston, in arm., and w. Margt., dau. and sole h. of Robt. Yeo, Esq., **1591**, with 10 sons and 9 daus., qd. pl., mur. *Trans. of Exeter Soc.*, vol. v.

SAMPFORD PEVERELL. *Margt., w. of Sir Amias Poulet, and chil., 10 eleg. vv. cut in marble, Sir Franc. Vincent and Geo. Poulett, pos., **1602**.

SANDFORD. *Mary, only sister of Geo. Lord Carew, and widow of Walter Dourich, Esq., **1604**, lying on a tomb, and 4 chil., Thos. (m. Kath., dau. of John Stukely, Esq., of Afton), Dorothy (m. Thos. Peyton, of Iselham, Camb.), Elizth. (m. Geo. Trobrydge, Esq., of Trowbridge), and Mary (m. Wm. Limsey, Esq., of Colbye, Norf.) *Trans. of Exeter Soc.*, vol. v. pt. ii.

SHILLINGFORD. Sir Wm. Huddersfeld [1499-1500], and w.

Kath., dau. of Sir Wm. Courtnay [**1516**], in heraldic dresses, qd. pl., sm., mur., A.T., C., pp. 21, 30. *Oliver's Antiq. of Devon; Trans. of Exeter Soc.*, vol. v. pt. ii. pl. 12.

STAVERTON. John Rowe, Esq., son and h. of John Rowe, serjeant-at-law, **1592**, æt. 82, hf. eff., mur., outside C.

STOKE-FLEMING. I. John Corp, 1361, and [grand-dau.] Elyenore, **1391**, with canopy, Fr. inscr., curious, large, C., pp. 137, 164, 168. *Waller*, pt. viii.; *Trans. of Exeter Soc.*, vol. v. pt. ii. pl. 10. INSCR. II. Six Eng. vv., with sh., to old Elias Newcomm, **1614**.

STOKE-IN-TEIGNHEAD. I. A Priest, c. **1370**, once in a cross, now rel. in a slab with inscr. to John Symon, rector, and canon of Exeter, 1497, C., p. 57. INSCR. II. *Elizth., dau. of Thos. Tawley, Gent., of Dittisham, and w. of Francis, son of Francis Furlong, Gent., of Loddeswill, **1641**, in Fr., engr. on a heart, N.

TEDBURN ST. MARY. Edw. Gee, parson, and w. Jane, **1613**, with 1 son and 3 daus., 14 eleg. vv. and 14 Eng. vv., in wooden frame, mur., C. Edw. Gee was the author of a popular manual of devotion.

THORNCOMBE. *Sir Thos. Brook [1417-8 ?], not in arm., and w. Joan, dau. of Simon Hanape, of Glouc., and widow of Robt. Chedder, of Bristol [**1436-7**], both with SS. collar, marg. inscr. nearly all gone, loose, large, p. 208. *Trans. of Exeter Soc.*, vol. v. pt. iii. pl. 21.

TIVERTON. *John Greenway, mcht., and w. Joan, **1529**, Hy. Trin. and marg. inscr. lost, large. He founded the S.C. in 1517. *Trans. of Exeter Soc.*, vol. v. pt. ii.

TOR MOHUN. Wilmota, dau. and h. of John (?) Gifforde, Esq., of Yeo, and w. of Geo. Cary, Esq., of [C]ockington, **1581**, mutil., with 3 daus., 2 sons lost, C. *Trans. of Exeter Soc.*, vol. vi. pt. ii. pl. 13.

*WASHFIELD. I. Hen. Worth, Esq., **1606**, æt. 72, and w., with 1 dau., 10 eleg. vv., mur., N.A. INSCR. II. Alce, dau. of Wm. Frye, Esq., and w. of Philip Steynings, Esq., **1605**, æt. 72, had 9 sons and 5 daus., Geo. Montgomery, her son-in-law, pos., 18 Eng. vv. and 2 shs.

YEALMPTON. Sir John Crokker, "ciphorarius ac signifer" to Edw. IV., **1508**, N.A., p. 232. *Trans. of Exeter Soc.*, vol. v. pt. ii. pl. 13. Sir John distinguished himself in suppressing Perkin Warbeck's rebellion in 1497.

INSCRIPTIONS, &c.

BERRY POMEROY. Hen. Dypford, **1590**, had, by w. Elizth., a son and dau., p. 225. BICKLEIGH, near Plymouth. Nich. Slannyng, Esq., **1583**, æt. 59, 10 Eng. vv. COMBMARTIN. *Wm. Haucock,

Gent., **1587**. DODDISCOMBSLEIGH. *John Stephens, parson, and canon resident of Exeter Cath., **1559**. HARTLAND. *Alice, widow of Thos. Docton, Esq., **1619**, gave £20 to the poor, A.T. LOXHORE. *Rich. Carpenter, S.T.P., rector, **1627**, inscr. in form of a cross. *PILTON. I. Alex. Bret, Esq., **1536**. II. Robt. Bret, Esq., **1540**.

Dorsetshire.

BERE REGIS. —— Skerne and w. Margt. [Thornhull], who pos., **1596**, 8 Eng. vv., mur., A.T. *Hutchins's Hist. and Antiq. of Dorset*, 1796, vol. i. p. 88.

CAUNDLE-PURSE. I. Wm. Longe, Esq. (?), c. **1500**, w. and inscr. lost, N.C. II. Elizth., dau. and h. of Wm. Longe, Esq., **1527**, with flowing hair, sm., N.C. III. Rich. Brodewey, rector, **1536**, headless, very sm., C.

COMPTON VALENCE. Thos. Maldon, rector, rebuilder of Ch., c. **1440**, hf. eff., from which issue 2 scrolls with Lat. text from Ps. li. 1, worn, N.

CRITCHILL-MORE. †Isabel Uvedale, **1572**.

DORCHESTER, ST. PETER's. Joan de St. Omer, widow of Robt. More, **1436**, much worn, inscr. lost (?). *Hutchins*, vol. ii. p. 41.

EVERSHOT. Wm. Grey, rector, **1524**, with chalice and host.

*FLEET (old Church). I. Robt. Mohun, Esq., of Bothenhampton, in arm., and w. Margt., dau. and coh. of Steph. Hyde, **1603**, æt. 90, with 9 sons and 8 daus., mur., C. II. Maximilian Mohun, Esq. (son of No. I.), **1612**, æt. 48, in arm., and w. ——, dau. of John Churchill, Gent., of Corton, with 13 chil.

KNOWLE. John Clavell, Esq., **1572**, in arm., and 2 ws.; 1st w. with 3 sons and 1 dau., 2nd, Susan, dau. of Robt. Coker, of Mappowder, mur., N.A.

LYTCHETT MATRAVERS. I. Thos. Pethyn, rector, c. **1470**, in shroud, sm., C., p. 30. *Hutchins*, vol. iii. p. 23. INSCR. II. Margt. Clement, "generosa, specialis benefactrix reedificacionis hujus ecclesie," **1505**. A matrix of a very large fret (the arms of Maltravers), with marg. inscr. to Sir John Matravers, **1365**, N.A. *Gough*, vol. i. p. 117.

MELBURY SAMPFORD. I. Sir Gyles Strangwayes, **1562**, in tabard, N., p. 236. INSCR. II. Two Shs., with 14 and 13 quarterings, and inscrs. to Hen. Strangwayes, Esq., who "died at the syege of Bolleyne," and his w. Margt., dau. of Lord Geo. Rosse; and to Sir Gyles Strangwayse, and w. Jone, eldest dau. of John Wadham, Esq., of Meryfylde.

MILTON-ABBAS. I. Sir John Tregonwell, D.C.L. and a master of the Chauncerye, **1565**, in tabard, mur., A.T., N., p. 236.　INSCR. II. John Artur, monk, p. 87.

MORETON. *Jas. Frampton, Esq., son of Robt. Frampton, Esq., **1523**, with text from Ps. li. 1, on scrolls, mur., rel. 1733, S.A.

PIDDLEHINTON. I. Mr. Thos. Browne, parson for 27 years, **1617**, æt. 67, in hat, holding staff and book, very sm., with 12 eleg. vv., pecul., qd. pl., C.　INSCR. II. †John Chapman, **1494**, N.A.

PIDDLETOWN. I. Roger, son and h. of John Cheverell, Esq., **1517**, lower hf. of eff. lost, rel., C.　II. Christ. Martyn, Esq., son and h. of Sir Wm. Martyn, **1524**, in tabard, 7 Eng. vv., qd. pl., mur., S.C., p. 21.　III. Nich. Martyn, Esq., **1595**, in arm., with 3 sons and 7 daus., 4 of whom he left cohs., Elizth., Frances, Jane, and Anne; [he m. Margt., dau. and h. of John Wadham, of Meryfield], mur., A.T., S.C.

PIMPERNE. Mrs. Dorothy Williams, **1694**, curious, her husband, John (rector?), pos., qd. pl., mur., pp. 30, 56, 218, 222.

PUNCKNOWLE. *Wm. Napper, Esq., brother of Sir Robt. Napper, in arm., by his w. Anne, dau. of Wm. Shelton, Esq., of Onger Park, he had 6 sons, engr. c. **1600**, before his death, mur., S.A.

RAMPISHAM. Thos. Dygenys and w. Isabell, "gud benefactors to thys churche," both dec. **1523**, N.

SHAFTESBURY, ST. PETER'S. Inscr. to Stephen, son and h. of Nich. Payne, Steward of the Monastery, **1508**, worn, p. 252.

†SHAPWICK. I. Rich. Chernok, alias Hogeson, vicar, C.　II. Maria, h. of Lord de Champneys, and w. of John Oke, N.A.

STURMINSTER-MARSHALL. Hen. Helme, vicar, and founder of Baylye House [the vicarage], **1581**, inscr. in 6 Eng. vv., sm., A.T., C.

SWANWICK. I. Wm. Clavell (eff. lost) and ws. Margt. and Anne, c. **1490**, partly covd., sm., N.　INSCR. II. John Harve, **1510**.

WIMBORNE MINSTER. St. Ethelred, King of the West Saxons, martyr, "Anno Domini 873 [872?], 23 die Aprilis per manus dacorum paganorum occubuit," hf. eff., engr. c. **1440**, inscr. restored c. 1600 (?), N., pp. 45, 53, 74.　*Hutchins*, vol. ii. p. 544; *Carter's Anc. Sculpt. and Painting*, vol. ii. p. 57; *Introd.*, p. 74.　Matrices, p. 87.

WOLLAND. *Mary, [dau. of Robt. Williams, of Herrington, w. of Robt.] Thornhull, and then of [Lewis] Argenton, **1616**, inscr. in 12 Eng. vv. mur., C.

YETMINSTER. John Horsey, Esq. for the body to Hen. VIII., lord of the manor of Clifton, **1531**, and w. Elizth., lady of the manor of Turges Melcombe, sister and h. of Robt. Turges, Esq., the son and h. of Rich. Turges, Esq., with scrolls at sides, rel. (?), pp. 234, 235.

Durham.

AUCKLAND, ST. ANDREW. Fridesmond (Giffard), w. of Rich. Barnes, bp. of Durham, **1581**, a cross on qd. pl., sm.

BILLINGHAM. *Robt. Brerely, vicar, and prebendary of Norton, **1480**, C.

BRANCEPATH. I. Rich. Drax, priest, **1456**, in acad., hf. eff., worn, p. 84. II. †—— Claxton, Esq., in arm., much worn.

CHESTER-LE-STREET. †A Lady, 15th cent. Perhaps the brass of Wm. Lambton, Esq., **1430** (eff. lost), and w. Alice, S.A.

GREATHAM. *A Marg. Inscr. to Wm. de Midiltoun, "sacre pagine doctor," master of hospital, c. **1350**, C.

HOUGHTON-LE-SKERNE. *Dorothy, dau. of Rich. Chomeley, Esq. (3rd son of Sir Rich. Chomeley), and w. of Robt. Parkinson, Gent., of Whessey, **1592**, with her twins Rich. and Marmaduke, 6 Eng. vv., qd. pl., mur., C., p. 220.

HOUGHTON-LE-SPRING. Margery, w. of Rich. Belassis, of Pentknol, "remained widow 58 years, bestowing her whole time in hospitality & relief of the poore," **1587**, æt. 90, with 8 sons and 4 daus., qd. pl., mur., A.T., C.

NEWTON, LONG. †Sir Geo. Vane, **1679**.

SOCKBURN. *Shs. and inscrs. to 2 lords of the manor, Sir John Conyers, 1394, and Robt. Conyers, Esq., and w. Isabella, both dec. **1433**, North Porch.

SEDGEFIELD. *A Man and his w. as skeletons in shrouds, inscr. lost, N.A. *Engr.* —— (?). †Matrix of cross and inscr. to Andrew de Stanelai, master of Greatham, c. **1300**.

Essex.

ARKESDEN. A Man in arm. of the Cuttes family (?), c. **1440**, inscr. lost, A.T., N.C., p. 192. *Boutell's Series.*

ASHDON. A Man, in arm., and w., c. **1440**, sm., p. 190.

AVELEY. I. Ralph de Knevynton, **1370**, in arm., with canopy, qd. pl., small Flemish, C., pp. 20, 96, 149, 156, 160. *Waller*, pt. i.; *Fairholt's Costume*, p. 164. II. Elizth., eldest dau. of Edw. Bacon, Esq., and of his w. Helen, dau. of Thos. Littel, of Braye, Berks., **1583**, æt. 13 weeks, in swaddling clothes, mutil., sm., mur., N. FRAGS. III. *Two shs., with 6 sons and 2 daus., c. **1520** (Barrett family?), parents lost.   IV. Inscr., mutil., to —— Barrett, **1584**, and w. Christian, with 2 sons.

BADDOW, GREAT.   Jane, dau. of Edw. Lewkenor, Esq., and w. of John Paschall, Esq., **16**—, C., p. 33.

BARDFIELD, GREAT.   Wm. Bendlowes, once sole serjeant-at-law, **1584** (eff. lost), and 2nd w. Alionora, inscr. mur. in 42 eleg. vv., A.T., C.

BARKING. I. A Priest, with chalice, in acad., c. **1480**, worn, inscr. lost, p. 76.   *Views by J. R. Malcom*, intended as an Appendix to Lysons' Environs of London.   II. Thos. Broke, **1493**, and w. Alice, with a son and dau., N.   III. John Tedcastell, Gent., and w. Elizth., dau. of Wm. Mey, LL.D., **1596**, æt. 43, with 9 sons, 7 daus. lost, C., p. 219.   *Malcom.*   INSCRS., &c. IV. Seven sons, c. **1530**.   V. Elizth. (Powle), widow of —— Hobart, of Norfolk, **1590**, eff. lately gone, p. 260.   VI. Christ. Merell, citizen and goldsmith of London, **1598**, æt. 60, and his sister Anne Yardlye, a widow, 1579.

BENTLEY, LITTLE.   Sir Wm. Pyrton, captain of Guisnes, in Picardy, 1490, and widow Cath., **1501**, lower part of male eff. and inscr. (?) lost, C., p. 116.

BELCHAMP ST. PAUL'S.   †Elizth., dau. and coh. of Edw. Best, Esq., and she had by her 1st husband (John Buckingham), Edm., and Dorothy (dec.), and by her second (Wm. Golding), Edw., Elizth. (dec.), Margt., and Mary, **1591**, C.

BOCKING. I. John Doreward, Esq., son of Sir Wm. Doreward, **1420**, and w. Isabella, inscr. lost, S.C., p. 189.   II. *Oswald Fitch, C., **1612**.

BOREHAM.   Alse, w. first of Thos. Byng, of Canterbury, and then of Jas. Canceller, one of the gentlemen of the Queen's Chapel, **1573**, and chil. [Isaac (Byng, stationer of London), Margt., Annis, Jane, Mary, Alse].

BOWERS GIFFORD.   Sir John Giffard, **1348** (?), head and marg. inscr. lost, large, loose at the Rectory, pp. 153, 158, 260.   *Proceedings of Essex Arch. Soc.*, vol. i. p. 93; *Introd.*, p. 153.

BRADFIELD.   Joan, dau. and coh. of John Harbottel, Esq., and w. of Thos. Rysby, Gent., **1598**, æt. 60, C.

BRAXTED, LITTLE.   *Wm. Roberts, Esq., auditor to Hen. VII., **1503**, and 2 ws., Joyce, dau. of Edw. Peryent, Esq., and Margt., dau. of Sir Wm. Pyrton, with 5 daus., C.

†BRIGHTLINGSEA. I. John Beriff, **1496**, and 3 ws., 2 lost.   II. Maria Beriff, **1505**.   III. Margt. Beriff, **1514**.   IV. John Beriff, **1521**, and ws. Mary and Alice.   V. Wm. Beriff and w., **1527** (?).

VI. A Widow, and a maiden lady, **1542** (?), on a bracket c. **1400**.
VII. Wm. Beriff, **1578**.

BROMLEY, GREAT. I. [Wm. Bischopton, priest, **1432**,] under mutil. canopy, good, 4 Lat. vv. mutil., C. *Boutell's Series*. INSCR. II. John Hubbarde, **1537**, and ws. Agnes, Alice, Rose, Elizth., and sons John, Wm., John, C.

†CANFIELD, GREAT. I. John Wiseman, **1518**, and family.   II. Thos. Fytche, Esq., **1588**.

CANFIELD, LITTLE. I. Wm. Fytche, Esq. (eff. lost), **1578**, æt. 82, and ws. Elizth. (with 2 sons and 3 daus.) and Ann (with 4 sons). II. Ann, dau. of John Wiseman, of Felstead, m. 1st, Wm. Fyttche, Esq., and had Thos., Wm., Francis; 2udly, Raphe Pudsey, Esq., of Gray's Inn, **1593**, below is an eff. of a son in cloak, C.

CHESTERFORD, GREAT. I. A Lady (of the Holden family?), c. **1530**, pecul., S.A.   II. John, seventh son of Thos. Lord Howard, baron of Walden, and knt. of the garter, **1600**, æt. 12 days, in swaddling clothes, sm.   Some brasses (1532, 1524?), are sketched in Cole's MS., 5,806, fol. 65. b.   See also Weever, Fun. Mon., p. 624.

CHESTERFORD, LITTLE.   Geo. Langham, Esq., lord of the manor, **1462**, and widow Isabel, male eff. and inscr. lost, once on A.T., p. 194.   *Etching in* —— (?), 1792 (male eff.)   Cole (in MS. 5,806, fol. 31. b) sketched these brasses, and also those of Wm. Hasylden, Esq., 1480, and w. Elizth., 1476; in 1781 he saw some of them inlaid in the passage of the house of Mr. Rich. Reynolds, Market-hill, Cambridge!

CHIGWELL. I. A Civilian, with 7 sons and 7 daus., c. **1520**, w. and inscr. lost.   II. John Hodgson, **1620**, head gone, w. and inscr. lost.   III. Sam. Harsnett, vicar, "Indignvs Episcopvs Cicestriensis, Deindignior Episcop' Norwicensis, Demvm Indignissim' Archiepiscop' Eboracen," **1631**, in cope, marg. inscr., very large, C., pp. 25, 71, 74, 77, 222, 228.   *Ogbourne's Hist. of Essex*, p. 238; *C. C. Soc. Illustr.*, No. i. p. 29; *Waller*, pt. i.   INSCRS. IV. Robt. Rampston, who left 40s. yearly to the poor, **1585**.   V. *Thos. Coleshill, donor to Ch., **1598**.   Nos. I. and II. recently lost (?), p. 260.

CHINGFORD.   Robt. Rampston, Gent., left £6 yearly for bread to the poor, 1585, and w. Margt., **1590**, S.A., effs. stolen a few years ago, pp. 55, 127, 260.   *Introd.*, p. 127 (male eff.)

CHRISHALL.   I. Sir John de la Pole and w. Joan (Cobham), c. **1370**, under triple canopy, only a frag. of marg. inscr. in Fr. left, partly covd., N., pp. 33, 61, 91, 160.   *Boutell's Series*, front.   See Arch. Journ., vol. iv. p. 338.   II. A Lady, c. **1450**, sm., husband and inscr. lost, N.   III. A Civilian and w., kng., c. **1480**, pecul., N.

CLAVERING. I. —— Songar (?) (upper hf. gone), and w., c. **1480**, with 4 sons (1 a priest) and 9 daus., kng., sm., inscr. and chil. lost or covd.   II. Thos. Welbore, Gent., of Pondes, and w. Ursula, dau. of Silvester D'Anvers, Esq., of Dauntesey, Wilts., by Elizth., a dau. of Sir John Mordaunt, and only surviving sister of Sir John D'Anvers, **1591**, with 1 son and 5 daus., mur.   III. —— Day and w. Joan, **1593**, with 4 Eng. vv.   FRAG. IV. Three daus., c. **1520**, man, with 2 ws. and 3 sons, lost.

COGGESHALL. I. Two fem. effs., c. **1490**, inscr. lost.   II. A male and fem. eff., c. **1500**.   III. A Civilian and w., c. **1540**, p. 29. Perhaps John Paycock, 1533, and w. Joan.   IV. Thos., son of Robt. Peaycocke, **1580**, left 2 daus. Joan and Anne, 4 Eng. vv. and marg. inscr., p. 225. Nos. I. and II. were lately loose at the vicarage, they probably commemorate some of the Peacock fam. See Weever, Fun. Mon., p. 618.

COLCHESTER, ST. JAMES. I. John Maynard, clothier and alderman, **1569**, engr. c. 1584 (?)   II. Ales, w. of No. I., **1584**, S.A.

COLCHESTER, ST. PETER. I. *John Sayre, alderman, 1510, and w. Elizth., **1530**, with chil., S.A.   II. Agnes, dau. of John Woodthorpe, of Lavenham, with 4 sons and 5 daus., and 2 husbands, Aleyn Dister and Robt. Leache; she left money for the poor at the feast of Pentecost, **1553**, qd. pl., mur.   III. *John Sayers, **1563**, mur.   IV. Wm. Brown, Gent., and w. Margt., both dec. **1572**, with 6 sons and 2 daus., 6 eleg. vv., mur.   V. Rich. Sayer, **1610**, and 1st w. Alice (Spooner), with 1 son and 2 daus.; by his 2nd w. Ellen (Lawrence, widow), he had a dau. Jane.

CORRINGHAM. I. Rich. de Beltoun, rector, c. **1340**, hf. eff., C., p. 143.   II. A Civilian, c. **1460**, mutil., worn, sm., rel., inscr. lost, C.   INSCRS. III. Alice Greyve, **1453**, C.   IV. Thos. at Lee, " ffirmari' isti' Manerij," **1464**, and w. Margt., N.

CRESSING. *Dorcas Musgrave, dec. in child-birth, **1610**, reclining on an hour-glass, with infant in swaddling clothes, C.

DAGENHAM. *Sir Thos. Urswyk, recorder of London, chief baron of the exchequer, **1470**, and w. [—— Southworth?], with 4 sons and 9 daus. (the eldest a nun), marg. inscr. lost, pp. 89, 90. *Ogbourne*, pl. v. p. 58; *C. C. Soc. Illustr.*, No. III. p. 99.

DONYLAND, EAST (ruined Chapel). †Mary Marshall.

DUNMOW, GREAT. A Lady [Cockeine?], c. **1580**, husband and inscr. lost.

EASTER, GOOD. Margt., dau. of Edw. Buggx, Gent., and w. of Thos. Norrington, **1610**, with dau., mutil., N.

EASTON, LITTLE. I. Robt. Fyn, priest, born at Northborough, dec. c. **1420**, with 3 Lat. vv., C.   II. Hen. Bourchier, first earl of Essex, lord treasurer, knt. of the garter, **1483**, and his countess Isabel (Plantagenet), aunt of Ed. IV., coloured, fine, inscr. lost, A.T., C., pp. 104, 116, 117, 197. *Waller*, pt. xiv.

EASTWOOD. Thos. Borrovgh, yeoman, **1600**, æt. 45, and w. Mary; he had 10 chil., and left his w., Thos., Barnabas, John, Maria, Bridget, and Martha surviving.

ELMDON. I. A Civilian and 2 ws., c. **1530**, marg. inscr. with text from Job xix. 25, covd. by pews (?), pecul.   II. Thos. Crawley, Esq., **1559**, and w. (effs. lost or covd.), with 4 sons and 8 daus., S.C. He founded a school at Elmdon.

ELMSTEAD. Two Hands holding a heart with a scroll, c. **1500** (?), p. 108.

*ELSENHAM. I. Dr. Tuer, vicar, **1616**, C.   II. Anne, dau. of No. I., and w. of Thos. Fielde, **1615**, C.   INSCRS. III. John Waldene, Esq., lord of the manor, **1400**, C.   IV. Wm. Barlee, Esq., **1521**, and w. Elizth., effs. lost, mur., C.

FAMBRIDGE, NORTH. Wm. Osborne, 1590, and w. Anne, dau. of Wm. Walker [**1607**, æt. 72], head lost, with 8 sons and 8 daus., inscr. mutil., C.

*FAULKBOURN. I. Hen. Fortescue, Esq., **1576**.   II. Mary Darell, **1598**.

FINCHINGFIELD. I. John Berners, Esq., and w. Elizth., dau. of Simon Wysseman, Esq., **1523**, in heraldic dresses, A.T., S.C., p. 232. INSCR. II. Robt. Kempe, Esq., **1524**, and w. Anne.

FINGRINGHOE. *John Alleyne, **1610**, and dau.

FRYERNING. A Lady, c. **1560**, on reverse eff. of a widow, c. **1470**, loose, p. 46. Perhaps part of the brass of Leonard, 3rd son of Wm. Berners, Esq., 1563, and w. Mary, eldest dau. and h. of . . . . , Esq., of Shenfylde, Essex, with 2 sons (Wm.) and a dau. *Suckling's Essex*.

GOSFIELD. I. Thos. Rolf, lawyer, **1440**, in acad., "Es [Æs] dedit ip(s)e satis miseris q; vijs, maculatis [lepers], carc[er]e p(ro)stratis, et virginib; bona gratis, inter iuristas quasi flos enituit," 10 Lat. vv., A.T., C., pp. 85, 90. *Boutell's Series*. INSCRS. II. *Leonard Bernard, **1563**, C.   III. *Sir Rich. Ryche and w. Anne, marg. mutil., A.T., N.C.   Some shs.

HALSTEAD. I. Barth. Lord Bourgchier, **1409**, and 2 ws., Margt. (Sutton) and Idonea (Lovey) a widow, inscr. lost, large, S.A., p. 187. II. Elizth., dau. of John Coggeshall, Gent., and w. of John Watson, **1604**, with 2 sons and 3 daus., mutil., mur., C.

HAM, EAST. I. Hester, "the vartvovs Loveinge and obedyent wife of Frances Neve," citizen and mcht.-taylor of London, **1610**, æt. 58. II. Elizth., eldest dau. of Jas. Harvey, Esq., of Dagenham, and w. of Rich. Heigham, Esq., **1622**; she had 3 chil., Jas., Mary, Elizth. INSCNS. III. *Benefaction of Robt. Rampston, **1585**. IV. *Wm., son of Wm. Johnson, **1631**, æt. 1 week.

HAM, WEST. Thos. Staples, who left 20s. yearly to the poor, **1592**, and 4 ws., Anne, Margt., Denis, Alice, 20 Eng. vv., mur., S.A.

HARLOW. I. A Man, in arm., and w., c. **1430**, sm., S.Tr., p. 189. Erroneously ascribed to Robt. Druncaster [Symond?], 1490. II. Mr. Wm. Sumner, last tenant of John Reeve, last lord abbot of St. Edmunds Bury, he gave £10 6s. 11d. towards beautifying the Ch., **1559**, mutil., sm., inscr. lost, N.Tr. III. Edw. Bugge, the elder, Gent., and w. Janne, **1582**, with 3 sons and 2 daus., C., p. 240. IV. A Man and w., c. **1585**, sm., N.Tr. V. W. Newman, **1602**, with a figure of death, both standing, sm., mur., N. VI. John Gladwin the elder, **1615**, æt. 95, who "wth longe and tediovs sutes in lawe, wth ye Lord of the mannor of harlowe, did prove the Cvstome for the copie holds to ye greate benifitt of posteritie for ever," sm., now mur., N. VII. Rich. Bugges, Esq., son of Edw. Bugges, **1636**, in arm., holding a staff, and 2 ws. (in different costume), Vahan, dau. of Robt. Streinsham, Gent., and Elizth., dau. of Thos. Bowles, Esq., 4 Eng. vv., C. VIII. A Man and w. [—— Jocelyne], kng., sm., c. **1630**, mur. N.Tr. INSCNS. IX. Geo. Deryngton, yeoman, **1575**, æt. 70, mur., N. X. Margt., dau. of Nich. Cely, and w. of Robt. Lawson, Gent., **1617**, now placed beneath No. IV. Nos. I., II., III., and VII. have been removed from the floor and placed in wooden frames against the wall.

HATFIELD PEVERELL. I. †Three effs. under pews. INSCR. II. *John Alleyn, 1572, and 3 ws., with 3 sons and 4 daus. by 1st w., 24 Eng. vv., belonging to No. I. (?)

HEMPSTEAD. I. A Civilian, w. and inscr. lost, c. **1475**, N., p. 128. II. A Civilian, c. **1480**, with 5 sons and 2 daus., w. and inscr. lost, N. III. Thos. Huntingdon, Esq., **1492**, and w. Margt., dau. of Sir Wm. Tyrrell, of Beches in Rawreth, inscr. lost, N.C. IV. Wm. Mordant, chief prothonotary of court of common pleas, son of Wm. Mordant, of Turvey, Beds., **1518**, and w. Anne, youngest dau. and coh. of Thos. Huntington, with 10 sons; w. and 5 or 6 daus. lost, N. V. A Civilian and w., c. **1530**, with 4 sons and 5 (?) daus., inscr. lost, pecul., sm., N. INSCR. VI. Rich. Westley, **1518**, and w. Joan, N.C.

HEYBRIDGE. *John Whitacres, **1627**, N.

HEYDON. A Priest, c. **1490** (?), inscr. lost, N. Some brasses (c. 1460, 1520), now lost, are sketched in Cole's MS., 5,806, fol. 78. b.

HORKESLEY, LITTLE. I. Sir Robt. Swynborne, lord of the manor, 1391, and his son Sir Thos. Swynborne, "S' [Seigneour] de Hammys, Mair de Burdeux, & Capitaigne de ffronsak," **1412**, with collar of SS., each under a triple canopy, large and fine, marg. inscr. in Fr., A.T., C., pp. 45, 52, 187. *Suckling's Essex; Waller*, pt. iii. *Boutell's Mon. Br.*, p. 55 (eff.) II. Kath. Leventhorp, **1502**, in shroud, inscr. lost. *Publications of the Antiquarian Etching Club*, vol. iii. pl. 9. III. Dame Brygete Marnay, **1549**, and 2 husbands, Mr. Thos. Fyndorne, Esq., and John Lord Marnay [1524], in heraldic dresses, C., pp. 54, 57, 62. *Suckling's Essex*. INSCR. IV. John Swynborne, **1430**, and his brother Andrew, 1418, marg., effs. lost.

HORNCHURCH. I. A Civilian and 3 ws., c. **1590**, male and 1 fem. eff. and inscr. lost. II. Thos. Drywod, **1591**, æt. 57, and w. Anne, m. 28 years, with 8 sons and 3 daus., sm., marg. inscr. mutil. III. Thos. Hone, Gent., **1604**, æt. 63, and w., with 6 sons and 6 daus., sm. FRAGS., &c. IV. "Sire Boneface de Hart, chaunoine de Oste," a cross with 2 large hf. effs., all lost but 3 letters of Lomb. inscr., p. 139. V. A Sh., from brass of Thos. Scargile, Esq., **1475**, and w. Elizth. VI. Two shs., from brass of Kath. (Powlet), w. of Wm. Fermor, **1510**. VII. Inscr. to Mr. Geo. Reede, LL.B., vicar, **1530**, eff. in acad., lost. VIII. Jas. Pollexfen, born at Yeampton, Devon, B.C.L., fellow, auditor, and steward of St. Mary's Coll., Oxford; he m. Kath., dau. of Jas. and Alice Barefoote, of Northleigh, Oxon., and had 6 sons and 2 daus., **1587**, æt. 44, inscr. with 8 Eng. vv., eff. lost. IX. Sh. and inscr. to Peerce Pennaunte, Esq., servant to Ed. VI. and Queen Mary, and gent. usher for 32 years to Queen Elizth., **1590**, æt. 70. All these brasses are now in C.

HORNDON, EAST. *A Lady, c. **1450**, mur., vestry.

HUTTON. *A Man, in arm., and w., c. **1525**, with 8 sons and 8 daus., inscr. lost. *Suckling's Essex*.

ILFORD, LITTLE. I. Thos., son and h. of Sir John Heron, private treasurer of the king, dec. at Alderbroke, **1517**, æt. 14, C., p. 86. *Introd.*, p. 85. II. *Anne, only dau. of Barnard Hyde, Esq., of London, and his w. Anne, **1630**, æt. 18, with 6 Eng. vv. which her brother Barnard pos.; her infant brother Wm., 1614, was buried under the same stone; sm., partly covd. by clerk's seat, N.

*INGRAVE. I. Margt. [Fitz Lewis, **1457**?] marg. inscr. mutil. She seems to have been a dau. of Anne Montacute by her 2nd husband

John Fitz-Lewis; the 1st husband was Sir Rich. Hankford, and the 3rd John Holland, Duke of Exeter. Note by Rev. C. R. Manning. II. John Fitz-Lewis and 4 ws., in heraldic dresses, c. **1500**.

KELVEDON HATCH. I. A Civilian and w., c. **1560**, male eff. and inscr. lost, sm. INSCR. II. *Francis, dau. of Philip Waldegrave, and w. of John Wright, **1656**.

LAINDON. I. A Priest, c. **1480**, with chalice, inscr. lost. II. A Priest, with chalice and host, c. **1510**, sm., inscr. lost, p. 78.

LATTON. I. Sir Peter Arderne, chief baron, **1467**, and w. Cath. (?), A.T., C., pp. 90, 95, 210. *Gough*, vol. ii. pl. 85, p. 216; *Waller*, pt. iv.; and *Drummond's Hist. of Noble British Families.* II. John Bohun, Esq., and w. Anne, dau. of Sir Peter Arderne (?), c. **1485**, with 3 sons and a dau., inscr. lost, C., p. 197. *Gough*, ibid. III. A Priest, c. **1520**, with chalice and host, and Evang. symbs., inscr. lost. IV. A Lady, c. **1560**, inscr. lost. V. Emanuell Woolloye, Gent., and w. Margt. (?), c. **1600**, inscr. lost. VI. Frances, dau. of Frances Roberts, Esq., and w. of Rich. Frankelin, Esq., of Willesdon, Middx., **1604**, æt. 23, and son and dau., "descended in the fourth generation from the Lady Jvdd."

LAVERS, HIGH. †Edw. Sulyard, cousin and h. to Sir Thos. Flemmyng, and w. Myrabyll, dau. and h. of John Compton, c. **1500**, with 4 sons and 1 dau., C.

LAYER MARNEY. *A Man, in arm., of the Swynborne family (?), c. **1430**. *Suckling's Essex.*

LEIGH (near Rochford). I. Rich. Haddok, **1453**, and w. Cristina (with 7 sons and 3 daus.); also beside them their son John and his w. Alice, with 8 sons and 3 daus.; Rich. had also a w. Margt. *Antiq. Etch. Club*, vol. ii. pl. 51. II. Rich. Chester, mariner and an elder brother of the Trin. House, and master in 1615, dec. **1632**, and w. Elizth., m. c. 49 years, with 4 sons and 1 dau.; his surviving chil., Elizth., Geo., Robt., pos. *Antiq. Etch. Club*, vol. v. pl. 54 (male eff.) III. John Price, born at Cardiff, commander of several ships of war under Wm. III., **1709**, and w. Martha, dau. of Thos. Godman, Esq., of Bristol, 1696, (doubtful if eff's. engr. so late), p. 43. INSCR. IV. Robt. Salmon, **1591**, and w. Agnes, m. 32 years, and had 6 sons and 4 daus.

LEIGH, GREAT. I. A Priest, c. **1370**, only upper part of eff. left, loose, C. II. Ralph Shelley, rector, **1414**, hf. eff., head gone.

LEYTON, LOW. I. Ursula, only dau. of —— Gasper, **1493** (date modern), sm., 2 Lat. vv., p. 213. II. Tobias Wood, Esq., and w. Eliza, who dec. in child-birth, c. **1620**; with 7 sons and 5 daus.;

loose, inscr. lately lost.   INSCRS. III. †Lady Mary Kyngestone, **1557.**   IV. Robt. Rampston, **1585**, left 20s. yearly to the poor.

LITTLEBURY. I. A Civilian, c. **1480.**   II. A Priest, c. **1510.** with chalice and host.   III. A Civilian and w., c. **1510**, with scrolls.   IV. A Civilian, c. **1520**, pecul., 2 effs. and Hy. Trin. (?) lost, sm. The inscrs. of Nos. I.–IV. lost.   V. Jane, dau. of Gyles Poulton, Gent., of Desboroughe, Northants., and w. of Hen. Bradbuirye, Gent., **1578**, with chil., Wm., Mary, Anne, and Elizth. (daus. lost), C., p. 246.   VI. Anne, dau. and h. of Robt. Perkin, and w. of Thos. Byrch, Gent., **1624**, loose.   INSCR. VII. *James Edwards, "Satelles" of Hadstock, Hadham, and Littlebury, died of the plague, **1522.**

LOUGHTON. I. John Stonnard, **1541**, and ws. Joan and Cath. II. *Abel Guilliams, Gent. and mcht. of London, **1637**, æt. 42 (?), in arm., and w., with 8 chil., Wm., Robt., Frances, Robt., Rich., Chas., John, Geo., now under canopy, inscr. lost (?), qd. pl.

MARGARETTING. A Man, in arm. (head lost), and w., c. **1550**, with 3 sons, daus. and inscr. lost, C., p. 236. *Suckling's Essex.*

MESSING. *A Lady, c. **1530**, inscr. lost, C. *Suckling's Essex.*

*NETTLESWELL. I. Thos. Laurence, **1522**, in arm., and w. Alice, N.   II. John Bannister, Gent., **1607**, æt. 80, and w. Elizth., dau. of Edw. North, with 3 sons and 1 dau., C.

NEWPORT. I. Thos. Broad, **1515**, and w. Margery, with 2 sons, 2 daus. lost (?), marg. inscr. and Evang. symbs., S.A.   II. Geoff. Nightingale, Esq., and w. Kath., **1608**, they had 7 chil., Thos., Hen., Wm., Mary, Anne, John, and Elizth.   In Cole's MS., 5,806, fol. 29. b, is a sketch of a man and w., hf. effs., now lost.

OCKENDON, NORTH. I. Wm. Poyntz, Esq., and w. Elizabeth, a sister of Sir John Shaa, lord mayor of London, **1502**, with 6 sons and 6 daus., now mur., N.A., p. 232. *Suckling's Essex.*   II. Thomasyn, dau. of —— Badby, Gent., and w. of Robt. Latham, Gent., and then of Wm. Ardall, Gent., c. **1530**, inscr. mutil., N. INSCRS. III. "Johan bauchōn gist y cy…" **1323** (?), N.C.   See Anth. Wood's MS. in Ashmolean, C. 11, 8,551, fol. 21. b.   IV. John Poyntz, Esq., son and h. of Wm. Poyntz, Esq., patron of Ch., **1547**, with 4 shs., now mur., C.

OCKENDON, SOUTH. I. Sir Ingelram Bruyn, lord of the manor, **1400**, head lost, under canopy, large, C., pp. 92, 162.   II. Margt., w. of Edw. Barker, Gent., of Chiswick, Middx., **1602.**   INSCRS. III. Gilbert, eldest son of Rich. Salstonstall, of London, mcht.-adventurer, **1585.**   IV. Forty-four Eng. vv. to the same, mur.

ONGAR, HIGH. A Civilian, c. **1510.**   Some inscrs.

ORSETT. I. A Civilian, c. **1535**, sm., mur., C. FRAGS., &c. II. Thos. Latham, **1485**, and w. Jane (effs. lost), with 1 son and 2 daus. III. Six daus., c. **1520**. IV. Robt. Kinge, parson, **1584**, æt. 47, 4 Lat. and 8 Eng. vv.

PEBMARSH. A member of the Fitzralph family, c. **1320**, in arm., cross-legged, with sh. &c. mutil., fine, large, canopy and marg. inscr. lost, C., pp. 137, 150. *Waller*, pt. xiii.; *Boutell's Mon. Br.*, p. 37.

RALEIGH. A Civilian and w., c. **1420**, worn, inscr. lost, now in N.A. Probably John Barington, Esq., 1416, and w. Thomazina, 1420. See Appendix B.

RAWRETH. Edm. Tyrell, Esq., of Beaches and Ramesdon Barringtons, died at Whitestaple, Kent, **1576**, in arm., and w. [Coke], mutil., mur., S.A., p. 226.

RAYNHAM. A Civilian and w., c. **1500**, inscr. lost, N.

RETTENDEN. I. A Civilian and 2 ws., c. **1540**, with 3 sons and 4 daus.; a 3rd w., some chil., and inscr. lost. II. Rich. Cannon, Esq., who gave £5 yearly to the poor in lands, and £5 for bread every Sabbath-day to the poor of Hanningfellde, **1605**, N.A. III. Rich. Humfrie, Gent., half-brother to Rich. Canon, Esq. [**1607**], and 3 sons, kng., Rich., Wm., Edm.

ROCHFORD. Maria Dilcok, **1514**, sm., N.

RODING, HIGH. Thos. Fytche, **1514**, and w. Agnes, with 6 sons and 5 daus.

ROYDON. I. Thos. Colte, Esq., "Edwardi Regis consul honorificus," **1471**, and w. Joan [Trusbut] in mantle, both wearing collars, 8 Lat. vv., C., pp. 93, 194. *Gough*, vol. ii. pl. 95, p. 252. II. [John Colt], Esq., son of Thos. Colt, Esq. [**1521**], and ws. Elizth. (dau. of Sir John Eldrington, with 4 sons and 8 daus.) and Mary (dau. of Sir John Anbe, with 3 sons and 3 daus.), in heraldic dresses, marg. inscr. mutil., C. *Ibid.* III. A Civilian [Colt?], c. **1580**, inscr. lost. IV. Elizth., eldest dau. of Hen. Dinn, Esq., of Heydon, Norf., one of the 7 auditors of the exchequer, and w. of John Stanley, Gent., **1589**, with 5 chil., Hen., Beatris, Fraunces, and Rich. and Jane (dec.), qd. pl., mur.

RUMSEY, NEW. *Thos. Smith and ws., **1610**.

RUNWELL. Eustace Sulyard, Esq., 1547, and w. Margt. (Ayloffe), **1586-7**, they had 2 chil., Edw. and Wm.; by her 1st husband, Greg. Bassett, Esq., Margt. had a dau., Dorothy, m. to Anth. Maxey, Esq.

SAFFRON WALDEN. I. A Priest, c. **1430**, inscr. lost, S.C.A. Perhaps Thos. Boyd, or Byrd. II. *A Lady, c. **1440**, N.A. III. *A Lady, c. **1530**. IV. *Thos. Tanner, **1610**, and w. FRAG. V. Part of a male eff., c. **1470**.

SANDON. I. Patrick Fearne, late parson, and w., c. **1580**, mur., C. FRAG. II. Two scrolls and shs., effs. lost, C., p. 119.

SHOPLAND. Thos. Stapel, serjeant-at-arms, **1371**, in arm., Fr. inscr., partly covd., p. 160. *Antiq. Etching Club*, vol. ii. pl. 26.

SPRINGFIELD. A Man in arm., c. **1420**, inscr. lost, p. 190.

*STANFORD RIVERS. I. Thos. Grevile, child, **1492**, p. 173. II. Robt. Barrow, Esq., **1503**. III. A Man, in arm., and w., c. **1540**.

STEBBING. A Widow Lady, c. **1390**, inscr. lost, N.A., p. 167.

STIFFORD. I. Ralph Perchehay, rector, c, **1375**, hf. eff., C. II. A Priest, c. **1480**, in shroud, inscr. lost, N., p. 107. III. John Ardalle, Gent., lord of the manor, **1504**, not in arm., and w. Anne. IV. Wm. Lathum, Gent., lord of the manor, (son of Thos. Lathum, Esq., of North Okendon (dec.), the son and h. of Robt. Lathum, who m. the dau. and h. of No. III.), **1622**, and w. Susan, dau. of Symon Sampson, Esq., of Carsey, Suff., 1622. V. Ann, dau. of Thos. Lathum, Gent., **1627**, æt. 17, 8 Eng. vv., sm. VI. Elizth., w. of Thos. Lathum, Gent., **1630**, æt. 37, 8 Eng. vv., sm. Lomb. inscr. to David de Tillebery, C., p. 57.

STISTED. Elizth., dau. of John Glascock, Gent., of Roxewell, and w. of John Wyseman, Gent. (lord of the manor of Stisted, and son and h. of Wm. Wiseman, Gent., dec., son and h. of Thos. Wiseman, Esq., of Great Waltham), **1584**, with child, mur., C., p. 246.

STOCK. *Rich. Twedye, Esq., who founded 4 almshouses for 4 poor knights, **1574**, æt. 58, in arm., 8 Eng. vv., A.T., S.A.

*STONDON MASSEY. I. John Sarre, citizen of London, iron-monger, and mcht.-venturer, **1570**, and w., 16 Eng. vv., C. II. Rainold Hollingworth, **1573**, 12 Eng. vv., C.

*STRETHALL. I. A Priest, c. **1480**, in acad. INSCR. II. Thos. Abbot, parson, **1539**, on reverse, an inscr. to Margt. Sidney, "formosam mulierem religiosam," probably once with an eff. in shroud.

*TERLING. I. A Man and w., c. **1430**, hf. effs., male eff. and inscr. lost, N. II. A Man, in arm., and w., c. **1490**, S.A. III. Wm. Rochester, Esq., **1558**, and w. Elizth., 1556, 12 Eng. vv., mur., S.A., inscr. only (?). IV. John Rochester, Esq., **1584**, and 2 ws., with 12 chil., mur., S.A.

THAXTED. A Priest, c. **1450**, in acad., inscr. lost, p. 84.

*THEYDON GERNON. 1. Wm. Kirkaby, priest, **1458**, in cope, inscr. lost, N., p. 79. *Ogbourne's Essex*, p. 238. II. Ellen, dau. and h. of Francis Hayden, Esq., and w. of John Braunche, citizen and mcht. of London, **1567**, mur., C.

THORINGTON. *John Clare (eff. lost), and w.

THURROCK, GRAYS. A Civilian and 2 ws., the 2nd with 6 daus., a son and inscr. lost, c. **1510**, N.

THURROCK, WEST. I. Humph. Hoies, 1584 (eff. lost), and son Humph., **1585**, with 18 eleg. lines containing puns on the name Hay(s), *fœnum*, sm., p. 240.   INSCR. II. †Kath., dau. of Humph. Hoies, and w. of —— Redinge, **1591**.

TILLINGHAM. I. Lady Margt. Wyott, **1526**.   II. Edw. Wiot, Esq., **1584**, with 2 Lat. vv., mur., S.C.

TILTEY ABBEY. I. Gerard Danet, Esq., of Bronkynsthorp, Leic., counsellor of Hen. VIII., **1520**, and w., with 5 sons and 6 daus., C. II. Geo. Medeley, Esq., **1562**, in arm., and w. Mary, with 3 sons and 2 daus., marg. inscr., C.   III. Margt., w. of Geo. Tuke, Esq., of Layermarney, **1590**, with 3 sons, 3 daus., and 3 chil. in swaddling clothes, sm., C., p. 219.   INSCR. IV. Thos. of Thakley, abbot, c. **1460**, 4 Lat. vv. *Gough*, vol. i. pl. 20, p. 249.

*TOLLESHUNT DARCY. I. John de Boys, Esq., lord of the manor of Tolleshunt Tregoz, **1419**, mutil.   II. Anth. Darcy, Esq., justice of the peace, **1540**, large. Both brasses loose.

TOPPESFIELD. †John Cracherowd, **1513**, and w. Agnes.

TWINSTEAD. Isaac Wyncoll, Esq., and w. Mary, dau. of Sir Thos. Gaudy, of Gaudy Hall, judge of the king's bench, **1610**, with 5 daus., a son lost.

UPMINSTER. I. Roger Dencourt, Esq., **1455**, and w. Elizth., dau. of Hen. de la Felde; only eff. of w., in heraldic mantle, left, loose, p. 257.   II. Nich. Wayte (?), citizen and mercer of London, lord of the manor of Geynes, 1544, and w. Ellen, dau. of Robt. Deyncourt by his 1st w. Elizth., dau. of Jenkin Clarke, of Alveley, **1545**, only male eff. left, loose; on reverse, part of eff. of a bp. or abbot, 15th cent.   III. Geerardt, eldest son of Adrian D'Ewes (of the ancient family of "Des Ewes, Dynastarum ditionis de Kessel in ducatu Gelriæ"), by his 2nd w., Alice Ravenscroft, **1591**, in arm., inscr. lost, N.A., pp. 215, 236. *Weever's Fun. Mon.*, p. 653; *Suckling's Essex.* FRAGS., &c. IV. A Sh., part of the brass (?) of Mary (Engayne), w. of Sir Wm. Barnake (?), C.   V. Three shs. (one loose), with arms of Goldsmiths' Co., Latham, &c., N.C., p. 119.   VI. Palimpsest, with scroll and canopied work, loose.   VII. Two daus., c. **1620**, perhaps for Mary and Martha, 1624, daus. of Ralph Lathum, and his w. Mary, dau. of Hamlett and Elinor Clarke, N.C.   VIII. Grace, dau. of Wm. Lathum, Esq. (?), 1626, inscr. lost, loose.   IX. Inscrs. to Hamlett Clarke, Gent., and 2nd w., Alice, widow of Ralph Lathum, **1636**, and their chil., &c., mur., N.C.   The loose brasses were in the possession of Mr. Johnson, of Gaines, July, 1859.

WALTHAM ABBEY. I. Edw. Stacy, 1555, and w. Kath., **1565**, æt. 78; they had a son Francis; 12 Eng. vv., qd. pl., mur. II. Thos. Colte, Esq., 1559, and w. Magdalen, who pos., **1576**, and dec. 1591, with 6 sons and 4 daus., mur., p. 226.

*WALTHAM, GREAT. I. Geo. Everard, **1617**. II. A Civilian and 2 ws., c. **1600**.

WALTHAMSTOW. I. Sir Geo. Monox, lord mayor of London, **1543**, not in arm., and w. Ann, Hy. Trin. and inscr. lost, mur., S.A., pp. 119, 120, 242. *Ogbourne's Essex*, pl. 5, p. 58; *J. P. Malcolm's Views*. Sir Geo. built the tower and aisle of the Ch., and founded an almshouse near it. II. —— Hale, and w. ——, dau. of —— Porter, born at Grantham, dec. **1588**, 8 eleg. vv., eff. of w. mutil., but perfect when engr. by *Malcolm*. INSCRS. III. Hen. Crane, LL.B., vicar, **1436**. IV. Benefaction of 40s. yearly in Nov. to the poor, from Robt. Rampston, Gent., **1585**, mur., p. 55.

WARLEY, LITTLE. *Anne Hamner, **1592**, hf. eff.

WEALD, NORTH. *Walter Larder, **1617** (?), and w. Mary, with 3 sons, Walter, Sam., ——, and 2 daus., Annie, ——, inscr. mutil.

WEALD, SOUTH. I. A Civilian, c. **1460**, with 6 daus.; w., daus., and inscr. lost. II. *A Civilian and 2 ws., with 6 sons, c. **1540**. III. *Sir Anth. Brown, justice of com. pleas, **1567**, æt. 57 (eff. lost), and w. Joan, æt. 52, A.T., C. IV. *Robt. Picakis and Ellen Talbot, chil., **1634**, kng., with a small fish.

WENDEN. A Man in arm. (of the Loveney family?), c. **1410**, N., p. 188.

WENDEN-LOFTS. Wm. Lucas and w. Kath., c. **1450**, with 4 sons (the 1st an abbot) and 4 daus., pp. 74, 172.

*WILLINGHALE DOE. I. —— Torrell, Esq., N. II. [Anne, dau. of Humphrey Torrell, and widow of John Sackfild, Esq., of Buckhurst, Sussex,] **1582**, æt. 80, inscr. mutil., C. III. Dorothy, dau. of Sir Thos. Jocelin, and w. of Thos. Brewster, Esq., **1613**, C.

WIMBISH. I. Sir John de Wantone, **1347**, and w. Ellen, sm., in the head of a cross which is nearly all lost, inscr. gone, N.C., pp. 136, 149, 154, 158, 165, 166, 171. *Waller*, pt. xvi. *Boutell's Mon. Br.*, p. 119 (fem. and part of male eff.) II. Joan Wiseman, widow of —— Strangman, c. **1570**; on reverse an eff. of St. John, &c.; Flemish, a sm. portion (?) in possession of Rev. W. S. Simpson, London, p. 47.

WIVENHOE. I. Wm. Viscount Beaumount and Lord Bardolf, **1507**, with triple and super-canopy, side shafts gone, marg. inscr., large, C., pp. 114, 221, 232. *Waller*, pt. xi.; *C. C. Soc. Illustr.*, No. V. p. 165. II. Sir Thos. Westeley, priest, chaplain to

Rt. Hon. Lady and Countess of Oxenford, **1535**, with chalice and wafer, sm., N.   III. Lady Elizth. [Scroope, 2nd. w. of John de Vere, earl of Oxford, and widow of Wm. Viscount Beaumont, **1537**], in coronet and heraldic mantle, with triple and super-canopy, and marg. inscr., both much mutil., large, C. *C. C. Soc. Illustr.*, No. V. p. 185.

WHITTLE.   I. A Man in arm. [of the Hyde family], and w., c. **1500**, with 6 sons and 2 daus., inscr. lost, N.   II. Two men, in arm., and 2 ladies, partly covd.; to this belong (?) 3 groups of chil., 2 sons and 2 daus., 1 son and 5 daus., 7 sons and 2 daus.; the inscr., now lost (?), was in memory of Thomasi[n]a, the dau. and h. of Thos. Heveningham, jun. (son of Thos. Heveningham, sen., and his w. Thomasi[n]a), and w. successively of Thos. Berdefield, John Bedall, and Walter Thomas, Gent., **1513**, C., p. 232. *Suckling's Essex* (1 fem. eff.)   III. Constans, "meyden doughter" of John Berners, Esq., **1524**, sm., N.A.   IV. Wm. Pinchon, Esq., **1592**, and w. Rose, dau. of Thos. Reddin, with 6 sons and 3 daus.; male eff., daus., and inscr. lost, N.A.   Wm. was the son of John Pinchon, Esq., who m. Jane, dau. of Sir Rich. Empson, who was beheaded. See Lansdown MS., 874, fol. 83. a.   V. †Edw. Hunt, Gent., **1606**, and w., 1605, mur., N.A.   He gave 2 almshouses in Church-lane, and 20s. yearly to maintain them, also 10s., charged on land called Appesfield, in Chelmsford, yearly on Good Friday, to the poor.   VI. Edw. Bowland, Gent., 1609, and w. Joan, **1616**, C.   FRAG. VII. "Mercy" on a scroll, all that remains of a fine brass.   VIII. Two Shs., c. **1580**.

YELDHAM, GREAT.   *[Rich. Symonds, **1611**?], and w. [Elizth., dau. of Robt. Plume?], with 5 sons and 1 dau., mur., S.C.

INSCRIPTIONS, &c.

BROOMFIELD.   *Thos. Huntlye, **1613**, and w. Rachel, effs. lost.
FELSTEAD.   Thos. Ryche, child, **1564**, sm., eff. lost, p. 96.   HANNINGFIELD, EAST.   *Rich. Brydges, **1606**, C.   RAYNE.   *Lady Manners, **1572**, with sh.   ROXWELL.   *Thos. Younge, **1593**.   STANSTED MOUNTFITCHET.   Robt. de Bokkyngg, 1st vicar, **1361**.

The hf. eff. and curious inscr. (see Appendix B.) to Sir John Smythe, priest, **1475**, formerly at St. Mary's hospital, GREAT ILFORD, is now lost.   The hf. effs. of Robt. de Teye and w. Kath., both dec. Oct. 7, 1360, lately at MARKS TEY, are now lost; as are also those of Isabel Clovill and son John, **1361**, once at WEST HANNINGFIELD; the inscr. of the latter brass remains.   The brasses at LAMBOURN and DEBDEN (see the sketches in Cole's MS., 5,806, fol. 131) are lost.

Gloucestershire.

ABBENHALL. Rich. Pyrke, of Micheldean, **1609**, æt. 60, and w. Joan, dau. of John Ayleway, Gent., with their sons Thos. and Robt., C.

BERKELEY. [Wm. Frome, feodary of the Berkeley estates under Hen. VII., and escheator of the hundred of Berkeley, **1526**], head and feet gone, marg. inscr. mutil., now S.A., pp. 107, 230.

BISLEY. Kath., w. of Thos. Sewell, **1515**, with 5 sons and 7 daus., N.

BRISTOL, ST. JOHN'S. Thos. Rouley, mcht., and sheriff [in 1475], dec. **1478**, and w. Margt., with mcht.'s mk., and sh. with a roe (?), under moveable floor, N., p. 201.

BRISTOL, ST. MARY REDCLIFF. I. Sir John Juyn, recorder of Bristol, baron of the exchequer, chief justice of the king's bench, **1439**, marg. inscr. and 8 Lat. vv., Lady-chapel, p. 90.   II. Philip Mede, Esq. (?), **1475** (?), in tabard, and 2 ws., 1 in heraldic mantle, with demi-figure of our Saviour (?), inscr. lost, qd. pl., mur., A.T., N.A., p. 21.   III. John Jay, sheriff [in 1472], and w. Joan, c. **1480**, with 6 sons and 8 daus., canopy, mcht.'s mk. and fuller's bat (?) on shs., C.   IV. John Brook, serjeant-at-law, and justice of assize in west of England for Hen. VIII., also chief steward of the monastery of Glastonbury, **1522**, and w. Joan, a dau. and h. of Rich. Amerike, C., p. 90.   Incised slab of Wm. Coke, p. 130.

BRISTOL, ST. PETER'S. Robt. Lond, chaplain, **1461**, with chalice and host, C.

BRISTOL, ST. WERBURGH. I. Nich. Thorne, mcht., and mayor [in 1544], founder (together with his brother) of a school, 1546, æt. 50, and 2 ws. and chil.; by 1st w., he had Bridgett and John; by 2nd, Jane, John, Francis, Robt., Mary, Joan, Nich., Edw., 18 Lat. vv., engr. c. **1570**, mur.   II. Wm. Gyttyns, mcht., and one of the common council, **1586**, and w. Mary (who pos.), with 6 sons and 4 daus., qd. pl., mur.

BRISTOL, TEMPLE CHURCH. I. A Civilian [**1396**], hf. eff., 4 Lat. vv., marg. inscr. lost, N.A., p. 164.   II. A Priest, in cope, on reverse a lady in mantle, both engr. c. **1460**, rel., inscr. lost, pp. 47, 79.

BRISTOL, TRINITY, or BARSTAPLE ALMSHOUSE CHAPEL. I. John Barstaple, burgess, founder of almshouses, **1411**, canopy lost, sm., pp. 62, 96.   II. Isabella [Gayner?], w. of No. I., canopy lost, engr. c. **1411**, sm., pp. 53, 62, 96.

CAMPDEN, CHIPPING. I. Wm. Grevel, citizen of London, "flos mercatorum lanar' tocius Anglie," **1401**, and w. Marion, [dau. of Sir John Thornborough?], 1386, with canopy, mcht.'s mks., and marg. inscr. (the end of which was loose Jan. 1860), very large, C., pp. 138, 164, 169, 200. *Gough*, vol. ii. pl. iv. p. 10; *Bigland's Collections for Gloucestershire*, vol. i. p. 283; *Boutell's Series*, and *Weekly Register*, No. 7, p. 105. II. Wm. Welley, mcht., **1450**, and w. Alice, C., now within altar-rails. III. John Lethenard, mcht., **1467**, and w. Joan, N. IV. Wm. Gybbys, **1484**, and ws. Alice, Margt., Marion, with 7 sons and 6 daus., N. *Bigland*, vol. i. p. 284.

CHELTENHAM, ST. MARY'S. [Sir Wm. Greville, of Arle Court, justice of common pleas], **1513**, and w. [dau. of ——?] Sloughter, with 3 sons and 8 daus., marg. inscr. mutil., much worn, C., p. 91. (See Corrigenda.)

CIRENCESTER. I. A Wine-mcht. (?) and w. Margt., c. **1400**, under canopy, inscr. in 8 Lat. vv., mutil., head of male eff. and upper part of fem. eff. lost, large, much worn, N., pp. 129, 202. II. [Rich.] Dixton, Esq., **1438**, under canopy, marg. inscr. mutil., large, p. 192. *Bigland*, vol. i. p. 341; *Waller*, pt. xii. III. Robt. Page, wool-mcht., **1440** (?), and w. Margt., with 6 sons and 8 daus., canopy, marg. inscr. in 6 Lat. vv. (stating he repaired churches and roads) lost, p. 211. The date is given from Wood's MS. (D. 11. No. 8,517, fol. 29) at the Ashmolean Library. IV. Reginald Spycer, mcht., **1442**, and ws. Margt., Juliana, Margt., Joan, p. 211. V. Wm. Prelatte, Esq., a very special benefactor to the chapel [of Hy. Trin.], **1462**, and 2 ws., Agnes, widow of John Martyn, and Joan, dau. and h. of Rich. de Cobyndon, and widow of John Twynyho, Esq., of Cayforde, Somerset, p. 196. *Lysons' Gloucestershire Antiq.*, pl. 16. VI. Wm. Notyngham, 1427 (head gone), and w. Cristina, 1434, engr. c. **1470**, S.A., p. 45. VII. Ralph Parsons, **1478**, with chalice and host, much worn. VIII. A Priest, c. **1480**, in cassock, sin., inscr. lost, S.A., p. 77. *Introd.*, p. 77. IX. A Civilian and w., in mantle, c. **1480**, worn; another w., inscr., and chil. lost, S.A. X. John Benet, **1497** (head gone), and 2 ws., Agnes and Agnes, 1 w. and chil. gone, marg. inscr. nearly all lost, now in N. XI. A Civilian, c. **1500**, mutil., head restored, inscr. gone. XII. A Civilian and w., c. **1500**, with 4 sons (1 in acad.) and 3 daus., between them a pot of lilies mutil.; the w., daus., and lily-pot (which is loose) are now on the same slab as No. XIII.; inscr. lost, mur., St. Cath. C. Probably John Avenyng, 1501, and w. Alice, relations (?) of Bp. Ruthall, of Durham, born at Cirencester, whose mother's name was Avening. XIII. Two fem. effs. (one loose), c. **1530**, husband (?) and inscr. lost, rel., S.A., p. 241. *Introd.,* p. 241 (det.) XIV. Phillip Marner [clothier], **1587**, standing; he left a noble yearly for a sermon in Lent, and gave the interest (?) on £80 to 16 men in Cirencester, Burford, Abingdon, and Tetbury; mur., S.A., pp. 129, 215, 216. XV. Mr. John Gunter, 1624, æt. 89, buried at Kintbury, Berks., and w. Alice, **1626**, æt. 86; Jo. Plat, their son-in-law and executor, pos., St. Cath. C., p. 54. FRAGS., &c. XVI. An Angel and lily-pot, c. **1460**, man, w., and chil. lost, N.A., p. 105. XVII. Lower part of fem. eff., c. **1480**, part of the brass of a man and w., with 1 son and 4 or 5 daus., now lost, and No. XIII. inlaid on the slab, p. 53. XVIII. Hugh Norys, grocer, **1529**, and w. Joan, 8 Eng. vv., effs. lost, S.A. XIX. Hodgkinson Paine, clothier, Feb. 3rd, **1642**, 8 Eng. vv., with pun on name, S.A. He was slain at the taking of Cirencester by the royalists. Nos. II., III., IV., V., VII., XI. and XVII. have lately been placed at the east end of Trinity Chapel.

CLIFFORD CHAMBERS. I. Hercules Raynsford, Esq., lord of the manor, **1583**, æt. 39, in arm., and w. Elizth., dau. of Robt. Parry, Esq., with 2 sons and 1 dau., A.T., C. II. Elizth., dau. of No. I., and w. of Edw. Marrowe, Esq., of Barkswell, Warwickshire, **1601**, loose (?), p. 220.

DEERHURST. I. Sir John Cassy, chief baron of the exchequer, **1400**, and w. Alice, canopy, with SS. Anne and John Baptist (the latter lately stolen), marg. inscr., N.A., pp. 90, 105, 126, 168, 178, 206, 260. *Lysons' Glouc. Antiq.,* pl. 17; *Waller,* pt. xv. *Introd.,* p. 168 (det.) II. Elizth., dau. of Thos. Bruges, Esq., of Coverle, and w. of Wm. Cassey, Esq., of Whyghtfylde, and then of Walter Rowdon, Esq., **1525**, inscr. lost, N.A., p. 244. INSCR. III. Edw. Guye, Gent., **1612**; by his w. Frauncis, eldest dau. of John Gotheridge, Esq., he had 6 sons and 1 dau.

DOWDESWELL. A Priest, c. **1520**, in cope, with 2 Evang. symbs., inscr. lost, rel., p. 77.

DYRHAM. Sir Morys Russel [**1401**] and w. Isabel, with canopy (the pediments only left), 6 Lat. vv., large, S.A., pp. 94, 185. *Boutell's Series.*

EASTINGTON. I. Elizth., [dau. of Sir Wm.] Knevet [**1518**], in heraldic mantle, marg. inscr. mutil., C., p. 113. *Introd.,* p. 113. INSCR. II. Edw. Stephens, Gent., **1587**, æt. c. 64, and w. Joan, 1587, æt. c. 63; they left 3 sons and 2 daus., mur., S.A.

FAIRFORD. I. John Tame, Esq., **1500**, and w. Alice [Twynihow], 1471, marg. inscr., A.T., C., p. 199. *Bigland,* vol. i. p. 567; *Gent.*

Mag., vol. lvii. 1787, pt. ii. p. 345; *C. C. Soc. Illustr.*, No. IV. p. 115. John Tame, in 1493 founded the Ch., on purpose, it is said, to receive the painted glass captured by him in a vessel bound from the Low Countries to Rome. II. Sir Edmond Tame, **1534**, and 2 ws., Agnes [dau. of Sir Rich. Greville], with 2 sons and 3 daus., and Elizth. [Tyringham], in heraldic dresses, N.C., pp. 56, 97. *Bigland*, vol. i. p. 571. III. The same individuals as No. II., in heraldic dresses, but with 1 son only, mur., N.C., p. 56.

GLOUCESTER, ST. MARY DE CRYPT. John Cook, alderman, 4 times mayor [1501—1519], and founder of school, 1529, and w. dame Joan, **1544**, triple canopy with St. John Baptist, all lost but 2 pediments (a third lately stolen), inscr. lost, now fastened to a board in N.Tr., slab buried in C., pp. 89, 91, 105, 256, 260.

GLOUCESTER, ST. MICHAEL'S. Wm. Henshawe, bell-founder, [5 times] mayor [1503—1520], and ws. Alys, **1519**, and Agnes; male eff. and about 3 sons and 3 daus. lost, N., p. 130.

KEMPSFORD. Walter Hichman, **1521**, and w. Cristyan, with 4 sons, Thos., John (both lost), Robt., John, marg. inscr., C.

LECHLADE. I. A Wool-mcht. and w., **1450**, about 6 chil. and inscrs. lost. *Bigland*, vol. ii. p. 141. Perhaps the brass of John Towensend, wolman, 1458. See Harleian MS., No. 6,072, fol. 114. II. John Twinyhow (?), mcht., founder of a chantry, c. 1476, dec. c. **1510**; w., about 4 chil., inscr., &c., lost. *Ibid.*

LECKHAMPTON. Wm. Norwoodd, Esq., and w. Elizth. [dau. of Wm. Lygon, of Madresfield, Worc.], **1598**, æt. 50, with 9 sons and 2 daus., 6 eleg. vv., qd. ql., mur., S.A.

MICHELDEAN. Thos. Baynham, Esq., 1444, and 2 ws., Margery, dau. of Sir Rich. Hodye, and Alice, dau. of Wm. Walwyn, all lost but effs. of ws., which are loose, engr. c. **1485**.

MINCHINHAMPTON. I. A Civilian and w., c. **1500**, inscr. and other w. (?) lost. II. Edw. Halyday, **1519**, and w. Margery, with mcht.'s mk. III. John Hampton, Gent., 1556, and w. Elyn, in shrouds, with 6 sons and 3 daus. (the eldest, dame Alice), engr. c. **1510**, pp. 45, 87, 89. *Introd.*, p. 87 (dau.) IV. †Upper half of fem. eff., c. **1530**, loose. The brasses are now in the belfry; Nos. I. and II. are rel., perhaps incorrectly.

MINETY; see Wiltshire.

NEWENT. Roger Porter, Esq., **1523**, sm., S.C.

NEWLAND. A Man in arm., legs gone, and w., c. **1445**, with curious crest, a miner with candle in mouth, bag for ore at back, and pickaxe in hand, marg. inscr. nearly all lost, S.C., pp. 192, 209. *Antiq. Repert.*, 1808, vol. ii. p. 387. *Nicholls's Forest of Dean* (crest).

NORTHLEACH. I. A Wool-mcht. and w., c. 1400, large, once in N.A., rel. in N., p. 164. *Boutell's Series.* II. Thos. Fortey, wolman, repaired churches and roads, 1447 (head lost), Wm. Scors, tailor, 1420, and their w. Agnes (head lost), with 2 groups of chil., 2 daus. (3 (?) other chil. gone) and 2 sons and 4 daus., canopy and marg. inscr. mutil., N.A., pp. 129, 178, 179, 209. *Lysons' Glouc. Antiq.*, pl. 42. III. [John Fortey], wolman (made the roof of Ch.), 1458, under canopy, marg. inscr. mutil., with 6 mcht.'s mks. (one in private possession), large, N., pp. 92, 94, 129, 170. *Ibid.*, p. 41. IV. A Woolman and w., c. 1485, with 2 sons and 2 daus., mcht.'s mk. and marg. inscr., N.A., pp. 129, 180. V. [John Taylour], wolman, and w. Joan, c. 1490, with 8 sons and 7 daus., Evang. symbs., marg. inscr. mutil., Hy. Trin. lost, S.C. VI. Robt. Serche, 1501, and w. Anne, with 3 sons and 1 dau., N., p. 251. VII. Thos. Bushe, woolman and mcht. of the staple of Calais, 1525, and w. Joan, 1526, with canopy and marg. inscr., 3 or 4 sons and 2 or 3 daus. lost, N., pp. 118, 129. VIII. Wm. Lawnder, priest, c. 1530, in surplice (?), kng., marg. inscr. mutil., Hy. Trin. and B. V. M. lost, C., pp. 78, 100, 102, 224. INSCR., &c. IX. Wm. Bicknell, 1500, and w. Margt., 1493, founders of C. in 1489, all lost but 2 sons and 2 daus., S.C. X. Mawd Parker, [dau. of (?) ——] Thomas, 1584, had 10 chil., left 6 at her dec., in childbed; an acrostic, 20 Eng. vv., mur., S.C., p. 225.

OLVESTON. Morys Denys, Esq., son and h. of Sir Gylbert Denys, lord of the manors of Alveston and Irdecote, and his son Sir Walter Denys, 1505, in tabards, holding a scroll, mur.

QUINTON. Joan Clopton, widow of Sir [Wm. ?] Clopton, vowess, c. 1430, with canopy, and 8 eleg. vv. on marg. inscr., A.T., p. 251.

RODMARTON. John Edward, lord and patron of the manor, lawyer, 1461, C., p. 90. *Grose's Antiquities of England and Wales*, vol. i. pl. viii. fig. 2; *Gough*, vol. ii. pl. lxxv. p. 305; *Lysons' Glouc. Antiq.*, pl. 11.

SEVENHAMPTON. A Civilian, c. 1490, lately lost (?), feet and inscr. perhaps covd. by a step, C.

THORNBURY. Thos. Tyndall, 1571 (eff. lost), and w. [Avice, dau. of John Bodie], 12 Eng. vv., once on A.T., C.

TORMARTON. John Ceysyll, "famulus" of Lord John Sendlow, 1493, marg. inscr., N., p. 178. Sir John de la Riviere, c. 1350, lost, C., p. 123. *Introd.*, p. 124 (matrix).

*WESTON-UPON-AVON. I. Sir John Greville, lord of the manor of Milcot, 1546, C. II. Sir Edw. Greville, lord of the manor of Milcot, 1559, in arm., C.

WESTON-SUB-EDGE. Wm. Hodges, **1590**; he m. the dau. of Sir Geo. Throgmorton, of Kawghton [Coughton], and widow of John Gifford, Esq., of Weston-under-Edge.

WHITTINGTON. Rich. Coton, Esq., 1556, and w. Margt., **1560**, between them a child in swaddling clothes, a son (in cloak above) lost.

WINTERBOURNE. A Lady, c. **1370**, canopy and marg. inscr. lost, p. 168. *Boutell's Series.* Perhaps Agnes, w. of Sir Thos. de Bradeston, 1369-70; or Blanch, widow of Robt. Bradeston, 1391-2.

WORMINGTON. *Anne, eldest dau. of Rich. Daston, and w. of John Savage, Esq., of Nobury, Worc., **1605**, æt. 25, in childbed with infant, marg. inscr., p. 221.

WOTTON-UNDER-EDGE. Thos., 4th lord Berkeley, 1417, and w. Margt., dau. and h. of Gerard Warren, lord Lisle, **1392**, large, inscr. lost, A.T., N.A., pp. 2, 116, 160, 168. *Fosbrooke's Gloucestershire*, vol. i. p. 477; *Hollis's Monumental Effigies*, pt. iv. pl. 10; *Boutell's Mon. Br.*, p. 57. *Introd.*, p. 168 (det.) Rich. de Wotton, rector, c. 1320, kng. at a cross, with Lomb. inscrs. lost, matrix left, C., p. 141.

YATE. Alex. Staples, **1590**, and 2 ws., Avis, with 2 sons and 3 daus., and Elizabeth (who pos.) with 4 sons and 2 daus., 8 cleg. vv. "Rursus supremum tuba cum *tarantara* clanget, Spiritui iunget mortua membra Deus," qd. pl.

INSCRIPTIONS, &c.

COLD ASHTON. Thos. Key, rector, builder of Ch., c. **1500**, 6 cleg. vv., mur., C. CUBBERLEY. One Sh., all that remains of the brass of Sir Giles Bruges, c. **1511**, and w. Isabel, dau. of Thos. Baynham, with 3 sons and 4 (?) daus., mur., S.C. HEMPSTEAD. Nich., Hen., Roger, Nich. (jun.), Cecilly, Brigid, chil. of Arthur Porter, Esq., and w. Alys, **1548**, with sh., mur., Tower. QUEDGLEY. Fredeswid and Mary Porter, daus. of Arthur Porter, Esq., and w. Alys, **1532**, with sh., mur., C.

The brasses are lost at BISHOP'S CLEEVE, CHURCHDOWN, PAINSWICK, and ST. JOHN BAPTIST, GLOUCESTER. At CHURCHAM is the matrix of a large cross, 14th cent.

Hampshire.

ALTON. I. A Lady, c. **1510**, inscr. lost, N. INSCRS., &c. II. Three Daus., c. **1520**, N. III. Rich. Clarke, 1485, and dau. Margery, w. of Rich. Fylder, **1534**. IV. Christ. Wolaston, 1563 (date inserted), with rebus. V. Robt. Fry, "hedd Bailliffe," **1620**, "villicationis rationem reddidi," S.A.   VI. Elizth. Geale, **1638**, 2 Lat. and 2 Eng. vv., S.A. These brasses are now mur. at west end of Ch.

BARTON STACEY. *A Civilian and w., c. **1500**.

BASINGSTOKE. I. Robt. Stocker, **1606**, æt. 67, and w. Ursula, with 9 sons and 2 daus., now mur., N.   II. A Child, c. **1620**, sm., mur., C. To this belongs (?) an inscr. to John, son of Thos. Hilliard, Gent., 1621, mur., N.   INSCR. III. Roger Ryve, 6 Eng. vv., mur., N.

BRAMLEY. I. Gwen More, w. of John Shelford, Esq., "of the city of Harford," and mother to dame Elizth. Shelforde, abbess of Shaftsbury, **1504**.   II. Rich. Carter, **1529**, and w. Alys.

*BROWN CANDOVER. I. John Latihall, priest, c. **1520**, without stole, very sm.   II. —— Wylson, **1559**, and w. These brasses were lately loose and in the possession of Lord Ashburton (?).

CRONDALL. I. A Priest, c. **1370**, canopy and inscr. lost, large, C., pp. 67, 142. *Oxford Man.*, p. 26, and *Introd.*, p. 67.   II. John Gyfford, Esq., h. apparent of Sir Wm. Gyfford, **1563**, and w. Elizth., dau. of Sir Geo. Throkmarton, with 5 sons and 8 daus., w. and sons lost, mur., A.T., C.   III. John Eager, **1631**, a skeleton, with 4 Eng. vv., qd. pl., mur., S.A.

DEAN. *Nich. Ayliff, **1493**, and w.

DUMNER. *Wm. Atmore, alias Dumner, Esq., born 1508, comptroller of the chamber at London for above 50 years, and w. Henborough, dau. of Edm. Brydges, of London, c. **1580**, mur., C.

EVERSLEY. *A large Cross to Rich. Pendilton, servant to Giles [Lord] Dawbney, chamberlain to Hen. VII., **1502**, curious, C., pp. 96, 222.

FROYLE. John Lighe, Esq., **1575**, and w. [Margt., dau. of Thos. Saunders, of Uxbridge, and who m., 2dly, Sir Wm. Killigrew, of Cornwall], and child, eff. of w. lost at repairs in 1848, C.

HAVANT. Thos. Aileward, rector, **1413**, in cope, now mur., N.Tr., pp. 77, 183. *Introd.*, p. 182 (det.)

HEADBOURN WORTHY. John, son of Simon Kent, of Reading, and a scholar of Winchester, c. **1430**, sm., p. 86.

HECKFIELD. John Hall, **1514** (lost), and w. Elizth., builders of Chantry.

ITCHEN STOKE. Joan, w. of Mr. John Batmanson, doctor of Seville, **1518**; in possession of Lord Ashburton (?).

KIMPTON. Robt. Thornburgh, Esq., **1522**, and ws., Alys (with a son and dau.) and Anne (with a son and 6 daus.), mur., A.T., C., p. 102.

KINGSCLERE. I. Wm. Estwod, vicar, and parson of Newnom [Newnham], sm., **1519**. II. Ellen (?) Gobard, **1520** (?), sm., worn. INSCRS. III. *John Bossewell, Gent., and "notarye publique," **1580**. IV. Thirty-one hexameter lines to Sir —— Kingsmill and w. Constance (Goring), and chil., Wm., Rich., Roger, Edw., Hen., John, Geo. (twins), Andrew, Thos., Arthur, Constance, Jane (m. —— Cooper (?), Gent.), Anna, Kath. (m. Rich. Trenchard), Margt., Mary. V. *Elizth., w. of Jas. Hunt, Gent., of Popham, **1606**. The brasses are now in S.C.

MONKTON. *Alice Swayn, **1599**, æt. 98, and dau. Cath.

OAKLEY, CHURCH. Robt. Warham and w. Elizth., both dec. **1487**, with 4 sons (1st a priest, [afterwards Abp. Warham]), 2 or 3 daus. lost, p. 172.

ODIHAM. I. A Civilian (with gypcière and small dagger) and w., c. **1480**, C. II. A Lady, c. **1510**, and 9 daus., N.C. III. A Lady, c. **1520**, with a son and 5 daus. (?), N.C. IV. A Civilian, c. **1530**, N. V. A Man in arm., c. **1540**; his feet, 2 ws., and their chil. lost, A.T., N.C. The inscrs. of all the above brasses are lost. VI. Margt., 2nd dau. of Thos. Pye, Esq., **1636**, æt. 6 weeks, in swaddling clothes, C., p. 219. INSCR. VII. John Haydock, Esq., **1504**, and w. Elizth.; effs. and a cross between them lost, N.C.

PRESTON CANDOVER. *Kath. Dabridgecort, **1607**, C.

RINGWOOD. John Prophete (?), prebendary of Lincoln, dean of Hereford and York, **1416**, in cope, with SS. Michael, John Bapt., Peter, Paul—Wenefrida, Kath., Barbara (or Faith?), Margt., canopy nearly all lost, inscr. gone, large. *Gent. Mag.*, vol. lxxvii. 1807, pt. i. p. 1001.

SHERBORNE ST. JOHN'S. I. Raulin Brocas and his sister Margt., c. **1360**, hf. effs. with Fr. inscr., sm., pp. 139, 164, 166, 169, 213. *Introd.*, p. 134. II. Bernard Brocas, Esq., **1488** (?), in tabard, kng. to a cross which is now lost, below is a skeleton, marg. inscr. in 8 (?) Lat. vv., mutil., pp. 56, 93. III. John Brocas (?), in arm., c. **1490**, and 2 ws., 1st, Anne, dau. of Edw. Longford, with 2 sons and 3 daus.; and 2nd, Anne, dau. of John Rogers, with 5 sons and 1 dau., inscr. lost. IV. John Brocas, Esq. (son and h. of Wm. Brocas, Esq., who died at London 1483, and was buried at St. Bartholomew's, Smithfield), **1492**, in arm., kng., with Hy. Trin., sm. V. Wm. Brocas, Esq., of Beaurepair, 1505-6, sm., kng., he left 2 daus. and hs., Anne (dec. s.p.), Edith, m. Rauff Pexsall, Esq., and had 2 sons, John (dec.) and Rich.; Rauff pos., c. **1540**; p. 235. *Introd.*, p. 235 (det.) The brasses are now mur., in N.C.

L

SOMBOURNE, KING'S. Two Civilians, c. **1380**, inscr. lost, p. 163. *Introd.*, p. 164 (1 cff.)

SOUTHAMPTON, GOD'S HOUSE. †A Priest, c. **1500**, in cope, headless.

SOUTHWICK. *John White, Esq., "fyrst owner of the priory & manor of Suthwicke after ye surrender and departing of the Chanons from the same," 1567, and w. Kath. (only dau. of Wm. Pound, Esq., of Drayton, by his w. Mary, dau. and h. of Thos. Haynes, Esq., of the Isle of Wight), 1548, with 5 sons and 4 daus., engr. c. **1520**, marg. inscr., and with shs. subsequently added (?).

STOKE CHARITY. I. Thos. Wayte, Esq., **1482**, p. 104. II. Thos. Hampton, Esq., **1483**, and w. Isabella, 1475, with 2 sons and 6 daus., Hy. Trin.

SUTTON, BISHOP'S. A Man, in arm., and w., c. **1520**, inscr. lost.

THRUXTON. Lord John Lysle, lord of the manor of Wodynton in the Isle of Wight, and husband of Lady Elizth. Lysle, 1407, under fine triple canopy, marg. inscr., engr. c. **1425**, large, C., p. 189. *Gough*, vol. ii. pl. vii. p. 23; *Boutell's Series.*

WALLOP, FARLEY. *A Man and his w., c. **1500**. Perhaps John Wallop and w. Joan, dau. of Rich. Holte of Colrythe.

WALLOP, NETHER. Dame Maria Gore, prioress, **1436**, p. 87.

*WARNBOROUGH, SOUTH. I. Robt. Whyte, Esq., eldest son of John Whyte, **1512-3**, with a large band pointing to a scroll, mur., C. II. A Lady, now mur., with painted inscr. to Elizth., dau. of Sir Thos. White, and w. to Lord Chidioke Paulett.

WEEK. A figure of St. Christopher with inscr. to Wm. Complyn, **1498** (date filled in?), and w. Annes; he gave to the "frest dedycacion of ye Chvrch xl^s & to make nawe bellis to ye sam Chvrch x^l also gave to ye halloyeng of ye grettest bell⁻. vj^s. viiij*d*. & for ye testimonyall⁻ of the dedicacion of ye sam Church. vj^s. viij*d*.," mur., N., p. 106. *Proceedings of Arch. Inst. at Winchester*, 1845; *Arch. Journ.*, vol. iii. p. 84; *Boutell's Mon. Br.*, p. 140; *Oxford Man.*, p. 48; *Introd.*, p. 105.

WHITCHURCH. *Rich. Broke, **1603**, and w. Elizth.

WINCHESTER COLLEGE CHAPEL AND CLOISTERS. I. John Morys (?), first warden, **1413**, in almuce, inscr. lost, p. 79. II. John Wyllynghale, fellow, **1432**, in cope, hf. eff., worn, p. 81. III. Nich. North, fellow, **1445**, in cope, hf. eff., p. 81. *Lith. by E. Baijent.* IV. Robt. Thurbern, warden, **1450**, in fine cope, partly covd., inscr. in 8 Lat. vv. lost, large, pp. 76, 183. *Introd.*, p. 76 (part of eff.) V. Edw. Tacham, fellow, **1473**, in cope, hf. eff., p. 81. VI. John Taknell, fellow, **1494**, ¾ eff. VII. John Bedell, mayor of the city [in 1496], and formerly scholar of the college, **1498**, worn. *Lith. by F. J. Baijent.* VIII. Thos. Lyrypyn, priest, fellow, **1509**, ¾ eff. IX. John Gylbert, priest, fellow, **1514**, ¾ eff. X. John Erewaker, fellow, **1514**, ¾ eff. XI. John Barratte, B.A., fellow, **1524**, in acad., kng., sm., p. 85. XII. John White, warden, ob. 1560, in rich cope, inscr. in 20 eleg. vv., marg. inscr. lost, partly covd., large, engr. c. **1548**, pp. 75, 76, 95. John White was afterwards Bp. of Lincoln, translated to Winchester, deprived 1559, and was buried in the Cathedral. INSCRS. XIII. Wm. Clyff, 1st chaplain, "istius Capelle" [i.e. in the cloisters], **1433**. XIV. Wm. Ball, fellow, **1472**. XV. John Fylde, **1507**. XVI. John Curteys, fellow, **1509**. XVII. Rich. Skynner, fellow, **1514**. XVIII. John Hopkyns, conduct, **1514**. XIX. Wm. Erule (?), "in decretis bacallarij," fellow of New Coll., Oxford, and chaplain to the Bp. of Winchester, **1521**, eff. lost. XX. John Dere, M.A., fellow, **1527**. XXI. †—— Dolber, fellow, **1560**. XXII. Wm. Adkins, M.A., fellow, **1561**. XXIII. †Thos. Bass, fellow, and "vice custos," C. Jhonson pos., **1562**. XXIV. Edm. Hodson, clerk, fellow, **1580**. XXV. Thos. Jones, B.C.L., fellow, **1585**. XXVI. Thos. Davison, **1586**. XXVII. Thos. Geffres, B.A., **1605**. XXVIII. John Harris, **1658**. The brasses with effigies (except Nos. V., VI., IX., and X., which are now mur. in the cloisters) are on the floor of the ante-chapel. The inscriptions (except Nos. XXIII. and XXV.) are in the cloisters, and are all mur.; those from Nos. XXI. to XXVII. have each a few verses appended to them.

WINCHESTER, ST. CROSS. I. John de Campeden, warden of the hospital, [canon of Southwell, 1382], in cope, marg. inscr. with text from Job xix. 25—27, and Evang. symbs., very large, C., pp. 102, 144. *Carter's Anc. Sculpt. and Painting*, vol. ii. p. 46; *Boutell's Series; Old England*, No. 1,087. II. Rich. Harward (?), "decretorum doctor," warden, **1493**, in almuce, inscr. lost, rel., N. p. 79. III. Thos. Lawne, rector of Mottisfount, **1518**, Tower. INSCRS. IV. John Newles, a brother of the hospital, esquire, and servant for 30 years to Cardinal Beauford, **1452**, 8 Eng. lines, N. V. Wm. Saundres, chaplain, **1484**, S.Tr. VI. John, son of John Wayte and his w. Agatha, **1502**, S.A. of C., p. 57. VII. Elizth. Wroughton, "gentelwoman," **1551**, C. VIII. Alex. Ewart, a brother, **1569**, S.Tr.

YATELEY. I. Wm. Lawerd, **1517**, and w. Agnes, with 9 sons and 1 dau., N. II. Wm. Rygg, **1532**, and w. Tomysyn, with 4 sons and 7 daus., S.A. III. Elizth., dau. of Robt. Morflett,

1578; by her 1st husband, Edw. Ormeby, she had 4 sons and ... daus., by her 2nd, Andr. Smythe, she had 3 sons and 3 daus.; lower part of eff. gone, C. IV. A Civilian, c. **1590**, inscr. lost, N. INSCR. V. Joan, w. of John Hewlot, and dau. of Robt. Dyngele, C.

INSCRIPTIONS, &c.

ALDERSHOT. *Sir John Whyte, alderman, citizen, and grocer of London [pos. c. **1573**], with sh., mur., C. BENSTEAD. I. Susan, dau. of Rt. Hon. Wm. Lord Maynard. and w. of Nich. Bowell, Esq., **1644**, C. II. Rich. Cheyney, **1701**, æt. 66; left £100 to the poor. STRATFIELD-SAYE. Geo. Dabigecort, Esq., lord of the manor, **1558**; his son Thos. wrote the inscr., and pos., 8 Lat. vv.

The brass of a Man in arm., c. **1465** (Sir Reginald de Clerk?), formerly at HORDLE, and engr. by *Gough*, vol. ii. p. 386, is now lost. Also that at BISHOPSTOKE, to Wm. Button, Esq., **1590**, who m. Mary, dau. of Sir Wm. Kellwey, and had 8 chil., Ambrose, John, Frances, Edw., Hen., Dorothy, Cecile, p. 218. At WARBLINGTON is an incised slab to Raffe Smalpage, chaplain to Rt. Hon. Earl of Southampton, **1558**, mur., C., p. 30.

Isle of Wight.

ARRETON. Harry Hawles, "Longe tyme steward of the yle of Wyght," c. **1430**, head lost, 4 Eng. vv., S.C., p. 189. *Holloway's Walks round Ryde*, 1848, p. 152.

CALBOURNE. I. A Man in arm., c. **1380**, canopy lately lost, inscr. gone, A.T., p. 160. *A Tour to the I. of Wight, by C. Tomkins*, 1796, vol. ii. p. 55. II. *Dan. Evance, rector, **1652**, mur.

KINGSTON. Mr. Rich. Mewys, **1535**, with 4 sons, and a sh. nailed to a wooden frame.

SHORWELL. I. Sir Rich. Bethell, vicar, **1518**, in acad (?), C., p. 78. *Tomkins*, vol. ii. p. 77. *Introd.*, p. 78 (det.) II. Mrs. Elizth. Bampfield, 1615 (mother of 15 chil.), and Mrs. Gartrvde Percevall, **1619**, both ws. of Barnabas Leigh, Esq., who pos., qd. pl., mur.

At FRESHWATER are matrices of effs. in arm. and ladies under canopies.

Herefordshire.

BRAMPTON ABBOTTS. John Rudhale, Esq., **1506** (eff. lost), and w. Joan, sm., now mur., C.

BURGHILL. John Awbry, youngest son of Wm. Awbry, LL.D.,

and a master of Requests in ordinary to Queen Elizth., **1616**, æt. c. 78, and w. Rachell, a dau. of Rd. Danvers, Esq., of Totnum, Wilts., qd. pl., mur.

CLEHONGER. *—— Aubrey, Esq., and w., c. **1470**, left loose in a cupboard at the school-room after restoration of Ch.

COLWALL. *Anth. Harford, Esq., in arm., and w. Elizth., c. **1590**, and chil., qd. pl., mur.

HEREFORD CATHEDRAL. I. John Trilleck, bp., **1360**, with canopy, mutil., marg. inscr. lost, large, C., pp. 70, 78, 138, 142. *Gough*, vol. i. pl. xl. p. 111. *Oxford Man.*, and *Introd.*, frontispiece. II. A Priest, c. **1390**, in cope, in the head of a cross, the stem, finials, and inscr. lost. Perhaps for John Harold, dean, 1393, or Rich. de la Barr, canon, 1386; pp. 136, 144. *Boutell's Series*. III. A Priest in cope, c. **1430**, head lost, loose. Perhaps for Thos. Downe, canon residentiary, 1429; or for No. IX. IV. A Priest in cope, **1434** (?), inscr. in 6 Lat. vv. nearly all effaced. Perhaps for John Stanwey, dean. V. Rich. Delamare, Esq., **1435**, and w. Isabella, 1421, under fine canopy, with embattled entablature, large, Lady-chapel, pp. 176, 209. VI. A Priest in cope, c. **1480**, head and feet lost, loose. Perhaps for Thos. Chawndiler, S.T.P., chancellor of Oxford and dean of Hereford, 1490. VII. Sir Rich. De[labere], **1514**, and 2 ws., Anne, dau. of Lord Awdeley (with 1 son and 4 daus.), and Elizth., dau of Wm. Mores, late sergeant of the hall to Hen. VII. (with 10 sons and 6 daus.), marg. inscr., Eastern S.Tr., p. 233. VIII. Edm. Frowsetoure, S.T.P., dean, and prebendary of Barton Collwalle, **1529**, in cope and cap, triple canopy, with Hy. Trin., SS. Ethelbert, John Evang., Cath.—Hy. Trin (?), a Bp. (Thos. ?), Peter, Mary (?), 12 eleg. vv. and marg. inscr., worn, large, S.A. of C., pp. 77, 101, 102. INSCRS., &c. IX. Edm. Ryall, canon, **1428**, eff. lost, loose, N.Tr. X. A Bracket, loose. XI. Twelve Lat. vv. to Thos. Stanbury, bp., **1474**. XII. †Part of marg. inscr. to [Wm. Webb, archdeacon], **1522**. XIII. †Fragments of the canopy of Hen. Martyn (?), archdeacon of Salop, **1523**, S.A. of C. All the brasses not described as loose were temporarily placed in the S.A. of N. in 1859, except No. IV., which was then among a pile of gravestones and incised slabs (see p. 40) in the stone-yard; the loose brasses (except No. XII.) were in the hands of the clerk of the works. There was lately a brass of a Civilian, c. **1390**, in a cross mutil., now lost (?), pp. 136, 164. *Introd.*, p. 164. Also (?) a Man in arm., c. **1465**. See also brasses in private possession—J. B. Nichols, Esq. On a fine A.T. in N.Tr. is the matrix of the brass of Thos. Cantelupe, bp., **1282**, hf. eff., p. 134. In the crypt is an incised slab to Andrew Jones, mcht. (who repaired the charnel-house), c. 1497, and w. Elizth., p. 40. *Anonymous.* See also pp. 255, 258, 260.

LEDBURY. I. Sir Wm. Calwe, priest, c. **1410**, in acad., kng., eff. of St. Peter lost, sm., C., p. 77. *Gent. Mag.*, vol. lxiv. 1794, pt. ii. p. 1163. II. Thos. Caple, Esq., **1490**, now mur., C., p. 198. III. John Hayward, Esq., of Wellington, alias Prior's Court, co. Hereford, **1614**, in arm., qd. pl., now mur. INSCR. IV. Rich. Hayward, **1618**, 4 Eng. vv. An incised slab, pp. 40, 230.

LUDFORD. Wm. Fox, Esq. (founded the Aisle, and re-edified the Almshouse of St. Gyles), **1554**, in arm., and w. Jane.

*MARDEN. I. Dame Margt., w. of Sir Geo. Chute, dau. and sole h. of Thos. Welford, Esq., of Wisteston, dec. in childbed, **1614**, with 2 daus., Anne and Fraunces (dec.), C. INSCR. II. Hen. Wall, **1579**, 4 Eng. vv.

The brasses at BROMYARD are lost. At WEST HIDE is the matrix of a knight and lady.

Hertfordshire.

ALBURY. I. Thos. Leventhorp, Esq., twice high-sheriff, **1588**, and w. Dorothy, dau. and coh. of Wm. Barleo, Esq., of Aldbury, 1574, with 1 son and 5 daus., 6 Lat. vv. II. †John Scrogs, Gent., son of Frances Scroggs, Esq., **1592**, in arm., and w.; he left a son Edw., qd. pl.

ALDBURY. I. Sir Ralph Verney, **1546-7**, and w. Elizth., dau. of Edm. Lord Bray, in heraldic dresses, with 9 sons and 3 daus., marg. inscr. lost, once on A.T., C., p. 245. *Clutterbuck's Hist. and Antiq. of the Co. of Herts.*, vol. i. p. 287. *Lipscomb's Bucks.*, vol. i. p. 181. II. John, son of Hen. Davers, mercer of London, **1478**, very sm., C. INSCR. III. Inscr. erected by Edm., 3rd son of No. I., stating the removal, in 18 Elizth., of the bodies and tombs of Sir Robt. Whittingham, his dau. Margt., her husband Sir John Verney, and their son Sir Ralph Verney, from the monastery of "Ansheritche" to the S.Ch., built by Edm. Verney, in which his w., Dame Audrey Carewe, **1538**, is also buried, mur., p. 252.

ALDENHAM. I. A Civilian and w., c. **1520**, p. 239. II. A Civilian, c. **1520**, head gone. III. A Civilian and w., c. **1520**, with 2 sons and 6 daus. IV. A Civilian, c. **1520**, with 6 sons and 5 daus., w. gone. V. A Civilian and 2 ws., c. **1525**, with 1 son and 2 daus. VI. A Civilian (lost) and 3 ws., c. **1525**, with 4 sons and 1 dau., 4 sons and 8 daus., 1 son and 1 dau. (lost), sm. VII.

Jone Warner, c. **1535** [1538 ?], and dau., her husb. Wm., 1531 (?), lost, sm., inscr. mutil. VIII. A Lady, c. **1535**, sm., p. 243. IX. Lucas Goodyere [**1547**], in shroud, died in childbed with her son Edm., sm. X. Edw. Brisko, Gent., of Orgarhall, **1608**, and 1st w. Helen, by whom he had a son and h. Edw., who pos.; his 3 immediate ancestors were named Edw., and descended from the Briskoes, of Brisko and Crofton, Cumb., Esqs. INSCR. XI. Nich. Chowne, Gent., of the Haberdashers' Co., and w. Elizth., with 4 chil., c. **1580** (?), with 4 shs. The inscrs. of Nos. I.—VI., and VIII., are lost. Nos. I., II., IV., V., VI., X., have recently been floored over. The brass of John Long, 1538, and w. Margt., is lost. A rubbing is (?) in the possession of J. B. Nichols, Esq.

ARDELEY. I. Philip Metcalff, LL.B., vicar, **1515**, C. II. Thos. Shotbolt, Esq., **1599**, æt. 72, and w. Mary, 2nd dau. of Sir John Boteler, of Watton Woodhall, with 4 sons and 2 daus., C. Both brasses partly covd.

ASPEDEN. I. [Thos. Goodrich, **1500**], and w. Alice, inscr. mutil. II. Sir Robt. Clyfford, knight of the body to Hen. VII., and master of his ordinance, 3rd son of Thos. late Lord Clyfford, **1508**, and w. Elizth., late w. of Sir Rauffe Josselyn; in heraldic dresses, with 2 daus., mur., A.T., S.C.

ASTON. John Kent, servant to King Ed. VI., Queens Mary and Elizth., **1592**, æt. 72, and w. Mary, dau. of Thos. Saunders; they had 5 sons and 5 daus., N., p. 127.

AYOT, ST. LAURENCE. *Nich. Bristow, Esq., served Hen. VIII. and Queen Elizth., and w. Emme, with 8 sons and 4 daus., mur., Tower.

BALDOCK. I. A Lady, c. **1410**, lower part of eff., husband in mantle, and inscr. lost, p. 210. A rubbing of male eff. is in the possession of J. B. Nichols, Esq. II. A Civilian, mutil., c. **1420**, w. and inscr. lost, sm. Perhaps Wm. Vynter, 1416, and w. Margt., 1411, pp. 129, 130, 202. *Introd.*, p. 130. III. A Civilian and w., c. **1480**, inscr. lost. Perhaps Wm. Crane, 1483, and w. Margt. or Joane, p. 211. *Introd.*, p. 210 (det.) INSCR. IV. Rev. Edm. Pym, A.B., rector of Radwell, **1807**, placed below No. I. Inscr. lost, p. 181.

BARLEY. I. Andrew Willet, D.D., minister of Barley, and "magnum totivs veræ ecclesiæ ornamentvm," **1621**, æt. 59, 6 Lat. and 6 Eng. vv. Willet was the author of "Synopsis Papismi." INSCR. II. †Robt. Bryckett, Gent., **1566**.

†BAYFORD. I. A Man, in arm., and w. (lower part gone), c. **1550**. II. A Man in arm., 17th cent.

BENNINGTON. I. A Lady, c. **1570**, lower part, husb., and inscr. gone. II. †Some chil.

BERKHAMPSTEAD. I. [Rich. Torryngton, **1356**], and w. Margt. [**1349**], with canopy and marg. inscr. nearly all lost, large, N.Tr., pp. 61, 164, 169. *Clutterbuck*, vol. i. p. 305. *Boutell's Mon. Br.*, p. 107 (effs.) II. A Man in arm., c. **1365**, inscr. gone. Perhaps John Raven, Esq., 1395, S.A., p. 162. *Boutell's Series*. III. A Lady, c. **1370**, canopy and inscr. lost, N.Tr. Perhaps Margt. Briggs, 1374. *Boutell's Series*. IV. A Priest, c. **1400**, hf. eff. V. [Edm.] Cook, **1409**, with anelace, sm., S.C. VI. Rich. Westbroke, **1485**, N.Tr. VII. Kath., w. of Robt. Incent (the parents of John Incent, LL.D., a benefactor to the Chapel of St. John), **1520**, in shroud, sm., S.C. INSCRS. VIII. Six eleg. vv., 16th cent.; on reverse, part of brass to Thos. Humfre, of London, goldsmith, and w. Joan, dau. of Wm. Bayntun, brewer, c. **1500** (?), in shrouds (?), with 5 sons and 2 daus., and between them St. Michael weighing souls, qd. pl., little more left than part of inscr. with eff. of St. Jerome in initial letter, A.T., S.C., pp. 30, 46. IX. Robt. Incent, Gent., 1485, servant to Cecyle Duchess of York, engr. c. **1520**, p. 223.

BRAUGHING. I. *A Civilian and w., c. **1480**, inscr. lost. II. *A Civilian, c. **1490**, w. (?) and inscr. lost. III. Barbara, w. of Thos. Hanchett, Esq., dec. at Aldebury **1561**. INSCRS. IV. †Rich. Grene, Gent., **1561**. V. †Rich. Grene, Gent., **1610**.

BROXBOURN. I. A Priest, c. **1470**, with chalice, inscr. gone. Perhaps Robt. Ecton, vicar, 1474. *Boutell's Mon. Br.*, p. 99. II. [Sir John Say, 1478], head gone, and w. Elizth. [dau. of Laurence Cheyne], Esq., of Cambridgeshire, **1473**, in heraldic dresses, marg. inscr. mutil., A.T., C., pp. 112, 116, 197. *Waller*, pt. v. III. A Priest, c. **1510**, in acad., inscr. lost, C., p. 84. INSCRS. IV. Three Scrolls, 2 belonging to a priest in cope, hf. eff. lost; the 3rd to Peter Meedwyn, priest, **1465**, in acad., kng., sm., lost, N.C. A rubbing is in the possession of J. B. Nichols, Esq. V. Three Scrolls, parts of the brass of John Borrell, serjeant-at-arms to Hen. VIII., **1531**, and w. Elizth., with 8 sons and 3 daus., pecul., N.A., pp. 29, 115, 127, 234. *Antiq. Etch. Club*, vol. iii. pl. 56 (drawing reversed); and *Introd.*, p. 126 (male eff.) VI. Six Eng. vv., **1630**, with sh.

BUCKLAND. I. Alice, w. of John Boteler, **1451**, inscr. lost (?). II. Wm. Langley, rector, **1478**, in cope, with chalice and wafer, S.A., pp. 76, 79. III. John Gyll, **1499**, with 6 sons and 5 daus., inscr. now only (?) left, N., p. 260.

CHESHUNT. I. Nich. Dixon, rector for 30 years, benefactor to

Ch., rebuilder of C., "pipe subthesaurarius," baron of the exchequer, [canon of Lincoln], **1448**, eff. large (in cope?) lost, triple canopy, inscr. in 16 Lat. lines, C. *Boutell's Series* (canopy).   II. Wm. Pyke, **1449**, head gone, and w. Elena, worn, now loose, S.A.   III. Joan Clay (?), **1453**, Nor.-Fr. inscr. lost (see Appendix B), p. 178. IV. A Fem. eff., c. **1500**, loose.   V. *A Fem. eff., c. **1520**, loose. VI. Elizth. Garnett, w. of Edw. Collen, citizen and freemason of London, **1609**, æt. 33, kng., sm.   Inscrs. VII. Agnes, w. of John Luthyngton, Esq., **1468**.   VIII. Conscancia Vere, w. of John Parre, **1502**, C., belonging to No. IV. (?)

CLOTHALL.   I. John Vynter, rector, **1404**, C., p. 78.   II. John Wryght, "in decretis bacallarius," master of Trinity Hall, Camb., rector, **1519**, with chalice and wafer and Hy. Trin., C.   III. Thos. Dalyson, LL.B., parson of Ch., and master of St. Magd. Hospital, Clothall, **1541**, in cope, inscr. lost, C., p. 79.   IV. Anne, dau. of John Byll, Gent., of Asshewell, and w. of Wm. Bramfeld, of Clothall, **1572**; she had 6 sons and 10 daus., C.   V. Wm. Lucas, M.A., parson of Ch., **1602**, æt. 96, C.

DIGSWELL.   I. John Peryent, esquire for the body and [pennonbearer] to Rich. II., esquire of [Hen. IV. and] Hen. V., and master of the horse to Joan [Queen of England], at his feet a leopard, and w. Joan [dau. of Sir John Risain], **1415**, at her feet a hedgehog, large, marg. inscr. much mutil., C., pp. 33, 114, 188, 208, 209. *Gough*, vol. ii. pl. xxi. p. 43.   *Boutell's Mon. Br.*, p. 61; *Introd.*, p. 209 (dets.)   II. John Peryent, Esq., son of No. I., **1442**, in arm., inscr. lost, C., p. 189.   *Gough*, ibid.; *Boutell's Mon. Br.*, p. 69.   III. Wm. Robert, auditor of the bishopric of Winton, and w. Joyce, **1484**, in shrouds, with 2 sons, 2 daus. gone, sm. IV. *Thos. Hoore, citizen and mercer of London, **1495**, and w. Alice, with 4 sons and 8 daus.   V. A Civilian and w., c. **1530**, with 4 sons and 6 daus.   Inscrs. VI. Thos. Robynson, citizen and mercer of London, and w. Mary, **1492**, now under No. II., p. 50. VII. Robt. Battyll, **1557**, w. Margt. and son Wm., now under No. V., pp. 50, 226.

EASTWICK.   Robt. Lee, Esq., of Bagley, co. Chester, sewer to Ed. VI., Philip and Mary, and Queen Elizth., **1564** (eff. lost), and w. Joan, 8 Eng. vv. C.

ESSENDON.   I. Wm. Tooke, Esq., of Popes, Herts., "Auditor of the Courte of wardes and liveries," of which he was an officer 44 years, **1588**, æt. 80, and w. Alice, dau. of Robt. Barlee, Esq., late of Ribbesworth, Herts., m. 56 years, with 9 sons and 3 daus., mur., C. FRAG. II. Three shs. from the brass of Hen. Courtney, the elder and infant son of Hen. Marquis of Exeter, by his 2nd w. Gertrude, (dau. of Wm. Blount Lord Montjoy, by his 1st w. Elizth., dau. and coh. of Sir Wm. Say, which Elizth. was also buried here.)

FLAMSTEAD. I. John Oudeby, rector of Flamstead and Barughby [Barrowby], Lincolnshire, canon of St. Mary's Coll., Ware, and "camerarius ex p'te comitis Wau [i. e. Earl of Warwick] in Secio," **1414**, in cope, canopy lost, C., p. 115. II. A Civilian and w., c. **1470**, with 2 sons and 2 daus., scrolls and inscr. lost, pecul. These brasses were loose in the churchwarden's house, p. 250.

GADDESDEN, GREAT. I. Wm. Croke, **1506**, and w. Alice, dau. of Sir Wm. Faryngton, with 1 son (lost) and 3 daus., C. II. A Civilian and w., c. **1525**, inscr. lost, sm.

HADHAM, LITTLE. I. Rich. Waren, parson of Great Hadham, c. **1470**, in cope, sm., much worn. II. A Man, in arm., and w., c. **1485**, with 4 daus., p. 198.

HADHAM, MUCH. I. A Civilian and w., c. **1520**, inscr. lost. II. Clement Newce, Esq., citizen and mercer of London, 1579, and w. Mary, **1582**, with 8 sons and 9 daus., pp. 118, 120. III. Wm. Newce, Esq., **1610**, and 2 ws., by the former w. he had 6 sons and 7 daus. INSCRS. IV. * "Alban p'sone de Hadhm̄," C. V. *Joane Goldsmith, eldest dau. of Clem. Newce, **1569**.

HARPENDEN. I. Wm. Anabull, **1456**, and w. Isabella, worn, C. II. Wm. Cressye, Esq., 1559, and w. Grace (Johnson), a dau. of Robt. Darkenall, of Penshurst, Kent, 1571, mur., N.Tr.

HEMEL HEMPSTEAD. Robt. Albyn, in arm., and w. Margt., c. **1400**, Fr. inscr., once on A.T., now mur., pp. 160, 162. *The Topographer for* 1791, vol. iii. p. 244; *Clutterbuck*, vol. i. p. 422. *Introd.*, p. 159 (male eff.)

HINXWORTH. John Lambard, citizen, mercer, and alderman of London, **1487**, and w. Anne, with 4 sons (the eldest a priest) and 2 daus., marg. inscr., C. pp. 79, 196, 201, 241.

HITCHIN. I. John Pulter, draper, **1421** (only feet left), and w. Alice, with mcht's. mk., much worn, N. II. A Mcht. of the staple of Calais, **1452**, and w. Alice, with 4 sons and 6 daus., C. III. A Civilian and w., c. **1470**, about 5 sons and 4 daus. and inscr. lost., A.T., S.C. IV. John Beel (?) (eff. lost) and w. Margery, **1477** (?), in shrouds, with 4 sons and 4 daus., inscr. gone, S.C., p. 33. V. A Man and his w., in shrouds, c. **1480**, about 3 sons and 3 daus. and inscr. lost, A.T., S.C., p. 33. VI. Nich. Mattock, mcht. of the staple of Calais, citizen and fishmonger of London, and w. Elizth., **1485**, with 2 sons and 1 dau., all in shrouds, with Hy. Trin.; all lost but fem. eff., which is (like that at Yoxford, Suffolk, 1485) N.C.,

p. 33.   VII. A Man and his w., c. **1490**, in shrouds, with 3 sons and 5 daus., inscr. lost, N.C., p. 33.   VIII. Jas. Hert, B.D., vicar, **1498**, in cope, without almuce, inscr. lost, C., p. 132. *Boutell's Mon. Br.*, p. 103.   IX. A Civilian and w., c. **1535**; about 3 sons and 5 daus., Hy. Trin., and wives lost, pecul., N., pp. 29, 244. Inscrs., &c.   X. A Heart, all that is left of the brass of John Sperehawke, D.D., vicar, and canon of Wells, **1474**, stone lately removed (?), pp. 82, 108, 131. *Introd.*, p. 132 (eff.)   XI. John Pulter, Esq., 1485, engr. c. **1550**, with sh., A.T., N.C.   XII. Wm. Pulter, Esq., **1549**, with sh., N.C.   XIII. Arms of Pulter, N.C. The brasses Nos. III. and V. (or perhaps No. VII.) probably commemorate Thos. Abbot, mercer, and w. Joan, 1481, and their son Thos. Abbot, 1493, and w. Rubbings of 3 or 4 brasses of civilians and ws. (c. **1480** and c. **1530**, which were loose in the vestry several years ago) are in the possession of J. B. Nichols, Esq., p. 25.

HUNSDON.   I. Margt., w. of John Shelley, citizen and mercer of London, **1495**, in shroud, with Hy. Trin., N.   II. Jas. Gray, for 35 years park and house-keeper at Hunsdon, **1591**, æt. 69, with Death, &c., 6 Eng. vv., qd. pl., mur., N., pp. 130, 217. *Gent. Mag.*, vol. lxv. 1795, pt. i. p. 13.

ICKLEFORD.   Thos. Somer and w. Marion, c. **1400**, hf. effs., p. 164.

IPPOLYTS.   I. *Ryce Hughes and w. Alice, dau. of Thos. Kybworth, **1594**, æt. 29; they had 1 son and 2 daus.; 4 Eng. vv., qd. pl., mur., C.   Inscr. II. Robt. Poyidres (?), **1401**, and w. Alice, mutil., N.Tr.

KELSHALL.   Rich. Adane and w. Maryon, engr. **1435**, 12 Eng. vv., C., p. 180.

KNEBWORTH.   I. Simon Bache, treasurer of the household to Hen. V., and canon of St. Paul's, London, **1414**, in rich cope, with B. V. Mary, St. Peter, a Bp., St. Andrew—St. John Bapt., St. Paul, an Abp. (?), St. Jas. the Great, p. 76. *Clutterbuck*, vol. ii. p. 381. II. Rowland Lytton, Esq., **1582**, in arm., and ws. Margt. (Tate, who had a dau. Mary) and Anne (Carleton, who had Roland and Francisca), partly covd.   Inscr. III. John Hotoft, treasurer of the household to Hen. VI., and w., c. **1430**, marg. inscr. in Lat. vv. mutil., with shs. and effs. gone, once on A.T.

LANGLEY, ABBOTS.   I. Rauffe Horwode, **1498**, and ws. Elizth. and Joan, with 3 sons and 3 daus., sm., N.   II. Thos. Cogdell, yeoman, **1607**, æt. 83, and ws. Jane and Alice, N.   III. A Lady, c. **1570**; male eff., 3 sons (?), and inscr. lost, sm.   Inscr. IV. Robt. Nevyll, **1475**, and w. Elyn, eff. lost.

LANGLEY, KINGS.   I. †Rich. Newland, rector, **1497**, very sm.

II. Wm. Carter, **1528** (lost), and w. Alice, sm., partly covd.   III. John Carter, of Gifres, **1588**, and 2 ws., with 4 sons and 5 daus., and 5 sons and 4 daus., sm., S.C.   The rubbing of a Man, in arm., kng., and w., c. 1560, with 3 sons and 3 daus., is in the possession of J. B. Nichols, Esq.   A drawing of a brass to Margt. Cheyne, dau. of —— Skipwithe, 1578, with 5 chil., is in Add. MS., 9,063, in Brit. Mus.

LAYSTON.   †John Brande, **1527**, and w. Alys.

LETCHWORTH.   I. [Wm. Overbury], and w. Isabel, c. **1400**, hf. eff's., p. 164.   II. Thos. Wyrley, rector, **1475**, C., p. 107.

MIMMS, NORTH.   I. A Priest, c. **1360**, [perhaps Wm. de Kesteven, vicar, 1361,] with chalice covd. by paten, feet on a stag, under canopy, with SS. Peter, John Evang., Barth.—Paul, Jas. the Great, Andrew, resting on a bracket composed of a sh. between 2 lions, the stem lost, Flemish, C., pp. 22, 137, 143.   *Clutterbuck*, vol. i. p. 464; C. C. Soc. *Illustr.*, No. ii. p. 59.   *Boutell's Mon. Br.*, p. 21 (eff.) II. A Civilian, c. **1440**, legs and inscr. lost, sm., C.   III. Robt. Knolles, Esq. (eff. lost), and w. Elizth., **1458**, with 2 daus. headless, C., p. 172.   IV. Hen., eldest son of Wm. Covert, Esq., **1488**, in arm., C., pp. 197, 198.   *Introd.*, p. 197.   V. A Civilian and w., c. **1490**, with 4 sons and 6 daus., inscr. lost, sm., N.   VI. Thos., son and h. apparent of John Leucas, Gent., of Kent, **1531**, child, eff. covd. by step.   VII. Rich. Butler, Esq., in arm., and w. Martha (Olyff), c. **1560**, æt. nearly 20, with 36 Eng. vv. C., p. 236.   INSCR. VIII. Wm. de Bakthone, "Botyler al p(ri)nce," Fr. inscr., shs. lost, N.C.   There is an incised slab to Margt. Beresford (?), 1584, A.T., C., p. 40.

NEWENHAM.   I. A Civilian and 2 ws., c. **1490**, the 2nd w. with 1 son and 3 daus., inscr. lost.   II. Joane, dau. and h. of Hen. Cowlshull, Esq., son and h. of Robt. Cowlshull, of Beeford, Yorks., and w. of Jas. Dowman, **1607**, æt. 61, left 7 [8?] chil., Edw., Margt., Elizth., Jane, Anne, Constans, Mary, Susan, Susan.

OFFLEY.   I. John Samwel, **1529**, and 2 ws., Elizth. (with 1 son) and Joan.   II. A Civilian and 3 ws., c. **1530**, with 9 sons.

PELHAM, BRENT.   *Mary, 1625, and Anne, **1627**, æt. 27, ws. of Mr. Francis Rowley, with Eng. vv., sm., N.   In Cole's MS., No. 5,806, fol. 17. b, 18. b, are sketches of the brasses of a Lady, c. 1610, and of Ralf Gray, Gent., 1492 (not in arm.), and w. Anne.

PELHAM, FURNEUX.   I. A Civilian and widow, c. **1420**, dau. lost from beside mother, with canopy mutil., inscr. lost, p. 172. Perhaps the brass of John Barloe, 1420, and w. Joan, 1419.   II. *Robt. Newport, Esq., founder of Chapel, **1518**, and w. Mary [a dau. of

John Allington, of Horscheath, Camb.], with chil., inscr. lost, mur., N. INSCR. III. *John Newport, Esq., h. of No. II., marg. inscr. mutil., eff. lost.

RADWELL. I. John Bele, Gent., **1516**, not in arm., and 2 ws., Anne (with 2 sons) and Agnes, 2 daus. gone. II. Elizth., eldest dau. of Anth. Gage, Esq., of Stowe, Camb., and w. of John Parker, Gent., **1602**, æt. 27, C. Another now lost (?), p. 63.

REDBURN. I. Rich. Pecok, **1512**, and w. Elizth., with 4 sons, w. and 2 daus. lost, S.A., p. 132. II. Sir Rich. Rede, and w. Anne, **1560**, marg. inscr. lost, mur., once with A.T., the slab of which was converted into a hearth-stone. See Add. MS., 9,062, in Brit. Mus. FRAG. III. Eight daus., kng., c. **1490**.

RICKMANSWORTH. Thos. Day, **1613**, holding staff and book, and 2 ws., Alice, 1585, and Joan, 1598, 8 Eng. vv.

ROYSTON. I. Wm. Taverham, or Tabram, rector of Therfield, **1432** [or 1421], in acad., lower part of eff. and of canopy and inscr. lost, C., pp. 84, 256. *Boutell's Series*. II. A Plain Cross, inscr. gone, C., p. 222. *Gough* (?). III. A Civilian and w., c. **1500**, inscr. lost, N. INSCRS. IV. Eight Eng. vv., c. **1500**, loose, p. 181. V. Wm. Chamber, **1546**, ordained a yearly sermon to be preached on Rogation Monday by the collegers of St. John's, Camb., mur., N.A. A rubbing of the brass (now lost) of Robt. White, prior, 1534, is in the possession of J. B. Nichols, Esq., p. 75.

ST. ALBAN'S ABBEY. I. Thos. [de la Mare], abbot, ob. 1396, engr. c. **1360**, a Flemish brass, 9 ft. 3½ in. by 4 ft. 3¼ in., eff. in rich vestments, canopy very fine, with SS. Peter, Paul, Alban, and Offa, King of Mercia, founder of the monastery, in the upper part; below them SS. John Evang., Andrew, Thos., Jas. the Great, Bartholomew, Philip, and other figures, marg. inscr. unfinished, qd. pl., C., pp. 20, 34, 61, 101, 143. *Carter's Anc. Sculpt. and Painting*, vol. i. p. 29; *Clutterbuck*, vol. i. p. 67. *Boutell's Mon. Br.*, pp. 9, 11, 12, 13 (eff. and dets.) *Introd.*, p. 18 (dets) II. An Abbot, (John de la Moote, **1401** ?), upper part of eff. gone, on reverse of the remainder (which is loose), the lower part of a fem. eff., c. **1400** (?), canopy and marg. inscr. nearly all lost, 2 Lat. vv., C., pp. 47, 78. *Boutell's Br.*, p. 148. III. Thos. Fayreman, mcht. [of the staple] of Calais, **1411**, with anelace, and w., very much worn, S.C.A. IV. A Monk, c. **1450**, (perhaps Reginald Bernewelt, 1443), loose, inscr. lost, p. 86. V. [John Stoke, abbot, **1451**], eff. lost, with fine triple canopy, which had figures [of B. V. Mary and Child, Jesse, and St. Amphibalus?] above the pediments, and marg. inscr. in 16 Lat. vv., canopy and inscr. mutil. and partly covd., C., p. 109. *Gough*, vol. ii. pl. lxi.

p. 168. VI. Bartholomew Halsey, Esq. (upper part lost, lower loose), and w. Florens, c. 1465; 2 sons, 2 daus., and inscr. lost, C. VII. A Civilian, c. 1465, loose. VIII. A Civilian, c. 1470, head lost, loose. IX. Robt. Beauner, monk, who held various offices, (see Appendix B), c. 1470, C., pp. 86, 107. *Introd.*, p. 86. X. A Monk, c. 1470, hf. eff. (loose), inscr. lost, C., p. 86. XI. Sir Anth. Grey, son and h. of Edm. Earl of Kent, 1480, he m. Joan, dau. of Rich. Woodville, and "fourth hole suster" to Elizth., queen of Ed. IV., inscr. lost, C., pp. 116, 197. *The Topographer for* 1792, vol. iv., p. 118; *Gough*, vol. iii. pl. c., p. 269; *Boutell's Mon. Br.*, p. 73. XII. Rauff [Rowlat], mcht. of the staple of Calais, and w. Jane [1519], with 6 daus., eff. of w. and sons lost, marg. inscr. mutil., S.C.A. *Boutell's Mon. Br.*, p. 110. XIII. Thos. Rutlond, sub-prior, 1521, eff. and inscr. loose, marg. inscr. in slab, S.Tr., p. 86. INSCRS., &c. XIV. A Scroll, from a lost eff. of monk kng. at cross, with B. V. M. and St. John, C. XV. A Twisted Scroll, above a lost eff. of a priest, C. XVI. Wm. Stroder and w. Margt., 1517, loose, effs. lost, N.Tr. XVII. Hen. Grymbalde, chaplain, 1522, covd., C. XVIII. Mawde Harryes, 1537, 4 Eng. vv., loose, N.Tr. The loose brasses and No. I. are placed in Abbot Wheathampstead's Chapel. Nos. XVI., XVIII., and inscr. of No. XIII. were at the rectory in 1859. In Add. MS., 9,064, p. 122 a. is a sketch of the brass of a Civilian and w., c. 1500, once in N.A., now lost. Numerous matrices (see pp. 20, 57, 255), one in the S.Tr. is of a brass cross with a head at the centre (*Knight's Old England*, fig. 1,086, &c.); another was simply a head and inscr. An incised slab, with eff. and marg. inscr. to Abbot Ramryge, 1529, S.C.A., p. 40.

St. Alban's, St. Michael's. I. John Pecok and w. Maud, c. 1380 (?), under pews, S.A., p. 164. *Etching by A. White*, 1849. II. A Man in arm., c. 1380, fastened to a cupboard in the vestry, inscr. lost, p. 160. *Boutell's Mon. Br.*, p. 54. III. †A Civilian (?) in the head of a cross, c. 1400, w. (?) lost, uder pews, S.A., p. 136. *Gent. Mag.*, vol. lxxxii. 1812, pt. i. p. 321. INSCR. IV. Hen. Gape, 1558, and w. Florens, 6 Eng. vv., N., now in Ch. chest.

St. Alban's, St. Peter's. *Roger Pemberton, Esq., high-sheriff, founded by will 6 Almshouses for 6 poor widows, and left £30 yearly, from Shelton Manor, Beds., for their maintenance, 1627, æt. 72, and w. Elizth. (eff. lost), with chil., Ralphe (mayor), Robt., John, Elizth., Elizth., Tecla, on reverse of inscr. one to John Ball, brickmaker, 1515, left 10s. yearly for an obit. for himself, w. Elizth., and John and Chrystyan his parents, S.A. In the Add. MS., 9,063, pp. 203, 204, in the Brit. Mus., are drawings of the foregoing, and of these

4 brasses now lost:—A Priest, c. 1410, below was an inscribed Rose, now at the Bodleian, Oxford, C., p. 110.   John Atkyn, glover, 1449, and widow dame Joan, p. 129.   A Priest, c. 1460, with chalice, C.   Wm. Mitor, 1486, and w. Grace (eff. lost), N.A. The eff. (mutil.) of Sir Bertin Entwyssell, 1455, now lost, is engr. in *Nichols' Leic.*, vol. ii. pl. cxxix. p. 802.

ST. ALBAN'S, ST. STEPHEN'S. Wm. Robins, Esq., clerk of the signet to Ed. IV., **1482**, and w. Kath., with 4 sons and 5 daus., inscr. lost, S.C., p. 198.

SANDON. John Fitz-Geffrey, Esq., **1480**, with collar, and w. Elizth., with 6 daus., Agnes, Elizth., Elizth., Elienor, Jane, Margt.; the sons, [John], Wm., Thos. lost, N., p. 197.

SAWBRIDGEWORTH. I. John Leventhorp, Esq., **1433**, and w. Kath. (Twychet), 1431, large, inscr. lost, S.A., pp. 115, 189. *Waller*, pt. iv.; *Boutell's Mon. Br.*, p. 67.   II. Geoff. Joslyne, **1470**, and ws. Kath. and Joan, C.   III. John Leventhorp, Esq. (son of No. I.), **1484**, and w. Joan (Barrington), 1448, in shrouds, moved from S.A. to west end of Nave, an inscr. in 6 Lat. vv., now mur., S.A., pp. 107, 115.   IV. Thos. Leventhorpe, Esq., **1527**, and w. Joan, dau. of Geo. Dallison, Esq., and widow of Alex. St. John, of Thirby, Beds., in heraldic mantle, eff. of husband and inscr. lost, S.A.   V. Edw. Leventhorp, Esq., eldest son of No. IV., 1551, in arm., and w. Elizth., dau. of —— Barley, Esq., of Aldbury; their eldest son m. Mary, 2nd dau. of Sir Harry Parker, eldest son of Harry Lord Morlie, engr. c. **1600**, S.A., p. 45.   VI. Mary (Parker), w. of Edw. Leventhorp, Esq., who died at Rome 1566, their eldest son was John, engr. c. **1600**, moved like No. III., p. 247. *Introd.*, p. 247 (part of eff.)   INSCR., &c. VII. Wm. Chauncy, N.A. VIII. A Shield (another lately lost?), all that is left of the brass of John Chauncy, Esq., **1546**, and ws. Elizth. and Kath.   An incised slab, with eff. of Lady much defaced, 14th cent., is left in N.   See also brasses in private possession—Sir Sam. Meyrick.

SHENLEY. Mr. Raphe Allway, of Cannons, **1621**, and w. Dorothy, with daus., Mary, Anne, Dorothy, Elizth.

STANDON. I. †John Ruggewyn, Esq., **1412**, kng. on bascinet and camail, cross gone, C.   II. A Civilian, c. **1460**, inscr. lost. Probably John Curteys, stock-fishmonger of London, 1465.   III. [John Feld, alderman of London, and mcht. of the] staple of Calais, **1477**, in mantle, with 2 sons and a dau., and mcht.'s mk.; also his son John Feld, Esq. [1477?], in tabard, with 2 sons and 2 daus., marg. inscr. mutil., A.T., N.A., pp. 112, 118, 197, 201. *C. C. Soc. Illustr.*, No. II. p. 47; *Waller*, pt. ix.   IV. —— Wade, **1557**, in arm.,

8 Eng. vv., C., pp. 119, 236.   Inscrs., &c. V. Sir Wm. Coffyn, of the privy chamber to Hen. VIII., and master of the horse "to Jane ye most lawfull wyfe vnto ye aforsaid Kinge," and high steward of the liberty and manor of Standon, **1538**, with sh., C.   VI. Six Sons (and 4 daus.?) in shrouds, part of the brass of Philip Astley, Esq., **1467**, and ws., Lettis, Margt., Elizth., Alice.   VII. Rich. Emerson, **1562**, 8 Eng. vv.

STANSTEAD ABBOTS. I. A Civilian and w., c. **1540**, both on same plate, head of w. and inscr. lost, N., p. 62.   II. Wm. Saxaye, Gent., of Gray's Inn, (son of Hen. Saxaye, citizen and mcht.-venturer of London, and his w. Joyce, dau. of Robt. Trapper, of London, goldsmith), **1581**, æt. 23, C.   FRAGS. III. Two shs., 1 with arms of Rokesburgh, man, in arm., and w. lost.   IV. Evang. Symb. St. John, eff. lost, N.

STEVENAGE. Stephen Hellard, of the diocese of York, "in decretis Bacallarius," rector, canon of St. Asaph [ob. 1506], in cope, engr. c. **1500**, C.

TEWIN. Thos. Pygott, Gent., whose ancestors have lived at Tewin upwards of 300 years, **1610**, æt. 70; he left 2 daus., Rebekah, w. of Hen. Bull, Gent., of Hertford, and Elizth., w. of Beckingham Boteler, of Tewin, Gent., N.

WALKERNE. I. A Civilian and w., c. **1480**, inscr. lost, loose. II. Edw., son of John Humbarstone, Gent., **1583**, and w. Anna, dau. of Edw. Welche, with 5 sons and 3 daus., N.   III. Wm. Chapman, citizen and haberdasher of London, 1621, æt. 71, and w. Anne, **1636**, æt. 76, with 6 sons and 6 daus., loose.

WARE. I. A Lady, c. **1400**, worn, p. 169.   II. Elena, dau. of John and Margery Coke, and w. of Wm. Bramble (by whom she had a son Wm.), and afterwards of Rich. Warbulton, **1454**, p. 179. III. Wm. Pyrry, and ws. Agnes and Alice, each with 5 sons and 5 daus., engr. c. **1470**, in vestry.   Some brasses, now lost, are sketched in Add. MS., 9,062, in Brit. Mus.

WATFORD. I. Sir Hugh de Holes, justice, **1415**, large, mutil., marg. inscr. lost, pp. 62, 89, 90.   *Oxford Man.*, p. 39; and *Introd.*, p. 90.   II. Margt., w. of No. I., 1416, large, marg. inscr. lost, eff. seems engr. c. **1390**, p. 62.   III. Hen. Dickson, 1610, Geo. Miller, **1613**, Anth. Cooper, servants to Sir Chas. Morrison, and his widow Dorothy (who pos.), and their son Sir Chas., qd. pl., N.C. In the Lansdown MS., No. 874, fol. 69. a, in Brit. Mus., are sketches of Nos. I. and II. (with the inscrs.), also of other brasses now lost.

WATTON. I. Sir Philip Peletoot, **1361**, with single canopy, legs and canopy restored (the former stolen in 1837?), marg. inscr. in Fr. lost, N.C., pp. 53, 138, 160. *Clutterbuck*, vol. ii. p. 489. *Boutell's Mon. Br.*, p. 51 (eff.)   II. A Priest, c. **1370** (perhaps John Brigenhall, rector), 1375, in plain cope, large, canopy loose and much mutil., C., pp. 76, 138, 144. *Boutell's Series.*   III. A Civilian, c. **1450**, and w. (?), inscr. lost, S.A.   IV. Sir Edm. Bardolf, **1455**, w. Joan, 1438 (with 4 sons and 3 daus.), and kinsman Edm. Bardolf, Esq., all lost but eff. of w., S.C.   V. A Civilian and w. (?), c. **1470**, inscr. lost.   VI. John Butler, Esq., **1514**, and ws., Kath., dau. of Thos. Acton, Gent., Dorothy, dau. of Wm. Tyrrell, Esq., of Gypping, Margt., dau. of Hen. Belknap, Esq., 1513, all lost but male eff. and 5 shs., p. 232. The brasses have been lately rel.   The very small brass of Walter de Molinton and Jane de Gutecestri, c. **1400**, is lost.

WHEATHAMPSTEAD. I. Hugh Bostok and w. Margt. (Macry), c. **1450**, 6 Lat. vv., see Appendix B, N.Tr., p. 94. *Boutell's Mon. Br.*, p. 109.   II. John Heyworth, Gent., **1520**, and w. Elizth., with 4 sons and 5 daus.

WORMLEY. I. Edm. Howton, **1479**, and w. Annes, with 5 sons and 3 daus., C.   II. John Cok, yeoman, and w., c. **1490**, with Hy. Trin., marg. inscr. much mutil., lower part of male eff. gone, C., p. 132.   III. [Walter Tooke, Esq., of Popes, in Bishop's Hatfield, and w. Angelett (2nd dau. of Wm. Woodlife, lord of the manor, and citizen and mercer of London, and his w. Elizth., dau. of —— Fisher, who afterwards m. Edw. Saxilbie, baron of the exchequer), **1598**], with 8 sons and 4 daus., 4 Eng. vv., once on A.T., C., p. 225.   INSCR. IV. John Cleve, rector, **1404**, C. The inscr. of Edw. Sharnbroke, rector, and prebendary of St. Paul's, London, 1530, and the hf. eff. of Rich. Ruston, rector, 1457, engr. in *Introd.*, p. 181, were lost at the restoration of the Ch. about 16 years ago, pp. 181, 260.

WYDDIALL. I. John Gille, Esq., lord of the manor, **1546**, not in arm., and w. (whose eff. seems engr. c. 1520), with 8 daus., sons gone, p. 50.   II. *Margt. Plumbe, **1575**, hf. eff., large, mur., p. 218.   INSCR. III. Geo. Gyll, lord of the manor, **1568**; he had 2 ws. and 14 chil.

YARDLEY; see Ardeley.

INSCRIPTIONS, &c.

BARNET CHIPPING. †Elinor, w. of Edw. Taylor, Esq., and afterwards of John Palmer, Esq., of Kentish Town, **1558**.   HERTFORD, ALL SAINTS. Thos. Boose, **1456**.   HERTFORD, ST. ANDREW, or

NICHOLAS. Matrices, p. 130. †HERTINGFORDBURY. I. Phelipe and Isabel, daus. of Robt. de Louthe. II. Robt. de Louthe and w. Joan. Both inscrs. in Fr., and 14th cent.

Huntingdonshire.

DIDDINGTON. I. Wm. Tallard, **1505** (upper part gone), and w. Elizth. [dau. and coh. of John Anstye], in heraldic dresses, between 2 shafts, with our Bl. Lord, and SS. John Bapt., John Evang.— B. V. Mary and Child, Mary Magd., Cath., 6 Lat. vv., pecul., mur. *Gent. Mag.*, vol. xxxi. N.S., 1849, p. 149. II. [Alice (Wattes), widow of —— Tayllard], **1513**, with 3 chil., and B. V. Mary and Child, inscr. gone, pecul.

GODMANCHESTER. A Civilian and 2 ws., c. **1520**; ws., inscr., and chil. lost. *Fox's Godmanchester*, p. 298.

OFFORD DARCY. I. Sir Laur. Pabenham, 1400, and 2 ws., Elizth., one of the 3 daus. and hs. of John Engeyne, 1377, and Joan, dau. of Sir Giles Dawbeney, lower portions of effs. lost, engr. c. **1440**, S.A., pp. 189, 208. II. An Ecclesiastic, c. **1530**, in doctor's cap and acad., kng., pecul., p. 29. Two matrices of crosses with hf. effs.

SAWTREY. —— Moyne (not Stourton), **1404**, in arm., and w. Maria, marg. inscr. nearly all lost, large, C., pp. 87, 185, 205. *Boutell's Series. Arch. Journ.*, vol. ii. p. 388; *Boutell's Mon. Br.*, p. 64; *Oxford Man.*, p. 93; and *Introd.*, p. 206 (det.)

SOMERSHAM. A Priest with chalice and wafer, c. **1530**, pecul., pp. 29, 78.

STILTON. I. Rich. Curthoyse, yeoman, 1573, and w. Anne, **1606**; they had 6 chil., John, Thos. Wm., Ann, Isabell, Joane. II. Thos., 1590, and John, **1618** (sons of No. I.), their brother Wm. pos., sm., on same slab as No. I.

At ST. NEOT'S was a brass (see Introd., p. 128) to Thos. Lynde, yeoman of the crown to Hen. VIII., **1527**, and ws. Alice and Joan; he was "in the habit of a Yeoman of the Guard, with his Pole Axe, a Rose on his breast, and a Crown on his left breast or shoulder." See MSS., Visitation of Hunts., July 24, 1684, K. 7, p. 18, in the Coll. of Arms, quoted in G. C. Gorham's Hist. and Ant. of Eynesbury and St. Neots, vol. i. p. 160. In the same vol. (p. 159) is an engraving of a matrix of a cross with Lomb. inscr. to Joan la Gous(le); also engr. in *Gough*, vol. ii. pl. xviii. fig. 5, p. 247.

Ireland.

ST. PATRICK'S CATHEDRAL, DUBLIN. I. Robt. Sutton, dean, **1528**, in almuce, qd. pl. with initials, &c., mur., pp. 21, 41, 79, 222. *Mason's Hist. of Dublin Cath.*, p. 144. II. Geoffrey Fyche, dean, **1537**, in almuce, qd. pl. with "Virgin of Pity," &c., mur., pp. 21, 41, 79, 104, 132. *Ibid.*, p. 146. III. *Sir Edw. Fiton, of Saulworth, Cheshire, lord president of Connaught and Thomond 1569—1572, appointed treasurer and receyver-general in Ireland in 1573, **1579**, and w. Anne, dau. of Sir Peter Warburton, of Areley, Cheshire, 1573, m. just 34 years, with 9 sons and 6 daus., qd. pl., mur., p. 41.

For account of lost brasses, see page 42.

Kent.

ADDINGTON. I. Wm. Snayth, Esq., lord of the manor, and sheriff of Kent [in 1407], **1409**, and w. Alice, with canopy, now mur., S.C., p. 185. II. A Man in arm., c. **1415**, inscr. lost, N., p. 188. Probably John Northwood, Esq., 1416. Rubbings of the lost brasses of Thos. Chaworth, rector, c. 1470, hf. eff., with chalice, and of Robt. Watton, Esq., 1470, in helmet, and w. Alice (Clerk), are in the possession of J. B. Nichols, Esq.

ASH, near SANDWICH. I. Rich. [Roger?] Clitherow, Esq., c. **1440**, and widow Matilda (?), dau. of Sir John Oldcastle, 1457, with canopy, all lost but upper part of fem. eff. and pediment above, C. II. Jane, [w. of] —— Keriell, and dau. of Roger Cletherowe, c. **1460**, 7 Eng. vv. (see Appendix B), pp. 33, 211. *Introd.*, p. 211 (det.) III. Wm. Leus (?), **1525**, and w. Anys, sm., under pews, pecul., p. 214. IV. Christopher Septvans, alias Harflete, Esq., of Moland in Ash [1575], in arm., and w. [Mercy, dau. of Thos.] Hendley, Esq., of Otham, born 1530, dec. **1602**, 6 eleg. vv. and marg. inscr., several chil. gone, N.C., p. 237. V. Walter Septvanis, alias Harflet, Esq., of Cheker in Ash, born 1567, dec. **1642**, and w. Jane, dau. of John Challoner, Esq., of Fulham, born 1576, dec. 1626, with 6 chil., Thos., Wm., John, Jane, Mercy, Jone, 6 eleg. vv., N.C., p. 248. INSCR., &c. VI. John Brooke, of Brookestrete, **1582**, 14 Eng. vv. an acrostic. VII. Four Shields, with arms of St. Nicholas, &c.

ASHFORD. I. [Elizth.] "countesse Dathels," dau. of [Hen. Lord Ferrers, of Groby], **1375**, arms and feet gone, only pediment of canopy left, marg. inscr. mutil., large, C., pp. 126, 169. *Fisher. Introd.*, p. 167 (part of eff.) She married, firstly, David de Strabolgie, Earl of Atholl, and secondly, John Maleweyn, of Kent, and died at Ashford,—Weever, Fun. Mon., p. 275.   FRAGS. II. The head of a priest, c. **1320**, once in a cross (?), loose in Ch. chest, p. 135.   III. Sir John Fogge and 2 ws., Alice and ——, c. **1490**, all lost but head of male eff. and 8 Lat. vv., held by an angel, and stating he restored, and was a benefactor to, the Ch., and built the tower, A.T., N.C., pp. 111, 260.   IV. Thos. Fogg, Esq., serjeant porter to Hen. VII. and Hen. VIII., **1512**, and w. Elianor (effs. lost), with 2 daus., N.Tr., p. 50.

AYLESFORD. I. John Cosyngton, Esq., **1426**, and w. Sarra, helmet and mantling badly restored, N.A., p. 189.   INSCRS. II. Hen. Savell, Gent., servant to Sir Thos. Wiat, **1545**, C.   III. Hen., 4th son of Sir Hen. Crispe, **1594**, by his w. Anne, dau. of Thos. Cullpepper, of Aylesford, Esq., he had 5 sons and 1 dau., N.

BECKENHAM. I. Sir Humfrey Style, **1552**, in tabard, and 2 ws. in heraldic mantles, Brydgett, dau. of Sir Thos. Bauldry, lord mayor of London [in 1523], 1548 (with 6 sons and 3 daus.), and Elizth., dau. of Geo. Peryn, Esq. (with 1 son and 1 dau.), mur., C.   II. Dame Margt., w. of Sir Wm. Da(n)sell, **1563**, under moveable seats.   INSCR., &c. III. Wm. Danyell, alias Malham, rector, **1458**, shaft of canopy only left.   IV. Ellen, sister to No. II. (on same slab), **1609**, æt. 67, both daus. of John Berney, Esq., of Redham, Norf., by his 1st w., Margt., dau. of Wm. Reade, Esq., of Beckles, Suff.

BETHERSDEN. I. Wm. Lovelace, Gent., citizen of London, **1459**, not in arm., C.   II. Thos., son of Wm. Lovelace, serjeant-at-law, **1591**, sm., C.

BEXLEY. I. A Hunting-horn and a sh., inscr. and 2 shs. lost, 15th cent., N.C., p. 130. *Thorpe's Cust. Roff.*, pl. vii. fig. 1, p. 78. II. Thos. Sparrow, **1513**, 2 Eng. vv. on scroll, sm., C. *Ibid.*, pl. vi. p. 77.

BIDDENDEN. I. Margt. Goldwell, 1499, and 2 husbands, Laurence Hensell, 1452 (by whom she had Alice and Agnes), and John Goldwell, buried at Great Chart, 1499 (by whom she had Geoffrey), engr. c. **1520**, sm., p. 179.   II. John Mayne, Esq., sheriff, **1566**, in arm., and w. Margt., only dau. and h. of Ralph Jonson, Esq., with 6 sons and 8 daus., Anth., Walter, Elizth., Mary, Cecily surviving, mur., N.C.   III. *Wm. Boddindam (?), **1575**, æt. 63, and 2 ws., Juliana, by whom he had a son, Wm., and 5 daus., and ——.   IV. Rich. Allarde, alderman of Rochester, **1593**, æt. 60, and 3 ws., Helen (with chil., Hen., Rich., John, Anne, Mary, Elizth., effs. lost), Joan (with chil., Francis, Susan, and Phœbe), and Thomasin.   V. †John Evrenden, **1598** (?), æt. 60, and 2 ws., Jone and ——.   VI. Josiah

Scyliard, Gent., **1609**, æt. 61, and 2 ws., Judith (Boddendam), 1602, æt. 48 (with 4 sons and 2 daus.), and Anne, dau. of Thos. Austen (with 2 sons and 1 dau.) *Introd.*, p. 246 (det.)   VII. *Wm. Randolph, **1641**, and w., inscr. cut in stone, p. 240.   VIII. *J. H. Randolph, **1685**, æt. 56, and w. Elizth., dau. of John Best, Esq., of Canterbury, with 1 dau., p. 215.

BIRCHINGTON.   I. John Quek, **1449**, with anelace, and son, sm., N.C.   II. Rich. Quek, **1459**, inscr. lost, rel., N.C.   III. [Alys], w. of John [Cryspe the younger], **1518**, and dau., S.C.   IV. John Heynys, vicar of Monkton, **1523**, with chalice and wafer, C.   *Engr.* —— (?), 1818.   V. Margt., dau. and h. of Geo. Rotherham, Esq., and w. of John Cryspe the younger, **1528**, S.C.   VI. Margt., w. of John Cryppys the younger, **1533**, with chrysom child, S.C., p. 220. INSCR. VII. John Cryspe, Esq., and w. Agnes, **1533** (effs. lost), with 8 sons and 7 daus., N.C.

BOBBING.   I. Lord Arnold Savage, 1410, and widow Joan, canopy all gone except portions of the shafts, engr. c. **1420** (?), C., p. 190. II. Sir Arnald, son of Arnald Savage, **1420**, with SS. collar, head and feet lost, triple canopy with its groining ornamented with escallops, much mutil., N.C.   III. *A Fem. eff., 15th cent., in a pew, N.

BOUGHTON MALHERBE.   I. Nich. Wotton, Esq., lord of the manor, **1499**, not in arm., and w. Elizth., with 3 sons and 7 daus., kng., sm., C.   II. Sir Edw. Wotton (son of Sir —— Wotton), and his w. Dorothy (a dau. and h. of Sir Robt. Rede), **1529**, marg. inscr. mutil., C.

BOUGHTON-UNDER-BLEAN.   I. John Best the elder, **1508**, and w. Joan, sm.   II. Thos. Hawkins, servant to Hen. VIII., **1587**, æt. 101, in arm., 12 Eng. vv., N.C., p. 237.   III. Cyriac Petit, Esq., of Colkins, **1591**, æt. c. 80, and w. Florence, dau. of Robt. Chernocke, Esq., of Beds., 1568, æt. 35, with 5 sons (lost) and 4 daus., S.C. INSCRS. IV. John Colkyn, **1405**, with sh., N.   V. Elizth., dau. of No. III., and w. of John Driland, Gent., 2nd son of John Driland of Feversham, **1591**, eff. lost.

BOXLEY.   I. Wm. Snell, of All Souls' Coll., Oxon., and vicar, **1451**, in acad., C., p. 84.   *Fisher.*   II. Rich. Tomynw, Esq., **1576**, in arm., and w. Mary, a dau. of Sir Mathew Browne, of Bechworth Castle, Surrey, 12 Eng. vv., eff. of w. lost, N., p. 237.

BRABOURN.   I. Wm. Scot, Esq., **1434** (?), with canopy, inscr. lost, large, S.A., pp. 187, 191.   II. Dionisia, dau. of Vincent Finch, or Harbard, **1450**, with flowing hair, good, inscr. lost, S.C., p. 214. See Harl. MS., 3,917, fol. 77.   III. Sir Wm. Scott, **1527**, p. 232.

IV. Dame Elizth., w. of Sir Edw. Pownynges, **1528**. Nos. III. and IV. are loose at the Rectory.   Sir Robt. Gower, c. 1400, lost, p. 185.   A matrix, p. 57.

BREDGAR.   Thos. Coly, warden of the Coll. of Hy. Trin., **1518**, in acad., with chalice and wafer, N.A., pp. 75, 85.

BRENCHLEY.   I. Thos. Robert, senior, mercer, and ws., Elizth., Joan, Agnes, c. **1500**, with 7 sons and 4 daus., mcht.'s mk., N.A. II. A Civilian and w., c. **1540**, inscr. lost, S.Tr.

CANTERBURY, ST. ALPHEGE.   I. Robt. Gosebourne, "artibus instructor," and rector of Penshurst, **1523**, in acad., 6 Lat. vv., pp. 60, 96.   II. A Sh. and inscr. to Thos. Prude, "per quem fit ista columpna," mur.   *Gent. Mag.*, vol. xix. N.S., 1843, pt. i. p. 483.

CANTERBURY, ST. GEORGE.   John Lovelle, rector, **1438**, in cope, without almuce, S.A.

CANTERBURY, ST. MARGARET.   John Wynter, twice mayor, **1470**, he ordained a light for the altar, inscr. restored (?), p. 53.

CANTERBURY, ST. MARTIN.   I. Mich. Fraunces, Gent., and w. Jane, dau. of Wm. Quilter, Esq. (m. 4 husbands), both dec. Jan. 10th, **1587**, with 1 son and 5 daus., N.   II. Thos. Stoughton, Gent., of Ashe, Kent, **1591**, in arm., C., p. 237.   INSCRS. III. Bertha, w. of King Ethelbert, engr. 15th cent., mur., C.   IV. Stevyn Fawxs, **1506**, and w. Alys, N.

CANTERBURY, ST. MARY MAGDALEN.   I. Christopher Elcok, draper, **1492**, S.A., p. 239.   *Introd.*, p. 239 (det.)   II. Margt. Elcok, **1494**, N.   INSCRS. III. Joan, dau. of John Haccho, and w. of Hen. Lynde, of Canterbury, **1417**, eff. lost.   IV. Frag. of marg. inscr.

CANTERBURY, ST. MARY NORTHGATE.   Raff Brown, alderman and mayor, c. **1540**, pecul., mur., p. 215.

CANTERBURY, ST. PAUL.   Geo. Wyndbourne, Gent., **1531**, not in arm., and w. Kath., with 3 sons and 5 daus., pecul., S.A., p. 215.

CAPEL-LE-FERNE.   John Gybbis, **1526**, and w. Margt., with 4 sons, pecul., sm., p. 214.

CHALLOCK.   Thos. Thorston, **1508**, and w. Joan, sm., S.C.

CHART, GREAT.   I. A Notary, c. **1470**, inscr. lost, N., p. 128. II. Wm. Goldwelle, **1485**, and w. Avice; chil., Hy. Trin., and marg. inscr. with rebus, lost, A.T., N.C.   III. Wm. Sharp, **1499**, and 5 ws., N.   IV. Thos. Twesden, Gent., **1500**, not in arm., and w. Benedict, chil. lost, S.A.   V. John Toke, Esq., of Goddynton in Chart, **1513**, and 2 ws., Margt., dau. of John Walworth, of Suffolk, and Anne [dau. of John Engeham, Esq., of Syngleton in Chart], marg. inscr. mutil., chil. lost, N.C., p. 232.   VI. John Toke, Esq., son and h. of No. V., **1565**, æt. 69, and w. Cisley, dau. of Sir Thos. Kempe, 1559, æt. 69, with 11 chil., John, Frauncis, John, Nich., Barth., John, Rich., Mary, Elizth., Clare, Margt., daus. lost, N.C., p. 235.   VII. †Nich. Toke, Esq., **1680**, and 3 ws., or daus., below, all kng., marg. inscr., N.C., pp. 238, 248.

CHARTHAM. I. Sir Robt., son of Sir Robt. de Setvans, c. **1306**, cross-legged, with winnowing-fans on surcoat, ailettes and shield, large, marg. inscr. in Lomb. letters lost, C., pp. 34, 112, 146, 147, 148, 149. *Hollis's Mon. Effs.*, pt. i. No. 5; *Waller*, pt. ix.; *Boutell's Mon. Br.*, p. 35; *Introd.*, p. 146. p. 148 (det.)   II. Robt. London, rector, **1416**, in cope, sm., rel., C., pp. 50, 182.   *Oxford Man.*, p. 32; and *Introd.*, p. 76.   III. Robt. Arthur, rector, **1454**, in cope, C., p. 109.   IV. Robt. Sheffelde, M.A., rector, **1508**, in almuce, pp. 50, 79.   V. Jane Eveas, dau. of Lewys Clefforht, Esq., **1530**, pecul., sm., N., pp. 30, 214.   The inscrs. of Nos. II. and IV. are transposed.

CHELSFIELD. I. A Crucifix, with SS. Mary (lost) and John, and marg. inscr., much mutil., to Robt. de Brun, rector, **1417**, on the side of a coped tomb, C., p. 175.   II. Wm. Robroke, rector, **1420**, sm., C. *Fisher*.   III. †A Civilian (eff. lost) and w., c. **1480**, with 6 sons and 5 daus., C.   IV. Alice, dau. of John Bonavetur (?), and w. of Thos. Bray, **1510**, with 4 sons, 1 dau. lost. *Fisher*.

CHERITON. I. John Child, M.A., rector, **1474**, in acad., sm., C., p. 77.   II. Thos., son of Sir John Fogg, rector, **1502**, sm., C., pp. 96, 179.   III. Joane, w. of Robt. Brodnax, **1592**, æt. 39, sm.; she had 6 sons and 8 daus., C.

CHEVENING. *A Civilian, **1596**, æt. 61, and w., with 7 sons and 2 daus., inscr. lost.

CHISELHURST. Alan Porter, rector, **1482**, hf. eff., now mur., C. *Fisher*.

CLIFFE. I. Thos. Faunce, yeoman, **1609**, æt. 84, and 2 ws., Alyce (eff. lost, with 2 sons and 1 dau.) and Elizth. (with 1 son and 2 daus.), Thos., the eldest son, was mayor of Rochester in 1609, N.   II. Bonham Faunce, Gent., **1652**, æt. 55, and 2 ws., Elizth. and Mary, and a son and dau., inscr. lost (?), N.

COBHAM. I. Dame Jone de Kobeham, c. **1320**, with canopy, Fr. marg. inscr. in Lomb. letters lost, large, C., pp. 33, 137. *Gough*, vol. i. pl. xxxix. p. 106; *Waller*, pt. xii.; *Boutell's Mon. Br.*, p. 82; *Introd.*, p. 165.   II. Sir John de Cobham, **1354** (head lost), with canopy, and marg. inscr. in Fr., large, C., pp. 140, 158, 160.   III. John de Cobham, founder of a college at Cobham, 1407, holding church; canopy and marg. inscr. in Fr. nearly all lost, engr. c. **1365**,

large, C., pp. 43, 123, 140, 158, 160. *Thorpe, Cust. Roff.*, pl. x. p. 89;
Bib. Topog. Brit., vol. vi. pl. ix. p. 42; *Gough*, vol. ii. pl. vi. p. 22;
Nichols' Leicestershire, vol. ii. pl. lxxvii. p. 442; *Boutell's Mon. Br.*,
p. 53.   IV. Sir Thos. de Cobham [**1367**], canopy and marg. inscr.
in Fr. mutil., large, C., pp. 62, 160. *Boutell's Series* (eff.)   V.
Margt. de Cobham, w. of Reynold, or Reginald, Lord Cobham (?),
1375, arms of eff. and inscr. lost, large, C., p. 169.   *Boutell's Series*.
VI. Dame Maude de Cobeham [w. of No. IV., **1380**], canopy and
marg. inscr. in Fr. much mutil., large, C., p. 62. *Gough*, vol. i.
pl. xxxix. p. 106; *Boutell's Mon. Br.*, p. 83.   VII. Margt. de Cobeham, dau. of [Hugh de Courtenay, 2nd] Earl of Devonshire, and w.
of [Sir John] de Cobeham the founder, **1395**, canopy with B. V.
Mary and Child above the finial, marg. inscr. in Fr., large, C.,
p. 104. *Boutell's Series*. She was sister to Sir Peter Courtenay
and to Abp. Courtenay, buried respectively at Exeter and Maidstone;
her dau. Joan married Sir John de la Pole (see the brass, c. 1370, at
Chrishall, Essex), and left an only dau. Joan (No. XIII.), who became
heiress to her grandfather, Sir John de Cobham (No. III.)   VIII.
Rauf de Cobham, Esq., **1402**, hf. eff. holding inscr., C., p. 185.
Boutell's Series, and *Chr. Mon.*, p. 151; *Ant. Etch. Club*, vol. ii.
pl. 14.   IX. Sir Regenald Braybrok, husband of Lady Joan de
Cobham [No. XIII.], dec. at Myddelburgh, in Flanders, **1405**, with
sons, Robt. (eff. lost) and Reginald, canopy with Hy. Trin., marg.
inscr., large, C., pp. 62, 185. *Gough*, vol. ii. pl. v.* p. 22.   X. Sir
Nich. Hawberk, husband of Lady Joan de Cobham, died at Cowlyng
Castle, **1407**, with son John, fine triple canopy, with B. V. Mary and
Child, Hy. Trin., and St. Geo., marg. inscr., large, C., pp. 62, 105,
115, 149, 172, 185. *Gough*, vol. ii. pl. vi. p. 22. *Boutell's Mon. Br.*,
pp. 178, 235 (cffs.)   XI. Wm. Tannere, priest, 1st master of the
College, **1418**, in almuce, hf. eff., C., p. 79. *Boutell's Series*.   XII.
Reginald de Cobham, priest, c. **1420**, in cope, on a bracket with
sm. triple canopy; stem, inscr., and head of eff. lost, N.A., p. 173.
Boutell's Series.   XIII. Joan Lady Cobham, wife of Sir Reginald
Braybrook, in mantle, **1433**, with 6 sons and 4 daus., large, C.,
p. 62. She married 5 husbands, Sir Robt. de Hemenhale, Sir Reg.
Braybrooke, Sir Nich. Hawberk, Sir John Oldcastle (burnt as a
Lollard 1419), Sir John Harpedon (see Westminster Abbey, 1457).
XIV. John Gladwyn, master of the Coll., c. **1450**, in cope, partly
covd., N.   XV. John Sprottle, priest, master of the College,
1498, in cope, inscr. lost, C.   XVI. Sir John Broke, baron of
Cobham (eff. lost), and w. Lady Margt., dau. of Edw. [Nevill, Lord
Burgaveny], **1506**, with 8 sons and 10 daus., canopy with Hy. Trin.,

marg. inscr. mutil., C., p. 102. XVII. Sir Thos. Brooke, Lord Cobham, kinsman and h. of Sir Rich. Beauchampe, **1529**, and [1st] w. Dorothy [dau. of Sir Hen. Heydon], with 7 sons and 6 daus. [Sir Thos. m. 2ndly, Dorothy, dau. of Sir Wm. Calthorpe, and widow of —— Southwell; and 3rdly, Elizth. Harte, and had no issue by either]; marg. inscr. mutil., C., pp. 235, 243. FRAGS. XVIII. John Ger[rye], priest, fellow of the Coll., **1447**, in the head of a cross, all lost but a finial and the stem bearing the inscr., N.A., p. 173. *Gough*, vol. ii. pl. liii. p. 149. XIX. Wm. ——, master of the Coll., hf. eff. and half the inscr. lost, C. The loose portions of the brasses were rel. several years ago by J. G. Nichols, Esq., and C. Spence, Esq., at the expense of —— Brooke, Esq., of Ufford, Suffolk, the representative of the male line of Brook, Lord Cobham. Copper-plate engravings (unused) of the brasses of the Cobham family are in the possession of J. G. Nichols, Esq.

COWLING. I. Feyth, dau. of Sir John Brooke, lord of Cobham, **1508**, sm., N. INSCRS. II. Thos. Wodycare, Gent., **1611**, m. Mary, dau. of Wm. Lynch, Gent., and had 1 son and 3 daus. III. Sybell, dau. of Gilbert Thurston, of London, and w. of Matthew Sparks, rector for 28 years, **1639**, æt. 67, p. 225.

CRANBROOK. I. A Civilian, c. **1520**, with a child in swaddling clothes, n.cht.'s mk. with initials T. S. *Gough*, vol. ii. pt. i. pl. xii. p. 228. II. A Civilian and w., c. **1640**, kng., inscr. gone.

CRAY, ST. MARY. I. Rich. Abery (or Avery), **1508**, and ws. Joan, Agnes, Elynor, sm., C. II. Elizth., w. of Geo. Cobham, brother to the Rt. Hon. Lord Cobham, and formerly w. of John Hart, Gent., by whom she had the Rt. Worshipful Sir Percival Hart, **1544**. III. Rich., son of John Manning, Gent., **1604**, and w. Rachael, dau. and coh. of Wm. White, of Hampsteed, Middx., m. 39 years, dec. s.p., C. IV. Mrs. Philadelphia, w. of Benj. Greenwood, Esq., and 2nd dau. of the late Sir Geo. Merttins, president and treasurer of Christ's Hospital, **1747**, æt. 46 years and 7 days, engr. c. 1775 (?), qd. pl., N., pp. 43, 248. V. Benj. Greenwood, Esq. (son of Augustus Greenwood, of Lancaster, mcht.), **1775**, æt. 81, with one hand pointing to a ship, the other to a skull, qd. pl., N., pp. 43, 240. INSCRS. VI. Isabell Cossale (eff. lost), mother of Wm. Obson, 16th cent., N. VII. Rich., son of Thos. Manning, **1605**, 6 Eng. vv., C.

CUDHAM. *Alys, w. of Water Waleys, and sister of John Alegh, Esq., of Addington, Surrey, justice of quorum, **1503**, with 6 sons and 3 daus. *Gent. Mag.*, vol. lxxiv. 1804, pt. ii. p. 901.

DARTFORD. I. Rich. Martyn and w. ——, **1402**, canopy and marg. inscr., large, C., p. 200. *Introd.*, p. 200 (male eff.) II.

Agnes, dau. of John Appelton, w., 1st, of Wm. Hesill, baron of the exchequer of Hen. VI.; 2ndly, of Robt., brother of Sir Thos. Molyngton, baron de Wemme, a widow, **1454**, C. III. Wm. Rothele, **1464**, and ws. Beatrix and Joane, all lost but eff. of 2nd w., S.C. IV. Rich. Burlton, Gent., and w. Kath., **1496**, curious Eng. inscr. (see Appendix B.), S.C. V. A Civilian, **1508**; w. Elenor and marg. inscr. lost, S.C. VI. Wm. Death, Gent., "once Prynsipall of Staple Inne, and one of the Attorneys of the Comon Pleas at Wesminster," **1590**, æt. 63, and ws. Elizth., then æt. 40 (with 10 sons, one held in her arms, and 6 daus.), and Anne, N., p. 220. VII. Upper part of fem. eff., c. **1590**. VIII. Captain Arthur Bostocke, Gent., **1612** (eff. lost), and w. Frances, 2nd dau. of Francis Rogers, Esq., by whom he had 2 sons and 4 daus., C. INSCRS. IX. John Hornley, B.D. [**1477**], 12 eleg. vv., eff. in acad. gone. He was president of Magdalen Hall, Oxford. X. John Beer, Esq., 1572, and ws. Alyce and Joan, and son and h. Hen., who m. Anne, widow of Rich. Howlett, Gent., and had a son Wm. dec., Hen. dec. **1574**, S.C.

DAVINGTON. I. John Edwards and w. Anna, a relation of Lord Wotton, **1613**, æt. 63, with 1 son and 3 daus. (2 infants), qd. pl., mur. II. Kath., dau. of Edm. Lashcford, alias Lyshford, Gent., **1616**, æt. 25, qd. pl., mur.

DEAL, UPPER. I. Thos. [Baker, **1508**?], and w., with 4 sons, w. and daus. under a pew, inscr. mutil. II. *Thos. Boys, Esq., son of John Boys, Esq., of Fredfielde in Nonington, attended Hen. VIII. at the siege of Bullen, receiver of Guynes, mayor of Calais, made captain of Deal Castle 1551, dec. **1562**, æt. 60, in arm., mur.

DITTON. Rowland Shakerley, Gent., son and h. of Frauncys Shakerley, Esq., of Brookecourte, fellow of Grayes Inn, **1576**, in arm., eff. covd (?), C., p. 97.

DOVER, ST. JAMES. Vincent Huffam, priest, and w., with 1 son and 1 dau., c. **1600**, inscr. in 8 Lat. lines by I. G. and W. R., S.C., p. 230.

DOVER, ST. MARY'S. I. Wm. Jones, Gent., **1638**, æt. 75, and w. Kath., 1636, æt. 72, m. 49 years, and had 1 son and 9 daus., C. INSCR. II. Thos. Elwood, "omnibus quinque portuum muneribus functi." **1604**, 10 eleg. vv. and 5 Greek lines, his son pos.

DOWNE. I. Thos. Petle and w. Isabella (eff. lost), c. **1420**, sm. II. Jacob Verzelini, Esq., born at Venice, dec. 1606, æt. 84, and w. Elizth., "borne in Andwerpe, of the Auncient howse of Vandbvren and Mace," dec. **1607**, æt. 73, m. 49 years and 4 months, with 6 sons and 3 daus., large, C., p. 247.   INSCRS. III. John Bederenden, citizen, "pannarius and camerarius" of London, **1445**, C.   IV. John Maning, **1543**, and w. Agnes, dau. and coh. of John Petle de Trowemer.

*EASTRY.   I. Thomas Nevynson, Esq., provost-marshall and scoutmaster of East Kent, captain of the light horses of the lathe of St. Augustines, **1590**, in arm., and w. Ann, dau. of Rich. Tebolde, Esq.; they had 6 sons and 4 daus.   INSCR. II. Sir Roger Nevison, **1625**, with sh.

EDENBRIDGE.   John Selyard, Gent., of Brasted, **1558**; by his w. Alice he had 4 chil., John, Frauncis, Wm., Mary, C.

ERITH.   I. Roger Seneler, "seruiens Abbatis & Conuentus de Iesens" [Lesnes], **1425**, sm., S.C.   II. John Ailemer, **1435**, and w. Margery, S.C.   III. Emma, dau. of John Walden, alderman of London and mayor of the staple of Calais, and w. of John Wode, citizen of London and mcht. of the staple of Calais, **1471**, S.C., p. 25. IV. John Mylner, **1511**, and ws. Margt. (eff. lost) and Benet, S.C. V. Edw. Hawte, Esq., **1537**, and w. Elizth., with 3 or 4 sons (lost) and 1 dau., S.C.   FRAGS., &c. VI. Felice atte Cok, Fr. inscr., N.A.   VII. Two Shs. from the brass of Ralph Criel, Esq., **1447**, and w., C.   VIII. A Sh. with arms of Wode, and 3 sons, c. **1500**, parents and c. 3 daus. lost, S.C.

FARNINGHAM.   I. Wm. Gysborne, vicar, **1451**, hf. eff., C.   II. Alys Taillor, **1514**, sm., N.   III. *Wm. Petham, **1517**, and w. Alice (eff. lost), N.   IV. *Thos. Sibill, Esq., **1519**, and w. Agnes.

FEVERSHAM.   I. Seman [Tong, born at Thrughleigh, baron of the cinque-ports], **1414**, æt. 80, eff. all lost but feet (stolen within the last 30 years by workmen?), canopy and marg. inscr. partly covd., large, S.C., p. 176.   II. Wm. Thornbury, c. **1480**, in cope, canopy nearly all lost, 12 Lat. vv., C.   III. John Redborne, vicar, **1531**, with chalice and wafer, C., p. 179.   IV. Hen. Hatche, mcht.-adventurer, and a great benefactor to the Ch., **1533**, and w. Joan, with large canopy, marg. inscr., S.Tr.   V. Rich. Colwell, mayor of Feversham [**1533**], and ws. Agnes (with 2 sons and 3 daus.) and Agnes (with 3 sons and 1 dau.), marg. inscr. mutil., and 4 Eng. vv., S.A., pp. 120, 132, 224.   VI. A Mcht., c. **1580**, with mcht.'s mk. and initials S. N. B., inscr. lost, N.A., pp. 119, 120. VII. John Haywarde, mayor, **1610**, with 3 sons (Wm. the eldest dec.) and 3 daus.; he m. Anna, dau. and coh. of Thos. Cole; S.Tr. INSCRS. VIII. Edw. Thomassom, mayor, **1494**, and ws. Emota and Margaret, rel., S.Tr.   IX. Edw. Blakwell, Esq., lawyer, **1572**, with texts, C.   X. †Wm. Saker, jurat, **1594**, S.Tr.

FORDWICH. Aphra, dau. of Thos. Norton, Esq., and w. of Hen. Hawkins, Gent., **1605**, æt. 21, N., p. 246. *Introd.*, p. 246.

GOODNESTONE. I. Wm. Boys, **1507**, and w. Isabella, with 5 sons and 3 daus., Hy. Trin., N.   INSCRS. II. *Thos. Engeham, Esq., and w. Elizth., both dec. **1558** (effs. lost), with 2 sons and 5 daus., 7 Eng. vv.   III. †Vincent Boys, Gent., **1568**, æt. 36, and w. Mary, dau. of John Honeywood, Esq.; left 3 sons and 4 daus.   IV. Thos. Warren, Esq., chief customer of Sandwich, **1591**, æt. 80.

GOUDHURST. I. John, son of John Bedgbery, or Begebure, **1424**, in arm., canopy, inscr. lost, S.A., p. 189.   II. A Man in arm., c. **1490**; w., 6 chil., and inscr. lost, canopy much mutil. and partly covd., A.T., S.C. Perhaps Sir John Culpeper, 1480, and w. Agnes (Bedgebury).   III. —— Culpeper, in arm., and w., c. **1520**; w., 3 sons, 3 daus., and inscr. lost.

GRAVENEY. I. Dame Joan [de Feversham and son John?], c. 1370, hf. effs., canopy nearly all lost, marg. inscr. in Fr. mutil., N.A., pp. 134, 137, 163.   II. Robt. Dodde (eff. lost), and his son[-in-law] Rich. de Feversham, lord [of the manor], **1381**, in arm., loose (?), marg. inscr., A.T., S.C., p. 160.   III. John Martyn, justice of the court of common pleas, **1436**, and w. Anna [Boteler, 1458], holding hearts, canopy and marg. inscr., very large and fine, N.A., pp. 21, 89, 94, 107, 126. *Boutell's Series. Introd.*, p. 176 (det.)   INSCRS., &c. IV. Joan, dau. of Rich. de Faversham [No. II.], and [w. of John Boteler], of Graveney [**1408**], eff. lost, mutil. marg. inscr. and canopy left, S.A.   V. Thos. Borgeys, Esq., **1452**, eff. lost, marg. inscr., N.A.; he m. Anna, widow of John Martyn, and grandau. of No. IV.

HALLING. I. Silvester (dau. of Robt. Dene, Gent., and his w. Margt. Whyte), born Dec. 18th, 1554, m. Wm. Dalyson, Esq., June 29th, 1573, and afterwards Wm. Lambarde, Gent., 1583, dec. **1587**, leaving Silvester and Maximilian Dalyson, Multon and Margt. Lambord, and Gore and Fane, sons and twins, curious, qd. pl., mur., N., p. 221.   INSCR. II. Shs., one with 5 wounds to John Colard, for 37 years one of the king's clerks of the exchequer, and w. Margery, c. **1470** (?), C., p. 102.

*HALSTEAD. I. Wm. Burys, Esq., lord of the manor, **1444**, N. II. Wm. Petley, **1528**, and w. Alys, C.

HALSTOW, HIGH. I. †Wm. Groby, rector, **1399**, in ordinary dress, and his father Wm., 1396, hf. effs., partly covd., p. 63. II. Wm. Palke, minister, **1618**, and w. Ann, lower part of eff. of w. gone, sm., p. 230.

HARDRES, UPPER. I. John Strete, rector, **1405**, in acad., kng. to a bracket supporting the eff's. of SS. Peter and Paul, C., pp. 77, 173. *Waller*, pt. vii. II. Thos. Harderes (mutil.), 1572, and his brother John, **1575** (eff. lost), sons of Rich. Harderes, Esq., and his w. Mabell, sm., S.C.   INSCRS. III. Geo. Hardres, Esq., **1485**, S.A. IV. Dorothy Hardres, dau. of Sir John Preston, **1533**, S.A.   V. Mabell, dau. of Sir Thos. Wrathe, and w. of Rich. Hardres, Esq., **1579**, and chil., Thos., Thos., Roger, John, Peter, Mary, Jane, S.A.

HAWKHURST. John Roberts (?) and w., c. **1495**, with 6 sons and 6 daus., mcht.'s mks. and initials. *Bib. Topog. Brit.*, vol. ix.

HAYES. I. John Osteler, rector, c. **1460**, hf. eff., C. *Fisher.* II. Sir John Andrew, priest, c. **1470**, sm., C., p. 25. *Fisher.* III. Sir John Heygge, parson, **1523**, sm., C.   INSCRS. IV. Robt. Garet, rector of Hayes and Chiselhurst, notary public **156-**, dec. 1566 (?). *Fisher.*   V. John Hoare, rector for 18 years, **15[84?]**, æt. 83, 8 Eng. vv., C.

HERNE. I. Peter Halle, Esq., and w. Elizth., dau. of Lord Wm. Waleys and Dame Margt., dau. of Lord John Seynclere, c. **1420**, N.C., p. 166. *Waller*, pt. vii.; *Boutell's Mon. Br.*, p. 62.   II. John Darley, vicar, c. **1450**, in acad., mutil. marg. inscr. and 6 Lat. vv., C., pp. 82, 126. *Duncombe's Hist. of Herne*, pl. viii. p. 98, in *Bib. Topog. Brit.*; *Waller*, pt. xiii. III. Christiana, w. of Matthew Phelip, citizen, goldsmith, and mayor [in 1464] of London, **1470**, in mantle, with rosary, pecul., N.C., pp. 30, 171, 211. *Duncombe*, ibid.; *Boutell's Series.*   IV. Elizth., w. of Sir John Fyneux, **1539**, 10 Eng. vv., pecul., C., pp. 215, 243. She was converted to the protestant faith by Ridley, who was vicar of Herne.   V. John Sea, Esq., of Underdowne in Herne, **1604**, and 2 ws., Martha, dau. of Thos. Hammond, Esq., of St. Albans in East Kent (with 6 sons and 3 daus.), and Sara, eldest dau. of Thos. Boys, Gent., of Barfreston (with 1 son and 1 dau.), chil. lost, N.C.   INSCRS. VI. Antony Loveryk, Esq., **1511**, and w. Constance, N.C.   VII. Andrew [Benstede (?), vicar 1511—1531], 2 Lat. vv., N., p. 92.

HEVER. I. Margt., w. of Wm. Cheyne, **1419**, in mantle, N., pp. 104, 170. *Gough*, vol. ii. pl. xxiv. p. 53; *Knight's Old England*, No. 1,630, &c.; *Boutell's Series.*   II. Sir Thos. Bullen, knt. of the garter, earl of "Wiltscher & Ormunde," **1538**, large, A.T., N.C., pp. 223, 233. *Thorpe's Cust. Roff.*, pl. xix. p. 115; *Waller*, pt. xii.; *Knight's Old England*, No. 1,421; *Eng. Cyclopædia, Arts and Sciences*, vol. ii. p. 303, &c.   III. Wm. Todde, schoolmaster to Chas. Waldegrave, Esq., **1585**; his friend Wm. Napper, Gent., of Puncknowle, Dorset, pos., mur., C. *Knight's Old England*, No. 1,631. INSCRS. IV. John Cobham, Esq., of Devonshire, **1399**, and w. Joan, "dame de leukenore," and their son Renaud, with sh. V. Sybbill, dau. of Roocke Green, Esq., of Sampford, Essex, **1614**. A matrix of a very small cross to Hen. (?), son of Sir Thos. Bwllayen, inscr. lately (?) lost, N.C.

HOATH. I. Isabella Chakbon, head gone, c. **1430**, C. II. Antony Maycot, **1532**, and w. Agnes, with 2 sons and 5 daus., eff. of w. palimpsest, sm., N.

HOO, ST. WERBURGH. I. John Brown, vicar, c. **1410**, hf. eff., C. II. Rich. Bayly, vicar [**1412**], head gone, marg. inscr. mutil., large, C., p. 181. *Introd.*, p. 181 (det.) III. A Civilian, c. **1430**, inscr. gone, C., p. 202. IV. Stephen and Rich. Charlis, **1446**, N. V. Thos. Cobham, Esq., **1465**, and w. Matilda, inscr. lost, S.A., p. 194. VI. Dorothy, w. of John Plumley, **1615**; her son Jas. pos., C. VII. Mr. Jas. Plumley, lived at the parsonage, **1640**, and w. Anna, with 7 chil., Jas., Wm., John, Sara, Mary, Anna, Elizth., C. INSCR. VIII. John Beddyll, **1500**, N.

HORSEMONDEN. I. [John de Grovehurst], priest, c. **1340**, with inscr. on his breast stating he gave [in 1338] the manor of Leveshothe to the abbat and convent of Beghame for a chaplain for the Ch. of Horsmonden and chapel of Leveshothe, canopy mutil., marg. inscr. gone, C., p. 143. *Thorpe's Cust. Roff.*, pl. xxiii. p. 121; *C. C. Soc. Illustr.*, No. vi. p. 195; *Boutell's Series;* and *Arch. Journ.*, vol. vi. p. 90. II. Joane, dau. of Jeffry Berry, of Midley, and w. of John Austen, **1604**, æt. 36, leaving 9 chil., John, Jeffry, Benj., Robt., Joane, Francis, Peter, Thos., Robt.; her husband pos., N.

HORTON KIRBY. John Browne, Esq., **1595**, æt. 28, and w. Elizth., dau. of Launcelott Batherst, Esq., m. only 3 months, the w. pos.

IGHTHAM. I. Sir Rich. Clement, in tabard, and 1st w. Anne, dau. of Sir Wm. Catesby, of Northants., **1528**; w. and lower part of male eff. lost, C. II. Jane Dirkin, w. of John Cradock, Gent., **1626**, she had 3 chil., Dorothy (m. Rich. Amherst, Esq., and had Dorothy and Jane), Nevill, Elizth. (m. John Howell, Gent.), N., p. 248. INSCRS. III. Geo. Multon, Esq., justice of the peace, **1588**, æt. 85, and w. Agnes, dau. of Thos. Powell; they had 2 sons and 2 daus., N. IV. Dame Dorothy, only dau. and h. of Chas. Bonham, Esq., w. of Sir Wm. Selby, **1641**, C. There is a curious mur. monument to the same. See Arch. Journ., vol. xiii. p. 416. V. Two vv. to 3 infant brothers, C. VI. Four eleg. vv.

KEMSING. Thos. de Hop, priest, c. **1320**, hf. eff., C., p. 143. *Boutell's Series.*

LEE. I. Mrs. Isabell, dau. of Thos. Hatteclyf, Esq., and w. to Mr. Nich. Annesley, Gent., **1582**. II. Nich. Ansley, 33 years servant to Queen Elizth., he died serjeant of her cellar, **1593**, æt. 58, in arm., 6 Eng. vv. *Gent. Mag.*, vol. lxxxii. 1812, pt. i. p. 529. The brass of Elizth. Couhyll, 1513 (p. 214), now lost (?), is engr. in *Malcom's Views*.

LEEDS. Wm. Merden, **1509**, and w. Alice, with 1 son and 1 dau., sm.

LEIGH. I. A Shroud in a tomb, and fem. eff. summoned by an archangel, c. **1580**, qd. pl., sm., C., p. 56.   INSCRS. II. *Thos. Chanu, Esq., **1407**, and w. Christina, now (1860) in Ch. chest.   III. John Stace, of Hollenden, **1539**; his cousin and h. John Stace pos.   IV. John Stace, of Moreden, eldest son of John Stace, of Hollenden, **1590**, C.   V. *John Stace, of Hollenden, **1591**, had 3 sons and 2 daus., he left his son Geo. his h., mur., C.

LINSTEAD. I. Elizth., dau. and sole h. of Rich. Parke, Esq., of Kent, and w. of John Rooper, "she ledd her lyfe most vertuously and ended the same most Catholykely, whose soule God p'don," c. **1570**, with 1 son and 2 daus.   II. *John Worley, Gent., of Skuddington in Tonge, **1621**, and w. Alice, C.

LULLINGSTONE. I. Sir Wm. Pecche, **1487**, 6 eleg. vv., engr. c. 1530 (?), C., pp. 30, 32, 171, 179, 194. *Introd.*, p. 194 (det.)   II. Mrs. Alice Baldwyn, "late gentilwoman to the ladi Mary princes of Englond," **1533**, sm., C.   III. Elizth., w. of John Hart, Gent. (by whom she had a son, Sir Percyvall Hart), and afterwards of Geo., brother to the Rt. Hon. Lord Cobham, **1544**.   INSCR. IV. Lord John de Rokesle, **1361**, with sh., C.   *Fisher* (?).

LYDD. I. John Motesfont, LL.B., vicar, **1420**, in acad., inscr. reversed, marg. inscr. with Lat. vv., mutil., C., p. 84.   II. John Thomas, **1429**, N.   III. Thos. Godefray [of Romney, **1430**], and w. [Joan, dau. of —— Tamworth], with canopy, worn, now in N.   IV. A Civilian, c. **1510**, inscr. lost, sm., N.   Perhaps Robt. Cokenham, or Cokyram.   V. A Civilian, c. **1530**; w., chil., and inscr. lost, N.   VI. Thos. Harte, yeoman, "sūtyme Baylye" of Lydd, **1557** (loose), and w. Malyn, N., p. 244. *Introd.*, p. 244 (fem. eff.)   VII. Peter Godfrye, **1566**, and w. Joue [dau. of John Eppes], 1556, with 5 sons, 4 daus. lost, N.   VIII. Thos. Bate, jurat, **157[0?]**, æt. 72, 16 Eng. vv., he left 4 chil., N.   IX. A Civilian and w., loose, c. **1590**, inscr. lost. Perhaps Wm. Dallet, thrice bayliff, 1598, æt. 48, with 5 sons and 3 daus.   X. John Berrey, chosen jurat in 1558, five times baylif, **1597**, æt. 82, 4 Eng. vv., N.   XI. Clement Stuppeny, chosen jurat 1565, seven times baylif, **1608**, æt. 83, 8 Eng. vv., A.T., covd. by a table, S.C.   XII. Laurence Stuppenye (son of No. XI.), formerly jurat and bayliff, **1613**, N.

INSCRS. XIII. Mary, only dau. and h. of Thos. Partridge, Gent., of Iden, Sussex, 1st w. of Thos. Godfrey, Esq., 1580, had a son Peter, engr. c. **1600**. XIV. John, fourth son of Thos. Godfrey, Gent., student at a school near Doane, and at Hart's Hall, Oxford, **1612**, æt. 18. XV. Robt., infant son of Rich. Godfrey, Gent., **1616**, C. Ch. visited July, 1858; the loose brasses were then in the vestry.

MAIDSTONE, ALL SAINTS. I. Thos. Beale, twice mayor, **1593**, and 2 ws., Joan and Alice, and with 6 sons and 2 daus. surviving of 21 chil.; also his ancestors, Wm., 1534, and w. Joan; Robt., 1490, and w. Agnes; John, 1461, and ws. Agnes and Alice; Wm., 14..., and w. Kath.; John, 1399, and w.,—with their chil., engr. very sm. in 6 tiers each of 3 divisions; qd. pl., mur., p. 3. II. Rich. Bees[ton?], **164[0?]**, and w. Elizth., dau. of John Raw..., with 4 sons and 3 daus. kng., qd. pl., inscr. cut in stone. Some fine matrices, one a coped priest under a triple canopy, p. 138.

MALLING, EAST. I. Thos., son of Robt. Selby, **1479**, and w. Isodia, C. II. Rich. Adams, vicar, prebendary "magne misse" in the monastery of West Malling, **1522**, in almuce, with chalice and wafer, sm., C., pp. 76, 79.

MALLING, WEST. I. Wm. Millys, **1497**, sm., N. II. Wm. Skott, Gent., **1532**, sm., N. III. Elizth., dau. of Sir Anthony Babington, and w. of Geo. Perepoynt, Esq., **1543**; lower part of eff., 3 or 4 sons, 2 or 3 daus., and inscr. lost; on reverse of a sh. part of a canopy, C., pp. 48, 115, 244. *Introd.*, p. 244. See Harl. MS., 2,129, fol. 130 a.

MARGATE, ST. JOHN'S. I. Nich. Canteys, **1431**, with flowing beard and anelace, S.A., pp. 62, 202. *Waller*, pt. ii. II. A Heart and scrolls for Thos. Smyth, vicar, **1433**, C., p. 107. *Gent. Mag.*, vol. lxvii. 1797, pt. ii. p. 641; *Oxford Man.*, p. 114; and *Introd.*, p. 263. III. John Parker, **1441**, and w. Joan, N., p. 53. IV. Peter Stone, **1442**, with anelace, sm., N C. V. John Daundelyon, Gent., **1445**, inscr. restored, N.C., pp. 53, 192. *Gent. Mag.*, vol. lxiii. 1793, pt. ii. p. 791; *Waller*, pt. xiv.; *Boutell's Mon. Br.*, p. 70; *F. Delamotte's Ornamental Alphabets*. VI. Rich. Notfelde, **1446**, a skeleton, restored, N., pp. 53, 171. VII. Sir Thos. Cardiff, vicar for 55 years, **1515**, sm., C. *Lewis's Hist. of Tenet*, p. 100; *Gent. Mag.* (see No. II.) VIII. —— Cleybroke (?), c. **1600**, in arm., inscr. lost, covd., S.C., p. 237. *Oxford Man.*, p. 105, and *Introd.*, p. 237. INSCRS. IX. Alex. Norwood, 1557, and his son Alex., 1583 with Joan his w., **1605**, C. X. Roger Morris, **1615**, p. 129. Perhaps another brass under the pews.

MEREWORTH. I. John de Mereworth, **1365-6**, or **1370-1**; legs of eff., shafts of canopy, and greater part of canopy gone; large, S.A., pp. 140, 160. *Thorpe's Cust. Roff.*, pl. x. p. 89, fig. 1 (incorrectly assigned to Sir Nich. Hawberk). II. Wm. Shosmyth, citizen and "pelliparius" of London, **1479**, and w. Juliana, chil. and inscr. lost, sm. III. Sir Thos. Nevell, a councillor of Hen. VIII., **1542**, not in arm., mur., p. 102. *Drummond's Noble Brit. Fam.*, vol. ii. INSCRS. IV. Shs. and inscrs. to his ancestors, placed, in **1583**, by Sir Thos. Fane and his w. Maria Nevill, mur.

MILTON-NEXT-SITTINGBOURNE. I. A Man in arm., c. **1470**, chil. and inscr. lost, S.C. II. *John Norwood, Esq. (?), **1496** (?), in tabard, and w. loose. III. *Thos. Alcfe, Esq., **1539** (eff. lost), and w. Margt., 8 Eng. vv., mur., C.

MINSTER, ISLE OF SHEPPEY. Sir John de Northwode, cross-legged, with shield, &c., and w. Joan (Badlesmere), c. **1330**, C., pp. 22, 53, 149, 150, 165, 166. *Stothard's Mon. Effigies*, p. 50; *C. C. Soc. Illustr.*, No. vi. p. 205; *Boutell's Mon. Br.*, pp. 42, 44; *Introd.*, p. 23.

MONKTON. I. A Priest, c. **1460**, inscr. lost, N. Perhaps John Spycer, vicar. *Boutell's Series.* INSCR. II. Lebbic Orchard, **1580**, on same slab as No. I.

NEWINGTON. I. Wm. Monde, **1488**, and John Sayer, N.A. II. Lady Norton, w. of John Cobham, Esq., of Kent, **1580**, with 2 sons, 6 Eng. vv., C. III. Frannces Holbrok, Gent., **1581**, and 2 ws., with 4 sons and 6 daus. and 1 son and 2 daus., C. IV. Mary, widow of Edw. Brooke, alias Cobbum, Esq., **1600**, C. Two Shs.

NEWINGTON-JUXTA-HYTHE. I. †A Lady, c. **1480**, hf. eff., p. 172. II. Thos. Chylton, **1501**, in shroud, and w. Thomasina, with 2 sons and 1 dau, N.C., p. 97. *Antiq. Etching Club*, vol. i. pl. 27. III. John Clerk, vicar, **1501**, with chalice and wafer, sm., N.A. IV. Rich. Ryege, **1522**, and ws. Alice, Joane, Kath., S.A. V. Hen. Brockman, Esq., of Bichborough, lord of the manor, **1630**, in arm., and w. [Helen, dau. of Nich. Sawkins], and 7 chil. [Wm., Zouch, Margt., Helen, Elizth., Mary, Agnes], marg. inscr., S.A. INSCRS. VI. Margt., dau. of Humf. Clerke, Esq., and w. of Wm. Brockman, **1610**, æt. 73. VII. Helen, dau. of No. V., and w. of John Strout, clerk, æt. 25, dau. Helen æt. 6 weeks, and son Hen. æt. 3, all dec. **1628**.

NORTHFLEET. I. [Peter de] Lacy, rector, prebendary of the prebend of Swerdes in Dublin Cath. [**1375**], canopy all lost but part of the pediment, marg. inscr. mutil., large, loose, C. *Thorpe's Cust. Roff.*, pl. xxviii. p. 135; *Boutell's Series.* II. Wm. Lye, rector, **1391**, hf. eff., inscr. lost, loose, C. *Thorpe* (ibid.) III.

[Wm. Rikhill, Esq., eldest son of Sir Wm. Rikhill], and w. Kath. [**1433**], legs of male eff. and nearly all the marg. inscr. lost, loose, N.A., p. 208. *Thorpe*, pl. xxx. p. 136. INSCR. IV. Margt., w. of Wm. Baron, citizen and dyer of London, **1429**, they had a son Nich., C., loose. In *Thorpe* (pl. xxix. p. 136) is engr. the slab of Wm. Hesill, baron of the exchequer, 1425, and w. Agnes.

ORPINGTON. I. Thos. Wilkynson, M.A., prebendary of St. Wulfram at Ripon, rector of Harrow-on-the-Hill and Orpington, **1511**, in cope. *Thorpe's Cust. Roff.*, pl. x. fig. 2, p. 137. II. †A Priest under pews. Perhaps John Gower, LL.B., vicar, 1522, N.C. *Thorpe*, pl. xxvi. fig. 1, p. 128. INSCR. III. Wm. Gulby, Esq., **1439**, with sh., C.

PECKHAM, EAST. I. A Civilian and w., c. **1525**, inscr. lost, sm., N. INSCR. II. Rich. Etclesley, rector, **1426**, C., p. 76. The eff. in almuce, with chalice, now lost, is engr. in *Thorpe's Cust. Roff.*, pl. x. fig. 3, p. 89.

PEMBURY. Elizth., eldest dau. of Nich. Rowe, Esq., of Hawckwell, **1607**, æt. nearly 8 years, C.

PENSHURST. I. A Sm. Cross to Thos., son of Sir Thos. Bwllayen, c. **1520**, repaired (?), S.C., p. 222. II. Pawle Yden, Gent., son of Thos. Yden, Esq., **1514**, not in arm., and w. Agnes, with 1 dau., S.C., p. 223. *Thorpe Cust. Roff.*, pl. xxxi. p. 141. INSCRS. III. Walter Darnowll, **1507**, and ws. Joan and Annes (effs. lost), with 4 sons and 3 daus., N. IV. Sir Wm. Sydney, chamberlain and steward to Ed. VI. when Prince, lord of the manor, **1553**, S.C. V. Margt., dau. of Sir Hen. Sydney and his w. Mary, **1558**, æt. 1¾ years, S.C. VI. John Paswater, steward to Sir Thos. and Sir Hen. Cheyney, **1577**, and w. Elizth., mur., C. VII. Wm. Darkenoll, parson, **1596**, æt. 78, 11 Eng. vv. VIII. Bridget, æt. 6 months, and Alice, æt. 2 years and 4 months, both dec. **1599**, daus. of Sir Robt. Sydney and his w. Barbara, S.C.

PLUCKLEY. I. †John Dering, Esq., **1425**, sm., marg. inscr. in 6 Lat. vv. mutil., N. *Weever's Fun. Mon.*, p. 292; *Ant. Repert.*, vol. iii. p. 169. II. Rich. Malemayns, Esq., **1440**, much worn, N. III. A Man in arm., Rich. Dering, Esq., 1544-5 (?), under a trefoil arch, sm., qd. pl., engr. c. **1600** (?), S.A., p. 52. *Ant. Repert.*, vol. iii. p. 149. IV. A similar eff. to No. III., not on qd. pl., p. 52. V. Julyen Deryng, gentylwoman, **1526**, pecul. The brass of Rich. Deryng and 2 ws., c. 1470, now lost, is engr. in *Weever's Fun. Mon.*, p. 293.

PRESTON, near FAVERSHAM. I. Valentine Baret, 1440, in arm., and w. Cecilia, **1442**, p. 190. II. Wm. Mareys, esquire to Hen. V.

and to Cardinal Hen. [Beaufort], **1459**, pp. 132, 195.   III. †Thos. Finch, Esq., **1615**, and w. Bennet, dau. and h. of Wm. Maycott, of Feversham, 1612, partly covd., C.

RAINHAM.   I. Wm. Bloor, Gent., **1529**, not in arm., pecul., C., p. 28.   II. John Norden, Esq., and ws. Joan (with about 7 chil. lost), Agnes (with 2 sons), Elleyn (with 2 sons), Elizth., c. **1580**, effs. of first 3 ws. lost.

RINGWOULD.   I. Wm. Abere, **1505**, and ws. Alys and Ann, with 2 sons and 3 daus.; all lost but inscr., chil., and upper part of one w.; sm., N.   II. John Upton, **1530**, pecul., sm., C., p. 215.   INSCR. III. Elizth., w. [of Robt. Gaunt, **1550**?].

ROCHESTER, ST. MARGARET'S.   I. Thos. Cod, vicar, **1465**, in cope, hf. eff., engraved on both sides, 9 Lat. vv., restored, inlaid in a copper plate, now mur., pp. 34, 48, 79. *Boutell's Series*, and *Chr. Mon.*, p. 154.   INSCR. II. Sir Jas. Roberts, priest, **1540**, a chalice lost, C., p. 125.

ROMNEY, NEW.   I. Thos. Lamberd, **1510**, 8 Eng. vv.   II. *Thos. Smyth, jurat, **1610**, æt. 68, and w. Mary, with daus. Elizth. and Mary, N.C.

ROMNEY, OLD.   John Ips. and w. Margt., sm., c. **1520**.

ST. LAURENCE, THANET.   I. Nich. Manston, Esq., **1444**, with collar of SS, now mur., N.A., p. 189. *Waller*, pt. xiv.   II. A Lady, c. **1490**, inscr. lost, now mur., N.A.   INSCRS., &c. III. Four Shs. with arms of Manston, fem. eff. (if not No. II.) lost. IV. Sir Adam Sprakeling, son of Robt. Sprakeling, Gent., **1610**, æt. 58, leaving 17 chil., Robt., Adam, John, Hen., Hen., Chas., Thos., Judeth, Elizth., Kath., Mary, Annis, Kath., Marg., Franc., Margt., Hanna.   V. Adam Sprakeling, Gent., 2nd son of Sir Adam Sprakeling, dec. **1615**, leaving 4 chil., Robt., Hen., Kath., Rebecca.   The inscr. (now lost?) of John Pawlyn, 1462, and w. Margery, is engr. in *Gent. Mag.*, vol. lxxi. 1801, pt. ii. p. 1,097.

ST. MARY-IN-THE-MARSH.   I. Matilda Jamys, **1499**.   II. Wm. Gregory (son of No. I.), **1502**.

ST. NICHOLAS, THANET.   Valontyne Edvarod, Gent., 1559, and 2 ws., Agnes (with 4 sons and 2 daus.) and Joane, **1574** (with 3 sons and 6 daus. lost); and Thos. Parramore, 2nd husband of Joane, with 1 son and 1 dau. lost, N.C., p. 54.

ST. PETER, THANET.   I. Rich. Colmer, "carpentarius," **1485**, and w. Margt.   II. Nich. Esstone, **1503**, and w. Alice, sm., S.A. Several shs.

SALTWOOD.   I. John Verien, rector of Sandherst, c. **1370**, hf. eff., C.   II. Thos. Brokhill, Esq., **1437**, and w. [Joan?], marg. inscr.,

N.A., p. 190.   III. An Angel, hf. eff. holding a heart, with sh. and inscr. for Dame Anne, w. of Wm. Muston, **1496**, C., p. 108.

SANDWICH, ST. CLEMENT. I. A Mcht., c. **1490**; w., 1 son, and inscr. gone; with canopy, much worn, N.   INSCRS. II. Geo. Rawe, Gent., mayor and customer of the town, mcht.-adventurer, and haberdasher of London, and w. Sara, both dec. **1583**, they had 7 sons and 5 daus., C.   III. Elizth., w. of Nich. Spencer, Gent., customer of Sandwich, **1583**, S.C., p. 57.

SEAL.   I. Lord Wm. de Bryene, lord of the manors of Kemsing and Sele, **1395**, marg. inscr., large, C., p. 162. *Boutell's Series; Ant. Etch. Club*, vol. iii. pl. 17.   INSCR. II. John Tebold, alias Theobauld, Gent., **1577**, eff. lost, S.C.   There was a brass here to Thos. Brenton, Bp. of Rochester, 1389. See Weever, Fun. Mon., p. 325.

*SELLING, near FAVERSHAM. I. A Civilian, c. **1530**, w. and inscr. lost.   FRAG. II. Some chil., c. **1530**, parents gone.

SHELDWICH. I. Lord Rich. Atte Lese, **1394**, and w. Dionisia (lower part of eff. gone), with canopy, C., pp. 160, 168. *Boutell's Series*. II. John Cely, Esq., **1426**, and w. Isabella, S.C., p. 190.   III. Joan, w. of Wm. Mareys, **1431**, hf. eff. in shroud, C., pp. 107, 171.

SHORNE.   I. John Smyth, **1457**, and w. Marion, hf. effs., sm., with scroll.   II. A Lady, c. **1470**, headless, loose.   III. A Chalice and wafer for Thos. Elys, vicar, **1519**, C., pp. 125, 223. IV. Elynor, only dau. and h. of John He[arnd]en, Gent., of Shorne, w. of Edm. Pagge, Gent. (by whom she had Thos., Wm., Jas., Hearnden, Edm., Geo., Lyonell, John, Elizth., An, Benett, Dorithie, Annes), and then of John Allen, Gent., **1583**.   INSCRS. V. Frag. of inscr. of Wm. Pepyr, vicar, **1468**, eff. lost, C.   VI. Thos. Sharpe, lawyer, **1493**, N.   VII. *Edm. Thomas, **1558**, loose. VIII. *Geo. Page, Gent., **1639**, and w. Elizth., dau. of John Somers, of St. Margt.'s, Rochester, C.   IX. *Geo. Haysden, Gent., **1670**. Edmund Page and w., lost, p. 30.

SNODLAND. I. Roger Perot, **1486**, sm., N.   II. Edw. Bischoptre and w. Margt., both dec. **1487**, sm., N.A.   III. Wm. Tilghman the elder, **1541**, and ws. Isabell and Joane, sm., N.

SOUTHFLEET.   I. Joan, dau. of Sir John Reskemer, of Cornwall, and w. of John Urban, Esq., **1414**, on a bracket, with inscrs. above and below it, p. 55. *Boutell's Mon. Br.*, p. 123; and *Gent. Mag.*, vol. xxx. N.S. 1848, p. 604.   II. John Urban, Esq., **1420**, not in arm., and w. Joan, dau. of Sir John Reskymmer, a cross between them lost, p. 55.   III. John Tubney, rector, archdeacon of St. Asaph's, and chaplain of John Lowe, bp. of Rochester [**1457**?], in cope, hf. eff., C. *Boutell's Mon. Br.*, p. 114.   IV. Thos. Cowrll, c. **1520**, in shroud, very sm.   V. John Sedley, an auditor of the king's exchequer, and w. Elizth., c. **1520**, with 2 sons and 4 daus., Hy. Trin. lost, marg. inscr. mutil., on a sm. inscr. "Dyg not w^t yn too flote of this tombe," A.T., p. 53.   INSCR. VI. John Sedley, Esq., 1581, and w. Anna, dau. of John Colepeper, Esq., of Aylesford, **1594**, p. 53.

STAPLE. A Civilian of the Lynch family (?), c. **1510**, inscr. gone.

STAPLEHURST. A Civilian and 2 ws., c. **1580**, all lost but eff. of one w., A.T., S.C., p. 245.   *Introd.*, p. 246.

STOKE. *Wm. Cardiff, priest, **1415**, head gone.

STONE. I. John Lumbarde, rector, **1408**, sm. eff. in the head of a cross, on which the inscr. and text from Job, "Credo quod," &c., are engr., C., pp. 174, 181.   *Gough*, vol. ii. pl. xi.* p. 28; *Boutell's Series; Cresy's Stone Ch.; Introd.*, p. 174.   INSCRS. II. Sir John Dew, priest (?), c. **1530**, C.   III. Robt. Chapman, Esq., mcht.-venturer, draper, freeman of London, owner of Stone Castle, **1574**, 8 Eng. vv. and 4 shs., C., p. 119.   IV. Wm. Carew, Esq., freeman of the Drapers' Company, owned Stone Castle, æt. 70.

SUNDRIDGE. I. Roger Isly, lord of the manors of "Sondresshe and ffrenyngham," **1429**, in arm., C.   II. Sir Thos. Isley, **1520** (?), and w. Elizth., dau. of Sir Rich. Guldeford, 1515 (?), with 10 sons and 3 daus., inscr. lost, C., p. 232.   See Harl. MS., 3,917, fol. 73.

SUTTON, EAST. Sir Edw. Filmer, 1629, in arm., and w. Elizth., dau. of Rich. Argall, Esq., **1638**, with 18 chil., Robt., Edw., John, Thos., Reginald, Thos., Rich., Hen., Augustin, Mary, Margt., Elizth., Judeth, Kath., Anne, Jane, Susanna, Sarah, qd. pl., C., p. 238. *Waller*, pt. xv.

TEYNHAM. I. John Frogenhall, Esq., **1444**, with collar of SS., inscr. gone, S.Tr., pp. 187, 189.   II. *Robt. Heyward, **1509**, a dau. and a child in swaddling clothes lost, his parents Wm. and Kath. are buried close by.   III. *Wm. Wreke, **1533**, sm., C.

THANNINGTON. Thos. Halle, Esq., **1435**, C., p. 198.

TROTTERSCLIFFE. Wm. Crofton, Gent., B.C.L., of Grey's Inn, **1483**, not in arm., and w. Margt., 148-.

TUNSTALL. I. Ralph Wulf, rector, **1525**.   II. A Lady, c. **1590**, inscr. lost.   INSCRS. III. Margt., dau. of Sir Jas. Crowmer, w. of John Rycyls, h. of the manor of Eslyngham, **1496**.   IV. Hen. Guyldeford, Esq., captain of Artclyffe Fort, near Dover, third son of Sir John Guyldeforde, of Kent, **1595**, æt. 57.   V. Christopher Webbes, B.D., president of St. John's Coll., Camb., rector, son of John Webbes, Esq., of Gillingham, Kent, had 16 chil., **1610**, æt. 63, his w. Kath. pos.

ULCOMBE. I. Wm. Maydeston, Esq., **1419**, canopy, marg. inscr.

mutil., A.T., N.A., p. 189.   II. Ralph Sentleger, Esq., **1470**, and w. Anne, N.A., p. 197.

WESTERHAM. I. Rich. Hayward, **1529**, and w. Anne, with 5 sons and 3 daus. N.   II. Thos., son of John Potter, Gent., **1531**, p. 239. *Introd.*, p. 239.   III. John Stacy, **1533**, and ws. Margt. and Joan, sm., loose at the vicarage.   IV. Two Civilians, c. **1545**, sm.   V. Wm. Myddilton, Esq., **1557**, and ws. Elizth. and Dorothe.   VI. *Wm. Stace, **1566**, and ws. Jone (with 2 sons and 1 dau.), and Alice (with 5 sons and 7 daus.), chil. lost (?), p. 63.   VII. Sir Wm. Dye, parson of Tattisfylde, **1567**, S.A., p. 230.   INSCRS. VIII. John Lovestede, c. **1450**.   IX. Rich. Potter, **1511**.   X. Rich. Potter, Esq., **1563**, and ws. Elizth., Anne, Alice, had 20 chil., left 3 sons and 10 daus., on reverse base of a column and a sh. below it, Flemish, loose, p. 47.   XI. Six Daus., c. **1520**, on reverse a head with scroll, background diapered with quatrefoils, loose, p. 48. XII. Seven Sons, loose, c. **1540**.

WICKHAM, EAST. I. John de Bladigdone and w. Maud, c. **1325**, very sm., hf. effs., in a cross mutil., loose, pp. 136, 162, 165. *Fisher* (?); *Boutell's Chr. Mon.*, p. 125; *Oxford Man.*, p. 74; *Introd.*, p. 135.   II. Wm. Payn, yeoman of the guard, **1568**, and ws. Elizth., Joan (eff. lost, with 1 son), and Joan (with 2 sons), now mur., pp. 127, 226. *Thorpe's Cust. Roff.*, pl. li. p. 257 (male eff.)

WICKHAM, WEST. I. Wm. de Thorp, rector, **1407**, sm., C. *Fisher*.   II. Sir John Stokton, priest, **1515**, sm., C. *Fisher*.   An incised slab of a priest, c. 1370, hf. eff., p. 40.

WOODCHURCH. I. Nichol de Gore, priest, c. **1320**, sm. eff., surrounded with Fr. Lomb. inscr. in 2 vv., in a cross, stem lost, C., pp. 135, 142, 143. *Paley's Man. of Goth. Arch.* (front.); *Boutell's Series; Introd.*, p. 135.   II. *Thos. Harlakinden and w. Elizth. (dau. of Robt. Watno, Esq., of Warminghurst), **1539**, S.A.   INSCRS. III. Roger Harlakynden, Esq., son of Wm. Harlakynden, Esq., **1523**, S.A.   IV. Martin Harlakinden, Esq., **1584**; by his w. Deborah, dau. of Thos. Whetenhall, he left an only child, Deborah, S.A.   V. *A large Sh. on the tomb of —— Waterhouse.

WROTHAM. I. Thos. Nysell, **1498**, and w. Alice, with 5 sons and 5 daus., N.   II. John, son of John Burgoyn (of Impington, Camb., Esq.), c. **1500**, sm., N.   III. Thos. Pekham, Esq., and w. Dorathea, **1512**, N.   IV. Reynold Pekham the elder, esquire for the body to Hen. VIII., **1525**, and w. Joyce [Colepeper], 1523, in heraldic dresses, N.   V. A Man in arm., c. **1530**, w. and inscr. lost, p. 232. *Introd.*, p. 232. Perhaps Jas. Peckham, Esq., 1533, and w. Agnes.   VI. Wm. Clerke, Esq., **1611**, æt. 76, in arm., and

w. Ann, dau. of Hugh Carthright, Esq., of Ossington, Notts., with 2 sons and 10 daus., p. 237. *Introd.*, p. 237 (det.)   VII. Elizth., youngest dau. of John Norton, Esq., of Boughton Monchelsea, and w. of Hen. Crispe, Gent., **1615**, with 5 sons and 4 daus., p. 247. *Introd.*, p. 247 (part of eff.)   INSCR. Jas. Pekham, Esq., **1500**, and w. Margt., dau. of Thos. Burgoyn, Esq., of Impington, Camb., with 4 sons and 5 daus., all effs. lost but the daus., N.   An incised slab, a Civilian and w., with 1 son and 6 daus., mur., 16th cent.   The brasses of John Sundressh, priest, 1426, and Thos. Gawge, D.D., chancellor of York, 1470, loose in the vestry coalhole in 1768, are now lost; the former is engr. in *Thorpe's Cust. Roff.*, pl. xxvi. fig. 2, p. 128.

WYE.   John Andrew, Thos. Palmere, and their w. Alice, with 3 sons and 8 daus., c. **1440**, 4 Lat. vv., mutil.   *Hist. and Topog. of Wye*, 1842, p. 66.

INSCRIPTIONS, &c.

BENENDEN.   Edm. Gibbon, "ye principall fovnder of ye free scole of Benninden, & gave the livinge that thereto belongeth," **1607**. C. BROMLEY.   Isabella, w. of Rich. Lacer, mayor of London [in 1345], **1361**.   BURHAM.   Robt. Ware, **1506**, and w. Joan, N.   *CHIDDINGSTONE.   I. Rich. Streatfield, **1601**, æt. 40 (an iron plate?). II. Margt. Waters, widow first of John Reeve, **1638**; her dau. Fraunces, w. of John Seyliard, pos.   COLDRED.   Wm. Fyntch, Gent., **1615**, and w. Bennet, dau. and h. of Christopher Hunniwood, Gent., and 7 chil.   CUXTON.   I. Master John Buttyll, chaplain to Prince Edw. [dec. 1568], engr. c. **1540**; on reverse, portions of small figures under canopies, Flemish (?), 15th cent., eff. lost, A.T.. S.C., p. 47.   II. John ——, woolpacker of London, and w. (?) Katheryn ......, Chryst churche, **1545**; on reverse, portions of 2 inscrs., one to Adam (?) Atte Sterre, **1395**, and [w. Ma?]riona, 139-, loose.   DARENTH.   John Crepehege and w. Joan, mur., N. *Gough*, vol. ii. pl. xx. p. 249.   EWELL.   Rich. Lamynge, yeoman, **1597**, æt. 46, and w. Thomazen, dau. of Edw. Merewether, and 6 chil.   FOLKESTONE.   Hen. Philpot, Gent., thrice mayor, **1603**, æt. 59, and w. Judith, with 9 chil.   GILLINGHAM.   John Bregge, vicar, c. **1420**.   Several brasses are lost (p. 104) : one was a Priest in a cross, with a marg. inscr. to Wm. Beaufitz, 1433; rubbings of it and of another (a Man, in arm., and w.) are in the possession of J. B. Nichols, Esq.   HIGHAM.   I. Robt. Hylton, yeoman of the guard to Hen. VIII., **1523**, 8 Eng. vv., mur., N.C.   II. Elizth., dau. of Sir Wm. Crayford, and w. of Wm. Boteler, Esq., of Rochester, **1615**, æt. 32, and 4 chil., mur., N.C.   HYTHE.   John

Bredgman, jurat, **1581**, 4 Eng. vv., "he gatt 3 sutes of ye crowne, the mortmaine fayer & Mayraltie for Heythe...he was the Baylye last & Mayer first," N.　LEWISHAM.　Geo., son and h. of Wm. Hatteclyff, Esq. (treasurer of the king's land in Ireland, and a clerk of the household accounts), **1514**, C. Eff., now lost, engr. in *Thorpe's Cust. Roff.*, pl. xxvi., fig. 3, p. 128.　MEOPHAM.　John Folham, vicar, **1455**, p. 257.　MERSHAM.　Two Lat. vv. on a scroll, eff. lost. RIPPLE.　I. Thos., son of John Warren, Esq. (son of Wm. Warren, Esq., chief customer of Sandwich, &c.), **1591**, æt. 80.　II. John Warren, Esq., son of No. I., **1612**, æt. 50; he had 12 chil.　ROLVENDEN. *Inscr. of Dedication of Chantry, **1444** (see Appendix B.), S.C.　SANDWICH, ST. PETER'S.　*Thos. Gilbert, Gent., searcher of Kent, **1597**, æt. 37, and w. Kath., dau. of Robt. Fylmer, of East Sutton, and 9 chil.

At SWANSCOMBE is a brass under pews.

The brasses are lost at GREENWICH (p. 127), LOWER HARDRES (p. 236), MINSTER IN THANET (p. 87), SPELDHURST, ROCHESTER CATHEDRAL (p. 62), and RECULVER. The brass of John Sandewey, Esq., and w. Joan, c. 1480, once at the latter Ch., is engr. in *Bib. Topog. Brit.*, vol. i. pl. x. p. 165.

Lancashire.

CHILDWALL.　†Sir R. Norreys and w., c. **1510**, mur.

MANCHESTER CATHEDRAL.　I. Jas. Stanley, bp. of Ely, warden of the coll. of Manchester, **1515**, lower part lost, rel., pp. 55, 70, 73. *The Ch. of the People*, vol. iv. p. 101, July, 1859.　II. †A Man in arm., sm.　III. †Sir John de Bryan, wife (head gone), and chil., c. **1465**, much mutil.　IV. Anth. Mosley, mcht., **1607**, æt. 70, and w. Alice, with 8 chil., Oswald, Francis, Edw., Rich., Rowland, Helen, Alice, Anne, qd. pl., mur.　V. Oswald Mosley, Esq., of Ancoates, **1630**, æt. 47, and w. Anna, with 8 chil., Nich., Edw., Oswald, Sam., Francis, Anne, Margt., Mary, qd. pl., mur.　FRAG. Two pediments of canopies, c. **1480**, belonging to brasses of the Ratcliff family (?).

MIDDLETON.　I. Edm. Assheton, rector, **1522**, holding chalice and wafer, pecul., C., pp. 29, 78.　*Boutell's Series.*　II. John Laurence, Esq., Rich. Radclyffe, Esq., of Towre, Thos. Bothe, Esq., of Hakensall, and their w. Alice, **1531**, one male eff. lost, pecul.　III. Rich. Assheton, Esq., lord of the manor, **1618**, æt. 41, and w. Mary, dau. of Thos. Venables, baron of Kinderton, with 8 chil., Rich., Rodolph, John, Jas., Wm., Thos., Dorithea, Maria.　IV. Ralph Assheton, Esq., **1650**, æt. 45, in arm., with scarf, and w. Elizth., dau. of John Kaye, Esq., of Woodsome, Yorks., and 6 chil. (2 in shrouds), Rich., Ralf, John, Elizth., Mary, Anne, curious, p. 238. *Chetham Society's Publications* (?).

ORMSKIRK. A Man in a tabard, with arms of the Scarisbrick family, c. **1500**, large, p. 199.

SEFTON. I. Margt., dau. of Sir Rich. Molyneux, w. first of John Dutton, Esq., and then of Wm. Buleley, Esq., she founded and endowed a chantry, **1528**, with double canopy, p. 92. *Engr.* —— 1822 (?). II. Sir Wm. Molineux, lord of the manor, 1548, æt. 65, in arm., and 2 ws., Jane, only dau. and h. of Rich. Rugge, of Salop. (who had Rich., Jane, Anne), and Elizth., dau. and h. of Cuthbert Clifton, Esq. (who had Wm., Thos., Anne), engr. c. **1570** (?), curious, pp. 52, 53, 113, 122. *Waller*, pt. xiii. III. *Sir Wm. Molyneux, in arm., son of No. II., **1568**, and 2 ws.

WHALLEY ABBEY. *Raffe Caterall, Esq., **1515**, and w., with 21 chil., mur. *Illustrated Itinerary of Lancashire*.

WINWICK. I. Peers, son and h. of Sir Thos. Gerard, **1492**, in tabard, with 1 son, triple canopy mutil. He m. Margt., dau. of Sir Wm. Stanley, of Hatton. and h. of Sir John Bromley. *Waller*, pt. xii. II. Lord Peter Legh, died at "Lyme in Hanley," **1527**, in arm. with chasuble over it, and w. Ellen, dau. of Sir John Savage, buried at Bewgenett, 1491, in heraldic mantle, marg. inscr., about 4 sons and 5 daus. lost, Leigh Chapel, pp. 63, 90, 91. *Waller*, pt. v.; *C. C. Soc. Illustr.*, No. iii. p. 93. *Introd.*, p. 91 (male eff.)

INSCRIPTIONS, &c.

ECCLES. *Inscr. and sh. to Wm. ——, 16th cent. PRESTWICH. *Inscr. and sh. to Isaac Allen, 17th cent.

Leicestershire.

AYLESTONE. *Wm. Heathcott, parson, **1594**, holding a book, marg. inscr. with 12 eleg. vv., C., p. 230. *Nichols' Leicestershire*, vol. iv. pl. 13, p. 30.

BARWELL. I. Mr. John Torksay, B.D., 1613, and w. (who pos. **1614**), with 1 son, 4 daus., and an infant dec., qd. pl., mur., C., p. 216. *Nichols' Leic.*, vol. iv. pl. 76, fig. 18, p. 477. *Nichols' Hinkley* in *Bib. Topog. Brit.*, vol. vii. p. 427. II. †Rich. Breton, Gent., of Elmisthorp (son of Robt. and Alice Breton), **1659**, æt. 60, and w. Elizth., dau. of Jas. Bayley, Esq.; they had 3 sons and 4 daus., mur., C. *Ibid.*

Q

BOSWORTH, HUSBAND'S. †Mr. Rice Jemlae, rector, **1648**, æt. 68, holding a book. *Nichols' Leic.*, vol. ii. pl. 81, fig. 18, p. 467.

BOTTESFORD. I. [Hen.] de Codyngtoun, rector, prebendary of Oxtoun and Crophill in Southwell Coll. Ch., **1404**, in cope, with SS. Peter, John Evang., John Bapt., Cath.—Paul, Jas. the Great, a Bp., Margt., fine triple canopy with B. V. Mary in centre pediment, marg. inscr. mutil., large, C. *Nichols' Leic.*, vol. i. pl. 33, p. 98. II. John Freman, rector, c. **1440**, in cope with initials, head and 3 scrolls lost, 6 Lat. vv., C. *Nichols' Leic.*, vol. i. pl. 22, fig. 13, p. 9. INSCR. Abr. Fleming, rector of S. Pancras, London, died here **1607**, æt. 56.

DONINGTON, CASTLE. [Robt.] Staunton, Esq., and w. Agnes, **1458**, with 4 sons and 3 daus. standing beside their parents, fine groined canopy and marg. inscr. both mutil., A.T., S.C., p. 196. *Nichols*, vol. iii. pl. 109, fig. 18, p. 782; *Boutell's Series. Arch. Journ.*, vol. vi. p. 91 (effs.) *Gent. Mag.*, vol. lx. 1790, pt. ii. pl. iii. p. 1,181 (male eff.)

HINCKLEY. †A Civilian and 2 ws., c. **1490** (one eff. and inscr. lost). *Nichols' Leic.*, vol. ii. pl. 117, fig. 22.

HOBY. †A Man, in arm., and w., mutil., c. **1490**, inscr. lost, S.A., covd. by pews. *Nichols*, vol. iii. pl. 39, fig. 28, p. 267.

LEICESTER, WIGSTON'S HOSPITAL. Wm. Fysshcr, first master of the hospital founded in 1473 [a mistake (?) for 1513] by Wm. Wigston, mcht., four times mayor of the staple of Calais, c. **1540**, in shroud, marg. inscr. *Nichols' Leic.*, vol. i. pl. 34, p. 495; *Bib. Topog. Brit.*, vol. viii. pl. 45, p. 927.

LOUGHBOROUGH. I. †Giles Jordan, fishmonger of London, and w. Margt., c. **1480** (?). II. Thos. Marchall, mcht., **1480**, and w. Agnes, with 6 sons and 6 daus., pecul., p. 30. INSCRS., &c. III. Robt. Frye, rector, "privati fuit is subcustos nempe sigilli" [**1435**], 4 Lat. vv., eff. lost, marg. inscr. mutil. IV. Part of shaft of a large double canopy to Gilbert Meringe, Gent., **1481**, and w. All these brasses are engr. in *Nichols' Leic.*, vol. iii. pls. 121, 122, pp. 897, 901; and *Bib. Topog. Brit.*, vol. viii. pl. 69, p. 1,381.

LUTTERWORTH. I. John Fildyng, 1403, and w. Joan, **1418**, N.A. *Nichols' Leic.*, vol. iv. pl. 38, p. 263. II. A Civilian, with short knife (feet gone), and w., c. **1470**, inscr. lost, pecul., nailed to a board. Perhaps John Renolds, mcht., 1473. This brass and 3 others (a Civilian and w., c. 1530, and a Lady, c. 1500) are engr. in *Nichols' Leic.*, vol. iv. pl. 40, p. 263. Some of these brasses were stolen about 1836 by a man who was transported for the offence. No. II. was preserved by Mr. Hilpack, the parish clerk.

MELTON MOWBRAY. A large inscribed Heart, with inscr. to Crystofer Tonson (or Gonson), 1498, and w. Elizth., parents of Wm. Tonson, of London, esquire for the body to Hen. VIII., and of Barth. (?) Tonson, vicar of the Ch., who pos. **1543**.

SAXELBY. Wm. [Brokysbi, patron] of the Ch. [**1523**], in arm., and 2 ws., all lost but eff. of one w. and part of marg. inscr., pecul., partly covd., S.A. *Nichols' Leic.*, vol. iii., pl. 60, fig. 5, p. 403.

SCALFORD. I. A Civilian, c. **1520**, kng.; w., a cross above, Hy. Trin. below, about 5 sons and 6 daus., and marg. inscr. all lost, now in vestry. *Nichols' Leic.*, vol. i. pl. 54, fig. 27, p. 315. INSCRS. II. Edw. Darker, Gent., **1651**, æt. 85, and w. Anne, they had 15 chil. III. Jas. Bardsey, B.D., son of Edm. Bardsey, D.D., and his w. Sara, **1651**, æt. 37.

SHEEPSHED. Thos. Duport, Esq., **1592**, æt. 78, in arm., and w. Cornelia (Belknapp), m. about 50 years, with 3 sons and 4 daus. (surviving out of 13 chil.), qd. pl., mur.

SIBSON. John Moore, M.A., rector, prebendary of Osmonderley, **1532**, in almuce, with scrolls from hands to eff. of our Lord above, pp. 79, 102. *Nichols' Leic.*, vol. iv. pl. 147, fig. 23, p. 954.

STAPLEFORD. Geoff. Sherard, Esq., and w. Joyce, dau. of Thos. Assheby, Esq., of Lovesby, **1492**, N., p. 198. *Nichols' Leic.*, vol. i. pl. 63, p. 340; *Gough*, vol. ii. pl. cxxix. p. 372.

STOKERSTON. I. John Boville, **1467**, in arm., head gone, and w. Isabella (Murdac ?), in mantle, holding hands, inscr. lost, large, S.C., p. 194. *Nichols' Leic.*, vol. ii. pl. 132, fig. 31, p. 820. II. A Man., in arm., and w., c. **1490**, upper part covd.; 8 sons and 2 daus. and inscr. lost. *Ibid.*, fig. 30. Perhaps Hen. Southill, 1485, and w., or John Southill and w. Elizth., 1493.

SWITHLAND. Agnes Scot, "*antrix* deuota domino ferrers vocitata," c. **1455**, 4 Lat. vv.

THURCASTON. *John Mershden, rector, canon of Windsor, **1425**, in cope (lower part gone), canopy, C. *Nichols' Leic.*, vol. iii. pl. 140, fig. 9, p. 1,058.

WANLIP. Sir Thos. Walsch, lord of the manor, and w. Kath., who built the Ch. of "Anlep" and hallowed the Ch. yard, **1393**, marg. inscr. in Eng. (see Appendix B.), C., pp. 160, 168, 169. *Nichols' Leic.*, vol. iii. pl. 146, fig. 29, p. 1,097; *Waller*, pt. xiv.

WYMONDHAM. Sir Morys Barkeley (eff. lost) and w. Margery, **1521**, marg. inscr. mutil., S.Tr.

INSCRIPTIONS, &c.

STOKE GOLDING. *Thos. Brooksby, **1684**.

The brasses are lost at the following Churches: BITTESWELL (Wm. Townysynd, Esq., and w. Mabyll, c. 1500. *Nichols' Leic.*, vol. iv. pl. 14. fig. 10, p. 45), HUNGERTON (Mary Cave, 1510, p. 214. *Nichols' Leic.*, vol. iii. pl. 41, fig. 21, p. 282), PECKLETON (—— Vincent, Esq. (?), c. 1540. *Nichols' Leic.*, vol. iv. pl. 140, p. 872), SHEEPEY MAGNA (p. 258), STANFORD (Four brasses of the Cave family, p. 125. *Nichols' Leic.*, vol. iv. pl. 52, p. 356). The brass of Thos. Chaworth, Esq., 1458, and w. Isabella, once at LAUND ABBEY, is in private possession. It is engr. in Nichols' Leic., vol. iii.

Lincolnshire.

ALGARKIRKE. Nich. Robertson, mcht. of the staple of Calais, **1498** (with signet ring at end of rosary), and ws. Isabella and Alice, (1458, buried at St. Botolph's, Boston), with hf. effs. of B. V. Mary and Child, 4 Lat. vv., other inscr. lost (?), pecul., Belfry.

ASHBY PUERORUM. I. Rich. Lytleburye, Esq., of Stancsbye, 1521, in arm., and w. Elizth., dau. of Sir Edm. Jenney, of Knodshall, Suffolk, 1523, engr. c. **1560** (?). II. A Man (Littlebury?), in arm., and w., with 10 chil., Humfrey, Thos., Wm., John, Robt., Edm., Elizth., Jane, Anne, Mary.

BARTON-UPON-HUMBER. Simon Seman, vintner, alderman of London, **1433**, marg. inscr. and Evang. symbs., large, C., pp. 129, 200, 210.

BIGBY. I. Elizth., dau. of Sir Wm. Tyrwhyt, of Kettylby, and w. of Wm. Skypwith, Esq., son and h. of Sir John Skypwith, of Ormesby, Linc., c. **1520**. II. Edw. Naylor, "a faithfull and painefull minister of God's word," rector 16 years, **1632**, and w., with 2 sons and 5 daus., 4 eleg. vv., qd. pl., mur., p. 230.

BOSTON. I. Walter Pescod, mcht., a benefactor to the guild of St. Peter, **1398**, and w., each under a triple canopy, a super-canopy and its shafts composed of niches with 14 SS., of which there remain Peter, John Evang., Jas. the Great, Matthew, Philip, Simon—Thos., Bartholomew, Jas. the Less, Jude; lower part of male eff., w., Hy. Trin. (?), and marg. inscr. lost; large, N.A., pp. 131, 137, 164, 165. II. A Priest, c. **1400**, in cope, with SS. John Bapt., Peter, Thos., Jude (?), John Evang. (?), Paul, Andrew, Bartholomew, inscr. lost, worn, large, C., pp. 28, 105. III. A Civilian (only the feet left) and 2 ws., c. **1400**, on a bracket with canopy; the stem, inscr., and lower part of one w. lost; sm., S.A., pp. 28, 137, 171. IV. A Lady, c. **1460**, head, feet, and inscr. lost, on reverse part of the eff. of a widow, c. **1390**, loose, p. 46. V. A Civilian and w., c. **1480**, with Evang. symbs., much worn, loose, S.A. VI. Thos. Lawe, "senator Bostoniensis," thrice mayor, 1657, æt. 71, a bust, his son Thos. pos. **1659**. *P. Thompson's Boston, &c.*, p. 196. FRAGS., &c. VII. Two Sons and 7 daus., c. **1490**, parents lost, S.A. VIII. Portions of large canopies with 3 effs. of mourners, c. **1500** (?), of foreign design, man and w. lost, much worn, large, N., p. 22. IX. Portion of shaft of canopy with 2 sm. effs., partly covd. by font, two entablatures and part of triple canopy belonging to it (?), c. **1500** (?), like No. VIII., loose, man and w. lost, p. 22. X. Nine Sons, c. **1500**, loose. XI. Two Hands, N., p. 23. XII. Inscr. to Mr. Robt. Townley, alderman, comptroller of the port, and w. Joane; m. 28 years, had 2 sons and 4 daus.; both dec. **1585**; by her first husband, Rich. Skepper, Gent., Joan had 2 sons and 1 dau. The loose brasses are kept in the library. Matrices, pp. 23, 33, 39. In the Add. MS. by Kerrich (No. 6,732, pp. 20, 21), in the Brit. Mus., are notices of some brasses now lost.

BROUGHTON. A Man, in arm. (Rydford?), and w. (—— Strange?), c. **1370**, partly covd., triple canopy and inscr. lost, C., pp. 107, 160. *Boutell's Series.*

BURTON COGGLES. *Sir Humphrey Cholmeley, **1620**, and w.

BURTON PEDWARDINE. *A Lady, c. **1631**. A matrix of the brass of Alice (Longchamp), w. of Roger de Pedwardyn, 1330, hf. eff., with Lomb. inscr., A.T., N.C. Of her husband it is said, "Ecchiam de Burton Pedwardyn cum capella beæ Mariæ integerrime construxit, excepto le South Isle cum Capella Sci Nicholai Epi, constructis per Parochianos ejusdem villæ." Harl. MS. 6,829; note by Rev. C. R. Manning.

BUSLINGTHORPE. Sir Rich., son of Sir John de Boselyngthorpe, c. **1310** (earlier?), hf. eff., with sh., and marg. inscr. in Lomb. letters, N., pp. 107, 146, 148, 150. *Waller*, pt. x.; *Boutell's Mon. Br.*, p. 113, and *Chr. Mon.*, p. 146; *Introd.*, p. 150.

COATES, GREAT. I. Isabella [Kelke], w. of Roger Barnardiston, Esq., c. **1420**, in mantle, pecul., N., p. 28. II. *Sir Thos. Barnardiston, son of Thos. Barnardiston, dec., of Milkkylcotes, Linc., **1503**, and w. Elizth., dau. of Geo. Newport, of Pelham, Herts., with 8 sons and 7 daus., the Resurrection, marg. inscr., C., pp. 103, 226.

CONISHOLME. John Langholme, Esq., **1515**, and w. Anne, with 5 sons and 9 daus., marg. inscr., N.

COVENHAM, ST. BARTHOLOMEW. John Skypwyth, Esq., **1415**, pecul., C., p. 28.

CROFT. A Man in arm., c. **1310**, hf. eff., N., pp. 146, 149. *Boutell's Mon. Br.*, p. 114, and *Chr. Mon.*, p. 147.

DRIBY. *Jas. Prescot, Gent., **1583**, and w. Alice, mur., N.

EVEDON. *A Civilian and w., c. **1600**, with 5 sons and 8 daus., nailed to the front of a gallery. To this belong (?) a sh. and inscr. to Dan. Hardeby, Esq., J.P., 4 Eng. vv., his 4 sons and 8 daus. pos.

FISKERTON. A Priest, c. **1490**, in cope, pecul.

GRAINTHORPE. A fine large cross, c. **1380**, stem and marg. inscr. nearly all lost, C., p. 135. *Boutell's Series*, and *Chr. Mon.*, p. 43.

GUNBY. I. *A Knight of the Massyngberd family and w., c. **1405**, with collars of SS., with canopy mutil., marg. inscr. replaced by one to Sir Thos. Massyngberde [**1552**], and w., large, N., pp. 149, 185. *Boutell's Series*. II. Wm. Lodyngton, justice of the common pleas to Hen. V., **1419**, with anelace, feet on a leopard, canopy, once on A.T., C., p. 90. *C. C. Soc. Illustr.*, No. vi. p. 199.

HAINTON. I. John Heneage, **1435**, and w. Alice, N.C. II. Sir Thos. Henneage, son and h. of John Henneage, Esq., and chief gentleman of the privy chamber to Hen. VIII., **1553**, in tabard, (head lost), and w. Kath., dau. of Sir John Skipwith, with dau. Elizth., w. of Lord Willoughbye, of Parham, in heraldic dresses, mur., A.T., C. INSCR. III. John Henn'age, Esq., **1530**, and w. Kath., mur., N.C.

HALTON HOLGATE: Bridgett, dau. and h. of Thos. Thorey, and w. of John Rugeley, **1658**, æt. 21, qd. pl., N.

HARRINGTON. John Copledike, Esq., son and h. of Sir John Copledike, **1585**, in arm., and w. Anne (Etton), 1582, mur., C.

HATCLIFFE. *A Man, in arm., with collar of SS., and w.

HOLBEACH. 1. *A Man, in arm. (head gone), and w., c. **1420**. INSCR. II. †Joan, dau. of Sir Rich. Leake, and w. of Thos. Welby, Esq., **1457**, N.

HORNCASTLE. I. Sir Lionel Dymoke, **1519**, with 2 sons and 1 or 2 daus. (on reverse of a sh. an eff. playing on a violin, Flemish), pecul., mur., N.A., pp. 30, 47, 56. II. The same in shroud, head lost, with 6 Lat. vv., much worn, pecul.

INGOLDMELLS. Wm. Palmer, **1520**, with a "stylt," or small cross-handled staff, beside him, pp. 29, 123.

*IRNHAM. I. Sir Andrew Luttrell, **1390**, with canopy, large, N.C., p. 160. *C. C. Soc. Illustr.*, No. iv. p. 143; *Proceedings of Arch. Inst. at Lincoln*. II. A Man in arm., c. **1430**, C.

KELSEY, SOUTH. A Man, in arm., and w. with her head on a cushion, c. **1410**, pecul., N., pp. 28, 186, 188, 208. *Boutell's Series.*

LAUGHTON. A Man in arm., c. **1400**, with fine triple canopy, large; inscr. subsequently added to Wm. Dalison, sheriff, eschaetor, a J.P. and quorum of the co. of Lincoln, 1546 (?), and his son Geo., **1549**, A.T., S.A., pp. 53, 138, 139, 160. *Boutell's Series; Introd.*, p. 161.

LEADENHAM. Rt. Hon. Lady Elizth., dau. of the Rt. Hon. Earl of Lincoln, Lord Clynton and Saye, and w. of John Beresforde, Gent., **1624**, æt. 32; she left Thos., Mary, Fynes, qd. pl.

LINCOLN, ST. BENEDICT'S. *John Becke, mayor 1617, and w. Mary, **1620**, with chil., mur.

LINWOOD. I. John Lyndewode, woolman, **1419**, and w. Alice, m. 43 years, with canopy, and 4 sons and 3 daus. also under sm. canopies, 10 Lat. vv., large, p. 172. These were the parents of the author of the "Provinciale." II. *John Lyndewode, son of No. I., woolman, **1421**, with anelace, canopy mutil., large, p. 202. A matrix of a sm. cross-legged eff. (Sir Hen. ......) in arm., with ailettes, on a bracket, p. 146.

MABLETHORPE, ST. MARY. Elizth., dau. of Geo. Fitz William, Esq., and his w. Elizth., dau. of Thos. Barneston, of Great Coates, **1522**, C., p. 214.

NORTHOPE. A Civilian and 2 ws., c. **1600**.

NORTON DISNEY. *Wm. Disney, in arm., and w. Margt., with 9 chil., Rich., Wm., Thos., Francis, Anne, Mary, Margt., Kath., Briget; below Rich. Disney [**1578**?], in arm., and 2 ws., Nele, dau. of Sir Wm. Husoy, with 7 sons and 5 daus. (Sara, Ester, Judeth, Judeth, Susan), and Jaune, dau. of Sir Wm. Ayscoughe, all hf. effs., on reverse a Dutch inscr., qd. pl., mur., fastened with hinges, pp. 47, 218, 236. *Gough*, vol. i. p. 122. A Matrix of a cross-legged eff. in arm.

ORMSBY, SOUTH. I. A Lady in mantle, c. **1420**, pecul., C., p. 28. II. Sir Wm. Skypwyth, **1482**, and widow Agnes, with 1 son and 2 daus., canopy, C., p. 198.

PINCHBECK. Margt. [Carr], w. of John Lambart, **1600** (?), qd. pl., with 27 shields arranged genealogically from Wm. I., qd. pl., mur., C., p. 3. *Gent. Mag.*, vol. lxi. pt. ii. 1791, pl. iii. p. 916 (a sh.)

RAUCEBY. Wm. Styrlar, vicar, canon of Shelford, **1536**, sm., now in vestry.

SALMONDY. *A Civilian, 15th cent., much worn, N.

SCOTTER. Marmaduke Tirwhit, Esq., 4th son of Sir Wm. Tirwhit, **1599**, æt. 60, and w. Ellen, dau. of Lionel Reresby, Esq., m. nearly 40 years, with 5 sons and 5 daus., qd. pl., mur., N.

SCRIVELSBY. I. A Man, in arm. (head gone), and w., c. **1430**, canopy much mutil., inscr. lost, pp. 189, 208.   II. Sir Robt. Demoke, bart., **1545**, A.T., N.A., p. 233. He was champion at the coronation of Hen. VIII.

SLEAFORD. I. *A Civilian and w., with 7 sons and 3 daus., c. **1520**, male eff. and inscr. lost, C.   INSCRS. II. Three Lat. vv., eff. of a priest lost, S.A., p. 140.   III. *Rich. Pykeworth, mercer, **1557**, with mcht.'s mk., N.A.

SOMERSBY. Geo. Littlebury, **1612**, mur., C.

SPILSBY. I. Margery [dau. of Wm. Lord Zouch, of Harringworth, and] w. of Robt. de Wylughby, Lord of Eresby [**13**]**91**, in mantle, with head on cushions, marg. inscr., large, N.C. *Boutell's Series.* *J. Simpson's List of Sepulchral Brasses* (frontispiece).   II. A Man in arm., of the D'Eresby family, and w., c. **1410**, under fine triple canopy, its shafts and the inscr. lost, C., pp. 28, 160, 171, 185, 187, 188, 208. *Boutell's Series.* Probably the brass of Wm. Lord Willoughby D'Eresby, 1409, and his 1st w. Lucy, dau. of Roger Lord Strange, of Knokyn, or his 2nd w. Joan, 2nd dau. of Thos. Holland, Earl of Kent.

STALLINGBOROUGH. *Sir Wm. Ayscugh and w. Margery, c. **1510**, C.

STAMFORD, ALL SAINTS. I. John Browne, mcht. of the staple of Calais, 1442, in gown with full sleeves and mantle, standing on two woolpacks, and w. Margt., **1460**, large, inscr. detached between two mcht.'s mks., now mur., N.A.   II. Wm. Browne, son of No. I., founder of the hospital and builder of the steeple, **1489**, and w. Margt., dau. of John Stoke, Esq., of Warmington, Northants., canopy half lost, 12 eleg. vv., large, engr. c. **1460**, S.C., pp. 115, 201. *Peck's Annals of Stamford*, lib. xiv. p. 67, pl. D.   III. Margt., dau. of John and Elizth. [dau. of No. II.] Elmes, of Hendole [Henley?] upon Thames, **1471**, sm., S.C., p. 25.   *Peck*, pl. C.   IV. [John Browne, son of No. I.], **1475**, in alderman's mantle, and widow Agnes, 9 Lat. vv., now mur., N.A., p. 203.   V. A Civilian and w., c. **1490**, inscr. gone, loose. Perhaps Christopher Brown and w., 1518 (?).   VI. Hen. Wykys, vicar, **1508**, in cope, head gone, worn, loose, p. 79.   INSCR. VII. Alice Bredmeydew, sister of Wm. Browne, **1491**, loose. The loose brasses are in the possession of the Rev. C. Nevinson, Warden of Brown's Hospital, to whom the author is indebted for information respecting the foregoing brasses.

STAMFORD, ST. JOHN'S. I. Nich. Byldysdon, alderman, and w. Kath., **1489**, with 4 sons and 5 daus., pecul., now mur., S.C. *Peck*, pl. A.   II. Hen. Sargeaunt, rector, **1497**, worn, inscr. lost, loose in Ch. chest, C.   *Peck*, pl. B.   INSCR. III. *Wm. Gregory, mcht., and w. Agnes, now mur., S.C.

STOKE ROCHFORD. I. *Hen. Rochforth, **1470**, in arm., with helmet.   INSCR. II. Mastr. Olyver Sent John, esquire to the Duchess of Somerset, **1503**, and w. Elizth. (Bygod).

TATTERSALL. I. Hugh de Gondeby, supervisor of Ralph do Cromwell, **1411**, worn, now mur., p. 128.   II. Baron Ralph Lord Cromwell, founder of the College, **1455**, with cloak over armour, head and w. Mary, 1454, gone, canopy much mutil., with SS. Cornelius (?), Geo., Maurice (in arm.), Peter (in cope and crossed stole), misplaced, large, now mur., C., pp. 91, 195.   *Gough*, vol. ii. pl. lxii. p. 172.   III. Wm. Moor, "micuit more mitis morigeratus," B.D., 2nd provost of the Coll., canon of York, rector of Ledenham, **1456**, 12 Lat. vv., now mur., C., p. 96.   IV. *Joan (Stanhope), widow of Humphrey Bourchier, Lord Cromwell, **1479**, in mantle, with mutil. canopy, and SS. Mary, Christopher, Dorothy, Geo., Anna (?), Edmund, large, now mur. against roodscreen, N., pp. 175, 214. *Gough*, vol. ii. pl. xcviii. p. 267.   V. Lady Matilda [Stanhope], widow of Sir Robt. Willughby, niece of Ralph Lord Cromwell, and a special benefactor to the Coll., **1497**, with canopy, with SS. Thos Cant., Christopher, John Evang., Michael, Anna, Helena, Syra (?), Elizth., large, now against roodscreen, N.   *Gough*, vol. ii. pl. cxvii. p. 329.   VI. A Priest [Provost Warde?], c. **1510**, in cope, with 12 Apostles, inscr. lost, large, now mur., C., p. 105.   *Gough*, vol. ii. pl. lxvi. p. 179.   VII. Wm. Symson, chaplain to Edw. Hevyn (?), **1519** (eff. engr. c. 1480?).

THEDDLETHORPE, ALL SAINTS. Robt. Hayton, Esq., **1424**, pecul., S.C., pp. 28, 188. *Boutell's Series*.

WALTHAM. I. Joan Waltham, **1420**, with her son and dau., three hf. effs., N., p. 205. *Introd.*, p. 205 (det.)   INSCR. II. John Waltham and w. Margt., parents of John bp. of Salisbury, engr. c. **1420**, now on oak board. This inscr. was probably laid down in accordance with the directions contained in the will of the bishop: see the abstract in Kite's Brasses of Wiltshire, p. 97.

WINTERTON. John Rudd, **1504** (eff. lost), and 2 ws., marg. inscr., C.

*WINTHORPE. I. Rich. Barowe, mcht. of the staple of Calais, **1505**, and w.   II. Robt. Palmer, **1515**.

WRANGLE. *John Reed, mcht. of the staple of Calais, and w.

Margt., both dec. **1503**, 12 Lat. vv. and marg. inscr. in Eng. vv., mutil., p. 180.

INSCRIPTIONS, &c.

CAISTOR. John Ousteby, **1461**, and w. Joan, with 2 Evang. symbs. HARLAXTON. Wm. Strood and w. Agnes, both dec. Feb. 19th, **1498**. HECKINGTON. Wm. Cawdron, "baylyf of Hekyngton," **1544**. LINCOLN CATHEDRAL. A Mitre and sh. from the tomb of Bp. Russell, **1494**, loose in the library. See also p. 255. SCREDINGTON. Wm. Pylet, **1403**. WELBOURN. †Nich. Baylye, **1557**.

The brasses are lost at BRACEBOROUGH (p. 223) and GREAT GRIMSBY (p. 115). At KINGERBY there was a hf. eff. of a Man in arm., with sh. on the arm; and at NEWTON, near Folkingham, is the matrix of a small eff. in episcopal vestments.

Middlesex.

ACTON. Humfrey Cavell, Esq., **1558**, mur.

BRENTFORD, NEW. *Hen. Redmayne, chief mason of the king's works, **1528**, and w. Jone, with 2 daus., Hy. Trin. lost, mur., N. *Faulkner's Brentford*, p. 60.

CHELSEA. Lady Jane Gvyldeford, duchess of Northumberland, sole h. to the Rt. Hon. Sir Edw. Guyldeford, knight of the garter, &c., **1555**, in heraldic mantle, with 8 sons (lost) and 5 daus., mur. *Faulkner's Chelsea*, p. 98.

COWLEY. Walter Pope, yeoman, **1502**, and w. (either Joan his 1st w., or Alys his 2nd w.), sm., C. INSCR. *—— Collins, C.

DRAYTON, WEST. I. A Civilian, c. **1520**, inscr. lost, sm. II. Jas. Good, M.D., native of Dimock, Glouc., fellow of Magd. Coll., Oxford, **1581**, æt. 54, and w. Joan, dau. of Edw. Glinton, alderman of Oxford, m. 28 years, with 6 sons and 5 daus., 4 eleg. vv. allusive to name. INSCR. III. Rich. Roos, citizen and mercer of London, **1406**, and dau. Anna, and Anna dau. of Thos. Roos.

EALING. Rich. Amondesham, or Awnsham, mercer, mcht. of the staple of Calais, and w. Kath., c. **1490**, with 3 sons and 6 daus., mur. *Faulkner's Brentford*, p. 60.

EDGEWARE. Anth., eldest son of John Childe, goldsmith, and his w. Elizth., **1599**, æt. 3 weeks, in swaddling clothes, mur.

EDMONTON. I. John Asplyn, Godfrey Askew, and their w. Elizth., c. **1500**, sm. II. Nich. Boone and w. Elizth., c. **1520**, 8 Eng. vv. The male eff. was lately in the hands of the schoolmaster.   III. Edw. Nowell, Esq. (the son of Hen., son of Chas., the 4th son of Roger Nowell, of Little Merley, Lanc.), **1616**, and w. Mary, dau. of Wm. Isham, of Ilbruess (?), Somerset, **1600**, and 4 chil., Hen. (dec.), Isham, Edw., and Kath.

ENFIELD.   I. Joyce, a dau. and h. [of Sir Edw.] Charlton, lord Powes, and [Eleanor] lady Marche [the dau. of Thos. Holland, earl of Kent and first the w. of Roger Mortimer, earl of March], and w. of Sir [John Tiptoft], **1446**, in heraldic mantle and coronet, with fine triple canopy, marg. inscr. partly covd., engr. c. **1470** (?), large, A.T., N.C., p. 178.   *Gough*, vol. ii. pl. xlix. p. 137; *Nichols' Leic.*, vol. ii. pl. xiv. p. 41; *Boutell's Series; Trans. of Lond. and Middx. Arch. Soc.*, vol. i. p. 80.   II. Wm. Smith, served Kings Hen. VIII. and Edw. VI., Queens Mary and Elizth., and left 20s. quarterly to the poor, **1592**, and w. Jone, 2 sons and about 4 daus. lost, S.A. *Robinson's Enfield*, p. 51.   INSCRS. III. *Robt. Rampston, left 40s. yearly to the poor, **1585**.   IV. Jesper Nicoles, of St. Sepulchre's, London, left £50 to the poor, **1614**.   V. Anne, dau. of Rich. Gery, Esq., of Bushmead, Beds., **1643**, 10 Eng. vv.

FINCHLEY.   I. Rich. Prate, **1487** (eff. lost), and w. Joan, very sm.   II. Simon Skudemore, Gent., **1609**, æt. 83, and w. Jeane (Edwards), they had 1 dau., Elizth., C.   III. Nich. Luke, Gent. (2nd son of Walter Luke, Esq.), and w. Elizth. (dau. of No. II.), buried at Aversle, Hunts., with 3 sons and 3 daus., male effs. lost, sm., on same slab as No. II.   IV. Thos. White, citizen and grocer of London, **1610**, and 3 ws., Mary (with 5 chil., Abr., Anth., Jone, Mary), Mary (with 4 chil., Thos., Martha, Ann, Elizth.), and Honnor (with 4 chil., Thos., John, Sam., Hanna), qd. pl., mur., N.A., pp. 119, 120.   INSCRS. V. Wm. Blakwell and son Rich., c. **1500**, worn.   VI. An extract from the will of Thos. Sanny, of the Estend of Fyncheley, **1509**, who directed, after the death of his w., that the house called Fordis and Stowkefeld should yearly pay 40s. to priests to sing for his and his relations' souls, also a noble for repairs of the house, for highways, for the poor and charity, and "that thys be gravyn in a stone of m'bul that all men mey know hit," mur., C., p. 3.   VII. Wm. Godolphin, **1575**, eff. lost, rebus, sh., and 6 Eng. vv. ending, "Barnes flayeth to hem shall never dye."

FULHAM.   I. Margt. Svanders, a native of Ghent, w. of Gerard Hornebolt, the celebrated painter, and mother of Susan, the w. of John Pareker, the king's bowyer, **1529**, hf. eff. in shroud, two angels holding inscr., initials of husband (?) G. O., on a lozenge plate, Flemish, mur., Tower, pp. 20, 26, 133, 257. *Etched by J. Simco*,

1794; *Faulkner's Fulham*, p. 99; *Lithograph by L. Defferez, Ghent.* INSCR. II. Augustus Parker, **1590**, æt. 63, with mcht.'s mk. Faulkner engraves (pp. 67, 71, 78) the brasses (now lost) of Wm. Harvey, vicar, 1471; Sir Sampson Norton (?), 1517; and Sir Wm. Butts, chief physician to the king, 1545.

GREENFORD, GREAT. I. A Priest, c. **1450**, hf. eff., inscr. lost. Perhaps Simon Hert, rector, 1452. II. A Lady, c. **1480**, inscr. lost. III. Thos. Symons, rector, 2 Lat. vv., c. **1515**, now mur. He resigned in 1518. IV. Rich. Thorncton, **1544**, and w. Alys (eff. lost).

GREENFORD, LITTLE, or PERIVALE. I. Hen. Myllet, **1500**, and ws. Alice (with 3 sons and 6 daus.) and Joan (with 3 sons and 3 daus.), very sm., N. II. A Civilian, c. **1590**, inscr. lost, sm., now mur.

HACKNEY. I. Christopher Urswic, almoner of Hen. VII., eleven times ambassador, dean of York and Windsor, archdeacon of Richmond, he refused the bishopric of Norwich, **1524**, æt. 74, in cope, A.T., p. 227. *Engr.* —— (?) 1812; *Waller*, pt. ii.; *Introd.*, p. 228. II. John Lymsey [Esq., one of the six clerks of the court of chancery], **1545**, and w. Margt. [with 3 sons (now lost), Edw., Robt., Thos.], marg. inscr. mutil., pp. 50, 230, 244. *Introd.*, p. 231, restored from an early drawing. III. Arthur Dericote, Esq., of the Drapers' Co., **1562**, in arm., and 4 ws., Mary, Eme, Margt., Jone (with 2 sons), 12 Eng. vv., mur. IV. Mr. Hughe Johnson, vicar for 45 years, a benefactor to the poor of Hackney, and of Macclesfield, where he was born, **1618**, æt. 72, hf. eff., mur., p. 216. Alice Ryder, lost, p. 130. Nos. II. and III. are in the Tower of the old Ch. Woodcuts of all the brasses have been engr. for J. R. D. Tyssen, Esq., F.S.A.

HADLEY. I. Philip and Margt., chil. of Walter Grene, Esq., and his w. Elizth., and Margt. Somercotes, all three dec. Sept. 16th, **1442**, sm., male eff. lost, the rest of the brass now placed in different parts of the Ch. II. Wm. Turnour, **1500**, and w. Joan, with 4 daus., p. 212. *Introd.*, p. 212 (det.) III. John Goodeyere, Gent., 1504, and w. Joan, engr. c. **1495**, male eff. and chil. lost, p. 45. IV. A Civilian and w., c. **1520**, inscr. lost. V. Wm. Gale, Gent., M.A. Oxon., **1614**, æt. about 40, and w. Anne, dau. of Roger Bragge, Gent., with 2 sons Wm. and Nich. (dec.) INSCRS., &c. VI. Walter Tornor, **1494**, and w. Agnes, on same slab as No. II. VII. Anne (Goodere), w. of —— Walken, Eng. vv., 16th. cent., mur. VIII. Wm. Gale, citizen and barber chyrvrgion of London, a second time master of his Co. at his decease, **1610**, æt. about 80, and ws.

Elizth. (with 5 sons and 8 daus.) and Susan, inscr. and chil. only left.

HAREFIELD. I. Editha, w. of Wm. Newdegate, **1444**, sm., now mur. II. Geo. Assheby, Esq., a clerk of the signet to Hen. VIII., **1514**, and w. Rose [Eden], with 4 sons and 3 daus., engr. c. **1540**. III. Wm. Assheby, Gent., and w. Jane, **1537**, with 1 son and 7 daus., p. 97. IV. John Newdegate, serjeant-at-law, **15..**, and w. Amphilisia, dau. and h. of John Nevell, Esq., 1544, with 9 (?) sons and 7 daus., partly covd., A.T., pp. 90, 125. V. John Newdegate, Esq., **1545**, not in arm., and w. Anne, with 7 sons and 5 daus., mur., C. INSCR. VI. Geo. Assheby and w. Margt., both dec. **1474**, mur. The brasses (except No. V.) are in the Breakspear Chapel.

HARLINGTON. I. John Monemouthe, rector, c. **1430**, hf. eff. II. Gregory Lovell, Esq., lord of the manor and patron of the Ch., **1545**, and w. Anne, dau. of David Bellyngham, Esq., a son and dau. lost, A.T., C., p. 244. *Introd.*, p. 245 (det.)

HARMONDSWORTH. I. Two Civilians, one much mutil., also 6 sons and 6 daus., c. **1600**, loose in chest. INSCRS. II. Agnes Urmestone, widow, **1614**. III. Leonard Davies, pastor, **1623**. IV. Dan. Baukys, Gent., **1665**, and ws. Mary and Elizth., with 9 sons and 10 daus.; by Elizth. he had 2 sons and 4 daus.

HARROW. I. Edm. Flambard, in arm., and w. Elizth., c. **1370**, on a bracket with canopy, all lost but the pediments and male eff. which is loose, C., pp. 137, 138, 160. *Grose's Antiq.*, 1773, vol. i. pl. vi. (the fem. eff. was then left). II. John Flambard, c. **1390**, in arm., 2 Lat. vv., worn, large, C., pp. 93, 160. *Ibid.*, pl. vii. III. Simon Marcheford, canon of Sarum and Windsor, rector, **1442**, in cope, head and inscr. gone, rel., C. IV. A Priest, c. **1460**, in acad., hf. eff., inscr. lost, C., p. 77. V. [John] Byrkhed, priest, **1468**, in cope, with SS. B. V. Mary, Peter, John Evang., Rich., Paula—John Bapt., Anna, Laurence, Nich., Brigitta, head gone, canopy fine but mutil., as is the marg. inscr., C., p. 70. *J. P. Malcom's Views*, 1799. *Introd.*, p. 70 (det.) *Trans. of Lond. and Middx. Arch. Soc.*, not yet published (det.) VI. Geo. Aynesworth, **1488**, and 3 ws., Agnes (with 5 sons and 6 daus.), Isabella, Joan (with 2 sons), mur., S.Tr. VII. [Wm. Wightman], **1579**, in arm., and w. Etheldreda, m. 31 years, lived 27 years in the rectory, left 4 out of 5 chil. surviving, marg. inscr., p. 237. VIII. John Lyon, of Preston, Harrow, yeoman, left lands to a corporation for a free grammar school for the poor, for poor scholars at the universities, repairing highways, &c., **1592**, and w., mutil., now mur., p. 260.

IX. A Civilian and lady, c. **1600**, inscr. lost, lately loose.   X. John Sonkey, Gent., son of Thos. Sonkey, of Lanc., **1603**, inscr. lately lost (?), C.   Inscrs. XI. Thos. Downer, **1502**, and ws., mutil. XII. Dorothye, dau. of Wm. and Kath. Bellamy, of Uxenden, Harrow, and w. of Anthony Frankyshe, Gent., of Water-strafford, Bucks., **1574**, and 5 chil., Gerratt, Jone, Mary, Fraunces, Jone, also 10 Eng. vv. on a separate plate; on reverse of the former plate, part of an inscr. and figures wearing hoods and holding books; on reverse of the latter, part of the face, shoulders, &c., of a lady resting on a cushion and eff. of St. Paul, both plates Flemish. *Trans. of Lond. and Middx. Arch. Soc.*, not yet published.

Hayes.   I. Robt. Levee (or Lence), rector, c. **1370**, C.   II. Walter Grene, Esq., c. **1450**, marg. inscr., A.T., N.A., p. 193. *Waller*, pt. xiv.   III. Thos. Higate, Esq., **1576**, in arm., and w. Elizth. (mutil.), with 5 sons and 4 daus., 6 Eng. vv., A.T., S.A., p. 237.   Inscr. IV. Robt. Burgeys, rector, **1421**.

Hendon.   John Downner and w. Joan, with their son John, **1515**, eff's. of parents lost or covd., N.A.

Heston.   I. A Lady in childbed, with dead infant, ministering angel, &c., c. **1580**, qd. pl., C., pp. 102, 221.   Perhaps Constance, w. of Mardocheus Bownell, vicar, 1581.   II. *Rich. Awnsham, parson, **1612**.

Hornsey.   I. John Skevington, c. **1530**, a child in shroud, 2 Eng. vv., sh. lost, very sm., p. 220.   *Engr.* —— (?).   A John Skevington (perhaps the father) was sheriff of London in 1520.   Inscr. II. Rich. Ruggenale and ws. Isabella and Alice, c. **1420** (?).   An incised slab, p. 40.

Hillingdon.   I. John Lord Le Strange, lord of Knocking, Mahun, Wasset, Warnell, Lacy, and Colham, 1477, and w. Jagnette, sister of Elizth. [Woodville] Queen of England, and only child Joan, who pos. **1509**, with double canopy, inscr. lost, large.   *Gough*, vol. iii. pl. cxxviii. p. 370.   *Introd.*, p. 221 (det.)   II. Hen. Stanley, Esq., **1528**, inscr. lost (see Appendix B.), p. 232.   *Introd.*, p. 232. III. Drew Saunders, Gent., mcht., **1579**, and w., with mcht.'s mk., C., p. 118.   IV. John Atlee, high constable of Elthorne hundred for 36 years, **1599**, S.A.   Inscrs., &c. V. Six Sons and 3 daus., c. **1560**, rel., S.A.   VI. Anne, dau. of Myles Wilson, of Bristol, **1569**, 10 Eng. vv.   VII. Wm. Gomsall, citizen and ironmonger of London, **1597**, left 1 son and 2 daus.

Ickenham.   Edm. Shorditche, Esq., lord and patron of the Ch., **1584**, in arm., and w., with 2 sons and 1 dau., 8 Eng. vv., C. Some others under pews.

ISLEWORTH. I. A Man in arm., c. **1450**, beneath an inscr. to Wm. Chase, Esq., serjeant to Hen. VIII. and of his hall and woodyard, **1544**; on reverse of inscr. a Saint under a canopy, Flemish, now mur., pp. 50, 193. *Aungier's Hist. of Syon, Isleworth, &c.,* p. 162; and *Introd.,* p. 192. II. Margt. Dely, nun, **1561**, very sm., now on a pew-door, N.A., p. 89. *Aungier,* p. 146. III. A Civilian, c. **1590**. INSCRS. IV. Fraunces, dau. of Edw. Holland, Esq., of Denton, Lanc., and servant to the countess of Derby, **157–**; on reverse some scroll-work, 16th cent., Flemish, p. 47. V. Kath., w. of Rich. Cox, mcht.-taylor, **1598**, æt. about 48, she left 4 chil., Edw., Laurence, Margt., Jane, inscr. and sons only remain. The brasses (except No. II.) are in the vestry.

ISLINGTON, ST. MARY. I. A Man, in arm., and w., c. **1535**, of the Fowler family (?), sm., now mur., S.A. *Lewis's Hist. of Islington,* p. 230. II. Hen. Savill, Esq., and w. Margt., dau. of Thos. Fowler, Esq., **1546**, æt. 19, now mur., N.A., p. 245. *Ibid.* FRAG. III. A Pediment of a canopy, c. **1440**, now over No. I.

KINGSBURY. John Shephard, **1520**, and ws. Anne (with 7 sons and 3 daus.) and Mawde (with 5 sons and 3 daus.)

LONDON, ALL HALLOWS' BARKING. I. John Bacon, citizen and woolman of London, **1437**, and w. Joan, with scrolls encircling a heart, N.A., pp. 107, 128. *Boutell's Chr. Mon.,* p. 115 (det.) II. Thos. Gilbert, citizen and draper of London, mcht. of the staple of Calais, 1483, in mantle, and w. Agnes, widow of John Saunders, citizen and draper of London, mcht. of the staple of Calais, **1489** (date filled in?), with 7 sons and 5 daus., finely engr., mur., A.T., N.A., p. 179. The inscr. which no doubt belongs to this brass is now on the floor. III. The Resurrection, painted, with 2 scrolls, c. **1510** (?), A.T., S.A., p. 103. *Godwin and Britton's Churches of London.* IV. John Rusche, Gent., **1498**. V. Christopher Rawson, mercer, mcht. of the staple of Calais, **1518**, and ws. Margt. and Agnes, S.A. VI. Andr. Evyngar, citizen and salter of London, and w. Ellyn, with 1 son and 6 daus., Virgin of Pity, c. **1535**, qd. pl., Flemish, N., pp. 20, 104, 120. *Waller,* pt. vi. VII. [Mr. Wm. Thinne, Esq., a master of the household to Hen. VIII.], **1546**, in arm., and w., marg. inscr., much mutil., rel., S.A., pp. 117, 235, 245. He edited, in 1532, the first complete edition of Chaucer's works, with the exception of the "Ploughman's Tale." VIII. Wm. Armar, Esq., servant for 51 years to Kings Hen. VIII. and Edw. VI., Queens Mary and Elizth., governor of the pages of honour, free of the city of London and of the Clothworkers' Co., **1560**, in arm., and w., with 3 sons and 2 daus., 12 Eng. vv., qd. pl., mur., S.A. IX. Roger James, brewer, **1591**,

æt. 67, leaving his w. Sara and 8 sons and 1 dau., p. 120.   INSCRS.
X. Wm. Tonge, Fr. inscr. around a sh., c. 1370, p. 120.   XI.
Thos. Vyrly, vicar, 1454, N.A.   XII. A Figure under a canopy
incised on a blue stone, the head and hands apparently engraved or
enamelled on a copper plate, the whole of foreign work and nearly
effaced, N.A., p. 23.   No. XI. and two wings (?) are now inlaid in
the slab.   XIII. Geo. Snayth, Esq., auditor to Wm. Lawd,
late abp. of Cant., born at Durham 1602, dec. 1651, N.A. See also
p. 223.

LONDON, ST. ANDREW UNDERSHAFT.   I. Nich. Leveson, mercer,
sheriff of London [in 1534], mcht. of the staple of Calais, 1539, in
mantle, and w. Denys, 1560, with 8 sons and 10 daus., mur.   II.
Simon Burton, citizen and wax-chandler of London, thrice master of
the Co., a governor of St. Thos. Hospital, 29 years com. counsellor,
benefactor to the poor, 1593, æt. 85, and ws. Elizth. (with 1 son and
3 daus.) and Ann ; his dau. Alyce Coldock pos., qd. pl., mur.   FRAG.
III. Eight Daus., c. 1570, and 2 shs., mur., pp. 118, 119.   Perhaps
part of the brass of David Woodroffe, haberdasher, 1563.

LONDON, ST. BARTHOLOMEW THE LESS.   Wm. Markeby, Gent.,
1439, not in arm., and w. Alice.   *Gough*, vol. ii. pl. xl. p. 120.

LONDON, ST. CATHERINE, REGENT'S PARK.   Wm. Cutinge, a benefactor to Gonville and Caius Coll., Camb., St. Katherine's, East
Dereham, Norton Fitzwarren, &c., 1599, and w̄., mur.

LONDON, ST. DUNSTAN-IN-THE-WEST.   I. Hen. Dacres, citizen
and mcht.-taylor of London, in mantle and scarf, and w. Elizth.,
1530, mur.   II. †Margt. Talbot, 1620, qd. pl., mur.

LONDON, GREAT ST. HELEN, BISHOPSGATE.   I. A Civilian, mutil.,
and w., c. 1465, inscr. lost, N., p. 200.   II. Thos. Wylliams, Gent.,
1495, not in arm., and w. Margt., S.A.   III. John Leenthorp, Esq.,
one of the four "hostiarii" of the chamber to Hen. VII., 1510, N.,
pp. 113, 194, 199, 232.   *Oxford Man.*, p. 90 ; and *Introd.*, p. 198.
IV. Robt. Rochester, Esq., serjeant of the pantry to Hen. VIII., 1514,
N., p. 117.   V. A Lady in heraldic mantle, c. 1535, inscr. lost,
rel., S.A., p. 113.   INSCR. VI. Robt. Cotesbrok, 1393, Fr. inscr.
A printing from the eff. of Joan (?), w. of Rich., son and h. of
Robt. Lord Poynings, 1420, in mantle, formerly in this Ch., is
preserved in the Brit. Museum.   It is engr. (reversed) in *Grose's
Antiq.*, vol. i. pl. v. fig. 1.

LONDON, HOLY TRINITY, MINORIES.   Constantia, eldest dau. of
Sir Thos. Lucy, jun., and his w. Constantia, 1596, æt. about 11,
10 eleg. vv., sm., nearly effaced.

LONDON, ST. MARTIN OUTWICH.   I. Nich. Wotton, rector, LL.B.,

1482, in acad., rel., p. 77.   II. An Ecclesiastic in doctor's dress, c. **1500**, inscr. lost, p. 82.   FRAG. III. Seven Sons, 2 scrolls, and shs., part of the brass of Hugh Pemberton, **1500**, and w. Kath., mur., p. 119.

LONDON, ST. MARY MAGDALEN, OLD FISH-STREET.   Thos. (?) Berrie, he "xii penie loaves to xii poore foulkes geve everie sabathe day for aye," **1586**, 10 Eng. lines, qd. pl., mur., p. 3.

LONDON, ST. OLAVE, HART-STREET.   I. John Orgone, **1584**, and w. Ellyne, not kng., with mcht.'s mk. on woolpack, 6 Eng. vv., very sm., now mur., p. 180.   INSCR. II. *Mr. Thos. Morley, Gent., clerk of the Queen's storehouse of Deptford, and officer of the navy, **1566**, 4 Eng. vv., mur., N.A.

LONDON, WESTMINSTER ABBEY.   I. John de Waltham, bp. of Salisbury, lord high treasurer, **1395**, with B. V. Mary on orphrey of chasuble, lower part of eff. lost at the last coronation (?), three side niches mutil. only remain of a fine triple canopy, marg. inscr. lost, large, worn, Confessor C., pp. 63, 101, 138, 139. *Dart's Westmonasterium*, 1742, vol. ii. pl. 92, p. 46 (brass perfect). *Moule and Harding's West. Abbey*, pl. iv. p. 15; *Kite's Brasses of Wiltshire*, pl. xxxi. p. 94.   II. Robt. de Waldeby [S.T.D., bp. of Ayre in Aquitaine, abp. of Dublin, bp. of Chichester], abp. of York, **1397**, canopy, marg. inscr. in 10 Lat. vv. mutil., worn, C. of St. Edm., pp. 63, 115. *Dart*, vol. i. pl. 20, p. 127; *Moule*, pl. v. p. 17.   III. Alianore de Bohun, eldest dau. and a h. of Humfrey de Bohun (earl of Hereford, Essex, Northampton, and constable of England), and w. of Thos. of Woodstock, son of Ed. III., duke of Gloucester, earl of Essex and Buckingham, and constable of England [**1399**], in widow's attire, fine triple canopy, marg. inscr. in Fr., large, A.T., C. of St. Edm., pp. 89, 139. *Dart*, vol. i. pl. 19, p. 124; *Gough*, vol. i. pl. lx. p. 159; *Penny Mag.*, vol. xiii. 1844, No. 812; *Moule*, pl. vi. p. 20; *Sandford's Geneal. Hist. of Eng.*, p. 232; *Pict. Hist. of England*, vol. ii. p. 232; *Old England*, No. 1312; *Kelke's Sep. Mon.*, p. 16; *Trans. of Lond. and Middx. Arch. Soc.*, vol. i. p. 68.   IV. Sir John Harpedon, **1457**, chamfer inscr. lost, engr. c. 1445 (?), once on A.T., N.A. of C., p. 190. *Gough*, vol. ii. pl. xxi. p. 43; *Moule*, pl. vii. p. 25; *Bloxam's Mon. Arch.*, p. 189; *Boutell's Mon. Br.*, p. 66.   V. [Sir Thos. Vaughan, private treasurer to Edw. IV. and Prince Edw., **1483**], feet gone, marg. inscr. much mutil., C. of St. John Bapt. *Gough*, vol. ii. pl. xcvi. p. 255; *Moule*, pl. ix. p. 31.   VI. John Estney, abbot, **1498**, fine triple canopy, inscr. lost, large, once on A.T., N.A. of C., p. 64.   *Dart*, vol. ii. pl. 67, p. 1; *Gough*, vol. ii. pl. lxxxi. p. 210; *Moule*, pl. x. p. 34.   VII. Sir Humfrey Stanley, one of the bodyguard to Hen. VII., **1505**, C. of St. Nich., p. 232.

Moule, pl. xi. p. 38; *Boutell's Mon. Br.*, p. 78.   VIII. Wm. Bill, S.T.D., dean, provost of Eton, master of Trin. Coll., Camb., and chief almoner to Queen Elizth., **1561**, in gown and hood, 10 eleg. vv., marg. inscr., A.T., C. of St. Benedict. *Moule*, pl. xii. p. 43. INSCRS., &c. IX. A few Lomb. letters of marg. inscr., a cross surrounded by mosaic work lost, to a son of Wm. de Valence, end of 13th cent. (?), now covd., Confessor C. *Trans. of Lond. and Middx. Arch. Soc.*, vol. i. p. 42.   X. Frag. of canopy and marg. inscr. to [Sir John Golofre, **13**]**96**, S.A. of C., p. 116.   XI. John Wyndsore, a great warrior in his youth, h. to his uncle Sir Wm., dec. on Easter-eve, **1414**, eff. lost (left in Dart's time), 10 Lat. vv., worn, N.A. of C.   XII. Sir Humfrey Bourgchier, descended from Ed. III., son and h. of John Lord Barnes [Berners], and "cironomon menso" (cup-bearer) to Elizth., Queen of Ed. IV., slain on Easter-day at the battle of Bernett [**1471**], while fighting for Ed. IV., eff. lost; 14 Lat. vv., water-bougets, shs. left, large, A.T., C. of St. Edm., pp. 93, 114. *Gough*, vol. ii. pl. lxxxvi.* p. 220; *Moule*, pl. viii. p. 28.   XIII. Sir Thos. Parry, treasurer of the household, and master of the court of wards and liveries to Queen Elizth., **1560**, eff. and inscr. lost, 4 shs. left, S.A. of C.   XIV. Hen. Ferne, S.T.D., 8th son of Sir John Ferne ("Civitati Eboranensi a secretis"), master of Trin. Coll., Camb., bp. of Chester for 5 weeks only, **1661**, æt. 59, mitre, shs., and marg. inscr., C. of St. Edm., p. 123.   XV. Hen. Killigrew, S.T.P., prebendary, **1699**, C. of Hen. VII. The brass of Thos. of Woodstock, 1397, now lost (see p. 117), is engr. in *Dart*, vol. ii. pl. 89, p. 46, and *Sandford*, p. 230; it consisted of several small figures in tiers under canopies, arranged round the eff. of the deceased. The slab remains in the Confessor C.   The entire brass of Edm. Kirton, D.D., abbot, 1466 (p. 111), is engr. by *Dart* (vol. ii. pl. 71).   The triple canopy (now lost) alone remained in Gough's time, and is engr. in his *Sep. Mon.*, vol. ii. pl. lxxxi. p. 210.   Matrices, p. 87. See also Appendix A.   In a MS. at the Ashmolean Library, Oxford (D. 4. 8,518, fol. 392), is a sketch of the brass of a Man in arm., formerly in the N.Tr., and probably the memorial of Robt. Haule, who was murdered there in 1378 while resisting a band of armed men sent by John of Gaunt to force him from the sanctuary.

LONDON, WESTMINSTER, ST. MARGARET. —— Cole, a burgess in Parliament, **1597**, and w. Margt. (who pos.), with 1 son and 2 daus., 46 Eng. and 2 Lat. vv., qd. pl., mur. In *Weever's Fun. Mon.* (pp. 494, 495), are engravings of the brasses of Dame Mary Bylling (w. of Sir Thos. Bylling, chief-justice), 1499, and of her second husband Wm. Cotton.

MIMMS, SOUTH. I. Thos. Frowyk, Esq. [**1448**, and widow Elizth.], with 6 sons and 13 daus., 12 Lat. vv., legs of male eff. lost, much defaced, Tower, pp. 94, 193.   INSCRS. II. Hen. Frowyk, Fr., with 4 shs. *Boutell's Chr. Mon.*, p. 109.   III. Roger Hodsden, **1606**, and w. Jone, with 5 sons and 5 daus.   A Sh., p. 119.

NORTHOLT. I. Hen. Rowdell, Esq., **1452**, sm., p. 193.   II. John Gyfforde, in arm., and w. Susan who died in childbed, **1560**, æt. 30, with 9 sons and 3 daus., 6 Eng. vv., loose, on reverse of daus. about 8 sons kng., sm., pp. 48, 226, 235.   III. Isaiah Bures, vicar, M.A. of Balliol Coll., **1610**, æt. 64, his w. Kath. pos., mur., C.

NORWOOD. I. Matthew Hunsley (or Horsman?), Gent., **1618**, æt. 35, his w. Elizth. pos.   II. Francis Awsiter, Esq., **1629**, æt. 67; by his w. Frances, dau. of Laur. Horseman, Esq., he had 4 chil., Rich., Elizth., Mary, Anne; 4 Eng. vv.

PINNER. Anne, dau. of Eustace Bedingfeld, Gent., **1580**, in swaddling clothes, buried by her grandmother Margery, widow of John Draper, of London, p. 221.

RUISCLIP. I. John Hawtrey, Esq., J.P., **1593**, æt. 68, in arm., and w. Bregget, p. 246.   II. Abr. Kent, citizen and alderman of London, and w. Mary, dau. of Mr. Rich. Living, of Ruislip, **1609**, 8 Eng. vv., worn, partly covd. by stove, N.

STANWELL. Rich. de Thorp, rector, **1408**, hf. eff.   *Gent. Mag.*, vol. lxiii. 1793, pt. ii. pl. iii. fig. 2, p. 994.   Thos. Windsor, Esq., 1485, lost, p. 56.

TEDDINGTON. *John Goodyere, **1506**, and w. Thomasin, sm., S.A.

TOTTENHAM. I. John Burrough, Gent., and w. Elizth., **1616**, with 2 sons and 1 dau., sm.   II. Lady Margt., dau. of Sir Edw. Barkham, Lord Mayor [in 1621], and w. of Sir Anth. Irby, of Boston, Linc., **1640**, and daus. Jane, Margt., Jane, all dec., kng., qd. pl.   INSCH. III. Thos. Hymyngham, **1499**.   In *Sperling's Ch. Walks in Middx.* (front.), is an engraving of the brass of Walter Hunt, priest, 1419, hf. eff., holding a book with a chalice on it; and in *Robinson's Hist. of Tottenham* are engravings of the brasses of Thos., son of Geo. Hymingham, 1512, and of Umfray, son of Wat Povy, of London, 1510-11.   These brasses are now lost.

WILLESDON. I. Barth. Willesden, comptroller of the great roll of pipe, **1492**, and ws. Margt. and Margt., with 4 daus., one w. and inscr. lost, C.   II. Margt. Roberts, dau. of Robt. Fyncham, Esq., **1505** (?), with 3 sons and 3 daus., N.   III. Wm. Lichefeld, LL.D., vicar, residentiary of St. Paul's Cath., **1517**, in cope and cap, C. IV. Edm. Roberts, Esq., of Neasdon, **1585**, in arm., with 2 ws., Fraunces, dau. and h. of Rich. Welles, Esq., of Hertford (with 2 sons and 4 daus.), and Fayth, dau. and h. of John Patenson, Gent., of London (with 2 sons and 1 dau.), 16 Eng. vv. and 2 cleg. vv., probably palimpsest, C.   V. Jane, w. of John Barne, Esq., **1609**, m. 49 years and 7 months, and 2 daus., Mary, w. of Franc. Roberts, Esq., of Wilsdon, and Elizth., w. of Edw. Altham, of Latton, Essex, eff. of one dau. lost, C.   Nos. I., II., III. are now mur. in C.

INSCRIPTIONS, &c.

BROMLEY ST. LEONARD'S.   Roger ———, citizen and goldsmith of London, **1556**, and w., mutil., and sh. (?)   CRANFORD. Nich., son of Thos., and brother of Mardocheus Bownell, parson, **1581**, eff. lost, C.   LITTLETON.   I. Lady Blanche, w. of Sir Hugh Vaughan, "who lyoth buryed at Westmynst'," **1553**, with sh.   II. Two Roses inscribed "Jhu—M'cy," c. **1460** (?), on same slab as No. I., p. 111.   SAVOY CHAPEL.   I. Thos. Halsey, "leghnes epūs, In basilica scti petri Romæ nationis Anglicor' penitenciari'," and Gavan Dowglas, "natione scotus, Dunkelley præsul, patria sua exul," **1522**, Gawin Douglas was the well-known poet who died of the plague in London.   II. *Wm. Chaworthe, **1582**, mur.   TWICKENHAM. Rich. Burton, chief cook to the king, **1443**, and w. Agnes, N.A., p. 115.

The brasses are lost at ST. MARY'S, CLERKENWELL (see pp. 73, 87), and CHISWICK (p. 260): the brass of Wm. Bordall, principal vicar of Chiswick, 1435, in cope, is engr. in *Faulkner's Brentford*, 1845, p. 320, the eff. (now lost) was in the possession of the churchwarden, the canopy and inscr. were then gone.   The brass of Sir Thos. Leigh, 1545, formerly at SHOREDITCH, is engr. at p. 51 of *H. Ellis's Hist. and Antiq. of St. Leonard's, Shoreditch*, 1798; see also supra, p. 253.   In *Dugdale's Hist. of St. Paul's Cathedral* are engravings of several brasses formerly in existence in the old Cathedral, p. 77. At ST. BOTOLPH, ALDERSGATE-STREET, is an incised stone, painted and gilt, and liable to be mistaken for a brass: it commemorates Sir John Packington, in arm., and widow Anne, 1563, with one dau., engr. c. 1620 (?).

Monmouthshire.

ABERGAVENNY.   I. Maurice Hughes, vicar, master of the free school, **1631**, he left surviving his w. Joan (dau. of Rice Harbert, Esq., of Couldbrooke, son and h. of Sir Wm., the son and h. of Sir Rich. Harbert), and 1 son Robt., a clerk, and a dau. Cath., C.   II. Margt., dau. of Wm. Herbert, Esq., of Coulebrooke, dec., and w. of John Robertes, Gent., **1632**, with child in swaddling clothes; she left a son Herbert; pecul., sm., qd. pl., mur., S.C.   INSCR. III.

John Morgon, Gent., son of Evan Morgon, **1587**, æt. 42, with mercers' arms.

LLANGATTOCK-NIGH-USK. Zirophœniza, dau. of Wm. Mathewe, Esq., of Radyr, Glamorgan, and w. of Andrew Powell, Esq., **1625**, qd. pl., mur.

MATHERNE. Philip Williams, **1562**, æt. 71, and w. Alice, **1567**, æt. 62, 4 Eng. and 2 Lat. vv., their son Hen. pos. **1590**, p. 141.

USK. I. A Welsh inscr. (see Appendix B) in 2 lines, c. **1400** (?), perhaps end of 15th cent., p. 41. *Coxe's Monmouthshire*, p. 418. II. Inscr. to Margt. Baskervyle, 2nd w. of Hen. Rumsey, **1613**.

Norfolk.

ACLE. I. John Swanne, **1533**, head gone, sm. II. Thos. Stones, minister of the Ch. for 43 years, **1627**, æt. 73, hf. eff., sm.

†ALDBOROUGH. I. Clement Herward, Esq., **1427**, N. II. Rich. Ricards, Esq., **1443**, N. III. Anne, w. of Clement Herward, **1485**, N.A.

ANTINGHAM, ST. MARY. *Rich. Calthorp, Esq., son of John Calthorp, of Cokthorp, Esq., 1554, in arm., and w. Anne, dau. of Edm. Hastyng, Esq., and widow of Robt. Raynnes, Esq., **1562** (eff. lost), with 19 chil., Hen., Geo., John, Anth., John, Thos., Edm., Wm., Geo., Martyn, Bartram, Mary, Elizth., Anne, Alice, Frances, the names of 2 sons and a dau. by the first husband not given, sm., N. *Engravings of Sepulchral Brasses in Norfolk and Suffolk by John Sell Cotman*, 1839, vol. i. pl. lxxiv. p. 39.

ATTLEBRIDGE. I. A Chalice and wafer for Geo. Cunynggam, vicar, c. **1525**, C., p. 125. INSCR. II. Wm., son and h. of Wm. Elys, a baron of the exchequer, c. **1530**, N.

AYLSHAM. I. Thos. Tylson, B.A., rector, c. **1490**, in almuce, with text from Job on scrolls, worn, C. II. Robt. Farman and w. Kath., c. **1490**, pecul., sm., worn, now in C. III. Rich. Howard, citizen and sheriff of Norwich, **1499**, and w. Cecilia, skeletons in shrouds, C., p. 61. IV. Thos. Wymer, worsted-weaver, a benefactor to the Ch., **1507**, in shroud, curious, p. 218. V. *A Man and w., much worn, C.

BACONSTHORP. *Alice Heydon, **1495**.

*BARNHAM-BROOM. I. Edm. Bryghteve (?), Gent., **1467**, hf. eff. II. John Dorant, **1514**, and w. Alice.

BARNINGHAM-NORWOOD. *—— Palgrave and w.

BARNINGHAM-TOWN. *John Wynter, Esq., lord of the manor, c. **1410**, inscr. mutil.

BAWBURGH. I. Robt. Grote, **1500**, and w. Agnes (eff. lost), pecul., sm., N. II. Thos. Tyard, S.T.B., vicar, **1505**, in shroud, pecul., C. III. A Chalice and wafer for Wm. Richers, vicar, **1531**, p. 125. *Introd.*, p. 125. IV. Philipp Tenison, S.T.P., archdeacon of Norfolk, rector of Hethersett and Foulsham, king's scholar of Trin. Coll., Camb., **1660**, æt. 48, a sm. eff. in shroud, curious, somewhat resembling the effs. at Dunston, Norfolk. On same slab as No. II. INSCR. V. Edm. Ryghtwys, S.T.P., vicar, rector of St. Mich. at Plea, Norwich, **1493**, eff. lost, C.

BEACHAMWELL ST. MARY. I. A Priest, c. **1385**, inscr. lost, rel., C. *Boutell's Series.* II. John Grymston, rector, **1430**, hf. eff.

*BEESTON-REGIS. I. John Deynes, **1527**, and w. Cath., A.T., N.A. INSCRS., &c. II. Two Evang. symbs., c. **1470**, a priest gone, C. III. Thos. Symson, priest, **1531**, N., p. 140.

BELAUGH. I. *Sir John Curson, **1471**, and w. Joan [Bacon], pecul., N., pp. 200, 212. *Cotman*, vol. i. pl. xxxii. p. 22. II. A Chalice and wafer for John Feelde, rector, **1508**.

BINTRY. 1. A Chalice for Thos. Hoont, chaplain, rector, **1510**, C. INSCRS. II. *Robt. Goodwin, **1518**, and w. Margt., N. III. *Edm. Ruth, **1526**, N. IV. Wm. Ruth, **1531**, N.

BLICKLING. I. A Bust of a Civilian, c. **1360**, inscr. lost, covd. by a pew, S.A., pp. 134, 162. *Anonymous; Introd.*, p. 134. II. *Sir [Nich.] Dagworth [lord of the manor], **1401**, marg. inscr. mutil., very large, S.C., pp. 160, 185. *Gough*, vol. ii. pt. ii. pl. i. p. 5; *Cotman*, vol. i. pl. xiii. p. 11; *Boutell's Series.* III. Roger Felthorp, **1454**, and w. Cecily, with 11 sons and 5 daus. standing before the parents, an early instance of pecul. style, sm., N. *Cotman*, vol. i. pl. xxiii. p. 19. IV. Cecilie, sister to Geoff. Boleyn, lord of the manor, **1458**, æt. 50, C., pp. 213, 223. *Gough*, vol. ii. pl. xl. p. 120. V. Anna, dau. of Wm. Boleyn, Esq., **1479**, æt. 3 years, 11 months, 13 days, pecul., C., pp. 173, 213. *Gough*, ibid.; *Cotman*, vol. i. pl. xxiii. p. 23. VI. Isabella [Boleyn], w. of Wm. Cheyne, Esq., of the Isle of Sheppey, **1485** [not 1482], pecul., C., p. 171. *Boutell's Series.* VII. Anne a Wode, second w. of Thos. Asteley, Esq., of Melton Constable, "masculu(m) et femella(m) ad partu(m) pe(pc)rit et post pariendi p(er)iculu(m) subito migrauit ad d(o)m(in)u(m)," **1512**, with twins, pecul., N., pp. 28, 220, 241. *Gough*, vol. ii. pl. xxxviii. p. 309; *Cotman*, vol. i. pl. li. p. 30; *Introd.*, p. 221. INSCRS. VIII. Agnes Appylyerd, w. to Robt. Phileppes, and to Wm. Reynald, **1484**, pecul., S.A. IX. *John Cok, **1503**. X. *John Catys, **1503**, N. XI. John Barker, S.A. XII. Geoff. Appelyerd. The dates of Nos. IX. and X. are in arabic numerals.

BRAMPTON. I. Robt. Brampton, Esq., **1468**, and w. Isabella [dau. of Simkin Cock, of Norwich], in shrouds, with B. V. Mary and Child (curious), 5 Lat. vv., sm., mur., C. II. John Brampton, Esq., **1535**, and ws. Tomasseyng [Jenny] and Anne [Brome] with 4 sons, pecul., pp. 233, 242, 243. III. Edw. Brampton, Esq., and w. Jone, dau. of Christopher Daubene, Esq., of Sharington, Norf., both dec. **1622**, m. 48 years, and had 6 sons, and 3 daus. (lost), mutil., mur., C. INSCRS. IV. Robt. Breton, Esq., **1479**; he m. Elizth., dau. of Thos. Brampton, Esq., mur., C. V. Emma, dau. of Robt. Brampton, Esq., and w. of Wm. Reymes, Esq., **1483**, mur., C. VI. Chas. Brampton, Esq., **1631**, mur., C.

BRISLEY. I. John Athowe, rector of Horningtoft, **1531**, with chalice and wafer, mutil., pecul., N.A., p. 79. *Cotman*, vol. ii. pl. ci. p. 49. INSCRS. II. Robt. Gogney, **1505**. III. *Robt. Mushunt, **1525**, and w. IV. Christopher Athowe, **1585**, æt. 72.

BUCKENHAM, OLD. I. A Chalice and host, c. **1530**, inscr. lost, N., p. 125. II. A Crane with scroll for Thos. Brown, c. **1500**, inscr. lost.

BURGH ST. MARGARET. John Burton, rector for about 28 years, **1608**, æt. 68, sm., C. *Cotman*, vol. ii. pl. civ. p. 50.

*BURLINGHAM, SOUTH. I. A Chalice and wafer for Wm. Curtes, **1540**. *Boutell's Mon. Br.*, p. 122. INSCRS. II. John Howlett, a chief constable of the hundred, **1615**, loose in Ch. chest, N. III. Wm. Smyth, clerk, **1639**, on same slab as No. I.

BURNHAM THORPE. *Sir Wm. Calthorp, lord of the manor and patron of the Ch., son of Sir Oliver Calthorp, and his w. Isabella, dau. [of Sir Barth. Bacon], **1420**, in SS. collar, canopy and embattled entablature, marg. inscr. mutil., large, pp. 114, 189. *Cotman*, vol. i. pl. xviii. p. 16.

BURNHAM WESTGATE. *John Huntely, **1503**, and ws. Mary and Anne, now in a frame in the vestry.

BUXTON. I. A Chalice and wafer for Robt. Northen, vicar, **1508**, C., p. 125. INSCRS. II. John Mannyg, c. **1500**, N.A. III. Cecily Abbys, widow, **1506**, N.A.

CATFIELD. A Chalice and host for Rich. Foo, rector of Thorpe, near Norwich [1477—1508], c. **1500**, p. 125. *Boutell's Chr. Mon.*, p. 111.

CLEY. I. A Civilian and 6 sons, c. **1460**; w., daus., and inscr. lost. II. John Symondes, mcht., 1508, and w. Agnes, **1512**, in shrouds, with 8 chil. detached, John, Aleyn, Raufe, Wm., Cecily, Anne, Agnes, Rose, 7 scrolls (of 9) inscribed "Now thus," inscrs. reversed, as the brass is at east end of S.C., p. 219. *Cotman*, vol. ii.

pl. cx. p. 52.   III. John Yslyngeton, S.T.P., c. 1520, in acad., with chalice, sm., p. 78. *Cotman*, vol. ii. pl. xcvi. p. 47.

CLIPPESBY.   I. Thos. Pallyng, 1503, and w. Emma, inscr. mutil., pecul. *Boutell's Mon. Br.*, pp. 88, 110.   II. John Clippesby, Esq., 1594, in arm., and w. Julian, with 1 son, Wm. (in shroud), and 3 daus., Audry, Frauncis, Julian, A.T., C. *Cotman*, vol. ii. pl. lxxxiv. p. 43.

COLBY.   *A Chalice and wafer, c. 1500.   Perhaps for Geoff. Walsh, rector, 1508.

COLNEY.   I. A Chalice and host for Hen. Alikok, rector, 1502, p. 125.   INSCR. II. *Robt. Pylcher, 1641, N.

CREAK, NORTH.   A Priest (?), c. 1500, in acad., with church on arm, triple canopy, 2 portions of it and of inscr. in 2 Lat. vv. loose, marg. inscr. lost, C., pp. 28, 123, 203. *Cotman*, vol. i. pl. xli. p. 26. *Introd.*, p. 123 (det.)

CREAK, SOUTH.   I. A Priest, c. 1400, in cope, hf. eff., inscr. lost. Perhaps John Felbrigg, prebendary of Wherwell and parson of Coltoshale, 1417.   II. John Norton, clerk, 1509, in cassock, plain albe, almuce and cope, with pastoral staff mutil., and father Rich., heads of both effs. gone, and mother Cristina, eff. lost, effs. of parents engr. c. 1470 (?), pp. 63, 74.

*CRESSINGHAM, GREAT.   I. Rich. Rysle, Esq., 1497, and w. Thomasine, pecul., p. 200.   II. John Eyre, Esq., a lawyer, and justice of the peace and quorum (?), in Suffolk and Norfolk [1507], in civilian costume, and w. Elizth. [dau. of Sir —— Barn]ardiston, eff. lost, inscr. mutil. *Cotman*, vol. i. pl. xlviii. p. 29.   III. John Aberfeld "in decretis bacc̄," rector [1518?], in almuce, sm., inscr. lost (?), p. 79. *Cotman*, vol. ii. pl. c. p. 49.   INSCR. IV. Wm. Smith, Esq., of Borowe Castle, Suffolk, 1596. The brasses were lately loose in Ch. chest.

DEREHAM, EAST.   I. Edm. Kelyng, vicar, 1479, hf. eff., very sm., pecul., C.   II. Etheldreda Castell, gentlewoman, 1486, pecul., N. FRAG. A Sh. bearing a scroll and bird, a priest and inscr. lost, for Hen. Edyal (?), 1503, C., p. 132. *Gent. Mag.*, vol. xxviii. N.S. 1847, p. 262.

DITCHINGHAM.   I. Philip Bosard, Gent., 1490, not in arm., and w. Margery, with 4 sons and 5 daus., pecul., C., p. 171.   II. Roger Bozard, Gent., 1505, not in arm., and son Wm., pecul., N.

DUNSTON.   *Clere Talbot, LL.D., and 2 ws. (in shrouds), —— and Anne, eldest dau. of Wm. Harborne, Esq., of Mundham, 1649, she left 3 daus. and cohs. by Wm. Sidnor her first husband, probably a palimpsest, inscr. and shs. cut in stone, C., pp. 53, 215. *Gough*, vol. ii. pl. xxxviii. p. 309; *Cotman*, vol. ii. pl. xcii. p. 46 (male eff.)

ELSING. Sir Hugh Hastings, builder of the Ch., **1347**, with shield on arm, head on cushion, legs lost, with fine canopy having St. Geo. in the centre, and two figures on brackets representing the coronation of the B. V. Mary, at the sides were 8 "weepers" in arm., Ed. III., Thos. Beauchamp earl of Warwick, Despencer (? lost), Roger Lord Grey of Ruthyn (lost), Hen. Plantagenet earl of Lancaster, Lawrence Hastings earl of Pembroke (lost), Ralph Lord Stafford, Lord St. Amand, all the effs. with their armorial bearings on their jupons, inscr. lost, large, perhaps of foreign execution, pp. 22, 105, 106, 115, 137, 139, 149, 152, 154, 156, 158. *Carter's Anc. Sculpt. and Painting*, vol. i. pl. 12, pp. 13, 37; *Cotman*, vol. i. pl. i. p. 1. *Waller*, pt. xv.; *Boutell's Series; Introd.*, p. 155 (dets.)

ERPINGHAM. I. John de Erpingham, lord of the manor, 1370, engr. c. **1415**, marg. inscr. nearly all lost, large, S.A., pp. 45, 188. *Cotman*, vol. i. pl. v. p. 6. INSCR. II. *Wm. Hobart, Gent., **1611**, S.A.

FAKENHAM. Hen. Keys, rector, archdeacon of Norfolk, c. **1428**, in cope, worn and mutil., marg. inscr. nearly all lost, canopy gone, C. The brass of Hen. Newman, rector of Pensthorpe (a chalice surrounded by 2 scrolls in the form of a heart), is lost, it is engr. in *Cotman*, vol. ii. pl. cv. p. 50.

FELBRIGG. I. *Symon de Felbrig, c. 1351, and w. Alice, buried at Herling (lower part of eff. lost), also Roger de Felbrig, dec. and buried in Prussia, c. **1380**, in arm., and w. Elizth., inscr. in Fr., C., pp. 160, 163, 203. *Cotman*, vol. i. pl. viii. p. 8. II. A Sh. (now lost) in a diaper, with inscr. to Geo. Felbrygg, Esq., of Tutyngton, **1411**, p. 120. *Boutell's Chr. Mon.*, p. 110; *Introd.*, p. 121. III. *Sir Symon Felbrygge, K.G., standard-bearer to Rich. II. [1443], with banner, and [first] w. Margt., a native of Bohemia [dau. of Primislaus duke of Teschen, and nephew to Winceslaus V. king of Bohemia], "domicella" of Anne queen of England, **1416**, in mantle, canopy, shs. with badge—a fetterlock, large, N., pp. 115, 117, 126, 188. *Gough*, vol. ii. pl. xlvii. p. 133; *Cotman*, vol. i. pl. xv. p. 13; *Boutell's Series; Weekly Register*, No. 5, p. 72. *Publ. of Norfolk and Norwich Archæol. Soc.*, vol. i. p. 356 (male eff.) IV. A Lady, c. **1480**, pecul., inscr. lost, sm., C., p. 213. *Cotman*, vol. i. pl. lvi. p. 31. V. Thos. Windham, Esq., third son of Sir Edm. Windham dec., 1599, in arm., 4 Eng. vv.; Sir John Windham, of Orchard, Somerset, pos. c. **1608** (?), N. V. Jane, dau. of Sir Edm. Windham dec., and w. first of John Pope, Esq., of Oxfordshire, next of Humphrey Coningsby dec., **1608**, æt. 67, 6 Eng. vv., Sir John Windham pos., C. *Cotman*, vol. i. pl. lxxxix. p. 45.

FELTWELL. Margt., w. of Francis Mundford, Esq., **1520**, pecul., mur., C. *Gough*, vol. ii. pl. xxxviii. p. 309; *Cotman*, vol. i. pl. liv. p. 31.

FINCHAM. I. A Fem. eff. in shroud, c. **1520**, pecul., sm., N. INSCR. II. Thos. Townsend, 16 eleg. vv., mutil., **15**[**70**].

FRANSHAM, GREAT. I. *Geoffrey Fransham, Esq. [**1414**], with canopy, marg. inscr. mutil., C., p. 188. *Cotman*, vol. i. pl. xvi. p. 15. II. *A Fem. eff. in shroud, pecul., c. **1500**, N. Probably the brass of Cecilia, w. of John Legge.

FRENZE. I. Ralph Blen'haysct, Esq., **1475**, pecul., C., p. 200. *Etching by Mrs. Hayles.* II. John Blen'hayset, Esq., **1510**, pecul., C., p. 200. *Cotman*, vol. i. pl. l. p. 29. III. Joan, widow of John Braham, Esq., "deo dicata," **1519**, N., p. 89. *Cotman*, vol. i. pl. liii. p. 30. IV. Thos. Hobson, c. **1520**, in shroud, pecul., sm., N. V. Jane, widow of John Blen'haysett, Esq., **1521**. *Cotman*, vol. ii. Appendix, pl. v. p. 60. VI. Geo. Duke, Esq., **1551**, eff. lost, and w. Anne, dau. of Sir Thos. Blenerhaysett, with head on cushion, pecul., C., pp. 28, 54, 243. *Arch. Journ.*, vol. ii. p. 247; *Boutell's Mon. Br.*, p. 139; *Oxford Man.*, p. 16; *Introd.*, p. 55. INSCRS. VII. Sir Thos. Blenhaysette, **1531**, eff. in tabard, stolen since Cotman's time. *Cotman*, vol. i. pl. lxiii. p. 35 and front. VIII. Thomazine, dau. of Geo. Duke, Esq., and w. to Wm. Playters, son and h. of Thos. Platers, Esq., of Sotterley, **1560**. IX. Dame Margt., dau. of John Braham, Esq., of Wetheryngset, and widow of Sir Thos. Blen'hayset, **1561**; she had 2 sons, Thos., a priest, and John, also 5 daus., Elizth., Agnes, Anne [No. VI.], Margt., Kath., all married. X. *Mary, only dau. and h. of Geo. Blenerhaiset, Esq., eldest son of Sir Thos. Blenerhaiset; she m. first Thos. Culpeper, Esq., and next Franc. Bacon, Esq., buried at Petistree, Suff., **1587**, æt. 70.

FRETTENHAM. I. Alice Brunham, w. of Giles Thorndon, c. **1420**, 7 Eng. vv. (see Appendix B.), C., p. 179. II. A Lady, c. **1460**, inscr. lost, C. INSCR. III. Thos. Storme, Gent., **1531** (?), N.

†GUESTWICK. I. Rich. Athills, **1505**. II. A Chalice for John, son of Robert Robertson, vicar, **1508**.

HALVERGATE. I. A hf. eff. (fem.?) and inscr. to Robt. Swane, **1540**, and w. Al[ice], on reverse the bust of a monk and inscr. to "frater Willms Jernemut.." [Yarmouth?], pp. 48, 86. INSCRS. II. *Robt. Golword, **1543**, and w. Kath., on reverse 4 Eng. vv. to Elizth., dau. of Lord Bardolf, and w. of Thos. Lord Scalys, curious, 16th cent. III. John Deyman, 16th cent. The brasses were lately loose.

HARLING, WEST. I. Ralf Fuloflove, rector, **1479**, N. II. Wm. Berdewell, Esq., and w. Elizth., a dau. of Edm. Wychyngham, c. **1490**, pecul., N., p. 200. *Cotman*, vol. i. pl. xxxvii. p. 25. III. Wm.

Berdewell, Esq., patron of the Ch., and w. Margt., both dec. in one week, Jan., **1508**, pecul., N., p. 233. *Cotman*, vol. i. pl. xlix. p. 29.

HEACHAM.   A Man in arm., c. **1485**, inscr. lost, N.A., p. 197.

HEDENHAM.   I. A Chalice and wafer for Rich. Grene, rector, **1502**, p. 125.   *Introd.*, p. 178 (det.)   INSCRS. II. Ralf. Palmer, rector, **1530**, N.   III. John Richeman, N.   IV. John Camber, 16th cent., loose.   V. John Richeman, **1595**, 4 Eng. vv.

HEIGHAM.   Thos., second son of Thos. Holl, Esq., **1630**, perhaps a palimpsest, curious, sm., loose in Ch. chest, p. 215. *Cotman*, vol. ii. pl. xci. p. 45.

HELLESDON.   I. Rich. de Heylesdone and w. Beatrice, c. **1370**, hf. effs., Fr. inscr., N.C., pp. 140, 165. *Boutell's Series.*   II. Rich. Thaseburgh, rector, **1389**, N.C., p. 92. *Cotman*, vol. ii. pl. xciv. p. 47; *Boutell's Series.*   INSCRS. III. John de Heylesdon, **1384**, and w. Joan, patrons of the Ch. and founders of chantry, engr. c. **1420**, N.C.   IV. Alice Hellisdon, N.   V. Thos. Herte, N.

HINGHAM.   [John Longe], **1622**, æt. 69, and w. [Margt.], 1615, æt. 66, and son Robt. [who pos.], sm. eff. of son and some labels only left.   A Matrix, p. 125.

HOLM-BY-THE-SEA.   Herry Notingham and w., c. **1405**, "ȝat maden this Chircho stepull & quere, two vestmentȝ & belles they made also," 6 Eng. vv., sm., screwed to a board, mur., p. 179. *Gough*, vol. ii. pl lxxxvii. p. 230 ; *Cotman*, vol. i. pl. xiv. p. 12.

HONING.   Nich. Parker, Esq., **1496**, p. 199, C. *Cotman*, vol. i. pl. xliv. p. 27.

HUNSTANTON.   I. Edm. Grene and w. Agnes, c. **1490**, N. *Cotman*, vol. i. pl. xxxviii. p. 25.   II. Sir Roger L'Estrange [one of the body-guard to Hen. VII., son and h. of Hen. L'Estrange, Esq.], **1506**, in tabard with arms uplifted, on a bracket, above head shield with crest and lambrequin, a triple canopy having at the sides 7 effs. of his ancestors (father and son) in tabards under canopies, Sir Hamond, Hamond Esq., John Esq., John Esq., Roger Esq., John Esq., Herri, an 8th eff. is that of Sir Roger, a marg. inscr. (mutil.) gives his genealogy to Haymo L'Estrange, 14th cent., pecul., A.T., C., pp. 53, 154, 171, 175, 233. *Cotman*, vol. i. pl. xlvii. p. 28. INSCR. III. Hen. le Strawnge, **1485**, and w. Kath.   A Man in arm., c. 1485, lately lost (?), belonged to No. III. (?)   IV. *A Punning Inscr. on name to Sir Hamo le Strange, **1654**, æt. 71.

INGHAM.   I. Brian de Stapilton, son of Sir Milo de Stapilton, son of the founder [Sir Milo Stapleton], **1438**, in arm., and w. Cecilia, dau. of Lord Bardolph, 1432, with canopy and marg. inscr., all lost except portions of the canopies and inscr., C., p. 126. *Gough*, vol. ii.

pl. xlv.* p. 119; *Cotman*, vol. i. pl. xxii. p. 19 (with effs.)   II. Sir Milo Stapleton, son of No. I., **1466**, and 2 ws., Kath. (dau. of Sir Thos. Pool, son of Michael earl of Suffolk) and Elizth. (dau. of Sir Simon Felbrigg), triple canopy, all lost except portions of the canopy, pecul., C., p. 200. *Cotman*, vol. i. pl. xxx. p. 22 (with effs.)   Fragments of these brasses are in the keeping of the incumbent.   INSCR. III. *Lady Elizth., mother (or w.) of Lord Francis Calthorppe, **1536**. The brass of Sir Miles de Stapleton, 1364-5, and w. Joan, dau. of Sir Oliver de Ingham, founders of a priory, holding hands, canopy, marg. inscr. in Fr., is now lost, pp. 62, 91, 158, 168. *Cotman*, vol. i. pl. iv. p. 5. *Gough*, vol. i. pl. xlv. p. 119. *Stothard, Mon. Effs.*, p. 57 (effs.) *Introd.*, p. 158 (det.)   An impression from the original brass is in the Brit. Museum.   In *Cotman* (vol. i. pl. xx. p. 17) is an engraving of the brass of a Widow Lady, c. 1415, now lost, probably Ela (Ufford), w. of Sir Miles, son of Sir Miles Stapleton, 1418.

KETERINGHAM.   I. Sir Hen. Grey (son of Sir Thos. Grey, of Heton), and w. Jone, sister to the Duke of Norfolk, "that dyed at Venys" [1492], and w. Emma, dau. of Wm. Appleyard, Esq., engr. c. **1470**, pecul., all lost but fem. eff., now mur., C., p. 200. *Cotman*, vol. i. pl. xl. p. 25.   II. Thos. Hevenyngham, Esq., son and h. of Sir John Hevenyngham, **1499**, and w. Anne, dau. and h. of Thos. Yerde, Esq., in heraldic dresses, with 5 sons and 5 daus., pecul., mur., C., pp. 199, 212, 233. *Cotman*, vol. i. pl. xlvi. p. 28; *Publ. of Norfolk and Norwich Archæol. Soc.*, vol. iii. p. 285.   INSCRS. III. John, son of Rich. Colvyle, Esq., c. **1530**, in shroud, sm., p. 221.   IV. *Sir Rich. Wyrght [vicar, **1520**]. Nos. III. and IV. placed by No. I.

KIMBERLEY.   John Wodchows [1465], in arm., and w. Constancia [Gedding], engr. c. **1530**, pp. 45, 233. *Cotman*, vol. i. pl. xxix. p. 21.

KIRBY BEDON.   I. A Heart with 3 scrolls, c. **1450**, to one of the Rokewood family (?), inscr. lost, C., p. 107.   II. Wm. Dussyng and w. Kath., both dec. Feb. 10th, **1505**, in shrouds, N.   INSCRS. III. *John Osborne, **1532**.   IV. John Dussyng and w. [**1465** ?], N.

LANGLEY.   Robt. Berney, Esq., **1628**, æt. 79, C.

LODDON.   I. Two Hands holding a heart with scrolls, sh. with monogram for Dionysius Willys, **1462**, N., pp. 108, 133.   II. John Blomeville, Esq., and w. Dame Kath. [dau. of Sir Jas. Hobart], and widow of Sir Thos. Sampson, **1546**, in shrouds. *Cotman*, vol. ii. pl. cxi. p. 52.   III. Hen. Hobart, Esq., **1561**, in tabard, mutil., w. lost, A.T., N.C. *Cotman*, vol. i. pl. lxxiii. pp. 39, 233.   IV. Jas. Hobart, Esq., **1615**, æt. 91, and w. Francis, dau. of Sir Wm.

Drury, of Hawstead, Suff., 1609, m. 60 years, and had 8 sons and 6 daus., A.T., C., p. 224. *Cotman*, vol. ii. Appendix, pl. vi. p. 60. INSCRS. V. Anne, dau. of Sir John Fyneux, chief.justice, and w. of Hen. Hobart, Esq., **1530**, canopy, all lost but marg. inscr., A.T., N.C. VI. Nich. Gavell, Gent., **1518**, p. 179. VII. Roger Olynworthe, **1526**. VIII. Augnes Berry, **1529**, S.A. IX. John Gare and w. Margt., **15** ...

LYNN, ST. MARGARET. I. Adam de Walsokne, burgess of Lynn, **1349**, and w. Margt., born at Cley, under rich canopies, with souls, &c., above, and the twelve Apostles and attendant Prophets or SS. beside and between the effs., below them a rustic scene, broad marg. inscr. in Lomb. letters, very large, Flemish, much worn, especially in upper part, qd. pl., C., pp. 20, 33, 105, 162, 165, 166. *Cotman*, vol. i. pl. ii. p. 3. *Waller*, pts. iii., v.; *Introd.*, pp. 162, 165 (dets.) II. Robt. Braunche, **1364**, and ws. Leticia and Margt., under rich canopies, with souls, &c., above, and 8 weepers in male and female costume at the sides, beneath the "Peacock feast," marg. inscr. in Lomb. letters, very large, Flemish (about 8 ft. 8 in. by 5 ft. 5 in.), qd. pl., C., pp. 20, 33, 121, 150, 162, 165, 166, 167. *Gough*, vol. i. pl. xlv. p. 115; *Cotman*, vol. i. pl. iii. p. 4. *Carter, Anc. Sculpt. and Painting*, vol. ii. p. 13. *Old Eng.*, No. 1088 (det.) INSCRS. III. John Atkin, **1617**, with mcht.'s mk. IV. Francis Parlett, Gent., **1628**. The figure of Robt. Attelath, burgess of Lynn, **1376**, large, Flemish, is now gone, pp. 20, 33, 164, 257. The brass of Walter Coney, **1479**, with triple canopy, large, is engr. by *Gough*, vol. ii. pl. xcix. p. 268. Impressions of both these brasses are preserved in the Brit. Museum.

LYNN, WEST. Adam Owtlawe, chaplain, **1503**, pecul., S.C., p. 79. *Cotman*, vol. ii. pl. xcix. p. 49.

MATTISHALL. I. Geoff. Dene, c. **1510**. II. A Civilian [Wm. Brabant?] and w., **1540**, pecul., inscr. lost, worn. INSCRS. III. Florence Croshold, **1614**. IV. Francis Croshold, **1615**, 4 Eng. vv. V. Susanna Crossold, **1617**. The above were sisters and chil. of Arthur and Mary Croshold.

MERTON. I. Wm. de Grey, Esq., **1520** (?), in tabard, with 5 sons and 2 ws., Mary Bedingfield (with 3 daus.) and Grace Teye (with 2 daus.), inscr. and scrolls lost, mur., C., pp. 212, 233. *Cotman*, vol. i. pl. lv. p. 31. II. [Thos.] de Greye, Esq., son and h. of Edm. de Greye, Esq., **1562**, in arm., legs lost; he m. Anne, dau. and h. of Hen. Everode, Esq., of Linsted, Suff., and 2ndly, Temperance, dau. of Sir Wymonde Carewe, of Anthony, Cornwall, on reverse of part of inscr. the feet of a man, in arm., resting on a lion, c. **1390**, S.A., p. 233.

Inscrs. III. A Heart and 4 scrolls, all lost but 2 scrolls and inscr. to Alice, dau. of Thos. Bedygffeld, Esq., sister of Mary Grey, and w. of John, the eldest son of John Fyncham, **1474**, S.A.   IV. A similar brass, all lost but 3 shs. and part of a scroll, for Wm. de Grey, Esq., **1474**, and w. Christian, dau. of John Mannynge, Gent., of Great Ellingham, N.   V. Edm. de Grey, Esq., **1548**, and w. Elizth., dau. of Sir John Spelman, mur., C.   VI. Thos. de Grey, Esq., **1556**, and w. Elizth., dau. of Sir Rich. Fytzlewes, "after her decease [he] made hymselfe Preast and so lyved xlj yeres," mur., S.A., p. 90.   VII. Sir Robt. de Grey, son and h. of Sir Wm. de Grey, **1644**, and w. Elizth., a dau. and coh. of Wm. Bridon, Gent., of Ipswich, and had Wm. (dec.), Barbara, Ann, C.

METHWOLD. *Sir Adam de Clyfton, **1367**, armorial bearings on jupon, laminated sollerets, single canopy, mutil., inscr. gone, large, C., p. 257. *Publ. of Norfolk and Norwich Archæol. Soc.*, vol. vi. p. 18. This brass was sold to a tinker 1680; when recovered it was found broken up into upwards of 130 pieces, which had been lying ever since in the Ch. chest, and have lately been arranged by the Rev. C. R. Manning, rector of Diss.

METTON. *Robt. Doughty, **1493**, and w. Matilda.

MILEHAM. *Christopher Crowe, **1526**, and w. Christian, with 4 sons and 5 daus., S.A.

NARBURGH. I. Hen. Spelman, "Hospes" and recorder of Norwich, **1496**, in mantle, and [2nd] w. Ela [dau. of Wm. Narburgh], pecul., sm., now mur., C., p. 214. *Cotman*, vol. i. pl. xliii. p. 27. II. John Spelman, Esq., son and h. of Sir John Spelman, justice of the common pleas, **1545**; he m. Margt., a dau. of Sir Thos. Blen'hassett and his w. Margt., and had 2 sons and 2 daus., C., p. 235. III. Sir John Spelman, secundary justice of the king's bench, 1545, and w. Elizth. [dau. of Sir Hen. Frowick, of Middx.], **1556**, [in heraldic mantle], they had 13 sons and 7 daus., above is the Resurrection, mur., C., pp. 9, 91, 103. *Cotman*, vol. i. pl. lxix. p. 37. IV. John Eyer, Esq., receiver-general to Queen Elizth. in Norf., Suff., Camb., and Hunts., master of chancery, **1561**, in arm., and w. Margt., dau. of Sir Thos. Blen'haiset, of Frenze, and widow of John Spelman, Esq. [No. II.], 1558, mur., C. *Cotman*, vol. i. pl. lxxii. p. 39.   V. *John Spelman, Esq., **1581**, in arm., he m. Judyth, a dau. of Sir Clement Higham, and afterwards Kath., dau. of Wm. Saunder, Esq.; he left 5 chil., Clement and Robt. (by Judyth), and Robt., Francis, and Bryget (by Kath.), p. 237. *Cotman*, vol. i. pl. lxxxi. p. 42.

NECTON. I. Ismayne, w. of Wm. de Wynston, **1372**, Fr. inscr.

lost, N., p. 169. *Cotman*, vol. i. pl. vi. p. 7; *Boutell's Series*. II.
Philippa de Beauchampe [dau. of Hen. Lord Ferrers, of Groby],
widow of Gwy de Warewyk, **1383** (?), marg. inscr. lost, large, rel.,
C., p. 167. *Cotman*, vol. i. pl. ix. p. 9.   III. John Bacon, Gent.,
1528, sm., C.   IV. Robt. Goodwyn and w. Sabina, **1532**, with
7 sons, 3 daus. lost, pecul., N., pp. 29, 243. *Cotman*, vol. i.
pl. lxv. p. 36.   INSCRS. V. Wm. Curteys, notary, and w. Alice,
both dec. "v° Kalendas Marcij a° Jhū," **1499**, eff's. gone, pecul., N.,
pp. 96, 128. *Cotman*, vol. i. pl. xxxix. p. 25.   VI. Ethelburga,
dau. of Robt. Goodwyn, **1527**, eff. lost, N.

NORWICH, ST. ANDREW. I. John Gilbert, citizen, grocer, and
alderman of Norwich, and w. Avice, [both dec. **1467**], with 7 chil.,
canopies, effs. all lost but lower part of w. which is loose, inscr.
mutil., large, C.   II. A Civilian, in mantle, and w., c. **1500**, inscr.
lost (engr. by same artist as Narburgh, 1496), C., p. 214. Ascribed
by Blomefield to Wm. Layer and w., 1537, but probably for Robt.
Gardiner, mayor in 1490, 1499, 1506, dec. 1508, and w. *Cotman*,
vol. i. pl. lxvii. p. 37.   INSCRS., &c. III. *[Robt. Aylmer, alder-
man], **1493** [and w. Elizth.], eff's. lost, marg., N.   IV. *John
Holly, brewer, **1527**, and w. Elizth., effs., &c., lost, except 2 sons,
a scroll, and mcht.'s mk.   V. *John Underwood, titular bp. of
Chalcedon, 1541, cross, &c., all lost except a scroll and sh., pp. 103,
222. *Publ. of Norfolk and Norwich Archæol. Soc.*, vol. vi. p. 14.
VI. *Nath., son of Nath. Remington, **1617**, æt. 14, N.   VII.
*Wm. Jackson, master of King's Hospital, **1626**, N.   VIII. A
Sh., C.   The brass of John Clerk, mayor, 1527, now lost, is engr.
by *Cotman*, vol. i. pl. lx. p. 33.

NORWICH, ST. CLEMENT. I. Margt. Pettwode, widow, **1514**, pecul.,
N., p. 241. *Cotman*, vol. i. pl. lii. p. 30.   INSCR. II. Wm. Heyward, **1622** (Mary Kettell, **1651**, added), mur., N.

NORWICH, ST. GEORGE COLEGATE. I. Wm. Norwiche, mayor
[in 1461], founder of the chantry of St. Mary and All Saints 1463,
and w. Alice, **1472**, with a son between them, on a bracket, pecul.,
N.C. *Cotman*, vol. i. pl. xxviii. p. 21.   INSCR. II. Thos. Warryn,
alderman, **1514**, with mcht.'s mk., S.C.

NORWICH, ST. GILES. I. Robt. Baxter, mayor [in 1424, 1429],
1432, and widow Cristiana, N., p. 200. *Cotman*, vol. i. pl. xxi. p. 18.
II. Rich. Purdaunce, mayor [in 1430], **1436**, and widow "domina"
Margt. [1481], N., p. 200. *Cotman*, vol. ii. Appendix, pl. ii. p. 58.
III. A Chalice and wafer for John Smyth, chaplain, **1499**, S.A.
INSCRS. IV. Margt., w. of Robt. Landysdale, Esq., **1454**, N.   V.
Thos. Hervy and w. Clare, 16th cent., N.   VI. Francisca Bed-

ingfield, **1637**, 6 Eng. vv. with pun on name, her sister Elizth. pos., N.

NORWICH, ST. JOHN MADDERMARKET. I. Walter Moneslee [Mozeley?], **1412**, with anelace, and w. Isabella, worn, loose in Ch. chest, inscr. lately gone (?). II. John Todenham, c. **1450**, with scroll from hands; he had a w. Joan, sm., C'. *Cotman*, vol. i. pl. xxvi. p. 20. III. A Civilian, in mantle, and w., partly covd., c. **1470**, pecul., S.C., pp. 201, 212. IV. Wm. Pepyr, alderman, **1476**, and w. Joan, pecul., C. V. A Lady, c. **1510**, lower part covd., eff. of husband and his first w. lost, pecul., C. Part of the brass of Thos. Caus, mayor in 1495 and 1503, dec. **1506** [not 1560?], and ws. Joan and Helen. VI. John Terry, mcht., mayor [in 1523], he gave £400 to those in need, **1524**, and w. Lettys, with 2 sons and 2 daus., all on brackets, above 20 Eng. vv., pecul., C., pp. 28, 117, 118, 120, 175. *Cotman*, vol. i. pl. lviii. p. 32. VII. John Marsham, mayor [in 1518], **1525**, and w. Elizth., with crucifix at end of rosary, on a bracket; 4 sons, 8 daus., and inscr. lost, pecul., S.A., pp. 28, 111, 175, 226. *Cotman*, vol. i. pl. lix. p. 33. VIII. Robt. Rugge, Esq., alderman, twice mayor [in 1545, 1550], **1558**, and w. Elizth., with 4 sons, 3 daus. and mcht.'s mk. lost, a bracket loose, on its reverse part of a canopy, S.A. *Cotman*, vol. i. pl. lxx. p. 38. INSCRS. IX. John Martin, c. **1500**, in Ch. chest. X. Nich. Suttherton, alderman, mayor [in 1539], **1540**, on reverse part of a lady in mantle, c. **1440**, with a dau. beside her, loose, pp. 45, 89. XI. *Rich. Scottowe, alderman, 1616, and w. Mary, dau. of John Sutherton, alderman, **1619**; they had 2 sons and 3 daus.; on same slab as No. III. XII. John Melchior, **1657**, N. XIII. John Melchior, sen., **1707-8**, æt. 85, and Corn. Melchior, **1713**, æt. 47, N.

NORWICH, ST. JOHN SEPULCHRE. I. A Civilian and w., c. **1530**, inscr. lost, pecul., worn, C. II. John Browne, of Waltone, Gent. (son and h. of Phillip Brown and his w. Ann) [**1597**?], in arm., and sister Winifrid, holding hands, on same plate, two inscrs., each with 8 Eng. vv., loose in Ch. chest, p. 62. *Cotman*, vol. ii. pl. lxxxvi. p. 44. INSCR. III. John Chapman, **1621**, æt. 82, C.

NORWICH, ST. LAURENCE. I. [John Asger, mcht. of Bruges, mayor of Norwich in 1426, dec. **1436**], feet and an inscr. lost, 8 Lat. vv. left, N., pp. 93, 200. II. Geoff. Langeley [prior " istius loci," i. e. Horsham, near Norwich, **1437**], St. Faith above lost, marg. inscr. mutil., C., pp. 86, 175, 252. *Cotman*, vol. ii. pl. xcvii. p. 48. III. Thos. Childes, " clericus istius ecclesie," **1452**, a skeleton, inscr. lost, N., p. 171. *Cotman*, vol. ii. pl. cvi. p. 51. IV. A Civilian in mantle, c. **1500**, all covd. but head and shoulders, pecul., S.C. Said to be John Westgate, who was sheriff in 1520.   INSCRS. V. Robt. Asger, **1425**, with mcht.'s mk., N.   VI. Rich. at-the-jatys [Gates], **1427**, partly covd., N.   VII. Margt., w. of Robt. Leche, alderman, **1535**, S.C.   Part of a fem. eff., now lost, is engr. in *Cotman*, vol. ii. Appendix, pl. i. p. 57.

NORWICH, ST. MARGARET. Anne, dau. of Sir Thos. Blenerhayset, and w. first of Geo. Duke, Esq., of Brampton, and then of Peter Rede, Esq., of Gynnyngham, **1577**, A.T., C., p. 54. *Cotman*, vol. i. pl. lxxx. p. 42; *Arch. Journ.*, vol. ii. p. 247; *Boutell's Mon. Br.*, p. 139; *Oxf. Man.*, p. 16; *Introd.*, p. 55.

NORWICH, ST. MICHAEL COSLANY. I. Hen. Scolows, alderman, **1515**, and w. Alice, in shrouds, with mcht.'s mk. and Evang. symbs., now in N.C., p. 179.   INSCRS. II. Joan, w. of Rich. Ferrō, four times mayor, **1496**, now in N.C.   III. Rich. Ferrō, alderman, five times mayor [1473—1498], **1501**, "hora quasi .x. post meridiem," with mcht.'s mk., now in N.C., p. 223.   IV. Rich. Wallour, first chantry priest, **1505**, 5 Lat. vv., lately stolen (?), S.C., p. 60.   V. Thos. Coke, rector of Bodham, c. **1515**, chalice lost, now in N.C., p. 125.   VI. Helen and Elizth., daus. of Wm. Godfrey, sheriff, **1530**, now in N.C.   The brass of Joan, w. of Gregory Clerk, jun., citizen and alderman, 1513, has lately disappeared, p. 260.

NORWICH, ST. PETER MANCROFT. I. Peter Rede, Esq., "who hath worthely served not only hys prynce and cvntrey but allso the emperor Charles the 5th both at the conquest of Barbaria and at the siege of Tvnis as also in other places, who had given hym by the sayd emperovr for hys valiavnt dedes the order of Barbaria," **1568**, in arm., pecul.; on reverse of eff. and inscr. the upper part of a civilian, with scroll work, &c., 16th cent., Flemish, now in C., pp. 47, 52, 199, 233. *Cotman*, vol. i. pl. lxxvii. p. 41; *Introd.*, p. 52. INSCRS. II. Mary, dau. of [Christopher] Hudsoun, and w. of Wm. Bussie, c. **1600**, m. 18 years; the eff. was stolen in 1857, N.Tr.   III. *Rich. Anguish, **1616**, nearly covd., N.   IV. *Thos., eldest son of John Matthews, **1632**, N.A.   V. *Infant son of Rich. and Kath. Anguish, **1635**, S.C.   VI. John Dersley, **1708**, and w., C.

NORWICH, ST. PETER SOUTHGATE. I. A Priest, c. **1500** (Roger Clerk, 1487?), without stole or maniple, pecul., inscr. lost, nailed to the floor of pew, C. *Cotman*, vol. ii. Appendix, pl. iv. p. 59. INSCRS. II. Wm. Swan, rector [**1498**], C.   III. John Isbellys, N.

NORWICH, ST. STEPHEN. I. A Lady, c. **1410**, with inscr. to "Eel" (or Elena?) Buttry, prioress of Campesse, 1546, now in N.C., pp. 50, 87, 126, 210. *Introd.*, p. 210, and perhaps in *Cotman*, vol. ii. Appendix, pl. i. fig. A, p. 57.   II. Thos. Bokenham, **1460**, and w.

Christian, eff. gone, inscr. nearly all lost, worn, p. 28. *Cotman*, vol. i. pl. xxvii. p. 21. III. Robt. Brasyer, alderman and mayor [in 1410, dec. 1435], and w. Christian, engr. c. **1513**, N.A. IV. Rich. Brasyer, sen., alderman and mayor [in 1456, 1463], and son Rich., alderman and mayor [in 1510], **1513**, pecul., inscr. lost, N.A. V. Thos. Capp (or Capper), Doctor of Ecclesiastical law, vicar, **1545**, in cope, C. *Cotman*, vol. ii. pl. ciii. p. 50. INSCRS. VI. John Frankissh, Gent., **1498**, C., p. 179. VII. Robt. Burght, mayor [in 1504], **1516**, and w. Alice, effs. lost, N.A. VIII. Geo. Mingaye, Gent. (son of Wm. Mingaye, Esq., mayor [in 1561]), **1593**, N.C. IX. Wm. Mingaye, Esq., of Gray's Inn (son of Wm. Mingaye, Esq., mayor), **1607**. X. Mary, w. of Edw. Turflett, Gent., **1625**, N.A. XI. Hen. Mingay, Esq., of the inner Temple, **1632**. This inscr. and No. IX. are under pews, N.C. The brasses of John Danyel, 1418, and of Rich. Poryngland, vicar, 1457, in shroud, are now lost: they are engr. by *Cotman* (vol. i. pl. xvii. p. 15; vol. ii. pl. cvii. p. 51). The mcht.'s mk. of Walter Daniel, 1423, is in the Norwich Museum.

NORWICH, ST. SWITHIN. I. John Horslee, citizen and alderman, **1495**, and w. Agnes, 1504, pecul., inscr. lost, C. *Boutell's Mon. Br.*, p. 89 (det.) INSCRS. II. John Cok, chaplain, **1456**, N. III. John Staloñ, citizen and "barkere" (i. e. tanner), of Norwich, **1463**, S.C. IV. Peter Tilney, **1503**, N. V. Simon Bryght, **1514**, S.A. VI. Wm. Knyght, **1521**, N. VII. Rich. Clement, **1535**, N. VIII. Margt., w. of Thos. Baxter, **1619**, N. IX. Matthew Bridgis, **1625**, æt. 45, 6 Eng. vv. with pun on name, N.C.A.

ORMESBY, GREAT. I. A Lady, c. **1440**, hf. eff. holding a heart, altered by insertion of shading, &c., and inscr. (now lost) added to Alice, dau. of Sir Wm. Boleyn, and w. of Sir Robt. Clere, **1538**, C., p. 107. *Cotman*, vol. i. pl. lxvi. p. 36. II. Sir Robt. Clere, **1529**, marg. inscr. loose, each word divided by a sh., pecul., C., pp. 223, 233. *Cotman*, vol. ii. pl. lxii. p. 34; *Introd.*, p. 234. INSCRS. III. Robt. Mortymer, Esq., c. **1480** (?). IV. Three Scrolls with text from Job xix. 25, loose in Ch. chest, heart and inscr. lost, for Robt. Clere, **1446**.

OUTWELL. Rich. Quadryng, Esq., **1511**, pecul., now mur.

PASTON. Erasmus Paston [1538], and w. Mary [Windham, **1590**?], her eff. lost, they had 3 sons and 9 daus., 4 Eng. vv., on reverse of one sh. part of a Dutch inscr., **146**.., on reverse of the other a head on a mattress, Flemish, C., p. 47. *Cotman*, vol. i. pl. lxviii. p. 37.

PLUMSTEAD, LITTLE. I. A Civilian and w., c. **1480**, inscr. lost, C. II. Sir Edw. Warner, **1565**, æt. 54, in arm., 10 Eng. vv., p. 235.

Cotman, vol. i. pl. lxxvi. p. 40. INSCRS. III. Walter Burfford (?), rector " qui nouā fabricā istius cancelli fieri fecit," c. 1470, C. IV. *John Marker, 16th cent., N.

RAINHAM, EAST. I. *Geo., son of Roger Townshend, Esq., child, c. 1500. II. Robt. Godfrey, LL.B., rector of Reynham St. Mary, 1522, in acad. (?), pecul., sm., p. 78.

RAVENINGHAM. I. *Margt., w., first, of Hounfrey Castyll‾, and afterwards of Rauf Wyllughby, " Squier for kyng Rychard the thyrd' body," 1483, with collar of suns and roses, 8 Eng. vv., curious, pecul., C., p. 126. *Cotman*, vol. i. pl. xxxv. p. 24. INSCRS. II. Rich. Baspole and ws. Alice, Beatrice, Agnes, N., 16th cent. III. John Baspole and ws. Agnes, Elene, N.A.

REEDHAM. John Berney, Esq., 1473-4, and w. Elizth. (?), dau. of Osbert Mundeford, all lost but eff. of w., curious, pecul., S.C.

REEPHAM. I. *Sir Wm. de Kerdeston, 1391, and w. Cecilia (Brewes), in mantle, male eff. and canopy much mutil., marg. inscr. in 6 Lat. vv. lost, large, C., p. 160. *Cotman*, vol. i. pl. xii. p. 10. INSCRS. II. Margt. Camplyn, 1527, N.A. III. John Jeckes, 1577, N. IV. Mr. Rich. Heyward, 1608, æt. 68, S.A.

RINGSTEAD, LITTLE. Rich. Kegell‾, " arciū et decretor' inceptor," rector, "qui tectū isti' Cancelli totaliter fieri fecit," 1482, pecul., C., p. 78.

ROUGHAM. I. Sir Wm. Yelverton, justice of the king's bench, in arm., coif, collar of suns and roses, and w. Agnes (Brewes), c. 1470, inscr. lost (?), A.T., pp. 91, 116, 197. *Gough*, vol. ii. pl. lxxxvii. p. 230. II. †Wm. Yelverton, esquire for the body to Edw. IV., 1481, and w. Kath. (Spelman), with 7 sons, a dau. lost, engr. c. 1510 (?), pecul., N.C., p. 200. *Cotman*, vol. i. pl. xxxiv. p. 23. III. John Yelverton, 1505, Roger Yelverton, 1510, in shrouds, under canopy, very sm., pecul., qd. pl., C., pp. 221. *Cotman*, vol. ii. pl. cix. p. 52. IV. Wm. Yelverton, 1586, and 2 ws., Anne, dau. of Sir Hen. Fermour (eff. lost, with 6 sons and 4 daus.), and Jane, dau. of Sir Edw. Cocket (with 4 sons and 2 daus.), inscr. lost, C. *Cotman*, vol. ii. pl. lxxxii. p. 43. INSCR. V. John Swafham, vicar, 1499 (?).

SALL. I. Geoff. Boleyn, 1440, and w. Alice, 5 sons and 4 daus. lost, N. II. Thos. Roose, 1441, and w. Kath., with 8 sons and 4 daus. standing by their parents, on a bracket, canopy gone, N.Tr. This brass is similar to that at Blickling, 1454, and probably engr. about the same time by a local artist. III. John Funteyn, 1453, and ws. Alice, Joan, Agnes, with 2 sons and 1 dau.; all lost but eff. of 1st and 2nd ws., inscr., and a scroll; sm., now mur., N.Tr.

Blomefield, vol. vi. p. 234 (8vo. Ed. 1807); *Gough*, vol. ii. pt. ii. pl. xl. p. 120. IV. John Brigge [**1454**], in shroud, 6 Eng. vv. (see Appendix B.), S.A. *Gough*, vol. ii. pl. xxxviii. p. 309; *Cotman*, vol. ii. pl. cviii. p. 51. Inscrs. V. Simon Boleyn, chaplain, **1482**, chalice lost. VI. Thos. Hagham, chaplain, **1483**, with Evang. symbs., eff. lost, N. VII. *Margt. Cawke, **1486**. VIII. *Margt. Ryghtwys, **1500**. IX. *John Ryghtwys, **1504**. X. Wm. Funteyn, **1505** (?), and w. Margt. XI. *Hen. Hoddys, **1532**. XII. Simon Grene and w. Helwisia, rel. XIII. Geoff. Melman (?), worn, on reverse a head of a lady with braided hair on a cushion, Flemish, p. 47. XIV. *Peter and Margt. Crome. XV. *Cath. Good.

Scottow. *A Chalice and wafer for Nich. Wethyrley, chaplain, worn, S.A.

Sculthorpe. I. *Hen. Unton, "Gentilman, cirographorius" of the court of common pleas, **1470**, kng., p. 194. *Cotman*, vol. i. pl. xxxi. p. 22. II. John Hampton, **1521**, and w. Elizth., with 7 sons and 1 dau. Inscr. III. John Stebyrd and w. Margt., 15th cent., on a sh. a hammer surmounted by a crown and initials J. S.

Shernbourne. Sir Thos. Sherneborne, chamberlain to Queen Margt. (of Anjou), **1458**, and w. Jamima de Chorneys, maid of honour to the queen, in mantle, inscr. lost, C., p. 194. *Cotman*, vol. i. pl. xxiv. p. 20.

Sherringham. John Hook, **1513**, and w. Magdalene.

Shottisham, St. Mary. Edw. Whyte, Esq., loose, and w. Elizth. [Froxmere], both dec. [of the sweating sickness] July 8th, **1528**, pecul., C., p. 233, 243. *Cotman*, vol. i. pl. lxi. p. 34.

Snettisham. I. John Cremer, **1610**, and w. Anne, with 6 sons and 1 dau., 4 eleg. vv. *Cotman*, vol. ii. pl. xc. p. 45. II. †A Female eff., c. **1600**.

Snoring, Great. *Sir Ralph Shelton [**1424**], all lost but the head, and w. [Alice], dau. of Sir Thos. de Uvedale, with her arms— a cross moline—on her kirtle, marg. inscr. mutil., C., pp. 189, 190. *Cotman*, vol. i. pl. xix. p. 17.

Southacre. I. Lord John H[arsick], **1384**, and w. Kath., [dau. of Sir Barth. Calthorpe], with arms on dresses, marg. inscr. mutil., large, N.C., pp. 61, 112, 157, 159, 160, 166. *Gough*, vol. i. pl. lviii. p. 153; *Cotman*, vol. i. pl. x. p. 9; *Boutell's Series;* and *Introd.*, p. 157. II. Thos. Leman, rector, **1534**, in acad. (?), kng., with B. V. Mary and Child, pecul., loose, C. *Cotman*, vol. ii. pl. cii. p. 49. Frags. III. Two Hands holding a heart (on reverse the head of a civilian, c. **1400**); part of a scroll to [Sir Roger Harsicke] and w. Alice, c. **1450**, with Flemish letters on the reverse, pp. 48, 108.

SPARHAM. I. Wm. Mustarder, rector, c. 1490, pecul., N., p. 78. II. †Rich. Dykke, rector, 1539, N. INSCRS. III. Clement Wulvysby, 1497. IV. Wm. Follcard, Gent., c. 1500.

SPROWSTON. John Corbet, Esq., 1559, in arm. (upper part gone), and w. Jane [dau. of Ralph Berney, Esq.], with 4 sons and 6 daus., mur., N.A., p. 112. *Cotman*, vol. i. pl. lxxi. p. 38.

STALHAM. A Civilian and w., c. 1460, sm.

STOKESBY. I. Edmund Clere, Esq., 1488, and w. Elizth., dau. and h. of Thos. Charles, Esq., pecul., C., pp. 171, 200. *Cotman*, vol. i. pl. xxxvi. p. 24. II. Ann [dau. of Robt. Gygges, Esq., and widow of Sir Thos.] Clere, only lower part of eff. left, 10 Lat. vv., 1570, C. *Cotman*, vol. i. pl. lxxviii. p. 41. III. *Ann, w. of Thos. Clere, 1614, with 6 sons and 3 daus., C. INSCRS., &c. IV. *Thos. Gerard, "in decretis bacallarius," rector, 1506, eff. lost, C. V. *John Holte, S.T.B., rector, 1616, C. VI. *Chas. Clere, 1636, and w. Elizth. VII. *A Head of a fem. eff., c. 1600, in Ch. chest.

STRADSETT. Thos. Lathe, Esq., 1418, with collar, N., p. 188.

SURLINGHAM. I. John Alnwik, priest, benefactor to the Ch., 1460, in acad., 4 Lat. vv., rel., C., p. 84. *Cotman*, vol. ii. pl. xcviii. p. 48. II. A Chalice and wafer, c. 1520, mutil., for Rich. Louhauwys (?), rector, 1514, C.

SWAFFHAM. I. A Man in arm., c. 1480, worn, loose, w. and inscr. lost, pecul., p. 200. *Cotman*, vol. ii. Appendix, pl. iii. p. 58. INSCR. II. Thos., son of Arry Cannon, 1634.

SWANTON ABBOT. Stephen Multon, priest, 1477, pecul., sm., C.

TAVERHAM. *A Chalice and inscr. for John Thorp, priest, 1515.

THEMELTHORPE. †Wm. Pescod, 1505, sm.

THWAITE. *A Civilian and w., c. 1500, S.A.

TOTTINGTON. *Margt. Pory, 1598, æt. 54, and son (?) E. V.; her 2nd husband, Luke Vnger, pos., kng., N.A. *Gent. Mag.*, vol. lxxxix. pt. i. 1819, pl. 11, p. 113.

TROWSE. *———, w. of Roger Dalyson, 1585, C.

TRUNCH. A Heart with 2 scrolls, 16th cent., p. 108. See brasses in private possession—Mr. Bayfield.

TUDDENHAM, EAST. *A Civilian, with signet-ring at end of rosary, and 2 ws., c. 1500, inscr. lost, pecul. *Cotman*, vol. i. pl. xlii. p. 26.

TUDDENHAM, NORTH. A Cross bearing an inscr. for Francisca, dau. of Thos. Skippe, Esq., 1625, æt. 2, very sm., p. 222.

UPWELL. I. A Priest, c. 1430 [Wm. Mowbray, rector, 1428?], in cope, with good triple and super canopy, marg. inscr. lost, C., pp. 79, 176. *Cotman*, vol. ii. pl. xcv. p. 47. II. Hen. Martyn, rector of Yaxham, **1435**, in cope, now in C., p. 81. *Boutell's Series; Publ. of Norfolk and Norwich Arch. Soc.*, vol. ii. p. 110. In Cole's MS., 5,805, fol. 97 b, in Brit. Museum, is a sketch of a brass (now gone) exactly like No. II., but the head of eff. lost, to Wm. Whyttermote, rector of Yaxley, 1442, N.A.

WALSHAM, NORTH. I. A Chalice and wafer to Edm. Ward, vicar [**1519**?], p. 125.   II. Another to Robt. Wythe, chaplain, c. **1520**.   INSCRS. III. Margt. Hetercete, **1397**.   IV. Wm. Rous, **1404**.   V. Robt. Bradfield, 15th cent.   VI. *Robt. Grey, **1492**.   VII. Robt. Raunt, chief constable of the hundred of Twinstend, **1625**, æt. 60; by his w. Elizth. he had 2 sons and 6 daus., p. 119.   VIII. John Page, **1627**, æt. 59.

WALSINGHAM, GREAT. I. *Margt. Stoke, c. **1460**, hf. eff., loose, N.   II. Geoff. Porter, **1485**, with curious gypcière, and w., pecul., S.C.   III. Wm. Kemp, **1539**, and w. Margt., pecul., N.C., p. 28.   IV. A Civilian and w., c. **1540**, inscr. lost, pecul., p. 28. *Arch. Journ.*, vol. xiv. p. 94.   INSCRS. V. *John Child, **1517**.   VI. *Nich. Shotton, **1528**, and w. Margt.   VII. John Harte, **1529**, and w. Alice.   VIII. *Thos. Grandon, **1532**, chalice lost.   *Four others to Jacob Gresham, Cecily Gerald, Robt. Torold, Wm. Lawis.

WARHAM, ALL SAINTS. Wm. Rokewod, Esq., **1474**, pecul., sm., p. 200.

WHISSONSET. I. Wm. Boron (or Bozon), Esq., **1460**, pecul., engr. c. **1485**, p. 200.   II. Thos. Gybon, Gent., **1484**, pecul., p. 200.   III. Wm. Boron, Esq., **1489**, pecul., p. 200.   INSCR. IV. Rich. Bozoun, **1450**, 4 Lat. vv.

WITTON, near NORWICH. I. Dame Juliana Anyell, vowess, c. **1500**, sm., N.   INSCR. II. Nich. Dade, 16th cent., N.

WIVETON. I. Wm. Bisshop, priest, **1512**, with chalice and wafer, pecul., sm., p. 79.   II. A Skeleton in a shroud, c. **1540**, inscr. lost.   III. Geo. Brigge, late of Latheringsett, Esq., **1597**, æt. 53, and w. Anne; they had 2 daus., Margt., Sara.   INSCR. IV. A Memorandum of the bequest of Rauf Grenewey, citizen and alderman of London, **1558**, who left 13*d*. and 3*d*. in bread to 13 poor persons every Sunday. Thos. Grenewey, his executor, made over the rectory of Briston to trustees for the payment; with mcht.'s mk., Grocers' arms, and sh., mur.

WIGGENHALL, ST. MARY. A Heart surrounded by 4 scrolls (one lost), to Sir Robt., son of Edm. Kervile, c. **1450**, pp. 107, 108. *Boutell's Chr. Mon.*, p. 112.

WORSTEAD. I. John Yop, rector of Boton [**1404**?], hf. eff., worn, C.   II. A Civilian, c. **1500**, inscr. lost, C. *Cotman*, vol. ii.

Appendix, pl. vii. p. 61.   III. *Thos. Crymer, **1504**, in shroud, lost (?).   IV. John Alb'aster, **1520**, loose, very sm., N.   He and his w. erected the chancel-screen.   Inscrs. V. John Spicer, **1440**, 2 Lat. vv., C., p. 31.   VI. John Glaven, **1505**, and w. Isabella, N. VII. Thos. Whatts, "wursted wen'," **1506**, N.   VIII. John Carman, **1508**, with mcht.'s mk., N.   IX. Christopher Rauf (or Raut), **1538**, and w. Joan, C.   X. Roger Blome, S.C.A.

YELVERTON. I. Margt., youthful dau. of Thos. Aldriche, mayor of Norwich [in 1507], **1525**, very sm., S.A.   Inscrs. II. *Andr. Sparow, **1503**, N.   III. Thos. Holte and w. Beatrice, and her father Robt. Wolverton, Esq., c. **1530**, S.A.   IV. John Sparowe, C. V. *Thos. Blenerhayset, Gent., 4th son of Thos. Blenerhayset, of Barsham, **1590**, S.A.   VI. *John, son of Thos. Sparowe, 16th cent., C.

INSCRIPTIONS, &c.

BANHAM. *Dame Elizth. Mountencye, prioress [of the nunnery of St. George, Thetford], 16th cent., N.   BARSHAM, EAST. †—— Calthorpe, **1637**, on wall of a cottage.   BLAKENEY. I. John Calthorp, Esq., one of the founders "Epucal-" (?), **1503**, and w. Alice [Astley], with sh., N.   II. Wm. Rowd and w. Helen. III. Rich. Brown and w. Avice.   BROOM. Two Shs. and a scroll, effs. in shrouds (?) lost, mur., N.   *BURLINGHAM, NORTH, ST. ANDREW. I. Thos. Gylbert, **1508**, and w. Margt., N.A.   II. Robt. Frennes, **1527**, N.   III. John Blake, **1565**, and w. Kath.   BURLINGHAM, NORTH, ST. PETER. *Wm. Gillman, 6 Eng. vv., C., outside Ch.   CANTLEY. Hen. Hyldewell, **1519**.   CASTLE ACRE. Wm. Fuller, **1523**, not pecul., N.   CAWSTON. *Wm. Gurney, Gent., 1578, and w. Anne (Waytes), **1596**, with 1 son and 3 daus., effs. lost, S.Tr.   COLTISHALL. Robt. Postyl, N.   CROSTWIGHT. *Hen. Lessyngham, **1448** (?).   EASTON. Isabella Alberd.   ELMHAM, NORTH. I. Joan Fysscher.   II. Wm. Fysscher.   III. Thos. Smith, pastor, 1584—**1631**.   FELMINGHAM. Ursula Wychehynggam, c. **1530**, on reverse an inscr. to Wm. Elyes, chaplain, **1500**, in Ch. Chest, p. 48.   FORNCET. I. Thos. Baxter, and w. Margt., dau. of Wm. Drake, Gent., both dec. **1535**.   II. †Rich. Baxter and w. Isabella, **1485**.   FRAMINGHAM, EARL's.   Hen. Buntyng, N.   HELLINGTON. Sir Anth. Gaudy, **1642**, C., 6 Eng. vv.   HOLKHAM. Robt. Dockyng, **1458**, and w.   HOLME-HALE. Sir Esmon de Illeye [**1349**?], and w. Alice [Plumstead?], Fr., N.   HONINGHAM. Kath., w. of Rich. Vincente, **1544**.   Hoo. *John Dunham, **1467**, N. INTWOOD. Cicely, dau. of and h. of Edw. Shelton, Esq., of Brome, and w. of Wm. Hirst, Gent., **1619**, C.   KNAPTON. *Wm. Smyth,

1516, N. Lynn, St. Nicholas. I. Anne, dau. of Joseph and Isabell Raylie, **1627**, æt. 24 days. II. A Mcht.'s mk. Martham. Robt. Alen, vicar, **1487**, a heart (inscribed "post tenebras, spero lucem, laus deo meo"), stolen at the recent restorations, p. 108. Melton, Great. *John Harvy, **1519**, in a pew, N. Melton, Little. Dorothy, dau. of Robt. Marsham, Gent., and w. of Edm. Angwish, and her son Robt., both dec. **1604**. Moulton. I. John Holler, **1528**, and w. Cath., loose. II. Anne, dau. of Hen. Palmer, and w. of Jas. Underwode, loose.

Norwich. St. Benedict. *Peter Vertegans, "Gardyner," **1633**, N.A. The Cathedral. I. Ralf Pulvertoft, "custos caronelle" [Charnel-house, **1505**?], 9 Lat. vv., mur., Jesus Chapel. II. *Joseph, son of Edw. Hall [bp. of Norwich], **1642**, æt. 23, mur., C. Dutch Church. I. John Elison, 36 years pastor, **1639**, æt. 58, Lat., Dutch, and Eng. vv., his son John, mcht. of Amsterdam, pos., mur. II. Theoph. Ellison, son and successor for 36 years to his father, **1676**, æt. 67, rel. St. Ethelred. Wm. Ramsie, **1613**, æt. c. 80, C. St. George Tombland. I. John, son of Wm. Browne, alderman and his w. Judeth, **1621**, C. II. Lucian Lawes, sheriff, **1641**, and w. Elizth., Thos. their son pos., N. St. Gregory. I. John Wylby, "mercenarius," alderman, **1440**, and w. Matilda, pecul., N. II. Alice, w. of John Clerk, **1467**, S.A. III. Hen. Gunton, citizen, **1468**, and w. Margt., worn, N.A. IV. Thos. Alberd, citizen, **1510**, S.A. V. Robt. Bryon, **1531**, N.A. St. Helen. I. John Beteyns, 15th cent., S.A. II. Dan. Markon, **1627**, æt. 36, N. St. James. Wyborough, w. of Robt. Drake, **1618**, C. St. Julian. John Lulman, **1637**, æt. 58, N. St. Martin-at-Oak. *John Bungey, left a house to the parish, **1582**, and w. Agnes, mur., N. St. Martin-at-Palace. I. *John Tillys, Gent., 14 [90?], mutil., S.C. II. John, 2nd son of Raphe Shelton, Esq., of Brome, **1588**, æt. 33, 4 Eng. vv., loose. III. *John Powle, "inholder," **1620**, 6 vv., S.A. St. Mary Coslany. I. Hen. Mounteforth, "in decretis Doctor," curate, **1518**, 5 Lat. vv., C., pp. 60, 179. II. Ane (Clarke), w. of —— Claxton, had 9 sons and 5 daus., 12 Eng. vv., mur., **1605**, N.Tr. The brass of a Civilian and w., c. 1460, sm., now lost, is engr. by *Cotman* (vol. i. pl. xxv. p. 20); the head of a male eff. in the Norfolk and Norwich Museum is probably part of this brass. St. Michael-at-Plea. I. Barbara, w. of Wm. Ferrer, alderman and twice mayor [in 1562, 1575], **1588**, with skeleton, C. II. Mary, w. of Rich. Ferrer, **1605**, N.Tr. III. Anne, w. of Robt. Ferrer, twice mayor [in 1536], 1530; Wm. (her son) twice mayor, 1577; his son Rich. once mayor [in 1596], **1616**, A.T., N.C. IV. Dan. Heylett, M.A., incumbent, **1617**, æt. 27, 8 Eng. vv., C.

V. Tobyas de Hem, mcht., **1629**, æt. 41, N. VI. *An, dau. of Thos. Cory, alderman, **1634**, æt. 17, C. VII. *John Ward, B.A., of Eman. Coll., Camb., **1634**, C. ST. PETER HUNGATE. *Alice, w. of Augustine Scottow (?), **1596**, partly covd. ST. PETER-PER-MOUNTERGATE. I. John Barney, Gent., **1620**, with scroll, &c., C. II. *Robt., son of Owen Godfrey, Esq., of Hendringham, **1646**; perhaps a palimpsest, as there is the matrix of a chalice above, C. *ST. SIMON AND ST. JUDE. I. Hen. Gardener, priest, born at Catton, 2 Lat. vv., mur., N. II. John, son of Dan. and Jane Walters, **1619**, mur., C.

OXBURGH. [Wm. Schanckey, servant to Sir Thos. Bedingfyld, "olim ista per bene pulsans organa vigint' ann,"] **1521**, marg. mutil. C. PLUMSTEAD, GREAT. Rich. Zottys, **1502**, N. *PORINGLAND. I. Edw. Canwold, 1501, and w. Cecilia, **1503**, N. II. Wm. Body, N. RANWORTH. I. Roger Eryng, **1484**, N. II. Roger (?) ——, **1507**, worn, N. III. Robt. Bunne and w. Beatrice, c. **1520**, C. IV. Robt. Kynge, **1521**, N. V. Three Labels with text from Job (on reverse of one, part of inscr. to Thos. (?) Drye, citizen of Norwich, **1510**), c. **1530**, heart and inscr. lost, N., pp. 48, 108. *RINGLAND. I. John at Mere, chaplain, N. II. John at Mere, **1506**, and w. Elizth., N. ROCKLAND ST. MARY. Margt. Sendell, N. RUNTON. I. Agnes Maryet. II. Thos. Makke, **1497**. SANDRINGHAM. Wm. Cobbis, Esq., **1546**, and w. Dorothy, a dau. of Sir John Spelman, with 4 sons and 8 daus. SHIPDAM. *A Saint in brass, dug up in Ch. yard. *SLOLEY. I. Wm. Ward, chaplain, N. II. Adam Sparhawke, **1520**, C. Five others to Thos. and John Hardyngham, John Heynys, Wm. Thirkyld, Adam Ryall. STIFFKEY. Margt. Bramche, **1479**. STRATTON ST. MICHAEL. *John Cowall, rector, rebuilt C. in **1487** [dec. 1509]. SUFFIELD. I. Adam Symmondis, **1415** (?), and w. Agnes [Rugge]. II. John Symondys, **1453**, and w. Cecilia. III. Wm. and Joan Betynys, both dec. April 1st, **1460**. IV. John Theobald, **1467**. SWANTON-MORLEY. I. Robt. Rokysby, N. II. Thos. Baret and w. Margt., N.A. III. John Bone, S.A. TERRINGTON, ST. CLEMENT. John Coraunt, **1528**, and w. Joan, N. THORNHAM. I. Simon Miller, mcht., **1464**, with W. on sh. II. John Myller, **1488**, N. WALPOLE ST. PETER. Sir John Whetom, parson of Walpole and Leveryngton, **1537**. WALTON, WEST. *John Reppes, **1561**, and ws. Margt. (dau. and h. of Hen. Smith) and Thomasin (dau. of Thos. Denham), once on A.T., now mur., N.A. WELLS. *Thos. Bradley, rector, 1446—**1499**, built the C., mur., C. WITTON, near NORTH WALSHAM. I. Hen. Hemsley, vicar, [**1522**]. II.

x

Thos. Calke, **1519**.   III. *Thos. Parmeter, **1631**, and w. Frances, 1627, C.

Most of the inscrs. in this county which have no date affixed are generally of the early part of the 16th cent., and engr. by local artists.

The brass at HOCKWOLD is lost; it commemorated Amfelicia, dau. of Sir Humph. Coningsby, and w. of Sir John Tendall, **1532**, with 9 daus. kng., pecul., pp. 215, 243. *Gough*, vol. ii. pt. i. pl. xxxviii. p. 309; *Cotman*, vol. i. pl. lxiv. p. 36.   At WEST BRADENHAM was a brass cross with bust to Thos. de Cailey, rector, 1324; at REDENHALL, an eff., with canopy, to Wm. de Nieuport, 1326; at STRATTON ST. MARY, a brass to Sir Roger de Bourne, 1331; at HARPLEY, an eff., with canopy, to John de Gournay, rector, 1332. At EMNETH is a matrix of a Man in arm., cross-legged, c. 1290, with canopy; it is engr. in the *Publ. of the Norfolk and Norwich Archæol. Soc.*, vol. vi. p. 12, in illustration of a paper on "Lost Brasses," by the Rev. C. R. Manning, and supposed by him to commemorate Sir Adam de Hakebeach. In the same communication (at p. 21) are engravings of matrices of crosses in Norfolk, at NORTH PICKENHAM (Margt. de Wantone, c. 1320); PULHAM ST. MARY (Simon de Walpole, rector, 1331); EAST HARLING. The brass of Sir Ralph de Rochford, 1369, formerly at WALPOLE, is engr. in *Gough*, vol. ii. pl. iii. p. 8.

Northamptonshire.

ADDINGTON, GREAT. John Bloxham, first chaplain of St. Mary's Chantry founded by Hen. Veer, **1519**, with chalice and wafer, marg. inscr., Evang. symbs., A.T., C. *Churches of Northants.*, p. 100; *The Brasses of Northants.*, *by Franklin Hudson*, London, 1853; *Anastatic print.*

ALDWINCKLE. Wm. Aldewyncle, Esq., **1463**, not in arm. *Hudson.*

ASHBY CANONS. I. John Dryden, Gent., **1584**, inscr. lost, N. *Hudson.*   INSCRS. II. John, son of Sir John Dryden, bart., **1631**. III. Sir Erasmus Dryden, bart., **1632**, and w. Frances, 1630.

ASHBY, CASTLE.   Wm. Ermyn, rector, **1401**, in cope, with SS. Anna, Kath., Margt., Mary Magd., Elena—Peter, Paul, Andrew, Nich., Laur., inscr. lost, large, C., p. 67. *Waller*, pt. xi.; *Hudson.*

ASHBY ST. LEGER'S. I. Thos. Stokes, Esq., **1416**, not in arm., and w. Elena, with 4 sons and 12 daus., single canopy, Hy. Trin. (lost), sm., S.A., pp. 91, 172, 203. *Boutell's Series; Hudson.*   II. Wm. Catisby, Esq., Aug. 20th, 1485, and w. Margt. [dau. of Wm. baron Zouch, of Harrington], **1494**, in heraldic dresses, with 3 sons and 2 daus., fine canopy, pecul., C., pp. 59, 199. *Baker's Northants.*, vol. i. p. 249; *Hudson.* III. —— Catesby, in tabard, c. **1500**, kng., sm., S.A., p. 59. *Hudson.* Probably Geo. Catesby, Esq., **1505**. IV. Wm. Smyght, rector of Oxshylfe [Oxhill, co. Warw.], and Eldertoft (?), **1510**, in acad., head lost, pecul., S.A., pp. 29, 78. *Hudson.* INSCRS. V. Sir Wm. Catesby, " unus Trenchcatorum " to Hen. VI., **147**-, C. VI. Joan (dau. of Sir Thos. Barre (?) and his w. Alice, sister of John Lord Talbot), 2nd w. of Sir Wm. Catesby, and formerly w. of Rich. de la Bere (?), **1471**, C.

ASHTON. *Robt. Mariott, yeoman, and w., c. **1580**, with 9 sons and 6 daus., 12 Eng. vv., A.T., N.A. *Hudson.*

ASTON-LE-WALLS. *Alban Butler, Esq., **1609**, and 2 ws., Sybilla (dau. of Simon Rawlegh, Esq., of Thornborowe, co. Warw.), with 5 sons and 7 daus., and Isabella (dau. of John Odingesalls, Esq., of Long Itchington, co. Warw.), with 2 daus., mur., N. *Hudson.*

BARNWELL ST. ANDREW. Christopher Freeman, **1610**, æt. 51, and w., with 4 sons and 4 daus., 4 eleg. vv., sm., qd. pl., mur., C. *Hudson.*

BARTON, EARL's. *John Muscote, Gent., a prothonotary of the court of common pleas, **1512**, and w. Alice; 4 sons, 2 daus., inscr., Hy. Trin., and 3 Evang. symbs. lost, N. *Hudson.*

BARTON SEGRAVE. Jane, w. of Hugh Floyde, rector, **1616**, æt. 26, with 1 son and 1 dau., and 3 chil. dec., 6 Eng. vv., qd. pl., mur.

BLAKESLY. Matthew Swetenham, " Portitor Arcus" and Esquire to Hen. IV., **1416**, with SS. collar, C., p. 189. *Hudson.*

BLATHERWYCKE. Sir Humph. Stafford, Esquire for the body to Hen. VIII., son and h. of Sir Humph. Stafford, **1548**, and w. Margt. [Tame] (upper part of eff. lost), with 6 sons, now mur. *Hudson.*

BLISWORTH. Roger Wake, Esq., lord of the manor, **1503**, and w. [Elizth., dau. of Sir Wm. Catesby], with 7 sons and 3 daus., Hy. Trin. lost, marg. inscr., A.T., S.A. *Hudson.*

BODDINGTON. *Wm. Procter, rector of Boddington and Brington, **1627**, C. *Hudson.*

BRAMPTON, CHURCH. Jone, w. of James Furnace, **1585**, a skeleton, inscr. reversed, worn, sm., qd. pl., N. *Hudson.*

BRAMPTON-BY-DINGLEY. I. *A Man, in arm., and w. in mantle, head gone, c. **1420**, canopy mutil., inscr. lost. *Hudson.* II. *Simon Norwiche, Esq., **1468**, and w. Isabella, 1467 (eff. lost), with B. V. Mary and Child. *Hudson.*

BRINGTON, GREAT. A Priest, c. **1340**, in cap, hf. eff. on a bracket, stem and marg. inscr. lost, rel., C., pp. 137, 142. *Oxf. Man.*, p. 63; *Boutell's Chr. Mon.*, p. 139; *Hudson; Introd.*, p. 143.

BURTON LATIMER. I. *A Man [Rich. Boyvill?] and w., in

shrouds, c. **1500**, with 9 sons and 8 daus., male eff. (fem. effs. ?) and inscr. lost. *Hudson.* II. Margt., w. of Thos. Bacon, and dau. of Geo. Francklyn, Esq. (who pos.), **1626**, with child in swaddling clothes, 6 Eng. vv., mur., p. 25. *Hudson.*

CHACOMB. Hy. Trin., arms of city of London, mcht.-adventurers', mcht.'s mk., monogram, and inscr. to Myghell Fox, citizen and grocer of London, and patron of the Ch. [ob. 1569, engr. c. **1543**], and ws. Mary [Eddes] and Clemons [Hawtyn], with chil., Rich., Anth., John, Anne, Alice, Jone, Alys, C., p. 102. *Hudson.*

CHARWELTON. I. Thos. Andrewe, jun., Gent., and w. Emma, dau. of Rich. [Knyh]tley, Esq., **1490**, with 4 sons and 7 daus. under sm. canopies, marg. inscr. and 4 Lat. vv., pecul., N.A., p. 29. *Hudson.* II. Thos. Andrewe, mcht. [dec. 1496], and w. Margery [dau. and h. of Rich. Clarell, Esq.], engr. c. **1490**, with 5 sons and 3 daus., double canopy with 4 pediments and sm. canopies over chil., mutil., marg. inscr. and 6 Lat. vv., pecul., N.A., p. 29. *Baker,* vol. i. p. 302; *Hudson.* III. Thos. Andrewes, Esq., **1541**, and w. Agnes [Newport], male eff. engr. c. **1510** (?), N.A., pp. 41, 230. *Hudson.*

CHIPPING WARDEN. I. Wm. Smarte, rector, **1468**, sm., C. *Hudson.* II. Rich. Makepeace, yeoman, **1584**, æt. 68, and w. Dorothy, with 6 sons (lately lost) and 9 daus., N. *Hudson.*

COTTERSTOCK. *Robt. [Wyntryngham], canon of Lincoln, prebendary of Ledyng, and provost of the chantry of Cotterstock, **1420**, in cope, on a bracket, canopy and marg. inscr., C., p. 173. *Hudson.*

CRANFORD, ST. ANDREW. I. *John Fossebrok, Esq., **1418**, and w. Matilda, "sicca antrix" to Hen. VI., now mur., pp. 189, 208. *Hudson.* II. John Fosbroke, Esq., **1602**, æt. about 80, and 2 ws.; by his 1st w. —— he had 4 sons and 4 daus., by his 2nd w. Awdre, 1589, he had 4 sons and 12 daus.; he had above 70 grandchildren which he relieved, and portioned 18 chil., now mur., sm. *Hudson.*

CRANSLEY. *Edw., son and h. of Geo. Dalyson, Esq., **1515**, and w., S.A.

*DENE. I. Sir Edm. Brudenell [eldest son of No. II.], **1581** (?), in arm., and 2 ws. [Agnes, dau. of John Bussey, and Etheldred, dau. of Thos. Fernly], and dau. [Etheldred], 6 eleg. vv., qd. pl., mur., N.A. *Hudson.* II. Sir Thos. Brudenell, 1558, and w. Elizth. [dau. of Sir Wm. Fitz-William], their son Thos. pos. **1586**, A.T., S.C., pp. 62, 237. *Hudson.* III. A Man, in arm., and w., c. **1600**, mur., S.A. *Hudson.* Probably John Brudenell, Esq., 1606, and w.

DODFORD. I. John Cressy, Esq., **1414**, and w. Cristina, N.C., p. 188. *Boutell's Series; Hudson.* II. Wm. Wylde, Esq., **1422**, and widow Cecilia, mother of Cristina Cressy, N.C., p. 189. *Hudson.*

III. *Bridget, 2nd w. of John Wyrley, Esq., **1637**, sm., now under pews, N.C.

EASTON NESTON. Rich. Fermer, Esq., mcht. of the staple of Calais, **1552**, in arm., and w. Anne, dau. of Sir Wm. Browne, knt., [lord mayor of London in 1513], marg. inscr., A.T., C. *Hudson*.

FAWSLEY. I. Thos. Knyghtley, Esq., second son of Sir Rich. Knyghtley, **1516**, in tabard, and w. Joan, dau. and h. of Thos. Burneby, Esq., N., p. 107. *Hudson*. II. *Sir Edm. Knyghtleye, 1542, in arm., and w. Ursula [dau. of Sir Geo. Vere], sister of the Rt. Hon. John earl of Oxford, **1557**, with 6 daus., Jane, Isabell, Jane, Joan, Jane, Joane, marg. inscr. and 18 eleg. vv., N. *Hudson*.

FLOORE. I. Thos. Knaresburght, Esq., 1450, and w. Agnes, **1498**, B. V. Mary and Child lost, loose, C., p. 199. *Hudson*. II. Hen. Michell, Esq., **1510**, and w. Phillipa, with Hy. Trin., loose and worn, pecul., C. *Hudson*. III. A sm. Cross, loose and mutil., with inscr. for Alyce, dau. of John Wyrley, Gent., and his w. Dorothe (dau. and h. of John Wake, Esq.), **1537**, C., p. 222. *Hudson*.

GEDDINGTON. I. Hen. Jarmon, with small knife, and w. Anna (much mutil.), c. **1480**, pecul., N.A., p. 202. *Hudson*. INSCR. II. *Thos. Maydwell, **1628**, and w.

GREEN'S NORTON. I. Sir Thos. Grene, **1462**, and widow Matilda (dau. of John Throckmarton, Esq., under treasurer of England), with 3 sons (lost), Thomas, ——, John, and 1 dau. Elizth., marg. inscr., large, once on A.T., C., p. 194. *Baker*, ii. p. 65; *Boutell's Series*; *Hudson*. The inscr. states that Sir Thos. was son and h. of Sir Thos. Grene, by Philippa, dau. of Robt. Lord Ferrairs, of Charteley, by his w. Elizth., the dau. of Thos. Lord Spencer. Sir Thos. (the father) was son and h. of Sir Thos. Grene, by his w. Maria, dau. of Rich. Lord Talbot and his w. Ankeret, the dau. and h. of John Lord Strange, of Blakemere. II. A Fem. eff., c. **1490**, husband and inscr. lost, sm., once on A.T., N.A. *Baker*, ii. p. 65; *Hudson*.

GRENDON. A widow Lady betw. 2 men in arm., c. **1480**, inscr. lost, p. 197. *Hudson*.

HARROWDEN, GREAT. [Wm. Harwedon, Esq.], **1433**, and widow Margery, dau. and h. of Sir Giles Seynt-John, canopy lost, marg. inscr. mutil., C., p. 190. *Hudson*.

HEMINGTON. Thos. Mountagu, Gent., **1517**, not in arm., and w. Agnes [dau. of Wm. Dudley, of Clopton]. *Hudson*.

HEYFORD, NETHER. I. Sir Walter Mauntell, **1487**, and w. Elizth., a dau. and h. of John Abbot, Esq., marg. inscr., large, A.T., C., pp. 62, 198. *Hudson*; *Arch. Journ.*, vol. ix. p 300. INSCR. II. John Mauntel and w. Elizth., c. **1400**, Fr., with 2 shs., once lost, the other with arms of Heyford, and on reverse the arms of Wm. Montacute, earl of Salisbury, 1344 or 1397, engr. in *Arch. Journ.*, vol. ix. p. 300; see also the communication (at p. 385) by W. S. Walford, Esq., A.T., C.

HIGHAM FERRERS. I. Laurence de St. Maur, rector [**1337**], with fine canopy and super-canopy having niches containing the Deity (?) with soul, SS. Peter, Andrew, Paul, Thos.; at the sides, S. John Evang., an Angel, SS. John Bapt., Stephen, a Bp., St. Mark — SS. Luke, 4 effs. lost (the 4th S. Christopher), Matth., large, A.T., C., pp. 106, 137, 138, 143. *Gough*, vol. ii. pl. cxviii. p. 332; *Hudson. Boutell's Mon. Br.*, p. 95 (eff.) II. A Large Cross with Deity at intersection and Evang. symbs. at the extremities (S. Mark restored) for Thos. Chichele, **1400**, and w. Agnes [dau. of Wm. Pyncheon, Gent.], N.C., pp. 106, 173. *Stemmata Chicheleana*, Oxf., 1765, p. 1; *Gough*, vol. ii. pl. xxviii. p. 80; *Specimens of Anc. Ch. Plate, Sep. Crosses, &c.; Churches of Northants.*, p. 17; *Oxf. Man.*, p. 79; *Boutell's Series*, and *Chr. Mon.*, p. 42; *Introd.*, p. 175. Abp. Chicheley was the eldest son of Thos. and Agnes Chicheley. III. [Wm. Chichele, sheriff and alderman of London, **1425**, and w. Beatrice, dau. of Wm. Barret, Esq.], in mantle, with canopy, marg. inscr. in 12 Eng. vv. [see Appendix B], mutil., the other inscr. lost, large, N.C., p. 200. *Stemm. Chich.* (front.); *Gough*, ibid.; *Boutell's Series*. IV. Editha [widow of John] Chaunceler, mcht. of Kensham, c. **1435** (?), head mutil., N.A. *Gough*, vol. ii. pt. iii. p. 333; *Hudson*. V. Hen. Denton, chaplain of Chelston, **1498**, with chalice and wafer, S.A. *Churches of Northants.*, p. 18; *Gloss. of Architect.*, Art. Brasses; *Arch. Journ.*, vol. iii. p. 139; *Boutell's Mon. Br.*, p. 99; *Oxf. Man.*, p. 23; *Hudson; Introd.*, p. 64. VI. Wm. Thorpe, mercer, **1504**, and widow Marion, with 6 sons and 6 daus., N.C., p. 118. *Gough*, see No. I. VII. A Heart inscribed Jhc̄, c. **1510** (?), above matrix of Hy. Trin. (?), N.C., p. 107. *Boutell's Mon. Br.*, p. 124; *Hudson*. VIII. Arthur Sotheryn, **1518**, inscr. lost, sm., N.A. *Hudson*. IX. Rich. Wylleys, warden of the College [**1523** ?], in cope, C. *Gough*, see No. IV.; *Boutell's Series; Hudson*. X. A Civilian, c. **1540**, worn, w. and inscr. lost, pecul. *Hudson*. XI. A Civilian, c. **1540**, w. and inscr. lost. *Hudson*.

HORTON. Roger Salisbury, Esq., **1491**, and ws. Emma (with 1 son and 2 daus.?) and Anne (with 1 dau.), chil. lost, C. *Hudson*.

KELMARSH. Morrys Osberne, Gent., **1534**, not in arm., and ws. [Grace and Alyce], with 8 sons and 9 daus., one w. and upper part of the other lost, inscr. mutil.

KETTERING. Edm. Sawyer, **1631**, æt. 69 (?), in arm., and w. Anne, dau. of Edw. Goodman, Gent., of Blaston, Leic., they had 15 chil., qd. pl., mur.

LOWICK. Hen. Grene, Esq., of Drayton, **1467**, in tabard, and widow Margt., **1460** (?), head on cushion, 9 scrolls inscribed Da gliam Deo (one lost), marg., A.T., S.A., p. 115. *Gough*, vol. ii. pl. lxxxiv. p. 215; *Hudson*.

MARHOLM. *Sir Wm. Fytzwillyams, **1534**, and w., in heraldic dresses, mur., A.T.

NASEBY. I. John Olyver, jun., **1446** (head lost), and widow Agnes, inscr. and scrolls lost, N.A. *Hudson*. FRAG. II. *A Sh. and crest of John Shukbrugh, Gent., **1576**, and w. Joan.

NEWBOTTLE. *Peter Dormer, of Lee Grange, Bucks., son of Geoff. Dormer, Esq., of West Wycombe, **1555**, and 2 ws., the former with 8 sons and 11 daus., mur., A.T., C. *Hudson*.

NEWNHAM. *Rich. Catesby, Esq., **1467**, and w. Letitia (in mantle), with hands joined, all lost but eff. of w. and sh. with motto, now mur., S.A., p. 115. *Hudson*.

NEWTON-BY-GEDDINGTON. I. *John Mulsho, Esq., not in arm., and w. Joan, **1400**, sm. effs. kng. to a cross, with S. Faith in the head, marg. inscr. recently restored, pp. 136, 261. *Gough*, vol. ii. pl. lxxiii. p. 195. II. Margt., dau. of Francis Tanfield, Esq., of Gayton, and w. of Maurice Tresham, **1604**, æt. 66, qd. pl.

NEWTON BROMSHOLD. I. Wm. Hewet, rector, **1426**, sm., C., p. 78. *Hudson*. II. Roger Hewet, chaplain, **1487**, C. *Hudson*.

NORTHAMPTON, ST. SEPULCHRE. Mr. Geo. Coles, left £11 yearly to the town for pious uses, **1640**, and ws. Sarah (with 2 sons and 1 dau.) and Eleanor (with 7 sons and 2 daus.), hands joined, also two clasped hands with 8 Eng. vv. alluding to this emblem of firm friendship, marg. inscr., p. 62. *Hudson*. *Gent. Mag.*, vol. lxxxii. 1812, pt. ii. p. 609 (effs.)

NORTON. *Wm. Knyght, 1501 (?), and w. Kath., **1504**, special benefactors to the Ch., N. *Hudson*.

*ORLINGBURY. I. Wm. Lane, **1502** (?), and w. INSCR. II. John Max, **1450**.

PAULERSPURY. Sir Hen. Mylnar, parson [**1512**], with chalice and wafer, eff. lately lost (?), C., p. 260. *Hudson*.

POTTERSPURY. Agnes, w. of Cuthbert Ogle, lieut. of Whittelwood Forest, **1616**, she "beareth ye armes of the Mandleys, out of which house she Descended," pecul. (?), sm., S.A. *Hudson*.

PRESTON DEANERY. *Sir Clement Edmonds, secretary to Jas. I., æt. 58, in arm., and w. Maria, a t. 52, both dec. **1622**, sm.

†RAUNDS. I. John Tawyer, **1470**, and w. Margt., with 4 daus., sons gone. II. Wm. Gage, Esq., **1632**, left to the poor £10 for 40 years, his brother John pos., mur.

ROTHWELL. I. Wm. de Rothewelle, archdeacon of Essex, prebendary of Croprydi (?) [Croperdy, a prebend of Lincoln], Ferryng, and Yalmeton [**1361**], in cope, head on a cushion supported by 2 angels, Fr. inscr., rel., C., pp. 104, 144. *Bridges's Northants.*, vol. ii. p. 56; *Waller*, pt. v.; *Hudson. Gent. Mag.*, vol. lvii. 1787, pt. ii. p. 759 (inscr.) II. Edw. Saunders, of Haryngton, first founder of chantry, **1514**, and w. Joan. *Hudson.* III. Owen Ragsdale, founder of hospital, qd. pl., mur., C. *Hudson.*

SPRATTON. Robt. Parnell, **1474** (or 1464), and w. Joan, with 5 sons and 4 daus., worn and mutil., C. *Hudson.*

STAVERTON. *Thos. Wylmer, Gent., **1580**, and w. Elizth. (Crudye), with 6 sons and 4 daus., mur., N.C. *Hudson.*

STOKE BRUERNE. *Rich. Lightfoot, rector for 23 years, **1625**, æt. 63, his son and h. pos., qd. pl., mur., C. *Hudson.*

SUDBOROUGH. Wm. West, 1390, and w. Joan, **1415**; also on the same stone, on one plate, sm., John West, chaplain, Wm. West, marbler, Alice, w. of Rich. Mason, and 5 sons and 3 daus. of Wm. and Joan West, now mur., N.Tr., pp. 63, 65, 211. *Hudson. Introd.*, p. 65 (John West).

SULGRAVE. *Laur. Wasshington, Gent. [1584] (head lost), and w. Anne [dau. of Robt. Pargiter], **1564** (eff. lost), with 4 sons and 7 daus., N. *Hudson.* They were ancestors (in the 6th remove) of Geo. Washington, first President of the United States.

TANSOR. John Colt, rector, **1440**, C.

THORP MALSOR. †Thos. Maunsell.

WAPPENHAM. I. A Man in arm., c. **1460**, lower hf. of eff. lost, inscr. and 4 shs. lost, N., p. 196. *Gent. Mag.*, vol. lxiii. 1793, pt. ii. pl. 11, p. 1,163; *Hudson.* II. Sir Thos. Billyng, chief justice of the court of common pleas, **1481**, and w. Kath. [dau. of Roger Gyfford, of Twyford, Bucks.], with 5 sons and 4 daus. all lost but one dau., lower part of effs. of parents gone, 6 scrolls lost out of 16 inscribed " Jhū mercy, Lady helppe," inscr. loose, S.A., pp. 90, 252. *Hudson.* III. Constancia, w. of John Butler, Esq., and sister of Hen. Vere, Esq., **1499**, sm., S.A. *Hudson.* IV. A Man, in arm., and w., c. **1500**, inscr. lost, sm., S.A. *Hudson.* Probably Thos. Lovett, Esq., 1492, and 2nd w. Anne (Drayton), and placed by No. V. V. Thos., son of Thos. Lovett, Esq., in arm. [dec. 1542], and w. Elizth. [dau. of John Butler], c. **1500**, sm., S.A. *Hudson.* INSCR. VI. Thos. Lovett, Esq., of Astwell, **1586** (eff. lost); by his

w. Elizth. [dau. of Rich. Fermor, Esq.] he had a dau. Jane, who m. John Shirley, Esq., S.A.

WARKWORTH. I. Sir John Chetwode, lord of the manor, 1412, Fr. inscr., legs mutil., S.A., p. 188. II. John Chetwode, son of No. I., 1420, Fr. and Lat. inscr., C., pp. 178, 189. *Hudson.* III. Margery, dau. of Sir John Chetwode, and w. of John Brounyng, Esq. (dec. and buried at Melbury), she died the same year as her husband, 1420. IV. Amabilla, w. of Sir John Chetwode, and afterwards of Sir Thos. Straunge, 1430, inscr. in Fr. and Lat., now in S.A., p. 178. *Hudson.* V. Wm. Ludsthorp, Esq., 1454, he m. Lady Elizth., dau. of Sir John Chitwode, C., p. 197. Nos. I., III., and V. are buried in the Ch., p. 259.

WELFORD. *Francis Saunders, "legum Anglie apprenticius," lord of the manor, 1585, æt. 71, in arm., and 3 ws., the 1st with 2 sons and a dau., the 2nd with an infant, the 3rd with 1 son and 4 daus., a motto allusive to name, "Franck et saine counseil," 4 eleg. vv. cut in stone, qd. pl., mur., A.T. *Hudson.*

WOODFORD, near THRAPSTONE. *Symon Malory, Esq., the elder, c. 1580, in arm., A.T., C. *Hudson.*

WOODFORD CUM MEMBRIS. *Nich. Stafford, vicar, c. 1425, C. *Hudson.*

INSCRIPTIONS, &c.

ABINGTON. *Three Daus., remains of the brass of Wm. Mayle (?), 1536, and w. Margt., 1557, with 13 chil., Hen., Nich., Thos., Peter, Rich., Wm., Robt., John, Christopher, Arthur, Ales, Annes, Joan. BRIXWORTH. Edw. Saunders, Esq. (son of Franc. Saunders, of Welford), lord of the manor, 1630, æt. 8, 4 Lat. vv. In the *Gent. Mag.*, vol. lxxx. 1810, pt. i. p. 321, are engravings of matrices of crosses to Adam de Tauntone, 1334 (hf. eff.), and Simon Curteis, 1328 (?). DODDINGTON. Wm. de Pateshull, 1359, Fr., a cross lost. ISHAM. *John Boyville, Esq., 1493, worn, eff. lost.

The brasses are lost at BRAUNSTON (Hen de Barneby, rector, 1391 ?), KING'S SUTTON (Thos. Weston, 1525, and ws. Agnes, Elizth., Agnes), and TOWCESTER. In PETERBOROUGH CATHEDRAL was a cross-legged eff. in arm. to "Senour Gascelin de Marham;" it had been "lately divorced from the marble" when Gunton's Hist. of the Ch. was published in 1786.

Northumberland.

NEWCASTLE-UPON-TYNE, ALL SAINTS. *Roger Thornton, mcht., 1429, and w. "domicella" Agnes [Wanton], 1411, in mantle, with

7 sons and 7 daus., two fine triple canopies, with soul, 12 apostles, 6 saints, &c., marg. inscr., Flemish, large, now mur. in Vestry, p. 20. *Brand's Hist. of Newcastle*, vol. i. p. 382; *Hodgson's Hist. of Northumberland*, vol. i. pt. ii. p. 312.

At St. Andrew's, Newcastle, are the feet of a Man in arm., being a fragment of the brass of Sir Adam (?) de Atholl and his w. Mary, **1387**; also at Hexham, *Inscr. and shs. to Robt. Ogle, son of Ellen, dau. of Sir Robt. Bertram, **1404**, eff. and canopy gone, S.C.A.

Nottinghamshire.

Clifton. I. Sir Robt. Clyfton, founder of a college of three chaplaincies, **1478**, p. 197. *Thoroton's Notts., by Throsby*, vol. i. pl. 6, p. 112. II. Sir Gervase Clyfton, son and h. of No. I., completed the college, dec. at London, **1491**, buried at Clyfton by his 2nd w. Agnes, dau. of Sir Robt. Constable, of Flamborough, p. 198. *Ibid.* III. Geo. Clifton, Esq. (son and h. of Sir Gervis Clyfton and his w. Wynyfrid), **1587**, æt. 20 years and 7 months, and w. Wynyfreide (dau. of Sir Anth. Torold and his w. Anne, a dau. and h. of Sir John Constable, of Kynukton), with 1 son, Gervis (eff. lost), p. 240. *Ibid.* IV. †A Lady, c. **1570**, nailed to a board.

Darlton. *A Man, in arm., and w., c. **1510**, inscr. lost.

Markham, East. Millicent, w. of Sir Wm. Meryng [**1419**], marg. inscr. mutil., pp. 207, 208. *Thoroton*, vol. ii. p. 232; *Introd.*, p. 208.

Newark. I. Alan Fleming, mcbt., **1361**, under fine groined triple canopy, with the Soul, S. Peter, and other figures (39 in all, including male and female figures in niches at the sides), marg. inscr., Evang. symbs., mcbt.'s mk., very large, Flemish, qd. pl., measuring 9 ft. 4 in. by 5 ft. 7 in., worn, now mur., pp. 20, 39, 141, 162, 165, 168, 203. *Fowler's Newark* (?). *Boutell's Mon. Br.*, p. 19 (eff.) II. A Civilian, c. **1540**, inscr. lost, sm. III. Wm. Phyllypott, mcbt., **1557**, and w. Elizth. (eff. lost), now mur. *Fowler* (?). Inscrs., &c. IV. Robt. Whitecoumbe, mcbt. of Calais, **1447**, with mcbt.'s mk., C. V. John Burton, D.D., vicar, **1475**. VI. Robt. Browne, Esq., alderman of the Guild of the Hy. Trin. in the Ch., constable of the Castle, receiver to Cardinal Wulcy and to John Longlond bp. of Lincoln, sheriff of Notts. and Derbyshire, keeper of the rolls in Notts. and district of Kesteven, Lincolnshire, **1532**, and w. Agnes, marg., on A.T., with shs. at the sides, C. VII. Robt. Kyrkbye, master of the Song school for 42 years, appointed by its founder

Thos. Magnus, **1573**, and w. Elizth., **1566**. VIII. Thos. Lund, once mayor, **1715**, with skeleton, hour-glass, &c.

STANFORD. A Priest, c. **1400**, holding chalice, inscr. lost.

STRELLEY. Sir Robt. Strelly, **1487**, and w. Isabella, **1458**, in mantle, pp. 126, 170, 198. *Thoroton*, vol. ii. p. 225.

WOLLATON. A Man in arm., and w. in mantle, c. **1470**, inscr. lost (?), pp. 113, 195. *Thoroton*, vol. ii. p. 225 (?). Probably Sir Rich. Willoughby, 1471, and w. Anna, 1467, dau. of Simon Leek.

The brass of Wm. Breton, 1595, formerly at ANNESLEY, was probably lost in 1811 when the Ch. was repewed, p. 130.

Oxfordshire.

ADDERBURY. I. A Man in arm., with collar, and w., c. **1460**, inscr. lost, C., p. 194. II. Jane, w. of Geo. Smyth, dec. Feb. 30, **1508**. INSCR. III. Roger Well¯s, mcht., benefactor to the Ch., and ws. Joan and Agnes.

ASTON ROWANT. I. Ralph Compoite, 1437, and w. Isabella, **1441**, inscr. lost, sm., N. II. A Man and his w., c. **1470**, with 5 daus., all lost but the lower part of the w., the daus., and a sh., N. A Matrix, p. 146.

BAMPTON. I. Thos. Plymmyswode, vicar, c. **1420**, in surplice and almuce, hf. eff., C., p. 79. II. Robt. Holcot, M.A., "venerabilis ac scientificus vir," vicar, **1500**, in cope, sm., C., p. 76. III. Frances, dau. of Sir Thos. Gardner, of Peckham, Surrey, and w. of Sir Thos. Hord, of Cote in Bampton, **1633**, æt. 36, p. 248.

BARFORD, GREAT. Wm. Foxe and w. Joan, **1495**, with 5 sons, sm.

BRIGHTWELL-BALDWIN. I. John Cottusmore, chief justice, **1439**, and w. Amice, very sm., kng., 26 Lat. hexameters, Hy. Triu. lost(?), mur., pp. 56, 90, 171. II. The same persons with fine canopy, no inscr., large, pp. 56, 90, 208. INSCRS. III. John the Smith, c. **1370**, 7 Eng. vv., N.A., p. 141. IV. *John Carleton [**1547**], came from Walton on Thames [c. 1500], and w. Joyce, and 8 chil., Anth., Geo., Wm., John (dec. at Bologna s. p.), Edw., Anne (m. Rowland Litton), Kath. (m. Francis Blunt, Esq., brother to Lord Mountjoy), Jane (m. Erasmus Gaynsford, Esq.), N.C. V. Anth. Carleton and w. Anne (dau. of Thos. Perient, Esq., of Digswell, Herts.), **1562**, and chil. John and Joyse, N.C.

BRIGHTWELL-PRIORS. Rich. Crook, sen., **1549**, 7 Lat. and 4 Eng. vv.; below is a similar inscr. to Rich. Crook, jun.: Robt. Hallei pos.

BRIGHTWELL-SALOME. "Mores Johñ," rector, **1492**, sm., C.

BROUGHTON. Lady Philippa Byschoppesdon, **1414**, large, marg. inscr., p. 208. *Boutell's Series. Introd.*, p. 208 (det.)

BURFORD. I. John Spycer, **1437**, and w. Alys, kng. to a bracket (with the B. V. Mary and Child under a sm. canopy now lost), 12 Eng. vv. (see Appendix B.), pp. 33, 102, 175, 179, 202. II. *John Osbaldeston, Gent. of the upper court in Chadlington, **1614**, and w. Grace, dau. of Humf. Ashfeild, Esq., of Hethrop, 1611, with 10 sons and 2 daus., of which they left 4 sons and 1 dau. surviving them, qd. pl., mur., S.C.

CASSINGTON. 1. A Cross fleury for Roger Cheyne, esquire to the king [**1414**], p. 173. *Oxf. Man.*, p. 79; *Kelke's Sep. Mon.*, p. 16; *Boutell's Series*, and *Chr. Mon.*, p. 102; *Introd.*, p. 175. II. Thos. Nele, Hebrew professor at Oxford, æt. 71, in shroud, 8 eleg. vv., engr. **1590**, qd. pl., mur., pp. 44, 95.

CHALGROVE. I. Reginald Barantyn, Esq., **1441**, C., p. 192. II. Drugo Barantyn, Esq., and ws. Joan, 1437, and Dame Beatrix, **1446**, C., p. 192. INSCR. III. †Thos., son of Thos. Barentyne, Fr., 14th cent., mutil.

CHARLTON-UPON-OTMOOR. Thos. Key [rector, canon of Lincoln], chaplain to John [Chedworth, bp. of Lincoln], **1475-6**, in cope, marg. inscr. mutil., now in C.

CHASTLETON. I. Kath., dau. of Wm. Willington, Esq., of Barson, Warwickshire, and w. of Anth. Throkmorton, **1592**, with 5 sons and 5 daus., sm., N. II. Edm. Ansley, Gent., **1613**, and w., with 7 sons and 3 daus., sm., N. INSCR. III. Wm. Bankes, Esq., of Winstanley, Lanc., son of Wm. Bankes by his w. Sarah, youngest dau. of Walter Jones, Esq., of Chastleton, **1676**, æt. 46.

CHECKENDON. I. John Rede, servant to the king [**1404**], triple canopy and marg. inscr. mutil., C., p. 164. *Boutell's Series.* II. Soul borne by two angels for Walter, son of Sir Wm. Beauchamp, c. **1430**, C., p. 107. *Boutell's Series.* III. Anna, dau. of John Gaynesford, Esq., of Crowhurst, Surrey, and his w. Kath., and w. of Rich. Bowett, Esq., **1490**, upper part of eff. covd., C. INSCR. IV. Cecilia, w. of John Rede, **1428**, eff. lost, C.

CHESTERTON. *Wm. Mawnde, Gent., **1612**, and w. Anne, C.

CHINNOR. I. A floriated Cross with the head of a priest in the centre, c. **1320**, stem and marg. Lomb. inscr. lost, C., p. 135. *Oxf. Man.*, p. 60; *Boutell's Series*, and *Chr. Mon.*, p. 124; *Introd.*, p. 135. II. John Hotham, "magister in theologia," rector, **1361**, in acad. and cap, hf. eff., large, C., p. 144. *Boutell's Series.* He was provost of Queen's Coll., Oxford. III. "Monsr. Reginald Malyns," in arm., and 2 ws., c. **1385**, Fr. inscr., partly covd., large, N.A., pp. 160,

169. IV. "Mouns' Esmoun de Malyns," son of No. III., in arm., and w. Isabel [**1385-6**?], hf. offs., Fr. inscr., N., p. 160. V. Alex. Chelseye, rector, **1388**, holding chalice and wafer, hf. eff., large, C. VI. A Man and his w. of the Malyns family (?), c. **1390**, hf. effs., male eff. and inscr. lost, N. VII. [John Cray, esquire to Rich. II., **1392**], marg. inscr. nearly all lost, large, N., p. 160. *Boutell's Series.* VIII. Robt. Atte Heelde (all lost except the feet), and w. Kath. (headless), c. **1410**, a son lost, S.A. IX. Nich. Atte Heel[d, son of No. VIII., and w. Margery], c. **1410**, eff. of w. lost, inscr. mutil., on same slab as No. VIII. X. Reginald Malyns, Esq., **1430**, head and legs lost, N. XI. Folke Poffe, **1514**, and 2 ws., one w. and inscr. lost, sm., N. INSCRS. XII. Adam Ramoseye, c. **1400**, Fr., a cross or eff. lost, N., p. 140. XIII. John Cristemas, son of John esp'u' (?), c. **1400**, Fr., N. A rubbing of a brass of a civilian, c. 1480, with gypcière, collar, hood, and anelace, once in the S.A., is in the possession of the Archæol. Institute.

COTTISFORD. A Man, in arm., and w., with 8 sons and 5 daus., c. **1500**, inscr. lost, mur.

CROWELL. Sir John Payne, parson, **1469**, hf. eff., 8 Eng. vv., now mur., C., p. 25.

CROWMARSH GIFFORD. Wm. Hyldesley, Gent., **1576**, head and legs lost; by his w. Margt. he had 13 chil., and left surviving Walter, Edm., Franc., Wm., Mary, Cyseely, Margt., Kath., N.

CUXHAM. John Gregory, **1506**, and ws. Petronilla (with 3 sons and 1 dau.) and Agnes, sm., N.

DEDDINGTON. I. A Civilian, c. **1370**, hf. eff., inscr. lost, p. 163. *Gent. Mag.*, vol. lxv. 1795, pt. ii. p. 737. II. †John Higgins, Gent., **1641**, mur. INSCR. III. *Wm. Byllyng, mcht. of the staple of Calais, **1533**, and w. Elizth., 1522, effs. lost, mur., A.T., N., now loose in Ch. chest.

DORCHESTER. I. Sir John Drayton, **1411**(?), with SS. collar, belt ornamented with trefoils slipped, part of the arms of Drayton (?), and w. Isabella [St. Amand?], canopy, inscr. in 10 eleg. vv., large; the whole brass is lost except part of the male eff., whose legs are gone, S.A., pp. 104, 188. *Gent. Mag.*, vol. lxvi. pt. i. 1796, p. 105; *Boutell's Series. Introd.*, p. 116 (det.) II. Sir Rich. Bewfforeste [abbot], c. **1510**, in cope, 2 Eng. vv., C., pp. 74, 76. *Addington's Dorchester Ch.*, p. 15; *Waller*, pt. xv.; *Oxf. Man.*, p. 32; *Introd.*, p. 75. III. A Lady, c. **1490**, sm., inscr. lost, S.A. IV. [Wm. T]anner (eff. lost), Rich. Beweforest, and w. Margt. [**1513**], 5 sons and 2 daus. lost, inscr. mutil., sm., S.A. V. A Sh. with arms of [Rich. ?] Drayton, c. **1450**, eff. lost, S.A. VI. A Mcht.'s mk.,

S.A. Matrix of brass of John de Sutton, abbot, 1349, C., pp. 57, 123. *Gough*, vol. ii. pl. vi.; *Addington*, p. 14; *Oxf. Man.*, p. 56; *Boutell's Chr. Mon.*, p. 54; *Introd.*, p. 57. Matrices, p. 135. *Gough*, ibid.

EWELME. I. Thos. Chaucer, Esq., lord of the manor and patron of the Ch., 1434, and w. Matilda [dau. and coh. of John Burghcrst, of Ewelme], **1436** (?), in mantle, marg. inscr. restored, A.T., S.C., pp. 25, 53, 190. *Gough*, vol. ii. pl. xxxvi. p. 106; *Napier's Swyncombe and Ewelme*, p. 44. Thos. Chaucer was son of the Poet, and had a dau. Alice, who married Wm. De la Pole, duke of Suffolk, and with him founded the hospital at Ewelme. II. John Bradstane, rector, **1458**, hf. eff., N. III. Hen. Morecote, rector, **1467**, hf. eff., N. IV. Wm. Branwhait, master of the almshouse, 1498, engr. c. **1460**, hf. eff., S.A. V. John Spence, B.D., master of the almshouse, **1517**, in acad., S.A., p. 85. VI. Thos. Broke, Esq., serjeant-at-arms to Hen. VIII., **1518**, and w. Anne [Bulstrode], N. *Napier*, p. 338. *Introd.*, p. 212 (det.) VII. †Cath. Palmer, **1599**, and chil., mur. INSCRS. VIII. John Saynysbery, rector, **1454**, hf. eff. lost, S.A. IX. Simon Brayles, chaplain to Alice duchess of Suffolk, and rector of Chedesey, Somerset, **1469**, N. X. Thos. Vernon, Esq., son of Sir Rich. Vernon, **1471**, N.A. XI. Robt. Esmund, Esq., **1474**, N.A. XII. Hen. Lee, fuller and citizen of London, and buried there in "Abdechyrch," and w. Alice, buried here, **1494**, S.A. XIII. John Bacheman, **1513**, N.A. XIV. Anne, w. of John Froste, **1585**, 8 Eng. vv., S.C.

GARSINGTON. Thos. Radley, Gent., **1484**, and w. Elizth., with 5 sons and 5 daus., worn, very sm., now mur. *Arch. Guide to Churches round Oxford*, p. 344. Matrix, p. 135.

GLYMPTON. *Thos. Tesdale, Esq., a benefactor to Balliol Coll. and Abingdon School, born at Stanford Deanlye, Berks., 1547, dec. **1610**, his w. Maude pos., C.

GORING. I. Elizth. ———, **1401**, canopy and Eng. marg. inscr. mutil., N.A., pp. 168, 205, 206. *Oxf. Man.*, p. 94; *Introd.*, p. 207. II. A Civilian and w., c. **1600**, with 3 sons and 5 daus., inscr. lost, C. INSCR. III. Hen. de Aldryngton, **1375**, Fr., N.A.

HAMPTON POYLE. John Poyle, Esq., **1424**, and w. Elizth., S.A., pp. 189, 210. *Introd.*, p. 190 (det.), p. 210 (fem. eff.)

HANDBOROUGH. Alex. Belsyre [first president of St. John's Coll., Oxford], **1567**, recumbent, in shroud, 4 eleg. vv., and translation in 4 Eng. vv.; Thos. Nele (see Cassington, Oxon.), his nephew, pos.; qd. pl., mur., C.

HARPSDEN. I. A widow Lady, c. **1460**, sm., inscr. mutil. II.

A Man, in arm., and w., c. **1480**, inscr. lost.   III. Walter Elmes, rector, **1511**, sm.   IV. Sara, dau. of Roger and Anne Allanson, of London, and w. of John Webb, rector, **1620**, æt. 25, with chil. Wm. and Anne.

HASELEY, GREAT.   I. Thos. Buttler, rector, **1494**, in almuce, C., p. 79. *Weare's Haseley Ch.*, p. 79.   II. Wm. Leynthall, lord of the manor of Lachford, **1497**, in shroud, 3 sons and 3 daus. lost (?), S.A.   III. *Julian, w. of Sir Rich. Fowler, of Rycote, **1527**, N.A.   IV. Mary, dau. of Sir Wm. Barrentyne, and w. of Anth. Huddleston, Esq., **1581**, C.   INSCR. V. Nich. Englefield, Esq., serjeant of the counting-house to Rich. II., **1415**.

HEYTHORPE.   John Aschefeld, Esq., **1521**, and w. Elenor, with 4 sons and 4 daus., A.T., C. Above is a painted window with effs. of the same persons.

HOLTON.   I. Wm. Brome, builder of Chapel and benefactor to Ch., **1461**, in arm., now mur., S.C., p. 196.   II. Wm. Brome, **1599**, æt. 10, sm., now mur., S.C.

IPSDEN.   "Master Thamas Englysche," in arm., and w. Isbell, both dec. **1525**, sm.; on reverse of male eff. the upper part of a lady, with surplice sleeves, c. **1420**; on reverse of fem. eff. part of inscr. in Lat. vv., "......t Stapilton (?) sponsa Johis, Eu John morte ruit . heres tenerisq; suo annis, [e]t plures nati . pat' huc missale legauit, Sint (?) dūo (?) grati . deus oīes santificauit, ..." now fixed down, C.

ISLIP.   *Robt. Banks, Gent., 1605 (with 8 sons and 10 daus.), Hen. Norrys, Esq., **1637** (with 1 son, Hen.), and their w. Susanna, 1634, qd. pl., mur., C.

KIDDINGTON.   *Walter Goodere, rector, **1513**, N.

KINGHAM.   *Cath. James, **1588**, and chil., mur.

LEWKNOR.   John Alderburne, c. **1380**, hf. eff. with fylfot ornament, inscr. lost, a part left in 1845 before the restoration of the Ch., rel., C., p. 260. *Boutell's Series*, and *Chr. Mon.*, p. 153.

LILLINGSTONE LOVELL.   I. Two Hands holding a bleeding heart inscribed "Jhc̄," for John Merstun, rector, **1446**, p. 107.   II. Thos. Clarell, Esq., patron of the Ch., 1471, with collar, not in arm., and w. Agnes, with 1 son and 2 daus. kng., engr. c. **1460**, martlets (part of the arms of Clarell) are at the feet of the effs., sm., pp. 45, 116. III. Wm. Rysley, Esq., **1513**, not in arm., and w. Agnes.

MILTON, GREAT.   *Two Effs. and inscr. to Wm., John, Wm., and Elizth., children of Robt. and Kath. Edgerley, 16th cent., mur., S.A.

NOKE.   Wm. Manwayringe, Gent., of Eastham, Essex, 1529,

Hen. Bradshawe, Esq., chief baron of the exchequer, 1553, and their w. Joan, dau. and coh. of John Hurste, of Kingston-on-Thames, **1598**; she built the chapel, and left lands and rents to the poor of Noke, and of Halton and Wendover, Bucks., qd. pl., mur., pp. 54, 89, 91.

NORTHLEIGH. *A Man in arm., c. **1415**, large, pp. 189, 260.

NORTON, CHIPPING. I. John Stokes, mercer, and w. Alice, c. **1450**, with mcht.'s mks., worn, sm. II. John Yonge, wolman, **1451**, and w. Isabell, large, pp. 128, 202, 211. *Introd.*, p. 202 (male eff.) III. A Civilian, c. **1460**; feet, w., and inscr. lost. Perhaps Wm. Acylton, Gent., 1457, and w. Alice. IV. John Pergett, ironmonger, **1484**, and w. Agnes, with 5 sons and 7 daus., mcht.'s mks. *Introd.*, p. 131 (det.) V. A Lady, c. **1500**. Probably Agnes Tanner, 1503 (see Appendix B.) VI. John Ashefyld, Esq., **1507** (eff. lost), and w. Margt., with 4 sons, 1 dau. and Hy. Trin. lost. VII. Rich. Tante, **1530**, and w. Elizth., all lost but fem. eff. INSCR. VIII. Wm. Lyveryche, John Tanner, Thos. Benet, **1531**, and their w. Anne, effs. lost; 6 sons and 8 daus. belonging to this (?) were lately left. Nos. I., II., III., V., VII., and VIII., which 15 years ago were loose in the churchwarden's house, are rel. in N.A., and all misplaced except No. I. Nos. IV. and VI. are at west end of the Over Norton aisle. The inscrs. to No. VII.; Thos. Grene, 1465, and w.; Isabella Stokys, 1458, have disappeared. See Appendix B., and Introd., p. 260.

NUFFIELD. Beneit Engliss', c. **1360**, hf. eff., Fr. inscr., p. 163.

ODDINGTON. Ralph Hamsterley, rector, fellow of Merton Coll., engr. c. **1500** [dec. 1518], a skeleton in shroud eaten by worms, pp. 44, 55, 218. *Dunkin's Bullington and Ploughley*, vol. ii. p. 101.

OXFORD, ALL SOULS' COLL. I. Philip Polton, B. Can. L., archdeacon of Gloucester, **1461**, in cope, head gone, kng., sm., p. 76. *Kite's Mon. Brasses of Wilts.*, p. 28 (eff.) He built the N.A. of St. Aldate's Ch., Oxford, and was the son of Thos. and Edith Polton, whose brass is at Wandborough, Wilts. II. Rich. Spekynton, LL.B., fellow, commissary and official of Buckyngham, **1490**, in acad., sm., p. 77. III. David Lloyde, LL.B., and Thos. Baker, S.C.L., both dec. Dec. 24, **1510**, in acad., hf. eff's., pp. 34, 85. The brasses are in the ante-chapel.

OXFORD, CHRIST CHURCH. I. John Fitzal[eyn, **1452**], sm., once in C., now in N.C. *Fisher.* II. Edw., son of Hugh Courtenay, brother of the earl of Devon, c. **1460**, sm., now in N.C., p. 202. *Gough*, vol. ii. pl. vii. p. 117; *Fisher; Introd.*, p. 201. III. James Coorthopp [canon of Ch. Ch. and dean of Peterborough,

1557], in almuce, marg. inscr. mutil. and 12 eleg. vv., N.C.A., pp. 79, 227. *Oxf. Man.*, p. 34; *Introd.*, p. 80. IV. Hen. Dow, sent as a student to Ch. Ch. by Queen Elizth., dec. at his brother's at All Souls' Coll., **1578**, æt. 21, in acad., his parents Robt. (cutler of London) and Lettice Dow pos., mur., N.Tr. V. Thos. Morris, M.A. [**1584**], 4 eleg. vv., mur., N.C.A. VI. Stephen Lence, M.A., of London, benefactor to the Ch., **1587**, æt. 34, in acad., ¾ eff., 6 eleg. vv., Arnold Harbart pos., mur., S.C.A. VII. John, son of Geo. Bisshop, bookseller of London, **1588**, æt. 18, 8 eleg. vv., qd. pl., mur., N.C.A. VIII. Thos. Thornton, M.A. (?), educated at Westminster and Ch. Ch., **1613**, æt. 37, his brother Geo. pos., qd. pl., mur., N.C.A. INSCRS. IX. Robt. Kyng, S.T.P., first bp. of Oxon. [**1557**], marg., A.T., moved from C. to S.A. of C. X. Thos. Palmer, "quondam a ratiouibvs edi Christo fundatæ," **1558**, æt. 57, had 5 sons and 5 daus., 6 eleg. vv. A Matrix, A.T., N.Tr., p. 129.

OXFORD, CORPUS CHRISTI COLL. John Claimond, first president and especial benefactor of the Coll. [ob. 1537], an emaciated eff. in shroud, 12 eleg. vv. and mutil. marg. inscr., engr. c. **1530**, now in ante-chapel, pp. 44, 95.

OXFORD, HOLYWELL CHURCH. I. Agnes, w. of Thos. Hopper, physician and once fellow of New Coll., and her dau. Jane, both dec. **1625**, kng., her son Robt. pos., qd. pl., C. II. Eliza, third w. of Mr. Thos. Franklin, dec. in childbirth, **1622**, æt. 33 (?), in bed, with 4 chil., 6 Eng. vv., curious, qd. pl., mur., S.A., p. 221.

OXFORD, MAGDALEN COLL. I. Ralph Vawdrey, M.A., chaplain, **1478**, hf. eff. II. Thos. Sondes, scholar of Divinity, son of Wm. Sondes, Esq., of Trewlegh, Kent [**1478**], marg. inscr. mutil. III. Wm. Tibarde, S.T.B., first president [**1480**], in cope, head and lower part of eff. lost, 12 eleg. vv., marg. inscr. mutil., rel. It is most probable that the eff. is of much later date [c. 1530 ?], and incorrectly assigned to Wm. Tibarde. IV. John Perch, M.A., and "Bacallarius Physico," chaplain to the bp. of Winchester, fellow, c. **1480**, in cope, lower part gone, 14 eleg. vv. and mutil. marg. inscr., rel. V. A Master of Arts (?), c. **1480**, inscr. lost, loose, p. 85. *Introd.*, p. 85 (det.) VI. A Figure similar to No. V., mutil., loose, p. 85. VII. An Ecclesiastic, c. **1480**, hf. eff., loose, p. 84. *Oxf. Man.*, p. 37 ; *Introd.*, p. 84. One of these three effs. is probably that of John Goolde, M.A., 1473. VIII. Geo. Jassy, c. **1500**, hf. eff., 4 eleg. vv. *Fisher.* IX. Thos. Mason, M.A., fellow, **1501**, p. 85. *Ibid.* X. Walter Charyls, M.A., fellow, **1502**, ¾ eff., head lost, loose, sm., p. 85. *Ibid.* XI. Wm. Goberd, B.A., archdeacon of Salop, **1515**, in almuce, p. 79.

Ibid. XII. Nich. Goldwell, M.A., fellow (not an ecclesiastic), **1523**, B. V. Mary and Child lost, sm., p. 85. *Ibid.* XIII. Arthur Cole, S.T.B., president, canon of Windsor, **1558**, on reverse a priest, in chasuble &c., inscr. to Robt. Cobbe, citizen and tailor of London, **1506**, and w. Marg., and part of another inscr., recently repaired, pp. 81, 227. *Waller,* pt. xiii. INSCRS. XIV. †John Cary, fellow, **1515**, nearly effaced, loose. XV. John Bentley, M.A., 6 eleg. vv., loose. All the brasses are now placed on the floor at the sides of the ante-chapel, the effs. are in acad. except Nos. III., IV., XI., and XIII.

OXFORD, MERTON COLL. I. Rich. de Hake[bourn]e, [or Hagbourn], rector of W(o)lford [co. Warw., c. **1310**], a hf. eff., on the head of a large floriated cross, marg. inscr. in Lomb. letters, all lost except the eff., now in N.Tr., pp. 135, 142. *Gough,* vol. ii. pt. i. pl. vii. p. 117; *Boutell's Mon. Br.,* p. 115, and *Chr. Mon.,* p. 137. II. A Priest, **1372** (?), in acad. (?), sm., in the head of a cross which is nearly all lost, marg. inscr. gone, N.Tr., p. 136. *Boutell's Man. of Archæology,* pl. 7, p. 134. III. John Bloxham, B.D., warden, [dec. 1387], and John Whytton, rector of Wodeton, benefactor to the Coll., who pos. c. **1420**, two effs., in acad., under small canopy supported on a bracket with a long shaft, rel., now in C., pp. 45, 77, 82, 175, 176. *Gough,* vol. ii. pt. i. pl. vii. p. 117; *Ingram's Memorials of Oxford,* vol. i.; *Gloss. of Arch.; Boutell's Series; Introd.,* p. 83. IV. John Kyllyngworth, M.A., **1445**, in acad., hf. eff., S.Tr., p. 84. V. Hen. Sever, S.T.P., warden and especial benefactor to the Coll., and a descendant of the founder, **1471**, in cope, with SS. —— (bp.), Jas. the Great, Jas. the Less, Paul, John Bapt., John Evang., Barth., Thos., triple canopy mutil. and partly restored, large, now in C., p. 53. *Ingram,* vol. i.; *Bloxam's Mon. Arch.,* p. 203; *Gloss. of Arch.* (early editions). *Boutell's Series* (eff.) VI. A Priest, in acad., holding chalice and wafer, hf. eff., c. **1520**, Tower, pp. 76, 85. Probably John Bowke, 1519. INSCRS. VII. Wm. Bysse, "consors" of the Coll., **1510**, Tower, p. 179. VIII. Nich. Marshe, M.A., **1612**. IX. Robt. Beseley, M.A., **1623**. Lomb. letters, lately lost (?), p. 139. Matrix of the brass of Thos. Harper and Ralph Hamsterley, 1518, pp. 55, 91. Numerous other matrices, from which most of the brasses have been stolen since the time of Anthony à Wood.

OXFORD, NEW COLL. I. Rich. Malford, warden, **1403**, in cope, inscr. lost. II. [Thos. Cranley, warden, abp. of Dublin, **1417**], with fine triple and super-canopy, 8 Lat. vv., and 8 others on a marg. inscr. nearly all lost, large, pp. 73, 93, 176. *Gough,* vol. ii. pl. xxiii.* p. 50; *Waller,* pt. xvi.; *Boutell's Series. Introd.,* p. 69 (eff.) III.

John Desford, "Juris Canonici Bacallari'," canon of Hereford, **1419**, in cope, hf. eff.   IV. Wm. Fryth, B.D., fellow, **1420**, in cope (?), hf. eff., partly covd.   V. John Lowthe, fellow, "juris civilis p'fessor," **1427**, in acad., p. 82. *Waller*, pt. xi.   VI. Wm. Hautryve, fellow, "decretor' doctor," **1441**, in acad., p. 82. *Ibid.*   VII. Geoff. Hargreve, fellow, S.T.S. (Sacre Theologie Scolaris), **1447**, in acad., p. 84. *Ibid.*   VIII. Walter Wake, S.T.S., fellow, **1451**, in acad., hf. eff., p. 84. *Fisher.*   IX. Thos. Hylle, S.T.P., fellow, benefactor to the Coll., **1468**, in acad., 2 Lat. vv., pp. 82, 96, 103. *Waller*, pt. xi.   X. Thos. Flemyng, LL.B., fellow, **1472**, an emaciated eff. in shroud, sm.   XI. [Rich. Wyard, "Bacca]larij Juris," fellow, **1478**, in acad., pp. 84, 103.   XII. John Palmer, B.A., fellow, **1479**, in acad., p. 84.   XIII. Walter Hyll, M.A., S.T.S., warden, **1494**, in cope.   XIV. John Frye, fellow, S.T.S., **1507**, with chalice and wafer, hf. eff. *Fisher.*   XV. John London, M.A., S.T.S., scribe of the university, **1508**, in acad., p. 85.   XVI. A Notary, c. **1510**, inscr. lost, sm., p. 128.   XVII. John Rede, B.D., warden, **1521**, in cope.   XVIII. John Yong, titular bp. of Callipolis [a city of Thrace], warden, [dec. 1526], engr. c. **1525**, head lost, large, pp. 70, 71, 73, 78. *Boutell's Series.*   XIX. Walter Bailey, "cui Doricastrensis patria fundus erat. Wicchamicis didicit iuuenis quam sumptibus artē Grandior hanc lector regius edocuit," physician to Queen Elizth., **1592**, æt. 63, 10 eleg. vv. and 6 others on mutil. marg. inscr., his brother Wm. pos., p. 57.   XX. Hugh Lloyd, fellow, chancellor to the bp. of Rochester, master of Winchester Coll., D.C.L., &c., **1601**, 10 Lat. vv., qd. pl., mur.   XXI. Anth. Aylworth, born at London, educated at Winchester, fellow of New Coll. [regius professor of medicine 15 years], **1619**, æt. 72, in cap and hood, marg. inscr. mutil., p. 86. He left 2 sons, Martin and Anth.   Inscrs., &c. XXII. A Scroll, all that is left of the brass of Hugh Holes (son of Sir Hugh Holes, justice of England), fellow, **1430** [or 1480], in acad. XXIII. Nich. Osylbury, S.T.B., warden, **1453**, eff. in cope lost. XXIV. A Sh., part of the brass of Dr. Thos. Gascoigne, **1457**, eff. lost.   XXV. *Thos. Hopper (son of John Hopper, Gent., of Loxley, Warwick.), fellow, donor of 500 books to the library, a medical practitioner in Oxford 20 years, **1623**, æt. 56, with a circle, triangles, &c., curious, Agnes his sister pos. and dying, R. H., fellow, completed it, mur.   The brasses are now in the ante-chapel on the floor at the north side, except those which are mur., p. 33.

OXFORD, QUEEN'S COLL. I. Dr. Robt. Langton, enlarged the chapel, c. **1518**, in cope and cap, inscr. lost, pp. 62, 77, 132. *Gough*, vol. i.

pl. xxxvi. p. 102; *Boutell's Series.* II. Hen. Robinson, 18 years provost, restorer of the college, and 18 years bp. of Carlisle, **1616**, æt. 63, curious, 4 eleg. vv., the Coll. pos. in token of gratitude, qd. pl., pp. 30, 54, 72, 216, 230. III. Hon. Airay, S.T.P., provost, **1616**, æt. 57, curious, 8 eleg. vv., Christopher Potter, fellow, pos., qd. pl., pp. 30, 96, 216, 230. These brasses are now preserved in the bursary.

OXFORD, ST. ALDATE. I. Lewis and Griffin Owen, brothers, and of the family of Owen of Penmynyth, M.A. of Ch. Ch., 1597, **1607**, 10 eleg. vv., mur. II. Arthur Strode, of Devon, a member of the Middle Temple, and of Broadgate's Hall [afterwards Pembroke Coll.], **1612**, æt. 23, 4 eleg. vv., qd. pl., mur. III. Nich. Roope, of Devon, B.A., of Broadgate's Hall, **1613**, æt. 27, in acad., 6 eleg. vv. alluding to the name of the Hall, qd. pl., mur.

OXFORD, ST. JOHN'S COLL. I. [Robt.] Harte, born at London, brought up in Kent, educated at Oxford, and dec. there 1571, æt. 24, 6 Lat. vv. II. Robt. Shingleton, of Leicestershire, M.A., fellow, **1577**, æt. 28, 10 eleg. vv. III. John Glover, M.A., fellow, student of medicine, senior proctor, **1578**, æt. 35, 2 Lat. vv., his friends, Rodolph Huchinson and Thos. Mainwaring, pos. INSCR. IV. *Hen. Price (son of John Price, dyer, of London), fellow, B.D., **1600**, æt. 38, eff. lost (?). The brasses are mur. in the ante-chapel.

OXFORD, ST. MARY MAGDALENE. I. Wm. Smith, M.A., fellow of Merton, and a very skilful physician, **1580**, æt. 58, in hood, 16 eleg. vv., mur., p. 86. INSCRS. II. Philip(a) Caxston, widow, **1514**, mur., S.A. III. Jane, dau. of Thos. Basset, Esq., of Hince, Staffordshire, 2nd w. of Robt. Fitzherbert, Esq., of Tissington, Derbyshire, **1574**, mur. Impressions of the brasses (now lost) of Robt. Abdy, priest in cope, 1494, and of Alice, w. of Rich. Hamden, 1524, are in the Craven Ord collection in the Brit. Museum.

OXFORD, ST. MARY-THE-VIRGIN. I. Edm. Croston, native of Lancashire, incumbent of Biggleswade, **1507**, in almuce, with St. Cath., Hy. Trin. lost, 16 eleg. vv., mur., Tower, pp. 79, 100, 132. II. Edw. Chernock, of Brasenose Coll., a son and h. of Robt. Chernock, Esq., of Lancaster, **1581**, 14 eleg. vv., qd. pl., mur., N.A. III. Malina Boys, **1584**, æt. 70, with 7 sons and 5 daus., 10 Lat. vv., Anth. and her other chil. pos., mur., S.A. INSCR. IV. Wm. de Haukesworth, S.T.P., "tercius p'positus huius ecclie," **1349**, C. He was 3rd provost of Oriel Coll. V. *Nich. Quarne, **1598**, mur., C. Matrix of a cross brass on A.T. to Adam de Brome, 1st provost of Oriel, 1332 (?).

OXFORD, ST. MICHAEL. I. Ralph Flexney, alderman, **1578**, and

2nd w. Kath., 1567, by whom he had Thos., Rich., and 7 daus., Thos. pos., qd. pl., p. 216. II. John Pendarves (eldest son of Sam. Pendarves, Esq., of Cornwall), commoner of Exeter Coll., **1617**, æt. 17, 4 eleg. vv., p. 218. INSCR. III. Anna, dau. of Wm. Goodwin, dean of Ch. Ch., and w. of John Prideaux, rector of Exeter, regius professor of divinity, **1627**, and 2 chil. The brasses are now mur. in N.C.

OXFORD, ST. PETER-IN-THE-EAST. I. *Wm. Robertson, "pincerna" of Queen's Coll., **1487**, and w. Joan, worn, sm., now mur., N.Tr. II. Simon Parret, Gent., M.A., fellow of Magdalen Coll., twice proctor, 1584, æt. 71, and w. Elizth., dau. of Edw. Love, Esq., of Aynhoe, Northants., **1572**, æt. 42, with 9 sons and 10 daus., qd. pl., mur., N.A. III. Rich. Atkinson, alderman, five times mayor, J.P. and quorum, **1574**, in mantle, and 2 ws., —— (with 5 sons and 6 daus.) and Annes (chil. lost), A.T., N.C. IV. Rich. Ratcliff, M.D., **1599**, æt. 54, and w., 4 eleg. vv., qd. pl., mur., N.C. V. †John Chyttock, citizen and draper of London, and Rich. Hawnsard, Esq., of Lincolnshire, on reverse 2 Lat. vv.

OXFORD, ST. PETER-LE-BAILEY. I. John Sprunt, mayor, **1419**, head gone, worn. II. A Lady, c. **1420**, inscr. lost. III. A Civilian (Geo. Box?) and w., c. **1640**, kng. INSCR. IV. Wm. Parkar, LL.B., **1510**. The brasses are now mur.

ROLLRIGHT, GREAT. Jas. Batersby, LL.B., rector, **1522**, with chalice and wafer.

ROTHERFIELD-GREYS. I. Sir Robt. de Grey, lord of the manor, **1387**, canopy, marg. inscr., large, C., p. 160. *Boutell's Series; Hewitt's Ancient Armour*, vol. ii. pl. 28, p. 168. INSCR. II. Joan, w. of John Hasteyngs, Esq., **1537**.

SHIPLAKE. John Symonds and w. Jone, c. **1540**.

SHIPTON-UNDER-WYCHWOOD. Elizth., dau. and h. of Thos. Tame, and w. of Edm. Horne, Esq., **1548**, recumbent, in shroud, sh., 12 Eng. vv., qd. pl., mur., N.A.

SHIRBURN. I. Rich. Chamburleyn, Esq., of "Cootys," Northants. [**1493**], and w. Sybyll, dau. of Rich. Fowler, chancellor of the duchy of Lancaster, dec., with 4 sons and 3 daus., Hy. Trin., mur., C. INSCR. II. Wm. Bouldre, **1498**, and w. Joan, N.

SOMERTON. Mr. Wm. Fermoure, Esq., lord of the town, patron of the Ch., and a "Clarke of the Crowne in the Kyng' Benche," temp. Hen. VII., VIII., **1552**, in arm., and w. Elizth., dau. of Sir Wm. Norrysse, S.C.

*SOULDERN. I. Thos. Warner, parson, **1508** (or 1514), p. 79. II. John Throckmorton, child, c. **1620**.

STADHAMPTON. *John Wylmot, **1508**, and w., N.A.

STANTON HARCOURT. I. Thos. Harecourt, Esq., **1460**, not in arm., and Nich. Atherton, Esq., 1454, not in arm., below 3 very sm. effs. [Geo., Alys, and Isabell Harcourt], sm., S.C.   II. Elen, w. of John Camby, **1516**, with a son and dau., C.   III. Hen. Dodschone, vicar, **1519**, C.   A Sh., 1293 (?) (lately lost?), p. 120. *Arch. Guide*, p. 178; *Oxf. Man.*, p. 55; *Introd.*, p. 121.

STOKE LYNE. Edw. Love, Gent., not in arm., and w. Alys, **1535**, with 5 sons and 3 daus., mur., C., pp. 104.

*STOKENCHURCH. I. Robt. Morle, **1410**, in arm., Fr. inscr., N., pp. 140, 188.   II. Robt. Morle, **1412**, similar to No. I., N., pp. 140, 188.

STOKE TALMAGE. I. John Adene, **1504**, and w. Joan.   II. John Pettie, Esq., **1589**, in arm., and w. Elizth., a dau. and h. of Thos. Snapp, Gent., by whom he left surviving, John, Leonard, Maximilian, Christopher, Geo., Mary, Joan, Anne, Alice, Phillippa, p. 237.

SWINBROOK. I. John Croston, Esq., and 3 ws., the first w. with 2 sons and 2 daus., c. **1470**, 6 Lat. vv., C., p. 197.   II. Anth. Fetyplace, Esq., **1510**, in tabard, C.   INSCRS. III. *Alys Feteplas, **1530**, N.   IV. *Symond Feteplas, c. **1530**, N.   V. *Alex. Feteplace, **1616**, N.

TEW, GREAT. I. [John Wylcotes, **1410**?], in arm., and w. Alice [Raynsford?], canopy, marg. inscr. in Lat. vv. mutil., large, C., pp. 186, 187, 205. *Boutell's Series. Introd.*, p. 186 (eff.)   II. Wm. Bosby, **1513**, and w. Agnes, marg. inscr. lost, rel., C., p. 224. FRAG. III. Hy. Trin., c. **1500**, loose, the only remains of the brass of Wm. Reynesford, Esq., lord of the manor, and w., with canopy.

THAME. I. Thos. Quatremayn, of North Weston, and w. Kath. (dau. of Guy de Breton and his w. Joan, a dau. and h. of Thos. de Grey, son of Sir Robt. lord de Grey, of Retherfeld), both dec. 1342, and their son Thos. Quatremayn, 1396 (lower part of eff. lost), and his w. Joan, on a bracket, engr. c. **1420**, marg. inscr. nearly all lost (see Appendix B.), A.T., S.Tr., pp. 45, 188, 208. *Introd.*, p. 189 (det.)   II. Rich. Quartremayns, Esq., councillor to Rich. duke of York and Ed. IV., founder of a "chauntrie .vj. pore men and a fraternyte In the Worshipp of Scynt Cristofere to be relevid in p(er)petuyte," and w. Sibil [dau. of Nich. Englefeld] (head gone), in mantle, with 1 son in arm., c. **1460**, marg. inscr. in 10 Eng. vv., A.T., S.Tr., p. 194. *Boutell's Series. Introd.*, p. 195 (eff.) Rich. Quartremayns and w. founded Ricot Chapel.   III. A Civilian and w., c. **1500**, with 3 sons and 6 daus., worn, Hy. Trin. and inscr. lost, N.

IV. Geoff. [Dormer, mcht. of the staple of Calais], 1502, and ws. [Margery] (with 5 sons lost, and 8 daus.) and Alice (with 7 sons and 5 daus.), mcht.'s mk., Evang. symbs., marg. inscr. mutil., A.T., N.Tr.   V. Cristofre Bridgman, 1503, and w. Mawde, with 12 chil., Cristofre, John, Edw., Geoff., Rich., Wm., Thos., Edw., Nich., Thos., Joan, Joan, nearly covd., N., p. 203.   VI. Walter Pratt [1508], and w. Isabell, with 3 sons and 3 daus., Evang. symbs., inscr. reversed, worn, N.   VII. *Sir John Clerk, of North Weston, who took Louis of Orleans, duke of Longueville, marquis of Rotuelm prisoner, at the tourney (?) of Bomy (?) by Terouane, Aug. 16th, 5th Hen. VIII., dec. 1539, in tabard, mur., A.T., C.   VIII. [John G]aley, Gent., 1543, not in arm., head lost, and w. Joan, cff. lost, sm., C.   IX. Edw. Harris, M.A., fellow of New Coll., first master (for 30 years) of the school at Thame founded by John Williams, 1597, æt. 63, mur., C.   Rubbings of the brass of a Civilian, 16th cent., and of an inscr. to John Benet, c. 1460, now lost, are in the possession of the Arch. Institute.

WATERPERY.   I. Isabell Beaufo, c. 1370, sm., mutil., Fr. inscr. lost, p. 169.   *Introd.*, p. 168 (part of eff.)   II. Walter Curson, Esq., 1527, and w. Isabell, dau. of Robt. Saunders, Esq., of Harrington, Northants., both buried at the Augustin Friers Ch. at Oxford, with 8 sons, 9(?) daus. lost, marg. inscr. with text from Job xix. 25—27 mutil., other inscr. lost, palimpsest, large, N., pp. 48, 111, 242, 244, 252.   *Architectural Guide*, pt. iii. p. 253; *Proceedings of Oxf. Arch. Soc.*, 1845; *Oxf. Man.*, p. 16; *Introd.*, p. 49. III. A Man in arm., c. 1530, mutil., w. and inscr. lost, S.A.

WATLINGTON.   I. Wm. Frankeleyn, 1485, and w. Sibill, 3 sons and 1 dau. lost, N.   II. Wm. Gibsson, 1501, and w. Matilda, in shrouds, inscr. lost (see Appendix B.), S.A.   III. Jerem, eldest son of Robt. Ewstes, "who gave ye trebell Bell that hangeth in this Steppell" [1587], and John Ewstes, brother of Jerem, 158[8], only one eff., S.A.

WHITCHURCH.   I. Thos. Walysch, "valectus trayer Ducis Laucastrie Henrici quarti quinti sexti Regum," c. 1420, in arm., and w., inscr. half gone, C., p. 189.   II. Roger Gery, "in decretis bacularius," vicar, procured the sanction of John bp. of Lincoln to the union of the rectory and vicarage of the Ch., 145-, with chalice and host, once on A.T., now mur., C.   III. *Peter Winder, curate, 1610, mur., outside C., pp. 5, 230.   INSCR. IV. Thos. Percyvalle, rector, 1533 (?), N.

WITNEY.   I. Rich. Wenman, 1500, and ws. Anne (with 3 sons and 3 daus.) and Christian (with 2 daus.), scrolls to Hy. Trin., arms of the staple of Calais, marg. inscr. lost (?), partly covd., A.T., N.C., p. 224. II. Rich. Ayshcome, Gent., of Lyford, Berks., gave £200 to the poor, **1606**, æt. 55, C.

WOODSTOCK. Rich. Bailly, citizen and haberdasher of London, and chairman of Woodstock, **1441**, sm.

YARNTON. *Wm. Fletcher, alderman, **1826**, A.T., p. 43.

INSCRIPTIONS, &c.

BICESTER. I. Wm. Staveley, Esq., "Dūs de Bygnell," 1498, and w. Alice (dau. and h. of Sir John Fraunces and his w. Isabella, dau. and h. of lord Hen. Plesyngton), **1500**, now mur., C. II. Roger Moore, Esq., 1551, and w. Agnes, dau. and h. of John Husye, Esq., and chil., engr. c. **1650** (?), mur., A.T., C. III. Wm. Hortt, alias Hart, Gent., **1584**, and w. Eme, dau. of Mr. (?) Ashton, Esq., of Crostone, Lanc., with 5 sons and 4 daus., mur., C. IV. Humph. Hunt, **1601**, and w. Elizth., with 5 sons and 3 daus. BLOXHAM. *John Griffith, **1635**, with sh. LAUNTON. Sir Matthew Shawe, priest, c. **1520**, very sm., eff. lost, C. The Matrix of the brass (a Greek cross fleury, bearing the inscr.) of Mr. Rich. Glasyer, priest, 16th cent., is left in the N.A., p. 222. A sketch, taken May 27, 1660, is given in Harleian MS., 4,170, fol. 30. An Inscr. lately at HOOKNORTON is in private possession (see Appendix B.); in the same Ch. there is a matrix of a brass to Dame Isabell de Plessi, p. 259. MINSTER LOVELL. *Three Scrolls, one mutil.

The brasses are lost at BENSINGTON (?) (Thos. Freeman and chil., c. 1550), BLACKBOURTON, BUCKNELL, ENSHAM, HENLEY-ON-THAMES, MAPLEDURHAM (Sir Robt. Bardolfe, 1385), ALL HALLOWS', OXFORD (p. 128), STANDLAKE (Joan, w. of John Gaunte, 1465), STEEPLE BARTON (Wm. Fox and ws. Alice, Isabel, with 20 chil.), WESTON-ON-THE-GREEN (p. 221). A Rubbing of a brass of a Man in arm., with Hy. Trin., c. 1520, formerly mur. at CARFAX CH., OXFORD, is in the possession of the Arch. Institute.

Rutlandshire.

BRAUNSTON. *Kenelme Cheseldyn, Esq., of Uppingham (descended from Anne, dau. and h. of Lord Brooch), **1590** (?), and w. Winefrid, dau. of Francis Say, Gent., of Wilby, Northants.; he had 11 sons and 3 daus., and left a son Edw.

CASTERTON, LITTLE. Sir Thos. Burton, lord of the manor of Tolthorp, and patron of the Ch. [1381], and w. Margery [Greenham?], "in eius sinistris," in mantle, marg. inscr. mutil., engr.

c. **1410**, pp. 45, 116, 185, 205. *Blore's Rutland*, pl. ii. p. 12; *Boutell's Mon. Br.*, p. 55.

LIDDINGTON. I. Helyn, w. of Robt. Hardy, Gent., **1486**. II. Edw. Watson, Esq., J.P., **1530**, and w., with 5 sons (headless) and 10 daus., marg. inscr. lost (?), C.

MANTON. *INSCR. to Wm. Villers, LL.B., master of the chantry, and brother of Elizth. and Thos. Villers, draper of London, and Thos. Neuton, once an apprentice of Thos., afterwards master of the chantry, all benefactors to the same.

Scotland.

GLASGOW CATHEDRAL. A Man in arm., of the Mynto family, **1605**, qd. pl., mur., N., p. 41.

For an account of other brasses see Introd., p. 41. The author is indebted to Mr. George Barclay, son of Mr. Barclay, Sheriff-clerk of Fife, for a notice of a very interesting incised slab, apparently of foreign work, discovered in 1839 a few inches under the pavement, at the Ch. of CREICH, in Fifeshire, being perhaps purposely concealed. It measures 6 ft. 7. in. by 2 ft. 8 in., and bears the effigies of a Man in arm., and his w. in surplice sleeves, turned towards her husband; both eff's. have rich triple canopies of different design over their heads only; the heads and hands were inlaid with white marble (?); at the side is an inscr. to "David . Berclay de lmre . dul . de . prisayi" (?), and w. Helena de Douglas, 1421.

Shropshire.

ACTON BURNELL. Lord Nich. Burnell, lord of the manor of Holgot, **1382**, canopy, large, A.T., S.Tr., pp. 28, 31, 92, 138, 159, 160. *Arch. Journ.*, vol. ii. p. 329; *Boutell's Mon. Br.*, p. 54; *Oxf. Man.*, p. 70; *Introd.*, p. 138.

ADDERLEY. I. An Ecclesiastic in episcopal vestments, c. **1390**, head and inscr. lost, large, pp. 72, 73, 78, 125. II. Sir Robt. Nedeham, **1556**, in arm., and w. Agnes, dau. of John Maynwaring, Esq., of Pever, **1560**, with 7 sons and 2 daus., C. INSCR. III. John Podmore, rector, **1673**, æt. 73.

BURFORD. Dame Elizth., w. of Mons. Esmon de Cornewaylle, c. **1370**, eff. and marg. inscr. in Fr. mutil., large, C., pp. 53, 167, 169. *Introd.*, p. 167.

DRAYTON. Rowland, youthful son and h. of Judge Corbet, c. **1580**, 8 eleg. vv., qd. pl., mur., C.

SHROPSHIRE—SOMERSETSHIRE.

Edgmond. Francis Younge, Esq., **1533**, in shroud, and w. Margt., with 9 sons, 5 daus. and inscr. lost (see Appendix B.), N., pp. 102, 218.

Glazeley. Thos. Wylde, Esq., **1599**, and w. Elizth., dau. and h. of Rich. Cooke, Esq., with 4 sons and 2 daus.

Ightfield. I. Dame Margery Calveley, dau. of Wm. Maynwaryng, of Ightfeld, and w. of Philip Egerton, c. **1495**, with 4 sons and 4 daus. beside her eff., mutil. triple canopy, with S. John Bapt. on central finial, marg. inscr., large. II. "The Good" Wm. Maynwaryng (second son of Hawkyn Maynwaryng and Margt. his w., dau. and h. of Gryffyn Waren and lady, of Ightefelde), a special benefactor to the Ch., **1497**, head lost, large, p. 202.

Middle. I. A Man in arm., c. **1490**, pecul. II. Arthur Chambre, patron of the Ch., **1564**, and w., with 2 chil. (?), inscr. lost (?). Frag. III. Seven Sons (Corbet family?), c. **1530**.

Tong. I. Sir Wm. Vernon, constable of England (son and h. of Sir Rich. Vernon, treasurer of Calais), **1467**, and widow Margt., dau. and h. of Lord Robt. Pypis and Spernores, with 7 sons and 3 daus. (2 others lost), marg. inscr., pp. 113, 197. *Waller*, pt. xi. II. Ralph Elcok, a brother of the coll., born "in villa Slapfordie in com. Cestric," **1510**, in almuce, pecul., worn, now mur., p. 79.

Wenlock, Much. Rich. Ridley (son and h. of Raynold Rydley, Gent., of Lynley, and his w. Alice Leighton, who before was the w. of Thos. Mownsloe, Gent., of Caughley, and had by him 1 son and 5 daus.), twice bayly, **1592**, and w. Eleanor, dau. of John Sydenham, of Chilworthy, Somerset, who pos., mur., C.

†Withington. I. John Olney (?), **1515** (?), in arm., and w., with 7 chil., partly covd. by a pew. II. Adam Grafton, parson of Ch., chaplain to Ed. V. and Prince Arthur, archdeacon of Stafford, warden of the Battellfield, dean of St. Mary's Coll., Salop, **1530**, in cope.

INSCRIPTION, &c.

Onibury. Dorothy Pitt, **1633**. The brasses formerly at Shrewsbury are lost (?), see pp. 91, 257, 258.

Somersetshire.

Axbridge. Roger Harper, mcht., and w. Joan, both dec. **1493**, kng., S.C.

Backwell. *Rice Davies, Esq., re-edified the Chapel, **1638**, and w. Dorothe, dau. of Morice Rodney, Esq., sister and coh. to Sir Geo.

Rodney, 1604, with 3 sons (dec.) and 3 daus., Joan, Elizth., Margt., qd. pl., mur., N.C.

BANWELL. I. A Civilian and w., c. 1480, inscr. lost, sm., N. II. Master John Martok, physician, 1503, in cope, now in C., pp. 53, 75. The same name is engraved on the brass lectern at Merton Coll., Oxford. III. John Blandon, 1554, and w. Elizth., w. and head of male eff. lost, sm., N. INSCR. IV. Thos. Morse, 1608, on same slab as No. III.

BATH ABBEY. †Sir Geo. Ivy, of West Kington, Wilts., 1639, and w. Susanna (Hide), with 6 chil., mur., S.A.

BECKINGTON. I. John Seyntmour, Esq., 1485, and w. Elizth., C., p. 197. II. *John Compton, mcht., 1510, and w. Edyth, partly covd.

BRISTOL, TEMPLE CHURCH. See Gloucestershire.

BURNETT. John Cutte, mayor of Bristol [in 1566], 1575, and w. Joan, with 12 chil., Robt., Wm., Rich., John, Nich., John., Thos., Matt., Anne, Susan, Mary, Brigit, 6 cleg. vv., mcht.'s mk., qd. pl., mur., S.A., p. 120.

CHEDDAR. I. Sir Thos. Cheddar, 1442 (?), inscr. lost, A.T., C., pp. 25, 62, 190. *Introd.*, p. 190 (det.) II. Isabell Cheddar, widow of No. I. (?), c. 1460, inscr. lost, C., p. 62.

CHEDZOY. A Man in arm., c. 1490, inscr. lost, large, C., p. 198. Perhaps of the Layton or Yea family.

CHURCHILL. Raphe Jenyns, Esq., 1572, in arm., and w. Jane, 5 sons and 3 daus. lost, S.A., pp. 236, 245. *Introd.*, pp. 236, 245 (dets.)

COSSINGTON. John Brent, Esq., lord of the manor, 1524 (in arm. like the eff. at Wrotham, p. 232), and w. Mawd, dau. of Sir Water Pansfote, marg. inscr., C.

CREWKERNE. Thos. Golde, Esq., 1525, kng., sm., rel.

CROSCOMBE. *Wm. Bisse, 1625, æt. 66, and w., with 9 sons and 9 daus., 14 cleg. vv., mur., S.A.

DUNSTER. John Wyther and w. Agnes, their eldest son John buried with them, 1497, engr. c. 1520, N. Perhaps the inscr. does not belong to the effs. *Gent. Mag.*, vol. lxxvii. 1808, pt. ii. p. 877.

FIVEHEAD. *A Lady, c. 1580, inscr. lost.

HEMINGTON. *John Bawfelde, 1528, sm.

HINTON ST. GEORGE. †Adam Martin and w. Elizth., with 5 sons and 5 daus., 12 Lat. vv., temp. Queen Elizth., mur., S.A.

HUTTON. I. John Payne, Esq., 1496, and w. Elizth., with 4 sons and 7 daus., inscr. now mur., C., p. 116 (see Corrigenda). II. Thos. Payne, Esq., 1528, and w. Elizth., with 8 sons and 3 daus., Hy. Trin. lost. pecul., mur., C.

ILMINSTER. I. Sir Wm. Wadham and mother (or w. in widow's attire), c. 1440, each under a triple canopy with embattled entablature, 8 Lat. vv. and mutil. marg. inscr., large, A.T., N.Tr., pp. 176, 192. *Boutell's Series* (male eff.) II. Nich. Wadham, Esq., of Merefeild, Somerset, founder of Wadham Coll., dec. 1609, in arm., and widow Dorothie, 1618, æt. 84, very large, A.T., N.Tr., p. 237.

ILTON. *Nich. Wadham (son of Sir Nich. Wadham, captain of the Isle of Wight), 1508, in shroud, C.

LANGRIDGE. I. Elizth., widow of Robt. Wallche, Esq. [No. II.], 1441, N. INSCR. II. Robt. Walsshe, Esq., 1427, a cross with eff. in the head lost, C.

LUCCOMBE. *Wm. Harrison, Esq., 1615.

LYDIARD, BISHOP'S. *Nich. Grobham, 1585, and w. Eleanore, 1594, with 5 chil. (surviving), Rich., John, Geo., Joan, Grace, mur., S.A.

MINEHEAD. Joan ——, w. (?) of ——, justice of England, 1440, in mantle, lower part of eff. gone, canopy and marg. inscr. mutil., pp. 166, 209.

PETHERTON, SOUTH. I. A Man in arm., of the Dawbeney family, and w. in mantle, c. 1430, canopy, large, inscr. lost, A.T., S.Tr., pp. 190, 209. II. Lady Maria, dau. of Simon Leek, Esq., of Notts, and w. of Sir Giles Daubeney, 1442, in mantle, worn, S.Tr. INSCR. III. Wm. Sands, Gent., 1670.

PORTBURY. *Sara, w. of Walter Kemish, Gent., 1621, æt. 38, with 2 daus., Elizth. and Fraunces, and 2 infant sons dec., Roger and Francis, sm., mur., N.A.

ST. DECUMANS. I. †[Sir John Wyndham], born in Norfolk, served the king of France, [1574], and w. Elizth. Sydnam, 1571, m. 42 years, and had 7 sons and 6 daus., 56 Eng. vv., A.T., N.A. II. John Windham, Esq., son and h. of No. I., 1572, æt. about 56, in arm., and w. Florence, a dau. of John Wadham, Esq., of Merefield, sister and coh. to Nich. Wadham, 1596, æt. 58; they had one child, Sir John, who pos.; 6 Eng. vv., lately restored (?), N.A., pp. 224, 237.

SHEPTON-MALLETT. Wm. Strode, Esq., of Barington, in arm., and w. Joan, only dau. of Edw. Barnard, Esq., of Downside, 1649, æt. 42, m. 28 years, with 9 chil., Wm., Edw., John, Geo., Essex, Barnard, Jane, Elizth., Joan, 6 other sons and 1 dau. dec., with Death, &c., curious, qd. pl., mur., N.C., pp. 218, 238.

STOGUMBER. Margery, dau. of Rich. Chamberlayne, alderman of London, and w. of Edm. Windham, Esq., of Kensford, 1585, she left 8 chil., Thos., Edm., John, Zach., Frauncis, Geo., Hugh, Margt., pecul. (?)

SWAINSWICK. Edm. Forde, Esq., **1439**, not in arm., with anelace, above eff. 3 scrolls with text from Job xix. 25, 26, once on A.T. (?), C., p. 203.

TINTINHULL. I. John Heth, rector of Tintinhull and Chisleborough, canon of Sarum, **1464**, in cope, ¾ eff., 2 Lat. vv., C. INSCR. II. John Stone, rector, **1416**, C.

WEARE. John Bedbere, c. **1500**, 3 Eng. vv., N.

WEDMORE. I. Geo. Hodges, Esq., c. **1630**, qd. pl., mur., N.C., p. 238. *Introd.*, p. 238. INSCR. II. Capt. Thos. Hodges, Esq., slain at Antwerp, **1583**, with heart, &c., mur., N.C., pp. 109, 122.

WELLS, ST. CUTHBERT. Francis Hayes, Gent., **1623**, æt. 34, very sm., mur., C.

YEOVIL. I. Martin Forester, monk (?), c. **1460**, hf. eff., 2 Lat. vv. on scroll, on lectern, pp. 56, 87. II. Gyles Penne, Gent., not in arm., and w. Isabell, **1519**, C.

INSCRIPTIONS, &c.

SOUTH BARROW. †Rich. de Morice, p. 225. TAUNTON, ST. MARY'S. *Bernard Smith, **1696**, mur. WELLS CATHEDRAL. I. Thos. [Cornish], bp. of Tyne, **1513**, eff. lost, mur., A.T., N.C.A. II. Arthur Lake, D.D., bp., **1626**, with mitre, sh. lost, S.C.A., p. 123. Matrix, on slab composed of three pieces, p. 2. There is an incised slab to B.) Bitton, 1264 or 1274.

The brasses are lost at NEWTON ST. LOE.

Staffordshire.

†ABBOTS-BROMLEY. A Civilian, sm.

AUDLEY. Sir Thos. de Audeley, son of Jas. Audele, "seignour de Helegh de rouge chastell," **1385**, Fr. inscr., large, C., p. 160.

BIDDULPH. Wm. Bowyer, Esq., of Knypersley, patron of Ch., 1602, and w. Ann, dau. and coh. of Wm. Heywood, Gent., of Stonylowe, **1603**, m. 51 years, with 8 sons and 7 daus., and 2 sons by Ann's former husband, Wm. Grosvenor, Esq., of Bellaport, qd. pl., mur.

BLORE. Wm. Basset, Esq., lord of the manors of Blore and Langeley [**1498**], not in arm., head gone, and widow Joan, a dau. and h. of Rich. [Buryn, Esq., son and h. of Sir John Buryn], marg. inscr. mutil., N.C.

CLIFTON-CAMPVILLE. A Lady (widow?), c. **1360** (or earlier), hf. eff. on a bracket; stem, canopy, and marg. inscr. lost, p. 137. *Boutell's Chr. Mon.*, p. 139.

HANBURY. I. The head of a Cross, c. **1390**; eff., inscr., finials, &c.,

lost, C., p. 136.   II. A Priest, c. **1480**, in cope, worn, loose, inscr. lost, C.

KINVER. Sir Edw. Grey, son and h. of Humfrey Grey, Esq., **1528**, and 2 ws., the 2nd w. with 7 sons and 10 daus., marg. inscr., pecul. (?), A.T., C., pp. 29, 243.

LEEK. *John Ashenhurst, **1597**, and 4 ws., with 17 chil.

MADELEY. *John Egerton, Esq., **1518**, not in arm., and w. Ellen.

OKEOVER. Wm. Lord Zouch [dec. 1462], and 2 ws. (?), Alice, dau. and h. of Rich. Lord Seym[our], **1447**, and ———, canopy, marg. inscr., altered into a memorial to Humfrey Oker, Esq. [**1538**], and w. Isabell, with 13 chil., Philyp, Rauf, John, Wm., Roger, Nich., Robt., Thos., Jone, Elizth., Margery, Mare, Dourathe, pp. 50, 51, 260. *Waller*, pt. xvi. This brass was stolen about three years ago and broken in pieces, those composing the male and one of the fem. effs. (not the palimpsest, which has flowing hair) have not been recovered.

RUGELEY. *John Weston, sen., Gent., **1566**; by his w. Cecily, dau. and h. of John Ford, Gent., he had Rich. and John.

STOW. *Thos. Newport, steward of the household to Walter, 6th earl of Essex, **1587**.

TRENTHAM. Sir Rich. Leveson, of Lylleshall, Salop, 1559, in arm., and w. Mary, dau. of Sir Edw. Fyton, of Gawsworthe, spent her widowhood and was buried at Trentham, dec. at Battersea, Surrey, **1591**, with 1 son and 2 daus., Sir Walter (in arm., who m. Anne, dau. of Sir Andr. Corbet), Mary (m. Geo. Curzon, Esq., of Croxall), Anne dec. in infancy, mur., S.C.

The brasses are lost at BREWOOD (Margt., w. of Sir Edw. Grevill, of Milcote, 1574), STAFFORD, ST. MARY (p. 94), and WESTON-UNDER-LYZIARD (John Mytton, Esq., 1499. and ws. Agnes and Joan, 1475, and inscr. to John Mytton, Esq., 1532, and w. Constance).   In a MS. by Dugdale (F. 1. or N. 11. fol. 1546) is a sketch, taken in 1639, of a brass at WALSALL to Mons. Roger Hillary, chief justice of the court of common pleas, c. **1370**, in arm., and w. Kath., with canopy.

Suffolk.

ACTON.   I. Sir Robt. de Bures, **1302**, cross-legged, in chain mail, with shield on arm, &c., marg. inscr. in Lomb. letters lost, large, N.C., pp. 146, 147, 148. *Gough*, vol. i. pl. xlii. p. 113; *Engravings of Sepulchral Brasses in Suffolk, by John Sell Cotman*, London, 1838, pl. i. p. 1; *Waller*, pt. ii.; *Boutell's Mon. Br.* (front.) *Introd.*, p. 148 (det.) II. Alyce, dau. and h. of Sir Robt. de Bures, and widow of Sir Edm. Bryan, **1435** (?), triple canopy mutil., inscr. lost, large, N. *Boutell's Series.* III. Hen. Bures, Esq., **1529** (or 1539), inscr. lost, N.C., pp. 29, 234. *Introd.*, p. 234. IV. Edm. Daniel, 1569, and w. Margt., **1589**, with 5 sons and 6 daus., sm., S.C. V. John Daniel, c. **1590**, sm., S.C.

ALDEBURGH. I. Emma Foxe, c. **1570**, with 7 sons and 7 daus., 16 Eng. vv. (see Appendix B), sm., p. 94. II. John James, **1601**, æt. 50, and w. Joan, m. 26 years, with 2 sons and 3 daus., mcht.'s mk., 16 Eng. vv., qd. pl., sm. III. Wm. Bence, a chief burgess, **1606**, æt. 57, and w. Mary (Blome), she left 4 chil., Robt., John, Thos., Mary, 12 Eng. vv., N. IV. Alex. Bence, **1612**, and w. (eff. lost), with 9 sons and 2 daus. V. John Bence (son of Alex. Bence), four times bailiff, **1635**, æt. 54, and 2 ws., Mary (with 5 chil., John, Alex., Edm., Mary, Elizth., then living) and Elizth. FRAG. VI. Three Sons, c. **1520**.

AMPTON. I. A Mcht. and w. (of the Cosset family?), c. **1480**, kng., with 7 daus., inscr. lost. II. †Joan Heigham, **1611**. FRAG. III. †Two Daus., kng., c. **1490**.

ASH, CAMPSEY. Sir Alex. Inglisshe, parish priest of the Ch. [**1504**], with chalice and wafer, canopy mutil., marg. inscr. lost, C.

ASH BOCKING. Edm. Bockinge, Esq., **1585**, æt. 57, in arm., and 2 ws., Frances, dau. and h. of Sir Thos. Tey (with dau. Frances, m. to John Harvy, Esq., of Acworth), and Mary, dau. and h. of Thos. Payne, Esq., of Gt. Dunham, Norf. (with dau. Kath., æt. 8), now in wooden frame, mur., N., p. 225.

ASSINGTON. A Man, in arm., and w., c. **1500**, inscr. lost, pecul., pp. 199, 242. *Introd.*, pp. 199, 243 (male eff. and det.)

BARHAM. I. Robt. Sowthwell, Esq., "apprenticius ad leges," J.P., **1514**, not in arm., and w. Cecily, a dau. of Thos. Sheryngton, Esq., of Barsham, dec., with marg. inscr., chil. lost, C. INSCR. II. Frances, eldest dau. of Thos. Hynson, of Tawstock, Devon, and w. of Robt. Southwell, Gent., **1607**, æt. 29, with 7 chil., John, Thos., Robt., Francis, Margt., Susan, Anne.

BARNINGHAM. Wm. Goche, rector, **1499**, in acad., pecul., sm., C., p. 82.

BARROW. I. Sir Clement Heigham, twice reader at Lincoln's Inn, speaker of the parliament and chief baron of the exchequer to Queen Mary, **1570**, in arm., and 2 ws., 1st [Anne, dau. of Thos. Monings], with 1 son, in shroud, and 5 daus., 2nd [Anne, dau. of Geo. Waldegrave, Esq., and widow of Hen. Bures, Esq.], with 3 sons

(lost) and 2 daus., 44 Eng. vv., mur., A.T., C. *Cotman*, pl. xxviii.
p. 18; *Gage's Thingoe*, p. 22. II. John Crosyer, parson, left
"almose" to the poor [**1569**], 22 Eng. vv. mutil., mur., p. 230.

BARSHAM. A Man in arm., c. **1415** (Sir Robt. Suckling?), with
collar of SS., inscr. lost, large, C., pp. 186, 188. *Suckling's Memorials of Suffolk*, vol. i. p. 42; *Introd.*, p. 186.

BELSTEAD. A Man, in arm., and 2 ws., c. **1520**, pecul., inscr.
lost, N.C., p. 243. Probably John Goldingham, Esq., 1518, and ws.
Joan and Thomasyn.

BENHALL. I. Edw. Duke, Esq., **1598**, and w. Dorothy, dau. of
Sir Ambrose Jermine, with 10 sons and 6 daus. II. Ambrose
Duke, Esq., 1610, in arm., and w. Elizth., a dau. and h. of Bartram
Colthorp, Esq., **1611**; they had 1 son and 2 daus.

BERGHOLT, EAST. *Robt. Alfounder, Gent., **1639**, æt. 50, p. 240.
Cotman, pl. xlvi. p. 27.

BILDESTON. Wm. Wade, Esq., high constable of the hundred,
1599 (eff. lost), and w. Alice Boggis, with 6 chil., Wm., Robt., Alice,
Anne, Joane, Mary, N.

BOXFORD. I. David, son of Joseph Birde, **1606**, æt. 22 weeks, in
a cot, qd. pl., sm., C., p. 219. INSCRS. II. Wm. Doggett, mcht.-
adventurer, citizen and mcht. of London, and free of E. India Co.,
1610, æt. 53, and w. Avis, dau. of Thos. Lappadge, Gent., with
6 sons and 6 daus., shs., p. 118. III. †Wm. Birde, pastor,
1599.

BRADLEY, LITTLE. I. Thos. Underhill, Esq., **1508** (?), not in
arm., and w., kng., inscr. cut in stone (?). II. A Man in arm.
[Thos. Knighton, Esq.?], c. **1530**, kng., with 2 sons and 1 dau.;
head of male eff., w., and inscr. lost, pecul., p. 234. III. [John]
Daye, printer, **1584**, and 2nd w. Als [dau. of —— Lehunte, by ——
Knighton], with 6 sons and 5 daus. and 2 chil. in swaddling clothes,
14 Eng. vv. (see Appendix B.), mur., pp. 96, 120. *Gent. Mag.*,
vol. cii. 1832, pt. ii. p. 417. IV. John Le Hunt, Esq., **1605**, and
w. Jane, eldest dau. of Hen. Colte, Esq., of Cundish, Suff.; they had
1 son and 2 daus.; pecul. V. Thos. Soame, Gent., 1606, æt. 64,
in arm., and w. Elizth., dau. of Robt. Alington, Esq., of Horseheath,
Camb., with 5 sons and 2 daus., w. pos., **1612**, qd. ₁ l., mur.

BRAISEWORTH. Alex. Newton, Esq., **1569**, in arm.; he m.
Anne, dau. of Sir Humfre Wyngfeld, p. 236. *Cotman*, pl. xxvii.
p. 17.

BREDFIELD. Leonard Farrington, **1611**, and w. Elizth., dau. of
Geo. May, of Walton, dec., with 6 sons and 2 daus , sm., mur., N.

BRUISYARD. I. A Civilian, c. **1520**; w., chil., and inscr. lost.

II. Mich. Hare, Esq., **1611** (eff. lost?), and 2 ws., Elizth. (Hobert) and Mary (Brudenell).

BRUNDISH. I. Sire Esmound de Burnedissh, parson of Castre Ch., c. **1360**, Fr. inscr., A.T., N. *Waller*, pt. iii.; *Boutell's Series.* II. John Colby, **1559**, in arm., 4 Eng. vv., C.   III. John Colby, Esq., 1540, in arm., and w. Alice, **156**.., with 4 sons and 9 daus. (3 lost), sm., N.   IV. Francis Colby, Esq., in arm., and w. Margt., dau. of Lord Wentworth, c. **1570**, head of w., inscr. (and male eff.?) lost. V. Thos. Glemham, youth [**1571**?], 8 Eng. vv., kng., C.

BURGATE. Sir Wm. de Burgate, **1409**, and w. Alianora, dau. of Sir Thos. Vyzsdelon, canopy, marg. inscr., large, A.T., C., p. 185. *Gough*, vol. ii. pl. xii. p. 29; *Proceed. of Bury and West Suffolk Arch. Inst.*, vol. i. p. 211.

BURY ST. EDMUNDS, ST. MARY. I. Jenkyn Smyth, with Yorkist(?) collar, and w. Marion, c. **1480**, kng., inscr. lost, S.C.A., p. 171. *Boutell's Series.*   II. John Fynexs, archdeacon of Sudbury [1497—**1514**], in almuce, 2 Lat. vv., pecul., N.A., p. 79.   INSCRS., &c. III. Thos. and Alice ——, **1513** (?), worn.   IV. Edm., eldest son of Hen. —— (?), **1575**, 12 Eng. vv.   V. Wm. Fairclyffe, **1601**. VI. Geo. Este, "concionator," **1601**, æt. 36, his w. pos., p. 30. VII. Eliza Juell, **1609**, æt. 46, 4 hex. vv.   Several shs. (p. 103) and frags.

CARLTON. I. A Civilian, c. **1480**, w. and inscr. lost. *Cotman*, pl. xiv. p. 11.   II. A Civilian, c. **1490**, w. and inscr. lost. *Ibid.*, pl. xx. p. 14.

CHATTISHAM. John Revers (eff. lost) and w. Mary, **1592**, with 3 sons and 7 daus.

COOKLEY. Wm. Broune, 1587, buried in "Reindam" Ch., and w. Margery, 1594, with 4 sons and 4 daus., their son, Rich., pos. **1595**, N.

COOLING. Robt. Higham, Esq., 1571, æt. 45, and w. Margt., **1599**, æt. 75, with 5 sons and 5 daus.

DARSHAM. I. Anne, w. of Eustace Bedingfeild, Esq., of Holmehale, Norf., **1641**, æt. 80 years and 7 months, C., p. 248. *Cotman*, pl. xlvii. p. 28; *Suckling*, vol. ii. p. 225.   INSCRS. II. Wm. Garard, 2 Eng. vv., in a pew, N.   III. Marion Reve, N.

DEBENHAM. A Man in arm., c. **1425**, and w. (probably John Framlingham, 1425 (or 1424), and w. Margt.), hf. effs., inscr. lost, C., p. 189. *Cotman*, pl. xi. p. 10.

DENHAM. I. Anth., 3rd son of Sir Edm. Bedingfeld, **1574**, C. II. Two Hearts united at the points for Wm. Selfte, inscr. lost, qd. pl., sm.

DENSTON. I. Hen. Everard, Esq., and w. Margt., dau. of Sir Robt. Broughton, **1524**, in heraldic dresses, pecul., inscr. lost, p. 29. *Cotman*, pl. xxv. p. 16. II. A Lady of the Drury family, c. **1530**, pecul., inscr. lost, pp. 29, 33, 243. *Ibid*, pl. xviii. p. 13.

DEPDEN. Geo. Waldegrave, Esq., of Smallbridge (with 5 sons and 2 daus.), Sir Thos. Jermyn, of Rushebroke (with 2 sons), and their w. Anne, dau. of Sir Robt. Drewry, of Halstead, **1572**, in heraldic dresses, mur., p. 56.

EASTON. I. A Man in arm., c. **1425** (perhaps John Brook, 1426), inscr. lost, now in C., p. 189. *Cotman*, pl. ix. p. 9. II. John Wingfeld, Esq., a son of Thos. Wingfeld, of Gt. Dunham, Norf., dec., **1584**, in arm. *Ibid.*, pl. xxxiv. p. 22. III. Radcliff, dau. of Sir Gilbert Gerrarde, of Bromley Gerrard, Staffordshire, master of the rolls, and his w. Anne, and w. of Thos. Wingfeld, Esq., **1601**, p. 247. *Ibid.*, pl. xxxvi. p. 23.

EDWARDSTONE. †Benj. Brand, Esq., and w. Elizth., with 6 sons and 6 daus., "all nurs'd with her vnborrowed milk," c. **1620**.

ELLOUGH. Margt., w. of Christofer Playtors, Esq., and w. of Arthur Chewt, Gent., **1607**, æt. 55 (?), worn, C.

EUSTON. I. A Civilian and w., c. **1480**, pecul., inscr. lost, N. II. A Civilian (lower part lost) and w. (partly covd.), c. **1520**, pecul., inscr. lost, p. 239. III. A Lady, c. **1520**, pecul., sm., inscr. lost. IV. —— Rokewood, in arm. (lower part lost), and 2 ws., c. **1530**, one w. and inscr. lost, pp. 234, 243. INSCRS. V. Mr. Wm. Foter, rector, **1524**. VI. Gerard Sothil, Esq., **1528**.

EYKE. I. John Staverton (?), baron of the exchequer, and w., c. **1430**, marg. inscr. nearly all lost, p. 90. *Cotman*, pl. xii. p. 10. II. Hen. Mason, M.A., of Camb., a minister, **1619**, æt. 66, p. 230. *Ibid.*, pl. xliii. p. 26.

FORNHAM, ALL SAINTS. Thos. Barwick, Gent., for many years professor of medicine at Bury St. Edmunds, **1599**, æt. 83, 4 eleg. vv., his grandsons and hs. pos., lower part lost, p. 216. *Introd.*, p. 240.

FRESSINGFIELD. Wm. Brewes, Esq., son and h. of Sir Thos. Brewes, **1489**, and w. Elizth., C., pp. 179, 198.

GAZELEY. A Chalice, c. **1530**, inscr. lost, p. 125.

GORLESTON. A Man in arm. of the Bacon family, cross-legged, with sh. on arm, c. **1320**; legs of eff., canopy, and marg. inscr. lost; now mur., N.A., pp. 137, 150, 260. *Cotman*, pl. ii. p. 3; *Stothard*, p. 48; *Suckling*, vol. i. p. 372; *Boutell's Mon. Br.*, p. 36; *Introd.*, p. 152.

HADLEIGH. I. Thos. Alabaster, clothier, **1592**, æt. about 70, under arch, qd. pl., mur., S.A. II. Anna [Alabaster, first] w. of

John Still [D.D., rector of Hadleigh, and afterwards] bp. of Bath and Wells, 1593, 4 Lat. vv. and mutil. inscr. in arch over eff., S.A. III. John Alabaster, clothier, twice mayor, 1637, æt. 76, under arch; he was married 52 years to his w. Mary, and had 2 sons and 9 daus. IV. Rich. Glanfield and w. Elizth., both dec. 1637, "per annos pene bis denos quater juncti," hf. effs., 6 Lat. vv., their son, Rich. "Pembrochianus presbyter," pos., pp. 62, 218. INSCRS. V. Twenty Eng. vv. to Rowland Taillors, D.C.L., parson of Hadleigh, martyr, 1555, engr. c. 1560 (?); on reverse, head and shoulders of a Civilian resting on a pillow, part of a Flemish brass, c. 1500, mur., N., p. 46. *Rev. H. Pigot's Hist. of Hadleigh*, 1860, p. 61. VI. Thos. Parkins, clothier, 1577, æt. 50, 6 Eng. vv., N. VII. †Wm. Foorthe, Esq., 1599, and w. Dorothie, dau. and coh. of Rich. Harvy, Gent., of Worlingworth, 1581; they had 5 chil., Philip, Edw., Wm., Nichol., Elizth. (married to Mr. Poyntel, mcht. of London). VIII. Nich. Strutt, clothier [1601?], æt. 51; he had 9 chil. IX. Alice, w. of Thos. Moswell, 1605, S.A. X. Bridgget, 3rd dau. of Robt. Rolfe, Esq., of Hadley, and w. of Rich. Champeneis, Esq., of Bexley, Kent, 1617, and Thos. her 2nd son, S.A. XI. Edw. Alston, 1628, æt. 12, C. A Matrix (see Addenda). *Pigot*, p. 61.

HALESWORTH. I. John Everard, 1476, hf. eff., pecul., p. 172. II. John Browne, c. 1580, æt. 80½ years, (had 65 grandchildren, left 54 surviving), and w., with 6 sons, 10 daus. and inscr. mutil., male eff. and lower part of fem. eff. lost, on reverse of inscr. part of the eff. of a Civilian, c. 1530, Flemish, p. 47. This brass is now (?) in private hands, part of it was found, c. 1823, in the river Waveney, between Flixton and Bungay. INSCRS. III. Wm. Fyske, 1512. IV. Joan, w. of John Crosse, Gent., 1644, and Mary, 1645, both daus. of Jacob Keble, Gent., now covd. (?)

†HAWKEDON. I. A Civilian and w., c. 1510, with 2 sons and 5 daus., pecul., inscr. lost. *Cotman*, pl. xxi. p. 15. II. Edm. Plume, 1639, and w.

HAWSTEAD. I. A Lady, c. 1530, inscr. lost, pecul., sm., C., pp. 29, 33. *Gage's Thingoe Hundred*, p. 460. Perhaps the brass of Ursula, 4th dau. of Sir Robt. Drury, and w. of Giles, son of Sir Giles Allington. II. †Roger Drury, Esq., 1498 (?), inscr. lost, sm. III. Sir Wm. Drury, 1557, in arm., and 2 ws. [Jane, dau. of Sir Wm. St. Maur, 1517, and Elizth., dau. and coh. of Hen. Sothill], the 1st w. with 1 child (lost), the 2nd with 13 daus., 4 sons lost, 10 Eng. vv., pecul. (?), A.T., S.A., pp. 33, 51, 63, 234, 236. *Gage*, p. 468. FRAGS. IV. A Child, c. 1500. and shs. with arms of Drury, part of the brass of (?) Roger Drury, Esq., 1495, and ws., Agnes, Felice, Anne.

HOLBROOK. A Man in arm., c. 1480, and w., with 6 sons and 5 daus.; w., daus., and inscr. lost, p. 197.

HONINGTON. I. Geo. Duke, Gent., 1594, C.   INSCR. II. †Anne, w. of Augustine Curteis, Gent., 1585, eff. lost.

IPSWICH, ST. CLEMENT. I. John Tye, mcht. and portman, 1583, æt. 58, and ws., Ales (with 2 sons and 3 daus.) and Julyan (with 3 sons and 6 daus.), worn, C. II. Wm. Cocke, 1607, æt. 69, and w. Joane, dau. of Wm. Peare (eff. lost), with 3 sons and 3 daus., worn, C.

IPSWICH, ST. MARY QUAY. I. Thos. Pownder, mcht. and bayly of Ipswich, 1525, and w. Emma, with 2 sons and 6 daus., marg. inscr., Flemish, qd. pl., C., pp. 20, 139. *Shaw's Dresses and Decorations; Wodderspoon's Memorials of Ipswich* (front.) *Introd.*, pp. 18, 131 (dets.)   II. Hen. Toolye, portman, bequeathed to "wayes & pore" his lands, tenements, and annual rents, 1551, and w. Alice, 1565, with 1 son and 2 daus., 13 Eng. vv., mur., A.T., N.A. *Wodderspoon*, p. 338. III. ——, w. of Christopher Merell, 1583, inscr. lost (?), S.A. INSCRS. IV. Alice, w. of John Tymperley, Esq., 1485, C.   V. Augustin Parker, 1590, æt. 63, with mcht.'s mk.

IPSWICH, ST. MARY TOWER. I. A Notary, c. 1475, canopy and inscr. lost, large, pp. 92, 128. *Waller*, pt. i.; *Boutell's Mon. Br.*, p. 112; *Gent. Mag.*, vol. xxx. N.S. 1848, p. 606; *Wodderspoon*, p. 343. II. *A Civilian and 2 ws., c. 1500, inscr. lost, C.   III. Robt. Wymbyll, notary, Thos. Baldry, mcht., and their w. Alys, 1506, with 4 sons and 5 daus., S.A., pp. 118, 128, 204. *Introd.*, pp. 128, 203 (eff. and det.)   IV. *Thos. Drayle, mcht., and 2 ws. (head of first lost), on a bracket mutil., the 1st w. with 2 sons and 3 daus., a child of 2nd w. lost, pecul., N.A. *Wodderspoon*, p. 361.

IPSWICH, ST. NICHOLAS. I. Wm. Style, 1475, and w. Isabella; chil., Hy. Trin., and Evang. symbs. lost, pecul., N.   II. A Civilian, c. 1500; w., inscr., &c., lost, N. Probably the brass of Wm. Stiles and w. Margery.   III. A Civilian and w., c. 1600, inscr. lost, N.

IPSWICH, ST. PETER. John Knapp, mcht. and portman of Ipswich, 1604, and w. Martha, with 4 sons and 8 daus. *Cotman*, pl. xxxviii. p. 24.

IXWORTH. I. A Man in arm., c. 1415, and 2 ws. in mantles, inscr. lost, large, p. 188.   II. Rich. Codington, Esq., "the ffirst Temporall Lorde of this manor of Ipworth after the Suppressyon of the Abbye which he had of o^r souereigne lorde kinge Henrye the eight in Exchaunge for the mano^r of Codington now called Nonsuche in the Countie of Surrey," 1567, and w. Elizth. (Jenour) with her chil., John and Dorothy, by her first husband, Thos. Bucknham, mur., C. *Proceed. of Bury and West Suff. Arch. Inst.*, vol. i. p. 102.

KENTON. John Garneys, Esq., **1524**, and w. Elizth., in heraldic dresses, with 6 sons and 9 daus., crucifix mutil., qd. pl., S.A., pp. 52, 222.

KETTLEBURGH. Arthur Pennyng, Gent., **159[3]**, æt. about 65, and 2 ws., mutil., C.

KNODISHALL. John Jenney, Esq., **1460**, with 1 son and 2 ws., Maud, dau. of John Bokele, Esq. (eff. with 2 chil. lost), and Margt., C.

LAKENHEATH. A Civilian and w., c. **1530**, pecul., inscr. lost, sm., pp. 243, 244.

LAVENHAM. I. Thos. Spryng, "qui hoc vestibulū fieri fecit In vita sua," **1486**, and w. Mergaret, with 4 sons and 6 daus., all the effs. in shrouds, mur., Vestry, p. 171. II. Allaine Dister, clothier, left a small sum to the poor yearly at Whitsuntide, 1534, and w., with 3 sons and 3 daus., 12 Eng. vv., engr. c. **1570**, qd. pl., mur., N.A. III. Clopton, son and h. of Sir Simon Dewes and his w. Anne, dau. of Sir Wm. Clopton [**1631**], æt. 10 days, a chrysom child, C., p. 221.

LETHERINGHAM. Sir John (?) de Wyngefeld, lord of the manor, **1389**, with arms on jupon, inscr. lost (?), large, now mur., N.A., p. 160. *Cotman*, pl. v. p. 6; *Boutell's Series*. See also brasses in private possession, &c.—Bodleian Library, Oxford; J. B. Nichols, Esq.

LIDGATE. A Priest, c. **1380**, head and feet gone, once in the head of a cross, sm.

LIVERMERE, GREAT. I. A Female figure in shroud, c. **1500**; head, husband (?), and inscr. lost. INSCR. II. Kath., w. of John Chetham, Gent., **1577**, 3 Eng. vv., C. The curious brass of a Man in arm., with helmet, and w., c. **1480** (said to be Hugh de Bokenham and w. Joan), pecul., now lost (?), is engr. in *Ant. Repertory*, 1807, vol. iii. p. 341; an impression is in the Brit. Museum.

LOWESTOFT. I. A Civilian, c. **1490**, and w., with 4 sons and 3 daus., mcht.'s mk. and initials N. H., w. and inscr. lost. II. A Civilian and 2 ws., c. **1530**, with 3 sons, pecul., 2nd w. and inscr. lost. INSCR. III. Thos. Annott [**1577**], æt. 90, 8 eleg. vv. mutil., eff. pierced by Death lost, S.A., p. 218. Rubbings of a Civilian, c. 1545; mcht.'s mks. with initials R. C., c. 1450; A. C. C., c. 1500; W. P.; frags. of canopies, c. 1420; and inscr. to Margt. Parker, 1507, now lost (?), are in the Brit. Museum.

MELFORD, LONG. I. Two maiden Ladies of the Clopton family, c. **1420**, eff. of one and inscr. lost, N.C.A., p. 205. *Boutell's Series. Introd.*, p. 205 (det.) II. A Civilian of the Clopton family,

c. **1420**, marg. inscr. lost, N.C.A. Perhaps this brass commemorates Thos. Clopton, 1420, son of Wm. Clopton, 1416, and his w. Margt., 1424, and No. I. two daus. (Margt. and ——) of the same persons. III. A Lady of the Clopton family in heraldic mantle, c. **1480**, canopy mutil., inscr. lost, N.C.A., p. 113. IV. A Brass similar to No. III. Perhaps for Margt., dau. and h. of Elias Fraunceyes, Esq., and 2nd w. of Wm. de Clopton, 1424 (or 1444?), and engr. c. **1480**, p. 113. *Boutell's Mon. Br.*, p. 92 (eff.) V. Francis Clopton, Esq., son and h. of Wm. Clopton, Esq., **1577**, in arm., inscr. lost, N.C.A., p. 237. *Introd.*, p. 236. VI. *Roger Martyn, **1615**, æt. 82 (?), and 2 ws. [Ursula, dau. of Sir Thos. Jermyn, of Rushbrooke] (with 4 sons and 2 daus.), [and Margt., dau. of Walter Bowles, Esq., of Pembrokeshire] (with 2 sons and 2 daus.), S.C.A. VII. *Rich. Martin, **1624**, æt. 65, and 3 ws., the 1st w. with a dau. (?) in swaddling clothes and 2 sons, over 3rd w. the arms of Mannock, sm., S.C.A. Inscr., lost, p. 94.

MELTON. *A Priest in acad., and civilian (feet lost) and lady, c. **1430**, canopy much mutil., inscr. gone, pp. 63, 211. *Cotman*, pl. xiii. p. 11.

MENDHAM. I. Cecilia, dau. of Thos. Felton, Esq., and w. of No. II., **1615**, she had 6 sons and 2 daus., C. II. Rich. Freston, Esq., **1616**, C. III. *Rich. Freston, Esq., **1634**, C. INSCR. IV. Wm., son of Jas. Hobart, Esq., **1641**, æt. 3.

MENDLESHAM. I. John Knyvet, Esq. (?), **1417**, large, inscr. lost, partly covd., S.A., pp. 156, 188. INSCRS. II. Barnaby Barker, **1617**, æt. 54. III. John, son of No. II., **1629**, æt. 34.

MICKFIELD. I. Peeter Preston, 1616, and w. Thomasine, **1617**, they had 5 sons and 2 daus., sm., C. INSCRS. II. Francisca, dau. of Thos. Dade, Esq., of Tannington, and his 1st w. Agnes, **1615**. III. Peter Preston, son of No. 1., **1631**, æt. 25.

MIDDLETON. I. A Civilian and w., c. **1500**, inscr. lost, sm. *Cotman*, pl. xxii. p. 15. II. Anth. Pettow, yeoman, **1610**, æt. 54; his w. Francis, dau. of Thos. Bishope, of Kelleshall, yeoman, pos. *Ibid.*, pl. xxxix. p. 25.

MILDENHALL. I. Sir Hen. Warner, **1617**, in arm., and w. Mary, dau. of Sir Robt. Wingefeild, of Letheringham (eff. lost); their son Edw. married Mary, dau. of John Wentworth, Esq., of Gosfeild, Essex, and dec. **1618**, C. INSCRS. II. Mr. Rich. Baggoott, **1424**. III. Mary Warner, w. of No. I., **1601**. In *Hollis's Mon. Effs.*, pt. iii. No. 8, is an engraving of the brass (now lost) of a Man in arm., c. 1390, with badge, a crown and lion (or dog).

MONEWDEN. I. Thos. Reve, 4th son of Wm. Reve, Gent., of

Monewden, a senior fellow of Gonville and Caius Coll., Camb., where he continued 20 years, he left a pension for a "lerned devyne;" to preach an annual sermon on Sept. 3rd.; dec. **1595**, æt. 35, in hood, mur., C.   Inscr. II. Wm. Reve, **1587**, and w. Rose; they had 10 sons and 5 daus., he left 11 surviving; 18 Eng. vv., effs. lost.

NETTLESTEAD. A Man in arm., c. **1500**, inscr. lost, sm., N.

NEYLAND.   I. A Man and his w., c. **1440**, with canopy, all lost but the canopy, which is mutil., N.A.   II. A Civilian and 2 ws., c. **1480**, canopy; all lost except a pediment of canopy and portion of marg. inscr., S.A.   III. John Hacche, and w. E......, dau. of John Hamond, with book under arm, c. **1485**, canopy much mutil., effs. lost except upper part of fem. eff., frags. of marg. inscr. lately lost, N.   IV. A Civilian and w., c. **1500**, canopy, marg. inscr. nearly all lost, N.   V. Rich. Dinn (?) and w. Joan (?), c. **1520**, mcht.'s mk., much worn, N.A.   VI. Pediment of canopy, c. **1520**. INSCR. VII. †Frag. of marg. inscr. to ...... Sekyn and w. Joan, **1475**. Weever (Fun. Mon., p. 771) records inscrs. to John Ewel, fuller, 1436, and w. Agnes [No. I.?]; Geo. Hamund, weaver, 1530, and Thomasin Hamund, ..., 1548.

OCCOLD.   Wm. Corbald and w. Joan, c. **1490**, 6 Lat. vv., pecul., N.

ORFORD.   I. A Civilian and w., c. **1500**, pecul. (?)   II. A Civilian, c. **1510**, with mcht.'s mk., sm., N.   III. A Civilian, c. **1510**, C. IV. A Lady, c. **1510**, with 6 sons and 6 daus., N.   V. A Civilian and w., c. **1520**, with Hy. Trin., C.   VI. A Civilian, c. **1520**, sm., N.A.   The inscrs. of all the foregoing are lost.   VII. Roger Sawyer, justice, Jas. Coo, mayor, and their w. Bridgett, **1580**, with 3 sons and 1 dau. by her 1st husband, fem. effs. lost (?).   VIII. Bridgett (Smith), had 6 chil. by her 1st husband, Robt. Coverdall, and 1 son and 2 daus. by her 2nd, Robt. Bence, **1605**, æt. 65; and below, her dau. Jone (Bence), who had by her husband, Robt. Wheatley, salter of London, 1 son and 3 daus., buried at "St. Buttolphes without Allgate," London, 1603, æt. 28, 8 Eng. vv. and marg. inscr., p. 225.   IX. John Coggeshall, **1640**, and w., with 5 sons and 2 daus., inscr. lost (?), qd. pl., mur.   FRAG. X. †Three sons and seven daus., c. **1490**, parents lost.

OULTON.   I. Sir Adam (?) de Bacon, rector, large, C., p. 142. *Cotman*, pl. iii. p. 5; *Boutell's Mon. Br.*, p. 95; *Suckling*, vol. ii. p. 39; *Introd.*, p. 142.   II. John Fastolff, Esq., 1445, and w. Kath., **1478**, C., p. 197. *Suckling*, vol. ii. p. 40.   INSCR. III. Wm. Bedyngfeld, rector, **1503**.   Nos. I. and II. were stolen in Feb. 1857, p. 260.

PAKEFIELD. I. John Bowf and w. Augnes, both dec. **1417**(?), with 2 sons and 9 daus., worn, 8 curious Eng. vv., now mur., S.A. II. Rich. Folcard, "rector Medietatis isti' ccclīē in parte australi," **1451**, in acad., hf. eff., now mur., S.A. *Suckling,* vol. i. p. 284.

PETTAUGH. John (?) Fastolfe, **1549** (?), and w., with 2 sons and 4 daus., inscr. lost, sm.

PETTISTREE. Frances Bacon, 3rd son of Edm. Bacon, Esq., of Hesett, dec., **1580**, and 2 ws., 1st, Elizth. (Cotton, of Barton, Suff.), by whom he had a dau., Elizth., and 2nd, Mary, dau. and h. of Geo. Blenerhaysett, Esq. *Cotman*, pl. xxxiii. p. 22.

PLAYFORD. [Sir Geo. Felbrigg, **1400**], with arms on jupon, canopy all lost but shafts, marg. inscr. in Fr. mutil., large, rel., C., pp. 160, 162, 176. *Gough*, vol. ii. pl. xlvii. p. 134; *Cotman*, pl. vi. p. 6; *Boutell's Series; Hewitt's Anc. Arm.*, vol. ii. No. 26, p. 159.

POLSTEAD. I. A Priest, c. **1440**, inscr. lost, loose in vestry. II. A Civilian and w., c. **1490**, with 5 sons, partly covd., daus. and inscr. lost.

RAYDON. I. A Lady, c. **1480** (perhaps sister of No. II.), head and inscr. lost, very sm., N.   INSCR. II. Thos., son of Thos. Reydon, **1479**, sm., eff. lost, N.

REDGRAVE. *Anne, dau. and coh. of Hen. Bures, Esq., and widow of Edm. Butts, Esq., **1609**, "a second Anna," having lived 7 years in wedlock and 61 in widowhood, 8 Eng. vv. and marg. inscr., C.

RENDHAM. †A Chalice for Thos. Knyg (Kyng?), vicar, **1523**.

RINGSFIELD. Nich. Garneys, Esq., built Redsham Hall [dec. 1599], and w. Anne, dau. of Chas. Clere, Esq., of Stokesby, in heraldic dresses, engr. c. **1600** (?), qd. pl., mur., pp. 52, 222. *Suckling*, vol. i. p. 69.

ROUGHAM. Sir Roger Drury [dec. 1410], and w. Margery [dau. and h. of Sir Thos. Naunton], **1405**, large, N.A., pp. 185, 205. *Gent. Mag.,* vol. lxxxiii. 1813, pt. ii. p. 17; *Cullum's Hawstead*, p. 127; *Introd.*, p. 184.

RUSHBROOKE. *Thos. Badby, Esq., of Bury St. Edmunds, one of the queen's receivers, son and h. to Wm. Badby, of Layermarney, **1583** (eff. ?) mur.

SAXHAM, GREAT. *John Eldred, born at New Buckingam, in Norfolk, alderman of London, travelled to Babilon, Egypt, Arabia, and the Holy Land, æt. 80, 6 Lat. and 8 Eng. vv., one inscr. below a stone bust; his son and h., Revett, pos., **1632**; A.T., C., pp. 118, 120. *Gage's Hundred of Thingoe*, p. 114.

SIBTON. I. Edm. Chapman, **1574**, æt. 70, and w. Margt. [Revett], with 8 sons and 5 daus., 16 Eng. vv., mur.   *Cotman*, pl. xxx. p. 20.

II. John Chapman, alias Barker, **1582**, æt. 52, and w. Julyan, with 3 sons and 3 daus.   III. Edm. Chapman, alias Barker, Gent., **1626**, æt. 64, and w. Marryan [dau. and h. of Geo. Vesey, Gent.], with 8 sons and 5 daus., qd. pl., mur.   INSCRS. IV. John Chapman, formerly Barker, **1475**.   V. Edm. Chapman, **1501**.   VI. Robt. Chapman, alias Barker, 1511, engr. c. **1600**.   VII. Thos. Copland, **1595**, æt. 83, and w. Ollive, 1589, æt. 68.

SOTTERLEY. I. Thos. Playters, Esq., patron of Ch., and w. Anne, a sister and h. of Roger Denneis, Esq., of Tannington, both dec. **1479**, inscr. lost, C., pp. 61, 196, 212. *Cotman*, pl. xv. p. 11; *Suckling*, vol. i. p. 89; *Oxf. Man.*, pp. 89, 96; *Arch. Topogr. of Suff.; Introd.*, pp. 196, 211.   II. A Man in arm., c. **1480** (probably Robt. or John Bomsted, 1482 or 1479), pecul., inscr. lost, sm., C., p. 200. *Cotman*, pl. xvi. p. 12; *Suckling*, vol. i. p. 92.   III. Wm. Playters, Esq., son and h. of No. I., 1512 (eff. lost since 1843), and w. Jane, dau. of Sir Edm. Jenney, of Knotshall, they had a son, Christopher, and other chil., engr. c. **1580**, marg. inscr., A.T., C.   IV. Christopher Playters, Esq., **1547**, in arm., he had by his [first] w. Anne (dau. of Wm. Read, Esq., of Beccles) 5 sons and 4 daus., and by his 2nd w. Dorothie (dau. and h. of Wm. Aselack, Esq., of Carrow) a son Thos., curious, perhaps palimpsest, engr. c. 1580 (?), C., p. 52. *Cotman*, pl. xxvi. p. 17; *Suckling*, vol. i. p. 92.   V. Thos. Playters, Esq., patron of the manor, **1572**, in arm.; by his w. Elizth. (a dau. of Sir Thos. Jerman, of Rushebroke) he had 6 sons and 6 daus. *Cotman*, pl. xxix. p. 19; *Suckling*, vol. i. p. 92.   VI. Thomazen, a dau. and coh. of Edm. Tyrrell, Esq., of Betches, Essex, and w. of Wm. Playters, Esq., **1578**, æt. 33, with dau. Susan, inscr. (with " On whose soule Jesus haue M'cy") now separated from eff., C., p. 246. *Cotman*, pl. xxxii. p. 21; *Suckling*, vol. i. p. 89.   INSCRS. VII. *Wm. Playters, Esq., **1584**, and 4 ws., Thomasine (Duke), Elizth. (Timperley), Thomasine (No. VI.), Mary (Drake), C.   VIII. †John Playters, Gent., **1609**.   IX. †Sir Thos. Playters, **1638**, æt. 73.

SOUTHELMHAM, ST. JAMES. I. A Civilian and w., c. **1500**, inscr. lost, N.   INSCR. II. *" Edm de flrevyll Squyer."

SOUTHOLT. Robt. Armiger, **1585** (lost), and w. Margt. (Sturging).

†STOKE-BY-CLARE. I. A Lady, c. **1530**, inscr. lost.   II. Ralph Turnor, **1609**, and w.   III. Alice Talkarne [Falkaner?], widow, eldest dau. of Robt., son and h. of Sir Giles Allington, **1605**.

STOKE-BY-NEYLAND. I. A Lady in mantle, c. **1400**, (perhaps Cath., w. of Sir Thos. Clopton, and afterwards of Sir Wm. Tendring, 1402), inscr. lost, p. 169. *Cotman*, pl. iv. p. 5.   II. Sir Wm. Tendring, **1408**, inscr. lost, large, pp. 62, 154, 185. *Cotman*, pl. viii.

p. 8; *Boutell's Series*; *Hewitt's Anc. Arm.*, vol. iii. No. 56,
p. 368. III. A Man, in arm., and w., all lost except the
pediments of a double canopy, c. **1425**, p. 176. *Introd.*, p. 176
(det.) Perhaps the brass of Sir John Howard, 1426, and w.
Alice (Tendring), see Weever's Fun. Mon., pp. 772. 3, where it
is inaccurately (?) engr. IV. Lady [Kath.], w. of John Howard,
duke of Norfolk, and mother of Thos. Howard, duke of Norfolk,
1452, in heraldic mantle, engr. c. **1535**, inscr. and 3 shs. lost, pp. 45,
113. *Weever*, p. 774; *Cotman*, pl. xxiv. p. 15 and front. V.
*Francis Mannock, Esq., **1590**, æt. 68, and 2 ws.; the 1st w. with
1 son and 5 daus., the 2nd w. with 1 son and 3 daus., 4 Lat. vv.,
effs. of parents lost, N.A. VI. Dorothy [dau. of Wm.] Sanders,
[Esq., of Welford, Northants.], and w. of Sir Francis Mannock,
bart., **1632**, æt. 42, m. 24 years, and had 4 chil., Francis, John, Wm.,
and Anne (an infant), mur., pp. 25, 248. *Cotman*, pl. xlv. p. 27.
INSCR. VII. †Wm., eldest son of Francis Mannock, and w., **1616**,
æt. 60. Three matrices of early brasses, one to Sir John de Pey-
tone, 1318 (?), cross-legged, canopy, Lomb. inscr. in Fr.; another
similar, probably to a w. of the foregoing, p. 137.

STONHAM-ASPAL. I. John Metcalfe (son of Mary, the dau. of
John and Elizth. Felgate), rector for 32 years, bequeathed lands for
charitable purposes, **1606**, C., p. 230. FRAG. II. Three Daus.,
kng., c. **1520**, fem. eff. and inscr. lost, C.

STOWMARKET. Ann Tyrell, **1638**, æt. 8½, in shroud, 20 Eng. vv., N.

STRATFORD, ST. MARY. Edw. Crane, **1558**, and w. Elizth.

STUTTON. I. †A Priest, **1413**, hf. eff. INSCR. II. John
Smythe, **1534**.

TANNINGTON. I. Anne, dau. of Rich. Cornwalys, of Shotley, 3rd
son of Sir John Cornwalys, of Broumehall, and w. of Thos. Dade,
Esq., **1612**. INSCRS. II. Thos. Dade, Esq., **1619**, æt. 63. III.
Mary, dau. of Hen. Wingfeild, Esq., of Croffield, and w. of Wm.
Dade, Esq., **1624**.

THURLOW, GREAT. A Man, in arm., and w. —— (Drury), c.
1530, with 9 sons, daus. and inscr. lost, pecul., pp. 29, 243. In
the Brit. Museum is a rubbing of a curious brass (now lost) of
a Man in arm. with helmet, and w. in mantle, c. 1465 (?), pecul.

THURLOW, LITTLE. A Man, in arm., and w., c. **1510**, pecul.,
inscr. lost, p. 233.

UFFORD. I. Symon Brooke, **1488**, and ws. Emota, Margt., Alice,
upper part of male eff. and inscr. lost. *Cotman*, pl. xix. p. 14. II.
Rich. Ballett, "First Goldsmith of the Balletts in London," **1598**,
æt. 76, a skeleton, 9 Eng. vv., qd. pl., mur., pp. 119, 225.

WALDINGFIELD, LITTLE. I. John Colman, 1506, and w. Kath., with 6 sons and 7 daus., iuscr. aud Evang. symbs. loose, p. 204. *Introd.*, p. 204 (male eff.)   II. *Robt. Appleton, 1526, and w. Mary, second dau. and coh. of Thos. Mountney, Gent., partly covd., pecul., pp. 29, 243. *History of Appleton Family*, published in America (?). *Introd.*, p. 243 (fem. eff.)   III. A Lady, c. 1530, with arms of Brewse on a sh., inscr. lost, pecul., sm., p. 29.   IV. John Wyncoll, clothier, 1544, pecul., p. 29.

WALTON. I. Wm. Tabard, 1459, and w. Agnes, sm., N.   II. *Wm. Simond, 1612, æt. 11, kng., with acrostic vv., much worn, sm., C.

WENHAM, LITTLE. Thos. Brewse, Esq., 1514, and w. Jane, with 2 sons and 3 daus., canopy, marg. inscr. mutil. at repairs to Ch. about 30 years ago, C., p. 233.

WICKHAM-BROOKE. Thos. Burrugh, Gent., 1597, æt. 66, and 2 ws., Elizth. (Burwell, with 2 sons and 1 dau.) and Brigette (Higham, with 3 sons and 3 daus.), qd. pl., mur., behind wooden grating.

WICKHAM-SKEITH. A Civilian and widow, c. 1530, with 3 sons and 3 daus., male eff. and inscr. lost.

WILBY. I. †A Priest, c. 1480, sm., inscr. lost.   II. A Civilian, c. 1530, with a hare running on a separate plate, inscr. lost. INSCRS. III. †Wm. James, rector, 1569, 4 Eng. vv.   IV. Joseph Fletcher, 1637, æt. 60, with punning Lat. and Eng. vv. referring to Truway, a former rector, buried under the same stone. Four inscrs. to the Bayles family, 1588 – 1639.

WOODBRIDGE. John Shorlond, 1601, æt. 7, 6 Eng. vv., sm., C. *Cotman*, pl. xxxvii. p. 24.

WORLINGHAM. I. Nich. Wrenne, Gent., 1511, not in arm., and w. Mary, S.C. *Cotman*, pl. xxiii. p. 15.   INSCR. II. Wather (Walter ?) Lecberd, c. 1500, N.

WORLINGWORTH. I. Four Sons, one a priest in acad., and 7 daus., c. 1520, kng., parents and inscr. lost, p. 78.   INSCR. II. †Jaspar Hussie, citizen of London, went to Worlingworth for change of air and there dec. 1624, æt. 44, 4 Eng. vv.

WRENTHAM. I. Ele, dau. of Robt. Ufford [and w. of Rich.] Bowet, 1400, 4 Lat. vv., p. 168. *Cotman*, pl. vii. p. 7.   II. Humphrey Brewster, Esq., 1593, æt. 67, in arm. *Cotman*, pl. xxxv. p. 23; *Boutell's Mon. Br.*, p. 80; *Penny Post*, 1855, p. 175.

YAXLEY. I. Andrew, son of John Felgate, Gent., of Stonham Aspall, 1598, and his only dau. Margt., w. of Robt. Felgate, "qui (*sic*) obiit in pvero partu," 1596, only one male eff. and inscr.

left, N. Inscrs. II. Alice. w. of Rich. Yaxle, 1474. pecul., C.
III. *Alice Pulvertoft. IV. *John Yaxle. 154...
YOXFORD. I. John Norwiche, Esq., 1428. and w. Matilda, 1418,
inscr. lost, partly covd. by pulpit, large, p. 189. *Cotman*, pl. x. p. 9.
II. Tomesina, a dau. of Wm. Sydney, Esq., and his w. Tomesina
Baryngton, and w. of Wm. Tendryng, Esq., 1485, in shroud, beside
her 3 sons and 2 daus. in shrouds and 2 daus. in gowns, 3 of these
effs. loose (?). large. C. *Cotman*, pl. xvii. p. 13. *Trans. of Exeter
Soc.*, vol. iii. (eff.) III. Anth. Cooke, dec. on Easter Monday,
1613, æt. 79, had 11 chil., left 10 surviving, 10 punning vv., p. 96.
Cotman, pl. xl. p. 25. IV. Christian, w. of John Foxe, 1618,
æt. 29, and son [Francis, 1619]. *Cotman*, pl. xli. p. 25. V. Joan,
eldest dau. of Sir Humfrey Weld. and w. of Sir Robt. Brooke, 1618,
æt. 38, C. *Cotman*, pl. xlii. p. 26 (part of eff.) Inscrs. VI.
Wm. and John, sons of Wm. Tendryng, Esq., now mur., N.A.
VII. Elizth., dau. of Thomesina Hopton, and w. of Thos. Knyvet,
Esq., 1471, now mur., N.A. VIII. John Skottow, 1511, and w.
Agnes, pecul., N. IX. John Coke, 1522, and w. Alice, pecul.
A Civilian, c. 1590, left in this Ch. (?)

INSCRIPTIONS, &c.

AKENHAM. Sissile, w. of Peter Joiy (or Tory?), c. 1500. BOXTED.
Rich. Poly, Esq. 1546, and w. Anne, C. BUNGAY, TRINITY CH.
Dame Margt. Dalenger, prioress [1497]. CLAYDON. Sam. Ayle-
mer, Esq., eldest son of John, bp. of London, 1635, marg., C. COVE,
NORTH. I. Thos. Sengylton, Gent., 1498, N. II. †Thos. Sigilthon,
alias Dunton, c. 1500, N. III. Wm. Manthorpe and w. Alice,
c. 1500, N. IV. Margery, w. of John Berney, Esq., 1548, N.
DALHAM. John Dunmow, rector of Dalham and prebendary of
Stoke, 1460, and parents. C. DENNINGTON. Thos. Hopton,
chaplain, c. 1480 (?). DRINKSTONE. †Wm. Twaytis, 1499, and
w. Elizth. DUNWICH, ALL SAINTS. See brasses in private
possession—Mr. Bayfield. †GLENHAM, LITTLE. I. Christopher
Glenham, 1549, m. a sister of Lord Wentworth, and had 9 chil.,
Arthur, Thos., Chas., Elizth., Anne, Mary, Kath., Margt., Maria,
engr. c. 1571. II. Thos. Glenham (son of No. I.), and w. Amy
(Parker), both dec. 1571; they had 3 chil., Hen., Thos., Elizth.,
22 Eng. vv. GRUNDISBURGH. I. John Awall, 1501, and w.
Margery, 6 Eng. vv. II. Anne, widow of Francis Manocke, Esq.,
of Stoke Nayland, 1610, and 1 son and 3 daus. III. Thos. Sullyard, Esq., 2nd son of Sir John Sullyard, of Weatherdyne, and w.
Bridget, dau. of No. II., 1612. The 3 brasses are now mur., S.A.

Heveningham. Mr. Roger Marpall, **1511**.   Ipswich, St. Stephen. Wm. Sherman, Gent., **1583**.   Metfield. *John Jermy, **1504**, and w. Isabella, dau. of John Hopton, Esq.   Shottisham. †Rose, dau. of Humph. Robertson, and w. of John Glover, parson, **1610**, 2 roses and 4 Eng. vv.   Snape. †Five Daus., c. **1480**, paren's, &c., lost.   Theberton. Kath. Pays, c. **1500**.   Wantisden. †Mary, w. of Rich. Wingfelde, Esq., **1582**.   Westhall. A long genealogical inscr. (from Thos. Plantagenet and Eleanor Bohun) to Nich. Bohun, **1602**, and widow Audrie (sister of Sir Edw. Cooke, attorney-general to Jas. I.), and 7 infant chil.   Woolverstone. Thos. Runtyng, rector, 15th cent.

Numerous inscrs. of the 17th cent. remain in various churches. At Wingfield are matrices of fine brasses of the Wingfield family; one also is at Dennington (Sir Wm. Wingfield, 1388, with canopy). At Hoxham is the matrix of an inscr. with a bird above. See also Introd., pp. 25, 256.

Surrey.

Addington. I. Thos. Hatteclyff, Esq., a master of the household to Hen. VIII., **1540**, he had a w. Anne, C., p. 230.   II. John Leigh, Esq., 1509, not in arm., and w. Isabell, dau. of John Harvye, Esq., of Thurley, Beds., and only sister of Sir Geo. Harvye, **1544**, with 2 sons and 3 daus., marg. inscr., A.T. recently removed, C.

Albury (Old Church).   John Weston, Esq., **1440**, p. 192.

Barnes. Edith and Elizth., daus. of John Wylde, Esq., and his w. Anne, "died virgyns," **1508**, sm., p. 214.   The brass of Wm. Mullebourne, Esq., 1415, is now lost, p. 187.

Beddington. I. Philippa, dau. of Nich. and Mercia Carreu, **1414**, and hf. eff's. of her brothers and sisters, Guido, John, John, John, John, Wm., Wm., Elienora, Lucia, Agnes, Agnes, Margt., Anna, marg. inscr., sm., N., pp. 172, 205.   II. A Cross for Margt. Oliver, servant to Nich. and Mercye Carru, **1425**, sm., p. 173. *Boutell's Series*, and *Chr. Mon.*, p. 40.   III. Nich. Carrew, Esq., lord of the manor, **1432**, "senex & plenus dierum," not in arm., and [2nd?] w. Isabella [Delamar, or Roet?]; they had a son Thos., canopy, marg. inscr., large, C., pp. 92, 203. *Lysons' Environs of London*, 1792, vol. i. p. 58; *Topogr. Hist. of Surrey, by E. W. Brayley and John Britton*, London, 1841, vol. iv. p. 62; *Boutell's Series.*   IV. A Civilian and lady, c. **1430**, inscr. lost. Perhaps Thos. Carew, Esq., 1430, not in arm., and sister Isabella, w. of Robt. Bukton, Esq., and afterwards of Brian Harsick, Esq., 1434, C. See Lansdown MS. (No. 874, fol. 41, b.) in Brit. Museum.

V. Roger Elmebrygge, Esq., "cui Rex concessit Surr' Sussex comitatus," **143**[7], p. 190. *Boutell's Series; Hewitt's Anc. Arm.*, vol. iii. No. 76, p. 445. VI. Kath., w. of Robt. Berecroft, Gent., and sister Elizth., widow of Wm. Barton, Gent., both dec. **1507**, sm., N. Inscrs. VII. Sir Rich. [Carew], **1520**, and w. Malyn, marg., effs. lost, A.T. VIII. Elizth. Boys, widow, servant to Sir Fraunces Carewe, **1599**. IX. Margt., w. of John Huntley, Gent., **1638**, æt. 74.

BETCHWORTH. I. Wm. Wardysworth, vicar, **1533**, with chalice and wafer, C. Inscrs., &c. II. Thos. Morsted and w. Alianora, c. **1460**. III. A Mcht.'s mk. and initials W. H., on reverse arms of Fitz Adrian, from a tomb of the Frowick family (?). *Arch. Journ.*, vol. xii. p. 293; *Gent. Mag.*, vol. xliii. N.S. 1855, p. 270. IV. Rich. Powlesden, yeoman of Brockham, **1613**. V. Amy, widow of No. IV., **1614**; they had a dau. Jane.

BLETCHINGLEY. I. A maiden Lady, c. **1470**, inscr. lost, sm. II. A brass all covd. except 6 sons and 6 daus. and 2 shs., c. **1500**, N.Tr. III. Thos. Warde and w. Jone, **1541**, N.Tr.

BOOKHAM, GREAT. I. Elizth., dau. of Sir Edw. Seynt Johñ, and w., first, of Geo. Brewes, Esq., and then of Thos. Slyfeld, **1433**, sm., in a pew, C. II. Hen. Slyfield, Esq., **1598**, æt. 56, and w. Elizth., dau. of Rich. Buckfold, citizen of London, with 6 sons and 4 daus., S.A. III. *Robt. Shiers, Esq., of the inner temple, c. **1668** (?), under a pew, S.A., p. 125. *Brayley and Britton*, vol. iv. p. 479.

BYFLEET. Thos. Teylar, rector, canon of Lincoln, c. **1480** [dec. 1489], C., p. 79.

CAMBERWELL. I. A Man in arm., c. **1470**, with inscr. (now mur.) to Edw., son of John Scott, Esq., **1538**, S.A. *D. Allport's Hist. of Camberwell*, 1841, p. 140. II. Mighell Skinner, Gent., **1497**, not in arm., sm., N. *Ibid.*, p. 126. III. Rich. Skynner, **1507**, head gone, and w. Agnes (eff. lost), with 5 sons and 5 daus., mur., C., pp. 34, 258. *Ibid.*, p. 129. IV. John Scott, Esq., baron of the exchequer, **1532**, in arm., and w. [Elizth., dau. of No. III.], with 4 sons, 7 daus. lost, mur., C. *Lysons' Env. of Lond.*, vol. i. p. 77; *Allport*, p. 130. V. Mathye Draper, Esq., **1577**, and w. Seuce, dau. of Wm. Blackwell, Esq., of London, mur., C. *Allport*, p. 134. VI. John Bowyar, Esq., 1570, and w. Elizth., **1605**, with 8 sons and 3 daus.; by 2nd husband, Wm. Foster, Elizth. had also 1 son and 1 dau., mur., C. *Ibid.* Inscr., &c. VII. Margt., dau. of Matt. Keleatt, Gent., of Surrey, and w. of John Dove, **1585**; had 5 sons and 4 daus., mur. N. VIII. A Sh. for Thos. Muschamp, Gent., **1637**. Nos. II., VII., VIII., and inscr. of No. I. are now mur. in vestry; the eff. of No. I. is in private hands at Camberwell,

Nos. III., IV., V., VI., are in the possession of Mr. Acock, builder, Camberwell, p. 3.

CARSHALTON. I. Nich. Gaynesford, esquire for the body to Ed. IV. and Hen. VII., and w. Margt., one of the "Gentilwymmen" to the 2 Queens Elizth., with collar of suns and roses, c. **1490**, with 4 sons (the 2nd a priest), 4 (?) daus. lost, mur., coloured, A.T., C. *Lysons' Envir.*, vol. i. p. 128. II. Thos. Ellenbridge, Esq., J.P., "hostiarius" to Cardinal John Morton, abp. of Cant., **1497**, and w. Elizth. [Gaynesford?], with 3 (?) sons and 3 (?) daus., canopy, effs. stolen in 1837 (?), inscr. lost, C., pp. 104, 260. III. Joan, dau. of John Ellynbrege, Esq., and w. of Hen. Burton, Esq., **1524**, N.A. The upper part of the eff. of Walter Gaynsford, chaplain, 1493, with chalice, lately loose, is now lost (?), it is sketched in the Lansdown M.S. (874, fol. 132. b.) in the Brit. Museum, p. 260.

CHARLWOOD. Nich. Saunder, Esq., **1553**, in arm., and w. Alys, dau. of John Hungate, Esq., of Yorks. (parents of Sir Thos. Saunder, the king's rememberance' of the exchequer), with 4 sons and 6 daus., mur., C., p. 244.

CHEAM. I. A Frankelein, c. **1370**, with anelace, centre part of eff. and inscr. lost, S.A., p. 164. II. John Compton, 1450, and w. Joan, **1458**, hf. effs., inscr. covd., N. III. John Yerde (?), with collar, 1449, in arm., and w. Anna (widow of —— Fromonde?), 1453, engr. c. **1480**, inscr. lately (?) lost, very sm., the arms of the husband are those of Courtenay (?), S.C., p. 2. IV. Thos. Fromound, Esq., **1542**, not in arm., and w. Elizth., dau. and h. of John Yerde, Esq., with 6 sons and 4 daus., Hy. Trin., mur., S.A. *J. P. Malcom's Views.* INSCRS. V. Nich. Denys, Esq., **1518**. VI. Barth., son and h. of Thos. Fromoundes, Gent., **1579**, S.C.

CHIPSTEAD. *Kath. Roper, **1614**.

COBHAM. I. Fifteen Sons, loose, also the Adoration of the Shepherds, c. **1500**, the latter in possession of the clerk, and engr. in *C. C. Soc. Illustr.*, No. ii. p. 46; pp. 102, 260. II. A Man in arm., c. **1550**, on reverse a Priest, c. **1510**, with chalice and wafer, loose, pp. 45, 149, 235. *Brayley and Britton*, vol. ii.; *Introd.*, p. 46. Perhaps one of the brasses was to James Sutton, "baile" of the lordship, 1530, and w. Mawde.

COMPTON. Thos. Genyn (?), **1508**, and w. Margt., with 2 sons, 2 daus. lost, C.

CROWHURST. I. John Gaynesford, Esq., sen., **1450** (in arm., like the eff. at Isleworth, Middx., p. 192), A.T., C. *Boutell's Series; Hewitt's Anc. Arm.*, vol. iii. No. 80, p. 460. II. John Gaynesford, Esq., **1460**; he m. Anne, dau. of Rich. Wakeherst, A.T., N.C.,

p. 194.   INSCR. III. Anne, dau. of Sir Thos. Fynes, and w. of
John Gaynsford, Esq.   A *cast-iron* plate with sm. eff. in shroud,
and inscr. to Ane Forstr, dau. and h. of Thos. Gaynsford, 1591, with
2 sons and 2 daus.; she left 3 other daus. surviving, p. 1.

CROYDON. I. "Silvester Gabriel," **1512**, in cope, 6 eleg. vv., C.
II. Thos. Heron, Esq., **1544**, and w. Elizth., dau. and coh. of Wm.
Bond, clerke of the green cloth, with 4 sons and 7 daus., inscr. lost,
lately covd., C., p. 245.   III. Elizth., dau. of John and Clemence
Kynge, and w. of Samuell Fynche, by whom she had 3 sons and
2 daus., **1589**, æt. 21, N.   IV. A Civilian, c. **1600**, inscr. lost.
Perhaps John Packington, farmer of the parsonage, 1607, and w.
Anne, and son Hen., N.   V. A Civilian and w., c. **1630**, inscr. lost,
sm., N.A., p. 240.   *Introd.*, p. 240 (male eff.) Perhaps the brass
of Robt. Jackson, 1629, and w. Elizth.   INSCRS. VI. Giles Seymor,
1390, eff. and cross lost, N.   VII. Elye Davy, mercer of London,
1455, lately restored, A.T. He founded an almshouse at Croydon.

DITTON, LONG.   Rich. Hatton, **1616**, æt. 81, and w. Mary (dau.
of Geo. Evelyn, Esq., by his w. Rose), 1612, æt. 63, m. 56 years;
3 sons, 6 daus., and inscr. lost. *Manning and Bray's Hist. of Surrey*,
vol. iii. p. 21 (erroneously ascribed to Robt. Casteltunn, 1527.

DITTON, THAMES. I. Erasmus Forde, Esq., (son and h. of Walter
Forde, treasurer to Edw. IV. in his wars and "at ye wynnyng of
Barwyke," h. in descent to Sir Adam Forde), 1533, in arm., and w.
Julyan (a dau. and h. of Wm. Salford and his w. Elyn, dau. of Sir
Rich. Chawcey), **1559**, with 6 sons and 12 daus., mur., C. *Brayley
and Britton*, vol. ii. p. 421.   II. Cuthbert Blakeden, Esq., serjeant
of the confectionary to Hen. VIII., 1510, with 6 chil., Anne, Mary,
John, Cuthbert, Julyan, Kath.; John Boothe, Esq., one of the
ordinary gentlemen ushers to Hen. VIII. and Ed. VI., 1548, with
5 chil., Jane, Dorothe, Joan, John, Myllyseut; and their w. Julyan
(youngest dau. of No. III.), 1586, æt. 77, the w. pos. **1580**, now
mur., N.C., p. 45.   III. John Polsted, Gent., 1540, and w. Anne,
dau. of Robt. Wheeler, Gent. (in costume of the time she lived),
with 4 daus., Anne, Jane, Elizth., Julian; Julian pos. **1582**, æt. 73,
mur., N.A.   IV. Robt. Smythe, Gent., 1539, and w. Kath., dau. of
Sir Thos. Blounte, of Kinlett, 1549, kng., with —— sons and 3 daus.,
engr. c. **1587**, partly covd., C.   V. Wm. Notte, Esq., 1576, and w.
Elizth. (dau. of No. IV.), **1587**, kng., with 14 sons and 5 daus., on
same slab as No. IV.   VI. John Cheke, Gent., **1590**, æt. 73, and
w. Isabel, dau. of Wm. Seilearde, of London, with 6 sons, Roger,
Humfre, Anth., Robt., John, Wm., C.

EGHAM. Anth. Bond, Gent., "Citizen & writer of the Court

EWELL. I. Lady Jane, dau. of John Agmondesham, Esq., of "Ledered," Surrey, and w. of Sir John Iwarby, of Ewell, **1519**, in heraldic mantle, kng., once on A.T., C.   II. Margery, w. of John Treghstin, **1521**, N.   III. Lady Dorothe, dau. of Thos. Roberds, Esq., of Willesdon, Middx., w., first, of Allen Horde, Esq., bencher of the Middle Temple, and then of Sir Lawr. Taylare, of Doddington, Hunts., **1577**, æt. 70, with 10 chil. by her 1st husband, Thos., Edm. (dec. 1575), Alyn, Wm., John, Kath., Elizth., Mary, Dorothe, Ursula, N.   INSCRS. IV. John Tabarde and w. Joan. V. Edm. Dows, Gent., a clerk of the signet with Hen. VII., **1510**. A Sh.

†FARNHAM. I. Benedict Jay and w., c. **1580**, qd. pl., mur.   II. Sibil, dau. of Rich. Birde, Esq., and w. of —— Lloyd, **1597**, with chil., qd. pl., mur.

FARLEY. †John Brock, citizen and "pretor" of London, **1495**, and w., with 4 sons and 1 dau., sm., C. A John Brooke was sheriff of London in 1489.

GODALMING. I. Thos. Purvdebe (?), **1509**, and w. Joan.   II. John Barker, Esq., third son of Wm. Barker, Esq., of Sunning, Berks., **1595**, æt. 34, in arm.

GUILDFORD, ABBOTT'S HOSPITAL. I. Maurice Abbot, æt. 86, and w. Alice [Marsh], æt. 80, both dec. Sept. 25th, **1606**, m. 58 years, with 6 sons surviving, qd. pl., mur. They were the parents of Abp. Abbot.   INSCR. II. Baldwin Smythe, 12 Eng. vv., 16th cent.

HORLEY. I. A Lady, c. **1420**, with collar of SS., canopy, large, inscr. lost, another added to Joan, w. of John Fenner, **1516**, N.A., p. 50. *Boutell's Mon. Br.*, p. 87 (det.)   II. A Civilian [John Fenner?], c. **1520**, inscr. lost, C.

HORSHILL. I. Thos. Sutton, Gent., eldest son of John Sutton the elder, **1603**, æt. 38, p. 253.   II. Thos. Edmonds, citizen and carpenter to the chamber and one of the four "vewers" of the city of London, **1619**, and w. Ann, dau. of Wm. Frognall, citizen and fishmonger of London, with 5 sons and 2 daus., arms of London and Carpenters' Co.·   INSCR. III. John Aleyn, chaplain, 15th cent.

HORSLEY, EAST. I. A Civilian, c. **1400**, hf. eff., inscr. lost, C., p. 164. Probably Robt. de Brentyngham, brother (or father) of Thos., bp. of Exeter 1370—1394.   II. John Lowthe, bp. of Exeter, **1478**, 2 Lat. vv., mur., C., pp. 71, 73, 78, 171. *Brayley and Britton*, vol. ii. p. 67; *C. C. Soc. Illustr.*, No. iii. p. 85; *Boutell's Mon. Br.*, p. 102.   III. John Snellyng, **1498**, and w. Alys, with 6 sons and

5 daus., sm., C.   INSCR. IV. Thos. Snelling (smyth? erased), **1504**, and w. Jone (effs. lost), with 8 sons and 5 daus., Vestry.

KINGSTON-UPON-THAMES. I. Robt. Skern, "lege peritus... Regalis iuris viuens promouit honores," **1437**, with anelace, and w. [Joan] in mantle, 12 eleg. vv., once on A.T., C., p. 209.   *J. P. Malcom's Views; Manning and Bray*, vol. i. p. 368; *Brayley and Britton*, vol. iii. p. 37; *Fairholt's Costume*, p. 183. *Introd.*, p. 208 (det.) Joan Skerne was the dau. of Allice Perrers, mistress of Edw. III. and afterwards w. of Sir Wm. Wyndsore.   II. John Hertcombe, Gent., **1488**, not in arm., head gone, and w. Kath., 1477, kng., above matrix of our Blessed Saviour (?) in an aureole seated on a rainbow, sm., now mur., N.Tr., p. 257.

LAMBETH, ST. MARY. I. Lady Catharine, a sister and h. of John Broughton, Esq., and w. of Lord Wm. Howard (son of Thos., late duke of Norfolk); they left Agnes their only dau. and h., **1535**, in heraldic mantle, canopy and inscr. lost, p. 113.   *Allen's Lambeth*. II. Thos. Clere, Esq., **1545**, inscr. lost, pp. 95, 235.   *Ibid*.   At the siege of Montreuil, in France, Clere received a fatal wound while saving the life of his friend the illustrious earl of Surrey.

LETHERHEAD.   A Civilian; feet, w., and inscr. gone; c. **1470**, with 3 sons and 3 daus.

LEIGH. I. John Arderne, Esq., not in arm., and w. Elizth., both in mantles, c. **1440**, with 3 sons (one gone), Thos., John, IIen., and 3 daus., Anna, Brigitt, Susanna, inscr. lost, C.   *Drummond's Noble Brit. Fam.*   II. Susanna, dau. of John Arderne, Esq., and his w. Elizth., c. **1460**, sm., lately lost (?), C., p. 260.   *Ibid*.   INSCR. III. Rich. Ardern, Gent., **1499**, and w. Joan, with Hy. Trin., effs. lost, C.   *Ibid.*

LINGFIELD. I. A Lady of the Cobham family, c. **1370**, inscr. lost, large, N.C., pp. 33, 169.   *Introd.*, p. 169.   II. Sir Reginald de Cobham, lord of the manor of Steresburgh, **1403**, marg. inscr. with 10 Lat. vv., large, N.C., pp. 33, 185, 187.   *Waller*, pt. vi.; *Brayley and Britton*, vol. iv. p. 167; *Boutell's Mon. Br.*, p. 60.   III. Lady [Eleanor], dau. of Sir Thos. Colepeper, and w. of Sir Reginald Cobham, **1420**, in mantle, head gone, canopy, marg. inscr., N.C., pp. 33, 92.   IV. John Hadresham, **1417**, in arm., C., p. 188. *Boutell's Series.*   V. Kath. Stoket, c. **1420**, hf. eff., sm., N.A. VI. John Wyche, master of St. Peter's Coll., **1445**, hf. eff., C. VII. A maiden Lady, c. **1450**, inscr. lost, sm., C., p. 213.   VIII. Jas. Veldon, master of the Coll., **1458**, hf. eff., sm., S.C.   IX. John Swetecok, master of the Coll., **1469**, C.   *Boutell's Series*. X. John Knoyll, master of the Coll., **1503**, Hy. Trin. lost.   In

1846 the eff. of a Priest, c. 1440, head and inscr. gone, worn, sm., remained in N., p. 260. It perhaps commemorated John Acton, first master of the College.

MERSTHAM. I. John Ballard, **1464**, and w. Margt., sm., partly covd., C. II. John Elmebrygge, Esq., **1473**, not in arm., and 2 ws., Isabella (dau. of Nich. Jamys, lord mayor [sheriff? in 1423], 1472, with 7 daus., 4 (?) sons lost) and Anna, dau. of John Prophete, Gent., sm., A.T., N.C. III. John Newdegate, Esq., lord of the manor of [Harefield?], Middx., **1498**, C., p. 198. IV. Thos. Elmerigge, Esq., "alias dict' Thomas Elyngbrigge" (son and h. of Thos. Elmerigge), **1507**, and w. Joan, 3 sons and 3 daus. lost (?), N.C. V. Peter and Rich., sons of Nich. and Elizth. Best, of Alderstead in Merstham, 1585, **1587**, sm., S.C., p. 219. *Introd.*, p. 219.

MICKLEHAM. Wm. Wyddowsoun, patron of the Ch., citizen and mercer of London, and w. Jone, **1513**, A.T., N.C., pp. 203, 239, 241, 242. *Robinson's Mickleham. Introd.*, p. 241 (fem. eff.)

MOLESEY, WEST. A Man and his w., c. **1510**, in shrouds, inscr. and another eff. (?) lost, loose at the clerk's house.

NUTFIELD. Wm. Graffton and w., c. **1465**, sm.; they had a son John, C., p. 90.

OAKWOOD. Edw. de la Hale, Esq., **1431**, with collar of SS., inscr. reversed, sm., C., p. 189. *Gough*, vol. ii. pl. cxxiv. p. 358; *Brayley and Britton*, vol. v. p. 48.

OCKHAM. I. Walter Frilende, rector, builder of chapel, c. **1360**, hf. eff., now mur., C., p. 143. *Gent. Mag.*, vol. lxx. 1800, pt. i. p. 113; *Boutell's Series*, and *Chr. Mon.*, p. 153. II. John, son and h. of Wm. Weston, Esq., **1483**, in arm., and w. Margt. [Mitford], 1475, now mur., C., p. 198. INSCRS. III. John Wexcombe, mur., N.A. IV. Robt. Kellett, rector, **1525**, mur., C.

OXTED. I. John Ynge, rector, **1428**, upper part of eff. gone or covd., sm., C. II. Joan Haseleden, **1480**. III. Thos. Hoskins, Gent., 2nd son of Sir Thos. Hoskins, **1611**, æt. 5, "who Abovte a quarter of an houre before his dep'ture did of himselfe wthout any instruction speake thos wordes: & leade vs not into temptatiō bvt deliver vs from all evill, beinge ye last words he spake;" head gone; also Thos., 5th son of Sir Thos. Hoskins, **1611**, æt. half a year, sm., C. IV. A Son, c. **1620**, rest of brass lost or covd.

PEPPER-HARROW. I. Joan, widow of Wm. Brokes, Esq., patron of the Ch., and formerly w. of John Addirley, lord mayor [in 1442], **1487**, with Hy. Trin., mur., C., pp. 56, 171. II. A Cross to the same, C., pp. 56, 173.

PUTNEY. I. John Welbek, Esq., 1476, and w. Agnes, **1478**, eff. lost, N.A., p. 198. II. A Lady, c. **1585**, inscr. lost, N.

PUTTENHAM. Edw. Cranford, rector, **1431**, rel.

RICHMOND. *Mr. Robt. Cotton, an officer of the "remooving Wardroppe of Bedds" to Queen Mary, also a groom of the privy chamber to Queen Elizth., and w. Grace (Cawson), c. **1580**, with 4 sons and 4 daus., mur., C.

ROTHERHITHE. *Peter Hills, mariner, and one of the elder brethren of the Trinity House, **1614**, and 2 ws., much worn, qd. pl., mur., N.

SEND. *Laur. Slyffeld, Gent., **1521**, and w. Alys, sm.

SHERE. I. Robt. Scarclyf, rector, **1412**, C. II. Olever Sandes, **1512**, and w. Jone (eff. lost), "ye which made this wyndow & this auter," sm., S.A. III. John Redfford, **1516**, and w., with 4 sons and 2 daus., sm., S.A. IV. Sir John Towchet, lord of Awdeley, 1491, engr. c. **1525**, legs of eff. and inscr. lost, once on A.T., C., p. 232. *Gough*, vol. ii. pl. cxxiv. p. 358; *Manning and Bray*, vol. i. p. 525.

STOKE D'ABERNON. I. Sir John D'Aubernoun, **1277**, in chain mail, with enamelled sh. on arm, and holding a spear, Fr. marg. inscr. in Lomb. letters lost, large, C., pp. 12, 43, 139, 144, 147. *Waller*, pt. iii.; *Arch. Journ.*, vol. i. p. 209; *Brayley and Britton*, vol. ii. p. 462; *Boutell's Mon. Br.*, pp. 27, 28; *Oxf. Man.*, p. 66; *Gent. Mag.*, vol. xxx. N.S. 1848, p. 601; *Surrey Arch. Coll.*, vol. i. p. 234; *Introd.*, p. 145. II. Sir John D'Aubernoun, son of No. I., **1327**, with sh. on arm, finials and shafts of canopy lost, Fr. marg. inscr. in Lomb. letters nearly all lost, large, C., pp. 25, 137, 150, 153. *Stothard*, p. 60; *Brayley and Britton*, vol. ii. p. 462; *Boutell's Mon. Br.*, p. 41; *Surrey Arch. Coll.*, vol. i. p. 235; *Arch. Journ.*, vol. xv. p. 294; *Introd.*, p. 152, p. 139 (det.) III. A widow lady, lower part of eff. and inscr. lost, sm., loose, p. 209. *Introd.*, p. 209. IV. Elyn, dau. of Sir Edm. Bray and his w. Jane, **1516**, in shroud, loose (?), sm., N.C., p. 220. *Trans. of Exeter Soc.*, vol. iii. (front.) V. *Thos. Lyfelde, Esq., and w. Fraunces, youngest dau. of Sir Edm. and Lady Jane Bray, **1592**, æt. 70, with dau. Jane, w. of Thos. Vincent, Esq., inscr. tracing genealogy to Wm. the Conqueror, qd. pl., mur., N.C. INSCR., &c. VI. A Sh. (3 others and inscr. lost) for Sir Wm. D'Aubernoun, **1358**, C. VII. Eight Eng. vv. to Sir John Pynnoke, first priest of Sir John Norbery's chantry, **1521**, loose, N.C.

STREATHAM. I. Wm. Mowfurth, rector of Streatham and Mickleham, **1513**, now mur. INSCR. II. John Elslefeld, rector, c. **1420**.

TITSEY. Wm., son and h. of Sir John Gresham, late sheriff of Surrey and Sussex, **1579** [it should be 1578?], and w. Beatrys Gyboñe, and 7 chil., Jas., Wm., Thos., John, Mary, Elizth., Sysselley, mur., C., p. 226. The date has been subsequently added, and the beginning of inscr. altered from "Here lyethe" to "Near this place lyethe;" Ch. being rebuilt 1860.

THORPE. I. *John Bonde, **1578**, and w. Joan. II. Wm. Denham, citizen and goldsmith of London, **1583**, æt. 64, and w., with 5 sons and 10 daus., 8 Eng. vv. and inscr. on floor, qd. pl., mur., C., p. 119. *Brayley and Britton*, vol. ii. p. 252.

TOOTING. *Wm. Fitzwilliam, **1597**, and w. Elizth., 1582; their dau., Anne, pos.; qd. pl., mur. *J. P. Malcom's Views*.

WALTON-ON-THAMES. John Selwyn, "gent' Keeper of her Ma^{tis} Parke of Oteland' vnder ye right honorable Charles Howward Lord Admyrall of England," **1587**, and w. Susan, with 5 sons and 6 daus. (surviving), curious, dug up in S.A. (?), now on a board, mur., C., pp. 34, 47, 122. *Ant. Repert.*, ed. 1807, p. 1; *Brayley and Britton*, vol. iii. p. 328; *Illustrated London News*, vol. x. No. 268.

WANDSWORTH. Nich. ......, serjeant to king Hen. ..., **1420**, in arm., marg. inscr. mutil., much worn, p. 126.

WEYBRIDGE. I. Three Skeletons (a man and his 2 ws.?) head of one and inscr. lost, c. 1520, later inscrs. added, now in the possession of W. H. Hart, Esq., Folkestone House, near Streatham. II. Thos. Inwood the elder, yeoman, **1586**, and 3 ws., with 2 sons and 3 daus., 6 Eng. vv., qd. pl., mur., N. III. John Woulde, Gent., **1598**, and 2 ws., Adrye (widow of Thos. Streete, Esq., with 4 sons and 4 daus. by him), 1596, and Elizth. (eldest dau. of Wm. Notte, of Thames Ditton, and widow of Hen. Standish, Esq., of Esher, with 5 sons and 3 daus. by him), now mur., N. INSCR. IV. Fraunces, 1596; Dorothy, 1600; Thos., **1605**, chil. of Sir John and Lady Margt. Trevor.

WITLEY. *Thos. Jonys, a sewer of the chamber to Hen. VIII., c. **1525**, and w., with 3 sons.

WOKING. I. †Hen. Purdan, **1523**, and w. Joan, with 3 sons and 4 daus., male eff. and inscr. lost, sm., C. II. John Shadhet, **1527**, and w. Isabell, chil. lost, sm., S.A. The brass of Gilbert Gilpyn, 1500, is lost, p. 130.

INSCRIPTIONS, &c.

CLAPHAM, ST. PAUL'S. †Wm. Tableer, **1401**, in Vestry. EFFINGHAM. John Aley, **1507**. GUILDFORD, HOLY TRINITY CH. †Hen. Norbrige, **1512**, and w. Ales, chief founders of the chantry in the

Lady chapel, mur., Porch.   HORSLEY, WEST.   I. Hen. Darckam,
1504, N.   II. Martin Whyth, **1506**, and w. Annes, N.   REIGATE.
A Memorandum of the erection of porch by John Skynner, Gent.,
1513 (see Appendix B.)

The brasses are lost at BATTERSEA, CRANLEY (? p. 104), HAM-
BLEDON, SOUTHWARK, and WIMBLEDON. At SANDERSTEAD was an
inscr. to Hen. Pollestede, Gent., of Pirllew, citizen and mcht.-tailor
of London, **1556** (?), on reverse an inscr. to Byckley Williams, **1467**;
it is said to be in the possession of a Mr. Glover.

Sussex.

AMBERLEY.   John Wantele, **1424**, in tabard, bare-headed, S.A.,
p. 190.   *Stothard; Boutell's Series; Hewitt's Anc. Arm.*, vol. iii.
pl. 67, p. 412.

ANGMERING.   Eden, dau. of Thos. and Ales Truelove, and w. of
John Baker, of Eglesden, **1598**, æt. 23, N.

ARDINGLEY.   I. *Rich. Wakeherst, Esq., 1457, not in arm., and
w. Elizth. dau. of Robt. Echyngham, 1464, engr. c. **1500**, canopy,
A.T., C.   *Boutell's Series; Sussex Archæological Collections*, vol. ii.
p. 312.   II. Rich. Culpepyr, Esq., son of Walter Culpepyr, of
Goudhurst, Kent, and w. Mary, dau. of Rich. Wakeherst, jun., **1504**
(upper part of eff. lost), canopy, C., p. 138.   III. Nich. Culpeper,
Esq., **1510**, and w. Elizth. [dau. of No. I.], with 10 sons and
8 daus., C.   IV. Elizth., dau. of Wm. Farnefold, Esq., of Steyning,
and w. of Sir Edw. Culpeper, of Wakehurst, Sussex, **1633**, C., pp. 25,
247, 248.   *Introd.*, p. 248.   V. Elizth., eldest dau. of Sir Wm.
Culpeper, of Wakehurst, and his w. Jane, **1634**, æt. 7, C., p. 25.

ARUNDEL.   I. Sir Adam Ertham, first master of the College [**1382**?],
in cope, hf. eff., Fr. inscr., p. 144.   *Tierney's Hist. and Antiq. of
Arundel*, p. 635.   II. Wm. Whyte, third master of the College,
1419, in almuce, inscr. lost, p. 79.   III. Thos. Salmon, Esq.,
"Vussher Cam'e" to Hen. V., **1430** (only centre of eff. left), and
w. Agnes, "[alias dict' dolyuer' nup' de Portugalia, principal' nup'
mulier illustris dūc Beatricis Comit ...," **1418**, with collar of SS.,
canopy, large, fine, pp. 125, 176, 208, 209.   *Tierney*, p. 637.   Beatrice
countess of Arundel and Surrey, was dau. of John I., King of
Portugal.   IV. Esperaunce Blondell, rector of Sutton, c. **1450**,
hf. eff.   V. John Baker, "socius" of the College, **1455**, inscr. lost,
p. 77.   VI. John Threel, marshal of the household to Wm., earl
of Arundel, **1465**, in arm., with collar of suns and roses, and w.
Joan, handmaid to Beatrix and Joan, countesses of Arundel, 1459

(eff. and inscr. lost), 10 Lat. vv., p. 196. The eff. of the w. is sketched in the Burrel MS. (5,699, Add. MS. in Brit. Mus., fol. 24. b.) VII. Robt. Warde, priest, ¾ eff., **1474**, pecul., N.C. One enamelled Badge (a horse galloping under an oak), out of 4, is left on the A.T. of John Fitzalan, 1421. *Gough*, vol. ii. pl. xxii. p. 45; *Dallaway's Sussex, by Cartwright*, 1832, vol. ii. p. 197. The brass of John Mundy, "submagister," 1506, with chalice, is sketched in the Burrell MS. (see No. VI.) See also p. 258.

BATTLE. I. John Lowe, **1426**, in arm., 12 hexameter vv., large, C., p. 188. II. Robt. Clere, dean, c. **1430**, feet on dog, 6 Lat. vv., C. III. Wm. Arnold, Esq., **1435**, hf. eff., N., p. 189. IV. Thos. Alfraye, 1599 (or 1589) æt. about 50 (eff. lost), and w. Elizth., dau. of Ambrose Comfort, **1600** (?), m. 31 years, left a son and dau., 14 Eng. vv., N. V. John Wythines, D.D., born at Chester, fellow of Brasenose Coll., and vice-chancellor of Oxford (?), dean of Battle for 42 years, **1615**, æt. 84, C., pp. 86, 230. *Grose's Antiq.*, 1773, vol. i. pl. ix. INSCR. VI. Elizth., widow of Thos. Haye, Gent., **1597**, N.A.

BODYHAM. I. John (?) Bodiham, c. **1360**, in arm., with arms on jupon; head, legs, and inscr. lost, pp. 157, 160. *Gent. Mag.*, vol. vii. N.S. 1837, pl. i. p. 262; *Sussex Arch. Coll.*, vol. ix. p. 281; *Arch. Journ.*, vol. xv. p. 95. II. Wm. Wetherden, vicar, "qui quidem non literatus uxorem duxit, qua mortua, se dedit studio literali & sacerdocij ordiëm suscepit," benefactor to the Ch., **1513**, in shroud, eff. of w. (?) lost, sm., pp. 63, 90. *Grose's Antiq.*, vol. i. pl. v. fig. 2; *Gent. Mag.* (see No. I., eff.) INSCR. III. Thos. Grove and w. Crestian, c. **1520**. The brasses are now mur. in Tower.

BILLINGHURST. *Thos. Bartlett, **1489**, and w. Elizth. [De Oakhurst?].

BREDE. I. Robt. Oxenbregg, Esq., 1487, nearly all lost, and w. Ann [Lyvelode], **1493**, in mantle, S.C. INSCR. II. Margt. and Kath., daus. of Robt. Oxenbregge, 15th cent.

BRIGHTLING. I. A Civilian and w., c. **1480**, inscr. lost. Perhaps John Batys, Gent., who gave the pavement, sedilia, and the lands called Levettys to the Ch., 1476, p. 254. II. Thos., child of Thos. Pius [Pye?], D.D., **1592**, kng., 6 Eng. vv., sm.

BROADWATER. I. John Mapilton, rector, chancellor to [Joan of Navarre] Queen of Hen. IV., **1432**, in cope, canopy, 8 Lat. vv., C., p. 131. *Dallaway's Sussex*, vol. ii. p. 36; *C. C. Soc. Illustr.*, No. vi. p. 211; *Boutell's Series; Weekly Register*, vol. i. No. iv. p. 57. II. A Cross, with the arms inscribed "Sanguis x̄p̄i Salua me,—Passio x̄p̄i Conforta me," for Rich. Tooner, rector, **1445**, found in taking up the pavement in 1826, inscr. lost, p. 173. *Boutell's Mon. Br.*, p. 118. INSCR. III. John Corby, rector, **1415**, now placed under No. II., its matrix is left in Ch.

BUXTEAD. I. Britell Avenel, rector, [**1408**], hf. eff. in diapered head of a floriated cross, marg. inscr. mutil., C., p. 173. *C. C. Soc. Illustr.*, No. V., p. 191; *Boutell's Mon. Br.*, p. 116, and *Chr. Mon.*, p. 123. Avenel was appointed canon of Windsor in 1385; he probably directed his brass to be made like that of Sir John de Lewes, parson, and founder of the C., c. 1330, the matrices of this and of another similar cross still remain. II. Deonicius Slon, priest, **1485**, with chalice, lower half loose, inscr. lost, sm., N.A. INSCRS., &c. III. Christine, mother of Robt. Savage, rector upwards of 24 years, c. **1450**, 8 Eng. vv. (see Appendix B.), C. IV. Part of the legs of a Man in arm., c. **1440**, loose. Probably a frag. of the brass of John Attewelle, 1437 (or 1438), and w. Joan. V. A Sh., part of the brass of John Warnett, of Furnivall's Inn, 1486, and w. Joan, **1496**, S.A. VI. Thos. [Smith], Esq., **1558**, and w., mutil., effs. lost, loose, S.A. The loose brasses were at the rectory, July, 1860.

CHICHESTER CATHEDRAL. Mr. Wm. Bradbridge, thrice mayor, 1546, and w. Alice, with 6 sons and 8 daus., their dau. Alice (widow of Mr. Franc. Barnham, sheriff of London in 1576), pos. **1592**, qd. pl., mur., S.A. of C. *Engr.* —— (?).

CLAPHAM. I. *John Shelley, Esq., **1526**, and w. Elizth., dau. of John Michilgrove, Esq., 1513, in heraldic dresses, Hy. Trin., C. *Dallaway*, vol. ii. p. 84. *Lower's Curiosities of Heraldry*, p. 38; *Journ. of Brit. Arch. Assoc.*, vol. i. p. 78 (fem. eff.) II. John Shelley, Esq., **1550**, and w. Mary, dau. of Sir Wm. Fitzwilliams, with 4 sons and 8 daus., mur. III. John, second son of John Shellie, of Michelgrove [**1592**], in arm., and w. Elinor, dau. of Sir Thos. Lovell, of Harling, Norf., with a son and a dau., inscr. cut in marble, qd. pl., mur., C.

CLAYTON. I. Mr. Rich. Idon, "parson of Clayton and Pykecum," **1523**, with chalice and wafer, sm., C. INSCR. II. Thos. a Wode, **1508**, N.

COWFOLD. I. Thos. Nelond [prior of the Cluniac monastery at Lewes, **1433**], in monk's habit, fine triple canopy, with B. V. Mary and Child and SS. Pancras and Thos. of Canterbury, marg. inscr. in 12 (?) Lat. vv. mutil., large, N., pp. 21, 86, 101, 176. *Dallaway*, vol. ii. p. 320; *Waller*, pt. viii.; *C. C. Soc. Illustr.*, No. iv. p. 133. II. †John a Gate and w. Jone (eff. lost), c. **1500**, inscr. mutil., loose at the vicarage.

CRAWLEY. I. A Lady, c. **1520**, inscr. lost, N.   INSCR. II. Wm. Blast, **1438**.

CUCKFIELD. I. —— Bowyer, c. **1590**, in arm., inscr. lost, now in S.A.   II. *Hon. Bowyer, Esq., **1614**, in arm., and w. Elizth., a dau. and h. of Thos. Vaux, of Katerum, clerk controller to Hen. VIII., with 3 sons and 2 daus., inscr. lost (?), qd. pl., mur., now in S.A.

ETCHINGHAM. I. Sir Wm. de Echingham, son of Sir Jas. Echingham, **1388** (or 1387), "entour my noet" (about midnight), head and canopy lost, Fr. inscr., and over head a Lat. inscr. (lately loose) stating he rebuilt the Ch., large, C., pp. 140, 160. *Ant. Repert.*, vol. iii. p. 188; *Boutell's Series; Arch. Journ.*, vol. vii. p. 266. II. Sir Wm. Echyngham, lord of the manor, 1412, and w. Joan [dau. and coh. of John Arundel, Lord Maltravers], 1404, in mantle, and their son Sir Thos., lord of the manor, **1444**, canopy, large, C., pp. 45, 190. *Ant. Repert.*, vol. iii. p. 188.   III. Elizth., eldest dau. of Thos. and Margt. Echyngham, 1452, and Agnes, dau. of Robt. Oxenbrigg [see Brede, Sussex, No. I.], **1480**, on reverse of inscr. "Hic iacet Thomas Austin filius Thome Aust[in] Quondam ciuis et merceri London qui obiit xxvj [die] mens' Maii A° dñi M°cccc°v° cui' aīc ppiciet' ds[amen], S.A., pp. 211, 213. *Introd.*, p. 213 (parts of effs.)   INSCRS. IV. Sir Thos. Echyngham, lord of the manor, **1485**, lately loose, eff. mur., and A.T. destroyed, C. V. ——, infant son of Sir Gyfford Thornhurst, bart., and his w. Susan, only dau. of Sir Alex. Temple, **1626**.

EWHURST. Wm. Crysford, c. **1520**, kng., sm., S.A.

FIRLE, WEST. I. Barth. Bolne, Esq., and w. Aleanora, both dec. **1476**, loose, p. 197. *Gage's Hist. and Ant. of Hengrave*, p. 227. II. Sir Edw. Gage, in arm., and w. Elizth. [dau. of John Parker, of Ratton, Sussex], 1569, engr. c. **1600**, A.T., N.C., pp. 226, 237. *Ibid.*, p. 236.   III. Thos. Gage, Esq., and w. Elizth. [dau. of Sir Thos. Guldeforde, of Hempstead-place, Kent], **1590**, with 1 son [John] (eff. lost) and 2 daus. [Mary and Elizth.], inscr. lost, effs. loose.   IV. John Gage, Esq., and ws. Elizth. [Littleton?] and Margt. [dau. of Sir Roger Copley, of Gatton, Surrey], **1595**, A.T., N.C., pp. 226, 237.   V. Mary, dau. of Wm. Lord Eure, m. 17¼ years to Sir Wm., eldest son of Sir Philipp, son and h. of Lord Wm. Howard, youngest son of the duke of Norfolk, **1638**, æt. 36, in shroud, loose in chest, N.   INSCR. VI. John Gage, K.G., constable of the Tower of London, &c., and w. Philippa, **1557**, mur., N.C. *Gage*, p. 230. In the inscrs. to the Gage fam., although the expression "qui obierunt" is used before the date, this probably refers to the decease of the husband only. Nos. I. and III., lately loose in the chest, were not seen when the writer visited the Ch., July, 1860. A rubbing of a Man in arm., c. 1590, loose in 1821, now lost, is in the possession of the Arch. Institute.

FLETCHING. I. Sir —— Dallingridge, with arms on jupon, and w. in mantle, c. **1380**, canopy, inscr. lost, large, A.T., S.Tr., pp. 138, 160. *Ant. Repert.*, 1808, vol. iii. p. 186; *Boutell's Series; Sussex Arch. Coll.*, vol. ii. p. 309. II. A pair of Gloves and inscr. for Peter Denot, glover, c. **1440** (?), p. 129. *Boutell's Chr. Mon.*, p. 97.

FRAMFIELD. *Edw. Gage, Esq., **1595**, and w. Margt., dau. of Sir John Shellie, of Michelgrove, with 3 sons and 5 daus., qd. pl., mur., S.C.

FRISTON. Thos. Selwyn, 1539, and w. Margery, **1542**, sm., N.

GORING. A Man, in arm., and w., c. **1490**, inscr. lost, once on A.T. (?), C., p. 198. *Gent. Mag.*, vol. lxxviii. 1808, pt. i. p. 121, where is also engr. the brass of John and Emme Cook (eff. gone), c. 1510, now all lost (?).

GRINSTEAD, EAST. I. Sir Thos. Grey, Rich. Lewkener, Esq., the elder, of Brambilletey, and their w. Dame Cath., dau. of Thos. Lord Scalis, and a lady-in-waiting to the Queens Elizth., ws. of Ed. IV. and Hen. VII., **1505** (eff. lost), A.T., N.A. Rich. and Cath. founded and endowed the Ch., and an almshouse of three parsons. II. A Civilian, c. **1520**, sm., inscr. lost. INSCR. III. Robt., only son of John and Anne Christian, of St. Gregories parish, London, **1660**, æt. 9, now below No. II.

GRINSTEAD, WEST. I. Philippa, dau. of David de Strabolge, earl of Athell, and w. of John Halsham, Esq., 1395, engr. c. **1440**, in mantle, canopy, marg. inscr. nearly all lost, S.C., p. 45. *Dallaway*, vol. ii. p. 314. *C. C. Soc. Illustr.*, No. ii. p. 39 (eff.) Philippa's first husband was Sir Ralph Percy; a brass to her mother remains at Ashford, Kent (No. I.) II. [Sir Hugh Halsham, **1441**, and w. Joyce [Colepepper?].] 1421, canopy and marg. inscr. mutil., A.T., S.C., p. 190. *Dallaway*, vol. ii. p. 314; *Boutell's Series*.

HASTINGS, ALL SAINTS. Thos. Goodenouth, burgess, and w. Margt., c. **1520**, C. An incised slab, p. 24.

HASTINGS, ST. CLEMENT'S. I. Thos. Wekes, jurat, **1563**, and w. Margt., with dau. Elizth., the two fem. effs. lost, N. II. John Barley, mercer, **1601**, æt. 49, with son Thos., 1600, æt. 19 (eff. lost), and dau. Alyce, 1592, æt. 7, N., p. 226. John Barley m. Mary, dau. of Robt. Harley. INSCR. III. Thos. Pierse, Esq., **1606**, N.

HENFIELD. I. Thos. Bysshopp, Esq., **1559**, sm., A.T., N.A., p. 226. II. Mrs. Ann Kenwellmersh, **1633**, æt. 68, and Meneleb, son of her dau. Mary Rainsford, **1627**, æt. 9, 8 Eng. vv. (see Appendix B.), pp. 247, 248.   INSCR. III. Elizth., w. of Geo. Raynsford, Gent., **1672**, æt. 58, 4 Eng. vv.

HORSHAM. I. Thos. Clerke, **1411**, in cope; head, feet, and inscrs. lost, p. 81. *Waller*, pt. x.; *Boutell's Mon. Br.*, p. 98.   II. A Lady, sm., c. **1515**. Perhaps part of the brass of Rich. Foys, 1513, and w. Elizth.

HOUGHTON. *Thos. Cheyne, Esq., **1486**.

HURSTMONCEAUX.   Sir Wm. Fienlez, **1402**, canopy, marg. inscr. in Fr. with "vj^{xx} iours de pardon" for saying a Pater Noster and Ave, large, C., p. 185. *Ant. Repert.*, 1808, vol. iii. p. 189; *Horsfield's Sussex*, 1835, vol. i. p. 556; *Boutell's Series.*

IDEN. Walter Seller, rector, **1427**, now mur., C.

ISFIELD. I. Edw. Shurley, Esq., son of John Shurley, Esq., and cofferer to Hen. VIII., **1558**, in arm., and w. Joan, dau. of John (?) Fenner, Esq., with 3 sons (2 lost) and 1 dau., S.C., p. 236.   II. Thos. Shurley, Esq., eldest son of Edw. Shurley, Esq., dec. at Lewes, **1579**, in arm., and w. Anne (dau. of Sir Nich. Pelham, of Lawghton, Sussex, and his w. Anne, sister to Sir Rich. Sackeville), 1571, C. INSCR. III. *John Shurley, Esq., chief clerk of the kitchen to Hen. VII., and cofferer to Hen. VIII., **1527**, eff. and B. V. Mary and Child lost, mur., S.C.

LEWES, ST. MICHAEL. I. —— Warren, in arm., c. **1430**, head and inscr. gone, C., pp. 114, 189. *Horsfield*, vol. i. p. 210.   II. John Braydforde, rector, **1457**, hf. eff., C. *Ibid.*

NORTHIAM. I. Sir Robt. Beuford, parson, **1518**, with 2 Evang. symbs., N.   II. Nich. Tufton, Esq., **1538**, not in arm., inscr. restored, N., p. 53. *Grose's Antiq.*, vol. i. pl. viii. fig. 1.

ORE. A Civilian, with anelace, and w., c. **1400**, canopy, bracket and marg. inscr. lost, pp. 137, 164, 167, 169. *Boutell's Series. Introd.*, p. 168 (det.)

POLING. Walter Davy, vicar, c. **1420** (?), hf. eff., C. *Dallaway*, vol. ii. p. 62.

PULBOROUGH. I. Thos. Harlyng, canon of Chichester, and rector of Ringwood and Pulborough, **1423**, in cope, canopy, marg. inscr., large, C. *Dallaway*, vol. ii. p. 360.   II. [Edm. Mille], Gent. [**1452**], not in arm., and w. [Matilda], inscr. mutil., C. *Dallaway*, vol. ii. p. 360.   III. Rich., son and h. of Edm. Mille, **1478**, p. 178.

RUSPER. I. John Kyggesfolde and w. AGLEYS, c. **1370**, hf. effs., N., p. 163. *Dallaway*, vol. ii. p. 379; *Boutell's Mon. Br.*, p. 117.   II. Thos. Challoner, **1532**, and w. Margt., with 1 son.

RYE. I. Thos. Hamon, thrice burgess for the parliament, six times mayor, long captain of the band, **1607**, his w. Martha pos., marg. inscr. mutil., C.   FRAG. II. Three Shs., c. **1600**, inscr. lost, C.

SHOREHAM, NEW.   A Civilian and w., c. **1450**, inscr. lost, N.

SLAUGHAM. I. John Covert, Esq., son of Wm. Covert, Esq., **1503**, canopy.   II. Rich. Covert, Esq., **1547**, and 3 ws., Elizth. (a dau. and h. of John Faggan (?), Esq., and his w. Elizth.), Elizth. (dau. of Sir Geo. Nevyle, Lord Burgevenie), and Jane (dau. of Wm. Ascheburnhame, Esq., of Burgevenie), with the Resurrection, mur., pp. 53, 103.   III. Lady Jane, dau. of John Covert, and w. to Sir Franc. Fleming, and afterwards to Sir John Fetyplace, **1586**, buried by her nephew and executor, mur.

STOPHAM. I. John Bartelot, treasurer of the household to Thos. earl of Arundel, 1428, not in arm., head restored, and w. Joan, dau. of Wm. de Stopham, engr. c. **1460**, pp. 30, 53, 202.   II. John Bartelot, "consul providus" to Thos., John, and Wm., earls of Arundell, 1453, in arm., head restored, and w. Joan, dau. and h. of John Leukenore, Esq., engr. c. **1460** (?), pecul., pp. 53, 196. III. Rich. Bertlot, Esq., marshall of the hall of the earl of Arundell, **1478**, with collar, and w. Petronilla [Sykeston?], 8 Lat. vv., p. 128. IV. Wm. Bartelot, Esq., **1601**, æt. 97, and w. Anne (Covert); they had a son Robt.; feet of male eff. and upper part of fem. eff. restored, pp. 53, 215. Beneath is now a kng. eff. of a son (?) in cloak, c. 1620 (?); perhaps not belonging to this brass.   V. Rich. Barttelot, Esq., patron of Ch. (grandson and h. to Wm. Barttelot [No. IV.], whose only son Robt., the father of Rich., was m. to Maria, eldest dau. of John Apsley, Esq., of Thakeham), **1614**, æt. 50, in arm., and 2 ws.—1st, Maria, dau. of Rich. Covert, Esq., of Slaugham, with 5 chil., Walter, Edw. (dec.), Wm., John (dec.), Anne (dec.); 2nd, Roesia, dau. of Rich. Hatton, Esq., of Thames Ditton, with 4 chil., Rich., Robt., Maria, Francisca (dec.), pp. 25, 237.   INSCRS., &c. VI. John, son and h. of Rich. Bartellot, **1493**, now below No. IV.   VII. John Barttelot, Gent., son of John Barttelot, Esq., 1525, engr. c. **1600**.   VIII. Maria, dau. of John Middleton, Esq., of Horsham, and w. of Walter Barttelot, **1626**, æt. 39, with 6 daus., Francisca, Mary, Anne, Jane, Elizth., and Barbara.   IX. Elizth., dau. and coh. of Walter Barttelot, and w. of Rich. Mille, Gent., of Greatham, **1644**.   X. Wm., 2nd son of Rich. Barttelot, **1666**.   XI. Walter Barttelot, Esq., **1702**, æt. 63. XII. Hen. Barttelot, Esq., of Fittleworth, **1710**, æt. 69.   XIII. Capt. Chas. Barttelot, **1738**.   XIV. Three groups of chil., c. **1620**, —2 sons, 3 sons and 2 daus., 3 sons and 1 dau.; the first two placed under Nos. I. and II.

STORRINGTON. *Hen. Wilsha, B.D., "alumnus" of Hen. Wilsha, of Lichfield, priest, chaplain to Hen. earl of Arundell, Lord Henry baron Mautravers, and Lord John Lumley, **1591**, æt. 84, his "cognati" pos., C., p. 230.

†THAKEHAM. I. Beatrix, mother of Wm. Apsley, Esq., **1515**. II. Thos., son of Wm. Apsley, Esq., **1517**.

TICEHURST. John Wybarne, Esq., dec. 1490 (eff. engr. c. **1370**), and ws. Edith [Hyde] and Agnes [1502], engr. c. **1510**, C., pp. 50, 160. *Sussex Arch. Coll.*, vol. viii.

TROTTON. I. Margarite de Camois, c. **1310**; 9 shs. on dress, canopy, Fr. marg. inscr. in Lomb. letters lost; large, C., pp. 22, 165. *Boutell's Mon. Br.*, p. 81. Sir John Camois had two ws., both of the name of Margt., one the dau. and h. of Rich. Folliott, dec. 1309-10, the other a dau. and h. of Sir John de Gatesden; she, together with her property, was granted, by a formal deed executed by her husband, to Sir Wm. Paynell, whom she married after her husband's decease. II. Thos. Baron Camoys, "providus Consul Regis & regni Anglie ac Strenuus Miles de Gartero," **1419**, and w. Elizth. [dau. of Edm. Mortimer, and widow of Hen. Percy], in mantle, with son, Sir Rich., sm. eff. standing beside his mother, fine canopy and super canopy, very large, A.T., C., pp. 26, 61, 117, 166, 172, 176, 189, 208, 253. *Dallaway*, vol. i. p. 224; *Boutell's Mon. Br.*, pp. 59, 127. *Introd.*, p. 26 (det.) Sir Thos. commanded the left wing of the English at Agincourt, and for his bravery was created Knight of the Garter.

UCKFIELD. John Fuller, Gent, gave 10s. yearly to the poor at each parish of Chiddingstone, Penshurst, Isfield, and Uckfield, **1610**, 4 Eng. vv. and text 1 John iii. 11, 12, 13, C.

WARBLETON. I. Wm. Prestwyk [dean of St. Mary's College in Hastings Castle], **1436**, in cope, with text from Job xix. 25, 26, on the orphrey, canopy, marg. inscr. in 11 Lat. vv. mutil., large, N.C., pp. 104, 106, 176, 182. *Boutell's Series; Sussex Arch. Coll.*, vol. ii. p. 309; *Introd.*, p. 177. INSCR. II. *John and Joan Prestwyk, parents of No. I., loose in chest.

WARMINGHURST. Edw. Shelley, Esq., one of the 4 masters of the household to Hen. VIII., Ed. VI., and Queen Mary, **1554**, and w. Joan, dau. and h. of Poll [Paul] Iden, of Kent, 1553, with 7 sons with initials, Ric., H., T., E., J., R., E. (?), and 3 daus. with their names, Elizth., Mary, Kate, inscribed on them, Hy. Trin. lost, mur., C.

WILLINGDON. I. John Parker, Esq., **1558**, in arm., his w. Joan dec. 1517, p. 236. INSCR. II. Thos. Parker, Esq., **1580**, and w. Elenor, dau. of Wm. Waller, Esq., of Grombridge.

WINCHELSEA. I. A Civilian, c. **1440**, feet lately loose, inscr. lost, C.   INSCR. II. Margt., w. of Jeremy Jorden, **1636**, æt. 63, and 3 daus., Margt., Alse, Martha, 6 Eng. vv.

WISTON. Sir John de Brewys, **1426**, marg. inscr., 4 Lat. vv., slab powdered with 31 scrolls (one lost) inscribed "Jesus mercy," large, S.C., pp. 179, 189. *Dallaway*, vol. ii. p. 154; *Boutell's Series*. *Boutell's Mon. Br.*, p. 66; *Penny Post*, 1855, p. 174; *Drummond's Noble Brit. Fam.; Hewitt's Anc. Arms and Arm.*, vol. iii. p. 426, No. 71 (eff.)   A fine matrix of a Man in arm.

INSCRIPTIONS, &c.

EASTBOURNE. †John Hyng, S.T.B., "proprietarius" of the Ch., treasurer of Chichester, **1445**, mur., C.   FINDON. Gilbert Frensche, **1374** (?), 3 Lat. vv.   LINDFIELD. I. Stephen Boorde, **1567**, and w. Pernell, with a skull; effs., with about 4 sons and 3 daus., lost, p. 222.   II. Joane, dau. of John Love, of Bishop's Bazing, w. of Abr. Allen, Esq., "Serieant Chyrurgeon" to King James, and then of Wm. Newton, Gent., impropriator of the Ch., **1655**.   III. Isaac, only son of Abr. Allen, Esq., and Joane (Love), **1656**, æt. 63. "Hee dyed at London a Prisoner to ye vpper-Bench, vpon an Accon for Wordes, most Falsely & Maliciovsly, by One single Witness sworne against Him, as he had often-tymes, & on his Death-bed Protested & Declared to severall Friends. Hee desired his Body might bee bvryed heere at Linfeild neare his mother."   NUTHURST. Thos. Frenshe, rector, **1486**, chalice lost.   RODMELL. *John de la Chambre, Esq., **1673**; on reverse, inscr. to John Broke and w. Agatha, dau. of John de Rademeld, and widow of Rich. Weyvyle, **1434**, benefactors to the Ch., mur., S.C.   STOUGHTON. Jas. Smyth, clerk, one of the "chapleynes perpetuall of the Hospital of ye Savoy in Strand," **1565**, mur., N.

At BURWASH is an iron plate, with a sm. cross with inscr. "Orate p annema Johne Colins," N., p. 1. *Boutell's Chr. Mon.*, p. 105. At PLAYDEN is a foreign incised slab to Cornelis Roetmanns (not Zoetmanns?), p. 24.   At BODECTON, or BURTON, were some brasses (now lost?) to the Goring family, 1551, 1553, 1558, one is sketched in the Burrell MS. 5,699, fol. 139. b.

Wales.

BEAUMARIS, ANGLESEA. Rich. Bulkley, mcht., and w. Elizth., c. **1530**, with 2 sons (one in almuce) and 1 dau., Hy. Trin., B. V. Mary and Child and St. John Evang., 6 eleg. vv., mur., C.

BETTWS, near NEWTOWN, MONTGOMERYSHIRE. *John ap Meredyth de Powys, vicar at the time the Ch. tower was built and three bells purchased, and contributor to the expenses of the same, &c., **1531**, with chalice, modern inscr. added, mur.

CLYNNOG, CARNARVONSHIRE. Wm., eldest son of Wm. Glynne, Gent., of Lleyar Carnarvon, and of his w. Jane, **1633**, æt. 2, sm., mur., p. 25. *Archæologia Cambrensis*, vol. i. p. 405.

DOLWYDDELAN, CARNARVONSHIRE. *Meredyth ap Ivan ap Robert, **1535**, in arm., kng.

HAVERFORDWEST, PEMBROKESHIRE. John Davids, Esq., 1651, æt. 51, his w. Sage dec. **1654**, æt. 62, qd. pl., mur.

LLANBEBLIG, CARNARVONSHIRE. Rich. Foxwist [notary?], **1500**, in bed holding a sh. with 5 wounds, he m. Joan, dau. of John Spicer, 8 eleg. vv., qd. pl., mur., pp. 102, 128. *Arch. Journ.*, vol. vi. p. 414; *Introd.*, p. 129.

LLANDOUGH, GLAMORGANSHIRE. Wenllan Walsche, w. of Walter Moreton, **1427**, C.

LLANRWST, DENBIGHSHIRE. I. †Sir John Wynn, of Gwydyr, **1620**. II. Lady Sydney, w. of Sir John Wynn, of Gwedyr, **1632**, a bust. III. Lady Mary, eldest dau. of Sir John Wynne, and w. of Sir Roger Mostyn, of Mostyn, Flintshire, 1657, æt. 31 (?); her son, John, pos. **1658**, a bust; p. 30. IV. Sir Owen Wynne, of Gwedyr, **1660**, æt. 68, a bust. V. Kath., eldest dau. of Maurice Lewis, Esq., of Estyniogg, **1669**(?), æt. 16, hf. eff. VI. Dame Sarah, dau. of Sir Thos. Middleton, of Chirke Castle, and w. of Sir Rich. Wynne, of Gwyddur, **1671**, part of eff., qd. pl. The brasses consist of lozenge-shaped plates, and are now framed and glazed in the S.C.

RUTHIN, DENBIGHSHIRE. I. Edw. Goodman, **1560**, 4 eleg. vv., p. 56. II. Edw. Goodman, burgess and mercer, 1560, æt. 84 (?), and w. Ciselye, **1583**, æt. 90, with 8 chil., Gallien, Gabriel, Godfrey, Dorothy, Kath., Fides, Clare, Jane, mur., N., p. 56.

SWANSEA, GLAMORGANSHIRE. Sir Hugh Johnys [see Appendix B], and w. Dame Mawde [Cradock], c. **1500**, with 5 sons (effs. lost) and 4 daus., the Resurrection, now mur., C., pp. 101, 103, 233. *Some Account of Sir Hugh Johnys and his Mon. Brass, by Bliss and Francis*, Swansea, 1845 (front.)

WHITCHURCH, DENBIGHSHIRE. †Rich. Middleton, **1575**, and w. Jane, 1565, now mur., S.Porch. *Pennant's Wales*.

See also p. 41, and brasses in private possession — Ven. Arch. Nares and J. D. Llewelyn, Esq.

Warwickshire.

ASTLEY. A Lady of the Astley family (?), c. **1400**, in mantle, lower part of eff. and inscr. lost, N. *Dugdale's Warwickshire*, 1656, p. 76. Other brasses, now lost, are also there engr.

ASTON. I. Thos. Holte, Esq., late justice of North Wales and lord of this town, **1545**, head lost, and w. Margery, with 1 son and 2 daus., marg. inscr., pecul., N.A., pp. 29, 91, 125, 243. *Dugdale*, p. 642. II. †Mary Loyd, **1680**, mur.

BAGINTON. Sir Wm. Bagot, **1407**, with arms on jupon, and w. Margt. (Whatton), in mantle (head restored), both with SS. collars, large, S.A., pp. 53, 185, 261. *Dugdale*, p. 155; *Boutell's Mon. Br.*, p. 56.

BARCHESTON. *Hugh Humfray, priest, **1530**, in acad.

BARTON. Edm. Bury, 1558, and w. Elizth., 7th dau. of Edw. Underhill, Esq., of Neather Etington, Warwickshire, who re-married Thos. Tawyer, Gent., of Raundis, Northants.; after his death she returned to Barton, and pos. **1608** (eff. lost), and 3 chil., Wm., John, Margt., C.

CHARLCOTE. I. John Marskre, chaplain, c. **1500**, with chalice and wafer, pecul., sm., N., pp. 29, 79. II. Edm., son of Thos. Wykham, Gent., c. **1500**, sm., N.

COLESHILL. I. Wm. Abell, vicar, **1500**, with chalice, pecul., sm., C., pp. 29, 79. II. Alice, dau. of Simon Digby, and w. of Robt. Clifton, Esq., **1506**, inscr. lost, pecul., C. *Dugdale*, p. 734. III. Sir John Fenton, L.B., vicar, official of Coventry, **1566**, C., pp. 125, 230. The brasses have lately been repaired by Messrs. Waller.

†COMPTON VERNEY. I. Anne, dau. of Rich. Verney, Esq., and w. of Master Edw. Odynsale, of Long Itchington (?), **1523**, N.C. *Dugdale*, p. 436. II. Rich. Verney, Esq. [**1536-7**], and w. Anne [dau. of Wm. Davers], with 9 sons and 5 daus., marg. inscr., N.C. *Ibid.* III. Geo. Verney, Esq., **1574**; he m. Jane, dau. of Wm. Lucy, Esq., of Charlcote. *Ibid.*

*COUGHTON. I. Sir Geo. Throkmorton and w. Kath., a dau. of Sir Nich. Vause, lord Harrowden, in mantle, c. **1510**, with 8 sons and 11 daus., A.T., C. *Dugdale*, p. 562. INSCR. II. Dame Elizth. Throkmorton, last abbess of Denye [in Cambridgeshire], and aunt to Sir Geo. Throkmorton, **1547**.

COVENTRY, ST. MICHAEL'S. I. Maria Hinton, **1594**, æt. 30, with

4 infant chil., 6 hexameter vv., mur. II. John Whithead, mayor, and 2 ws., the first with 1 son and 3 daus., the second with 3 sons and 2 daus., c. 1600, 10 eleg. vv., mur., p. 120. III. Ann, w. of Wm. Sewell, vintner, 1609, æt. 46, 6 Eng. vv., mur., C. *Bloxam's Mon. Arch.*, p. 254.   In the S.A. is a matrix of a Civilian and w., c. 1380, canopy.

EXHALL, near ALCESTER. *John Walsingham, Esq., 1566, in arm., and w. Elenor, dau. of Humphrey Ashefeld, Esq., of Heythrop, Oxon., A.T., C.

HALFORD. *Hen. Kymycher, rector, 1484.

HAMPTON-IN-ARDEN. A Civilian, c. 1500, pecul., inscr. lost, sm., p. 29. Perhaps the brass of Rich. Stokys, salter (or Brokes, bailiff?), and w. Isota, p. 180.

†HARBURY. I. Alice Wagstaff, 1563. II. Ann Wagstaff, 1624. III. James Wright, Gent., 1685.

HASELEY. Clement Throkmorton, Esq., 3rd son of Sir Geo. Throkmorton, 1573, in arm., and w. Kath., eldest dau. of Sir Edw. Nevell, by whom he had 6 sons and 7 daus., partly loose, two portions of the inscr. palimpsest, A.T., C. *Dugdale*, p. 496.

HILLMORTON. A Lady, c. 1410, in mantle, with scroll from hand, inscr. lost, in a pew, now covd. (?)

IPSLEY. *Nich. Hubbaud, Esq., 1558, and w., A.T., N.

ITCHINGTON, LONG. *John Bosworth, yeoman, 1674, and ws.

MEREVALE. Robt. Lord Ferrers, of Chartley, 1412 (?), and w. Margt. [Spencer], in mantle, inscr. lost, large, C., p. 188. *Gresley's Forest of Arden; Boutell's Series.*

MERIDEN. †Elizth. Rotton, 1633, inscr. only (?) with anagram.

MIDDLETON. I. Rich. Byngham, a justice of the king's bench, 1476, and widow Margt., pecul., p. 90. *Dugdale*, p. 758. Margt. Byngham was dau. of Sir Baldwin Freville, and first the w. of Sir Hugh Willoughby. INSCR. II. Dorothy, dau. of Sir Hen. Wiloughby, and w. of Ant. Fitzherbert, 1507, mur., C. *Ibid.*

NAPTON. *John Shuckburgh, Gent., 1624.

PACKINGTON, GREAT. *John Wright, vicar, 1527, N.

PRESTON BAGOT. *Elizth., 2nd dau. of Rich. Knightley, of Burge Hall, Staffordshire, and w. of Wm. Randoll, "legis consiliarius," head gone.

SOLIHULL. Wm. Hyll, Gent., 1549, and ws. Isabell and Agnes, with 7 sons (lost?) and 11 daus., pecul., N., pp. 29, 243. *Dugdale* (?), p. 691.

SHUCKBURGH, SUPERIOR. I. *Margt., dau. of Thos. Shukburgh, and w. of John, son and h. of John Cotes, Esq., of Honingham,

c. **1500**, eff. loose. *Dugdale*, p. 208. II. Tomas Shukburghe, Esq., lord of the manor, **1549** (or 1560?), in arm., and w. Elizth., pecul., pp. 29, 233, 243. *Ibid.* III. *Anth. Shukburgh, Esq., **1594**, in arm., and w. Anne, with 3 sons and 5 daus (?). *Ibid.*

SUTTON COLDFIELD. I. Barbara, dau. of Ralph Simonds, Gent., and w. of Roger Eliot, rector, **1606**, æt. 24, with 2 chil., Raphael and Elizth. II. Josias Bull, Gent., **1621**, æt. about 50, with 5 chil., Josias, Hen., Geo., John, Ann, by his w. Kath. Walshe, widow, dau. of Wm. Botlier, Esq., of Tyes, Essex.

TANWORTH. *Margt., dau. of Simon Ralegh, Esq., of Farnborough, and w. of Andrew Archer, Esq., **1614**, mur., C.

TYSOE. †Thos. Mastropp, priest, **1465**, C.

UFTON. Rich. Woddomes, parson, patron, and vossioner of the Ch. and parish, **1587**, and w. Margery, with 7 chil., Rich., John, John, Anne, Jone, Elizth., Ayles, qd. pl.

WARWICK, ST. MARY. I. Thos. de Beauchamp, earl of Warwick, 1401, with arms on jupon, and countess Margt., dau. of Wm. Lord Ferrers, of Groby, **1406**, in mantle, with arms on kirtle, large, canopy and marg. inscr. lost, rel., once on A.T., now mur. S.Tr., pp. 28, 185. *Dugdale*, p. 324; *Gough*, vol. ii. pl. xi. p. 5; *Waller*, pt. vi. II. Thos. Oken, **1573**, and w. Jone, now mur., N.Tr., p. 226. INSCR. III. Mistress Cisseley Puckering, **1636**, p. 225. Four brasses, now lost, are engr. in *Dugdale*, p. 348.

WARWICK, ST. NICHOLAS. Robt. Willardsey, first vicar, **1424**, p. 260.

WELLESBOURNE. Sir Thos. le Strannge, constable of Ireland [**1426**], with SS. collar, marg. inscr. restored, C., pp. 187, 189. *Dugdale*, p. 440.

†WESTON-UNDER-WEATHERLEY. I. Anne, dau. and h. of John Huggefford, lord of Edmondescot, **1497**, C. *Dugdale*, p. 201. INSCRS. II. Margt., dau. of Sir Thos. Englefeld and his w. Elizth., dau. of Sir Robt. Throgmorton, and w. of Sir Edw. Saunders, **1563**, 14 eleg. and 10 Eng. vv. III. Joyce Tomer, **1566**, 4 Lat. and 4 Eng. vv., mur., C.

WHATCOTE. Wm. Auldyngton, parson, [**1511**?], with chalice, head lost, eff. loose in chest, sm.

WHICHFORD. Nich. Asheton, B.D. of Cambridge, chaplain of the earl of Derby, rector, formerly vicar of Kendall, near Great Leaver, Lanc., **1582**, A.T., C., p. 230.

WHITNASH. I. A Civilian and w., c. **1500**, inscr. lost, now mur., C. Probably Benedict Medley, clerk of the signet to Hen. VII., 1503, and w. Agnes (?). II. Rich. Bennet, M.A., **1531**, with chalice and wafer, pecul., now mur., C., pp. 29, 78.

WIXFORD. I. Thos. de Cruwe, Esq., builder of Chapel, and w. Juliana, **1411**, in mantle, canopy and marg. inscr. with the badge —a foot, large, A.T., S.C., pp. 188, 189. *Dugdale*, p. 633; *C. C. Soc. Illustr.*, No. v. p. 155. II. Rise, 4th son of Rise Griffyn, Esq., of Brome, Warwickshire, **1597**, æt. ¾ of a year, qd. pl., mur.

WOOTTON-WAWEN. John Harewell, Esq., **1505**, and w. Dame Anna, widow of Sir Edw. Grey, with 5 sons and 5 daus., engr. c. 1520 (?), marg. inscr., A.T., C., p. 232. *Dugdale*, p. 603.

WROXHALL. *A Lady, c. **1430**, now mur., said to have been originally in Brailes Church, but no matrix corresponding to it remains there.

INSCRIPTIONS, &c.

RYTON ON DUNSMOOR. I. Rich. Wylmer, farmer, **1527**, and w. Joan (effs. lost), with 6 daus., sons lost, 8 Eng. vv., pecul., N. II. Moses Macham, minister, **1712**, æt. 63, 6 Eng. vv., p. 222. STRATFORD-ON-AVON. Anne [Hathaway], w. of Wm. Shakespeare, **1623**, æt. 67, 6 eleg. vv., C.

In Dugdale's Warwickshire are engravings of several brasses now lost (as at EMSCOTE, to the Hugford family, effs. with hands joined), but the costume of the figures is very inaccurately represented.

Westmoreland.

KENDAL. *Alan Bellingham, Esq., **1577**, mur., N.A.

Wiltshire.

ALDBOURNE. Hen. Frekylton, chaplain, **1508**, beside him a chalice (the bowl lost) and book, sm., C., p. 125. *The Mon. Brasses of Wiltshire, by Edw. Kite*, 1860, pl. xiv. An incised slab to John Stone, priest, 16th cent., p. 40.

ALTON PRIORS. I. Agnes, w. of Wm. Button, **1528**, N. II. Wm. Button, Esq., 1580, æt. 64, eff. rising from an altar-tomb at the summons of an angel with "the key of David" [Rev. iii. 7] as a trumpet, 6 Eng. vv.; he left, by his w. Mary, dau. of Sir Wm. Kellwey, 8 chil., Sir Ambrose, Wm. (m. Jane, dau. of John Lambe, of Coulston), John, Francis, Edw., Hen., Dorothie (m. John Drake, Esq., of Mount Drake, Devon), Cecilie (m. Sir John Mewys, of Kingston, I. of Wight). Sir Wm., grandchild to the first, and son and h. to the latter Wm. Button, pos. [c. **1620**?], mur., A.T., C., p. 218. *Kite*, pl. xxv.

BARFORD ST. MARTIN. *Alis Walker, **1584**, æt. 44, with 7 sons and 4 daus., 12 Eng. vv. ending "such is the fickle state of man, th' vncertaine lott of life, noe sooner spūne by Lachese hands, but cutte w¹ Atrops knife," her eldest son Thos. pos., mur., S.Tr.

BEDWYN, GREAT. I. John, son and h. of Sir John Seymoure and his w. Margery, a dau. of Sir Hen. Wentworth, **1510**, not in arm., now mur., C., p. 252. *Kite*, pl. xv. INSCRS. II. Thos. Dogeson, vicar, **1501**, eff. lost, N.Tr. III. [Edw.] Semer, [Lord] Beauchamp [son of Edw., earl of Hertford, and Lady Kath.] Grey [**1612**], had 3 sons and 1 sister, 2 eleg. vv., now mur., C.

BERWICK BASSET. Wm. Bayly, "legauit ecclie solidos centū semp' manere," **1427**, hf. off., N. *Kite*, pl. vii.

BRADFORD-ON-AVON. I. Thos. Horton, founder of chantry, and w. Mary, c. **1530**, mcht.'s mk., sm., N.A., p. 44. *Kite*, p. 51 (mcht.'s mk.) II. Anne, only dau. and h. of John Yewe, Gent., of Bradford, and w. of Gyfford Longe, Gent., **1601**, with daus. Anne and Cath., N., p. 247. *Kite*, pl. xxvii.

BROAD BLUNSDEN. A Lady, **1608**, with 2 daus., marg. inscr. mutil.

BROMHAM. I. Elizth., dau. [of Gerard Braybrooke] and [w. of Wm. Beauchamp] Lord St. Amand, [and afterwards of Sir Roger Tocotes], c. **1490**, in mantle coloured, marg. inscr. mutil., Hy. Trin. lost, mur., S.C., pp. 9, 212. *Kite*, pl. ix. II. John Baynton, Esq., son and h. of Sir Robt. Baynton, the cousin and h. of Rich. Beauchamp, Lord St. Amand, **1516**, marg. inscr., S.C. *Kite*, pl. xvi. III. Sir Edw. Baynton, dec. (?) **1578**, in arm., and 2 ws.; 1st, Agnes (Ryce), **1574**, with 3 chil., Hen., Anne, Elizth. (eff. lost), she had 10 other chil. dec.; 2nd, Anne (Pakyngton), 8 Eng. vv., mur., A.T., S.C. *Kite*, pl. xxiv.

BROUGHTON GIFFORD. An Altar-tomb with a Herald and Death standing behind it, for Robt., 2nd son of Hen. Longe, Esq., of Whaddon, Wilts., **1620**, æt. 46; by his w. Millesaint he had 4 sons, Robt., Edw., Hen., Posthumus, 6 Eng. vv. (see Addenda), qd. pl., mur., N., pp. 30, 217. *Wilts. Archæol. Mag.*, vol. vi. p. 48; *Wilkinson's Hist. of Broughton Gifford*, p. 116; *Kite*, pl. xxix.

CHARLTON. Wm. Chaucey, Gent., who edified the chapel, **1524**, and w. Marion [Dunch?], now mur., N.C. *Kite*, pl. xix.

CHISLEDON. *Frauncis Rutland, Esq., son and h. of Nich. Rutland, Esq., of Mitcham, Surrey, **1592**, and w. [Mary], dau. of Thos. Stephens, Esq., with 4 sons and 2 daus., effs. of chil. lost, sm., C. *Kite*, p. 73 (male eff.)

CLIFFE-PYPARD. A Man in arm., of the Quintin family, c. **1380**, inscr. lost, S.A., p. 160. *Boutell's Series*; *Kite*, pl. ii.

COLLINGBOURNE DUCIS. Edw., 4th son of Wm. Saintmaur, earl of Hertford, and his w. Lady Francis [Devereux], **1631**, æt. 11 months, 6 Eng. vv., sm., C. *Engr.* —— (?), *a Tale for Children* (front.); *Kite*, p. 88.

COLLINGBOURNE KINGSTON. Constantine Darell, Esq., eff. lost, and w. Joan, **1495**, in mantle, chil. lost, C.

DAUNTSEY. I. Sir John Danvers, lord of the manor, and patron of the Ch. in right of his w., **1514**, and w. Anne, marg. inscr., A.T., C., pp. 56, 233. *Kite*, p. 53 (female eff.) II. Dame Anne, dau. of Sir John Dauntesey, and w. of Sir John Danvers, c. **1535**, with Hy. Trin., diapered background, 12 Eng. vv. (see Appendix B.), qd. pl., mur., C., pp. 21, 56. *Kite*, pl. xx. An incised slab to John Delvale, Esq., and w., 15th cent., p. 40.

DEANE, WEST. *Geo. Evelyn, Esq., eldest son of Sir John Evelyn, **1641**, æt. 6, sm., C. *Kite*, p. 90.

DEVIZES, ST. JOHN. John Kent, sen., a benefactor to the town, **1630**, and w. [Mary Wyatt], S.C. *Kite*, pl. xxx.

DRAYCOT CERNE. Sir Edw. Cerne [**1393-4**], and widow Elyne [1419 ?], Fr. inscr., C., pp. 61, 149, 160, 167. *Boutell's Series; Kite*, pl. iii. *Introd.*, p. 167 (det.) An engraving of the brass (now lost) of Philippe de Cerne, dau. of Sir Edw. by his first w. Philippa, is given in *Kite's Mon. Brasses of Wilts.*, pl. iv., from a sketch by Aubrey.

DURNFORD, GREAT. *Edw. Younge, Esq., son and h. of John Younge, Esq., and of his w. Mary, one of the 4 daus. and cohs. of Thos. Trapnell, Esq., of Monckton Farley, **1607**, and w. Joane, eldest dau. of Laur. Hide, Esq., of West Hatche, with 6 sons and 8 daus., qd. pl., mur., A.T., C. *Hoare's Wilts.*

FOVANT. Geo. Rede, rector of the Ch. at the time of the building of the new Tower in **1492**, in acad., with the Annunciation, qd. pl., mur., C., pp. 21, 77, 105, 203. *Hoare's Wilts.; Kite*, pl. xiii.

LAVINGTON, WEST. I. John Dauntesay, Esq., justice, **1559**, æt. 44, in arm., he m. 2 ws., by the first he had 5, by the 2nd 7 chil., 14 Eng. vv., on reverse an inscr. in Dutch, S.C., pp. 47, 235. *Kite*, pl. xxi. INSCR. II. *Margt., 2nd w. of No. I., **1571**, 20 Eng. vv., on reverse an inscr., date 1552; the daus., Maria and Dulcia, pos. III. John, Walter, Robt., Peter, sons of John Auncell, sen.

LAYCOCK. Robt. Baynard, Esq., **1501**, and w. Elizt. [Ludlow], in heraldic dresses, with 13 sons, the 2nd a priest, and 5 daus., S.Tr., p. 78. *Kite*, pl. xi.

MERE. I. John Bettesthorne, lord of the manor of Chadenwyche, founder of chantry, **1398**, in arm., 2 Lat. vv., large, S.C., pp. 96, 140, 160, 162. *Hoare's Wilts., Hundred of Mere*, pl. iii. p. 12;

Boutell's Series; Kite, pl. v.   II. A Man, in arm., and w., c. **1415**, all lost but upper part of male eff., large, S.C., p. 188. *Hoare* (ibid.); *Kite*, pl. viii.   Mr. Kite (p. 31) conjectures this to be the brass of Sir John Berkeley, 1426-7, and w. Elizth., only dau. and h. of No. I., who died before her husband.

MINETY.   [Nich. Poulett, Esq.], in arm., and w. [Mary, dau. of Thos. Hungerford], c. **1620**, with 4 chil., Ames, Elizth., Mary, Edight, inscr. covd. (?), qd. pl., mur., N.A.

NEWNTON, LONG.   I. John Erton, rector, **1503**, inscr. reversed, now in N., p. 78. *Kite,* pl. xii.   INSCR. II. Nich. White, "qui primo obtinuit de monast'io Malmesburie sepultura mortuor' fieri in hac ecclia Et Cimiterio ciusdm̄," c. **1500**, now on same slab as No. I.

OGBOURNE ST. GEORGE.   Thos. Goddard, **1517**, and w. Joan, a son and dau. lost, N.C. *Kite*, pl. xvii.

PRESHUTE.   John Barley, **1518**, and w. Maryon, with 7 sons and 3 daus., S.A.   *Kite*, pl. xviii.

SALISBURY CATHEDRAL. I. [Robt. Wyvil, bp. for 45 years, "Int' enim alia beficia sua minima Castrum d̄co ecclīē de Schirebon̄ p' ducentos annos et amplius manu militari violent' [occupatum eidem ecclīē ut pugil] intrepidus recup'auit, ac ipī ecclīē chaccam de la Bere restitui pēurauit," **1375**, hf. eff. standing in a castle, &c., with champion before the gate, marg. inscr. mutil., large, N.E.Tr., pp. 73, 122. See also Addenda. *Gent. Mag.*, vol. lvii. 1787, pt. ii. p. 949; *Nichols' Leic.*, vol. ii. pt. ii. pl. cxxix. p. 802; *Hutchins' Dorset*, 1815, vol. iv. p. 122; *Carter's Anc. Sculpt. and Painting*, vol. i. p. 42; *Waller*, pt. ix.; *Kite*, pl. i.   II. Edm. Geste, S.T.P. of Camb., bp. of Rochester and high almoner for 12 years, bp. of Sarum for 5 years, bequeathed an immense number of books to the Ch., **1578** [a mistake for 1576]; Giles Estcourte, Esq., one of his executors, pos.; N.E.Tr., pp. 125, 216, 229.   *Life of Bp. Guest by H. G. Dugdale, Esq.*, 1840 (front.); *Kite*, pl. xxiii. Bp. Guest was the prominent person in the review of the Com. Prayer-book, made under the direction of Secretary Cecil in 1559.   Matrices of several brasses: Bp. Bingham, 1246, a hf. eff. with crosier, placed on a cross, N.A.C., p. 134. *Boutell's Chr. Mon.*, p. 138; *Kite*, p. 6.   Bp. York, 1256, hf. eff., S.C.A., p. 134.   Walter Lord Hungerford and w. (*Gough*, vol. ii. pl. lvii.), and Robt. Lord Hungerford, 1463 (*Ibid.*, pl. lxxix.), the slabs powdered with sickles, a badge of the family.

SALISBURY, ST. THOMAS. *John Webbe, mayor [in 1561], **1570**, and w. Anne, dau. of Nich. Wylford, citizen and mcht.-taylor of ―― (?), with 3 sons and 3 daus., marg. inscr. mutil., C.   *Kite*, pl. xxii.

SEEND.   John Stokys, **1498**, and w. Alys, sm., N.A. *Kite*, pl. x.

*Stockton. I. Elizth., [1st] w. of Hierom Poticary, clothier, **1590**, æt. 35, with 1 son and 4 daus., 12 Eng. vv., qd. pl., mur., S.A. II. Hierome Potecary, **1596**, æt. 52, and [2nd] w., with 2 sons and 2 daus., 14 hexameter vv.; his son, Christopher, pos.; mur., S.A.

Tisbury. I. A Civilian and w., c. **1520**, chil. and inscr. lost, S.A. II. Laur. Hyde, Esq., of West-Hatch, son of Robt. Hyde, **1590**, and w. Anne, dau. of Nich. Sibell, Esq., of Chimbhams, Kent, with 10 chil. [Robt., Laur., Hen., Nich.], Hamonet and Edw. both dec. young, [Elizth., Susannah, Avice, Joan], 6 eleg. vv. and mutil. marg. inscr., qd. pl., C. *Hoare's Wilts.; Kite*, pl. xxvi.

Upton Lovell. A Priest, c. **1460**, hf. eff., C. *Kite*, p. 32. Perhaps Thos. Marchaunt, 1462, or John Garton, 1469.

Wandborough. I. Thos. Polton and w. Edith, both dec. **1418**, hf. effs., 12 Lat. vv. stating that they had 8 sons and 8 daus., and left 14 "nummos" to the "curate" for celebrating an obit (?) "post ortū matris dni dnica die sequente, Ellermis de & Halle plase Wanbergh retinento," S.A., p. 209. *Kite*, pl. vi.   Inscr. II. An inscr. desiring prayers for Thos. Polton and w. Edith (dec.), for their son Philip, archdeacon of Gloucester, dau. Agnes, and 14 other of their chil.; for Robt. Everard, vicar, and all his parishioners who began the bell-tower in **1435**, mur., Tower.

Westbury. Thos. Bennet, Gent., **1605**, and w. Margt., eldest dau. and coh. of Thos. Buriton, Esq., of Streatley, Berks.; the w. pos., N.C. *Kite*, pl. xxviii.

Wilton. *John Coffer, Gent., servant for 38 years to Sir Wm. and Hen. Herbert, earls of Pembroke, **1585**, æt. 77, and w. Phelipe, dau. of Gilbert Synclere, Esq., 4 Eng. vv., mur., p. 225. *Kite*, p. 66 (male eff.)

Wokingham. See Berks.

Woodford. *Gerrard Erington, Esq., of Heale, **1596**; he m. Margt., dau. of Wm. Green, Esq., of [Stanlinche] Heale, mur., S.A.

INSCRIPTIONS, &c.

Alton Barnes. Wm. Budd, LL.B., fellow of New Coll., rector, **1685**, æt. 56.   Amesbury. Editha, w. of Robt. Matyn, 147-, now covd. (?), C.   Bishopstone-near-Salisbury. *John Wykham, rector, **1417**, C.   *Everley. I. John Neet, rector, **1429**. II. Susanna, w. of Christopher Tesdale, rector, **1650**.   III. Mary, dau. of Wm. Prater, and w. of John Samuel, of Lavington, **1671**. All loose in vestry.   Hinton, Broad. Wm. Parish, of Cotermersh, 1447, Thos. Paris, 1610; Thos. Paris, S.T.B., fellow of C. C. Coll., Oxon. (abnepos of Thos.), "titulum avulsum, Restitui curavi,"

1687. Laverstock. *Ant. Ernley, Esq., **1530**, and w. Margt., N. Melksham. See brasses in private possession — Rev. E. Wilton. Pitton. *Edw., 2nd son of Sir John Zouche, **1580**, mur., C. Salisbury, St. Edmund. *Anne Venard, "a mother thrice," **1586**, 18 Eng. vv., effs. of chil. lost, S.A. Steeple Ashton. Peter Crooke, gave 20s. to the Ch. and 40s. yearly to the poor, **1633**, mcht.'s mk. *Kite*, p. 89. Stourton. *John Winford, rector, **1473**, C. Winterslow. *Dorothy, w. of —— Stanesbye, 6 cleg. vv., **1587**, mur., C. Wishford, Great. Thos. Bonham, Esq., patron of the Ch., **1473**, and w. Edith, 1469, effs. lost, with 9 chil. detached, all gone but 2 daus. and part of a son, N., p. 172.

The brasses are lost at Bishopstone near Swindon, Hilmarton, and Wroughton. In *Kite's Mon. Brasses* (pp. 10, 11) are engravings of two matrices at Ramsbury, one a cross with hf. eff. above it, and Lomb. marg. inscr. (see Appendix B.), c. 1330; the other, c. 1450, to Wm. Darell, Esq., and w., with Hy. Trin., shs., crests, &c.

Worcestershire.

Alvechurch. Philip Chatwyn, gentleman usher to Hen. VIII., **1524**, in arm., p. 233.

Birlingham. *Thos. Harewell, 1603, and w., **1617**, qd. pl., mur., C.

Blockley. I. Philip Worthyn (?), M.A., vicar, **1488**, in acad., kng., marg. inscr., B. V. Mary and Child lost, pecul., C., pp. 24, 77, 125. *Bigland's Gloucestershire*, p. 216. II. Wm. Jombharte (?), LL.B., rector of [Stretton (?) on the] Fosse, c. **1500**, kng., marg. inscr. nearly all lost, Hy. Trin. gone, pecul. (?), C., p. 78. *Ibid.* (where it is incorrectly ascribed to Wm. Neele).

Broadway. Anth. Daston, **1572**, æt. 66, in arm., 10 hex. vv., now mur., C.

Bushley. Thos. Payne, who first obtained permission to bury in the Ch., **1500**, and w. Ursula, inscr. restored, 11 sons and 4 daus. lost, p. 92.

Chaddesley Corbet. *Thos. Forest, park-keeper of Dunclent Park, and w. Margt., c. **1500**, with 5 sons and 6 daus., marg. inscr. mutil., N., p. 178.

Daylesford. *Wm. Gardiner, Esq., of Layham, Surrey, **1632**, æt. 26; by his w. Ann, dau. of Simon Hastings, Esq., he had a son Wm.; 7 Eng. vv. on marg. inscr., C., p. 240. Ch. being rebuilt 1859.

FLADBURY. I. John Throckmorton, Esq., under treasurer of England, **1445**, and widow Alianora [Spiney?]; marg. inscr. mentioning their son Thos., lately restored, A.T., N., pp. 53, 191. *Introd.*, p. 191 (male eff.)   II. Thos. Mordon, LL.B., treasurer of St. Paul's, London, rector, **1458**, in cope with initials on orphrey, hf. eff., C., p. 48. *Nash's Worcestershire*, vol. i. p. 449.   III. Edw. Peytoo, Esq. [**1488**], and w. [Goditha, dau. of Thos.] Thokmerton, Esq., with 4 sons and 1 dau.; effs. of w. in mantle, chil., and part of inscr. lost, N. *Dugdale's Warwickshire*, ed. 1730, vol. i. p. 477.   IV. Wm. Plewme, M.A., rector, **1504**, sm., C. *Nash*, vol. i. p. 449.   INSCR. V. Godyth, dau. of Wm. Bosom, w. of Robt. Olney, Esq., and mother of Margt., the w. of Thos. Throgmerton, 5 Lat. vv., N.

HANLEY CASTLE. †Rich. Lechmere, Gent., **1568**, and widow Margery, with 9 chil., Rich., Edm., Frances, Joane, Elianor, Mary, Frances, Mary, Wineford, S.A.

KIDDERMINSTER. Sir John Phelip, "Henricus quintus dilexerat hunc ut amicus....Audax & fortis apud Harffleu Johñ bene gessit, Et Baro vim mortis paciens migrare recessit," **1415**, in arm., Walter Cookesey, Esq. [**1407**], and their w. Matilda [Harcourt], all with SS. collars, canopy mutil., 8 Lat. vv., large, worn, C., pp. 32, 187, 188, 208. *Nash*, vol. ii. p. 49; *Napier's Swyncombe and Ewelme*, p. 33. *Introd.*, p. 187 (det.)

LONGDON. *Wm. Brugge, Esq., of Estington, Worc., son and h. of Thos. Brugge, Esq., of Dimmocke, Glouc., **1523**, and w. Alyce, dau. and h. of Wm. Estington, Esq., lord of the manor of Estington, loose, inscr. lost.

MAMBLE. John Blount, Esq., and w. Kath. [Corbet], c. **1510**; effs. of their son Sir Edw., knt. of the body to Hen. VIII., 9 other sons, 7 daus., and inscr. lost (?), C.

STOCKTON. *Wm. Parker, **1508**, and ws. Sibill and Elizth., effs. of ws. lost, N.

*STOKE PRIOR. I. Hen. Smith, citizen and draper of London, he left to this parish in which he was born £100 for purchase of land, 40s. of the rent of which was for 4 or 6 sermons to be yearly preached by strangers, and the rest for the schooling of poor boys, **1606**, mur. II. Robt. Smith, Esq., citizen and draper of London, free and twice governor of the Mcht.-Adventurers' Co. at Antwerp and Middleborough, **1609**, æt. 75, and 2 ws., Tomasin, dau. of Arthur Dericote, Esq., of Hackney (with 11 sons and 6 daus.), and Susan, dau. of Sir Rich. Pipe, lord mayor [in 1578], mur., N.C.

STRENSHAM. I. Robt., son of Thos. Russel, lord of the manor,

c. **1390**, in arm., marg. inscr., C., pp. 149, 160. *Nash*, vol. ii. p. 393; *Boutell's Series*. II. [Sir John Russell, lord of the manor], dec. at Letheryngham, Suff., **1405**, he had 3 ws., Elizth., Margt., Augnes, canopy, marg. inscr. mutil., C., p. 185. *Nash*, vol. ii. p. 393. III. †Robt. Russell, Esq., lord of the manor, **1502**, and w. Elizth. [Baynham], perhaps covd. by pews, C. *Ibid.* IV. Sir John Russell, **1556**, and w. Edethe [Umpton], **1562**, "the naturall father & mother of Sir Thomas Russell knight theyr onlie sone," in heraldic dresses, mur., A.T., C., p. 236. *Ibid.*

TREDINGTON. I. *Rich. Cassey, rector, "ecclesiæ Henrici quinti quondam fuit ipse sacerdos," canon of York [**1427**], in cope, marg. inscr. in Lat. vv. mutil., C. II. *Hen. Sampson, rector, **1482**, in almuce, kng., C., p. 79. III. †A Lady, loose. Part of the brass (?) of Wm. Barnes, Esq., 1561, and w. Alice, dau. of Thos. Middlemore, of Edgbaston.

YARDLEY. *Wm. Astell, Simon Wheler, and their w. Isabella, dau. of Simon Norwich, **1598**, qd. pl., mur.

INSCRIPTIONS, &c.

EVESHAM, ALL SAINTS. I. Robt. Wyllys and w. Agnes, c. **1520**, effs. lost, sm., N. II. A Scroll, c. **1520** (?); civilian, w., and chil. lost, N. BREDON. John Prideaux, born at Stoford, Devon, Sept. 17th, 1578, fellow, and for nearly 30 years rector of Exeter Coll., Oxford, regius professor of divinity for upwards of 26 years, five times vice-chancellor, chaplain to Prince Hen. and Kings James and Chas., consecrated bp. of Worcester at Westminster Dec. 19th, 1641, dec. **1650**, æt. 72, with mitre and 4 shs., C., p. 123.

The brasses are lost at BROMSGROVE and also at MIDDLE LITTLETON, unless the brass of Thos. Smith, founder of the S.Ch. at the latter place, is under pews.

Yorkshire.

ALDBOROUGH, near BOROUGHBRIDGE. Wm. de Aldeburgh, c. **1360**, in arm., arms on jupon, with sh., on bracket, pecul. (?), large, now mur., N.A., pp. 28, 107, 112, 156, 159, 160. *Oxford Man.*, p. 70; *Gent. Mag.*, vol. xxxiv. N.S. 1850, p. 44; *Waller*, pt. xvii. (not yet published); *Introd.*, p. 156.

ALLERTON MAULEVERER. Sir John Mauleverere, **1400**, with arms on jupon, and w. Elianora, dau. of Sir Peter de Midelton, pecul., sm., qd. pl., pp. 28, 62, 154, 162. *Arch. Journ.*, vol. v. p. 68; *Anastatic Drawing Soc.*, vol. for 1859.

Aughton. *Rich. Ask, Esq., and w. Margt., 15th cent., C.

Bainton. *Roger Godcale, rector, with chalice.

Beeford. [Thos.] Tonge, rector [LL.B., **1472**], in cope, marg. inscr. mutil., C., pp. 77, 81, 125. *Hist. and Ant. of the Seignory of Holderness, by Geo. Poulson, Esq.*, 1840, vol. i. p. 255.

Bolton-by-Bolland. Hen. Pudsey, Esq., lord of the manor, builder of chantry, **1509**, and w. Margt., 1500, in heraldic dresses, mur., S.C. *Whitaker's History of Craven*, p. 106.

Brandsburton. I. Wm. Darell, rector of Halsham Ch., **1364**, hf. eff., head gone, on bracket, Fr. inscr., and marg. inscr. mutil., C., p. 137. II. Sir John de St. Quintin, lord of the manor, **1397**, head gone, and w. Lora, 1369, marg. inscr. nearly all lost, pecul. (?), very large, now under seats, C., pp. 28, 58, 107, 160, 162. *Poulson*, p. 280; *Boutell's Series*.

Burgh Wallis. †Thos., son of Sir Wm. Gascoign, **1554** (?), inscr. lost, N.

Burton, Bishop. I. A Chalice for Peter Johnsun, vicar, **1460**, pecul., C., p. 125. II. Joan, a dau. and h. of John Bolnie (?), and w. of Ralph Rokeby, Esq., **1521**, with chil., Wm., Agnes, Rose, their effs. lost. III. *Lady Isabell, dau. of Rich. Smethelaye, Esq., **1579**, and 2 husbands, Sir John Ellerker (who had a son, Wm.), in arm., eff. lost, and Christopher Estoft, Esq., one of the queen's "honorable covncell established in the northe," 1566, pecul., mutil., C., pp. 30, 214.

Catterick. I. Wm. Burgh, Esq., son and h. of John Burgh, 1442 (his w. Matilda dec. 1432), and Wm. Burgh, Esq., son and h. of the said Wm., **1465** (his w. Elena dec. 1446), pecul., pp. 28, 195, 196. *Whitaker's Hist. of Richmondshire*, 1823, vol. ii. p. 28. II. Wm. Burgh, Esq., one of the founders of the chantry, **1492**, and w. Elizth., p. 97. *Ibid.* Inscr. III. John de Burgh, Esq., **1412**, and w. Kath.

Cottingham. I. Nich. de [Luda (Louth), rector], builder [of Chancel in 1374, prebendary of Beverley], **1383**, in cope; canopy, super-canopy, and marg. inscr. in 8 Lat. vv. mutil.; large, rel. and restored, C., pp. 25, 92, 144, 259. II. John Smyth, **1504**, and w. Joan, N.

Cowthorpe. *Brian Rouclyff [baron] of the exchequer, founder of Ch., **1494**, and w. Joan (Ughtred), holding a church between them, below it an altar with sh. and inscr., "Orate p. aīa Johīs Burgh armigeri," canopy, with scrolls on the pediments, chess rooks, &c., marg. inscr. mutil., C., pp. 90, 123. *Waller*, pt. vii.

Harpham. I. Sir Thos. de St. Quintin [lord of the manor], and

w. Agnes [Warren (?), **1418**], canopy, marg. inscr. mutil., pecul., large, C., pp. 28, 125, 185, 187, 188. *Boutell's Series; Gent. Mag.*, vol. xxx. N.S., 1848, p. 602. *Introd.*, p. 185 (male eff.) II. Thos. St. Quintin, Esq., lord of the manor, **1445**, with collar, pecul., C., pp. 28, 192. *Boutell's Series; Hewitt's Anc. Arm.*, vol. iii. pl. 79, p. 452.

HOWDEN. I. A Man in arm., c. **1480**, a sm. part of canopy left (with inscr. on reverse?), inscr. lost, loose, p. 195. INSCR. II. Peter Dolman, Esq., counsellor-at-law, **1621**, on reverse lower part of a civilian, c. **1520**, p. 48.

HULL, HOLY TRINITY. Rich. Byll, alderman, **1451**, and w., hf. effs., 8 Lat. vv., mcht.'s mk., and Evang. symbs., C.

HULL, ST. MARY. John Haryson, scherman and alderman of Hull, **1525**, and 2 ws., Alys and Agnes, with 3 sons, Thos., John, Wm., Hy. Trin. defaced, early instance of qd. pl., mur.

KIRBY MOORSIDE. *Lady Brooke, **1600**, with 6 sons and 5 daus., kng.

LAUGHTON-EN-LE-MORTHEN. †John Mallevorer, Esq., of Lettwell, Yorks., c. **1600**, 8 Eng. vv., eff. of w. (?) lost.

LEAK. John Watson, auditor to Lord Skroope, and w. Alice, c. **1530**.

*LEEDS, ST. PETER. I. Sir John Langton, **1459**, and w. Eufemia, in mantle, pecul., now mur., C., pp. 28, 195. *Antiquities of Leeds, by Jas. Wardell*, 1853, pl. v. II. John Langton, Esq., son and h. of No. I., both dec. on the feast of St. Lambert, bp. and martyr, **1464**, much worn and mutil., C. III. A Chalice for Thos. Clarell, vicar, **1469**, now mur., C., p. 125. *Wardell's Leeds*, pl. vi. IV. John Massie, **1709**, and family, mur., N.C. Seven Effs. rough from oxidation, and about thirty plates with arms and inscrs.

LONDESBOROUGH. *Margt. Lady Threckeld, widow of John Lord Clifford, **1493**, C.

MARR. John Lewis, Esq. (son and h. of Robt. Lewis, Gent.), justice of peace and quorum for the West Riding, recorder of Doncaster, **1589**, æt. 46, and w. Mary, dau. of Lionell Reresbye, Esq., of Thriburgh, with 2 sons and 4 daus.

OTLEY. I. ―― Palmerson (last of the family), **1593**, recumbent eff., above it a curious genealogical tree, with arms of Frauncis, Hadnall, Corbett, &c., 6 eleg. vv., qd. pl., mur., p. 3. II. †Hen. Thoresby, bencher of Lincoln's Inn, and a master of the Chancery, son and h. of Wm. Thoresby, Esq., and w. Ann, a dau. of Mr. John Scroope, youngest brother of Lord Scroope, of Boulton, c. **1640**; Hen. Thoresby left money to the poor and for two sermons yearly, mur.

OWSTON. Robt. do Haitfeld [1417], and w. Ade, **1409**, both with SS. collars, Fr. inscr., N.A., pp. 61, 116.

RAWMARSH. †John Darley, Gent., of Kilnhirst, younger son of Wm. Darley, Esq., of Buttercrambe, **1616**, æt. 75, and w. Alice, a dau. of Christopher Mountfort, Esq. (who pos.), m. 47 years, with 8 chil., Thos., Wm., Frauncis, John, Benedicta, Elizth., Ann, Mary (whose son John Ellis became the h.), 8 Eng. vv., mur., C.

RONALD KIRK. John Lewelyne, rector, founder of chantry and of a chapel on a bridge (?) over the Tees, c. **1470**, in cope, head gone, marg. inscr. mutil., C., pp. 77, 81. *Whitaker's Richmondshire*, vol. i. p. 131.

ROTHERHAM. Robt. Swifte, Esq., **1561**, æt. 84, and first w. Anne, 1539, æt. 67, with 4 chil., Wm., Robt., Anne, Margt., qd. pl., mur., A.T., N.C., p. 226. *Lith. by Mr. F. W. Hoyle.*

ROUTH. Sir [John Routh], and w. [Agnes] with surplice sleeves, both with SS. collars, c. **1410**, canopy and inscr. mutil., large, C., pp. 187, 188. *Poulson's Holderness*, vol. i. p. 399.

ROXBY CHAPEL. *Thos. Boynton, Esq., **1523**.

SESSAY. *Thos. Magnus, archdeacon of the East Riding, parson of the Ch., **1550**, in cope, with scroll from hands, p. 227. *Engr.* —— (?).

SHERIFF HUTTON. †Mary Hall, **1657**.

SKIPTON. See brasses in private possession—Mr. Tufton.

SPROTBOROUGH. Wm. Fitz William, Esq., lord of the manor, dec. at Hathilsay, **1474**, and widow Elizth., dau. of Sir Thos. Chaworth, pecul., C., p. 195. *Rev. Joseph Hunter's South Yorks.*, 1828, vol. i. p. 345. *Introd.*, p. 195 (det.)

TANFIELD, WEST. I. A Man in arm., c. **1480**, inscr. lost, p. 195. II. Thos. Sutton, M.A., canon of West Chester, c. **1480**, in cope, C. *Whitaker's Richmondshire*, vol. ii. p. 174.

THIRSK. I. A Priest between 2 angels (?), hf. eff., much worn. INSCR. II. Robt. Thoresby (?), rector of Goseworth and ......, **1419** (?), worn.

THORNTON WATLASS. A shrouded Eff. on A.T., between two cypresses, with initials G. F., **1669**, mur.

TOPCLIFFE. [Thos. de] Topclyff, 1362, with anclace, and w., **1391**, both in mantles, canopy with souls, angels, &c., marg. inscr. mutil., qd. pl. 5 ft. 9. in. by 3 ft. 1 in., Flemish, on reverse are some unfinished portions of brasses, rel., pp. 39, 164, 167. *Waller*, pt. xvi.

WATH. I. Rich. Norton, chief-justice of the king's bench, **1420**, and w. Kath., 1418 (?), in mantle, much worn, under pew, S.Tr.,

p. 90. *Whitaker's Richmondshire*, vol. ii. p. 184. II. Rich. Norton, in arm., and w. Isabella (Tempest), they dec. [of the plague?] Sept. 30th and 20th, **1433** (or 1438?), inscr. and eff. of w. lost, pecul. Yorkshire artist, S.Tr. *Ibid.* FRAG. III. Arms of Ward, on matrix of brass of Sir John Norton and w. Margt., dau. of Sir Roger Ward, of Guiseley and Givendale, Yorks., both dec. **1520**, S.Tr.

WELLWICK. *Wm. Wryght, Esq., of Plewland, **1621**, and w. Anne, 1618, m. 50 years, N.A. *Poulson's Holderness*, vol. ii. p. 512.

WENSLEY. I. Sir Simon de Wenslagh, rector, engr. c. **1360** (?), with chalice on breast, head on cushion, fine Flemish, marg. inscr. lost, C., pp. 22, 39, 61, 143. *Whitaker's Richmondshire*, vol. i. p. 373; *Waller*, pt. vii.; *Boutell's Mon. Br.*, p. 20. INSCR. II. Oswald Dykes, rector for 20 years, **1607**, on same slab as No. I.

WENTWORTH. Mich. Darcy, only son of John Lord Darcy, of Aston, **1588**, in arm., and w. Margt., dau. of Thos. Wentworth, Esq., of Wentworth Woodhowse, with 3 chil., John, Anne, Margt., qd. pl., mur.

*WINESTEAD. I. A Man in arm. [Sir Robt. Hildyard?] (lower part gone), and w. mutil., c. **1540**, with 7 sons and 7 daus. (two gone), marg. inscr. lost, C. *Poulson's Holderness*, vol. ii. p. 479. II. Wm. Retherby, rector, builder of Ch., **1418**, C.

WYCLIFFE. I. *Ralph, only son of Wm. Wickliff (who pos.), **1606**, æt. 14, kng., qd. pl., C. *Whitaker's Richmondshire*, vol. i. p. 199. INSCR. II. Roger de Wyclif, lord of the manor, and w. Kath., C., 15th. cent.

YORK, ALL SAINTS, NORTH-STREET. I. Thos. Atkinson, tanner, sheriff of York, **1642**, æt. 72, large, hf. eff. INSCR. II. Thos. Clerk, "clericus" of the city and county of York, and w., both dec. Feb. 16th, **1482**. III. Three Evang. symbs. The brasses are now all on the same slab, S.A.

YORK MINSTER. I. Wm. de Grenefeld, abp. and lord chancellor, **1315**; canopy, with saints at the sides, and inscr. lost; large, the lower part of eff. stolen about 1829, A.T., N.Tr., pp. 71, 142. *Waller*, pt. iv. II. Elizth., dau. of Sir Edw. Nevell, one of the privy chamber to Hen. VIII., w. of Thos. Eynns, Esq., dec., and one of the gentlewomen of the privy chamber to Queen Elizth., **1585**, hf. eff., holding an open book with the texts Ps. cxix. 30, 54, mur., S.A. III. Jas. Cotrel, Esq., born at Dublin, about 20 years served the queen's council in the north "testes examinando," **1595**, hf. eff., pecul., mur., S.A., p. 218.

*York, St. Cross. I. A Civilian, c. **1600**, in official dress (?) with cap and signet-ring, hf. eff., qd. pl., mur., inscr. lost. Inscr. II. Hen. Wyman, mayor, 1411, and w. Agnes, dau. of John Basden, **1416**. III. Mcht.'s mk. and shs., p. 120.

York, St. Martin-le-Grand. I. Christopher Harington, goldsmith, **1614**, hf. eff., N., p. 119. Inscr. II. *Thos. Colthurst, Gent., **1588**, and w. Kath., dau. of Rich. Anslie, Gent.

York, St. Michael Spurrier-Gate. I. A Chalice for Wm. Langton, rector, **1466** (not 1463), C., p. 125. *Boutell's Series*, and *Chr. Mon.*, p. 111. Inscr. II. *Wm. Hancok, apothecary, **1485**, and w. Elen, 1470. III. Wm. Wilson, pecul., 15th cent.

INSCRIPTIONS, &c.

Ainderby. *Wm. Saleys, rector, confessor of John Lord Scrope. A Matrix, p. 123. Barmston. *Thos. Baske, cit'zen and fishmonger of London, **1505**, and w. Joan. Beverley Minster. *Rich. Ferrant, **1560**. Cayton. *Inscr. with Evang. symbs., worn, C. Coningsborough. †Nich. Bossvell, founder of chantry, **1523**, mur., p. 60. Flamborough. *Sir Marmaduke Constable, served in France with Ed. IV. and Hen. VII., was at the "winnyng" of Berwick and at Brankiston (Flodden), c. **1530**, 26 Eng. vv., C. Hornby. *Three Scrolls (heart lost?) and inscr. for Christopher Conyers, Esq., and w. Elena, **1443**, S.A. Kilnwick Percy. *Thos. Wood, c. **1570**(?), 12 Eng. vv. (see Appendix B.) Kirklington. †John Wandyssford, Esq., **1463**, and w. Alianor. Masham. Christopher Kay, 1689, and Mrs. Jane Nicollson, **1690**. Middleham. Thos. Bernham, frater ordinis ......, 15th cent., much worn, C., p. 87. Nunkeeling. *Geo. Acklam, **1629**. Ripley. I. Rich. Kendale, M.A., rector, **1429** (?). II. Kath., w. of Sir Wm. Ingelby, **1500**. III. John Ingelby, Esq., lord of the manor, **1502**. Sheffield. *Elizth., dau. of Thos. [Butler, 7th] earl of Ormond, and his w. Lore (w. of [John Blount] Lord Mountjoye), **1510**. Stanwich, St. John. †Emma, w. of Sir Ralph Pudsay, **1485**. Tickhill. †Wm. Estfeld, steward of the seignory of Holderness and of the honour of Tickhill with Queen Philippa, and of the lordship of Heytfeld with Edm. duke of York, **1386**, and w. Margt., mur., A.T., C.

At Sandal Parva was a mur. brass to Wm. Rokeby, rector, afterwards abp. of Dublin, 1521. The brasses are lost at Badsworth (p. 140), Thornton Abbey (p. 123), and Wighill.

Private Possession, Museums, &c.

ASHRIDGE HOUSE, BUCKS. I. John de Swynstede, rector [prebendary of Lincoln], **1395**, large. *Anastatic-printing.* II. A Rose and inscr. for John Killyngworth, **1412**, p. 110. *Anastatic Drawing Soc.*, vol. for 1859; *Introd.*, p. 110. These brasses were originally at Edlesborough, Bucks.

MR. BACK, NORWICH. A Clergyman (?), c. **1600**, with hood, 2 ft. long; said to have come from Staplehurst Ch., Kent, but perhaps from St. Peter Mancroft, or some other church in Norwich.

MR. BAYFIELD, NORWICH. I. A Lady, c. **1530**, very sm., from St. Edmund, Norwich. *Cotman*, vol. i. pl. li. p. 32. II. Four Daus., c. **1440**. III. Inscr. to Walter Bownyng (?) and w. Melicent (?), **1473**, on reverse part of marg. inscr. and sh., Flemish, from Trunch, Norfolk, p. 26. *Boutell's Mon. Br.*, p. 149. IV. Inscr. to Anne, w. of Thos. Randolf, **1536**; on reverse part of a Lady in mantle, Flemish, c. **1500**; from St. Paul or St. James (?), Norwich. V. Inscr. to Thos. Cooper, bayly [**1576**], who had 1 son and 6 daus., 4 Eng. vv., mutil., from All Saints', Dunwich. VI. Two sm. frags. of inscrs., with Flemish engraving on the reverse.

REV. F. T. J. BAYLY, BROOKTHORPE, GLOUC. A Civilian, c. **1535**, kng., sm., p. 128.

BODLEIAN LIBRARY, OXFORD. I. A Rose bearing an inscr., c. **1410**, from a brass formerly at St. Peter's, St. Albans, p. 110. *Gough*, vol. ii. pt. i. p. 335. II. A Man in arm., c. **1490**, from Letheringham, Suffolk, p. 200. Perhaps Wm. Wyngefelde, Esq., 1481. *Gough*, vol. ii. pt. ii. pl. xi. p. 28. III. Inscr. to Sir John de Wyngefeld, lord of the manor [**1389**?], mutil., also a sh. with arms of Wingfield impaling Hastings, from Letheringham. *Ibid.* Actual impressions from these plates are given in Gough's Sep. Mon.

BRITISH MUSEUM. I. The Head of a bishop or abbot, c. **1360**, under fine canopy, with soul, saints, &c., part of a large quadrangular foreign brass obtained from some continental church by the late Mr. A. W. Pugin, pp. 18, 20, 74. *Boutell's Series; Gent. Mag.*, vol. xxx. N.S., 1848, p. 600. II. Thos. Qvythed, "magest' Terci' isti' collegii," c. **1460** (?), hf. eff. of a priest surrounded by inscr., on a circular plate, sm., on reverse a pair of compasses; from Eton Coll. (?) III. A Civilian, c. **1480**, mutil. IV. Head of a female eff., c. **1490**. V. Upper part of a man in tabard, c. **1550**, head gone. Perhaps for Ralph, fifth son of Sir John Fitz William, of

Sprotborough, or Thos., fifth son of Sir Wm. Fitz William, of Gainspark; see the notice by Mr. Walford in Arch. Journ., vol. xii. p. 82. VI. Three Evang. symbs. on reverse of one part of a sh. Printings of brasses now lost (see p. 250), from Marlow, Bucks.; Broxbourne, Herts.; St. Helen's, London; Ingham, Norfolk; St. Mary Magdalen, Oxford; Great Livermore, Suffolk, &c., are preserved in the Printroom. Notices of these brasses will be found in the List.

CASSIOBURY HOUSE, HERTS. A Civilian and w., c. 1530, p. 128.

CHICHESTER MUSEUM. *Two hands holding a heart inscribed "ihc," from a tomb in the Cathedral.

MR. HEN. DAY, IPSWICH. *Two Shs. from St. Mary Tower Ch.

H. N. DIAMOND, ESQ. (?) Upper part of a man in tabard, c. 1520, with arms of Brewse, &c. Probably from some Ch. in Sussex (Earnley ?).

—— EDLIN, ESQ., CAMBRIDGE. I. The B. V. Mary kng. at a desk, c. 1470 (?). *Anastatic Drawing Soc.*, vol. for 1855. II. A Man in arm., c. 1530, pecul., 19 in. III. A Lady, c. 1530, pecul., 17½ in., belonging (?) to No. II.

C. FAULKNER, ESQ., DEDDINGTON, OXON. Inscr. lately at Hooknorton, 1497 (see Appendix B.), p. 259.

MR. FISHER, NORWICH. A Sh., from Toft Monk's, Norfolk.

A. W. FRANKS, ESQ., BRITISH MUSEUM. Inscr. to John Bowes, rector of Aldebury, 1517.

GOODRICH COURT, HEREFORDSHIRE. A Man in arm., c. 1480, p. 197. Said to be from Sawbridgeworth, Herts.

REV. H. B. GREENE, LONGPARISH, HANTS. A Man in arm., of the Compton fam., and w., c. 1500, qd. pl., formerly at Netley Abbey, pp. 21, 115.

J. J. HOWARD, ESQ., LEE, KENT. A Shield.

REV. F. G. LEE, LUNSFORD, near MAIDSTONE. A Priest with chalice, c. 1520, 15 in., p. 124. Purchased near Aylesbury.

J. D. LLEWELYN, ESQ., PENLLEGARE. Mathew Johnes, of Nydvevch, 1623, and w. Mary, 1631, 10 oleg. vv.; their son, Marmaduke Matthewes, pos.; on it are scratched the words "Ex Rapacibus Sacralegiorum manibus fœliciter (?) M....ne, recuperavit 1660," qd. pl.

LYNN MUSEUM. Two Shs., from Blackburgh Priory, 15th cent.

REV. C. R. MANNING, DISS. I. Inscr. to Simon, second son of John Throkmarton, of Southelmham, in Suffolk, second son of Thos. Throckmarton, of Throkmorton, Worcestershire, 1527. II. Inscr. to Margt., dau. of John Throkmarton. III. Inscr. to Alice, w. of Wm. Bumpsted, Gent.

*—— MARLBOROUGH. Four Eng. vv. to Robt. Weare, "otherwise

Browne," seven tymes mayor, **1570**, from SS. Peter and Paul, Marlborough. See Kite's Br. of Wilts., p. 59.

MUSEUM OF ŒCONOMIC GEOLOGY, LONDON. Lodewyc Cortewille, **1504**, and w. Dame Colyne Van Caestre, 1496, large, Flemish, qd. pl., pp. 20, 261.

REV. O. NARES, ARCHDEACON OF BRECON. A Priest, c. **1370**, hf. eff., found in the ruined chapel of St. Nonita, near St. David's.

HON. R. C. NEVILLE, AUDLEY END, ESSEX. I. A Finial, c. **1380**. II. Eight Sons, c. **1450**. III. Two Sons and 6 daus., c. **1520**. IV. A Son, c. **1580**. V. Two Evang. symbs. VI. An Inscr., "Te ergo quesimus tuis famulis subveni, quos presioso sanguine redimisti." VII. Mcht.'s Mk. and initials G. (or T.) L.

J. B. NICHOLS, ESQ., LONDON. I. Rich. Rudhall, "decretorum Doctor," sub-collector to the Pope, archdeacon of Hereford and canon residentiary, **1476**, in cope, with mutil. canopy, and SS. Kath., Geo., Rich., Ethelbert, John Bapt., Leonard (?), Michael, inscr. lost, p. 77. II. A Man in arm., c. **1480**, with arms of Heveningham. III. John Stockton, mayor of Hereford, **1480**, inscr. lost, p. 132. IV. Mr. Rich. Burghchyll, "instructor gramatice istius Civitat'," **1492**. V. Alice, w. of Wm. Curteys, notary, **1499**, from Necton, Norfolk. VI. A Priest, with chalice and wafer, c. **1520**; to it belongs (?) an inscr. to Wm. Lyster, rector: a person of this name resigned the vicarage of Roydon, Essex, in **1499**. VII. Portions of the canopy of the brass of Wm. [not John] Porter, S.T.B., warden of New Coll., Oxford, canon residentiary of Hereford, **1524**, p. 104. VIII. John Bell, bp. of Worcester, **1556**, lower part of eff. and inscr. lost, from St. James', Clerkenwell, pp. 71, 73. IX. Wm. Wilson, Gent., of Wellsbourne, Lincolnshire, dec. at Windsor Castle, **1587**, and w., with sh., inscr. lost. X. Inscr. to Wm. Hotale, Esq., **1432**. XI. Inscr. to Thos. Themylthorp, **1526**, and w. Joan. XII. Inscr. to Alice Samson, pecul. XIII. Inscr. to John Thomson, B.D., prebendary of Windsor, chaplain in ordinary to Queen Elizth., **1571**, æt. 51, 10 Eng. vv., mutil. XIV. Inscr. to Anth. Russhe, S.T.D., dean of Chichester, canon of Windsor, chaplain to the Queen, **1577**, æt. 40. XV. Various Frags., five daus., c. **1480**, shs. with mcht.'s mks. and with initials N. H., portions of canopies, &c. XVI. †An Inscr. to one of the Naunton family, with figures of a thirsting hart and dying swan, 17th cent., from Letheringham. *Nichols' Leic.*, vol. iii. pt. i. pl. lxxv. p. 515 (printed from the actual brass). Nos. I., III., IV., VII., and X. are from Hereford Cathedral; Nos. IX., XIII., and XIV. from St. George's Chapel, Windsor.

NORWICH MUSEUM. Two Frags., from St. Mary Coslany, and St. Stephen's, Norwich (see the List, pp. 152, 146).

OXFORD ARCHITECTURAL SOCIETY. A Lady, c. 1530, sm., probably by a Suffolk artist.

†—— SMITH, ESQ., RADBROOK, near SHREWSBURY. I. A Civilian, c. 1520. II. A Civilian, c. 1520. III. A Lady, c. 1520. IV. A Civilian and w., c. 1530. See "Notes and Queries," vol. xi. p. 499. See p. 258.

CHRISTOPHER SMYTH, ESQ. (?) A Lady in heraldic mantle, kng., c. 1540; on reverse the head of a female Saint under a canopy, Flemish.

SOCIETY OF ANTIQUARIES. I. A Crown Keeper in arm., pecul., 20¼ in., c. 1480, pp. 127, 196. *Proceedings of Soc. of Antiq.*, vol. iv. 1857, p. 71. *Introd.*, p. 127 (det.) II. A Lady in hat, c. 1590, 16½ in., feet lost. III. Inscr. to Margt., dau. of Edm. Dawtrey, Esq., w. of Sir John Erncle, chief justice of the common pleas, 1518, 16 in. by 5 in. IV. A Sh., on reverse some sons, c. 1470.

MR. TUFTON, SKIPTON CASTLE. A Man in tabard, mutil., Hy. Trin., and 2 shs., c. 1560, pecul., part of a mur. brass once at Skipton Church, probably to Hen., 2nd earl of Cumberland, 1569, and 2nd w. Anne, dau. of Lord Dacres. Two Shs., each surmounted by an earl's coronet with arms of Clifford and Russell, for Margt., w. of Geo., third earl of Cumberland. See Arch. Journ., vol. vii. pp. 304, 305.

MESSRS. WARNER, JEWIN CRESCENT, LONDON. I. A Man in arm., c. 1480, 2 ft. ¾ in. *Introd.*, p. 197. II. A Civilian, c. 1510, 15¼ in. III. Upper part of a lady, c. 1520, 16¼ in. IV. Seven Sons (one a priest), c. 1520. V. A Dau., c. 1620. VI. Inscr. to Anna, w. of Robt. ——. VII. Inscr. to Thos. Tye, Gent., 1646, 15½ in. by 8½.

REV. E. WILTON, WEST LAVINGTON, WILTS. Two Shs., one with arms of Dauntesey, on reverse part of a man in arm., and lady, kng., c. 1600; the other with arms of Sadler, on reverse part of inscr. with 4 Lat. vv. *Kite's Br. of Wilts.*, p. 82.

See also the account of brasses at Wavendon, Bucks. (Addenda); Crowan, Cornwall; Upminster and Wimbish, Essex; Northleach, Glouc.; Clehonger, Hereford; Laund Abbey, Leic.; Edmonton, Middx.; Queen's Coll., Oxford; Halesworth, Suffolk; Camberwell, Cobham, Sanderstead, Weybridge, and West Molesey, Surrey. A Sh., with the arms of Carew imp. Chapman, probably from Stone, Kent, is in the possession of Mr. Thos. Bateman, Youlgrave, Derbyshire.

236 PRIVATE POSSESSION, MUSEUMS, &c.

The writer has been unable to ascertain the localities of the following brasses:—A Civilian and w., c. **1480**, with a hand pointing to a scroll, "Lerne to dee & lif eu'." A Man, in arm., and w., in heraldic dresses, arms on a cross, 5 mullets pierced, and a chev. betw. 3 birds' legs, an escutcheon of pretence. *Jane (Coltropp), w. of Sinolphus Bell, Esq., **1631** (?), æt. 62, with chil., mur., from Norfolk (?). Dorothy Alleine, **1584**, æt. 3, head gone, sm., 10 Eng. vv. beginning "A litle impe here buried."

APPENDIX A.

A LIST OF SOME MODERN BRASSES, ENGRAVED PRINCIPALLY BY MESSRS. JOHN HARDMAN AND CO., OF BIRMINGHAM, AND MESSRS. J. G. AND L. A. B. WALLER, OF LONDON.

The dates indicate the year of decease, the initials (H., W.) are those of the artists; brasses of which the design is not stated are chiefly inscriptions on tablets, with crosses, armorial bearings, monograms, &c.

Bedfordshire.—HAWNES. John Baron Carteret, 1849, cross, &c. (W.)

Berkshire.—FINCHAMSTEAD. Rev. Edw. St. John and w., 1850-1. (W.) WEST-SHEFFORD. Rev. Thos. Ashley, 1851. (W.) SULHAM. Mary, w. of Rev. John Wilder, M.A., 1856. (W.) THEALE. Mrs. Sophia Sheppard, eff. (H.) WANTAGE. A Cross. WARGRAVE. Col. Raymond White, 1844, angels with chalice, sword, and inscr. (Engr. by Mr. J. Wykeham Archer, London.) WINDSOR, ST. GEORGE'S CHAPEL. Duchess of Gloucester, 1859, cross. (Engr. by Mr. F. Skidmore, Coventry.)

Bucks.—ETON COLL. CHAPEL. Rev. J. G. Mountain, cross; also brass shields, &c., of the memorial of the Crimean Officers. (H.) MARLOW. Lady Morris, 1842, cross.

Cambridgeshire.—CAIUS COLL., CAMBRIDGE. Dr. Davy, 1840, eff. (A.) ELY CATHEDRAL. Geo. Basevi, Esq., 1845, eff. and canopy. (W.); Prior Crauden, cross and eff. (H.) FEN DRAYTON. Rev. Geo. Shaw and w., 1845, effs. kng. at a cross. (W.) FOULMIRE. Anna Maria Blackburne, 1843, cross. (A.)

Cheshire.—ST. JOHN'S, CHESTER. Rev. W. Massie, cross. (W.) TARPORLEY. Lieut.-Gen. Egerton. (H.)

Cornwall.—KENWYN, TRURO. Jas. L. Kirkness, Esq., 1848. (W.) PENROSE. Rev. John Rogers, 1856. (W.)

Cumberland.—CARLISLE CATHEDRAL. Rev. Walter Fletcher, angels with scroll. (H.) IRTHINGTON. Robt. Bell. (H.) WETHERAL. Hen. Howard, Esq., and w., cross. (H.)

Derbyshire.—ASHBOURN. Constance M. Watts Russell, 1847, cross. (W.)

Devonshire.—BARNSTAPLE. Thos. Salmon, Esq., and w., 1818—1847, cross. (W.) BICTON. John Baron Rolle, cross. (H.) DARTMOUTH. Three inscrs. to the Hunt family, 1800—1849. (H.)

GITTESHAM. Rev. Thos. Putt, 1814. (W.) HEAVITREE. Rev. A. Atherley, off., 1857. (W.) KITLEY. Edm. P. Bastard, Esq., and w., 1833-38. (W.) MAMHEAD. Sir Robt. Wm. Newman, bart., 1848; Sir Robt. L. Newman, bart., 1851. (W.)

𝔇𝔬𝔯𝔰𝔢𝔱𝔰𝔥𝔦𝔯𝔢. — MELBURY. Brig.-Gen. Thos. Fox Straugways, K.C.B., 1854. (W.) MORETON. Jas. Frampton, Esq., and w., 1844, 1855. (W.) CAUNDLE-PURSE. Lieut.-Col. Huddleston, off. kng. (H.) SHERBOURN ABBEY. Walsingham Gresley, 1633, cross; Countess of Bristol, 1658, cross; Earl Digby, 1656, off. (W.)

𝔊𝔩𝔬𝔲𝔠𝔢𝔰𝔱𝔢𝔯𝔰𝔥𝔦𝔯𝔢.—BRISTOL, SS. LEONARD AND NICHOLAS. Rev. John Eden, 1840. (W.) MITCHELDEAN. (W.) NEWENT. —— Onslow. UPPER SLAUGHTER. Rev. Francis Edw. Witts. (W.)

𝔥𝔞𝔪𝔭𝔰𝔥𝔦𝔯𝔢.—BIGHTON. Ensign Rich. G. Deane. (W.) HART-LEY WESPALL. Rev. John Keate, D.D., 1852, cross with Agnus Dei. (W.) HIGHFIELD. Col. E. J. Crabbe, crucifixion, with bust, &c. (H.) LAVERSTOCK. John Portal, Esq., 1848, tablet held by angels. (W.) PORTSWOOD. Harriet Louisa, w. of Col. Crabbe, 1848, off.; Arthur Brandon, architect, 1847, cross (see Leicester). (W.) RYDE, I. OF WIGHT. Lieut. Kent, R.N., ship and inscr. (H.) STANSTED. Mrs. Amelia Harriet Dixon, 1816, cross; Capt. Geo. Wilder, R.H.A., 1856, cross. (W.)

ℌ𝔢𝔯𝔢𝔣𝔬𝔯𝔡𝔰𝔥𝔦𝔯𝔢.—HEREFORD CATH. Geo. Terry, Esq., and others, cross. (H.)

ℌ𝔢𝔯𝔱𝔣𝔬𝔯𝔡𝔰𝔥𝔦𝔯𝔢.—ESSENDON. Cornet H. F. Dimsdale, cross; T. R. C. Dimsdale, Esq., angels holding scroll. (H.) WARE. Rev. Hen. Coddington, 1845, off. (W.) WATFORD. Hon. Randolph Capel, 1857. (W.)

𝔍𝔯𝔢𝔩𝔞𝔫𝔡.—ARMAGH. Rev. Rich. Allott, cross. (H.) CLONDRO-HID, co. CORK. Lieut.-Col. Kyle, off. at base of cross. (H.) KILLARNEY CATH. (R. C.) Valentine, earl of Kenmare, off. in robes, rich canopy; Cath., countess of Kenmare, crucifixion and kng. off. (H.)

𝔎𝔢𝔫𝔱.—ALLINGTON. Tablet to the Bartholomew family, 1730—1810; Hon. John W. Stratford and w., 1827, 1850. (W.) BROMLEY (?). Lieut.-Gen. Sir Greg. H. B. Way, 1844. (W.) ELTHAM. Lieut. Leon. N. Malcom, 1854. (W.) PENSHURST. Hon. Viscount Hardinge, 1856. (W.) ROCHESTER CATH. Capt. Cooper, 1858. (W.)

𝔏𝔞𝔫𝔠𝔞𝔰𝔥𝔦𝔯𝔢.—BOLTON (?). Rev. Thos. Rimmer, 1848, chalice and inscr. (H.) GARSTANG. Ensign Geo. Weld, crucifixion and St. George. (H.) GRIMSAGH CHAPEL. Wm. Cross, Esq., and w., 1827, 1849, cffs. with canopy and figures of Justice, Mercy, and Charity. (W.) LANCASTER. (R. C.) Thos. Coulston and others, cross with kng. off.; Wm. Whiteside. (H.) MANCHESTER, SALFORD, ST. JOHN'S. (R. C.) Dan. Lee, Esq.; John Leeming, Esq.; crosses. (H.) PRESCOTT. Geo. Case, Esq., and w., 1836, cross. PRESTON, ST. GEORGE'S CHAPEL. Joseph S. Aspden, Esq., cross enclosing angel with scroll. (W.) RAINHILL. (R. C.) Barth. Bretherton, Esq., crucifixion, B. V. Mary, and St. John; Hon. Gilbert Stapleton. (H.) WARRINGTON. Thos. Lyon, Esq., 1859, cross. (W.) WORSLEY. Hon. Granville Egerton, 1851, cross. (W.)

Leicestershire.—LAUNDE ABBEY. Edw. and Maria Dawson, 1845. (W.) LEICESTER, ST. MARY'S. Arthur Brandon, architect, cross. (W.)

Lincolnshire.—BOSTON. Rev. John Cotton. (H.) LINCOLN, ST. ANN'S. Humph. Sibthorp, Esq., 1815, entombment; Susannah Sibthorp, 1826, Rebecca at the well. (W.) SLEAFORD. Wm. Welby, Esq. (H.)

Middlesex.—KENSAL GREEN CEMETERY. Lady Frances Cole, 1847, cross. (W.) LONDON, ST. ANDREW'S. Vicesimus Knox, Esq., bencher of Lincoln's Inn, eff. (H.) LONDON, HY. TRINITY, SLOANE STREET. Louisa Grace Cornwall, 1856. (W.) WESTMINSTER ABBEY. Dr. Monk, bp. of Gloucester, 1856; eff. with canopy; Sir Robt. T. Wilson and w., effs. with canopies; Robt. Stephenson, Esq., C.E., eff. with circles shewing locomotive engine, Menai tubular bridge; John Hunter, Esq., inscr. with canopy, &c. (All by H.)

Monmouth.—LLANOVER. Mrs. F. L. H. Berrington, cross, copied from that at St. Columb, Cornwall. (H.)

Norfolk.—FELTWELL. Rev. Wm. Newcome, 1846, eff. under triple canopy. (W.)

Northamptonshire.—CARLTON. Lady Palmer, cross. (H.) GRAFTON UNDERWOOD. Lady Gertrude Fitzpatrick, 1841, kng. eff. with cross and canopy. (H.) OVERTON LONGVILLE. Rev. Sam. Rogers, cross. (H.) PRESTON DEANERY. Rev. Sam. Parkins, 1855, cross with The Good Shepherd. (W.)

Northumberland.—FELTON (R. C.) Miss Laura E. Riddell, kng. eff. among lilies. (H.) HOWICK. Chas. earl Grey, 1845, cross. (W.) MORPETH. Rev. John Bolland, angels with scroll. (H.) NEWTON. Sam. Cook, Esq. (H.)

Nottinghamshire.—COTGREAVE. Ven. Archdeacon Browne. (H.) ELSTON. Rev. Hen. R. Harrison, cross. (H.)

Oxfordshire.—MAGDALEN COLL., OXFORD. Rev. Dr. Routh, 1855, eff. and canopy. (H.)   OXFORD. Rev. T. B. Seymour, eff.; Mrs. Wrangham, inscr. and canopy. (H.)   OXFORD, ST. MARY MAGD. ——, eff. and canopy.

Rutland.—OAKHAM. J. E. Jones, 1833, cross. (W.)

Scotland.—BEAULY, INVERNESSHIRE. Hon. Geo. S. Fraser, cross. (H.)   CUMBRAE COLL. CHAPEL. W. A. Robertson, Esq., kng. eff. (H.)   DUNKELD. Rev. John Skinner, dean, 1841, The Last Supper. (W.)   POLTALLOCK. Neill Malcolm, Esq., cross. (H.) ROSSLYN CHAPEL. Harriett Countess Rosslyn. (H.)

Shropshire.—SHREWSBURY. Lieut.-Col. Warren, The Resurrection. (H.)

Somerset.—BATH. H. E. Carrington, Esq. (H.)   KINGWESTON. Wm. Dickenson, Esq., and w., 1837, 1844, and Hen. Dickenson, child, 1842, crosses. (W.)   KNOWLE. Rev. John Allen, cross. (H.)   MELLS. Rev. John Bishop, and w., 1806-23, effs. and canopies; Rev. Thos. Paget, 1783, eff. with canopy; Rev. Thos. Burt and w., 1805, 1823, effs. with canopy. (All by W.)   MILVERTON. Rev. Thos. Trevelyan, 1848, cross. (W.)   WELLS CATH. Dr. Rich. Bagot, bp. of Bath and Wells, 1854, cross, pastoral-staff, &c.; Dr. Edm. Goodenough, dean, 1845, cross, &c. (W.) WELLS, ST. CUTHBERT. Rev. Hen. W. Barnard, vicar, 1855, The Good Shepherd, &c.; also in the CATH. a cross to the same. (W.) YEOVIL. Capt. Prowse. (H.)

Staffordshire.—ALTON (R. C.) John, 16th earl of Shrewsbury, eff. in robes, 1852, with canopy. (H.)   ASTON. Humph. Stanley, rector, 1557, cross; Rev. John Sneyd, rector, 1835, cross and hf. eff. (W.)   BREWOOD. Rev. Wm. Richmond, eff. with canopy. (H.) HANDSWORTH (R. C.) Rev. Dr. Moore, kng. eff. (H.)   LICHFIELD CATH. Thos. Wm., earl of Lichfield, eff. in robes, with canopy. (H.)   Lieut.-Col. Peter J. Petit, 1852, eff. on a diaper. (W.) SANDON. Dudley, first earl of Harrowby, 1847. (W.)   STOKE-UPON-TRENT. Thos. Minton, Esq. (H.)

Suffolk.—BURY ST. EDMUNDS, ST. MARY'S. Arthur Walsham, 1854. (W.)   FLIXTON. Members of the Adair family, 1859, angel holding scroll. (W.)

Surrey.—ALBURY. Five crosses with inscrs. to Malcolm Hen., Arthur Hen., Hen., Hen., and Lady Henrietta Drummond. (H.) HAM. Admiral Sir Hyde Parker, C.B., and w., 1854; Capt. H. Parker, R.N., 1854. (W.)   SOUTHWARK, ST. GEORGE'S CATH. (R. C.) Wm. Bernard, Lord Petre, 1857, cross; Geo. Hodges, 1843. (H.)   Rev. John Whebb, dec. at Balaclava 1854, battlefield, &c.   WINDLESHAM. Rev. Edw. Cooper and ws., 1807, cross. (W.)

Sussex.—CATSFIELD. Serjeants Bridgland and Powell, Corporal Finlay, and Private Beeney, 1855. (W.)   CHICHESTER (R. C.) Anth., earl of Newburgh, cross. (H.)   LEWES. Dr. G. A. Martell, 1853. (W.)

Wales.—ABERGELE. Rev. Rich. Jackson, cross. (H.)   GRESFORD. Rev. Christopher Parkins and w., 1843, effs. with canopy. (W.)   Lady Broughton, angels holding scroll. (H.)   HAVERFORDWEST. Eliza, Baroness Milford; Rich., Baron Milford. (H.)   LLANILAR. John Williams, Esq., inscr., canopy, &c. (H.)   MACHYNLLETH. Mrs. Jane Gilbertson, 1810, kng. eff. (W.)   NORTHOP. Rev. Rich. Howard and daus., kng. effs. (H.)   RUTHYN. Ven. Archdeacon Newcome, cross. (H.)   TREFIR, ABERDOVEY. Three chil. of Capt. Thruston, R.N., effs. (W.)

Warwickshire.—COUGHTON. Sir Thos. Throckmorton, bart., cross. (H.)   COVENTRY, HOLY SACRAMENT CH. Wm. F. Patterson, Esq., and w., 1843, cross. (W.)   DUNCHURCH. Elizth., w. of Rev. John Sandford, archdeacon of Coventry, cross; Dan. Augustus, their son, cross. (W.)   KENILWORTH (R. C.) Lieut. G. W. Turville, cross. (H.)   LEAMINGTON (R. C.) Mrs. E. Bisshopp, cross. (H.)   NEWNHAM REGIS, LORD SCOTT'S CHAPEL. Mrs. Audrey Leigh, eff. with canopy. (H.)   OSCOTT COLL. (R. C.) Rev. bp. Milner, eff. (H.)   RUGBY SCHOOL CHAPEL. Mrs. J. F. Cartwright, cross. (H.)   RUGBY (R. C. CH.) Captn. Hibbert, w., and chil., kng. effs. (H.)   SHERNBOURN. Sam. Ryland, Esq.

Wiltshire.—ASHTON, ROOD. Mrs. M. A. Long, inscr. and canopy. (H.)   BISHOPSTOKE. Geo. Markham, 1846.   BOWOOD. John R. Seymour, Esq. (W.)   BURBAGE. Rev. J. Shepherd Gale. (W.)   CALNE. Markham Heale, Esq., cross.   DEVIZES, ST. JOHN'S. Mary Maskell, 1847, cross. (W.)   KNOYLE. Hen. Seymour, Esq. (W.)   SALISBURY CATH. John Britton, Esq., 1857, angels holding inscr. under canopy. (H.)   Dr. Francis Lear, dean, 1850. (W.)   Louisa Mary, w. of Edw. Denison, bp., 1841.

Worcestershire.—CLAINES. Capt. Sanderson, R.N. (H.)   CORTON. John Merry, Esq., cross. (H.)   DODDERHILL. W. H. Ricketts, Esq. (H.)   DUDLEY (R. C.) Rev. Geo. Fox, eff. with canopy. (H.)   HANLEY (R. C.) Valentine Brown, earl of Kenmare, crucifixion and kng. eff.; Thos. C. Hornyhold, Esq., kng. eff. (H.)   KIBBISFORD. Capt. F. W. Ingram, 1843, eff. with canopy. (A.)   KIDDERMINSTER. Joseph Lea and others. (H.)   MADRESFIELD. John Reginald, earl Beauchamp. (H.)   MALVERN. Rev. Franc.

Dyson, kng. eff. (H.) SPETCHLEY. Robt. Berkeley, Esq., kng. eff.; Mrs. Berkeley, angels with scroll. (H.) STOURBRIDGE (R. C.) Rev. Mich. Crewe, eff. (H.) WORCESTER CATH. Rev. Canon St. John, cross. (H.)

Yorkshire.—ECCLESFIELD. J. K. Booth, Esq., M.D. HAREWOOD. Wm. Lascelles, 1851, cross. (W.) MIRFIELD. Thos. Wheatley, Esq., cross. (H.) THIRSK. Wm. Hen., viscount Downe, 1856, cross. (W.) YORK MINSTER. Officers of the 19th Regt. who fell in the Crimean War, 1854-5, resurrection, angels, warriors of Holy Scripture, &c. (H.)

MISCELLANEOUS.

SIMLA, UPPER INDIA. Col. A. S. H. Mountain, C.B., 1854. (W.) FEROZESHAH. Officers of Lord Hardinge's staff who fell there and at Moodkee, inscr. surrounded with English and Indian weapons, trophies, elephants, &c., brass now destroyed (?). (A.) *Lithographed by Mc Lean.* In NEW ZEALAND are several brass tablets engraved by Messrs. Waller, and one in the cemetery at FUNCHAL, MADEIRA. A fine brass of a Lady, with canopy, containing the works of Mercy, &c., executed by the same artists, obtained a Prize Medal in the Exhibition of 1851. *Engr.* ——. See also BLEWBURY, BERKS.; YARNTON, OXON.

APPENDIX B.

A SELECTION OF INSCRIPTIONS FROM MONUMENTAL BRASSES, ARRANGED CHRONOLOGICALLY.

c. 1330. RAMSBURY, WILTS. (from Kite's Mon. Brasses of Wilts., p. 10). Marginal.

✠ SOVTZ . CESTE . PERE . LETTERE . OV . LATON . GIST . WILL'M . LA . SEINT . IOHN . DE . RAMM . ESBVRY . PERSONE . ET . FUR . POR . SA . ALME . PRIER . ORASON . QARANT . IOVRS . ASSVRON . DE . P'DON.

1393. WANLIP, LEICESTERSHIRE.

Here lyes Thomas Walsch knyght lorde of anlep and dame kat'ine his wyfe whiche in her tyme made the kirke of Anlep and halud the kirkyerd first in wurchip of god and oure lady and seynt Nicholas that god haue her soules and mercy anno dñi Millmo CCC nonagesimo tercio.

c. 1400 (?). USK, MONMOUTHSHIRE.

Nole clode yt [yr?] ethrode yar llcyn aduocade llawnhade llundcyn A barnour hede [bede?] brcynt apile (?) ty nebaro ty hauabe (?) Seliff sunuoeir suma seadam yske cy (?) alk(?)uske Deke kummode doctor kymmen llen a luc i llawn o leue.

This inscr. is rather indistinctly cut, and difficult to divide into words. The sense is probably as given in the following translation, which is partly taken from one by the Rev. — Evans, of St. Woolos, printed in Coxe's Monmouthshire, p. 419 :—

Here is the grave of the learned doctor, a completely learned advocate of London. He judged according to the privileges of the country (?), [or Baron of the villages of] Ty Nevaro ty Havalic. A Solomon in science; it is here at Usk that he sleeps; pleasing in counsel (?), an eloquent doctor, the place where he shone (?) was full of light.

c. 1410. EMBERTON, BUCKS., now mural.

Orate p aïa Mri Iohis Mordon als andrew quond᷑ᵐ Rectoris istī' ecclīe qui dedit istī ecclīe portos missal᷑. ordinal᷑ p͞s oculi in erat' ferr' manual᷑ p͞essonal᷑ & ecclīe de Olney catholicon legend' aur' & portos in erat' ferr' & ecclīe de Bulle= morton portos in erat' ferr' & alia ornam͞eta. qui obiit   die mens'   Añ° dñi M°CCCC°x   cuius aīe p͞iciet' deus Am͞eⁿ.

---

[a] For an account of the books mentioned in the above inscr. as being given to different churches in cases of open iron-work (Introd., p. xi.) see Maskell's Anc. Liturgy of the Ch. of England, preface; Johnson's English Canons, pt. ii. pp. 318—320, Oxf. 1851. The *portos, porteaus*, or *Portiforium* was another name for the Breviary, so called from its being written in a portable form. The *Pupillas Oculi*, by Johannes de Burgo, contained Rules and Directions for the administration of the Sacraments. The "Golden Legend" contained the Acts of the Saints, arranged in suitable order for reading on their several festivals.

On a scroll from the mouth of the effigy,—

Jon prey𝔥 the sey for ħ a pat' nost' & an auc.

1418. SHELFORD, GREAT. CAMBRIDGESHIRE, now lost, taken from Harl. MS., 2,129, fol. 131. b., or 169. b.

Hic Jacet dñs Tho. Patesley, quondam rector istius Eccle, et pbendarius de north muskam, in Ecclia Collegij de Southwell, qui istam Eccliam cum cancello et campanili eiusdm sumptibus suis pprijs fieri fecit, et ipsam (?) libris, vestamentis, imaginibus vitreis picturis, et pluribus ornamentis multipliciter decorauit, qui migrauit ad deum blt' die octob' Anº 1418.

c. 1420. THAME, OXFORDSHIRE, now nearly lost; taken from Cottonian MS. Cleopatra, C. iii. fol. 3. b., in Brit. Museum; and Anth. à Wood's MS. B. 15, 8,586, in Ashmolean Library, Oxford.

[Hic iacent Thomas Quatremayn de North Westenne Kath'rna(?) vxor eius que fuit filia Guidonis Breton et Johē vxor' eius filie et heredis] Thoē de Grey filij Roberti dñi de Grey Retherfeld' militis [qui obierūt vj die innij Anno dñi millesimo CCC xlij. Similiterq; hic iacent Thomas filius predicti Thome Quatremayn et Johanna vxor eius qui quidem Thomas obijt vj die Maij Anno Dñi millesimo CCC lxxxvi. quorum aīabz; pficietur Deus amen].

c. 1420. RALEIGH, ESSEX, now lost; from Harl. MS., 5,195, fol. 188. b.

Orate pro aiabus Johis Barington armigeri & Thomazinæ vxis eius expectantiū miam Dei qui quidm Johes obijt 8. die mensis Novembris Aº Dnī 1416 & pdēa Thomazina obijt xv die mensis Septembris Aº Dñi 1420, Quorū alabus propicietur Deus amen.

c. 1420 (?). FRETTENHAM, NORFOLK.

O cryst ihū pyte and mercy haue
On alys brunham that whylom was the wyff
Off gylys thorndon whych her y graue
And her deffende fro werre off fendys stryff
Make her partable of eternal lyff
By the Mercyt of thy passion
Whych wyth thy blood madyst our redēpcion.

c. 1420. THORNBOROUGH, BUCKS.

Hic iacet Willm̄s Bartoñ qui ob ſt in ſesto Translacōis Sti Benedicti Abb'tis Anno dñi Millo . CCCº lxxxixº et Regni Regis Rici Scdi . xiij . incipiente quando dies dñicalis accidit sup' lrām . C . hora bespar" Cuius aīe pficietur dš Amen.

1425. HIGHAM FERRERS, NORTHANTS. The lost portions are supplied from Gough's Sep. Mon.

✠ Such as ye be . such wer' we
Such as we be [such shal ye be
L'erneth to deye that is the lawe
That this liſ . yow to wol drawe

Sorwe or gladnesse nought letten age
But on he cometh to lord & page
[Wherfor for us that ben goo
Preyeth as other] shall for you doo
That god of his benignyte
On vs haue mercy & pite
And nought rememb' ou[r wykednesse]
Sith he vs bought of his goodnesse. Amē.

1437. Burford, Oxon.

...... quidem John͠es obiit in bigilia Purificacōis beatissime Virginis Marie. Anno domini Millīmo CCCC⁰ Tricesimo. Septimo. Quor" anime & omniū fideliū defunctor" per misericordiam dei. in pace requiescant Amen.

I pray yow all for charite
hertely that ye pray for me
To oure lord that syttith on hye
ful of grace & of mercye
The wiche Rode. soler b in this chirche.
vpon my cost y dede do wirche
wt a laumpe brenyng bright
to worschip god boye day & nyght
And a gabulwyndow dede do make.
En helth of soule & for crist' sake
Now Jhū that dydyst on a tre
on vs haue mercy and pite. Amē.

The former inscription is marginal, the latter is beneath the kneeling effigies of the deceased and his wife; from their hands issue scrolls, inscribed—

Mary moder mayde cler' haue m'cy on me Jon͠ Spycer',
And on me Alys his wyff. lady for thi joyes fyue.

1444. Rolvenden, Kent.

fundata fuit Hec Capella in die Scōr" Tiburcij & Valeriani Martir' p' Edwardū goldeford Armigerū in honore Scī Anne & Scē Katerine virginis A⁰ dn͠i M⁰ccccxliiijo.

1448. South Mimms, Middx.

[Hic iacet Thomas Frowick Armig. qui obiit 17 Mens. Februar. 1448 & Elisabetha vxor eius que ob—— 1100—— ac pueri corundem quorum animabus propitietur altissimus. Amen.]

Qui iacet hic stratus Thomas Frowyk vocitatus
Moribus et natu gestu victu moderatu
Vir generosus erat generosa qʒ gesta colebat
Nam quod amare solet generosi plus qʒ frequentant
Aucupiū uolucrū venaticium qʒ ferarum
Multum dilexit . vulpes foueis spoliauit
Ac taxos caueis . breuiter quecumqʒ propinquis

---

b Soler means a loft, or garret. See Gloss. of Arch., 1850, vol. i. p. 430.

> Entulerant dampna pro posse fugaberat ipsa
> Enter eos eciam si litis cerneret vmq{a}m
> Accendi faculas medians extinxerat ipsas
> ffecerat et pacem . cur nūc pacis sibi pausam
> Det deus et requiem que semp' permanet Amen.

The former inscription, now lost, is supplied from Weever's Fun. Mon., p. 592; the latter remains beneath the effigies of the deceased.

c. 1450. WHEATHAMPSTEAD, HERTS.

> Hic pater hic mater . soror hic iacet . hic quoq; frater
> Pastoris pecorum Prothomartiris angligenarum
> Vostok hugo patri . Macry margareta q; matri
> Nomen erat . simile genitus trahit a genitore
> Vinc qui pertransis . rogo femina vir puer an sis
> Vt pariter recubant . in pace precare quiescant.

c. 1450. MORLEY, DERBYSHIRE.

ffor the Sowles of Rafe Godyth Thom{as} Elizabeth Cecill and John & of theyr' Successores & for all crysten Sowles De p'fundis &c' pater noster & sancte Maria et ne nos: reqē et' nam &c' Dūe exaudi oracoēm: b{t} p{is} orisō Enelina dūe &c Johis Estathm ordeynd p{is} to be said & more writen in other diuers bokis.

c. 1450. BUXTEAD, SUSSEX.

> Here lyth grauen vnder thys stoon :
> xpine Sauage bothe flessh and boon,
> Rob't huyre sone was persoñ heere :
> moore than xxiiij yeere,
> Cryst godys sone born of a mayde :
> to xpine and Rob't huyre sone foresaide
> That owt of ys world ben passed vs frō :
> g{a}unte thy m'cy and to vs also.   Amē.

1453. CHESHUNT, HERTS., inscription and effigy now lost; copied from a rubbing in the possession of J. B. Nichols, Esq.

Ecy gist Damoiselle Jehanne Clay qui trespassa lan de grace M. CCCC. liij le xxij{o} jour de Octobre jour saint melony (?) euesque [c].

1454. SALLE, NORFOLK.

> Here lyth Johñ Brigge vndir this Marbilston
> Whos sowle our lorde ihū haue mercy vpōn
> ffor in this worlde worthily he lyued many a day
> And here his bodi ys beryed and cowched vndir clay
> Lo frendis fre what euyr ȝe be . pray for me y pow pray
> As ȝe me se in soche degre . So schall ȝe be a nothir day.

---

[c] The festivals of St. Mark, bp. and martyr; St. Mello, bp. of Rouen; and St. Moran, fell on Oct. 22nd.

APPENDIX B.

1455. Taplow, Bucks.

Here lyth Rychard ye sone and ye Eyre,
Of Robard Manfeld Squyer & Kateryne his wyfe
wyth Isabelle hys Suster bothe young & feyre:
That at xix. yeer of age. he leftc hys lyfe.
Wyth yong John his brother be the seconde wyfe:
The yeer' full complete of cristis in carnacyon
Rychard. dyde. yt. vj. day. of. Aprill . M. CCCC . I. & . v,
God reward her' soulys wyt eternall saluacyon.

On three scrolls from the effigies—

Jhū heven kyng . graunte us grace
En heven to have a place
And the trinite graunte us ther' to be.

1458. Chipping Norton, Oxon. (now lost).

Hic iacet Isabella quondam vxor Roberti Stokys . que obijt viij⁰ die Marcij . A⁰ . dñi M⁰ . CCCC⁰ . lviij⁰ Cui' aīe piciet' de' amen.

c. 1460. Ash, near Sandwich, Kent.

Prey for the sowle of Jane Keriell
Ye ffrendis alle that forth by pass
En endeles lyff perpetuell
That god it grawnte m'ey and grace
Roger Cletherowe hir fadir was
Thowgh erthe to erthe of kynde reto'ne
Prey that the sowle in blisse soio'ne.

1465. Chipping Norton, Oxon. (now lost).

Hic iacet Thomas Grene marchant qui obijt vij⁰ die Mens' Maij A͞no d͞ni M⁰ CCCC . lxv⁰ . et Margareta vx' ei' quor" aīabz picietur deus.

c. 1470. St. Alban's Abbey, Herts.

Hic iacet ffrater Robertus Beauner quondam hui' Monasterij Monachus qui quadraginta sex annis continuis & vltra ministrabat diu'sis officijs maioribus & minoribz couent' monasterij p'scripti vidclicz. En officijs bercij (?) p'oris Coquarij Reffectorarij & Enffirmarij Et in officijs subreffectorarij & su͞eru͞ couent' Pro cui' a͞ia ffratres carissimi ffunde p'ces dignemini ad iudicem altissimu͞ piissimu͞ diuu͞ Ih͞u cristu͞. vt concedat sibi suor' veniam peccator' amen.

1472. Upton, Bucks., inscription now lost; copied from a rubbing taken April 6th, 1819, in possession of the Archaeological Institute.

Orate p' a͞iabus Willi Bulstrode & Agnetis vxis eius filie Willi Porrys de bray ac pro A͞iabz Rici . Robti . Isabelle . Joh͞is . Willi . Edmu͞di . Agnetis . Thome . Rogeri . henrici & georgij libor' p'd͞cor" Willi Bulstrode et Agnetis que quidm Agnes mat' obijt xj⁰ die Aprilis Anno d͞ni M⁰ CCCC⁰ lxxij⁰ et A͞no Regni Reg' Edwardi quarti xj⁰ et p'd͞cus Willm͞s Bulstrode pater etatis l. (?)

1475. GREAT ILFORD, ESSEX, brass now lost; inscription copied from an impression in the possession of J. B. Nichols, Esq.

Here lieth ye body of Sir John Smyth sūtyme maist' of this place a good house holder a ffyne man large in almys he did worship to alle hys kynne all' ye felowship was ye merver pᵗ s' Johñ Smyth was inne . E pay to God haue mercy oñ hys soule & all Cristeñ, he passed to god ye xjᵒ day of Nouēber in the yere of Grace A Mᵒ CCCC lxxv for charite say a pat' nost' ad.

1496. DARTFORD, KENT.

O pytefull creatur c'cernyng erthly sepulture
Of katryn burlton subterrat ix day wᵗ yn June
Thowsand iiij C lxxxvjᵗʰ yer accurrent
wᵗ rychard burlton Jantilmā spows to the katryn
Expired thowsand bc
wᵗ hyer thus cumbent ask criest mā gᵃᶜᵉ yᵗ is ingent
wher thorow y prayour of theys twen schall he be savyour.

1497. HOOKNORTON, OXON., now in private possession, see p. cclix.

Orate pro aīabʒ Johīs Byshoppe et Isabellē vx' eius ...... quidm Johēs obijt vicesimo nono die Mīs' Maij Anno do...... Millmo CCCCᵒ nonagesio septimo quor' aīabus piciet' d......

1497. BASILDON, BERKS.

Hic iacet Johēs Clerk & lucia vx' eins qui quidē Johēs obijt vjᵒ die Julij Aᵒ dñi Mᵒ CCCC lxxxvijᵒ quor" aīabʒ ac aīabʒ pucror" suor" piciet' dē' amen.

c. 1500. SWANSEA, GLAMORGANSHIRE.

Pray for the sowle of sir Hugh Johnys and dame Mawde his wife which s' Hugh was Made knight at the holy sepulcre of oure lord ihū crist in the city of Jerusalem the xiiij day of August the yere of oure lord gode Mᵗ CCCC xlj And the said sir Hugh had cōtynuyd in the werris ther long tyme byfore by the space of fyve per' that is to sey Ageynst the Turkis and sarsyns in the p'tis of troy grecie and turky vnder Johñ yᵗ tyme Emprowe of Constantynenople and aftir that was knight marchall of frawnce vnder John duke of som'set by the space of ffyve yere And in likewise aftyr that was knight Marchall of England vnder the good John duke of Norfolke which John gvave vnto hym the manor of landymor to hym & to his heyrˢ for eu'more appon whose soullis ihū haue mercy.

1501. WATLINGTON, OXON., inscription now lost; copied from a rubbing in the possession of the Archaeological Institute.

Orate pro aīabus Willī Gibsson et Matilde vxoris eius qui quidem Willms obijt xᵒ die augusti anno dñi Millmo quingintesimo primo quorū animabus picietur deus amē.

1503. CHIPPING NORTON, OXON., inscription now lost.

Hic iacet Agnes Tanner quodā vxor Willmī Tanner ātea vxor Nicholai Dyar de Abyndon que q'dē Agnes obijt ixᵒ die Junij Aᵒ dñi Mᵗ vᶜ iijᵒ cui' aīe propicietur deus amen.

1513. REIGATE, SURREY.

Memorand' qᵈ in Anᵒ dñi Mᵒ CCCCCᵒ xiij Johẽs skynner Gentilman tam cũ decem libris p aĩa Rici knyght & cũ quadraginta solidis p aĩa Willi laker Ac cũ xviijˢ bjᵈ p aĩa Alicie holmeden Necnõ cũ xijˢ iiijᵈ p aĩa georgij longevile p' ipm̃ Johem̃ skynner disponend' qᵃm cũ Ciijˢ de p̃iis suis denariis p aĩabʒ parent' suor" I Honore dei omipotẽtis istud vestibulũ fecit edificari q°r" omniũ aĩar" pfciẽt' de'.

1528. HILLINGDON, MIDDX., inscription (now lost) copied from Harl. MS., No. 6,082, art. 4, p. 14.

Heere lieth Henry Stanley esquire, son of Thomas late erle of Derby, & of Anne Countesse of Derby, brother to Edward erle of Derby. wᶜʰ Henry deceassed the 29 day of June aᵒ 1528.

1533. EDGMOND, SHROPSHIRE, inscription (now lost) copied from Harl. MS., No. 2,129, Plut. liv. E. fol. 194. b. (or 145).

Of yᵉ charity ye shall pray for yᵉ soulls of ffrancis Yonge sometymes of Capnton Esqʒ sonẽ & heire of Sʳ Willm̃ Yonge kᵗ: & dame margᵗᵗ his wife dau of Rich: Eyton Esqʒ wᶜʰ ffrancis depted this worlo yᵉ last day of march yᵉ yeare of our Lo: m. cccc. xxx. iii. & for yᵉ sol of Ane late wife to ffrancis dau: of Rich chorlton of Appley Esqʒ & Elisabet his wife doughter to Willm̃ Maynwaryng of Eghtfeld Esq, wᶜʰ Anẽ deceassed xxiiii day of August yᵉ yeare of our Lord. M. be vij, of whos souls Jhũ haue mercy Amen.

c. 1535. DAUNTESEY, WILTS.

What bayleth yᵗ Riches or what possession
gyftes of high nature nobles in gentry
dattenes depuryoᵈ or pregnant pollycy
sith prowes sith power haue their p'gressiõ
ffate it is fatall on selff ssuecession
that world hath no thing yᵗ smellith not freaItie
where most assuraunce is most vnsuertie
here lieth dame Anne the lady of dauntesey
to sir John danvers spowse in coniunction
To sir John dauntesey by lyne discencion
Cosyn and heire whose herytage highlye
fastely be firmed in Criste his mancion.

c. 1500 and 1543. HALVERGATE, NORFOLK.

Here restyth yᵉ body of elisabeth yᵉ wyf of thoᵃˢ yᵉ lord scalys yᵉ worthy
Cwplũ ᵉ yᵉ dowt' of yᵉ nobyl lord bardolf I hys dayes ryth dowghty
To qwose sowle ihũ sende yᵉ droppys of yᵗ plentcuows mercy
So yᵗ aftyr yis owilatory sche abyde wyth yᵉ holy I yᵗ p'petuel glory.

On the reverse has been engraved this later inscription :—

Pray for the Soule of Roba'd Golword & Kate'ine his wyfe on whois Souls Jesu haue m'cy Aᵒ dñi Mᵒ CCCCCᵒ xliij Et p quibʒ tenentur f.

ᵈ Refined. ᵉ Whilom. (orare) tenetur," or "tenentur," for
ᶠ The desiring prayers "pro quibus whom the deceased are bound to pray,

c. 1570 (?). KILNWICK PERCY, YORKS.[g]

Thomas Wood Gentilman who in warfare hath be
He fought in Scotland in Royall Armyes thre
Lyeth now buried in this grave hereunder
Of Bulloign when it was English Clerk comptroller
Of the ward Court sixe and twenty yeres together
Depute Receyvor of Yorkshire once escheter
Clerke of the Statut in London noble cytye
Collector of Selby with tenne pound yerely ffe
For thought wordes or deeds which to God or man were yll
Of bothe he askt forgyveness with glad hart and will
He buylt th'owse hereby and this churche brought in good case
God grant his wyfe and sonnes to passe a godly pace Amen.

c. 1570. ALDEBURGH, SUFFOLK.

To you that lyfe posses great troubles do befall
Wher we that slepe by Deathe do feel no harme at all.
An honest life dothe bringe a ioyful Deathe at last
And lyfe agayne begins when Deathe is overpast.
My loving ffoxe farewell god guyde the wt his grace
Prepare thyselfe to come and I will geue the place
My children all adewe and be right sure of this
You shallbe brought to Dust as Emme ffoxe yor Mother is[h].

1581. BURNHAM, BUCKS.

The life I lead, may witnesse of my deathe
Hope in my Christ, and faithe hath saved mee
O happye I whilst yet I haled breathe
More now yea happye in the best degre
As first I liude full fourescore yeeres to dye
So last I dyed to liue eternally
Ensue that sample which I haue Begone
You that liue yet bee fathers to the poore
Enforce your selues to dooe as I haue doounc
Remember Jesus allso hath a doore.

---

i. e. their relations, benefactors, or persons injured by them, though not unfrequently found in wills, is of rare occurrence on brasses. Instances of this expression are nearly confined to inscriptions engraved by Norfolk artists, as at Salle, 1453; West Harling, c. 1490; Worstead, 1538; and formerly at Merton, 1474 (see Gent. Mag., vol. xcv. 1825, pt. ii. p. 13). The same peculiarity occurs also on the Flemish brass at Lynn, 1364; at Morley, Derbyshire, 1403; and on an original inscription, now palimpsest, at Eton, Bucks., to Walter Haugh, 1505, and wives, which, however, probably came from Norfolk.

[g] From a written copy kindly furnished by the Vicar, the Rev. M. A. Lawton.

[h] Owing to the indistinctness of the rubbing in the collection of the Oxford Architectural Society, this inscription was printed incorrectly at page 142 (No. 360) in the Manual of Monumental Brasses. From a similar cause, a modern brass at St. Chad's, Birmingham (No. 32), has the date given 1439, instead of 1839. The brass of Elizth. Horne, 1548 (No.

1584. Little Bradley, Suffolk.

Heere lies the Daye that darknes could not blynd
when popish fogges had ouer cast the sunne
This Daye the cruell night did leaue behynd,
To view and shew what bloudi Actes weare donne
he set a Fox to wright how Martyrs runne
By death to lyfe : Fox venturd paynes & health :
To giue them light Daye spent in print his wealth.

But God with gayn returnd his wealth agayne
And gaue to hym : as he gaue to the poore,
Two wyues he had pertakers of his payne
Als was the last encreaser of his stoore,
who mourning long for being left alone
Set vpp this toombe, her self turnd to a Stone[1].

1633. Henfield, Sussex.

HERE LYETH THE BODY OF M^{rs} ANN KENWELLMERSH A VERTVOYS & WOORTHY MATRON OF PIETIE WHO DYED IN THE 68th YEER OF HER AGE ANNO DÑI : 1633. HERE ALSOE LYETH THE BODY OF MENELEB RAINSFORD HER GRANDCHILD THE SONNE OF HER DAVGHTER MARY WHO DEPARTED HENCE ON THE 21st DAY OF MAY ANNO DÑI : 1627. IN THE 9th YEER OF HIS AGE.

GREAT JOVE HATH LOST HIS GANYMEDE I KNOW
WHICH MADE HIM SEEK AN OTHER HERE BELOW
AND FINDINGE NONE, NOT ONE LIKE VNTO THIS
HATH TA'NE HIM HENCE INTO ETERNALL BLISS
CEASE THEN FOR THY DEER MENELEB TO WEEP
GODS DARLINGE WAS TOO GOOD FOR THEE TO KEEP
BVT RATHER IOYE IN THIS GREAT FAVOUR GIVEN
A CHILD IS MADE A SAINT IN HEAVEN.

1636. Landulph, Cornwall.

HERE LYETH THE BODY OF THEODORO PALEOLOGVS OF PESARO IN ITALYE DESCENDED FROM Y^e IMPERYALL LYNE OF Y^e LAST CHRISTIAN EMPERORS OF GREECE BEING THE SONNE OF CAMILIO Y^e SONE OF PROSPER THE SONNE OF THEODORO THE SONNE OF JOHN Y^e SONNE OF THOMAS SECOND BROTHER TO CONSTANTINE PALEOLOGVS THE 8TH OF THAT NAME AND LAST OF Y^e LYNE Y^t RAYGNED IN CONSTANTINOPLE VNTILL SUBDEWED BY THE TURKES, WHO MARRIED Wth MARY Y^e DAVGHTER OF WILLIAM BALLS OF HADLYE IN SOVFFOLKE GENT & HAD ISSVE 5 CHILDREN THEODORO IOHN FERDINANDO MARIA & DOROTHY & DEP'TED THIS LIFE AT CLYFTON Y^e 21th OF IANVARY 1636.

429), is at Shipton-under-Whychwood, Oxon.; that of Mary Huddleston, 1581 (No. 360), at Great Haseley, Oxon. The brass of Richd. Ratcliff, 1599 (No. 385), Oxford, is at St. Peter's-in-the-East.

[1] Alice Day probably remarried a person of the name of Stone.

1648. WING, BUCKS.

HONEST OLD THOMAS COTES, THAT SOMETIME WAS
PORTER AT ASCOTT-HALL, HATH NOW (ALAS)
LEFT HIS KEY, LODG, FYRE, FRIENDS AND ALL TO HAVE
A ROOME IN HEAVEN, THIS IS THAT GOOD MANS GRAVE
READER PREPARE FOR THINE, FOR NONE CAN TELL
BVT THAT YOV TWO MAY MEETE TO NIGHT, FAREWELL.

HE DYED THE 20th OF } SET VP AT THE APOYNTMENT
  NOVEMBER 1648   } AND CHARGES OF HIS FREND

                           GEO HOVGHTON.

APPENDIX C.

A LIST OF BRASSES OF FOUNDERS OF CHURCHES, CHANTRIES, &c., ARRANGED IN CHRONOLOGICAL ORDER.

1241. Ashbourn, Derbyshire.
c. 1330. Buxtead, Sussex.
1347. Elsing, Norfolk.
c. 1350. Tormarton, Glouc.
c. 1360. Ockham, Surrey.
c. 1362. Lower Gravenhurst, Beds.
c. 1365. Cobham, Kent.
1372. Lambourn, Berks.
1380. Morley, Derbyshire.
1383. Cottingham, Yorks.
1384. Hellesdon, Norfolk.
1388. Etchingham, Sussex.
1391. Wimmington, Beds.
1393. Wanlip, Leicestershire.
—— Mere, Wilts.
1401. Balsham, Camb.
1403. East Hagbourn, Berks.
—— Morley, Derbyshire.
c. 1405. Holm-by-Sea, Norfolk.
1407. Bag Enderby, Lincolnshire.
1408. Dartmouth, Devon.
1411. Trinity Almshouse, Bristol.
—— Wixford, Warwickshire.
1413. East Hagbourn, Berks.
1418. Great Shelford, Camb.
—— Winestead, Yorks.
1430. Little Marlow, Bucks.
1435. Wandborough, Wilts.
1437. Burford, Oxon.
c. 1440. Compton Valence, Dorset.
1444. Rolvenden, Kent.
1448. Cheshunt, Herts.
1454. Haddenham, Camb.
1455. Tattersall, Lincolnshire.
—— Croydon, Surrey.
1458. Northleach, Glouc.
c. 1460. Thame, Oxon.
1461. Holton, Oxon.
1465. St. Margt., Rochester (tower).
—— Callington, Cornwall.
1467. Latton, Essex.
c. 1470. Little Plumstead, Norfolk.
1472. St. Geo. Colegate, Norwich.
1475. St. George's Chapel, Windsor.
1478. Clifton, Notts.
1481. Biggleswade, Beds.
1482. Little Ringstead, Norfolk.
c. 1485. Lambourn, Berks.
1486. Lavenham, Suffolk.
1487. Stratton St. Michael, Norfolk.
1488. Wooburn, Bucks.
1489. Stamford, Lincolnshire.
c. 1490. Ashford, Kent.
1492. Fovant, Wilts.
1494. Cowthorpe, Yorks.
1498. Week, Hants.
1499. Wells, Norfolk.
c. 1500. Northleach, Glouc.
—— Cold Ashton, Glouc.
—— Fairford, Glouc.
—— North Creak, Norfolk.
1503. Blakeney, Norfolk.
1505. Lytchett Matravers, Dorset.
—— East Grinstead, Sussex.
1509. Bolton by Bolland, Yorks.
c. 1510. Over, Cheshire.
—— Lechlade, Glouc.
1512. Shere, Surrey.
—— Guildford, Surrey.
1513. Reigate, Surrey.
1514. Heckfield, Hants.
1516. Childrey, Berks.
1518. Pelham Furneux, Hants.
1520. Worstead, Norfolk.
1523. Coningsborough, Yorks.
1528. Sefton, Lancashire.
1529. Tiverton, Devon.
c. 1530. Bradford, Wilts.
1531. Bettws near Newtown, Montgomeryshire.
1538. Aldbury, Herts.
1542. Middle Claydon, Bucks.
1543. Walthamstow, Essex.
1544. St. Mary-de-Crypt, Gloucester.
1546. St. Werburgh, Bristol.
1554. Ludford, Herefordshire.
1557. Etwall, Derbyshire.
1559. Elmdon, Essex.
1573. St. Paul, Bedford.
1574. Stock, Essex.
1581. Sturminster Marshall, Dorset.
1592. Harrow, Middx.
1598. Noke, Oxon.
1600. Writtle, Essex.
1616. Queen's Coll., Oxford.
1617. Stapleford, Camb.
1618. Ilminster, Somerset.
1627. St. Peter's, St. Albans.
1638. Backwell, Somerset.

APPENDIX D.

A LIST OF TITLES, &c., FOUND IN INSCRIPTIONS ON BRASSES.

The numerical references are to the pages of the Topographical List of Brasses.

Abbas, abbot.
Abbatissa, abbess.
Aldermannus, alderman.
Antrix, nurse, 115, 156. ?
Apprenticius, apprentice, 177 ; ad leges, barrister (?), 183.
Archarius, archer.
Archas, archbishop.
Archidiaconus, archdeacon.
Archiepiscopus, archbishop.
Archilevita, archdeacon, 4 (Biggleswade).
Armiger, esquire.
Auditor, 11, 81, 128, &c.
Aurifaber, goldsmith.
Bacallarius, bachelor (legum, in artibus, decretis, sacræ theologiæ, &c.)
Bayly, 103, 232.
Baro, baron (scaccarii, of the exchequer, &c.)
Botyler, butler, 34.
Camerarius, chamberlain.
Cancellarius, chancellor.
Canonicus, canon.
Capellanus, chaplain, chantry priest.
Capitanius, captain, 47, 58.
Carpentarius, carpenter or coachmaker, 107.
Chairman, 176.
Chivaler, knight.
Ciphorarius, sword-bearer, 49.
C(h)irographorius, engrosser, 148, &c.
Cironomon mensæ, cup-bearer, 130.
Clericus, clerk (in orders, of the signet, crown kitchen, confectionary, spicery, &c.), 11, 25, 144, 173, 218, 230, &c.
Comes, earl.
Commissarius, commissary, 168.
Consiliarius, counsellor (regis, legis, &c.), 63, 217.
Constabularius, constable, 37, 135, 150.
Consul, counsellor, 61, 212, 213.
Contra(ro)tulator, comptroller, 131.
Coquarius, coquus, cook.
Custumarius, customer, collector of customs, 101, 108, 112.
Custos, warden, keeper, 152, 162.
Dapifer, an officer who placed the dishes on the royal table and tasted them.

Decanus, dean.
Domicella, damsel, maid of honour, 137, 161.
Domina, dame, lady (see Introd., p. lxxxix.)
Dominus, lord, lord of the manor, a title also applied to ecclesiastics (see Introd., p. xcvii.)
Eleemosinarius, almoner.
Episcopus, bishop.
Faber, smith.
Famulus, servant, 70.
Firmarius, farmer, tenant, 55.
Frater, brother, 251.
Fullo, fuller, 166.
Garden, warden, 15.
Generosa, gentlewoman, 199.
Generosus, gentleman, 104 (Margate), 148.
Hospes, 142.
Inceptor artium et decretorum, 147.
Infirmarius, officer of the infirmary of a monastery, &c.
Instructor (artibus, grammatice), 94.
Jurat, 103, 107.
Justiciarius, justiciary, justice (ad placita, de communi banco, &c.)
Magister, master (in artibus, in theologia, physice, in chancery, of the horse, &c.), 31, 88, 142, &c.
Major, mayor.
Marescallus, marshall, 16, 17, 212.
Medicus, physician.
Mercator, merchant (of the staple of Calais, &c.)
Mercenarius, tradesman (?), 152.
Mercerarius, mercerus, mercer.
Miles, knight.
Mulier, lady in waiting (?), 206.
Notarius, notary.
Officialis, official.
Ostiarius, or Hostiarius, doorkeeper, 18, 128, 199.
Pannarius, draper.
Patronus, patron (of church, &c.)
Pelliparius, tanner, 105.
Penitenciarius, penitenciary, 132.
Pennerarius, pennon-bearer, 81.
Persone, parson.

APPENDIX D. 255

Pincerna, cup-bearer, 9, 173.
Portitor arcus, bow-bearer, 155.
Portman, 188.
Prepositus, provost.
Prebendarius, prebendary.
Presbyter, priest.
Preses, presidens, president.
Presul, bishop.
Pretor, 201.
Prior.
Priorissa, prioress.
Proquæstor (aulæ), 14.
Professor (sacræ theologiæ, juris civilis, &c.)
Prothonotarius, prothonotary, 155.
Receptor, receiver, 38.
Refectorarius, an officer of the refectory.
Rememberancer of the exchequer, 199.
Residentiarius, residentiary (canon).
Sacerdos, priest, chaplain (?), 226.
Satelles, 60.
Scherman (of Hull), 228.
Scholaris, scholasticus, scholar (Sacræ Theologiæ, Juris Civilis, &c.)
Scoutmaster, 99.
Scriba, scribe, 171.
Searcher (of Kent), 112.
Seignour, lord.
Senator, 117.
Senescallus, steward.

Serjeant (of the cellar, counting-house, confectionary, pantry, &c.), 103, 128, 167, 200.
Serviens, servant, serjeant (ad legem, ad arma, scutellas, &c.), 26, 49, 11.
Sewer (Fr. *Essayeur*), a servant who tasted the dishes at the royal table, &c.
Signifer, standard-bearer, 49.
Sire, sir, a title of knights and ecclesiastics (see Introd., p. xcvii.)
Socius, fellow.
Subreffectorarius, an officer of the refectory.
Subthesaurarius, under-treasurer.
Supervisor, a surveyor, overseer, 7.
Thesaurarius, treasurer.
Trencheator, a carver at the royal table, &c., 155.
Usher (gentleman, of the chamber, &c.), 32, 38, 58, 200.
Valectus, valettus, valet, a title similar to esquire, serving-man, 16, 175.
Vexillarius, standard-bearer, 136.
Vicarius, vicar.
Vicecamerarius, 26.
Vice-cancellarius, vice-chancellor, 207.
Vicecomes, sheriff.
Vossioner, 218.
Votrix, vowess, nun, 150.
Yeoman of the crown, guard.

ADDENDA ET CORRIGENDA.

INTRODUCTION.

Page xix., line 12, for 1419 read 1483. Ibid., In the Archaeological Journal, vol. xvi. p. 210, is a description by Mr. J. G. Waller of a monumental brass at St. Mary's Hospital, Ypres, 1489, similar in design to that at St. Mary's, Lubeck; it consists of the inscription only, with the series of subjects illustrative of the Ages of life. A list of a few foreign brasses and incised slabs will be found at the end of this volume, in the prospectus of Mr. W. H. J. Weale's work on those monuments.

Page xxiii., bottom. In the chancel of the church of Ashby Puerorum, Lincolnshire, is a blue marble slab, forming a very interesting specimen of this style of foreign memorials. It represents an ecclesiastic, c. 1300, incised on the slab and habited in eucharistical vestments, of similar though plainer design to those on the well-known effigies, c. 1360, at North Mimms and Wensley (see p. xxii.) The hands are raised in the attitude of devotion, and a chalice is placed beneath them on the breast. The head, hands, chalice, and apparel at the bottom of the albe were engraved on plates of brass formerly inlaid in the slab, but are now lost.

Incised Slab with Matrices, c. 1300, Ashby Puerorum, Lincolnshire.

ADDENDA ET CORRIGENDA. 257

Above the figure is a canopy, consisting of four slender shafts supporting three tabernacles, each of which contained a small effigy of brass, probably that of a saint. These figures, as well as a marginal description of brass, are now lost, and the canopy so much defaced that its precise details cannot be distinctly made out; it is of like proportions to that on the slab at Boston, 1312 (described in the notes at pp. xxiii., xxiv.), but of less elaborate design, and is probably of about the same date. Sketches of memorials of the same description, from Boston Church, now much defaced, will be found in the Add. MS. by Kerrich, No. 6732, p. 20, in the British Museum, and it is not improbable that other slabs of the same kind may be discovered in Lincolnshire and the adjoining counties. An account of a similar memorial at Creich, in Fifeshire, is given at p. 177 of the List of Brasses. The brass plate inlaid in the slab at All Hallows' Barking, London (pp. xxiii., xxiv.), is perhaps a modern restoration.

Page xxviii., line 21, dele 'Tattershall, 1454.' Insert in paragraph just below, 'Early instances of the Norfolk peculiarities are at Sall, 1441, Blickling, 1454, Norfolk; also at St. Gregory's, 1410, and St. George's Colegate, 1472, Norwich.'

Page xxix., line 6, after 'Middleton, 1522,' add 'Lancashire; Compton Verney, 1523, 1536;' and in line 8, for c. 1545 read 1538. Line 12, for 'Bures, 1539,' read 'Acton, 1529 (?)'; make the same correction in the note at the foot.

Page xxx., line 5, for 1485, read 1487; line 7, for 1617, read 1631; line 23, for 1610, read 1616; first line of second col. of note, for 1636, read 1639.

Page xlvii., note, 2nd col., first line, for 'F. C. Carrington, Esq.,' read 'F. A. Carrington, Esq. (since deceased).'

Page xlvii., end of note d, add 'Others have lately been discovered at Cookham, Berks.; Harrow, Middx.; Wensley, Yorks.'

Page xlviii., note g, 'Other palimpsests are at Eton and Stone, Bucks.; Ipsley, Oxon.; Etchingham and Rodmell, Sussex; Lavington, Wilts., &c.'

Page l., lines 15, 16. The brass at Great Ormsby, Norfolk, belongs to the second class of palimpsests, the original effigy having been altered by shading, which is not represented in Cotman's engraving. Note i, 2nd col., line 17, for 'Herts., 1545,' read 'Herts., 1546.'

Page lii., lines 3 and 4. Sir Robert Swynborne was the name of the father, Sir Thomas that of the son; make the same correction at page clxxxvii., note n.

Page lvii., first paragraph. The slab of the brass of Sir Sampson Meverill, 1462, at Tideswell, Derbyshire, was used as an altar-slab. A stone bearing the matrix of a brass, c. 1320, marked with five crosses, exists at North Pickenham, Norfolk; see the List, p. 154. At Cookham, Berks., the altar-slab has lately been discovered: the crosses were of brass inlaid; two of them still remain.

Page lviii., last line of text, after 'from the church' add 'of Oulton, Suffolk.'

Page lxii., line 6, add 'Other examples are at Stokerston, Leicestershire, 1467; Newnham, Northants., 1467. In Owen and Blakeway's Hist. of Shrewsbury, vol. ii. p. 286, is an engraving of the brass (now lost) of a Man, in armour, and his wife, holding hands, under a triple canopy, c. 1400.

Page lxiii., line 9, after 'Shottesbrooke,' add 'Berks.'

Page lxvii., note f. At Tattershall, Lincolnshire, 1455, is a figure of St. Peter in cope and crossed stole.

Page lxx., note p; page lxxiii., 2nd col., line 3; page cxxxviii., line 17; page cxlii., line 24, for 'Trellick,' read 'Trilleck.'

Page lxxviii., line 6, after 1501, insert 'Great Coates, Lincolnshire, 1503 (on the second son of Sir Thos. Barnardston); and Whalley, Lanc., 1515 (on the eldest son of Raffe Caterall).' Last line but one, for 1522, read 1527, and insert 'St. Peter Southgate, Norwich, c. 1500.'

Page lxxix., note, 2nd col., insert '1542. John Lawrence, Burwell, Camb.'

Page lxxxiv., line 14, after 'Lydd, Kent, 1420,' insert 'Great Hadham, Herts., c. 1420.'

Page lxxxvii., line 4, and page ccvi., line 8, for 'Stourton,' read 'Moyne.'

Page lxxxix., line 5, before 'Westminster Abbey,' insert 'Necton, Norfolk, 1383;' and after, insert 'Quinton, Glouc., c. 1430;' also at line 14 add, 'At Witton, near Norwich, is the small brass of a vowess, c. 1500, and the figure of another among the children on a brass at Great Coates, Lincolnshire, 1503.'

Page xci., note, 1st col., line 1, for 'Wm. Sloughter,' read 'Sir Wm. Greville.'

Page xcii., line 2, insert 'At Broughton, Lincolnshire, c. 1370, are two effigies beneath a triple canopy.' Note k, line 2, after c. 1510, insert 'Fairford, Glouc., 1534; Aston, Warwickshire, 1545.'

Page xcvii., line 9, after 1537, insert 'Taplow, Bucks., 1540;' line 24, for 'Appendix E,' read 'Appendix D.'

Page cii., line 19, before 'Childrey,' insert 'Tideswell, Derbyshire, 1462.'

Page cvii., line 18, for 'Darrell, Bucks.,' read 'Lovell, Oxon.'

Page cviii., at bottom. The angel with the heart at Saltwood is engr. at p. 236. At end of note u, add 'At Hadleigh, Suffolk, is the matrix of a brass consisting of two hands holding a heart, with a single scroll issuing from it. The scroll having been mistaken for the indent of a snake, a comparatively modern tradition has arisen that the slab commemorated one Henry Mole, of Pond Hall, who died from the bite of an adder in the hand. See Rev. H. Pigot's Hist. of Hadleigh, 1860, pp. 60, 288.'

Page cxi., line 7, for 1460, read 1466.

Page cxiii., line 19, add, 'At Burton, Sussex, 1558, is a unique instance of a lady wearing a tabard.'

Page cxv., note q, dele 'Deerhurst, Gloucestershire, 1400.'

Page cxvi., line 30, for 1528, read 1496.

Page cxvii., line 1. The collar of mermaids may perhaps have been assumed by the earl of Berkeley in consequence of his successes over the French at sea, though his great naval victory over them at Milford Haven did not probably take place till after his monument was made at the death of his countess. See Rudder's Gloucestershire, p. 275.

Page cxx., line 15, for 1592, read 1591; and at line 17 add, 'The arms of the Carpenters' Company, Ar., a chevron (engr.) between three pairs of compasses expanded at the points sable, are at Horshill, Surrey, 1619.' Line 30 add, 'The arms of Ipswich are on brasses in the churches of that town.'

Page cxxii., note c. The name of the bishop's champion was John de Shawell: it was said that several rolls of prayers and charms were found in the coat of red sendal painted with the arms of the bishop, which he wore over a dress of white leather reaching to the thighs. See an interesting account of the trial in Kite's Mon. Br. of Wilts., pp. 15—18.

Page cxxv., line 8, for 'These kind of brasses,' read 'Brasses of this kind.'

Page cxxviii., line 11, insert 'All,' before 'Hallows.'

Page cxxx., line 5, for 'Working,' read 'Woking.'

Page cxli., end of line 8, add, 'and at St. Cross, Winchester, 1382.'

ADDENDA ET CORRIGENDA.

Page cxlvi., note i, add, 'also at Emneth, Cambridgeshire; Norton Disney, Lincolnshire.'

Page cl., end of line 12, add, 'The sollerets on the lately discovered effigy at Methwold, Norfolk, 1367, furnish another instance of this kind of defence.'

Page clxvi., lines 21, 22, dele 'Dartmouth, Devon, 1403; and Baginton, Warwickshire, 1407.'

Page clxxi., line 2, for 'Lovell, Oxon.,' read 'Dayrell, Bucks.'

Page clxxiii., line 12, for 1415? read 1445; at end of line 16 add, 'Thame, Oxon, c. 1420.'

Page clxxv., line 4, after 'e.g.' add, 'Salle, Norfolk, 1441; St. Geo. Colegate, Norwich, 1472.'

Page clxxvi., line 3, after 1433, add 'St. Alban's Abbey, 1451.'

Page clxxix., line 10, after 1489, add 'Hurley, Berks., 1492.' Line 13, after c. 1400, insert 'Goring, Oxon, 1401.' Last line but one, 'The inscription at Northleach was at the Mercers' Chapel at London on the tomb of John Riche, 1469; see Weever, Fun. Mon., p. 401.' In note x insert 'Blickling, Norfolk, 1503.'

Page clxxxiii., note f, 1st col., line 16, for 1411, read 1418; and line 21, after 'Bache,' insert 'with saints, &c.'

Page clxxxvii., note k, 1st col., line 5, after 'at,' insert 'Stevington, Beds., 1422.' 2nd col. of notes, after line 15, insert 'c. 1405. Robt. and Thos. de Frevile, Little Shelford, Camb.'

Page clxxxviii., line 13. Instead of the gauntlets not covering the last joints of the fingers, it is more probable that the marks of the finger-nails were imitated on the gauntlets.

Page cxciii., line 6, after 1448, insert 'Crowhurst, Surrey, 1450.'

Page cxcviii., 2nd col. of note, line 3, for 'Much,' read 'Little;' and line 16, after 'Kent,' insert 'Edw. Peytoo, Esq., 1488, Fladbury, Worcestershire.'

Page ccx., to note s add 'Stamford, Lincolnshire, 1460.'

Page ccxiii., line 13, for 1510, read 1480.

Page ccxiv., note x, line 5. The brass of Elizabeth Couhyll still exists, it has been relaid in the new Church at Lee. Other small brasses of maiden ladies with flowing hair are at Bletchingley, Surrey, c. 1470; Bobbing, Kent, 1496; Writtle, Essex, 1524; Yelverton, Norfolk, 1525; Caundle Purse, Dorset, 1527.

Page ccxv., 1st col. of note, line 1, after 1530, insert 'Selling, c. 1530.'

Page ccxvii., last line but two, for 'to (?),' read 'his.'

Page ccxxi., 2nd col. of note, line 15, after 1526, insert 'Sefton, Lanc., 1528.'

Page ccxxvii., note m, for 'Lovell, Oxon.,' read 'Dayrell, Bucks.'

Page ccxxx., 2nd col. of note, line 25, for 'Leicestershire,' read 'Lincolnshire.' Other instances of brasses of clergymen after the Reformation are at Sturminster Marshall, 1581, Piddlehinton, 1617, Dorset; Tedburn St. Mary, Devon, 1613.

Page ccxxxii., line 17, for '1527, Kent,' read '1524, Kent,' and add 'Cossington, Somerset, 1524.'

Page ccxxxiv., note d, for 1508, read 1507, and dele the rest of the note.

Page ccxliii., note n, line 5, for 'Salop,' read 'Staffordshire.'

Page ccxlv., line 12, and page cclii., 2nd col. of note, line 12, for 'Albury,' read 'Aldbury.'

Page ccli., first line, for 'bequeathed to,' &c., read 'purchased by the British Museum, at the decease of the late D. E. Davy, Esq.'

ADDENDA ET CORRIGENDA.

Page cclviii., end of line 4, add, 'A similar desecration took place at St. Nicholas, Great Yarmouth: "In this church there are a great many antient stones, whereon are no inscription, but matrices or moulds of various forms, wherein plates of brass have been fixed; all which plates were, by an order of an assembly in 1551, delivered to the bailiffs of this town, to be sent to London, to be cast into weights, measures, &c., for the use of the town." Swinfen's History and Antiquities of Great Yarmouth, 1772, p. 885, quoted in a paper on Lost Brasses by the Rev. C. R. Manning.'

Page cclxi., 2nd col. of note, line 6, for 'prête,' read 'prêtre.'

Some other errors of minor importance are corrected in the List.

LIST.

Bedfordshire.—HIGHAM GOBION. I. Kath., eldest dau. of Hen. Butler, Esq., of Brantfeld, Herts., and w. of John Browne, Esq., of Flamberts, Essex, 1602, æt. 37, with 8 sons and 6 daus. II. Jane, dau. of Sir Hen. Butler, 1603, and w. of Edw. Cason, Esq., with 2 chil., Julian (dec.) and Hen. WIMINGTON. No. III. is engr. in *Hewitt's Anc. Arms and Arm.*, vol. iii. No. 73, p. 433.

Berkshire.—BASILDON. John Clerk, 1497, and w. Lucy, sm., see Appendix B. BURGHFIELD. Correct, I. Nich. Williams, Esq., 1568, æt. 36, in arm., and 2 ws., Elizth., dau. of Robt. Hawkes, of Iver, Bucks. (eff. lost), and Mabel, dau. of Rich. Staverton, Esq., of Warfield, Berks., 1604, inscr. lost, 16 Eng. vv. left, now mur., C. INSCR. II. Reynolde Butler, yeoman, 1589, and w. Alice, 1612, and chil., Raynold 1565, Anne 1565, Alice 1561, John 1559, John 1562. COOKHAM. No. I., the w. is lost. No. III. On reverse of the lower part of the fem. eff. is part of a foreign brass, the top of the head of an eff., with diaper and portion of canopy. also part of an inscr. on the marg. inscr., 14th cent. (?) Add, No. V. Rich. Babham, Esq., 1527, and w., mur. An altar-slab with the crosses of brass inlaid, all lost but two, has been discovered at the late restorations. STANFORD DINGLEY. Add, II. John Lyford, citizen and mcht.-taylor of London, 1610, æt. 71; he was born at Stanford, and had 18 chil., N.A. III. A Civilian, c. 1620, kng., sm. WINDSOR, ST. GEORGE'S CHAPEL. No. II. is engr. in *Nichols' Leic.*, vol. ii. pt. i. pl. xv. p. 41.

Buckinghamshire.—ASTWOOD. For 'Chibnale,' read 'Chivnale.' CHICHELEY, No. I. On reverse of a sh. is part of an Eng. inscr. LECKHAMPSTEAD. Regenold Tylney, Gent., sole heir to the manor, second son of Ralph Tylney, citizen and alderman of London, 1506, below effs. of 3 of his sisters (?), Elsebeth, Johan, Johan, C., dele the description at p. 30, line 38. LUDGERSHALL. Line 1, dele 'and chil.;' the brass was engr. c. 1600. SAUNDERTON. Dele the comma at end of first line. STONE. No. II. On the reverse is an eff. and inscr. to Christopher Thorp, 1514 (?). Some brasses are said to have been lost at the late restorations. STOW. I. For 'Anna Saunders,' read 'Alice Saundres;' and line 3, for 'Pemston,' read 'Peniston.' THORNBOROUGH. I. Wm. Barton, 1389, and w., engr. c. 1420, see Appendix B. INSCR. II. John Crowche, chaplain, "qui quondā hic celebrauit p aīabȝ Johis Barton senioris et Junioris," 1473, "Ira dnicali C." TYRINGHAM. No. I. is now outside the Church. *WAVENDON. I. Rich. Saunders, Gent., and w. Elizth., 1596, with 4 sons and 3 daus., the fem. effs. lost, loose at the Rectory, 1860. INSCR. II. Rich. Saunders, whose ancestors are interred at Badlestone and Potsgrave, Beds., 1639, æt. 76; he had 4 ws., Elizth. (Charge), Frances (Fitzhugh), Beatrice (Annesly), Frances (Stanton). WOOTTON UNDERWOOD. The brass is mur., S.Ch., and the inscr. cut in stone.

ADDENDA ET CORRIGENDA.

Cambridgeshire.—CAMBRIDGE, ST. JOHN'S COLL. No. I. is probably the brass of Eudo de la Zouch, brother to Lord Zouch, canon of Sarum, chancellor of Cambridge, archdeacon of Hunts., 1414.

Cheshire.—WILMSLOW. One pediment of the canopy remains over the lady's eff.

Cornwall.—QUETHIOC. Perhaps the w. of No. II. was a Polwheele. TRURO. No. I. is perhaps the brass of Geo. Singleton, and w. Jane, dau. of John Trerise.

Cumberland.—CARLISLE CATH. No. 1. Add, '*Hutchinson's Hist. of Cumb.*, 1794, vol. ii. p. 603. A Lithographed facsimile has been published of No. II.

Derbyshire.—DRONFIELD. At end of No. II., insert '*Gent. Mag.*, vol. lxv. 1795, pt. i. pl. iii. p. 477 (male eff.)' BAKEWELL. Latham Woodroffe, Esq., secretary to John, earl of Rutland, 1648, standing, 2 Lat. and 4 Eng. vv., very sm., qd. pl. INSCRIPTIONS, p. 45, last line but one, at DARLEY, insert ' Maria, w. of Rev. John Potts, 1654 ;' and for ' HUCKNALL,' read ' HACKNALL.'

Dorsetshire.—WOLLAND. Line 1, for ' Herrington,' read ' Heringston.'

Essex.—*BERDEN. I. Wm. Turnor, 1473, and ws. Margt. and Margery, chil. lost, A.T., N.Tr. II. Thos. Thompson, Gent., and w. Anne, eldest dau. of John Alderscy, mcht. of London, dec. in childbed, 1607, æt. 31, with 9 sons and 4 daus., 4 Eng. vv., A.T., N.Tr. PEBMARSH. The brass is also engr. in *The Record of the House of Gournay, by Dan. Gurney, Esq., F.S.A.*, 1848, p. 439. TILTEY ABBEY. No. I. is engr. in *Nichols' Leic.*, vol. i. pl. xxv. p. 304, fig. 26. WIVENHOE. No. I. Enclose the date, 1507, in brackets; a representation of the Annunciation is lost from this brass. UGLEY, or OAKLEY. *Inscr. to Rich. Stock, 1568, and w., effs. lost.

Gloucestershire.—LECHLADE. No. I. For 1450, read c. 1450. QUINTON. The maiden name of the lady was probably Pyrrisford. Add, INSCR. Thos. de Rous, Esq, of Ragley, 1499, and w. Matilda, worn, effs. lost, C. TODENHAM. Wm. Molton, Esq., 1614, and w. Millicent, dau. of Gilse Spencer, Esq., of Nurthen, Warwickshire, 1604; out of 12 chil. he left 3 married daus., the 1st m. to Thos., son and h. to Sir Thos. Baufou; 2nd, to Rich., son of Walter Savage, Esq.; 3rd, to Wm. Willoughby, Esq., of Normanton, 12 Eng. vv., mur., C. WESTON-UPON-AVON. The effs. of Sir John Grevill and Sir Edw. Grivell arc in tabards, and in C. PAUNTLEY. Inscr. to Elizth., a dau. and one of the 6 cohs. of Thos. Whyttyngton, Esq., and w. of Sir Giles Pole, 1543, mur., S.C.

Herefordshire.—HEREFORD CATHEDRAL. No. XI. Correct, Twelve Lat. vv. to John Stanbury, Carmelite friar, bp. of Bangor, then of Hereford for 21 years. A matrix of a cross at HOLM LACY is engr. in *Gough*, vol. i. pl. iv. fig. 2, p. 109.

Hertfordshire.—ALBURY. No. I. is now mur.; No. II. is correct. BALDOCK. Add, No. V. A Man and his w., c. 1480, in shrouds, lately loose at the Rectory. HADHAM, MUCH. Add, No. VI. A Priest, c. 1420, in acad., with cap, hf. eff., inscr. lost. ROYSTON. No. II. is engr. in *Gough*, vol. i. pl. i. fig. 7, p. 108. *SHEEPHALL. Inscrs. to Geo. Nodes, 1564, and his w. Margery, 1582.

Kent.—BIDDENDEN. Correct, No. II. Wm. Boddingd(a)m, 1579, æt. 63, and 2 ws., Juliana (with 6 chil., Wm., Martha, Mary, Joan, Judith, Rabedigia) and Anne (with 2 daus. mutil., Anna, Joanna), engr. 1584. V. John Evrenden, 1598, æt. 60, and 2 ws., Jone m. 25 years (with 4 chil., Wm., Ferdinand, Isabell, and Phœbe, daus. lost), and Jane m. 7 years. VI. Add, ' 6 eleg. vv.' VII. Bernard Randolphe, Gent., 1628, æt. 72, and w. Jane, dau. of Wm. Boddenden, and sister to Sir Wm. Boddenham, 1619, æt. 48, with 6 chil., Bernard, John, Harbert, Edm.,

Elizth., effs. on qd. plates with head on cushions, p. 215.   VIII. Wm. Randolph, Gent., æt. 52, and w. Elizth., dau. of Stephen Curtis, Gent., of Tenterden, æt. 40, both dec. 1641, and left 8 chil., Barnard, Wm. (effs. lost), Elizth., Jane, Mary, Sarah, Susan, Margt., p. 240.   BOBBING. No. III. Correct, ' Joan, maiden dau. of Jas. Bourne, Esq., 1496, partly covd., sm., N.'   BRABOURN. No. III. For 1527, read 1524. The brasses are all rel. in C.; the canopy of No. I. is nearly all lost.   GOODNESTONE, referred to at p. 100, is near Wingham.   At Goodnestone, near FAVERSHAM, are inscrs. to Myldred Pyxe, 1572, and Thos. Pyxe, 1573, C.   GRAVENEY. The eff. of No. II. and part of the inscr. of No. IV. are loose in the chest.   In No. IV., for ' Boteler,' read ' Botiller,' and remove the brackets.   There is a matrix of a Man in arm., with one sh. (out of 4) left. Perhaps for John Martin, Esq., 1479, S.A.   Add, Inscr. to Jas. Napleton, farmer, of Graveney Court, 1625, N.A.   LEE. Add, No. III. Elizth. Couhyll, 1513, sm.   INSCR. IV. *Hen. Byrde, 1545; the brasses are rel. in the new church. MILTON. Correct, No. III. Thos. Alefe, Esq., h. of the manor of " Colsall sūtyme Rauff chechys," 1529, eff. with a son or sons lost, and w. Margt., with one dau., mur., S.C.   PRESTON, near FAVERSHAM. Nos. I. and II. are in C.   For No. III. read, ' Bennet, dau. and h. of Wm. Maycott, Gent., of Faversham, and w. of Thos. Finch, Gent., 1612, æt. 68, m. 46 years, and had a son dec. young, N.' Add, INSCR. IV. Peeter Jackson, minister for 30 years, 1616, his w. Thomasin pos. SALTWOOD. Part of No. III. is engr. at p. 236.   TEYNHAM. Nos. II. and III. are in N.Tr.; the 2 chil. of No. II. are left.   Add, IV. Wm., son of Wm. Palmer, of Horndon, Essex, and w. Elizth., both dec. 1639, marg. inscr., C.   WOODCHURCH. Correct, No. II. *Thos. Harlakynden, Esq., 1558, with 6 sons and 2 ws., Elizth., 1539 (with 3 daus.), and Margt. (with 1 dau.), once in C., loose at the rectory, Sept. 1860.

Lancashire.—WHALLEY ABBEY. Correct, ' Raffe Catterall, Esq., 1515, and w. Elizth., with 9 sons (the eldest a priest) and 11 (or 12) daus., mur.

Leicestershire.—HINCKLEY. Two (?) effs. are lost.   LOUGHBOROUGH. No. I. is left in N.Tr.; the male eff. lost, the w. and inscr. much worn and partly covd. Nos. II. and IV. are in N., No. III. is in C.   Add, V. Inscr. to Wm. Goodwine, 1592, æt. 80, S.Tr.   And end of INSCRIPTIONS, p. 116, read, *Nichols' Leic.*, vol. iii. pl. xlvi. fig. 7, p. 328.

Lincolnshire.—ASHBY PUERORUM. The chil. described as belonging to No. II. are those of No. I.   Correct, No. II. A Man in arm., c. 1560, probably a son of No. I., inscr., &c., lost. The brasses are now rel. and mur., N.   A foreign incised slab of a priest is engr. supra, p. 256.   BARTON-ON-HUMBER. Add, No. II. *A Lady, c. 1380, hf. eff., inscr. lost, N.   BROUGHTON. The central pediment of a triple canopy is left.   COATES, GREAT. No. I. For ' Barnardiston,' read ' Barnardston.' No. II. The effs. are kng., the male eff. is not in arm., the 2nd son is a priest, the 3rd dau. a nun (?), marg. inscr. is mutil.   HARRINGTON. Add, No. I. John Copuldyk, Esq., 1480, and w. Margt., all lost but fem. eff. which is loose, in mantle and pecul., C.   Add, INSCR. III. *Sir John Copledike, 1557, and w. Elizth. (Littlebury), 1552, effs. lost, mur., C.   HORNCASTLE. The 2 sons are mutil., and have part of a Flemish inscr. on reverse; there are 3 daus.   LINCOLN, ST. BENEDICT'S. Correct, John Becke, twice mayor, 1617, and w. Mary, 1620, with 10 chil., Robt., John, Thos., Edw., Roger, Augustine, Geo., and Mary, Martha, Mary (only 1 dau. on brass), qd. pl., mur., N.   A matrix of 2 crosses united by an inscr.   LINWOOD. In No. II. insert, ' 8 Lat. vv. mutil.'   SALMONBY. The date is c. 1445.   STALLINGBOROUGH. Correct, I. Sir Wm. Ayscugh and w. Margery, dau. of Sir Robt. Hylyarde, c. 1510, in heraldic dresses, pecul., sm., C. II. Wm. Ayscugh, Esq., son and h. of Sir Edw. Ayscugh, 1610, and w. Cath., dau. of Wm. Hennage, Esq., of Hainton, with 4 chil., Wm., Wm. (both dec.), Hester, Kath., no eff. of husband, C.   BAG ENDERBY. INSCRS. I. Thos. Enderby and w. Agnes, Fr., c. 1390.   II. Albin de Enderby, 1407, builder of Ch. and Tower. III. John Gedney, 1533, and w. Isabell, dau. of Edw. Grantham, of Dunham, 1536, engr. c. 1600. All in N.

Middlesex.—HARROW. No. VIII. is lithographed by *Netherclift.*

Norfolk.—BAWBURGH. Add, VI. Inscr. to Robt. Tylney and w. Isabella. FRENZE. No. X. is engr. in *Cotman*, vol. ii. pl. lxxxiii. p. 43.   HELLESDON. No. I. Add, ' *Record of the House of Gournay*, p. 380.'   STOKESBY. No. IV. The upper half of the eff. in acad. is loose in Ch. chest.   Add, VIII. Inscr. to Dorothy, dau. of John Berney, of Redham.   NORWICH, DUTCH CHURCH. At end of No. I., insert ' p. 30.'   BARSHAM, WEST. *Inscr. and sh. to Edw., son of Thos. Gournay, Esq., and his w. Martha, dau. of Sir Edw. Lewkenor, of Denham, Suff., 1641, æt. 33. *Cotman*, vol. ii. pl. xciii. p. 46; *Record of the House of Gournay*, p. 472. In the latter work (p. 408) is also engr. a matrix of a cross enclosing a sh. for Wm. Gurney; the matrix at HARPLEY (p. 154) is also engr. at p. 314 of the same work.

Monmouthshire.—USK. No. I. Add, '*Archæologia*, vol. ii. p. 20.'

Northamptonshire.—ASHBY ST. LEGERS. The brass of Sir Rich. Catesbye, 1506, in tabard, inscr. mutil., is under pews in N.A.   BURTON LATIMER. No. I. Rich. Boyvill, died c. 1510, and left a w. Gresyll.   CHARWELTON. No. I., for ' Knyhtley,' read ' Knyghtley.' The brasses are all in N.   DENE. The date of No. I. should be 1584 (?).   In No. II. the date of Sir Thos. Brudenell should be 1549, that of his w. 1557-8.   ORLINGBURY. No. I. is sm., the inscr. is lost. Correct, No. II. John, father of Hen. Max, rector, 1450.   MAIDFORD. Inscr. to John Wryght, 1518.

Nottinghamshire.—NEWARK. Nos. I. and III. are engr. in *A Hist. of Newark, by Wm. Dickinson, Esq.*, 1819, pp. 323, 324.

Oxfordshire.—OXFORD, CHRIST CHURCH. No. II. is engr. in *Gough*, vol. ii. pl. vii. fig. 3, p. 117.   SOULDERN. Add, *A Heart and scrolls.   WARDINGTON. *Inscr. to Hen. Frebody, Gent., 1444, loose.

Shropshire.—MIDDLE. No. I. is probably c. 1530, and engr. by a Warwickshire artist.

Somersetshire.—FIVEHEAD. For c. 1580, read c. 1565, and add ' rel., S.C.'

Staffordshire.—STONE. Thos. Crompton, Esq., of the honble. band of " Pentioners" to King Jas., in arm., and w. Etheldred, of the family of the Tussers of Rivenhall, c. 1600, with 4 sons and 2 daus., qd. pl., mur.; Thos. was son of Wm. Crompton, Esq., and his w. Kath., who and Lady Stannop (mother to John Lord Stannop, nephew to Anne duchess of Somerset) were brother's chil.

Suffolk.—RENDHAM. Dele ' Knyg.' The rest is correct.

Surrey.—*SANDERSTEAD. I. John Awodde, 1525, and w. Dyones, palimpsest, loose. INSCRS. II. Nich. Wood, 1586, on reverse Nich. Pury, 1585, loose.   III. Joan, w. of John Ounsted, Esq., 1587.   FARLEY. The brass is now mur.

Sussex.—ARUNDEL. No. III., for 1418, read 1448.   BILLINGSHURST. Correct, Thos. Bartlet, 1499, &c.   BODECTON, or BURTON. No. I. A Man in arm., c. 1525, inscr. lost, mur., A.T, N. Perhaps John Goring.   II. Sir Wm. Gorynge, a

Gent. of the privy chamber to Edw. VI., 1553, in arm., eff. lost, and w. Elizth., dau. of John Covert, of Slaugham, 1558, in *tabard*(!), with chil., Hen. (who m. Dorethe, a dau. and h. of Wm. Everard, Esq., dec., and had Wm., Edw., Barbare, Elizth.), Robt., dec. (who m. Mary, a dau. of Thos. Onley, Esq., and had Elizth.), —— (?) (who m. Mary, dau. of ——, Esq., of Pulborough,) 1557, Anne (w. first to Sir Geo. Delalind, of Dorset, and afterwards to Francis Browne, Esq., brother to Viscount Mountague), Thos., Edw., Custance, who dec. in their infancy, effs. of chil. all lost, mur., A.T., N. Dele the account at end of Sussex inscrs. HELLINGLY. A Lady, c. 1440, in mantle, marg. inscr. lost, large, C. HOUGHTON. Inscr. *only* to Thos. Cheyne, Gent., 1496, and w. Anna. PULBOROUGH. No. III. is now under the organ. SLINFOLD. I. Rich. Bradbryge, Gent., 1533, not in arm., and w. Denys, with 3 chil. (lost), John, Thos., Alis. II. A Lady, c. 1600, upper half and inscr. lost. INSCR. III. Edw. Cowper, Esq., 1678, æt. 38. Ch. rebuilding in 1860.

Warwickshire.—COLESHILL. Add to No. I., *Imperial Dictionary*. COMPTON VERNEY. No. I. is correct. No. II. The date should be 1536, the inscr. is mutil., the names and date lost. Correct, No. III. Geo. Verney, Esq., son of Sir Rich. Verney, 1574, in arm.; by his w. Jane, dau. of Wm. Lucy, Esq., of Charlcot, he had 1 son and 4 daus., engr. c. 1630. The brasses are in C. Nos. I. and II. are engr. by Warwickshire artists, No. III. by the same artist as those at St. Columb, Cornwall. HARBURY. The brasses are inscrs. only. ITCHINGTON, LONG. Correct, *John Bosworth, 1674-5, and ws. Ellinor and Isabella, with long inscr. detailing his charities to the parish, and directing loaves to be put for distribution on "the Communion Table Every Sabbath or Lord's day," qd. pl., mur., C. NAFTON. The monument is an incised slab, not a brass. A brass sh. left. TYSOE. Correct, I. Thos. Mastrupe, chaplain, 1463, sm., N.A. II. *Jane, eldest dau. of Robt. Gibbs, Esq., of Honnington, and his first w. Margery Pridiox, a dau. of Nich. Browne, 1598, hf. eff., rel., N.A. WESTON-UNDER-WEATHERLEY. No. I. Anne Huggesford was the w. of Gerard Danet, Gent.; the inscr. only now remains. The other two inscrs. remain.

Westmorland.—KENDAL. Correct, Alan Bellingham, Esq., 1577, æt. 61, in arm.; he m., first, Cath., dau. of Anth. Tucker(?), Esq.; and afterwards Dorothie, dau. of Thos. Sandford, Esq., by whom he had 7 sons and 8 daus., of which 2 sons and 1 dau. dec. before him; now mur. (?), N.A.

Wiltshire.—*HAM. John Hunt, 1590, æt. 90, and w. Christian; he gave £40 "to the marriage of poore maydens," at the advice of his w. he erected three almshouses at Thatcham, endowed them with £8 18s. yearly, and with house and land for their repairs, mur., N.

Worcestershire.—STRENSHAM. No. III. was loose in the vestry Oct. 1860; the inscr. is mutil. No. IV. There is an eff. of the son in arm. TREDINGTON. No. I. The marg. inscr. is nearly all lost and rel. inaccurately.

Yorkshire.—*HELMSLEY. I. A Man, in arm., and w., close of 15th cent., with 2 sons and 1 dau., worn, inscr. lost, S.Tr. Perhaps for Sir Robt. Manners(?), and w. Eleanor, dau. of Thos. Lord Roos. INSCR. II. Joan, w. of Wm. Chetwynd, 1410, "cui' aīa in sinu Abrahē requiescat amē," mur., C. THRIBERGH. †A Man in arm., 1466(?). Perhaps Arnald Reresby, 1485.

Several brasses of military effigies engraved in *Boutell's Series* will also be found in *Hewitt's Ancient Armour and Weapons in Europe*, vols. ii., iii.

INDEX TO THE INTRODUCTION.

Addresses, 87—89.
Abbots, vestments of, 69—72; brasses of, 73, 74, 123.
Academical habits, 81—85.
Acrostics, 225.
Agnus Dei, 104, 131.
Ailettes, 148.
Albe, 65, 66, 228, 229.
Aldermen, brasses of, 200, 201, 240.
Allegorical designs, 216, 217.
Almaine rivets, 234.
Almuce, or Amess, 75, 79.
Altar slabs, brasses inlaid in, 57.
Amice, 64, 65, 79.
Anagrams, 225.
Analysis of a brass, 20.
Anelace, 156, 202.
Angels, 66, 104, 139.
Annunciation of the B. V. Mary, 104.
Apostles, emblems of, 105.
Apparel, 64, 142.
Arabic numerals, 179.
Archbishops, insignia of, 69—73.
Arming-points, 150.
Arrière-bras, 150.
Artists, marks of, 25, 26, 30; modern, 261.
Austin Canons, dress of, 87.
Avant-bras, 150.

Bachelors of Divinity, Arts, and Law, dresses of, 82—85.
Badges, 113, 114.
Baguette, 186.
Banded mail, 149, 150.
Barbe, 167, 209.
Barons of Exchequer, &c., see Judges.
Bascinet, 153.
Basilard, 156.
Bawdric, 156.
Beards, 142, 154, 162, 202, 236, 239.
Belgium, brasses in, 19, 36, 261.
Bell-founder, brass of, 150.
Bishops, vestments of, 69—73; brasses of, 73, 74, 123.
Bliaus, 147.
Bonnegrace, 246.
Books, 125, 215.
Bracket-brasses, 33, 137, 173.
Brassarts, 150.

Brasses, interest and usefulness of the study of, 2—4; origin of, 5—13; manufacture of, 13, 14; Foreign, 14—23; English, 20, 21; artists of, 25—36; on the continent, 36—38; geographical distribution of, 39—42; earliest and latest, 43; criteria of date, 43—45; palimpsest, 45—51; copied, 52; restored, 53; duplicate, 54—56; used as Easter Sepulchres, 56, &c.; inlaid on Altar-slabs, 57; cost of, 57—61; subjects and classification of, 61; arrangement of figures on, 62, 63; ecclesiastical costume, &c., on, 63—89; legal costume on, 89, 90; canopies on, 91; inscriptions on, 92—100; emblems and devices on, 100—133; of the 14th cent., 133—169; of the 15th cent., 170—214; of the 16th and 17th cents., 214—248; rubbings of, 249; demolition of, 251—260; concluding remarks, 261—263.
Breastplates, 153.
Buskins, 68.
Busts, 134.
Butterfly head-dress, 171, 211.

Calvinists, destruction of French monuments by, 254.
Camail, 153.
Cambridgeshire, artists and brasses of, 29, 212, 214, 244.
Camisia, 65, 74, 77.
Canonical vestments, see Processional.
Canopies, 91, 92; 14th cent., 137; 15th cent., 175; 16th cent., 221.
Canting arms, 115.
Cap, professorial, 77, 81, 82, 229.
Cape, 82, 162.
Cassock, 77, 82.
Catacombs, 109, 131.
Cathedrals, spoliation of, 255.
Cervelière, 148, 152.
Chain-mail, 149.
Chalices, 3, 6, 123—125, 178.
Chamfer inscr., 92.
Channel Islands, matrices at, 42, 63.
Chapel-de-fer, 148.
Chasuble, 67, 68.
Chausses, 147.

Children, brasses of, 14th cent., 137; 15th cent., 172; 16th and 17th cent., 219.
Chimere, 230.
Chrysom, 220, 221.
Ciglaton, 153.
Cities, arms of, 120.
Civilians, 14th cent., 162—165; 15th cent., 200—204; 16th and 17th cents., 238—241.
Coif, 89.
Coif-de-mailles, 147.
Coins, 48, 109.
Cointisse, 149.
Collars, 116, 117, 186, 196.
Colobium, 70, 74.
Colour on brasses and slabs, 10, 112.
Contractions, 97—100.
Cope, 75—77, 228.
Copper-plate engravers, 30, 35, 216.
Coppersmiths, 26, 27.
Cost of brasses, 58—61.
Cote-hardie, 162, 168.
Couteau-de-chasse, 202.
Coutes, 158.
Crespine head-dress, 168, 205.
Crests, 113.
Crosses, stone, 5, 6; brass, 103; 14th cent., 135, 136; 15th cent., 173; 16th and 17th cents., 222; before inscr., 92.
Cross-legged effigies, 146, Addenda, 259.
Crown-keepers, 127.
Crozier, 72.
Crucifixion, representation of, 102; emblems of, 102.
Cuir-bouilli, 147.
Cuisses, 154.
Cullen or Cologne plate, 13, 27.
Cullum, Sir John, impressions of brasses taken by, 250, 257.
Cyclas, 153.

Dalmatic, 70, 74, 78.
Date, criteria of, 43—54; omission of, 45.
Deacons, dress of, 70.
Death, figures of, 112, 217, 218.
Defacement and demolition of brasses, 97, 251—261, Addenda, 260.
Demi-figures, 63, 134, 172, 218.
Demi-placcards, or placcates, 190.
Demysent, 242.
Denmark, brasses in, 38.
Devices, ecclesiastical, 100—112; heraldic, 112—121; professional, 6, 121—131.
Diapered backgrounds, 7, 9, 11, 18, 20, 22.
Doctors, brasses of, 19; dress of, 77, 81.
Dogs at feet, 125, 126, 137, 170.

Dominical letter, 95, 96.
Doublet, 239.
Dowsing, destruction of brasses by, 255, 256.
Duplicate brasses, 54—56.

Easter sepulchres, 56.
Ecclesiastics, costume of, 63—89; emblems of, 123—125; brasses of, 63, 123—125; 14th cent., 141—144; 15th cent., 181—183; 16th and 17th cents., 227—230.
Elizabeth, proclamation by Queen, 253, 262, 263.
Emaciated figures, 44, 56, 171, 218.
Emblems, see Devices.
Enamel, 7—12.
English Brasses, 20; Engravers, 21, 24—31.
Epaulières, 156.
Epitaphs, see Inscriptions.
Epomis, or Ephod, 65.
Errors on brasses, 34.
Eton scholar, dress of, 86.
Eucharistical vestments, 64—68; figures in, 14th cent., 141, 142; 15th cent., 181; 16th cent., 227.
Evangelistic symbols, 106, 222.

Fanon, 66.
Farthingales, 247.
Fermailes, 166.
Fifteenth cent., brasses of, 170—214.
Flemish and Foreign brasses, 7, 9, 13—24, 36—39, 46, 47, 72, 143.
Founders of churches, brasses of, 4, 13, 40, 123, 260, Appendix C, 253.
Fourteenth cent., brasses of, 133—169.
France, incised slabs of, 7, 9, 10, 68, 70, 75; brasses of, 9, 22, 26.
Frankelein, 163.
French inscriptions, 139, 178.
Frills, 235.
Fylfot, 109, 139, 142.

Gadlings, 158.
Gambeson, 148.
Garter, members of the order of, 81, 117.
Genealogical brasses, 3.
Genouillières, 147.
Germany, monumental effigies of, 7, 12, 137; brasses of, 12, 13, 18, 36—38; incised slabs of, 7.
Girdle, 65, 241.
Glass, painted, memorial windows of, 1, 56, 78, 97.
Gloves, 70, 129.
Goldsmiths, brasses engraved by, 30.
Gorget, military, 154; female, 165.
Groining, 138, 176.
Guarded spurs, 188.

INDEX TO THE INTRODUCTION.

Guige, 147.
Guilds, arms of, 117—120.
Gussets of mail, 159.
Gypcière, 203.

Habergeon, 156.
Halberds, 233.
Hands joined, 61, 62; held apart, 171; before inscrs., 92.
Hats, 246.
Hauketon, 148.
Haustment, 233.
Hawberk, 146.
Hearts, 107, 108, 178.
Heel-ball, 249.
Heraldic devices, 112—121; dresses, 112, 113.
Hood, ecclesiastical, 76, 77, 229; civil, 89, 162, 203.
Horned head-dress, 208, 211.
Horns on brasses, 130.
Humerale, 65.
Hunter, 129, 130.

Illuminated MSS., 31, 196, 239.
Incised slabs, 5—11, 23, 24, 30, 40, Addenda, 256.
Infulæ, 71.
Initials, 77, 132, 183.
Inscriptions, 92—100; 14th cent., 139—141; 15th cent., 178—181; 16th and 17th cents., 222—227.
Ireland, brasses in, 41, 42.
Iron slabs, 1.
Isleworth, brass works at, 14.

Jack-boots, 240.
Jambs, 150.
Judges, robes of, 89, 90; brasses of, 90, 125.
Jupon, 153.

Kennel head-dress, 212, 241.
Kentish engravers, 214.
Kirtle, 166, 205.
Knee-breeches, 240.
Knights, devices of, 125. See also Military brasses.

Ladies, 14th cent., 165—169; 15th cent., 204—214; 16th and 17th cents., 241—248.
Lamboys, 232.
Lames, 199.
Lance-rests, 194.
Latten, or Laton, 13, 26, 27, Addenda, 243.
Leaden plate, 1.
Leonine verses, 92, 181.
Lettern, effigy on, 56.
Limoges enamels, 7—9.
Lions at feet, 125, 137, 170.
Liripipes, 82, 162.

Lombardic characters, 139, 178.
London, artists of brasses at, 24, 28, 40.
Loose brasses, 260.

Mace, 126, 233.
Madeira, brass at, 39.
Maiden ladies, 205, 213, 214, Addenda, 259.
Mandyas, 77.
Maniple, 66.
Mantelletum, 81.
Mantle, judges', 89; civilians', 63, 200; ladies', 166; aldermen's, 200, 240.
Marks, artists', 25, 26; merchants', 130, 131.
Masters of Arts, dress of, 84, 85.
Matrices, 131.
Mayors, brasses of, 200, 201, 240.
Mentonière, 193, 195.
Merchant companies, arms of, 117—121.
Metallic rubber, 250.
Military brasses, 14th cent., 144—161; 15th cent., 184—200; 16th and 17th cents., 230—238.
Misericorde, 156.
Mitre, 71, 123.
Modern brasses, artists of, &c., 43, 261.
——— neglect of brasses, 257—260.
Monks, 86, 87.
Monograms, 104, 132.
Monumental effigies, classification of, 1.
Morse, 75, 77.
Mortality, emblems of, 111, 112, 222.
Moton, 191.
Mottoes, 115.
Moustaches, see Beards.
Mozetta, 81.
Mural brasses, 112, 171, 216.
Mythology, heathen, allusions to, 93.

Nebule head-dress, 167, 204.
Norfolk, artists and brasses of, 28, 170, 178, 199, 200, 212, 214, 233, 241, 242.
Notaries, 128.
Nuns, 89.

Obelisks, 6, 109.
Orarium, 66.
Ord, Craven, Esq., impressions of brasses by, 250, 257.
Orle, 185.
Orphrey, 64.

Palettes, 150.
Palimpsests, 45—51.
Pall, 72—74.
Pardon, grants of, 101, 140, 226.
Paris head-dress, 245.
Partlet, 243.
Parura, &c., 64, 65.
Pass-guards, 235.
Pastoral staff, 71; brasses of, 57, 123.

INDEX TO THE INTRODUCTION.

Pauldrons, 192, 236.
Pedimental head-dress, 212.
Pelican, 104.
Planeta, 67.
Plastron-de-fer, 153.
Pluviale, 77.
Poland, brasses in, 37, 53.
Poleyns, 147.
Pomander-box, 242.
Portcullis badge, 116, 242.
Portraits, 62.
Portugal, brasses in, 39.
Post reformation ecclesiastics, 227—229.
Posture of figures, 61, 133, 170, 215.
Pourpoint, 148.
Prioress, 87.
Processional vestments, 74—79; figures in, 14th cent., 144; 15th cent., 182, 183; 16th and 17th cents., 227, 228.
Professors, see Doctors.
Provincial engravers, 28—30, 79, 171, 214.
Pryck spurs, 147.
Punning inscriptions, 96; arms, 115.
Puritans, destruction of brasses by, 254.

Quadrangular plates, brasses composed of, 20, 21, 216.

Rebuses, 131.
Refixing brasses, 262.
Reformation, changes at, 222, 224, 228, 251.
Relief, monuments in, see Sculptured effigies.
Removal of brasses, 252.
Rerebraces, 150.
Resemblance of distant brasses, 24, 25; of male and female costume, 63.
Restoration of brasses, 53, 261.
Resurrection, representations of, 103.
Reticulated head-dress, 167.
Ring, 71, 89.
Rochet, 81, 166, 228.
Rosary, 203, 243.
Roses, 109—111, 176.
Roundels, 150, 186.
Rowell spurs, 153.
Royal vestments, 74; arms and badges, 115, 116.
Rubbings of brasses, 249.
Ruffs, 245.
Runic crosses, 5.

Sabbatons, 198, 232.
Saints, on canopies, 137, 175; on orphreys, 182; on crosses, 136; selection and invocation of, 100—102; emblems of, 104—106.
Salades, 195.
Sandals, 69.
Scale-work, 150, Addenda, 259.

Scarf, 229, 237, 241.
Scotland, brasses in, 11, 12.
Scrolls, 141, 179, 225.
Scull-cap, 63, 89, 229.
Sculls, 111, 222.
Sculptured effigies, 1, 2, 125, 126.
Seals, 4.
Serjeants at-law, 89; at-arms, 126, 127.
Shrouded brasses, 44, 56, 171, 218, 219.
Sideless dress, 166, 206.
Siglaton, 153.
Sir, title of priests, 97.
Skeletons, see Shrouded brasses.
Sollerets, 150.
Soul, emblem of, 106.
Spain, brasses in, 39.
Splints, 191.
SS., collar of, 116, 186.
Standard of mail, 196.
Stole, 66, 67, 74.
Stolen brasses, 51.
Stomacher, 247.
Student of Civil Law, dress of, 85.
Subdeacon, dress of, 68.
Suffolk, artists and brasses of, 29, 214, 254.
Superhumerale, 65.
Surcoat, royal, 74; military, 147; female, 166.
Surplice, 75, 228—229.
Surquayne, sosquenie, 166.
Swath-bondes, 219.
Sweden, brasses at, 38.
Symbols, see Devices.

Tabard, 112, 190, Addenda, 258.
Taces, 186.
Tapul, 196, 235.
Tassets, 236.
Tau-cross, 103, 232.
Tiles, effigies on, 1.
Tippet, royal, 74; academical, 82, 83; legal, 89; civilians', 162; ladies', 169.
Tonsure, 63.
Traditions respecting brasses, 42, 172, Addenda, 258.
Trinity, Holy, symbols of, 102.
Triptych, 11.
Trunk-hose, 236, 240.
Tuiles, 189.
Tuillettes, 196.
Tunic, royal, 74; ecclesiastical, 69, 78; civil, 162, 200.

Vambraces, 150.
Variations in wearing ecclesiastical vestments, 64, 67, 78—81.
Veil head-dress, 89, 166, 205, 241.
Verses, favourite, of the 14th cent., 140, 141; of the 15th cent., 179—181, of the 16th and 17th cents., 224—226.

Vervelles, 156.
Vestment, 228.
Vexillum, 72.
Virgin, annunciation of, &c., 104.
Vittæ, 71.
Vizor, 154.
Vuiders, 159.

Wales, brasses in, 41.
Wambais, 148.
Warwickshire, artists and brasses of, 28, 214, 233, 243.
Wheathampsted, Abbot, epitaphs by, 94.
Widows, attire of, 89, 209.

Wills, on brasses, 3; extracts from, 31, 50, 56, 58—61, 126.
Wimple, 166, 167.
Winchester scholar, dress of, 86.
Windsor, canons of, 81.
Wired head-dress. 171, 211.
Woolmen, brasses of, 128.

Yeoman of the Crown, 127; of the Guard, 127.
Yorkshire, artists and brasses of, 28, 186, 195.

Zigzag head-dress, 167.

INDEX OF NAMES.

ABBOTT, 62, 83, 157, 201
Abbys, 135
Abdy, 172
Abell, 216
Abere, 107
Aberfeld, 136
Acklam, 231
Acton, 89, 203
Acworth, 8
Acylton, 168
Adams, 28, 104
Adane, 83
Addirley, 203
Adene, 174
Adkins, 75
Agmondesham, 201
Ailemer, 99, 196
Aileward, 72
Airay, 172
Alabaster, 151, 186, 187
Alberd, 151, 152
Aldeburgh, 226
Alderburne, 167
Aldersey, 261
Aldewyncle, 154
Aldriche, 20, 151
Aldryngton, 166, 218
Alee, 5
Alefe, 105, 262
Alegh, 97
Aley, 205
Alfounder, 184
Alfraye, 207
Alikok, 136
Allanson, 167
Allarde, 92
Allen, Alleyne, 23, 56, 57, 113, 152, 201, 214, 236
Allington, 34, 35, 85, 184, 187, 193
Allway, 87
Alnwik, 149
Alston, 187
Altham, 132
Amerike, 66
Amherst, 102
Amondesham, 122
Anabull, 82
Anbe, 61
Anderson, 6
Andrew, 12, 15, 23, 101, 111, 156
Andrewes, 16

Anguish, 145, 152
Anne, 21
Annott, 189
Ansley, 102, 164, 231
Ansty, 35, 90
Anycll, 150
Appelton, 98, 195
Appleyard, 134, 140
Apsley, 212, 213
Archer, 218
Ardall, 60, 62
Arderne, 23, 59, 202
Argentine, 6, 32, 34
Argenton, 51
Armar, 127
Armiger, 193
Arnold, 207
Arthur, 95
Artur, 51
Arundell, 38, 39, 40, 41, 46, 209, 212, 213
Asger, 144, 145
Ashburnham, 212
Ashby, 115, 125
Ashenhurst, 182
Ashfield, 164, 167, 168, 217
Ashton, 9, 38, 112, 176, 218
Ask, 227
Askew, 122
Askowe, 30
Asplyn, 122
Astell, 226
Astley, 88, 134, 216
Astrey, 6
Atherton, 174
Athills, 138
Atholl, 91, 162
Athowe, 135
Atkinson, 173, 230
Atkyn, 87, 141
At Mere, 153
Atmore, 72
Atte Cok, 99
Atte Heeld, 165
Attelath, 141
Atte Lese, 108
Attelude, 11
Atte Spetyll, 7
Atte Sterre, 111
Atte Welle, 208
At the Gates, 145
Atwater, 30
Audeley, 181, 204

Aumberdene, 28
Auncell, 221
Aunes-fordhe, 10
Ann sly, 260
Austen, 93, 209
Avenel, 208
Avening, 67, 68
Avery, 97
Awall, 196
Awbrey, 25, 76, 77
Awdley, 7, 77
Awmarle, 38
Awnsham, 122, 126
Awodde, 263
Awsiter, 131
Ayleway, 66
Aylmer, 143
Ayloffe, 61
Aylworth, 171
Aylyff, 4, 72
Aynesworth, 125
Ayschombe, 13, 176
Ayscough, 119, 120, 263

Babham, 12, 260
Babyngton, 26, 42, 104
Bache, 83
Bacheman, 166
Bacon, 52, 127, 134, 135, 138, 143, 156, 186, 191, 192
Badby, 60, 192
Badlesmere, 105
Bagot, 190, 216
Bailey, see Bayley
Baker, 98, 168, 206
Bakthone, 84
Balam, 10
Baldry, 188
Baldwin, 19, 103
Ball, 75, 86
Ballard, 203
Ballett, 194
Balls, 251
Bampfield, 76
Bankes, 35, 125, 164, 167
Bannister, 60
Barber, 8, 10
Bardolph, 8, 64, 89, 138, 139, 176
Bardsey, 115
Barefoot, 12, 58
Barentyne, 164, 167

INDEX OF NAMES.

Barker, 10, 16, 23, 60, 134, 190, 193, 201
Barkham, 131
Barlee, 56, 78, 81, 87, 210, 222
Barloe, 84
Barnake, 63
Barnard, 3, 180
Barnardiston, 117, 119, 136
Barneby, 161
Barnes, 18, 52, 132, 226
Baron, 15, 106
Barr, 77, 155
Barratte, 75
Barrett, 52, 53, 106, 153, 158
Barrington, 61, 87, 196
Barrow, 62, 121
Barstaple, 66
Bartelot, 212
Bartlet, 207, 263
Barton, 14, 16, 29, 198, 260
Barwick, 186
Basden, 231
Baske, 231
Baskervile, 133
Baspole, 147
Bass, 75
Bassett, 39, 46, 61, 172, 181
Bate, 12, 103
Batersby, 173
Batherst, 102
Batmanson, 72
Battyll, 81
Batys, 207
Bauchon, 60
Bauldry, 92
Bawfelde, 179
Bayles, 195
Bayley, 29, 102, 113, 122, 171, 176, 220
Baynard, 221
Baynham, 60, 71, 226
Baynton, 80, 220
Beale, 104
Beauchamp, 3, 17, 97, 137, 143, 164, 218
Beaufitz, 111
Beaufo, 175
Beaufort, 20, 75, 107
Beaufoy, 261
Beaumount, 64, 65
Beauner, 66
Becke, 119, 262
Bedall, 65
Bedbere, 181
Bedell, 74
Bederenden, 99
Bedgbery, 100
Bedingfield, 131, 141, 142, 143, 153, 185, 191
Bedyll, 22, 102
Beel, 82

Beer, 98
Beeston, 104
Bekingham, 37
Belassis, 52
Bele, 85
Belknap, 89, 115
Bell, 42, 234, 236
Bellamy, 126
Bellingham, 125, 219, 264
Belsyre, 166
Beltoun, 55
Bence, 183, 191
Bendlowes, 53
Bennett, 67, 168, 175, 218, 223
Benstede, 101
Bentley, 170
Berde, 24
Berdefield, 65
Berdewell, 138, 139
Berecroft, 198
Beresford, 84, 119
Beriff, 53, 54
Berkeley, 22, 71, 115, 179, 222
Bernard, 9, 34, 56
Berners, 56, 65, 130
Bernewelt, 85
Berney, 92, 140, 147, 149, 153, 196, 263
Bernham, 231
Berry, 102, 103, 129, 141
Bertram, 162
Berwyk, 13
Beseley, 170
Best, 53, 93, 203
Beteyns, 152
Bethell, 76
Beton, 43
Bettesthorne, 221
Betynys, 153
Benford, 211
Bewforest, 165
Bewley, 42
Bicknell, 70
Bigbury, 46
Bignell, 29
Bilhemore, 6
Bill, 130
Billing, 130, 160, 165
Billingford, 31
Bingham, 217, 222
Birchemore, 24
Birde, Byrd, 36, 184, 201, 202
Bischopton, 54
Bishop, 33, 150, 169, 190, 210
Bisse, 170, 179
Blackhed, 25
Blacknall, 29
Blackwall, 45, 99, 123, 198

Blackwey, 36
Bladigdone, 110
Blake, 151
Blakeden, 200
Blakysley, 25
Blandon, 179
Blast, 209
Blenerhaysett, 138, 142, 145, 151, 192
Blighe, 13
Blodwell, 31
Bloor, 107
Blount, 22, 25, 200, 225, 231
Bloxham, 154, 170
Bluet, 38
Blundell, 10, 27, 206
Blunt, 5, 163
Bocking, 65, 183
Boddingdam, 92, 93, 261
Bodie, 70, 153
Bodiham, 207
Boggis, 184
Bohun, 59, 129, 197
Bokele, 189
Bokenham, 145, 189
Bole, 36
Boleyn, see Bullen
Bolne, 209, 227
Bomsted, 193, 233
Bon, 41
Bonavetur, 95
Bond, 200, 205
Bone, 42, 153
Bonham, 102, 224
Bonifant, 46
Boone, 15
Boone, 122
Boorde, 214
Boose, 89
Bordall, 132
Borgeys, 100
Boron, 150
Borrell, 80
Borrough, 56
Bosby, 174
Boscawen, 41
Bosom, 225
Bossewell, 73, 231
Bost, 23
Bostock, 89, 98
Bosworth, 217, 264
Boteler, see Butler
Bothe, 15, 38, 44, 112, 200, 201
Botlier, 218
Bouldre, 11, 173
Bourchier, 46, 56, 121, 130
Bourne, 154, 262
Boutrod, 23
Boville, 115
Bowell, 76

INDEX OF NAMES.

Bowett, 164, 195
Bowf, 192
Bowke, 170
Bowland, 65
Bowles, 57, 190
Bownell, 126, 132
Bownyng, 231
Bowyer, 181, 198, 209
Box, 173
Boyde, 61
Boynton, 229
Boys, 63, 98, 100, 101, 172, 198
Boyville, 155, 161, 263
Bozon, 150
Brabant, 141
Bradbridge, 208, 264
Bradbury, 60
Bradfield, 150
Bradford, 211
Bradley, 153
Bradshaw, 23, 29, 45, 168
Bradstane, 166
Bradstone, 35, 71
Bragge, 124
Braham, 138
Bramble, 88
Bramche, 153
Bramfeld, 81
Brampton, 155
Brande, 84, 186
Branwhait, 166
Brassie, 32
Brasyer, 146
Braunche, 62, 141
Braunstone, 37
Bray, 5, 6, 78, 95, 204
Braybrook, 10, 16, 96, 220
Brayles, 163
Bredgman, 112
Bredmeydew, 120
Bregge, 111
Brent, 179
Brenton, 108
Brentyngham, 201
Brerely, 52
Brereton, 37
Bret, 50
Breton, 113, 135, 163, 174
Brewes, 114, 186, 195, 198, 214, 233
Brewster, 64, 195
Brey, 3
Bridges, 65, 72, 146
Bridgman, 175
Bridon, 142
Brigenhall, 89
Brigge, 148, 150
Briggs, 80
Brinckhurst, 10
Brisko, 79
Bristow, 29, 79

Brocas, 11, 73
Brock, 201
Brockman, 105
Brodewey, 50
Brodnax, 95
Brokes, 217
Brokhill, 107
Brokysby, 115, 116
Brome, 135, 167, 172
Bromley, 113
Brond, 60
Brooch, 176
Brook, 49, 53, 66, 74, 91, 96, 97, 105, 166, 186, 194, 196, 214, 228
Broughton, 21, 30, 186, 202
Brounflet, 9
Brown, 51, 55, 64, 93, 94, 102, 120, 135, 144, 151, 152, 157, 162, 185, 187, 234, 260, 264
Browne-opp, 11
Browning, 18, 161
Brudenell, 19, 156, 185, 263
Bruges, 68, 71
Brugge, 225
Brugis, 22
Brun, 95
Brunham, 138
Bruyn, 60
Bryan, 108, 112, 152, 183
Bryckett, 79
Bryght, 146
Bryghteve, 133
Buckenham, 188
Buckfold, 198
Buckingham, 53
Budd, 223
Bugges, 55, 57
Bukton, 197
Bull, 88, 218
Bullen (Boleyn), 101, 102, 106, 134, 146, 147, 148
Bulstrode, 13, 24, 29, 166
Bungey, 152
Bunne, 153
Buntyng, 151
Bures, 131, 182, 183, 192
Burfford, 147
Burgate, 185
Burgeys, 126
Burgh, 227
Burghehyll, 234
Burgherst, 166
Burght, 146
Burgoyn, 9, 34, 110, 111
Buriton, 223
Burlton, 98
Burnedissh, 185
Burnel, 177
Burrough, 131, 195

Burton, 14, 16, 46, 128, 132, 135, 162, 176, 199
Bury, 216
Buryn, 181
Buryngton, 16
Burys, 100
Burwell, 195
Bushe, 70
Buslingthorpe, 117
Busshbury, 10
Butler (Boteler), 4, 8, 9, 14, 18, 23, 25, 79, 80, 84, 88, 89, 100, 111, 155, 160, 167, 231, 260
Buttell, 15
Button, 76, 219
Buttry, 145
Butts, 124, 192
Buttyll, 111
Byggins, 35, 39
Bygod, 121
Byldysdon, 121
Byll, 81, 228
Byng, 53
Byrch, 60
Byrkhed, 125
Byschoppesdon, 164

Caestre, 234
Cailey, 154
Calke, 154
Calthorpe, 97, 133, 135, 140, 148, 151
Calveley, 178
Calwe, 78
Camber, 139
Camby, 174
Camoys, 213
Campdene, 16, 75
Camplyn, 147
Canceller, 53
Cannon, 21, 61, 149
Cantelowe, 5
Cantelupe, 77
Canteys, 104
Canwold, 153
Caple, 78
Capp, 146
Carbonell, 19
Carbrok, 9
Cardiff, 104, 109
Carew, 47, 48, 78, 109, 141, 197, 198, 235
Carleton, 83, 163
Carlyll, 4
Carman, 151
Carmynolls, 40
Carmynow, 40
Carpenter, 50
Carr, 119
Carter, 9, 19, 72, 84
Cartwright, 111

INDEX OF NAMES.

Cary, 46, 49, 170
Casberde, 11
Cason, 260
Cassy, 68, 226
Castell, 136
Castyll, 147
Catesby, 24, 28, 154, 155, 159, 263
Catterall, 113, 262
Catys, 134
Caus, 144
Cave, 21, 24, 116
Cavell, 122
Cawdron, 122
Cawke, 148
Cawson, 204
Caxston, 172
Cely, 57, 108
Cerne, 221
Ceysyll, 70
Chakbon, 102
Challoner, 91, 211
Chamber, 85, 178
Chamberleyn, 8, 36, 173, 180
Chambers, 36
Champneys, 51, 187
Chann, 103
Chapman, 51, 88, 109, 144, 192, 193, 235
Charge, 260
Charles, 102, 149, 169
Charlton, 123
Chase, 127
Chatwyn, 224
Chaucer, 166
Chaunceler, 158
Chauncy, 87
Chawcey, 200, 220
Chawndiler, 77
Chaworth, 45, 91, 116, 132, 229
Cheddar, 49, 179
Chedworth, 164
Cheke, 200
Chelde, 23
Chelseye, 165
Cherneys, 148
Chernok, 51, 93, 172
Cheseldyn, 176
Chester, 27, 59
Cheswryght, 33
Chetham, 189
Chetwode, 161
Chetwynd, 264
Cheverell, 51
Chewt, 186
Cheyne, 13, 16, 21, 22, 34, 76, 80, 84, 101, 106, 134, 164, 211, 264
Chicheley, 158
Chichester, 46

Childes, 144
Chiverton, 41
Chivnale, 19, 260
Chomeley, 52, 117
Chorlton, 249
Christian, 210
Chubnoll, 9
Chudleigh, 47
Churchill, 50
Churmound, 18
Chute, 16, 78
Chylton, 105
Chyttock, 173
Claimond, 169
Clare, 26, 62
Clarell, 156, 167, 228
Clark, Clerk, 16, 24, 25, 63, 71, 76, 91, 105, 110, 143, 145, 152, 175, 211, 230, 248, 260
Clavell, 50, 51
Claxton, 52, 152
Clay, 81
Clement, 50, 102, 146
Clere, 146, 149, 192, 202, 207
Cleve, 89
Cleybroke, 104
Clies, 40
Clifford, 37, 79, 95, 228, 235
Clifton, 113, 142, 162, 216
Clinton, 119
Clippesby, 136
Clitherow, 91
Clopton, 25, 36, 70, 189, 190, 193
Clovill, 65
Clyff, 75
Cobbe, 8, 9, 170
Cobbis, 153
Cobham, 54, 95, 96, 97, 102, 103, 105, 202
Coblegh, 46
Cobyndon, 67
Cock, 89, 134, 135, 146, 188
Cockayn, 6, 42, 55
Cocket, 147
Cod, 107
Code, 40
Codyngton, 118, 188
Coffer, 223
Coffin, 41, 43, 88
Cogdell, 83
Cogenhoe, 21
Coggeshall, 56, 191
Coke, 35, 66, 88, 145, 196
Coker, 50
Cokyram, 103
Colan, 38
Colard, 100
Colby, 185

Coldock, 128
Cole, 99, 130, 170
Colepeper, 92, 100, 109, 110, 138, 202, 206, 210
Coles, 159
Coleshill, 8, 54
Colkyn, 93
Collen, 81
Collins, 122, 214
Collys, 22
Colman, 195
Colmer, 107
Colt, 61, 64, 160, 184
Colthorp, 184
Colthurst, 231
Coltrop, 236
Colvyle, 140
Colwel, 99
Coly, 94
Combe, 21
Comfort, 207
Complyn, 74
Compoite, 163
Compton, 22, 59, 179, 199, 233
Coney, 141
Coningsbie, 34, 154
Conquest, 6, 7, 30
Constable, 162, 231
Conyers, 52, 231
Cook, 69, 80, 178, 196, 197, 210
Cookesey, 225
Cookson, 26
Cooper, 73, 88, 232
Coorthopp, 168
Copland, 193
Copledike, 118, 262, 263
Copleston, 47
Copley, 209
Coraunt, 153
Corbald, 191
Corbet, 6, 19, 149, 177, 178, 182, 225, 228
Corby, 208
Cornew, 46
Cornish, 181
Cornwall, 177
Cornwalys, 194
Corp, 49
Cortewille, 234
Cory, 153
Coryton, 40
Cossale, 97
Cosset, 183
Cosworth, 38
Cosyngton, 92
Cotes, 30, 217
Cotesbrok, 128
Cotton, 26, 37, 44, 71, 130, 192, 204
Cottusmore, 163

N n

INDEX OF NAMES.

Couhyll, 103, 262
Court, 11
Courtenay, 39, 40, 47, 49, 81, 96, 168, 199
Coverdall, 191
Covert, 84, 212, 264
Covesgrave, 6
Cowall, 153
Cowlshull, 84
Cowrll, 108
Cox, 127
Crachcrowd, 63
Cradock, 102, 215
Crane, 64, 79, 194
Cranford, 204
Cranley, 170
Crawley, 56
Cray, 165
Crayford, 111
Creke, 36
Crokett, 10
Cromer, 148
Crepehege, 111
Cresswell, 13
Cressye, 82, 156
Criel, 99
Crispe, 92, 93, 111
Cristemas, 165
Crofton, 109
Croke, 82
Crokker, 49
Crome, 148
Crompton, 263
Cromwell, 121
Crook, 26, 163, 224
Croshold, 141
Crosse, 187
Croston, 173, 174
Crosyer, 184
Crowche, 260
Crowe, 142
Crowner, 109
Cruwe, 219
Crymer, 151
Cryseyan, 4
Crysford, 209
Curthoyse, 90
Curtis, Curteys, 9, 40, 75, 87, 135, 143, 161, 188, 234, 262
Curzon, 27, 44, 134, 175, 182
Cutinge, 128
Cutte, 179
Cuttes, 52

Dabridgecort, 73, 76
Dacres, 128
Dade, 150, 190, 194
Dagworth, 134
Dalenger, 196
Dallet, 103

Dallingridge, 210
Dallison, 81, 87, 100, 119, 149, 156
Danet, 40, 63, 264
Daniel, 146, 183
Dansell, 92
Danvers, 55, 77, 221
Darckam, 206
Darcy, 63, 230
Darell, 56, 221, 224, 227
Darkenall, 82
Darkenoll, 106
Darker, 115
Darley, 101, 229
Daston, 71, 224
Daubeney, 72, 90, 135, 180
Daubernoun, 204
Daunce, 10, 18
Daundelyon, 104
Dauntesey, 221, 235
Davers, 78, 216
Davids, 215
Davies, 125, 178
Davison, 75
Davy, 200, 211
Dawtrey, 235
Day, 55, 85, 184
Dayrell, 25
Death, 98
Decons, 17
De la Barr, 77
De la Bere, 155
De la Chambre, 214
Delalind, 264
De la Mare, 77, 85, 197
De la Moote, 85
De la Penne, 19
De la Pole, 35, 166
Dellvys, 38
Delvale, 221
Dely, 127
Dene, 100, 141
Denham, 153, 205
Dennis, 46, 70, 193, 199
Denot, 210
Denton, 20, 158
Dere, 75
Dericote, 124, 225
Dering, 106
Dersley, 145
Deryngton, 57
Desford, 171
Despencer, 137
Dethick, 42
Devereux, 221
Dew, 109
Dewes, 63, 189
Deyncourt, 63
Deynes, 134
Deynham, 138
Dickson, 88
Dilcok, 61

Dinn, 61, 191
Dirkin, 102
Disney, 119
Dister, 55, 189
Dixon, 80
Dixton, 67
Dockyng, 151
Docton, 50
Dodd, 38, 100
Dodschone, 174
Doe, 14
Dogeson, 220
Doggett, 184
Dolber, 75
Dolman, 228
Dorant, 133
Doreward, 53
Dormer, 4, 159, 175
Doughty, 142
Douglas, 132, 179
Dourich, 48
Dove, 198
Dowinan, 84
Downe, 77
Downer, 126
Dows, 201
Doyly, 19
Drake, 19, 151, 152, 193, 219
Draper, 131, 198
Drax, 52
Drayle, 188
Drayton, 160, 165
Driland, 93
Druncaster, 57
Drury, 27, 141, 186, 187, 192, 194
Dryden, 154
Drye, 153
Drywod, 58
Dudley, 157
Duke, 48, 138, 145, 184, 188, 193
Dumner, 72
Dunche, 18, 220
Duncombe, 25
Dunham, 151
Dunmow, 196
Dunton, 196
Duport, 115
Durcdent, 22
Dussyng, 140
Dye, 110
Dyer, 11, 248
Dygenys, 51
Dykes, 230
Dykke, 149
Dymoke, 118, 120
Dyneley, 16
Dyngele, 76
Dypford, 49
Dyve, 4

INDEX OF NAMES.

Eager, 72
Echingham, 206, 209
Ecton, 80
Eddes, 156
Edelen, 22
Eden, 125
Edgcomb, 23, 40
Edgerley, 167
Edmonds, 8, 159, 201
Edvarod, 107
Edward, 70
Edwards, 10, 60, 98
Edyal, 136
Egerton, 178, 182
Eglisfelde, 42
Elcok, 94, 178
Eldred, 192
Eldrington, 61
Eldysley, 14
Eliot, 218
Ellenbridge, 199
Ellerker, 227
Ellison, 152
Elmebrygge, 198, 203
Elmes, 120, 167
Elmor, 19
Elslefeld, 204
Elwood, 98
Elys, 108, 133, 151
Emerson, 88
Empson, 65
Enderby, 263
Engayne, 63, 90
Engeham, 94, 100
Englefield, 12, 167, 174, 218
English, 26, 37, 167, 168, 183
Entwysell, 87
Eppes, 103
Erchedeken, 38
Eresby, 120
Erewaker, 75
Erington, 223
Ermyn, 154
Ernley, 224, 233, 235
Erpingham, 137
Ertham, 206
Erton, 222
Erule, 75
Eryng, 153
Eryssy, 39
Esmund, 166
Essex, 13
Esstone, 107
Estbury, 14
Estcourte, 222
Este, 185
Estfeld, 231
Estington, 225
Estney, 129
Estwod, 73
Etclesley, 106

Etton, 118
Eure, 209
Evance, 76
Eveas, 95
Evelyn, 200, 221
Everard, 64, 185, 187, 223, 264
Everdon, 29
Everode, 141
Evrenden, 92, 261
Evyngar, 127
Ewart, 75
Ewel, 191
Ewstes, 175
Expence, 18
Eynns, 230
Eyre, Eyer, 19, 20, 43, 136, 142
Eyston, 14
Eyton, 249

Faggan, 212
Fairclyffe, 185
Faldo, 4, 8
Falkaner, 193
Fallywolle, 25
Fane, 105
Fanshawe, 43
Farman, 133
Farnefold, 206
Faryndon, 13
Faryngton, 82, 184
Fastolff, 191, 192
Faunce, 95
Fauxs, 94
Fayreman, 85
Fayrey, 5
Fazakyrley, 22
Feelde, 134
Felbrigg, 136, 137, 140, 192
Feld, 87
Felgate, 193, 195
Felthorp, 134
Felton, 190
Fenner, 201, 211
Fenton, 216
Fermor, 58, 147, 157, 161, 173
Ferne, 62, 130
Fernly, 156
Ferrant, 231
Ferrers, 143, 157, 217, 218
Ferror, 145, 152
Fettiplace, 12, 15, 16, 27, 174, 212
Feversham, 100
Field, 56
Fienlez, 211
Fige, 30
Fildyng, 114
Filmer, 109, 112
Finch, 5, 93, 107, 200, 262

Fisher, 4, 6, 89, 114, 151
Fitch, 53, 54, 61
Fitton, 16, 91, 182
Fitz Adrian, 198
Fitzalan, 168, 207
Fitz Geffrey, 87
Fitzherbert, 43, 44, 172, 217
Fitzhugh, 260
Fitzlewis, 58, 59, 142
Fitzralph, 61
Fitzwarren, 17
Fitzwilliam, 40, 119, 156, 159, 205, 208, 229, 232, 233
Flambard, 125
Fleetwood, 20
Fleming, 59, 114, 162, 171, 212
Fletcher, 176, 195
Floyde, 155
Fogg, 92, 95
Folcard, 149, 192
Folham, 112
Foljambe, 42
Foo, 135
Foorthe, 187
Forde, 25, 46, 47, 181, 182, 200
Forest, 224
Forester, 181
Forster, 12, 29, 200
Fortescue, 46, 47, 56
Fortey, 70
Fosbrook, 156
Foster, 198
Foter, 186
Fountain, 46
Fowler, 32, 127, 167, 173
Fox, 78, 156, 163, 176, 183, 196
Foxle, 11
Foxwist, 215
Foys, 211
Framlingham, 185
Frampton, 51
Francis, 20, 34, 94, 176, 190, 228
Franklin, 21, 23, 59, 156, 169, 175
Frankyshe, 126, 146
Fransham, 138
Frebody, 263
Freeman, 114, 155, 176
Frekylton, 219
Freme, 66
Frennes, 151
Frensche, 214
Freston, 190
Frevile, 35, 193, 217
Freychwell, 45
Frith, 171
Frilende, 203

INDEX OF NAMES.

Frogenhall, 109
Frognall, 201
Fromond, 199
Froste, 166
Frowsetoure, 77
Frowyk, 131, 143, 198
Froxmere, 148
Frye, 49, 71, 114, 171
Fulburne, 33
Fuller, 151, 213
Fulmer, 24
Fuloflove, 138
Funteyn, 147, 148
Furlong, 49
Fyche, 91
Fylde, 75
Fylder, 71
Fyn, 56
Fynderne, 11, 12, 58
Fynes, 200
Fyneux, 101, 141, 185
Fyntch, 111
Fyske, 187

Gabriel, 200
Gadburye, 6
Gage, 85, 160, 209, 210
Gale, 124
Galey, 175
Gape, 86
Garbrand, 21
Gardner, 20, 143, 153, 163, 224
Gare, 141
Garet, 101
Garnett, 81
Garneys, 189, 192
Garrard, 14, 17, 20, 185
Garton, 223
Gascoigne, 4, 5, 171, 227
Gasper, 59
Gate, 208
Gaudy, 63, 151
Gaunt, 107, 176
Gavell, 141
Gawge, 111
Gayner, 66
Gaynesford, 163, 164, 199, 200
Geale, 15, 72
Geddyng, 17, 140
Gedney, 263
Gee, 49
Geffreys, 75
Gerald, 150
Gerard, 113, 149, 186
Gernon, 36
Gerrye, 97, 123, 175
Gerveys, 39
Geste, 222
Gibbon, 111, 150, 205
Gibbs, 67, 94, 264

Gibson, 175
Gifford, Giffard, 21, 25, 26, 29, 43, 49, 52, 53, 71, 72, 136, 160
Gilbert, 75, 111, 127, 143, 151
Gille, 89
Gillman, 151
Gilpyn, 205
Gisborne, 99
Gittins, 66
Gladwin, 57, 96
Glanfield, 187
Glascock, 62
Glasyer, 176
Glaven, 151
Glemham, 185
Glenham, 196
Glinton, 122
Glover, 172, 197
Glynne, 215
Goad, 23
Gobard, 73, 169
Goche, 183
Goddard, 222
Godeale, 227
Godfrey, 33, 43, 103, 104, 145, 147, 153
Godolphin, 39, 123
Gogney, 135
Golde, 179
Golding, 53
Goldingham, 184
Goldington, 7
Goldsmith, 82
Goldwell, 92, 94, 170
Golofre, 130
Golword, 138
Gomfrey, 43
Gomsall, 126
Gonson, 115
Good, 122, 148
Goodenouth, 210
Goodman, 59, 159, 215
Goodrich, 33, 79
Goodryngton, 10
Goodwin, 29, 30, 134, 143, 173, 262
Goodyere, 79, 124, 131, 167
Goolde, 169,
Gore, 74, 110
Goring, 73, 263, 264
Gosebourne, 94
Gostwyk, 10
Gotheridge, 68
Gould, 47
Gournay, 154, 263
Gousle, 90
Gower, 8, 94, 106
Grafton, 178, 203
Grandon, 150
Grantham, 263
Gray, Grey, 5, 6, 23, 38, 50, 83, 84, 86, 137, 140, 141, 142, 150, 173, 174, 182, 210, 219, 220
Green, Grene, 28, 80, 102, 124, 126, 139, 148, 157, 159, 168, 223
Greenham, 176
Greenway, 22, 49, 150
Greenwood, 97
Gregory, 23, 121, 165
Grenefeld, 230
Grenville, 30, 38, 46
Gresham, 150, 205
Greville, 62, 67, 69, 70, 182, 261
Greyve, 55
Griffith, 176
Griffyn, 219
Grobham, 180
Groby, 100
Grosvenor, 181
Grote, 134
Grove, 207
Grovehurst, 102
Grymbalde, 86
Grymstone, 134
Guildford, 48, 109, 122, 209, 245
Guilliams, 60
Guise, 3
Gulby, 105
Gunby, 121
Gunter, 13, 14, 68
Gunton, 152
Gurney, 27, 151
Gutecestri, 89
Guye, 68
Gygges, 149
Gyll, 15, 80, 89

Hacche, 94, 191
Hacombleyn, 32
Haddok, 59
Hadnall, 228
Hadresham, 202
Haghain, 148
Haitfeld, 229
Hakebeach, 154
Hakebourne, 170
Hale, 64, 203
Hall, 4, 72, 101, 109, 152, 163, 229
Halsey, 86, 132
Halsham, 210
Halsted, 4
Halwell, 5
Halyday, 69
Hamden, 172
Hammond, 101, 191
Hamner, 64
Hamon, 211
Hampden, 11, 24, 27

INDEX OF NAMES.

Hampekons, or Hamperotis, 29
Hampton, 69, 74
Hamsterley, 168, 170
Hanape, 49
Hanbery, 21
Hanchett, 80
Hancock, 49, 231
Hankford, 59
Hansart, 34
Hanson, 21
Harbard, 93
Harbart, 169
Harborne, 136
Harbottel, 53
Harcourt, 174, 225
Hardeby, 118
Harderes, 101
Hardware, 38
Hardy, 177
Hardyngham, 153
Hare, 185
Harewell, 219, 224
Harflete, 91
Harford, 77
Hargreve, 171
Harington, 231
Harlakinden, 110, 262
Harlyng, 211
Harold, 77
Harpedon, 96, 129
Harper, 3, 178
Harris, 35, 75, 86, 175
Harrison, 4, 14, 180, 228
Harsick, 148, 197
Harsnett, 54
Hart, 58, 97, 103, 150, 172, 176
Harvey, 3, 4, 6, 51, 57, 124, 143, 152, 183, 187, 197
Harward, 75
Harwedon, 157
Haselle, 41
Haselwood, 16, 30
Hasseldene, 34, 54, 203
Hastings, 4, 133, 137, 173, 224, 232
Hatche, 99
Hathaway, 219
Hatteclyf, 102, 112, 197
Hatton, 44, 200, 212
Hauford, 32
Haugh, 23
Haukesworth, 172
Haule, 130
Hauley, 46
Hawberk, 96
Hawkes, 260
Hawkins, 93, 100
Hawles, 76
Hawse, 3

Hawtrey, 23, 131
Hawtt, 4, 99
Hawtyn, 156
Hay, 7, 207
Hayden, 62
Haydock, 73
Hayes, 181
Haynes, 74
Haysden, 108
Hayton, 121
Hayward, 78, 99, 110
Hearnden, 108
Heathcott, 113
Heies, 63
Heigham, 57, 183
Hellard, 88
Helme, 51
Hem, 153
Hemenhale, 96
Hemsley, 15
Hender, 40
Hendley, 40
Henneage, 118, 263
Hensell, 92
Henshawe, 69
Herbert, 132
Herleston, 15
Herne, 20
Heron, 58, 200
Hert, 83, 124, 139
Hertcombe, 202
Herward, 133
Hesill, 98, 106
Hetercete, 150
Heth, 181
Heveningham, 65, 140
Hevyn, 121
Hewet, 159
Hewke, 32
Hewlot, 76
Heydon, 20, 97, 133
Heyford, 158
Heygge, 101
Heylett, 152
Heyne, 10
Heynys, 93, 153
Heyward, 10, 109, 143, 147
Heywood, 181
Heyworth, 89
Hichman, 69
Hide, 179, 221
Higgins, 25, 165
Higham, 142, 185, 195
Highgate, 126
Hildsley, 19, 165
Hildyard, 230
Hill, 6, 17, 36, 40, 47, 171, 217
Hillary, 182
Hilliard, 72, 263
Hills, 204
Hinton, 216

Hirst, 151
Hitchcock, 3, 25
Hoare, 101
Hobart, 23, 53, 137, 140, 141, 185, 199
Hobbs, 17
Hobby, 30
Hobson, 138
Hoddys, 148
Hodges, 71, 181
Hodgson, 54, 75
Hodsden, 131
Hodye, 69
Hogeson, 9, 51
Holbrook, 32, 105
Holcot, 163
Holden, 54
Holes, 88, 171
Holl, 189
Holland, 120, 123, 127
Holler, 152
Hollingworth, 62
Holly, 143
Holmeden, 249
Holte, 74, 149, 151, 216
Hone, 58
Honeywode, 18, 100, 111
Hook, 148
Hoore, 81
Hop, 102
Hopkins, 75
Hopper, 169, 171
Hopton, 196, 197
Hord, 163, 201
Horman, 23
Horne, 173
Hornebolt, 123
Hornley, 98
Horsey, 24, 51
Horslee, 146
Horsman, 131
Horton, 220
Horwode, 83
Hoskins, 203
Hotale, 234
Hotham, 164
Hotoft, 83
Houghton, 30
Howard, 8, 54, 133, 194, 202, 205, 209
Howell, 102
Howlett, 98, 135
Howton, 89
Hubbard, 54, 217
Huchinson, 172
Huddersfield, 48
Huddleston, 35, 167
Huddye, 47
Hudson, 145
Huffam, 98
Huggeford, 218, 264
Hughes, 83, 132

INDEX OF NAMES.

Humbarstone, 88
Humfrey, 80
Humpton, 148
Hundon, 7
Hungate, 199
Hungerford, 27, 29, 222
Hunsley, 131
Hunt, 10, 15, 25, 65, 73, 131, 134, 176, 264
Huntingdon, 57
Huntington, 35, 57
Huntley, 135, 198
Hurst, 22, 24, 168
Hussey, 29, 119, 176, 195
Hutton, 33
Hyde, 12, 17, 34, 50, 58, 65, 223
Hylton, 111
Hymyngham, 131
Hyng, 214
Hynson, 183

Idon, 208, 213
Illeye, 151
Incent, 80
Ingelby, 231
Ingham, 140
Ingylton, 28
Inwood, 205
Ips, 107
Irby, 131
Isbellys, 145
Isbery, 10
Isham, 103
Isley, 109
Ivy, 179
Iwardby, 26, 27, 29, 201

Jackmain, 7
Jackson, 143, 200, 262
James, 107, 127, 167, 183, 195, 203
Jarmon, 157
Jarnegan, 39
Jay, 66, 201
Jeckes, 147
Jemlae, 114
Jennens, 14
Jenney, 116, 135, 189, 193
Jenour, 188
Jenyns, 179
Jermy, 197
Jermyn, 184, 186, 190, 193
Jernemuth, 138
Jocelyne, 57, 64, 79, 87
Johnson, 21, 57, 75, 82, 92, 124, 227
Johnys, 215
Joiy, 196
Jombharte, 224
Jones, 28, 75, 78, 98, 164, 205, 233

Jordan, 22, 34, 114, 213
Judd, 59
Juell, 185
Justice, 11
Juyn, 66

Kaye, 113, 231
Keate, 13, 14
Keble, 187
Kegell, 147
Kelleatt, 198, 203
Kellwey, 76, 219
Kelly, 41
Kelyng, 136
Kemish, 180
Kemp, 56, 95, 150
Kendale, 231
Kent, 14, 72, 79, 131, 221
Kenwellmersh, 210
Kerdeston, 147
Kervile, 150
Kesteven, 84
Key, 71, 164
Keys, 137
Kidwelly, 18
Killigrew, 38, 39, 40, 72, 130
King, 18, 30, 61, 153, 169, 192, 200
Kingdon, 41
Kingsmill, 73
Kingston, 11, 12, 27, 36, 60
Kirkaby, 62
Kirkeland, 43
Kirton, 130
Knapp, 188
Knaresburght, 157
Knatchbull, 20
Knevet, 68, 190, 196
Knevynton, 52
Knight, 146, 159
Knighton, 184
Kniveton, 44
Knolles, 84
Knoyll, 202
Knyghtley, 156, 157, 217
Kybworth, 83
Kyggesfolde, 211
Kyllyngworth, 170, 232
Kymbell, 8
Kymycher, 217
Kymyell, 39
Kynderton, 38
Kyrkbye, 162

Lacy, 105
Laeer, 111
Lake, 181
Laken, 11
Lamar, 7
Lambarde, 82, 100
Lambart, 119

Lambe, 219
Lamberd, 107
Lambton, 52
Lamynge, 111
Landysdale, 143
Lane, 159
Langham, 54
Langholme, 117
Langley, 44, 80, 144
Langston, 20
Langton, 47, 171, 228, 231
Lanyon, 39
Lappadge, 184
Larder, 64
Lasheford, 98
Latham, Lathum, 61, 62, 63
Lathe, 149
Latihall, 72
Latton, 11
Laud, 128
Launceleyn, 5
Lawe, 117
Lawerd, 75
Lawes, 152
Lawis, 150
Lawnder, 70
Lawne, 75
Lawrence, 31, 55, 60
Lawson, 57
Layer, 148
Layton, 179
Leache, 55
Leake, 42, 118
Lecberd, 195
Leche, 45, 145
Lechmere, 225
Ledewich, 26
Lee, 3, 21, 22, 36, 81, 166
Leck, 163, 180
Legge, 138
Legh, 37, 113
Lehunte, 184
Leigh, 76, 132, 197
Leighton, 178
Leman, 148
Lenee, 126, 169
Lentthorpe, 8
Lentton, 8, 13
Lessyngham, 151
L'Estrange, 139
Lethenard, 67
Letterford, 16
Leus, 91
Levec, 126
Leventhorp, 58, 78, 87, 128
Leveson, 128, 182
Levyng, 30
Lewelyne, 229
Lewes, 208
Lewis, 27, 215, 228

INDEX OF NAMES.

Lewkenor, 53, 210, 212, 263
Leyneham, 16
Leynthall, 167
Lichefeld, 131
Lighe, 72
Lightfoot, 160
Limsey, 48, 124
Lisle, 71, 74
Littell, 20, 52
Littlebury, 116, 120
Littleton, 209
Litton, 163
Living, 131
Lloyde, 168, 171, 201, 216
Lockton, 35
Lodington, 3, 118
Lond, 66
London, 95, 171
Longchamp, 117
Longe, Long, 50, 79, 139, 220
Longford, 73
Longlond, 162
Louhauwys, 149
Louthe, 90, 227
Love, 173, 174, 214
Lovelace, 17, 22, 92
Lovell, 94, 125, 208
Loveney, 64
Loveryk, 101
Lovestede, 111
Lovett, 160
Lovey, 56
Lowe, 108, 207
Lower, 41
Lowthe, 171
Lucas, 64, 81, 84
Lucy, 128, 216, 264
Ludlow, 221
Ludsthorp, 161
Luke, 5, 123
Lulman, 152
Lumbarde, 109
Lumley, 213
Lund, 163
Lupton, 23
Luthyngton, 81
Luttrell, 118
Lye, 105
Lyfelde, 204
Lyford, 260
Lygon, 69
Lynch, 97, 109
Lynde, 90, 94
Lyndewode, 119
Lyon, 125
Lyrypyn, 75
Lyshford, 98
Lyster, 234
Lytcot, 13, 16
Lytton, 45, 83
Lyveryche, 168

Mabeall, 30
Mace, 98
Macham, 219
Macry, 89
Madock, 37
Magnus, 163, 229
Mainwaring, 172
Makepeace, 156
Makke, 153
Maldon, 50
Malemayns, 106
Maleweyn, 91
Malford, 170
Malham, 92
Mallet, 27
Mallevorer, 228
Mallory, 34, 161
Malster, 33
Maltravers, 50, 209, 213
Malyn, 25
Malyns, 64, 165
Mandley, 159
Manfeld, 28
Manners, 65, 264
Manning, 97, 99, 135, 142
Mannock, 190, 194, 196
Manser, 27
Manston, 107
Manthorpe, 196
Manwayringe, 167,177,178
Manyngham, 27
Mapilton, 207
Marchaunt, 223
Marcheford, 125
Mareys, 106, 108
Marham, 161
Mariott, 155
Markeby, 128
Marker, 147
Marnay, 58
Marner, 68
Marowe, 42, 68
Marpall, 197
Marshall, 37, 43, 55, 114
Marsham, 144, 152
Marshe, 170, 201
Marskre, 216
Martin, 31, 51, 67, 77, 97, 100,144,149,179,190,262
Martok, 179
Maryet, 153
Mason, 160, 169, 186
Massie, 228
Massyngberde, 118
Mastrupe, 264
Mathew, 19, 133
Matthews, 145, 233
Mattock, 82
Matyn, 223
Maulaye, 4
Mauleverere, 226
Maunsell, 24, 160

Mauntell, 157
Mawnde, 164
Max, 263
May, 41, 184
Maycot, 102, 107, 262
Maydeston, 109
Maydwell, 157
Mayle, 161
Maynard, 55, 76
Mayne, 19, 22, 92
Meale, 25
Mede, 66
Medeley, 63
Medley, 218
Meedwyn, 80
Melchior, 144
Melman, 148
Mepertyshale, 8
Merden, 103
Mere, 12
Merell, 53, 188
Merewether, 111
Mereworth, 104
Meringe, 114
Merlawe, 17
Mershden, 115
Merstun, 167
Merttins, 97
Meryng, 162
Metcalf, 26, 32, 79, 194
Meverell, 45
Mewys, 76, 219
Mey, 53
Michell, 157
Michilgrove, 208
Middlemore, 226
Middleton, 52, 110, 212, 215, 226
Mille, 211, 212
Miller, 88, 153
Millys, 104
Mingaye, 146
Missenden, 26, 29
Mitchell, 9, 17
Mitford, 203
Mitor, 87
Mohun, 39, 40, 50
Molinton, 89
Molton, 261
Molyneux, 21, 113
Molyngton, 98
Molyns, 27
Moncke, 25
Monde, 105
Monemouthe, 125
Moneslee, 144
Monings, 183
Monkeden, 12
Monox, 64
Montacute, 58, 158
Montgomery, 49
Montjoy, 22, 82, 163, 231

INDEX OF NAMES.

Moore, 34, 115, 121, 176
Mordaunt, 55, 57
Mordon, 23, 225
More, 12, 16, 50, 72
Mores, 77, 163
Moresby, 42
Morflett, 75
Morgon, 133
Morice, 181
Morle, 174
Morley, 87, 129
Morris, 11, 12, 74, 104, 169
Morrison, 88
Morse, 179
Morsted, 198
Mortimer, 123, 146, 213
Morton, 199, 215
Mosley, 112
Mostyn, 215
Moswell, 187
Motesfont, 103
Mountague, 18, 157, 264
Mounteforth, 152
Mounteneye, 151, 195
Mountfort, 229
Mowbray, 4, 149
Mowfurth, 204
Mownsloe, 178
Moyne, 90
Mozeley, 144
Mugge, 17
Mullebourne, 197
Mullens, 27
Mulsho, 159
Multon, 102, 149
Mundford, 137, 147
Mundy, 207
Muschamp, 198
Muscote, 155
Musgrave, 55
Mushunt, 135
Mustarder, 149
Muston, 108
Myllet, 124
Mylner, 99, 159
Mynto, 177
Myrfin, 34
Mytton, 182

Nansegles, 21
Napier, 8
Napleton, 262
Napper, 51, 101
Narburgh, 142
Naunton, 192, 234
Nayler, 116
Nede, 28
Needham, 6, 177
Neet, 223
Nele, 164, 163
Nelond, 208
Neve, 57

Nevell, 83, 96, 105, 125, 212, 217, 230
Nevynson, 99
Newce, 82
Newcomm, 49
Newdigate, 7, 125, 203
Newland, 83
Newles, 75
Newman, 17, 137
Newport, 42, 84, 85, 117, 154, 156, 182
Newton, 184, 214
Nicoles, 123
Nicollson, 231
Nightingale, 60
Nodes, 4, 261
Noion, 33
Noke, 15
Norbery, 6, 204
Norbrige, 205
Norden, 107
Norreys, 112
Norrington, 55
Norrysse, 173
North, 60, 74
Northen, 135
Northwode, 48, 91, 105
Norton, 100, 105, 111, 124, 136, 229, 230
Norwiche, 143, 155, 196, 226
Norwoodd, 69, 104, 105
Norys, 68, 167
Notfelde, 104
Notingham, 67, 139
Notte, 200, 205
Nowell, 123
Nysell, 110

Oakhurst, 207
Obson, 97
Odingesalls, 155
Odynsale, 216
Ogle, 159, 162
Oke, 51
Oken, 218
Okeover, 43
Oker, 182
Oldcastle, 91, 96
Oliver, 159, 197
Olney, 178, 225
Olyff, 84
Olynworthe, 141
Onley, 264
Opy, 40
Orchard, 105
Orgone, 129
Ormeby, 76
Ormond, 45
Osbaldeston, 164
Osberne, 158
Osborne, 46, 56, 140
Osteler, 101

Osylbury, 171
Oudeby, 82
Ounsted, 263
Ousteby, 122
Overbury, 84
Owen, 172
Owtlawe, 141
Oxenbrigg, 207, 209
Oxford, 65

Pabenham, 90
Packington, 132, 200, 220
Page, 11, 67, 108, 150
Paine, 68
Paleologus, 41
Palgrave, 133
Palke, 100
Pallyng, 136
Palmer, 89, 111, 118, 121, 139, 152, 166, 169, 171, 262
Palmerson, 228
Pansfote, 179
Papley, 8
Pargiter, 160
Paris, 33, 34, 223
Parish, 223
Parke, 26, 103
Parker, 5, 13, 70, 85, 87, 104, 123, 124, 139, 173, 188, 189, 196, 209, 213, 225
Parkins, 187
Parkinson, 52
Parlett, 141
Parmeter, 154
Parnell, 160
Parramore, 107
Parre, 81
Parry, 68
Parsons, 67
Partridge, 104
Paschall, 53
Paston, 146
Paswater, 106
Patenson, 132
Pateshull, 161
Pattesle, 35
Paulett, 74
Paveley, 10
Pawlyn, 107
Pawson, 45
Payne, 9, 24, 34, 51, 110, 165, 179, 183, 224
Paynell, 213
Pays, 197
Peacock, 55, 85, 86
Peare, 188
Pecche, 103
Pecke, 12
Peckham, 22, 110, 111
Pedder, 5, 8

INDEX OF NAMES.

Pedwardine, 117
Peletoot, 88
Pelham, 211
Pemberton, 86, 129
Pen, 26, 27
Pendarves, 39, 41, 173
Pendilton, 72
Penhallinyk, 41
Peniston, 27, 260
Pennaunte, 58
Penne, 181
Pennebrygg, 15
Pennyng, 189
Penthelyn, 8
Pepyr, 108, 144
Percevall, 76, 175
Perch, 169
Perchehay, 62
Percy, 210, 213
Perepoynt, 104
Pergett, 168
Perkin, 60
Perot, 108
Perrers, 202
Peryent, 53, 81, 163
Peryn, 92
Perys, 3
Pescod, 116, 149
Peter, 48
Petham, 99
Pethyn, 50
Petit, 93
Petle, 98, 99, 100
Pettie, 174
Pettow, 190
Pettwode, 143
Pexsall, 73
Peyton, 34, 36, 48, 194
Peytoo, 225
Phelip, 21, 101, 225
Phileppes, 134
Philpot, 111
Phyllypott, 162
Picakis, 64
Pickering, 4
Pierse, 210
Pigott, 5, 6, 12, 18, 19, 22, 29, 31, 88
Pinchon, 65
Pitt, 178
Plantagenet, 56, 137
Plat, 68
Playdell, 14
Playters, 138, 186, 193
Plessi, 27, 176
Plesyngton, 176
Plewme, 225
Plompton, 43
Plumbe, 89
Plume, 65, 187
Plumleigh, 46
Plumley, 101

Plumstead, 151
Plymmyswode, 163
Poche, 33
Podmore, 177
Poffe, 165
Pole, 261
Pollard, 47
Pollexfen, 58
Polsted, 200, 206
Polton, 60, 168, 223
Polwheele, 261
Poly, 196
Pool, 140
Pope, 122, 137
Porte, 43
Porter, 64, 69, 71, 95, 150, 234
Portyngton, 9
Pory, 149
Poryngland, 146
Postyl, 151
Poticary, 223
Potter, 110, 172
Potts, 42, 261
Poulett, 48, 58, 222
Pound, 74
Povy, 131
Powell, 15, 102, 133
Powle, 53, 152
Powlesden, 198
Pownder, 188
Powys, 123, 215
Poyidres, 83
Poyle, 166
Poynings, 94, 128
Poyntel, 187
Poyntz, 60
Prate, 123
Prater, 223
Pratt, 175
Prescot, 118
Preston, 19, 32, 101, 190
Prestwyk, 213
Price, 59, 172
Prideaux, 48, 173, 226
Pridiox, 264
Primislaus, 137
Procter, 155
Prophete, 73, 203
Prude, 94
Prunes, 14
Puckering, 218
Pudsey, 54, 227, 231
Pulter, 82, 83
Pulvertoft, 152, 196
Purdan, 205
Purdaunce, 143
Pursglove, 45
Purvedebe, 201
Purvey, 5
Pury, 263
Pye, 73, 207

Pyke, 81
Pykeworth, 120
Pylcher, 136
Pym, 79
Pynchcon, 158
Pynchepole, 13
Pynfold, 5
Pynnoke, 204
Pypis, 178
Pyrke, 66
Pyrry, 88
Pyrrysford, 261
Pyxe, 262

Quadryng, 146
Quarne, 172
Quatremayn, 174
Quek, 93
Quilter, 94
Quintin, 220, 227, 228
Quythed, 232

Radelyffe, 112
Rademeld, 214
Radley, 166
Ragsdale, 160
Ralegh, 218
Rampston, 54, 57, 60, 64, 123
Ramryge, 86
Ramsey, 24, 152, 165
Randolf, 232, 261, 262
Randoll, 217
Rashleigh, 39
Ratcliff, 42, 112, 173
Rauf, 151
Raunt, 150
Raut, 151
Raven, 80
Ravenscroft, 63
Rawe, 108
Rawleigh, 155
Rawson, 127
Raylie, 152
Raynnes, 133
Raynsford, 68, 174, 211
Reade, Rede, 17, 29, 58, 85, 92, 93, 121, 145, 164, 171, 193, 221
Readman, 42
Redborne, 99
Reddin, 65
Redfford, 204
Redinge, 63
Redmayne, 122
Reeve, 57, 111
Remington, 143
Renolds, 114
Reppes, 153
Reresby, 120, 228, 264
Reskymmer, 108
Restwold, 20

INDEX OF NAMES.

Retherby, 230
Reve, 185, 190, 191
Revers, 185
Revett, 192
Reydon, 192
Reynes, 135
Reynald, 134
Reynell, 48
Reynes, 8, 21
Richardson, 35
Richeman, 139
Richers, 134
Ridley, 101, 178
Rikhill, 106
Risain, 81
Risdon, 47
Risley, 35
Rivière, 70
Robert, 81, 94, 215
Roberts, 53, 59, 101, 107, 131, 132, 201
Robertson, 116, 138, 173, 197
Robins, 87
Robinson, 42, 81, 172
Robroke, 95
Robyns, 18
Rochester, 62, 128
Rochforth, 121
Rodney, 178
Roet, 197
Roetmanns, 214
Rogers, 73, 98
Rok, 26
Rokeby, 227, 231
Rokesburgh, 88
Rokesle, 103
Rokewood, 110, 150, 186
Rokysby, 153
Rolf, 56, 187
Rolle, 41, 47, 48
Rolleston, 42
Rolond, 4
Roope, 46, 172
Rooper, 103
Roos, 12, 122, 147, 264
Roper, 199
Rosse, 50
Rotherham, 8, 92
Rothewelle, 160
Rotton, 217
Rouclyff, 227
Rouley, 66
Rous, 150, 261
Routh, 229
Rowd, 151
Rowdell, 131
Rowdon, 68
Rowe, 49, 106
Rowlat, 86
Rowley, 84
Rudd, 121

Rudhale, 76, 234
Rudyng, 4
Rufford, 22
Rugeley, 118
Rugge, 113, 144, 153
Ruggenale, 126
Ruggewyn, 87
Rumsey, 133
Rusche, 127
Rushe, 234
Russel, 68, 122, 225, 226
Ruston, 89
Ruth, 134
Ruthall, 26, 67
Rutland, 220, 261
Rutlond, 86
Ryall, 77, 153
Ryce, 220
Ryche, 56, 65
Rycyls, 109
Ryder, 124
Rydford, 117
Ryege, 105
Rygg, 75
Ryghtwys, 134, 148
Rypphingham, 36
Rysby, 53
Rysley, 136, 167
Ryve, 72

Sacheverell, 44
Sackfild, 64
Sackville, 34, 211
Sadler, 13
St. Amand, 137, 165, 220
St. Aubyn, 39
St. Clere, 101, 223
St. Ethelred, 51
St. George, 33
St. John, 28, 87, 121, 157, 198
St. Leger, 17, 48, 110
St. Maur, 158, 187, 221
St. Nicholas, 91
St. Omer, 50
St. Quintin, 227, 228
Saker, 99
Saleys, 231
Salford, 200
Salisbury, 31, 158
Salle, 10
Salmon, 59, 206
Salstonstall, 60
Sampson, 62, 140, 226, 234
Samwel, 84, 223
Sanders, 26, 194
Sandes, 180, 204
Sandewey, 112
Sandford, 264
Sanny, 123
Sargeaunt, 121

Sarre, 62
Saunder, 142, 199
Saunders, 7, 26, 27, 72, 75, 79, 123, 126, 127, 160, 161, 175, 218, 260
Saunterdon, 27
Savage, 24, 71, 93, 113, 208, 261
Savell, 92
Savill, 127
Sawkins, 105
Sawyer, 159, 191
Saxaye, 88
Saxilbie, 89
Say, 80, 82, 119, 176
Sayer, 105
Sayers, 55
Saynysbery, 166
Scalys, 138, 210
Scarclyf, 204
Scargile, 58
Scarisbrick, 113
Scelke, 26
Schanckey, 153
Scolffyld, 11
Scolows, 145
Scors, 70
Scott, 93, 104, 115, 198
Scottowe, 144, 153, 196
Scroggs, 78
Scrope, 24, 65, 228
Sea, 101
Sedley, 109
Seilearde, 200
Sekyn, 191
Selby, 102, 104
Selfte, 185
Seller, 210
Selwyn, 205, 210
Selyard, 99
Seman, 116
Sencler, 99
Sendell, 153
Sendlow, 70
Sengylton, 196
Senior, 45
Septvans, 91, 95
Serche, 70
Sever, 170
Sewell, 66, 217
Seyliard, 93, 111
Seymour, 179, 182, 200, 220 (see also St. Maur).
Seynelow, 44
Seys, 13
Shadhet, 205
Shakerley, 98
Shakespeare, 219
Sharnbroke, 89
Sharp, 94, 108
Shawe, 176
Sheepwash, 24

INDEX OF NAMES.

Sheffeld, 7, 95
Shelford, 72
Shelley, 59, 83, 208, 210, 213
Shelmerdine, 42
Shelton, 51, 148, 151, 152
Shephard, 127
Shepley, 19
Sherard, 115
Sherman, 48, 197
Sherneborne, 148
Sheryngton, 183
Shiers, 198
Shingleton, 172
Shirley, 161
Shorditche, 126
Shorlond, 195
Shosmyth, 105
Shotbolt, 79
Shotton, 150
Shukbrugh, 159, 217, 218
Sibell, 223
Sibill, 99
Sidney, 62, 106, 196, 215
Sidnor, 136
Simond, 195
Simonds, 218
Singleton, 261
Skelton, 10, 34
Skepper, 117
Skerne, 50, 202
Skevington, 126
Skinner, 75, 198, 206
Skippe, 149
Skipwith, 84, 116, 117, 119
Skudemore, 123
Slanning, 49
Sleford, 31
Slon, 208
Sloughter, 67
Slyfield, 198, 204
Smalpage, 76
Smalwode, 18
Smarte, 156
Smethelaye, 227
Smith, Smythe, 11, 17, 21, 23, 61, 65, 76, 104, 107, 108, 123, 135, 136, 143, 151, 153, 163, 172, 181, 185, 191, 194, 200, 208, 214, 225, 226, 227
Smyght, 155
Snapp, 174
Snayth, 91, 128
Snell, 93
Snellyng, 201, 202
Soame, 184
Somer, 83
Somercotes, 124
Somers, 108
Sondes, 169
Songar, 55

Sonkey, 126
Sotheryn, 158
Sothill, 186, 187
Southill, 115
Southwell, 34, 97, 183
Southworth, 55
Sparke, 20
Sparks, 97
Sparrow, 92, 151
Spekynton, 168
Spelman, 142, 147, 153
Spence, 27, 166
Spencer, 5, 45, 108, 157, 217, 261
Sperehawke, 83, 153
Spernores, 178
Spiney, 225
Spooner, 55
Sprakeling, 107
Spring, 20, 189
Sprottle, 96
Sprunt, 173
Spycer, Spicer, 67, 105, 151, 164, 215
Stace, 103, 110
Stacy, 64, 110
Stafford, 13, 47, 137, 155, 161
Stalon, 146
Stanbury, 77, 261
Standish, 205
Stanesbye, 224
Stanhope, 44, 121, 263
Stanley, 38, 52, 61, 112, 113, 126, 129
Stanton, 260
Stanwey, 77
Stapel, 62
Staper, 8
Staplehill, 47
Staples, 57, 71
Stapleton, 42, 139, 140, 167
Starky, 38
Stathum, 44
Staunton, 114
Staveley, 29, 176
Staverton, 12, 15, 16, 17, 186, 260
Stephens, 50, 68, 220
Stevyn, 33
Steynings, 49
Stickland, 10
Stiles, 188
Still, 187
Stock, 261
Stocker, 72
Stockton, 110, 234
Stodeley, 29
Stoke, 85, 120, 150
Stokes, 9, 23, 32, 154, 168, 217, 222

Stoket, 202
Stone, 104, 181, 219
Stones, 133
Stonnard, 60
Stonor, 30
Stopham, 212
Storme, 138
Stoughton, 16, 94
Strabolgie, 91, 210
Strachleigh, 47
Stradlinge, 41
Strange, 120, 126, 157, 160, 218
Stranginan, 64
Strangwayes, 50
Streatfield, 111
Streinsham, 57
Strelly, 163
Strete, 100, 205
Strode, 172, 180
Stroder, 86
Strood, 122
Strout, 105
Strutt, 187
Stukely, 48
Stuppeny, 103
Sturging, 193
Style, 26, 92, 188
Styrlar, 119
Suckling, 184
Sulyard, 59, 61, 196
Sumner, 57
Sundressh, 111
Sutherton, 144
Sutton, 22, 37, 56, 91, 165, 199, 201, 229
Swafham, 147
Swan, 36, 133, 138, 145
Swayn, 30, 73
Swetecok, 202
Swetenham, 155
Swifte, 229
Swynborne, 58, 59
Swynerton, 34
Swynestede, 232
Sydenham, 178
Sydnam, 41, 180
Syferwast, 11
Sykeston, 212
Sylam, 8
Symon, 49
Symond, 57
Symonds, 65, 124, 135, 153, 173
Symson, 121, 134
Synclere, 223

Tabard, 195, 201
Tableer, 205
Tabram, 84
Tacham, 74
Taillors, 187

INDEX OF NAMES.

Taknell, 74
Talbot, 64, 128, 136, 155, 157
Talkarne, 193
Tame, 68, 69, 155, 173
Tamworth, 103
Tanfield, 159
Tanner, 61, 96, 165, 168
Tante, 168
Tate, 83
Tauntone, 161
Taverham, 84
Tawbott, 17
Tawley, 49
Tawyer, 160, 216
Tayllard, 90
Taylor, 9, 13, 20, 70, 89, 201
Tebolde, 99, 108
Tedcastell, 53
Tempest, 230
Temple, 27, 209
Tendall, 154
Tendring, 193, 194, 196
Tenison, 134
Terry, 144
Tesdale, 166, 223
Tettersale, 17
Teye, 65, 141
Teylar, 198
Thakley, 63
Thaseburgh, 139
Themylthorpe, 234
Theobald, 108, 153
Thinne, 127
Thirkyld, 153
Thomas, 65, 70, 103
Thomassom, 99
Thompson, 234, 261
Thoresby, 228, 229
Thorey, 118
Thornborough, 67, 72, 99
Thorndon, 138
Thorne, 3, 66
Thornhill, 22
Thornhull, 50, 51
Thornhurst, 209
Thornton, 124, 161, 169
Thorp, 110, 131, 149, 158, 260
Thorston, 94
Threckeld, 228
Threel, 206
Throckmarton, 15, 29, 71, 72, 157, 164, 173, 216, 217, 218, 225, 233
Thurbern, 74
Thurloe, 25
Thurston, 97
Tibarde, 169
Tilghman, 108
Tillebery, 62

Tillys, 152
Tilney, 146
Timperley, 193
Tiptoft, 123
Tocotes, 220
Todde, 101
Todenham, 144
Toke, 94, 95
Tomer, 218
Tomynw, 93
Tong, 99, 128, 227
Tonson, 115
Tooke, 81, 89
Toolye, 188
Tooner, 207
Topclyff, 229
Torksay, 113
Tornay, 27
Torold, 150, 162
Torrell, 64
Torryngton, 80
Tory, 196
Tothill, 19, 36
Touchet, 204
Towne, 32
Townley, 117
Townsend, 69, 116, 138, 147
Trapnell, 221
Trapper, 88
Tredinnick, 38
Treffry, 39
Trefusis, 39
Tregasoo, 40
Treghstin, 201
Tregonon, 40
Tregonwell, 51
Tremnre, 39
Trenchard, 19, 73
Trenowyth, 39, 40
Trerise, 261
Tresham, 159
Trevanion, 40
Trevet, 16
Trevnwyth, 39
Trevor, 205
Trewinnard, 38
Trewonwall, 28
Trilleck, 77
Trobrydge, 48
Troughton, 24
Truelove, 206
Trumpington, 36
Truro, 41
Trusbut, 61
Trussel, 15
Truway, 159
Tubney, 108
Tucker, 264
Tuer, 56
Tufton, 211
Tuke, 63

Turflett, 146
Turges, 52
Turney, 27
Turnour, Turner, 124, 193, 261
Turpin, 31
Tusser, 263
Twaytis, 196
Twedye, 62
Twesden, 94
Twychet, 87
Twynyho, 67, 68, 69
Tyard, 134
Tye, 188, 235
Tyldsley, 20
Tylney, 22, 260, 263
Tylson, 133
Tymperley, 188
Tyndall, 33, 70
Tyrell, 28, 57, 61, 89, 193, 194
Tyringham, 21, 28, 69
Tyrwhyt, 116, 120

Ufford, 140, 195
Ughtred, 227
Umpton, 226
Underhill, 23, 184, 216
Underwood, 143, 152
Unger, 149
Unton, 13, 148
Upton, 107
Urban, 108
Urmestone, 125
Urswyk, 55, 124
Uvedall, 25, 50, 148

Valence, 130
Vandburen, 98
Vane, 52
Vaughan, 129, 132
Vause, 216
Vaux, 209
Vawdrey, 169
Veldon, 202
Venables, 38, 112
Venard, 224
Verdon, 42
Vere, 65, 81, 157, 160
Verieu, 107
Verney, 27, 78, 216, 264
Vernon, 166, 178
Vertegans, 152
Verzelini, 98
Vesey, 193
Vessy, 9
Villers, 177
Vincent, 116, 151, 204
Vipont, 42
Virgine, 25
Vynter, 79, 81

INDEX OF NAMES.

Vyrly, 128
Vyzsdelon, 185
Wade, 87, 184
Wadham, 50, 51, 180
Wagstaff, 217
Wake, 155, 157, 171
Wakeherst, 199, 206
Waldeby, 129
Waldegrave, 59, 101, 183, 186
Walden, 10, 56, 99
Waleys, 7, 97, 101
Waliston, 21
Walken, 124
Walker, 56, 220
Wall, 78
Waller, 17, 19, 213
Wallop, 74
Wallour, 145
Walpole, 153
Walrond, 11, 12
Walsh, 30, 115, 136, 180, 215, 218
Walsingham, 217
Walsokne, 141
Walters, 153
Waltham, 121, 129
Walworth, 94
Walwyn, 69
Walysch, 175
Wandyssford, 231
Wantele, 206
Wantone, 64, 153, 161
Warbulton, 88
Warburton, 91
Ward, 14, 121, 150, 153, 198, 207, 230
Wardysworth, 198
Ware, 111
Warham, 73
Warner, 31, 79, 146, 173, 190
Warnett, 208
Warren, 5, 8, 19, 71, 82, 100, 112, 143, 178, 211, 228
Warwekhyll, 9
Warwick, 143
Wasshington, 160
Water, 36
Waterhouse, 110
Waters, 111
Watno, 110
Watson, 56, 177, 228
Wattes, 90, 151
Watton, 91
Wayte, 8, 63, 74, 75
Waytes, 151
Weare, 233
Webb, 77, 167, 222
Webbes, 109

Wekes, 210
Welbek, 204
Welbore, 55
Welby, 118
Welche, 88
Weld, 196
Welford, 78
Welles, 7, 131
Welley, 67
Wellus, 163
Welsborne, 13
Wenman, 175
Wenslagh, 230
Wentworth, 20, 37, 45, 185, 190, 196, 220, 230
Were, 10
West, 26, 160
Westbroke, 80
Westgate, 145
Westlake, 17
Westley, 57, 64
Weston, 161, 182, 197, 203
Wetherden, 207
Wetheringset, 36
Wethyrley, 148
Weyvyle, 214
Whalley, 32
Whappelode, 20
Wharton, 30
Whatton, 216
Wheatley, 191
Wheeler, 21, 200, 226
Whelpdale, 42
Whetenhall, 110
Whetom, 153
Whitacres, 58
White, 24, 37, 41, 74, 75, 85, 97, 100, 123, 148, 206, 222
Whitecoumbe, 162
Whithead, 217
Whiting, 48
Whitlock, 7
Whittingham, 78
Whitwey, 14
Whyth, 206
Whyttermete, 150
Whytton, 170
Whyttyngton, 261
Wiat, 92
Wickliff, 230
Wideville, 4
Wier, 16
Wightman, 125
Wigley, 45
Wigston, 114
Wilde, 4
Wilford, 24
Wilkynson, 106
Willardsey, 218
Willesden, 131

Willet, 79
Williams, 11, 12, 28, 41, 48, 51, 128, 133, 175, 206, 260
Willington, 164
Willmott, 17
Willoughby, 44, 45, 118, 120, 121, 147, 163, 217, 261
Willys, 140
Wilsha, 213
Wilson, 72, 126, 231, 234
Winceslaus, 137
Winder, 175
Windham, 137, 146, 180
Winford, 224
Wingfeld, 184, 186, 189, 190, 194, 197, 232
Wiseman, 6, 54, 56, 62, 64
Wodbryge, 23
Woddoines, 218
Wode, see Wood
Wolaston, 71
Wolsey, 162
Wood, 16, 59, 99, 134, 208, 231, 263
Woodford, 10
Woodhall, 23
Woodhouse, 7, 140
Woodlife, 89
Woodroffe, 25, 128, 261
Woodstock, 129, 130
Woodthorpe, 55
Woodville, 86, 126
Woodyeare, 97
Woolloye, 59
Worley, 103
Worsley, 36
Worth, 49
Worthyn, 224
Wortley, 45
Wotton, 48, 71, 93, 98, 128
Woulde, 205
Wrathe, 101
Wreke, 109
Wrenne, 195
Wroughton, 75
Wryght, 81, 140, 217, 230, 263
Wulf, 109
Wulvedon, 41
Wulvysby, 149
Wyard, 171
Wyatt, 221
Wybarne, 213
Wyche, 202
Wychyngham, 138, 151
Wyddowsoun, 203
Wyghtham, 18
Wykham, 216, 223

Wykys, 120
Wylby, 152
Wylcotes, 174
Wylde, 156, 178, 197
Wylford, 222
Wylleys, 158, 226
Wyllynghale, 74
Wylmer, 160, 219
Wylmot, 174
Wyman, 231
Wymbyll, 188
Wymer, 133
Wynchcom, 19
Wyncoll, 63, 195
Wyndbourne, 94
Wyndsore, 13, 130, 131, 202

Wynn, 215
Wynston, 142
Wynter, 94, 133
Wyntryngham, 156
Wyott, 63
Wyrley, 84, 157
Wythe, 150
Wyther, 179
Wythines, 207
Wyvil, 222

Yardlye, 53
Yarmouth, 138
Yate, 11
Yaxle, 196
Yden, 106
Yea, 179

Yeate, 14
Yelverton, 147
Yeo, 48
Yerde, 140, 199
Yewe, 220
Ynge, 203
Yngleton, 28
Yngrame, 26
Yngrave, 26
Yop, 150
York, 13
Younge, Yonge, 13, 17, 65, 168, 171, 178, 221

Zottys, 153
Zouch, 32, 105, 120, 154, 182, 224, 261

Recently published, price 1s. 6d.

RULES FOR THE
GENDER OF LATIN NOUNS,

AND THE

PERFECTS AND SUPINES OF VERBS;

WITH AN APPENDIX,

CONTAINING

HINTS ON LATIN CONSTRUING, &c.

For the Use of Schools.

BY THE

REV. HERBERT HAINES, M.A.,

OF EXETER COLLEGE, OXFORD, AND SECOND MASTER OF THE
COLLEGE SCHOOL, GLOUCESTER.

THE object of this Compilation is to furnish the Pupil with such Rules, in English, for the Gender of Latin Nouns, and the Perfects and Supines of Verbs, as are easy to be learned and applied at an *early* stage of his progress, as well as sufficient for an advanced state of scholarship.

The Terminations of the Nominatives Singular in the several Declensions are adopted for a guide to the Gender of the Substantives, and the chief Exceptions are thrown into the form of memorial lines.

In the Rules for the Perfects and Supines, examples of the variations of the Compound Forms are printed in smaller type under the Simple Verbs, and those Perfects and Supines which are of rare occurrence are pointed out.

The English and Quantity of the Latin words has been carefully given throughout, and an Appendix has been added, referring chiefly to such points of Latin Construing as are usually confined to the labour of oral instruction.

LONDON: GEORGE BELL, 186, FLEET-STREET.

www.ingramcontent.com/pod-product-compliance
Lightning Source LLC
Chambersburg PA
CBHW031333230426
43670CB00006B/334